The Handbook of
Language Socialization

Blackwell Handbooks in Linguistics

This outstanding multi-volume series covers all the major subdisciplines within linguistics today and, when complete, will offer a comprehensive survey of linguistics as a whole.

Already published:

The Handbook of Child Language
Edited by Paul Fletcher and Brian MacWhinney

The Handbook of Phonological Theory, Second Edition
Edited by John A. Goldsmith, Jason Riggle, and Alan C. L. Yu

The Handbook of Contemporary Semantic Theory
Edited by Shalom Lappin

The Handbook of Sociolinguistics
Edited by Florian Coulmas

The Handbook of Phonetic Sciences, Second Edition
Edited by William J. Hardcastle and John Laver

The Handbook of Morphology
Edited by Andrew Spencer and Arnold Zwicky

The Handbook of Japanese Linguistics
Edited by Natsuko Tsujimura

The Handbook of Linguistics
Edited by Mark Aronoff and Janie Rees-Miller

The Handbook of Contemporary Syntactic Theory
Edited by Mark Baltin and Chris Collins

The Handbook of Discourse Analysis
Edited by Deborah Schiffrin, Deborah Tannen, and Heidi E. Hamilton

The Handbook of Language Variation and Change, Second Edition
Edited by J. K. Chambers and Natalie Schilling

The Handbook of Historical Linguistics
Edited by Brian D. Joseph and Richard D. Janda

The Handbook of Language and Gender
Edited by Janet Holmes and Miriam Meyerhoff

The Handbook of Second Language Acquisition
Edited by Catherine J. Doughty and Michael H. Long

The Handbook of Bilingualism and Multilingualism, Second Edition
Edited by Tej K. Bhatia and William C. Ritchie

The Handbook of Pragmatics
Edited by Laurence R. Horn and Gregory Ward

The Handbook of Applied Linguistics
Edited by Alan Davies and Catherine Elder

The Handbook of Speech Perception
Edited by David B. Pisoni and Robert E. Remez

The Handbook of the History of English
Edited by Ans van Kemenade and Bettelou Los

The Handbook of English Linguistics
Edited by Bas Aarts and April McMahon

The Handbook of World Englishes
Edited by Braj B. Kachru, Yamuna Kachru, and Cecil L. Nelson

The Handbook of Educational Linguistics
Edited by Bernard Spolsky and Francis M. Hult

The Handbook of Clinical Linguistics
Edited by Martin J. Ball, Michael R. Perkins, Nicole Müller, and Sara Howard

The Handbook of Pidgin and Creole Studies
Edited by Silvia Kouwenberg and John Victor Singler

The Handbook of Language Teaching
Edited by Michael H. Long and Catherine J. Doughty

The Handbook of Language Contact
Edited by Raymond Hickey

The Handbook of Language and Speech Disorders
Edited by Jack S. Damico, Nicole Müller, Martin J. Ball

The Handbook of Computational Linguistics and Natural Language Processing
Edited by Alexander Clark, Chris Fox, and Shalom Lappin

The Handbook of Language and Globalization
Edited by Nikolas Coupland

The Handbook of Hispanic Linguistics
Edited by Manuel Díaz-Campos

The Handbook of Language Socialization
Edited by Alessandro Duranti, Elinor Ochs, and Bambi B. Schieffelin

The Handbook of Intercultural Discourse and Communication
Edited by Christina Bratt Paulston, Scott F. Kiesling, and Elizabeth S. Rangel

The Handbook of Historical Sociolinguistics
Edited by Juan Manuel Hernández-Campoy and Juan Camilo Conde-Silvestre

The Handbook of Hispanic Linguistics
Edited by José Ignacio Hualde, Antxon Olarrea, and Erin O'Rourke

The Handbook of Conversation Analysis
Edited by Jack Sidnell and Tanya Stivers

The Handbook of English for Specific Purposes
Edited by Brian Paltridge and Sue Starfield

The Handbook of Spanish Second Language Acquisition
Edited by Kimberly L. Geeslin

The Handbook of
Language Socialization

Edited by

*Alessandro Duranti, Elinor Ochs,
and Bambi B. Schieffelin*

WILEY Blackwell

This paperback edition first published 2014
© 2014 John Wiley & Sons, Ltd

Edition History: Blackwell Publishing Ltd (hardback, 2011)

Registered Office
John Wiley & Sons Ltd, The Atrium, Southern Gate, Chichester, West Sussex, PO19 8SQ, UK

Editorial Offices
350 Main Street, Malden, MA 02148-5020, USA
9600 Garsington Road, Oxford, OX4 2DQ, UK
The Atrium, Southern Gate, Chichester, West Sussex, PO19 8SQ, UK

For details of our global editorial offices, for customer services, and for information about how to apply for permission to reuse the copyright material in this book please see our website at www.wiley.com/wiley-blackwell.

The right of Alessandro Duranti, Elinor Ochs, and Bambi B. Schieffelin to be identified as the authors of the editorial material in this work has been asserted in accordance with the UK Copyright, Designs and Patents Act 1988.

Wiley also publishes its books in a variety of electronic formats. Some content that appears in print may not be available in electronic books.

Designations used by companies to distinguish their products are often claimed as trademarks. All brand names and product names used in this book are trade names, service marks, trademarks or registered trademarks of their respective owners. The publisher is not associated with any product or vendor mentioned in this book.

Limit of Liability/Disclaimer of Warranty: While the publisher and author(s) have used their best efforts in preparing this book, they make no representations or warranties with respect to the accuracy or completeness of the contents of this book and specifically disclaim any implied warranties of merchantability or fitness for a particular purpose. It is sold on the understanding that the publisher is not engaged in rendering professional services and neither the publisher nor the author shall be liable for damages arising herefrom. If professional advice or other expert assistance is required, the services of a competent professional should be sought.

Library of Congress Cataloging-in-Publication Data
The handbook of language socialization / edited by Alessandro Duranti, Elinor Ochs, and Bambi B. Schieffelin.
    p. cm. – (Blackwell handbooks in linguistics)
Includes bibliographical references and index.
ISBN 978-1-4051-9186-9 (hardback) ISBN 978-1-118-77299-7 (paperback)
    1. Language acquisition–Social aspects.   2. Socialization.   3. Language and languages–Study and teaching.   I. Duranti, Alessandro.   II. Ochs, Elinor.   III. Schieffelin, Bambi B.
    P118.H3485 2012
    306.44–dc22

                                                                                    2011008792

A catalogue record for this book is available from the British Library.

Cover image: 'Jungle Abstract' by Collier Campbell, 1990. © Collier Campbell Lifeworks/Corbis
Cover design by Workhaus

Set in 10/12pt Palatino by Toppan Best-set Premedia Limited

1   2014

Contents

List of Illustrations

Notes on Contributors

Karin Aronsson is Professor of Psychology and Director of the Department of Child and Youth Studies at Stockholm University. Her research interests include bilingualism, informal learning, and language socialization practices in peer groups, family life encounters, and institutional arenas such as preschools, classrooms, and schoolyard settings, as well as clinical interviews. More recently, she has focused on informal learning and aesthetic practices of computer gaming. Her work has appeared in *Applied Linguistics*, *Childhood*, *Discourse & Society*, *Journal of Pragmatics*, *Language and Literature*, *Language in Society*, and *Text & Talk*.

Patricia Baquedano-López is Associate Professor in Language and Literacy, Society and Culture at the Graduate School of Education at the University of California, Berkeley. Her research centers on the study of language socialization and literacy practices in and out of schools. She examines learning and language use at intersections of ethnicity, race, class, and immigrant status. Her publications include the following articles: 'Language socialization: Reproduction and continuity, transformation, and change' (with Paul Garrett), 'Traversing the center: The politics of language use in a Catholic religious education program for immigrant Mexican children,' and 'Adaptation: The language of classroom learning.'

Steven P. Black is Assistant Professor in the Department of Anthropology at Georgia State University. He conducts research on the topic of HIV support and AIDS activism amid stigmatization, working with a Zulu gospel choir in which all group members are living with HIV in Durban, South Africa. He has also worked on creativity and communication in university jazz rehearsals in southern California. He has published in *American Anthropologist*, *Journal of Linguistic Anthropology*, and *Language in Society*.

Penelope Brown is a Fellow at the Center for Advanced Study (Wissenschaftskolleg) in Berlin and former senior researcher at the Max Planck Institute for Psycholinguistics in the Netherlands. She is co-author of *Politeness: Some Universals* *in Language Usage*, and co-editor of *Crosslinguistic Perspectives on Argument Structure: Implications for Learnability*. She has published numerous articles on language learning and language socialization, as well as on adult language usage, in the Mayan language, Tzeltal.

Matthew Burdelski is Associate Professor in the Graduate School of Letters at Osaka University. His research examines the ways first, second, and heritage language learners of Japanese in households, playgrounds, and classrooms become communicatively competent members of their social group. His research has appeared in journals including *Language in Society, Journal of Pragmatics, Multilingua*, and *Pragmatics and Society*.

Haruko M. Cook is Professor in the Department of East Asian Languages and Literatures at the University of Hawaii at Manoa. Her main research interests include discourse analysis, pragmatics, and language socialization. She is the author of *Socializing Identities Through Speech Style: Learners of Japanese as a Foreign Language* (2008) and a number of articles published in journals and edited volumes on Japanese sentence-final particles, honorifics and politeness, language socialization, and indexicality.

Lourdes de León is Professor and Researcher at the Center for Research and Higher Studies in Social Anthropology in Mexico City. She is the author of *La llegada del alma: Lenguaje, infancia y socialización entre los Mayas de Zinacantán*. She also edited, with Cecilia Rojas, *La Adquisición de la Lengua Materna: Español, Lenguas Mayas y Euskera*, and more recently *Socialización, Lenguajes y Culturas Infantiles*. Her publications delve into topics of early semantics and infant communicative socialization, and more recently into topics of attention, peer group, and family interaction among the Mayans.

Patricia A. Duff is Professor of Language and Literacy Education and Director of the Centre for Research in Chinese Language and Literacy Education in the Department of Language and Literacy Education at the University of British Columbia. Her books include *Case Study Research in Applied Linguistics* and the co-edited volumes, *Encyclopedia of Language and Education, Vol. 8: Language Socialization* and *Inference and Generalizability in Applied Linguistics*.

Alessandro Duranti is Distinguished Professor of Anthropology and Dean of Social Sciences at the University of California, Los Angeles. He has carried out fieldwork in (Western) Samoa and in the United States, where he studied political discourse, verbal performance, and everyday routine interactions (e.g. greetings). He has written on intentionality, agency, linguistic relativity, and, more recently, the role of improvisation in musical and verbal interactions. Honors include Guggenheim Fellow and Fellow of the American Academy of Arts and Sciences. His books include *From Grammar to Politics, Linguistic Anthropology* and *A Companion to Linguistic Anthropology*.

Ayala Fader is Associate Professor of Anthropology at Fordham University. She is the author of the award-winning book, *Mitzvah Girls: Bringing Up the Next Generation of Hasidic Jews in Brooklyn*, as well as numerous articles which have appeared in *American Anthropologist, Language in Society, Text & Talk*, and *Journal of Linguistic Anthropology* among others. Ayala has received many fellowships in support of her work, most recently from the National Endowment for the Humanities and the Jewish Memorial Foundation. She is currently conducting new research on social change and digital media among nonliberal Jews in New York.

Debra A. Friedman is Assistant Professor of in the Department of Second Language Studies at Indiana University, Bloomington. Her research involves the application of language socialization approaches to the study of language teaching and language classroom interaction, with a particular focus on the sociocultural, ideological, and political aspects of language education. Her work has appeared in *Applied Linguistics, Annual Review of Applied Linguistics*, and several edited volumes.

Heidi Fung is Research Fellow at the Institute of Ethnology, Academia Sinica, Taipei, Taiwan. She received her doctoral training in the Committee on Human Development at the University of Chicago. She was a visiting scholar at the Yenching Institute and the Graduate School of Education at Harvard University in 2000–2001. She has long been interested in how to situate human development in socio-cultural contexts. Her research involves the socialization of emotion, daily disciplinary and moral training practices, and childrearing beliefs across cultures. Recently, she conducted fieldwork in Taiwan and Vietnam to explore how socialization and family ties are practiced across borders and across generations by Vietnamese marriage migrants in Taiwan.

Inmaculada M. García-Sánchez is Assistant Professor of Anthropology at Temple University. Her research interests include language and the immigrant experience, language and culture in educational contexts, and language socialization in immigrant communities. Her work on immigrant children has been published in *Linguistics and Education* and *Child Language Brokering: Trends and Patterns in Current Research*. She was the recipient of the Council on Anthropology and Education's 2009 Outstanding Dissertation Award.

Paul B. Garrett is Associate Professor and Director of Graduate Studies in the Department of Anthropology at Temple University. His research focuses on the historical and contemporary sociocultural dynamics of language contact, particularly in Caribbean settings. His work has been published in *Annual Review of Anthropology, Journal of Pidgin and Creole Languages, Identities: Global Studies in Culture and Power, Language in Society*, and several edited volumes.

Marjorie H. Goodwin is Professor of Anthropology at the University of California, Los Angeles. Her work investigates how talk is used to build social organization within face-to-face interaction, with particular focus on the family and peer group. She is the author of *He-Said-She-Said: Talk as Social Organization among Black Children* and *The Hidden Life of Girls: Games of Stance, Status and Exclusion*, studies that combine the methodologies of long-term ethnography with conversation analysis.

Agnes Weiyun He is Professor of Applied Linguistics and Asian Studies at Stony Brook University. Her research interests are centered on discourse linguistics and language development in multicultural, intercultural and transcultural contexts. She has authored and edited three monographs and over forty research articles in edited volumes and refereed journals. Professor He's major honors include a Guggenheim Fellowship and a National Academy of Education Spencer Fellowship.

Shirley Brice Heath is Margery Bailey Professor of English and Dramatic Literature and Professor of Linguistics, Emerita, Stanford University. She is a linguistic anthropologist, documentary filmmaker, and specialist in longitudinal studies of community and family learning environments in under-resourced areas of Mexico, the United States, England, and Australia. Her books include *Ways with Words* and the co-authored books *The Braid of Literature* and *On Ethnography: Approaches to Language and Literacy Research*. Honors include AERA Distinguished Educator Award, Fellow of American Academy of Arts and Sciences, Guggenheim Fellow, and MacArthur Fellow.

Kathryn M. Howard is Associate Professor of Education at California State University, San Bernadino. Her work focuses on how multilingual children deploy a range of linguistic resources in educational contexts to enact multiple social identities and relationships, and how these communicative practices change over time. Her research among the Muang of Northern Thailand and Mexican immigrant children in the United States has been published in *Journal of Linguistic Anthropology*, *Journal of Sociolinguistics*, *Language in Society*, *Linguistics and Education*, and *Language & Communication*.

Michele Koven is Associate Professor of Communication and Courtesy Research Associate in Anthropology at the University of Illinois at Urbana-Champaign. Her research examines how bilingual daughters of Portuguese migrants raised in France enact and infer identities in a variety of discursive contexts. She is the author of *Selves in Two Languages: Bilinguals' Verbal Enactments of Identity in French and Portuguese*. Her work has appeared in *American Ethnologist*, *Ethos*, *Journal of Pragmatics*, *Language & Communication*, *Language in Society*, and *Text & Talk*.

Amy Kyratzis is Professor of Education at the Gevirtz Graduate School of Education, University of California, Santa Barbara. Her research follows children's peer groups using ethnography, talk-and-interaction, and sociolinguistics, and focuses on how children use language and co-construct peer group social organization, identities, and norms. Current research examines how Mexican-heritage children in a bilingual Spanish–English preschool use language and code-switching in peer play. Her research has been published in edited collections and journals including *First Language, Journal of Child Language, Multilingua-Journal of Cross-cultural and Interlanguage Communication,* and *Research on Language and Social Interaction.*

Shumin Lin is a Postdoctoral Scholar in the Department of Anthropology at the University of South Florida. She received her Ph.D. in 2009 from the Department of Educational Psychology at the University of Illinois at Urbana-Champaign. Her dissertation was entitled *Education at Last! Taiwanese Grandmothers "Go to School."* She is committed to understanding the role language plays in the processes of socialization across the lifespan and in the construction of social inequality. She approaches these problems from an interdisciplinary standpoint, drawing upon linguistic anthropology, cultural psychology, sociolinguistics, and communication. Her main research program examines elderly minority speakers' experiences of linguistic marginalization through their participation in contemporary communicative milieus in media consumption, senior adult education, and intergenerational communication.

Adrienne Lo is Associate Professor of Anthropology at the University of Illinois at Urbana-Champaign. She is the co-editor of *Beyond Yellow English: Toward a Linguistic Anthropology of Asian Pacific America* and co-editor of *South Korea's Education Exodus: The Life and Times of Early Study Abroad* (2014). Her recent research has examined the moral images attached to South Korean returnee students; discourses of multilingualism in the South Korean popular media; and gender and language learning in South Korea.

Ariana Mangual Figueroa is an Assistant Professor of Language Education in the Graduate School of Education at Rutgers University. Her research examines the language socialization experiences of multilingual Latino communities living in the United States. She is particularly interested in the ways in which juridical categories of citizenship status are negotiated, contested, and/or reproduced during everyday interactions between adults and children.

Peggy J. Miller is Professor of Communication and Professor of Psychology at the University of Illinois at Urbana-Champaign. Her research examines early socialization through the prism of everyday talk in families and communities. Focusing on personal storytelling, she has conducted comparative research across societies (Taiwan and the United States) and social classes (working class and middle class). She is the author of *Amy, Wendy, and Beth: Learning Language in South Baltimore,* co-author of *'Raise Up a Child': Human Development in an African-American Family,* and co-editor of *The Child: An Encyclopedic Companion.* She is currently studying self-esteem as a cultural ideal and child-rearing goal that circulates widely in contemporary US society.

Leslie C. Moore is Associate Professor in the Department of Teaching and Learning and the Department of Linguistics at The Ohio State University. Her research examines the social and cultural patterning of language and literacy development in communities whose members use multiple languages and participate in multiple schooling traditions. She has conducted research in northern Cameroon and among Somali immigrants and refugees in the United States. Her work has appeared in several reference works and in journals such as *Language Arts, Language & Communication, Social Analysis, Studies in African Linguistics*, and *Text & Talk*.

Angela M. Nonaka is Assistant Professor of Anthropology at the University of Texas. She has conducted extensive linguistic anthropological fieldwork in Thailand and Japan. Funded by the National Science Foundation, she participated in the EuroBABEL Village Sign project, the first systematic comparative study of 11 village sign languages around the world. Spanning more than a decade, her research on Ban Khor and Ban Khor Sign Language constitutes the most holistic and only long-term study of a village sign language and speech/sign community.

Elinor Ochs is UCLA Distinguished Professor of Anthropology and Applied Linguistics, Director of the UCLA Center for Language, Interaction, and Culture, and a Fellow of the American Academy of Arts and Sciences. Selected books include *Fast-Forward Family: Home, Work, and Relationships in Middle Class America* (2013), *Life at Home in the 21st Century: 32 Families Open Their Doors (2012)*, *Linguaggio e Cultura: Lo Sviluppo delle Competenze Communicative* (2006), and *Living Narrative* (2001).

Amy Paugh is Associate Professor of Anthropology at James Madison University. Her research investigates language socialization, language ideologies, multilingualism, and children and childhood in Dominica and Los Angeles, California. She is the author of *Playing with Languages: Children and Change in a Caribbean Village*. Her work has appeared in *Discourse & Society, Journal of Linguistic Anthropology, Language in Society, Text & Talk*, and *Time & Society*.

Kathleen C. Riley is Adjunct Assistant Professor at Queens College, City University of New York. She has conducted research in francophone multilingual communities in French Polynesia, Montreal, northern Vermont, and a suburb of Paris. Publications include 'To tangle or not to tangle: Shifting language ideologies and the socialization of Charabia in the Marquesas, French Polynesia,' 'Buying a slice of Anglo-American Pie: A portrait of language shift in a Franco-American family,' and 'Who made the soup? Socializing the researcher and shaping her data.'

Bambi B. Schieffelin is Collegiate Professor and Professor of Anthropology at New York University. Based on fieldwork in Papua New Guinea and New York

Haitian families, she co-pioneered, with Elinor Ochs, the field of language socialization. Her research interests also include language ideologies and language change, translation, missionization, and computer-mediated communication. Books include *The Give and Take of Everyday Life: Language Socialization of Kaluli Children* and the co-edited volumes *Language Ideologies* and *Consequences of Contact*. She is currently completing a book on Christian missionization in Bosavi, Papua New Guinea. Honors include Guggenheim Fellow, National Endowment for the Humanities Fellow, and the American Council of Learned Societies Fellow.

Olga Solomon is Research Assistant Professor in the Division of Occupational Science and Occupational Therapy at the University of Southern California. Her research examines how children and youths with autism engage in meaningful activities with family members, therapists, teachers, and peers in daily life and how interactional dynamics in clinical encounters affect diagnostic processes, interventions, and services. Her work has been published in *Annual Review of Applied Linguistics*, *Annual Review of Anthropology*, *Discourse Studies*, *Ethos*, and several edited volumes.

Laura Sterponi is Associate Professor at the University of California, Berkeley Graduate School of Education. Merging her graduate training in developmental psychology and applied linguistics, she is centrally concerned with the role of language and literacy practices in children's development and education. Her research toolkit is comprised of ethnographic and discourse analytic methods. Through analysis of language structures and sequential organization of interaction she discerns the interplay between sociocultural determinations and individual agency in development and education. Her work has been published in *Childhood*, *Discourse Studies*, *Ethos*, *Human Development*, *Journal of Child Language*, and *Linguistics & Education*.

Tanya Stivers is Associate Professor of Sociology at the University of California, Los Angeles. She studies social interaction in ordinary and healthcare settings with an interest in comparing interaction practices and structures across languages, cultures, ages, and racial/ethnic groups. She is the author of *Prescribing Under Pressure: Parent–Physician Conversations and Antibiotics* and co-editor of *Person Reference in Interaction: Linguistic, Cultural and Social Perspectives* and *The Morality of Knowledge in Conversation*.

Akira Takada is currently Associate Professor in the Graduate School of Asian and African Area Studies at Kyoto University, Japan. His academic interests include caregiver–child interaction, language socialization, and environmental perception. He has conducted field research in Botswana, Namibia, the United States, and Japan. His research has been published in *Cognitive Science*, *Language & Communication*, *Senri Ethnological Studies*, and in the edited volume *Hunter-Gatherer Childhoods: Evolutionary, Developmental, and Cultural Perspectives*.

Acknowledgments

The idea for this volume arose from a two-day University of California, Los Angeles (UCLA) symposium on language socialization, interaction and culture organized in 2007 by Alessandro Duranti and Elinor Ochs and sponsored by the Center for Language, Interaction and Culture (CLIC). We are very thankful to the participants for their inspiring presentations, to the UCLA students who helped in planning and running the symposium, and to those who assisted us in editing the chapters. In particular, we would like to acknowledge Robin Conley and Jennifer Guzmán for their attention to all of the details that made the gathering of so many people a smooth and pleasant experience; Merav Shohet and Inmaculada García-Sánchez for their editorial assistance on the first drafts; Karen M. Kuhn, Ruth Brillman, Aleksandra van Loggerenberg, and Rachel Flamenbaum for assistance during the final stages of production; and Heather Loyd for her dedication to this project for more than a year, during which time she provided vital editorial suggestions and kept track of the heavy traffic of drafts, comments, and urgent questions and changes. Danielle Descoteaux and Julia Kirk at Wiley Blackwell have been a pleasure to work with. Finally, we thank all the contributors for their commitment to this project, their patience with our requests, and, above all, their research. The harmonious combination of scholars of different generations represented in this collection gives us confidence that tradition and innovation will continue to keep language socialization the vibrant field that we want, need, and dream of.

Alessandro Duranti, Elinor Ochs, and Bambi B. Schieffelin

1 The Theory of Language Socialization

ELINOR OCHS AND
BAMBI B. SCHIEFFELIN

Scope of Language Socialization

Language socialization arose out of an anthropological conviction that language is a fundamental medium in children's development of social and cultural knowledge and sensibilities, a domain that the field of language acquisition does not capture. While the study of child language encompasses developmental pragmatics (Ochs and Schieffelin 1979), the scope of pragmatics tends to be limited to what Malinowski (1935) called 'the context of situation,' with an interest in verbal acts, activities, turns, sequences, stances, style, intentionality, agency, and the flow of information. Instead, the study of language socialization examines how children and other novices apprehend and enact the 'context of situation' in relation to the 'context of culture.' In so doing, language socialization research integrates discourse and ethnographic methods to capture the social structurings and cultural interpretations of semiotic forms, practices, and ideologies that inform novices' practical engagements with others. While language acquisition research privileges mother–child conversation as a site of observation, language socialization research extends the object of inquiry to the range of adult and child communicative partners with whom a child or other novice routinely engages in some capacity across socioculturally configured settings.

Language socialization also recognized a lacuna in anthropological studies of children across communities (Mead 1928; Whiting and Whiting 1975; Whiting and Edwards 1988), namely the paucity of attention to the role of language as integral to how children grow up to become members of families and communities. Mead concentrated on the psychocultural patterning of caregiving, weighing the effects of local culture on universal psychological and developmental forces in the transition from infancy to adulthood. The Harvard-based Six Cultures Project

The Handbook of Language Socialization, First Edition. Edited by Alessandro Duranti, Elinor Ochs, and Bambi B. Schieffelin.

systematically documented the sociocultural ecology of children's lives and children's behavior, inspiring research on how local theories and environments influence parenting and child development (e.g. Harkness and Super 1996; Rogoff 2003; Shweder, Mahapatra, and Miller 1987; Weisner 2002), but language practices were minimally addressed.

Drawing upon Gumperz and Hymes' (1964) paradigm of the ethnography of communication and the University of California at Berkeley's *A Field Manual for Cross-Cultural Study of the Acquisition of Communicative Competence* (Slobin 1967), language socialization research emerged in the 1980s to consider aspects of the sociocultural environment of children's communicative practices that were left out of linguistic, psychological, and anthropological studies. Suddenly, what children were told, by whom, and in what language variety or register became as important as the order by which particular sounds or syntactic constructions were being acquired. Adopting a cross-cultural and ethnographic perspective, language socialization scholars went to different societies around the world to document how, in the course of acquiring language, children become particular types of speakers and members of communities (Ochs and Schieffelin 2008; Schieffelin and Ochs 1986a, 1986b, 1996). Decades later, these scholars are teaching language socialization courses in anthropology, applied linguistics, education, psychology, and human development. The field has now expanded to include second language and heritage language socialization, literacy, and media socialization, as well as socialization across community settings.

The multidisciplinarity of language socialization research has allowed the field to understand how children and other novices come to create multiple, fluid, sometimes conflicting 'webs of meaning' (Geertz 1973) and the 'unconscious patterning of behavior' (Sapir 1929) that underpin social connectivity. To document the generation of cultural intuitions and common sense across social encounters is a very ambitious project that necessitates looking at micro-interactional and macro-societal and developmental processes. Attention to these dynamics and others draws from different kinds of linguistics, anthropology, sociology, psychology, education, and philosophy.

Contemporary scholarship considers language socialization to be a lifespan process that transpires across households, schools, scientific laboratories, religious institutions, sports, play, media use, artistic endeavors, medical encounters, legal training, political efforts, and workplaces, among other environments (Baquedano-López 2001; Baquedano-López and Mangual Figueroa, this volume; Duff and Hornberger 2008; Duranti and Black, this volume; Fader 2009, this volume; Garrett and Baquedano-López 2002; He 2003; Heath 2008, this volume; Kulick and Schieffelin 2004; Mertz 2007; Moore 2006, this volume; Philips 1982; Riley 2008; Stivers, this volume; Wortham 2005). Adults as well as children constantly encounter novel situations and challenges that summon the semiotically mediated involvement of more knowledgeable persons. In some cases, involvement is elicited, as when adults seek healers to illuminate a health-related or existential concern. In other cases, language socialization may be initiated by others, as when a supervisor at work or sports coach trains or corrects nonexperts.

Language socialization begins at the developmental point at which members of a community recognize that a person enters into existence and continues throughout the life course until a person is viewed as no longer a living social being. In the twenty-first-century United States, for example, some parents sing, speak, and read to their unborn baby. English language websites catering to expectant parents even advertise products that enhance this engagement. One site, for example, advises parents-to-be that 'your baby's senses are active by your fifth month. This is the time to start using your *Bébé Sounds Prenatal Talker.*' The mother is instructed to strap on a belt with a battery-operated microphone and 'speak into the microphone [...] in a normal voice [...] if you speak too loud it will disturb your baby.'[1] The site advises the mother and the father to alternate speaking in 'a loving tone' in five-minute intervals and to 'read a story [...] that you will also read to him/her after birth.' This practice is reported to help the baby to recognize family voices and enhance bonds between the unborn baby and the family. Lasky and Williams (2005), however, report that the fetus does not reliably respond to speech sounds until after 27 weeks and only then when given high levels of auditory stimulation, given the background noises in the womb and the fact that the cochlea matures at 31 weeks.[2] While fetuses eventually become familiar with the uterine version of their mother's speech, there is no evidence that they respond to their father's 'loving' voice or benefit from being read books across the abdominal wall. Alternatively, in other communities, infants are not routinely considered primary addressees until they produce recognizable utterances (Ochs 1988; Schieffelin 1990).

Language Socialization and Agency

Over the years the term 'socialization' (Parsons and Bales 1956) has been critically viewed as overly deterministic, unidirectional, and goal-oriented toward adulthood by many cultural psychologists, anthropologists, and sociologists (cf. Cole 1996; Prout and James 1997; Rogoff 2003; Vygotsky 1986; Zentella 2005). The same criticisms apply to the notion of 'enculturation,' which takes the view that children are passive recipients of the generation transmission of a localized culture (Boas 1911; Herskovits 1952). Boas (2004 [1932]: 144–5) set the stage for this perspective in his insistence that children's conformity to habits of speaking, acting, and thinking is instinctive and automatic:

> In childhood we acquire certain ways of handling our bodies. If these moves have become automatic, it is almost impossible to change to another style, because all the muscles are attuned to act in a fixed way . . . What is true of the handling of the body is equally true of mental processes. When we have learned to think in definite ways it is exceedingly difficult to break away and to follow new paths.

In this conceptual framework, cultural knowledge is reproduced in infancy through imitation and internalization without modification. More recently,

Bourdieu and Passeron (1990 [1977]) similarly assume that educators 'inculcate' and learners (drawing upon their developmental capacities) internalize implicit and explicit principles of practices, habitus, and cultural capitalism. The difference is that Bourdieu and Passeron (1990: 5) saw pedagogy as 'symbolic violence' and 'the imposition of a cultural arbitrary by an arbitrary power,' while Boas saw cultural transmission as predominantly seamless, necessary, and fruitful.

Our use of the term 'socialization' in 'language socialization' diverges from these usages and instead draws inspiration from Sapir's classic 1933 article 'Language,' which insisted that 'Language is a great force of socialization, probably the greatest that exists' (Mandelbaum 1958: 15), and his 1924 article 'Culture, Genuine and Spurious,' which argued for the conceptual and behavioral independence of the 'individual' and 'culture' (Sapir 1924: 411):

> [A] genuine culture refuses to consider the individual as a mere cog, as an entity whose sole raison d'etre lies in his subservience to a collective purpose that he is not conscious of or that has only a remote relevancy to his interests and strivings. The major activities of the individual must directly satisfy his own creative and emotional impulses, must always be something more than means to an end.

Reacting in part to the dispiriting effects of mechanization in modern life, Sapir proposes a view of 'genuine culture' as nurtured by society but ultimately arising internally from within the individual (1924: 421):

> The individual self, then, in aspiring to culture, fastens upon the accumulated cultural goods of its society, not so much for the sake of the passive pleasure of their acquirement, as for the sake of the stimulus given to the unfolding personality and of the orientation derived in the world (or better, a world) of cultural values.

A central tenet of language socialization research is that novices' participation in communicative practices is promoted but not determined by a legacy of socially and culturally informed persons, artifacts, and features of the built environment. Moreover, while many socializing situations involve older persons as experts and younger persons as novices, the reverse is also commonplace, especially as rapidly changing technologies and fresh perspectives render older modus operandi and ways of thinking inadequate (Goodwin 1996; Heath, this volume). Indeed, Margaret Mead (2001 [1950]) was one of the first to point out that older generations are often at a loss in raising their children to handle modern innovations and that children may guide their elders through the thickets of a brave new world. She depicted teachers who feel that each year they know less about children as if they were on 'an escalator going backwards' (2001 [1950]: 60). The antidote that Mead prescribed for teachers is to grow and learn with and from the children.

The agency of children and other novices has implications for the fixity and fluidity of habitus (Sterponi, this volume). As emphasized by Mead, predictability and plasticity coexist as polar societal necessities, thereby provoking an inherent tension in socializing encounters. It is tempting to stereotype 'traditional' communities as pulling novices in the direction of continuity, while postindustrial societies are pushing novices to break glass ceilings. Yet, these trajectories are desired endpoints in all communities, given that novelty and creativity are part of the human condition. As revealed by Schegloff (1986), even the seemingly simplest interactional routine (e.g. the beginning of a phone call) is far from automatic but instead a skillful interactional achievement. In Duranti and Black (this volume), the authors elaborate ways in which 'creativity is made possible by routinization . . . even though the degree of freedom of execution varies across situations and speech genres.' Analyzing spontaneous play, joking, formal instruction, and musical genres such as jazz and Indian classical music, where creativity is a key aesthetic value, they provide a framework in which repetition, daily routines, and imitation are necessary and sometimes arduous steps in the socialization of different kinds of 'patterned' improvisation and evaluated performance. In this spirit, Moore (this volume) indicates how repetition practices in Qur'anic and French schools in a Fulbe community in Cameroon demand far more cognitive agency than verbatim parroting of their mentors. Indeed, as Moore notes, repetition is always something more – creative and transformative. As they go about their lives, the Fulbe children's Qur'anic Arabic and French language practices resemble but are not replicas of those of their teachers. Indeed, Moore notes that Fulbe mothers even allow children to play with the sounds of Qur'anic verses. Similarly, Heath (this volume) reports that, while Pitjantjatjara youths in Australia imitate culturally rooted storytelling and sand-drawing practices, their stories are revised – that is, improvised – to relate to present-day events.

In line with the notion that individuals comprise multiple selves as they move through life experiences (Wittgenstein 1958), language socialization research holds that habitus is infused with fluidity across the life cycle as well as across generations. It has been widely noted that institutional experiences, most notably those transpiring in schools, draw children into transformative dispositions and practices (Bourdieu 1979). What is less noticed is that children and youths actively assume informal, age-appropriate, situated practical communicative competences and subjectivities that they then shed and that may 'atrophy' from disuse later in life. These habitus and their practical competencies may be integral to life stages, as when childhoods are nurtured through peer-constructed practices of play (Aronsson, this volume; Goodwin and Kyratzis, this volume). A life course may also be marked by shifting language socialization experiences that encourage the shedding of certain language forms in favor of the adoption of others, thereby having an impact on the historical vitality of a communicative habitus (Duranti 2009; Friedman, this volume; Nonaka, this volume). The contributors to this handbook bring to the fore how persons across the life cycle and across different generations are alike yet different, recognizable yet transformed, lending on-the-ground insight into how habitus and practice become durable, transposable, and restructured over time (Bourdieu 1979).

Regardless of when it transpires across the life course, language socialization is best viewed as an *interactional* rather than unidirectional process (Pontecorvo, Fasulo, and Sterponi 2001). That is, all parties to socializing practices are agents in the formation of competence. Valued knowledge, talent, virtue, action, and emotion are lodged in and nurtured through socially organized, fluid collaborative exchanges wherein displays of relative adeptness may shift among participants. This perspective resonates with Rogoff's (1990, 2003) idea that learning is collaborative and development is a dynamic outcome of children's active involvement in activities with others who guide their participation. Language socialization studies document the social and communicative positionings of children and other novices in different activity settings and the affordances of such positionings for situational and cultural competence.

Having laid down an argument for the agency of novices and for the interactional grounding of language socialization, we hasten to emphasize the social inequality in most expert–novice engagements (Lo and Fung, this volume; Miller, Koven, and Lin, this volume; Riley, this volume; Sterponi, this volume). Common to all socializing interactions is an asymmetry of knowledge and power. This asymmetry may last for the duration of an interactional turn or a lifetime. Whatever its tenure, experts and novices are distinguished precisely through an asymmetry of ratified knowledge, which is linked to the exercise of power over persons. The link between knowledge and power is exemplified by the well-known case of the panopticon, who exercises power by assuming a position that allows him to perceive everyone and everything (Bentham 1791; Foucault 1979). Think of the power implications of knowledge of religious and other texts, specialized lexicon, laws, rules, formulas, scientific findings, and eyewitness testimonials. In contrast to ratified knowledge, unratified knowledge does not yield a social advantage. Thus, Garfinkel (1967) bemoaned the attitude of psychology scholars who considered themselves as more knowledgeable about their research subjects than the subjects were about themselves, casting them as 'cultural dopes.' Similarly, Mehan's (1996) account of how a mother's experiential knowledge of her child is discounted in light of school psychologists' test results and expertise reveals the consequences of the distinction between ratified and unratified knowledge for the labeling of children as learning disabled. A similar phenomenon transpires when children's knowledge is viewed as less legitimate than that of an adult, as when adults speak for children (Stivers, this volume) or gloss their cries and unintelligible utterances in ways that match adult expectations. In these cases, power trumps knowledge.

The exercise of power over novices' communicative practices is ubiquitous. Schools in the US, for example, specify how children should tell stories for the class (Heath 1983; Michaels 1981; Miller, Koven, and Lin, this volume) and how they should read books – that is, alone and silently (Sterponi, this volume). During book-reading, children resort to counter-practices wherein they surreptitiously share the contents of their books, creating what Sterponi calls 'multi-vocal texts' with classmates in 'liminal spaces' out of the panoptical gaze of their teachers. This endeavor of school children resonates with Fader's insight (this volume) that '[c]hildren's autonomy is constrained in unique and temporary ways by adults. Their agency includes their capacity to reject or subvert the dominant moral discourse critical to the reproduction of their moral communities.' Even when adults and children engage in the seemingly neutral sphere of play, 'the child may challenge adult authority within the frames of the play. Yet, ultimately, adults tend to come out as winners as it were, in that they are stronger or more in the know' (see also Aronsson, this volume; Garrett, this volume; Paugh, this volume). Asymmetries in power are not limited to adult–child interaction; they also pervade socializing interactions among peers (Aronsson, this volume; García-Sánchez, this volume; Goodwin 2006; Goodwin and Kyratzis, this volume). Rather than benign means of enhancing skills, peer assessments and corrections can have the effect of degrading certain children who do not meet their standards as inadequate and marginal.

Becoming Speakers of Cultures

A further tenet of language socialization research is that, as children and other novices become fluent communicators, they also become increasingly adept members of communities. Their communicative efficacy in particular situations depends upon their grasp of shifting and enduring perspectives that give meaning and order to an array of relationships, institutions, moral worlds, and knowledge domains. The process of becoming a recognized member entails an accommodation to members' ideologies about communicative resources, including how they can be used to acquire and display knowledge, express emotions, perform actions, constitute persons, and establish and maintain relationships. That is, each of the speech communities relevant to the novice socioculturally organizes the situational parameters of the communication that surrounds him/her – who communicates what with whom in which style, genre, and code. Novices come to understand the social and cultural underpinnings of these parameters through their own and others' socially structured engagement in such situations. Stivers' study of pediatric visits in the United States, for example, indicates that children are primarily talked about and infrequently addressed during these visits, with most questions about the child's condition directed to parents (this volume). Yet, when a question is directed to them, children as young as two and a half years old can answer certain questions competently, indicating that they have some sense of the point of the medical visit. Stivers argues that doctors' questions indirectly socialize child patients into what constitutes medically relevant information (e.g. presence, severity, and duration of symptoms; general health condition) and what kind of response they or their parent are expected to provide.

Human beings are differentially apprenticed into and through linguistic codes and other semiotic systems, which parse environments, instantiate social actions, organize relationships, and evoke psychological states. Some of the ways in which semiotic forms accomplish these ends are universal and likely rooted in species-wide modes of thinking, feeling, and (inter)acting with the social and physical world. It is hard to imagine a community in which language socialization does not cultivate social competence in and through requesting, questioning, asserting, planning, storytelling, correcting, evaluating, confirming, and disputing, for example (Ochs 1996). Socialization into these common communicative activities facilitates social engagement not only within but also across linguistic communities, underpinning the globalization of institutions and perspectives. In this sense, language socialization into a community is language socialization into the human condition.

On the opposite side of the coin, language socialization is distinctly local and situated. Thrown into social situations from birth, human beings become attuned to socioculturally saturated linguistic cues that afford their sensibility to a fluidity of contexts. Infants not only become speakers of languages; they also become speakers of cultures. While anthropologists no longer view culture as homogeneous, bounded, and static, adults and children nonetheless 'are always trying to make sense out of their lives, always weaving fabrics of meaning, however fragile and fragmentary' (Ortner 1997: 9). Indeed, researchers immersed in the daily worlds of novices and experts, be they children and their caregivers or amateurs and professionals, can testify to the continued centrality of learning to interpret the situated social meanings of collective representations and to perform as expected in certain circumstances.

In a variety of participant roles (e.g. speaker, addressee, audience, overhearer), developing children and other novices are typically required to recognize how and when to produce kinds of requests, questions, assertions, plans, stories, corrections, evaluations, confirmations, and disputes. They learn how to express their emotions and constitute themselves as moral persons in public places to a greater or lesser extent. Moreover, while, universally, language socialization orients novices to the world around them, members of social groups use language and other semiotic resources to orient novices to notice and value certain salient and relevant activities, persons, artifacts, and features of the natural ecology. In making this point, we are not embracing linguistic determinism; rather, we simply note that the intertwining of language, society, and culture may begin in the womb and that language acquisition and socialization are interdependent developmental processes.

Transcending the Nature–Nurture Divide

Language socialization mediates the dualisms of nature and nurture, development and learning, individual and society, and mind and culture. The relation between neurobiology and culture has been a point of departure for cross-disciplinary dialogue, with considerable interest in the developmental transition into socially informed, protean selves capable of cooperating with others (Enfield and Levinson 2006; Richerson and Boyd 2004; Tomasello et al. 2005). This volume evidences the role of semiotic forms and practices as essential resources in this transition.

Going beyond the oppositionally framed debates of nature versus nurture surrounding the basis of acquisition, language socialization researchers have formulated a paradigm that assumes both nature and nurture as implicated. Language socialization assumes the biological immaturity of children, the social urgency for children to be nurtured by caregivers, and the universal cultivation of children's awareness of self and other. At the same time, it assumes that children's and other novices' social awakening is inextricably tied to their entry into social order and the cultural significance of their own and others' actions, demeanors, and signs (Heath 1983; Schieffelin and Ochs 1986a, 1986b; Schieffelin 1990). In this regard, language socialization research shares with cultural psychology the notion that each child's conception, birth, and growth is informed by the social and cultural histories of the communities with which their progenitors affiliate (Cole 1996).

As evidenced in the example of the *Bébé Sounds Prenatal Talker* depicted earlier, even before a child is born, he or she enters a social world, one that is culturally organized and shaped by ideas about personhood, sociality, and the complicated relationships between nature and nurture, however they are locally defined. While the lives of infants may seem relatively circumscribed, people and things, theories and practices – all embedded in time and place – explicitly and/or tacitly contribute to the emerging social and communicative competencies of the infant, as well as to the interactive moves of caregivers. While there are many universal practices observed in the first two years due to the obvious requirements of biological circumstances of infancy and caregiving, there is also significant variation in activities relevant to language socialization, both individually and collectively in any given community.

A case for this phenomenon is made in Takada's study of San mother–infant nursing interactions in Botswana (this volume). Takada finds evidence of the universal primacy of mutual involvement between nursing San infants and caregivers in Botswana, but, unlike nursing interactions observed elsewhere, San caregivers avoid gazing at the infant and do not pause while nursing to attend to a fussing infant, bowing to a San preference for continuous flow of rhythmic engagement, supplemented by songs and sounds. Similarly, Brown confirmed the establishment of caregiver–child joint attention to external entities in Tzeltal Mayan and Rossel Island (Papua New Guinea) communities. The study draws upon Tomasello et al.'s (2005) observation that the establishment of joint attention to entities with infants is ontogenetically and phylogenetically critical to the development of intersubjectivity as a platform for culture and that pointing is instrumental in achieving mutual gaze towards an object or event. Brown found that both Tzeltal and Rossel Islanders use pointing with infants to this end around the same developmental period, but that Rossel Islanders do so more frequently, for longer, and more affectively. Caregivers in both of these communities did not follow the preference for labeling objects that has been observed in studies of joint attention in other societies.

Language socialization research shares with cultural psychology a strong interest in the social 'niches' of human development, particularly how more knowledgeable members of social groups organize novices' transition into social and cultural competence (de León 1998; Lave and Wenger 1991; Rogoff et al. 2003). In the case of language socialization, preferred corporeal habitats of infants (e.g. carried on back, nested in front, or facing caregiver; swaddled; placed in cradle) organize communication between infants and others (de León, this volume; Ochs, Solomon, and Sterponi 2005; Solomon, this volume; Takada, this volume).

In addition, the built environment and household arrangements surrounding novices at all stages of life create certain communicative affordances and inhibitions for communication. For example, the open architecture of dwellings and the spatial plan of extended family compounds and villages in many places in the world promote multiparty engagements between very young children and others, while walled-off houses containing smaller nuclear families in other communities may afford dyadic exchanges.

This ecological distinction is a key cross-cultural distinction that organizes the extent to which infants and young children are positioned as addressees, over-hearers/observers, or messengers for others (de León, this volume; Schieffelin 1990; Solomon, this volume). De León's study of Zinacatecan Tzotzil families, for example, indicates a preference for involving infants in triadic exchanges and a dispreference for engaging them in dyadic proto-conversations, as observed in other communities (Bates, Camaioni, and Volterra 1979). The prevalence of multiparty versus dyadic communicative environments may also contribute to cross-cultural differences in the extent to which children are oriented to pay close attention to the social world around them, monitoring, learning, accommodating, and responding to situational contingencies (Garrett, this volume; Heath, this volume; Ochs and Schieffelin 1984, 1995; Paugh, this volume; Rogoff et al. 2003). It should be noted, however, that the distinction between multiparty and dyadic language socialization ecologies is by no means absolute or necessarily conducive to promoting keen attention to other people. Moreover, regardless of whether their home interactional environments are predominantly dyadic or multiparty, many young children across societies spend time outside their households in multiparty environments such as preschools and are brought to medical visits where they and their caregiver are differentially positioned in triadic interactions to inform and respond to the doctor (Stivers, this volume).

Language socialization research apprehends the role of nurture in children's emergent communication through systematic analysis of locally preferred and socially situated forms of participation, acts, and activities and their broader relation to social positionings, institutions, belief and knowledge systems, and aesthetic judgments. Language socialization studies take as central the idea that nurturing arrangements are motivated by a community's repertoire of shared and varied cultural beliefs about social reproduction, including personhood, sociality, emotions, knowledge, and human development, which are given materiality through language and other semiotic forms in everyday life. Language ideologies, for example, infuse and guide verbal input to children and other novices, profoundly affecting the form and content of communication in the presence of language-acquiring children (Paugh, this volume; Riley, this volume; Solomon, this volume).

Semiotic Resources for Socialization

Two important features distinguish language socialization as theoretical inquiry: (1) an analytic focus on speech, writing, gesture, images, music, and other signs as primary means and endpoints of the socialization process and (2) an ethnographic sensibility that accounts for the socializing force of these semiotic resources in terms of enduring and shifting socioculturally meaningful practices, events, situations, institutions, relationships, emotions, aesthetics, moralities, bodies of knowledge, and ideologies.

As originally defined, language socialization comprises 'socialization through the use of language and socialization to use language' (Schieffelin and Ochs 1986b: 163). A central goal has been to discern the role of language and other semiotic systems in the quotidian reproduction and innovation of social order and cultural knowledge, beliefs, values, ideologies, symbols, and indexes. Language socialization research has concentrated on the socializing affordances of grammar (e.g. evidentials), lexicon (e.g. kinship terms), phonology (e.g. exaggerated intonation), speech acts (e.g. directives), conversational sequences, genres, registers, channels (e.g. written, oral), and codes. It also attends to other expressive forms (e.g. gesture, corporeal demeanor and positioning, figurative representation) that enable and structure the process of becoming a competent communicator and member of one or more social groups. Cook (this volume) demonstrates, for example, that different Japanese morpho-syntactic forms repeatedly and effectively cue children and adult language learners into degrees of certainty of knowledge and the limits of imputing others' unexpressed subjective states. For instance, in interactions with learners (who demonstrate awareness), Japanese caregivers use bare verb forms to index kinds of knowledge, for example psychological states, that only subjective experiencers can access and express. Alternatively, they use particles (e.g. *deshoo*) to mark other knowledge, for example the tastiness of cuisine, that both the subject and others can have the authority to access and express. Similarly, Muang adults in Northern Thailand direct children's attention to lexical, grammatical, and embodied markers of politeness (Howard, this volume).

Language socialization brings linguistic anthropological perspectives (Duranti 1997) into the study of how linguistic and cultural competence emerges across lifespans and histories. These perspectives include the notion that signs are routinely and hence indexically linked to social contexts (Peirce 1931–58; Silverstein 1996). As such, signs are lampposts that point to facets of social worlds for children and other novices to recognize and refashion in coordination with other community members (Ochs 1990). Language socialization research also builds upon studies of linguistic and sociocultural heterogeneity and hybridity to analyze how children are socialized into forms of cultural capital (Bourdieu 1979) that privilege certain languages, dialects, registers, genres, and styles over others and the consequences for language maintenance and shift (cf. among others, Garrett and Baquedano-López 2002; Kulick 1992; Schieffelin et al. 1998).

The analysis of linguistic resources for socialization predominantly relies upon (1) systematic audio and visual documentation (e.g. recordings, photographs, maps) of embodied communicative practices in the context of the social life of communities, (2) collection of relevant texts and other artifacts, and (3) in-depth extensive ethnographic field observations and interviews, which are critical to gaining divergent and common understandings of complex situated relationships, symbols, and orientations. Language socialization research classically involves longitudinal data collection on socialization into/through and emergence of communicative practices over developmental time (Garrett and Baquedano-López 2002). While developmental time is associated with the early stages of life, it holds as well for the development of skills and ideas in the world of youths and adults. Language socialization research has also relied upon cross-sectional studies of novices in the context of families, schools, workplaces, and recreational and other settings (Goodwin and Kyratzis, this volume; Ochs and Taylor 1992; Stivers, this volume). Moreover, language socialization can be examined in the form of a single case study over a brief period of time (Aronsson, this volume; Aronsson and Cederborg 1996).

Attention to the details of temporally unfolding communication involving novices in relation to public webs of significance, including prevailing power asymmetries, is a hallmark of language socialization scholarship. These linked methodologies allow researchers to pursue the challenging Vygotskian concept that continuity and change transpire at interactional, diurnal, developmental, and sociohistorical levels. Language socialization studies tend to layer levels of analysis, looking at children and other novices' involvement in social life from the top down, looking into the organization of involvement itself for the socializing potentialities of semiotic forms and communicative arrangements, and looking up from micro-movements of bodies, gestures, and verbal acts to longer-term sociocultural and political implications. The threading of these methodologies provides crucial perspectives on the communicative roots of continuity, change, and marginalization in spheres such as religion, aesthetics, gender, peer and family relationships, classroom life, and ethnic diasporas.

Language Socializing Practices

At the risk of belaboring the obvious, language socialization does not boil down to a set of behaviors that are explicitly and intentionally oriented to enhance a novice's knowledge or skill. Emphasized throughout this volume are ways in which durative and emergent beliefs about speaking, acting, thinking, and feeling; the organization of communicative environments; the array of communicative activities, artifacts, and technologies available; the positioning of novices in interactional participant roles; and the socially differentiated accessibility of semiotic repertoires potentiate or hinder specific communicative and social habits and skills and evoke vital indexical meanings tied to context of situation and context of culture for novices of all ages. Language socialization rests upon the availability of these conditions and more.

Language socialization may transpire through explicit practices that express goals and instruct novices, yet vastly more pervasive is socialization through novices' routine participation in semiotically mediated practices, whose temporally unfolding structuring scaffolds and informs their experience, cuing them as to how they should initiate moves and interpret and respond to situational contingencies.

Bourdieu and Passeron (1990: 102) remarked on the distinction between explicit and implicit socialization, emphasizing the ubiquity of the latter:

> The pedagogic work of inculcation – together with institutionalization, which is always accompanied by a degree of objectification in discourse . . . is one of the major occasions for formulating and converting practical schemes into explicit norms . . . As is suggested by a reading of Plato's *Meno*, the emergence of institutionalized education is accompanied by a crisis of diffuse education, which moves directly from practice to practice without passing though discourse.

According to this perspective, educational institutions present rules and explanations in an attempt to objectify and codify knowledge, while all around novices acquire practical mastery without a whisper of objectifying discourses. Instead, Bourdieu emphasized the importance of hexis or corporeal involvement as the medium for gaining practical knowledge. In line with this position, Heath (this volume) argues that the body, especially vision, has for centuries been the seat of creative learning in the arts and sciences and that only recently have these enterprises been transformed into spoken and written verbal instruction in classroom settings. This distinction is not only historical but also cross-culturally consequential when indigenous ways of acquiring ecological knowledge through experiential keen observation contrasts with school-based expectations of learning through objectifying scientific discourse.

Between 'pedagogic inculcation' and 'diffuse education,' however, lies a range of language socializing affordances that are more or less overt and presuppositionally or declaratively codified than as projected by Bourdieu. Indeed, even gaining practical knowledge through corporeal immersion is not totally 'diffuse,' in that caregivers use pointing to deliberately orient children's bodies to entities or hold children up to engage them in rhythmic activities. Moreover, novices', especially children's, practical mastery is assisted by speech acts and activities that orient them to what matters in situations and life in general. As Riley (this volume) points out, in some speech communities, caregivers believe that children must be explicitly taught to speak correctly through prompting in everyday social engagements.

In other words, ordinary apprenticeship into practical logic is not immune to objectifying discourse. Novices engaged in both institutional (e.g. school) and informal conversational interactions are recipients of error-corrections, assessments, reminders, calling out and other attention-getting moves, prompts, commands, suggestions, requests, threats, warnings, insults, shaming, teasing, praise, confirmation, rhetorical and test questions, common sense and other evidential particles, proverbs, idioms, gossip, moralizing narratives, reported speech, explanations, and other metapragmatic discourse.

These speech acts and activities may occur before, during, immediately following, or some later time after the behavior that warrants the attention of others. In the throes of playing a fast-moving computer game, for example, Swedish children rapidly assess one other's moves, alerting them to 'what is risky, novel or noteworthy in the game [...] socializing each other into gamers' (Aronsson, this volume). And, in the midst of musical performances, performers and audience may evaluate novices' improvisational forays and aesthetic standards through comments, nodding, and laughter (Duranti and Black, this volume).

In Japanese households, caregivers also routinely monitor children in the midst of social practices, demonstrating and prompting young children how to appropriately use the body and language to greet and show appreciation during the appropriate moment (Burdelski, this volume). Similarly, in a rural Kam Muang community in Thailand, adult kin and teachers instill respect by referring to themselves with the address term/respect level that the child should use and correcting speech considered disrespectful (Howard, this volume). In a different part of the world, mothers in a New York Hasidic Jewish community also keep a watchful eye over their young daughters' demeanors and deploy praising, prompting, rote repetition, and ordering to apprentice them into 'a gendered ethical subjectivity' that includes delayed gratification, modesty, prayer, and acceptance of authority (Fader, this volume).

After a transgression has occurred, Taiwanese and South Korean caregivers and teachers frequently shame children to get them to reflect upon their transgression and its moral consequences (Lo and Fung, this volume). Sometimes entire narratives of a child's shameful actions are recounted in front of others, who are invited to join in explicit and elaborated shaming practices. The robust practice of using narrative to challenge children's behaviors is also common in working-class urban Euro-American households (Miller, Koven, and Lin, this volume). Yet, the endpoint is not so much to instill respect as to encourage the children to defend themselves against others, as part of developing the moral quality of 'hard individualism' (Kusserow 2004). In these and other communities, children are drawn into narrative interactions that problematize and give advice about life experiences (Ochs and Capps 2001). In some communities, narrative is used among peers to the same end of pointing out transgressions. As noted by Goodwin and Kyratzis (this volume), peers may use gossip and hypothetical and other kinds of narratives to 'police the local social landscape and make evaluative commentary to one another.'

Language Socialization and Speech Communities

Children's linguistic and social competence has been viewed as a dynamic system of development, but, in light of the social and cultural heterogeneity that prevails across the world's communities, language socialization research holds that (1) languages and communities are themselves also undergoing transformation, (2) children's linguistic and cultural production is influenced by this transformation, and (3) children themselves contribute to this transformation.

Given that most communities are characterized by heterogeneity of linguistic and cultural ideologies and practices, the linguistic and cultural lives of many children and adults lie in 'zones of contact' (Pratt 1991) between social and linguistic groups, which may be stable at times or fluid, leading to language shift, loss, and change. Arguing against utopian and idealized conceptions of unified speech communities with shared codes, conversational sequence preferences, and cooperative maxims, Pratt (1996: 6) presents contact zones as

> social and cultural formations [that] enter a long term, often permanent state of crisis that cannot be resolved by either the conqueror or the conquered. Rather the relationships of conquered/conqueror, invaded/invader, past/present, and before/after become the medium out of which culture, language, society and consciousness get constructed. That constructing . . . involves continuous negotiation among radically heterogenous groups whose separate historical trajectories have come to intersect; among radically heterogenous systems of meaning that have been brought into contact by the encounter; and within relations of radical inequality enforced by violence.

When Schieffelin entered the Bosavi (Kaluli) community in the 1970s to document language acquisition and socialization, she knew that the social and communicative practices she observed had been in place for at least twenty years before her arrival (Schieffelin 1990). But the 1970s ushered in a very dramatic change as a result of intensive missionization, which is one of the oldest and most pervasive language socializing institutions. Mission workers used translations to socialize Bosavi people into and through new genres such as sermons and literacy skills to read the Bible and other texts (Schieffelin 1996, 2000). Awkward translations cobbled from semantically distant Bosavi words attempted to codify and thereby impose ways of thinking and communicating that were indigenously unfamiliar and inappropriate (Schieffelin 2007). The power of the mission as a world-wide institution negotiated with the power of local institutions and meaning systems, with uneven consequences.

Postcolonial societies create sites of language shift, with language socialization interactions involving young children as the ground zero of linguistic transformation. Paugh (this volume), for example, demonstrates how the diminishing status of the Afro-French Creole in relation to English in Dominica (West Indies) is linked to a language socialization condition in which caregivers privilege English as the language of respect and discourage children from using the Creole, which is deemed vulgar. Garrett (this volume) proposes that micro-processual changes evident in language socialization practices 'may be, in some cases, one of the most important mechanisms of language shift.' His study of language socialization on the Caribbean island of St. Lucia ties the loss of Kwéyòl in favor of English among children to home and school socialization practices that position English as vital and Kwéyòl as inevitably acquired, which turns out not to be the case. While adults use Kwéyòl to preverbal infants, they insist that they switch to English once they begin to speak. Similar micro-processes of language socialization impact the vitality of the vernacular Kam Muang in Northern Thailand, in that village children are told to speak Thai to address their non-Muang classroom teachers and classmates as a sign of respect (Howard, this volume). Alternatively, Nonaka's analysis of a spontaneous sign language used in Ban Khor, Northern Thailand (this volume) and Friedman's study of the revitalization of Ukrainian (this volume) emphasize that continuation of local languages may be fueled through language socialization ideologies and practices that widely expose children to these codes and encourage their acquisition. Nonaka's study also reveals how government policies that may appear benevolent in fact undermine and endanger the robustness of such sign languages.

Immigration also portends zones of contact wherein children and youths become at once agents and targets of language socialization. As noted by Baquedano-López and Mangual Figueroa (this volume), the study of the language socialization of young immigrants entails 'processes and practices of continuity, identification, discontinuity, and dis-identification' as part of the experience of immigration. Violence comes in many guises for these children and youths, especially language practices by native-speaking peers to establish social barriers between 'them' and 'us.' García-Sánchez's study (this volume) of the exclusion of Moroccan immigrant children in Spain is a case in point. Spanish classmates used an array of embodied language practices to directly or indirectly negatively sanction and marginalize their Moroccan-born peers. On the agentive side, these and other immigrant children are themselves language socializers when they act as language and culture brokers for adults in their family and community, mediating encounters in medical, educational, and state institutions (Orellana 2008; Zentella 1997). Moreover, immigrant children can draw upon linguistic and cultural resources from their homeland and host country to improvise genres that build their hybrid identities (Baquedano-López and Mangual Figueroa, this volume). In addition to ethnic-minority children, children of fundamentalist religious groups and children who live in relative poverty may be monitored and corrected by inside members, who judge certain behaviors to be out of line with community expectations (Baquedano-López and Mangual Figueroa, this volume; Fader, this volume; García-Sánchez, this volume).

The field of linguistic anthropology abounds with studies of language forms that index and evoke social meanings, and language socialization studies evidence how novices are drawn into these meanings over the life course. As noted, the acquisition of languages is simultaneously coupled with language socialization practices that construct novices as certain kinds of situationally organized persons, with certain emotions, moral understandings, and beliefs, who engage in certain kinds of social and cognitive activities. Nowhere is this potential of language socialization more evident than in the worlds made desirable and to varying extents accessible through second language socialization (Duff, this volume). Second languages may, for example, usher in alternative subjectivities wherein interlocutors can revision their gendered self-construction and can engage in informal social relationships appropriate to certain second language situations. A twist in the interface of language learning and socialization into identity construction is the phenomenon of heritage language socialization, in which learners are expected to use the heritage code that displays them as suitable moral persons as envisioned by an idealized 'heritage culture' (He, this volume; Lo and Fung, this volume). Heritage and second language learners, like many caught in zones of contact, however, often manage multiple, morally conflicting selves and loyalties.

Conclusion

In summary, language socialization research examines the semiotically mediated affordances of novices' engagement with culture-building webs of meaning and repertoires of social practice throughout the life cycle. Language socialization also subscribes to the idea that a person may be an expert in one situation but a novice in another. Researchers view communicative practices involving novices as deeply sociocultural, in that:

*   novices are socially defined and positioned as certain kinds of members;
*   conversation and other discourse genres and practices are embedded in and constitutive of larger social conditions;
*   semiotic forms are complex social tools that are situationally and culturally implicative;
*   codes are parts of repertoires and morally weighted;
*   learning and development are influenced by local theories of how knowledge, maturity, and wellbeing are attained.

The Handbook of Language Socialization presents cross-cultural research on each of these themes. It captures children's and other novices' involvement in social life and cultural sense-making and the language socialization practices and frameworks that mediate their path to competence.

This volume is the product of a scholarly community that has grown through the kind of collaborative language socializing practices we have observed in our field sites. Scholars have drawn from one another's research to co-produce knowledge, allowing it to be transformed by a host of influences and ultimately to have a generative intellectual life of its own. When we returned from our respective fieldwork in Papua New Guinea and Western Samoa and began to draft 'Language acquisition and socialization: Three developmental stories' (Ochs and Schieffelin 1984), we considered the study of language socialization to be a germinal project. The collection of studies herein realizes the flourishing of this vision, with endeavors that have taken the field in creative directions.

NOTES

1   These quotes are taken from http://www.babyoffice.com, but *Bébé Sounds Prenatal Talker* is available on numerous websites.

2   Studies indicate that, as they mature, fetuses become attuned to the mother's voice and language (DeCasper and Fifer 1980). At 27 weeks the fetus responds sporadically to low-frequency tones and speech and requires high levels of auditory stimulation. Reliability increases as the fetus reaches 35 weeks (Lasky and Williams 2005).

REFERENCES

Aronsson, K. and Cederborg, A.-C. (1996) Coming of age in family therapy talk: Perspective setting in multiparty problem formulations. *Discourse Processes* 21: 191–212.

Baquedano-López, P. (2001) Creating social identities through *doctrina* narratives. In A. Duranti (ed.), *Linguistic Anthropology: A Reader*. 343–58. Oxford: Blackwell.

Bates, E., Camaioni, L., and Volterra, V. (1979) The acquisition of performatives prior to speech. In E. Ochs and B. B. Schieffelin (eds.), *Developmental Pragmatics*. 111–31. New York: Academic Press.

Bentham, J. (1791) *Panopticon*. London: T. Payne.

Boas, F. (1911) Introduction. In *Handbook of American Indian Languages*. Vol. BAE–B 40, P. I. Washington, DC: Smithsonian Institution.

Boas, F. (2004 [1932]) *Anthropology and Modern Life*. New Brunswick, NJ: Transaction Publishers.

Bourdieu, P. (1979) *Distinction*. Paris: Éditions de Minuit.

Bourdieu, P. and Passeron, J. C. (1990 [1977]) *Reproduction in Education, Society and Culture*. London: Sage.

Cole, M. (1996) *Cultural Psychology: A Once and Future Discipline*. Cambridge, MA: Harvard University Press.

DeCasper, A. J. and Fifer, W. P. (1980) Of human bonding: Newborns prefer their mothers' voices. *Science* 208: 1174–6.

de León, L. (1998) The emergent participant: Interactive patterns in the socialization of Tzotzil (Mayan) infants. *Journal of Linguistic Anthropology* 8(2): 131–61.

Duff, P. and Hornberger, N. (eds.) (2008) *Encyclopedia of Language and Education, Vol. 8: Language Socialization*. 2nd ed. New York: Springer.

Duranti, A. (1997) *Linguistic Anthropology*. Cambridge: Cambridge University Press.

Duranti, A. (2009) The relevance of Husserl's theory to language socialization. *Journal of Linguistic Anthropology* 19(2): 205–26.

Enfield, N. and Levinson, S. C. (eds.) (2006) *Roots of Human Sociality: Culture, Cognition, and Interaction*. Oxford: Berg.

Fader, A. (2009) *Mitzvah Girls: Bringing Up the Next Generation of Hasidic Jews in Brooklyn*. Princeton, NJ: Princeton University Press.

Foucault, M. (1979) *Discipline and Punish: The Birth of the Prison*. New York: Random House.

Garfinkel, H. (1967) *Studies in Ethnomethodology*. Englewood Cliffs, NJ: Prentice-Hall.

Garrett, P. B. and Baquedano-López, P. (2002) Language socialization: Reproduction and continuity, transformation and change. *Annual Review of Anthropology* 31: 339–61.

Geertz, C. (1973) Thick description: Toward an interpretive theory of culture. In *The Interpretation of Cultures*. 1–30. New York: Basic Books.

Goodwin, M. H. (2006) *The Hidden Life of Girls: Games of Stance, Status, and Exclusion*. Oxford: Blackwell.

Goodwin, C. (1996) Transparent vision. In E. Ochs, E. A. Schegloff, and S. Thompson (eds.), *Interaction and Grammar*. 370–404. Cambridge: Cambridge University Press.

Gumperz, J. J. and Hymes, D. (1964) The ethnography of communication. *American Anthropologist* 66(6) (special issue) 137–53.

Harkness, S. and Super, C. M. (eds.) (1996) *Parents' Cultural Belief Systems: Their Origins, Expressions, and Consequences.* New York: Guilford Press.

He, A. (2003) Linguistic anthropology and language socialization. In S. Wortham and B. Rymes (eds.), *Linguistic Anthropology of Education.* 93–119. Westport, CT: Praeger.

Heath, S. B. (1983) *Ways with Words: Language, Life and Work in Communities and Classrooms.* Cambridge: Cambridge University Press.

Heath, S. B. (2008) Language socialization in the learning communities of adolescents. In P. Duff and N. Hornberger (eds.), *Encyclopedia of Language and Education, Vol. 8: Language Socialization.* 2nd ed. 217–30. New York: Springer.

Herskovits, M. J. (1952) *Man and His Works.* New York: Knopf.

Kulick, D. (1992) *Language Shift and Cultural Reproduction: Socialization, Self, and Syncretism in a Papua New Guinean Village.* Cambridge: Cambridge University Press.

Kulick, D. and Schieffelin, B. B. (2004) Language socialization. In A. Duranti (ed.), *A Companion to Linguistic Anthropology.* 349–68. Malden, MA: Blackwell.

Kusserow, A. (2004) *American Individualisms: Child Rearing and Social Class in Three Neighborhoods.* New York: Palgrave.

Lasky, R. E. and Williams, A. L. (2005) The development of the auditory system from conception to term. *NeoReviews* 6: 141–52.

Lave, J. and Wenger, E. (1991) *Situated Learning: Legitimate Peripheral Participation.* Cambridge: Cambridge University Press.

Malinowski, B. (1935) *Coral Gardens and Their Magic.* New York: Dover.

Mandelbaum, D. G. (ed.) (1958) *Selected Writings of Edward Sapir in Language, Culture, and Personality.* Berkeley, CA: University of California Press.

Mead, M. (1928) *Coming of Age in Samoa.* New York: William Morrow.

Mead, M. (2001 [1950]) The school in American culture. *Society* 39(1): 54–62.

Mehan, H. (1996) The construction of an LD student: A case study in the politics of representation. In M. Silverstein and G. Urban (eds.), *Natural Histories of Discourse.* 253–76. Chicago, IL: University of Chicago Press.

Mertz, E. (2007) *The Language of Law School.* New York: Oxford University Press.

Michaels, S. (1981) 'Sharing time': Children's narrative styles and differential access to literacy. *Language in Society* 10: 423–42.

Moore, L. (2006) Learning by heart in Qur'anic and public schools in northern Cameroon. *Social Analysis: The International Journal of Cultural and Social Practice* 50(3): 109–26.

Ochs, E. (1990) Indexicality and socialization. In J. W. Stigler, R. Shweder, and G. Herdt (eds.), *Cultural Psychology: Essays on Comparative Human Development.* 287–308. Cambridge: Cambridge University Press.

Ochs, E. (1988) *Culture and Language Development: Language Acquisition and Language Socialization in a Samoan Village.* Cambridge: Cambridge University Press.

Ochs, E. (1996) Linguistic resources for socializing humanity. In J. J. Gumperz and S. C. Levinson (eds.), *Rethinking Linguistic Relativity.* 407–37. Cambridge: Cambridge University Press.

Ochs, E. and Capps, L. (2001) *Living Narrative: Creating Lives in Everyday Storytelling.* Cambridge, MA: Harvard University Press.

Ochs, E. and Schieffelin, B. B. (eds.) (1979) *Developmental Pragmatics*. New York: Academic Press.

Ochs, E. and Schieffelin, B. B. (1984) Language acquisition and socialization: Three developmental stories. In R. A. Shweder and R. A. LeVine (eds.), *Culture Theory: Essays on Mind, Self, and Emotion*. 276–320. Cambridge: Cambridge University Press.

Ochs, E. and Schieffelin, B. B. (1995) The impact of language socialization on grammatical development. In P. Fletcher and B. MacWhinney (eds.), *The Handbook of Child Language*. 73–94. Oxford: Blackwell.

Ochs, E. and Schieffelin, B. B. (2008) Language socialization: An historical overview. In P. Duff and N. Hornberger (eds.), *Encyclopedia of Language and Education, Vol. 8: Language Socialization*. 2nd ed. 3–15. New York: Springer.

Ochs, E., Solomon, O., and Sterponi, L. (2005) Limitations and transformations of habitus in child-directed communication. *Discourse Studies* 7(4–5): 547–83.

Ochs, E. and Taylor, C. (1992) Science at dinner. In C. Kramsch (ed.), *Text and Context: Cross-disciplinary Perspectives on Language Study*. 29–45. Lexington, MA: D. C. Heath.

Orellana, M. (2008) *Translating Childhoods: Immigrant Youth, Language, and Culture*. New Brunswick, NJ: Rutgers University Press.

Ortner, S. B. (1997) Introduction. In S. B. Ortner (ed.), *The Fate of 'Culture': Geertz and Beyond*. 1–13. Berkeley, CA: University of California Press.

Parsons, T. and Bales, R. F. (1956) *Family: Socialization and Interaction Process*. London: Routledge and Kegan Paul.

Peirce, C. (1931–58) *Collected Papers*. Cambridge, MA: Harvard University Press.

Philips, S. U. (1982) The language socialization of lawyers: Acquiring the cant. In G. Spindler (ed.), *Doing the Ethnography of Schooling*. 176–209. New York: Holt, Rinehart and Winston.

Pontecorvo, C., Fasulo, A., and Sterponi, L. (2001) Mutual apprentices: The making of parenthood and childhood in family dinner conversation. *Human Development* 44: 340–61.

Pratt, M. L. (1991) *Arts of the Contact Zone*. *Profession* 91: 33–40. Modern Language Association.

Pratt, M. L. (1996) Apocalypse in the Andes: Contact zones and the struggle for interpretive power. In *Encuentros, Vol. 15*. Inter-American Development Bank.

Prout, A. and James, A. (eds.) (1997) *Constructing and Reconstructing Childhood: Contemporary Issues in the Sociological Study of Childhood*. London: Routledge Falmer.

Richerson, P. J. and Boyd, R. (2004) *Not by Genes Alone: How Culture Transformed Human Evolution*. Chicago, IL: University of Chicago Press.

Riley, K. C. (2008) *Language socialization*. In B. Spolsky and F. M. Hult (eds.), *Handbook of Educational Linguistics*. 398–410. Malden, MA: Blackwell.

Rogoff, B. (1990) *Apprenticeship in Thinking*. New York: Oxford University Press.

Rogoff, B. (2003) *The Cultural Nature of Human Development*. Oxford: Oxford University Press.

Rogoff, B., Paradise, R., Arauz, R.M., Correa-Chávez, M., and Angelillo, C. (2003) Firsthand learning through intent participation. *Annual Review of Psychology* 54: 175–203.

Sapir, E. (1924) Culture, genuine and spurious. *Journal of Sociology* 29: 401–29.

Sapir, E. (1929) The unconscious patterning of behavior in society. In E. S. Dummer (ed.), *The Unconscious: A Symposium*. 114–42. New York: Knopf.

Sapir, E. (1933/1958) Language. In D. Mandelbaum (ed.), *Selected Writings of Edward Sapir in Language, Culture, and Personality*. 7–32. Berkeley, CA: University of California Press.

Schegloff, E. A. (1986) The routine as achievement. *Human Studies* 9: 111–51.

Schieffelin, B. B. (1990) *The Give and Take of Everyday Life: Language Socialization of Kaluli Children*. Cambridge: Cambridge University Press.

Schieffelin, B. B. (1996) Creating evidence: Making sense of written words in Bosavi. In E. Ochs, E. A. Schegloff, and S. A. Thompson (eds.), *Interaction and Grammar*. 435–60. Cambridge: Cambridge University Press.

Schieffelin, B. B. (2000) Introducing Kaluli literacy: A chronology of influences. In P. Kroskrity (ed.), *Regimes of Language*. 293–327. Santa Fe, NM: School of American Research.

Schieffelin, B. B. (2007) Found in translating: Reflexive language across time and texts. In M. Makihara and B. B. Schieffelin (eds.), *Consequences of Contact: Language Ideologies and Sociocultural Transformations in Pacific Societies*. 140–65. New York: Oxford University Press.

Schieffelin, B. B. and Ochs, E. (eds.) (1986a) *Language Socialization Across Cultures*. New York: Cambridge University Press.

Schieffelin, B. B. and Ochs, E. (1986b) Language socialization. *Annual Review of Anthropology* 15: 163–91.

Schieffelin, B. B. and Ochs, E. (1996) The microgenesis of competence: Methodology in language socialization. In D. Slobin, J. Gerhardt, A. Kyratzis, and J. Guo (eds.), *Social Interaction, Social Context and Language: Essays in Honor of Sue Ervin-Tripp*. 251–86. Hillsdale, NJ: Lawrence Erlbaum.

Schieffelin, B. B., Woolard, K., and Kroskrity, P. (eds.) (1998) *Language Ideologies: Practice and Theory*. New York: Oxford University Press.

Shweder, R. A., Mahapatra, M. and Miller, J. G. (1987) Culture and moral development. In J. Kagan and S. Lamb (eds.), *The Emergence of Morality in Young Children*. 1–82. Chicago, IL: University of Chicago Press.

Silverstein, M. (1996) Indexical order and the dialectics of sociolinguistic life. In R. Ide, R. Parker, and Y. Sunaoshi (eds.), *Third Annual Symposium About Language and Society (SALSA)*. 266–95. Department of Linguistics, University of Texas, Austin, TX.

Slobin, D. I. (ed.) (1967) *A Field Manual for Cross-Cultural Study of the Acquisition of Communicative Competence*. Language Behavior Research Laboratory, University of California: Berkeley, CA.

Tomasello, M., Carpenter, M., Call, J., Behne, T., and Moll, H. (2005) Understanding and sharing intentions: The origins of cultural cognition. *Behavioral and Brain Sciences* 28: 675–735.

Vygotsky, L. (1986) *Thought and Language*. A. Kozulin, transl. Cambridge, MA: MIT Press.

Weisner, T. (2002) Ecocultural understanding of children's developmental pathways. *Human Development* 45(4): 275–81.

Whiting, B. B. and Edwards, C. P. (1988) *Children of Different Worlds: The Formation of Social Behavior*. Cambridge, MA: Harvard University Press.

Whiting, B. B. and Whiting, J. M. W. (1975) *Children of Six Cultures: A Psycho-Cultural Analysis*. Cambridge, MA: Harvard University Press.

Wittgenstein, L. (1958) *Philosophical Investigations*. 2nd ed. G. E. M. Anscombe, transl. Oxford: Blackwell.

Wortham, S. (2005) Socialization beyond the speech event. *Journal of Linguistic Anthropology* 15(1): 95–112.

Zentella, A. C. (1997) *Growing Up Bilingual: Puerto Rican Children in New York*. Oxford: Blackwell.

Zentella, A. C. (ed.) (2005) *Building on Strength: Language and Literacy in Latino Families and Communities*. New York: Teachers College Press.

Part I   Interactional Foundations

From the moment a child is born, he or she enters a social and linguistic world, one that is culturally organized and shaped by local ideas about personhood, sociality, and communication. The lives of infants everywhere may seem relatively circumscribed, and caregiving practices in the first two years of life might appear to be universal due to biological circumstances. There is, however, significant cultural variation in the everyday activities of caregivers and infants and these variations are relevant to language socialization, both individually and collectively, in any given community. People and things, theories and practices, which are explicitly and/or tacitly embedded in time and place, contribute to the emerging social and communicative competencies of the infant, as well as to the interactive moves of caregivers and others that constitute this dynamic set of interactions, which in turn provides the foundations for engagement and participation.

The chapters in Part I direct our attention to the social worlds of prelinguistic infants and caregivers, asking what activities and practices are relevant, directly and indirectly, to the development of language and communication skills more broadly. What are the significant differences and similarities, not only in terms of forms but also of functions, meanings, and co-occurrence with other practices? To address these questions, Brown, Takada, and de León take comparative, cross-cultural perspectives. Using descriptive and theoretical material drawn primarily from middle-class, Euro-American studies of psychological and social development and caregiver interaction, they evaluate comparable types of social and verbal activities, detailing significant patterns and preferences based on their ethnographic studies. All highlight the importance of investigating the antecedents of language and sociality, identifying several that are essential to human interaction: socialization into and through joint attention using vocal, verbal, and nonverbal means; the cultural recognition and display of attention with infants; and the establishment of subjectivities and intersubjectivity. They point out the importance of looking at the frequency, sequencing, and coordination of both

The Handbook of Language Socialization, First Edition. Edited by Alessandro Duranti, Elinor Ochs, and Bambi B. Schieffelin.
© 2014 John Wiley & Sons, Ltd. Published 2014 by John Wiley & Sons, Ltd.

vocal and nonvocal interactional moves, demonstrating that they are socially embedded and infused with cultural significance.

The chapters in Part I also demonstrate that the early phase of caregiver–infant interaction requires particular modes of inquiry that are sensitive to methodological and interpretive issues that arise when investigating prelinguistic communicative activities. They offer critical frameworks that deploy multimodal forms of data collection and analysis to adequately consider comparisons across contexts, persons, communities, and histories that are relevant for studying patterns and differences and for evaluating what the patterns mean, and what difference these differences make, developmentally and culturally. What patterns or preferences hold across groups, and which ones might offer insights into the complex dynamic of cognitive, biological, and social factors? How do we as scholars balance our own theories with those of the people we are trying to understand? How important is the concept of developmental milestones? What role do attitudes toward precocity play in development? What are the implications for privileging verbal over motor development? These are some of the culturally based questions raised and responded to in these chapters.

Brown's 'The Cultural Organization of Attention,' (Chapter 2) evaluates possible universal developmental prerequisites for one of language's main functions: achieving referential communication. Referentiality presupposes the development of joint attention with a caregiver over a third object or event (Tomasello et al.'s 'referential triangle' (2005)) and the development of social referencing, when infants track the gaze of others, obtaining information about how to act on objects as well as how to direct others to their objects of interest through pointing and other indicative gestures. Highlighting the interactional dimensions of the organization of attention, Brown integrates a broad range of findings drawn from experimental studies as well as more naturalistic cross-cultural investigations. While pointing plays a significant role in achieving referential communication and is linked to labeling, interpretative difficulties remain, such as ascertaining prelinguistic infants' intentional behaviors. The claim that pointing is universal is further complicated by the fact that not all societies rely on pointing to direct attention to the extent documented in European and American contexts. Household organization and size may be factors in the patterning and deployment of joint attention. Infants growing up in large households where cultural preferences orient them toward facing and observing those around them become competent in sustaining multiple foci of attention, rather than the type of sustained joint attention patterns documented in households that privilege dyadic arrangements of caregiver and child.

Drawing on her comparative research among Tenejapa Tzeltal (Mexico) and Rossel Islanders (Papua New Guinea), Brown addresses a critical question raised by previous scholarship: does interactional variability due to cultural differences influence the developmental timeline of the referential triangle? She investigated socialization for communication in the 9–15-month period, in particular gaze following, index-finger point following and production, and the integration of gaze and vocalization with pointing to evaluate evidence for the 'nine-month revolution' (when the infant is said to demonstrate joint attention). Using mixed methodologies, both quantitative and qualitative, she analyzed videotaped recordings to determine infants' integration of gaze and pointing. Brown concludes that, while Tenejapa and Rossel Island communities share many characteristics – they are traditionalist, subsistence-based, small-scale, kin-based, rural, and use their vernacular languages in predominantly multiparty interactions – interactional style with infants is not one of them.

In contrast to the highly interactive spaces and caregivers' responsive verbal style that shapes the activities of Rossel Island infants, Tzeltal caregivers restrict the activities of infants and direct few responses to their preverbal vocalizations. Despite significant differences in the frequency of particular types of behavior sequences, caregivers in both communities nonetheless use canonical pointing with infants and at least some 9–15-month-olds follow others' points/gestures and sometimes initiate joint attention this way. Joint-attention episodes are more frequent, of longer duration, and more affectively marked in the Rossel Island community. In both communities, however, pointing is not exclusively used to achieve joint attention, nor do caregivers label the object of attention as is documented in postindustrial societies. Brown suggests that, despite the differences in interactional styles, there is no evidence that the highly active style of Rossel caregivers and infants supports earlier acquisition of the referential triangle compared to Tzeltal infants. Nor do the interactional and affective differences have a 'radical' effect on the emergence of pointing. Drawing on comparative studies, Brown concludes that developmental milestones are not notably affected by these differences in early interaction, nor do they seem to be affected by the absence of Baby Talk. Returning to the question of universals in interaction with infants, Brown proposes that gestural indicating, not just index-finger pointing, may be a candidate, but groups vary in terms of what may be the object of attention, and that labeling practices culturally vary as well.

Takada's 'Preverbal Infant–Caregiver Interaction,' (Chapter 3) also highlights processes through which infants acquire local cultural styles of joint attention. Based on ethnographic field research among several groups of San in Botswana (Southern Africa), Takada draws on video-recorded interactions of early nursing and socializing activities and interviews demonstrating the importance of conjoining micro-analyses of infant–caregiver bodily practices with their reported cultural significance. Two themes organize the chapter: the cultural formation of reciprocal accommodation to contingent infant behaviors, and the importance of musicality and rhythmicity coordinating early vocal and nonverbal communication in this community. Attending to 'micro-habitats' and 'material niches,' Takada closely observes the positioning of both mother and infant as well as the sequencing of their nonverbal behaviors. Takada outlines a trajectory of infants' developing coordination and behavioral and cognitive resources (including imitation), which eventually result in shared attention over objects and the development of intentionality, which is key to cultural learning.

Takada emphasizes the importance of reciprocal involvement, turn-taking, and other contingent responses for language socialization, locating their beginnings in San early nursing patterns. San mothers maintain very close contact with infants and nurse them on demand, even while simultaneously carrying out domestic tasks or socializing with others. Mothers also nurse infants to soothe them and do not gaze at them during this time. Assessing the assertion that turn-taking between sucking and jiggling is a fundamental, universal feature of mother–infant interaction, Takada finds that, while this is the case in Japan and the United States, it is rare among San. Mothers' soothing musical, verbal, and vocal practices with their newborns accompany holding the infant upright to encourage reflex walking or jumping movements. Even before the demonstration of intentional behaviors, the San infant is constituted as a participant. These practices also assist infants' developing coordination of movement and sound, a culturally valued skill. Older infants are rewarded for demonstrating skill in timing physical moves and vocalizations with others, which requires a sociocentric orientation. As Takada's scholarship suggests, these are very promising and integrative directions for cross-cultural comparison.

De León's 'Multiparty Participation Frameworks,' (Chapter 4) argues that participation frameworks and their interactional consequences are critical to understanding the organization of infants' communicative development, and thus must be carefully considered in order to understand children's language socialization. The participant role as overhearer in particular is significant for preverbal children in that it allows infants to develop participatory competence without necessarily being focal addressees. This participation framework augments the assumed centrality of the speaker–hearer (caregiver–infant) model of Euro-American middle-class households and foregrounds the ways in which critical skills such as observation, attention, and inference are enabled long before infants start using language.

De León's longitudinal linguistic and anthropological research in a Mayan community in Zinacantan (Chiapas, Mexico) conceptualizes the infant learner as adept at monitoring the verbal environment, a skill heightened in communities that do not prioritize dyadic infant–caregiver exchanges. Participant frameworks include not only face-to-face but also nested, side-by-side, and L alignments, all of which afford infants different types of social information. Zinacantecan families prefer configurations (nested, side-by-side, and L alignments) that position the infant for triadic interactions, similarly to numerous non-Western societies. In addition, while Mayan Zinacantec caregivers do not engage in proto-conversations with infants, they attribute intention to infants' gestures and vocalization. Moreover, caregivers are highly attuned to infants' physical needs, and these are glossed with explicit metapragmatic verbs ('she says'). Such interpretive actions, de León argues, help socialize the infant in her emergent participatory status as a quoted proto-speaker in triadic exchanges. As infants mature, local corporeal alignments are integral to the development of the referential triangle, (the 'nine-month revolution'), echoing a theme posed in Brown's chapter. Although the positioning of the infant as an addressee is thought to be central to developmental achievement, adults in Mayan communities minimally talk to nonverbal children. Young children's gestures and vocalizations are taken as indications of their interest in moving from peripheral to focal participation.

These chapters highlight the interactional foundations of communicative development, emphasizing the theoretical and methodological requirements for understanding the ways in which attention is socially organized, enabled, recognized, and coordinated in order to achieve joint attention, which is critical for social and linguistic development. The ways in which infants and young children 'learn how to learn' (Bateson 1972) depend on local theories of personhood, agency, teaching, and learning, as well as the social meanings and participation structures for participation in each community. As such, these constructs lay the groundwork for our understanding of processes of language socialization through the life cycle. The chapters in Part I provide interactionally grounded ethnographic and linguistic accounts for further generating, refining, comparing, and evaluating the variation as well as the similarities found in communicative activities and their consequences across human societies.

REFERENCES

Bateson, G. (1972) *Steps to an Ecology of Mind*. New York: Balantine Books.

Tomasello, M., Carpenter, M. Call, J. Behne, T., and Moll, H. (2005) Understanding and sharing intentions: The origins of cultural cognition. *Behavioral and Brain Sciences* 28: 675–91.

2   The Cultural Organization of Attention

PENELOPE BROWN

Introduction

Language socialization is the process of socialization into language through language and its use in interaction (Schieffelin and Ochs 1986). Research in language socialization focuses on particular interactional practices in different cultural settings, asking how these proceed in situated interaction and how they influence the development of children's communicative skills and their ability to think, feel, and interact like others in their social world. Its unique contribution is the combination of detailed analysis of naturally occurring interactions and ethnographically sensitive interpretations of the presuppositions and understandings underpinning language practices that shape the child's understanding of taken-for-granted cultural truths.

Despite the proliferation of research in the language socialization paradigm over the last 30 years, relatively little has focused on interaction with prelinguistic infants. Yet, how new social members are drawn into the interactional practices of their society during their first year and a half of life is critical to understanding the biological bases, learning, and cross-cultural variability of social interaction as well as the role of culture more broadly in children's social-cognitive and language development (see also de León, this volume; Takada, this volume).

Language use rests on a bedrock of uniquely human competencies in social interaction, which unfold during the first year of life (Clark 2001). Humans appear to be biologically preprogrammed for collaborative interactional abilities in a number of respects, which collectively Levinson (2006) has dubbed the 'interactional engine.' These abilities relate to cooperation, intentionality, reading others' minds, coordinating attention, and establishing common ground (Clark 1996; Tomasello 2008). Human communication builds on these structures for collaborating, both evolutionarily and ontogenetically (Tomasello 2008).

The Handbook of Language Socialization, First Edition. Edited by Alessandro Duranti, Elinor Ochs, and Bambi B. Schieffelin.

However, the evidence for universal underpinnings of interaction has to be reconciled with evidence for cultural specificity in interactional patterns, both in adult interaction and infant–caregiver interaction. This includes cultural differences in adult gaze patterns, conversational feedback mechanisms, and even in pointing behavior (e.g. Brown and Levinson 2005; Kita 2003, 2009; Rossano, Brown, and Levinson 2009). The anthropological and cross-cultural psychological literature on childhood provides abundant evidence for cultural variation in how infants are handled and socially engaged in their first year. Both the amount of interaction with infants and the features of the prelinguistic situation vary radically depending on social organization, household composition, socioeconomic activities of mothers and other caregivers, parental beliefs and cultural models, and ecological conditions – for example, mortality. These conditions influence the details of everyday experience for infants, from the physical arrangements of their handling (swaddling, feeding, degree of physical freedom) to the amount and nature of interactiveness: the positioning of babies as interlocutors whose 'utterances' are intentional communications, the amount of eye contact, turn-taking, and the kinds of participation structures into which an infant is drawn (de León 1998; see also de León, this volume). Interactional patterns are also influenced by adult beliefs about childhood and child rearing, including the contrast between child-centered versus situation-centered societies (Ochs and Schieffelin 1984) and, analogously, Lancy's (2008) distinction between gerontocracy (child-supported) and neontocracy (child-centered) societies.

Very little infancy research[1] has examined the contextualized sequential details of infant–caregiver interactions during the first year of life. Modern theories of infant development (e.g. Bruner 1975a, 1975b, 1982; Elman et al. 1996; Masataka 2003b; Tomasello 1999, 2008) emphasize the influence of particular interactional practices in the child's developing communicative skills, claiming that the child's entry into social understanding is grounded in communication with others and that the extent and nature of social interaction a child experiences influence the development of his or her social understanding. But these theories have not taken sufficiently into account the implications of the fact that interactional practices with infants widely differ and are culturally shaped by beliefs about what infants need and what they can understand at different ages.

The current focus of infancy research on joint attention (see e.g. Moore and Dunham 1995) provides the basis for a set of predictions that can be fruitfully examined in cross-cultural interactional data. The critical age for coordinating attention in infancy – identified in the extensive developmental literature for infants in postindustrial societies – is between about 9 and 15 months, when major social-cognitive abilities emerge, including awareness of the other as an intentional agent and joint attention with a caregiver over a third object or event, referred to as the 'referential triangle' (Tomasello 1999). Around 12 months there is an important developmental milestone: babies look where adults are looking reliably, use adults as social reference points (gaze at them to check what to do in uncertain situations), act on objects like adults do, and actively direct adult attention through indicative gestures and pointing (Carpenter, Nagell, and Tomasello 1998). All of these are (putatively) essential prerequisites for coordinated interaction and later for learning language. The argument is that joint attention, arising out of social processes that are more basic than language, creates a base for referential communication.

We simply do not know, however, how culture-specific this story is. How is the interactional organization of joint attention socialized in infants in different cultures? The resources for drawing an interlocutor's attention everywhere include speech, gaze, body touching and postures, pointing gestures, and other actions, but it is well known that there are cross-cultural differences in adult deployment of these resources,[2] so can we assume that they are deployed in comparable ways with infants everywhere? To answer these questions we need a more qualitative and comparative approach, one that can provide evidence of the process through which infants come to be able to coordinate attention in interaction in different cultural settings.

This chapter reports on recent steps in that direction, focussing on the prelinguistic period (to about 15 months of age) and on one type of cultural practice, the interactional organization of attention and how it is socialized in prelinguistic infants. The following discussion first sketches the developmentalist picture of infant social-communicative development in the first year, based largely on experimental studies in Europe, the United States, and Japan. This culminates in the 'nine-month revolution' during which several sociocognitive abilities come together as the infant comes to share attention jointly with others, as evidenced in pointing. The next section surveys recent research on how the coming-into-joint-attention process plays out in different cultural settings. The final section reports the author's findings on gaze and pointing behavior in infant–caregiver interaction in two nonindustrial societies, one in Mexico and one in Papua New Guinea, with radically different infant–caregiver interaction patterns.

Joint attention in prelinguistic infants has come into prominence as a research topic in the last two decades. Of course, the socialization of attention was a feature in the classic language socialization ethnographies (Kulick 1992; Ochs 1988; Schieffelin 1990), focussing on children beyond infancy. The socialization of attention goes on well beyond this early period, to be sure, sometimes with significant long-term effects (cf. Kulick 1992).[3] But the focus in this chapter is the crucial developmental step around the end of the first year, when infants get an understanding of others as intentional agents who can direct their (the infant's) attention and whose attention can in turn be directed by themselves, so that they can jointly share communication about some specific object or event.

Joint Attention in Infant–Caregiver Interaction in the First 12 Months

The developmentalist perspective

Laboratory research aimed at understanding cognitive development and the cognitive prerequisites for language has shown that infants during their first year develop the ability to engage with others in joint attention. They do not start out with this ability. The picture based on research in postindustrial societies (mainly the United States, Europe, and Japan) is as follows: newborns spontaneously orient to human faces and imitate facial expressions, for example tongue protrusion (Meltzoff and Moore 1977); they are also sensitive to eye contact (Farroni et al. 2002). By two months they contingently respond to smiles and the gaze of an interlocutor (Bigelow and Rochat 2006; Murray and Trevarthen 1985). This disposition forms a basis for turn-taking: Masataka, for example, stresses the importance of sequentially dependent responding between Japanese caregivers and infants in social interaction, leading to conversational turn-taking as an early milestone, with coordination first of infants' suckling and mothers' jiggling behavior followed by coordination of vocalization and gaze (Masataka 2003b: 44). The details of mother–infant coordination have been shown to be culturally variable (Gratier 2003; Gratier and Trevarthan 2008), but it is generally accepted that some form of interactive coordination occurs (see also Takada, this volume). This interdependence relies on the mother's attribution of intentionality to the infant's vocalizations, and response contingency, features that are clearly evident in data of American and Japanese interactions with infants. In these contexts, the infant develops from spontaneously showing certain behaviors and expressive resources to exploiting these in interactive sequences as (s)he gains control over them while they are shaped in interactive routines with caregivers (Masataka 2003b). In these interactions, the adults credit the infant with social qualities and communicative intentions. This orientation, it is argued, is a crucial first step for the infant's development of intentional communication, and indeed for cultural variation in their communicative behavior (Masataka 2003b).

By four months, Japanese infants extend their index fingers (without, however, extending the whole arm). At this age these movements are related to exploring and self-regulation of attention, and the rate of doing this index finger extension correlates with infants' speech-like sounds. By five months, the infants share elaborate episodes of face-to-face engagement with their caregivers. These engagements suddenly become less frequent as the infant turns his or her attention from caregivers to objects. By six months the infant can follow the mother's gaze to an object if the object is in front of the infant and is the first object in sight as (s)he turns to look. Meanwhile, the development of intentional control over vocalization leads to babbling by about six to seven months.

It takes an infant several months to master the triadic relation of infant–caregiver–object communication. Pointing is seen as crucial for the development of referential communication, providing a nonverbal procedure for picking out a referent in the environment for oneself and another person to focus on (Masataka 2003b: 230–1; see also Bruner 1995). Interlocutors need to be in a context of joint attention in order to interpret gestures and other communicative acts. Establishing that an infant is jointly attending is not all that easy, and important evidence for common ground and mutual awareness of joint attention over a referent is the infant's 'gaze' from referent to interlocutor and back (Bates et al. 1979). The infant's gaze links together a referential act (pointing) and its meaning *for* an interlocutor ('now attend to THAT'). When infants can do this reliably, we can be sure that they have a referential understanding of the behavior of others and (in some sense) an understanding that others have minds and intentions like their own.

In sum, there is a developmental progression wherein babies become sensitive to an increasingly wide range of social signals between birth and nine months (Carpenter et al. 1998). From six to ten months babies show the beginning of clearly intentional behavior toward others. During the 9–15-month period they progress from sharing to following to actively directing another's attention. From 10 months on their first words start to develop. Around 12 months these early abilities come together in the developmental milestone that involves awareness of the other as an intentional agent and joint attention with a caregiver over a third object or event (the 'referential triangle'); that is, attending to the same thing but with awareness that each other is attending. Pointing is a clear indication of this achievement, including pointing for a range of different motives, not just imperatively ('I want that') but also declaratively ('Look! That's there'). Infants point to provide information for others, to point out new and absent referents (i.e. their pointing is *referential*), and to align and share attitudes (see e.g. Butterworth 2003; Carpenter et al. 1998; Liszkowski 2005, 2006; Liszkowski et al. 2004, 2009; Liszkowski, Carpenter, and Tomasello 2007, 2008; Masataka 2003a; Tomasello 1999; Tomasello et al. 2005; Tomasello, Carpenter, and Liszkowski 2007).

On this general picture developmentalists are in agreement, though there is much dispute over the details.[4] Masataka (2003b: 241–2) summarizes the culmination of this developmental path in pointing and its significance for language as follows:

> In order to comprehend the meaning of caregivers' acts of pointing appropriately, infants must coordinate their attention to both caregivers and objects and learn the communicative functions of referring or requesting. Otherwise, a singular focus would result in either interpersonal engagement (as infants attend to caregivers) or in severing the communicative channel (as infants attend to objects restrictively) . . . Only with the development of this ability do infants become able to understand the meaning of referential messages such as 'Look at this' and requests such as 'Give me that.' . . . infants begin to use gestures composed of manual movements and gaze patterns as well as speech-like vocalizations, to [express] communicative intentions such as requests for and reference to objects.

Cross-cultural developmental research in Africa has found that Yoruba infants (Trevarthen 1988) and infants of the !Kung San (Bakeman et al. 1990) follow the same developmental path. Masataka, however, suggests that, in societies or families where interlocutors do not point for infants, rather than an emphasis on referential speech it may be a more holistic kind of communication that promotes the child's entry into language – a clear prediction of possible cultural differences.[5]

Implications of these processes for language acquisition

The link to language is based on the idea that infant pointing is achieved by virtue of a particular response by the adult to the infant's pointing: *labelling*. Labelling the object being pointed at helps the infant to learn the word, but more impor-tantly it leads to the understanding that others have communicative intentions (Masataka 2003b). A number of studies provide evidence that joint attention inter-actions do facilitate language learning (e.g. Carpenter et al. 1998; Tomasello and Farrar 1986; Tomasello and Todd 1983), showing clear links between joint attention and early vocabulary size, production of gestures, and length of conversations. This work rests on the early findings of Bruner and his colleagues, who argued that sociocommunicative routines scaffold the child's early language by providing him/her with an interpretable referential context via joint attention routines that help him/her to identify the adult's attentional focus and hence the intended referent (Bruner 1975a, 1975b, 1982, 1995; Ninio and Bruner 1978; see also Keenan and Schieffelin 1976). Brooks and Meltzoff (2008) also found a connection between infant gaze following and pointing and the infants' subsequent vocabulary devel-opment at age two. Childers, Vaughan, and Burquest (2007) reported on research in a rural community in Nigeria that showed that joint attention behavior among one-to-two-and-a-half-year-olds related to the development of both nouns and verbs, as reported by parents from a Child Developmental Index (CDI) checklist. In contrast, Masataka (2003b) found that the acquisition of the first five words among Japanese children is *not* correlated with the timing of the onset of pointing behavior, but the *type* of words in the vocabulary did correlate with pointing: common nouns (a positive correlation) and frozen phrases (a negative correlation). Kelly, Manning, and Rodak (2008) carry the argument about the relation between pointing gestures and speech into the child's second year, claiming that hand gestures significantly impact the brain's comprehension of speech and that the pointing gesture disambiguates indirect speech acts.

Interactional Studies of Attention Management and Infant Pointing, 12–18 Months

A related line of research focuses on joint attention in interaction in semi-natural but controlled 'free play' situations. Clark (2001) and Estigarribia and Clark (2007), for example, use such contexts to explore the establishment of 'common ground' (Clark 1996) and 'grounding' between American mothers and infants. Grounding, understood as 'the on-going process of establishing common ground in order to enable the joint projects of speaker and addressee in any exchange' (Clark 2001: 95), offers an 'opportunity space' for introducing new words and tracking the child's uptake of these new words. Clark (2001) analyzes grounding in adult speech to one-year-olds as they show unfamiliar objects, talk about them, and check on what the child means when their utterance is unclear. She finds that adults work to achieve joint attention, beginning with attention-getters (gaze, gestures, touch, attention calls, name). When the child is jointly attending, they use deictic terms to introduce words for new objects, using gesture and demon-stration to maintain the child's attention (Clark 2001: 95). The joint attentional focus makes the connection between label and object obvious; its embedding in an interactive activity motivates the child to learn and remember the label. Estigarribia and Clark (2007) offer a model of how gaze and gesture contribute to joint attention in exchanges between American mothers and children, though they concede that this process is open to cultural variability.

Another line of research more compatible with a language socialization approach looks at joint-attention interactional sequences involving somewhat older children in naturally occurring settings. In an exemplary study from a conversation analytic perspective, Wootten (1997) analyzes his own English daughter's initial entry into requesting, from 12 months to three years. He shows the child's developing ability after age two to tailor the form of her requests to understandings about how events will unfold that have been established in the prior discourse, and hence how this one child 'enters culture.' This analysis probes the effects of momentary 'local' sequential understandings in interaction on the child's developing cognitive and social abilities. In a critique of developmental studies in the cognitivist tradition, Wootten suggests adding to the question of cognitive prerequisites these questions: what are the publicly available forms of action through which knowledge is expressed and how have those forms of action evolved? Addressing these questions, he argues, yields insights into how the child comes to understand the content of others' minds and how she comes to understand the world in (more or less) the same way others do.

In this spirit, Kidwell (2003, 2005, 2009) and Kidwell and Zimmerman (2006, 2007) observed toddlers (age one to two and a half) in a large dataset of videotaped natural interaction in three Southern California daycare centers. In situations in which children were involved in sanctionable activities against another child (e.g. hitting, pushing, taking a toy away), these young children responded differently to types of caregiver gaze, differentiating 'the look' from 'a mere look' on the basis of their implications for whether or not the adult will intervene. The children adjust their conduct in relation to the caregiver's gaze, for example stopping or hiding sanctionable actions, indicating that one-to-two-year-olds are sensitive to features of the caregiver's gaze deployment – to its duration, fixation on a target, and relation to other activities of the caregiver. Kidwell and Zimmerman (2006) link these attention-organizing behaviors not just to the child's internal mental state or early understanding of intentionality (as developmentalists do). Rather, they argue that the children assess their own 'observability' via communicative resources that let the child 'read' the conduct of others and strategically adjust their own behavior. The early emergence of joint attention is one step on the way to a child's realization that their own actions can themselves be objects of attention.

Children's 'showing' actions are also sensitive to the activities of others (Kidwell and Zimmerman 2007). They position such actions at felicitous moments to get the attention of others and indicate their significance. Joint attention is fundamentally an interactional process, inseparable from the flow of social activity. 'Another's gaze shift constitutes a publicly available resource that offers participants opportunities to locate potentially relevant features of, and happenings in, the environment for their own attention and action' (Kidwell 2009: 148). Using the same daycare center data, Jones and Zimmerman (2003) argue that intentionality becomes visible in interaction between a 12-month-old child and a caregiver as the interaction unfolds. The child uses points and proto-words to orient to some feature of the environment in a way that makes a response by the caregiver relevant; the caregiver treats the child's behavior as intentional action directed to some end. Intentionality is thus *jointly achieved* by child and caregiver.

Studies of joint attention in a non-Western context look at the socialization of attention in a rather different way. Barbara Rogoff (Chavajay and Rogoff 1999; Rogoff et al. 1993) studied cultural patterns of attention management in San Pedro Guatemalan families and in US families in Salt Lake City, Utah, focussing on caregiver interactions with infants aged 14 to 20 months. Analyzing videotaped interactions in the home, they found that the Guatemalans were much more likely to attend to multiple events at once, keeping several attentional-interactional objects going simultaneously with a 'hummingbird' pattern of attention – with competing events smoothly attended to without the flow being interrupted. Salt Lake City attention patterns were much more single-focused. This pattern held both when the focus of attention was the toddler's activity and when it was adult interaction, suggesting that these are quite pervasive cultural practices. In short, the Guatemalans of San Pedro displayed a specific cultural preference in the deployment of attention in interaction. The authors suggest that the Guatemalans, with experience of many competing events in large households, have more practice in dividing their attention smoothly across multiple foci of attention. Attention to multiple foci are also facilitated by the Guatemalan cultural emphasis on keen observation as the basis for learning through 'intent participation' (Paradise and Rogoff 2009; Rogoff et al. 2003).

The big questions, of course, are these: does interactional variability across cultures matter developmentally? Can it influence the achievement of developmental milestones? The discussion below addresses this question through an ongoing comparative study conducted by the author on the integration of gaze and pointing in infant–caregiver interaction in two different social groups: the Tenejapa Tzeltal and the Rossel Islanders of Papua New Guinea (Brown 2007).

Comparative Study of Caregiver–Infant Interaction

Caregiver–infant interaction in Mexico and Papua New Guinea

This study addresses the question of whether the 'nine-month revolution' is affected by cultural differences in interactional style with infants. Video-recorded interactions between caregivers and 9–15-month-old infants in two nonindustrial societies were examined for evidence of infants' developing competence in engaging in joint attention episodes. One context is a Mayan society (Tzeltal) in Mexico, where interaction with infants during their first year is relatively minimal; the other is on Rossel Island (Papua New Guinea), where interaction with infants is characterized by intensive face-to-face communicative behaviors from shortly after the child's birth. Both societies are small-scale, rural communities based on kinship, with subsistence activities as the basic economic activity. Both are traditionalist and relatively isolated from the mainstream national culture, and the indigenous language prevails in the home (Tzeltal in the Mayan community; the Papuan language Yélî Dnye on Rossel Island). Inhabitants live in extended households: children have multiple caregivers (often child caregivers) and multiparty interactions are the norm, in contrast to the dyadic model familiar in studies of child–caregiver interaction in Anglo-American families. We are not, therefore, comparing an 'exotic' with a 'middle-class' society.

Differences in style of interaction with infants across these two speech communities are apparent even to a casual observer. Tzeltal infants are carried on the back in a shawl, are usually held, and are rarely set down for their first year. There are therefore strong physical restraints on their independent movement, and they have a restricted interactional space in which to operate. Living in small household compounds surrounded by fields, during their first year of life they have few interlocutors, and those they have tend to be relatively unresponsive to infants' preverbal 'utterances.' This is a society where interaction with infants is not a priority. Similarly to the Gusii of Kenya reported in LeVine et al. (1994), the chief goal of both mother and child caregivers is to soothe the infant and keep it calm, not to stimulate it. Adult interaction follows norms of restraint, nondemonstrativeness, and avoidance of eye contact, and this is also the case with infants; caregivers use body contact rather than social interaction to soothe. Adults do sometimes point for children, pointing out chickens and dogs, for example, but generally not with the aim of generating interactions but to distract the child or to instill fear as a basis for obedience.

By comparison, Rossel Island infants live in large hamlets of several households and spend a large proportion of time out of doors. They are carried in the arms or set down, or laid down to sleep, and they usually have a large public space to move around in and explore. They often have many interlocutors, including passersby through the village, who greet them and are generally responsive to infants' 'utterances.' In short, Rossel Islanders surround infants with interlocutors who actively engage them and are responsive to their 'utterances,' similarly to Anglo-American middle-class child-centered norms.[6]

Do these differences influence how infants learn to coordinate attention in interaction, and, ultimately, their pragmatic and linguistic development? During fieldwork over a number of years, I have observed social interactions with prelinguistic infants in both societies. The methods used are broad-ranging, including participant observation, video-recording of naturally occurring caregiver–child interaction, parental interviews, and systematic sampling of behavior and interaction with infants. The corpus contains 69 hours of video recordings of interactions with 33 Tzeltal infants and 73 hours with 44 Rossel infants in the age range up to 18 months, as well as many of their older siblings and cousins. Longitudinal samples for five Tzeltal children and six Rossel children were also collected across different contexts and over up to several years (I have used different subsets of this data in what is reported here). The overall aim of the project is to combine quantitative measures to probe the observed contrasts in amount and style of infant–caregiver interaction with ethnographic and conversation-analytic methods to examine the kinds of socialization for communication that occurs, the normal patterns of daily life affecting infants in the two societies, and cultural beliefs about children and parenting.

The analysis below focuses on the interactional management of joint attention in the 9–15-month period, including episodes of gaze following, index-finger point following and production, and the integration of gaze and vocalization with pointing. It asks whether there is any evidence that the different interaction practices have differential consequences in the children's development of communicative understanding.[7]

Baseline for infant activity: Five-minute samples

To establish a baseline of infant interaction, one-to-two-and-a-half-hour stretches of naturally occurring interactions of nine Rossel Island infants (five boys and four girls) and eight Tzeltal infants (four boys and four girls), either directly observed or in video recordings, were sampled at five-minute intervals, producing 'snapshots' of infant activity at different times of the day. The children were at comparable developmental stages and alert and available for interaction. The data for this measure are summarized in Table 2.1.

The kinds of activities the infants were engaged in during each snapshot – judged as their primary focus of attention at the instant sampled[8] – were coded as follows:

- BF: Attending to bodily functions (sleeping, eating, suckling, being clothed, being bathed, etc.).
- SO: socially oriented; interacting with other(s).
- PwO: playing with or manipulating an object by oneself.
- S-A: self-absorbed; doing nothing beyond looking around, moving around; just 'being.'
- CT: can't tell; for example, child not visible on camera.

These very general codes exhaustively categorize the activities captured in the five-minute sample 'snapshots.'

Table 2.1   Data for five-minute samples

	Number of Infants	Total Hours Sampled	Number of Datapoints (Sampled Every Five Minutes)
Rossel	9	38	482
Tzeltal	8	22	272

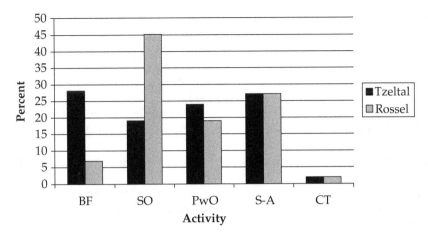

Figure 2.1   Results, five-minute samples, Tzeltal versus Rossel.

Figure 2.1 displays the relative frequencies of these activity types for Rossel and Tzeltal infants. There was a clear and dramatic difference in the two populations in the proportion of samples in which the infant was 'socially oriented' (primarily focussed on interacting or attempting to interact with someone) (Rossel 45 percent, Tzeltal 19 percent). The Tzeltal infants were much more often engaged in 'bodily functions' (eating, suckling, sleeping), although this is possibly an artifact of sampling times. There were no differences in the frequency of Rossel and Tzeltal infants playing with objects or being self-absorbed (doing nothing beyond observing the world).[9]

Interactional density

Several hours of videotaped data for these same infants were further analyzed for 'interactional density,' or the amount of interaction per unit time. Because measuring the density of interaction is fraught with difficulties, analysis focused on initiation of interactional sequences, where one participant makes an initiating move, a 'summons' to interaction, which is not necessarily responded to. The initiation of a 'sequence' was defined as a new focus of attention or new addressee about it, or new propositional content or attitude expressed to it.[10] In the discussion that follows we examine initiations in interactions involving two Rossel infants (aged 10–11 months) and three Tzeltal infants (aged 11–12 months).

The results of this measure are summarized in Table 2.2, which shows that there were twice as many interaction initiators per minute in the Rossel samples, compared with the Tzeltal ones.

A second question immediately arises: who is actually doing the initiating, the infant or the interlocutor? Table 2.3 shows that the Rossel and Tzeltal infants do not dramatically differ in the frequency with which they initiate interaction with

Table 2.2 Interaction initiators (per minute)

	Age Range	Number of Interaction Initiators in Samples	Range of Interaction Initiators per Minute	Mean Number of Interaction Initiators per Minute
Tzeltal (3 children, 3.5 hours)*	11–12 months	478	1.6–5.9	3.4
Rossel (2 children, 2 hours)	10–11 months	409	6.2–8.9	7.4

*More data for the Tzeltal infants was needed, to obtain a comparable number of interaction initiations.

Table 2.3 Infant- versus other-initiated interaction initiators

	Tzeltal	Rossel
Infant-initiated	1.9 per minute	2.3 per minute
Other-initiated	1.5 per minute	5.1 per minute

another person – 1.9 initiating moves per minute for the Tzeltal infants versus 2.3 per minute on average for Rossel. But Rossel caregivers initiate interaction with infants (in these samples) more than three times as often (per minute) as Tzeltal caregivers do! In other words, Rossel infants are interacting a lot more largely by virtue of the fact that others frequently initiate interaction with the infant. This finding supports the ethnographic observations of Rossels actively trying to interact with babies and the Tzeltal being much more restrained, waiting till the infant is ready and then responding to the infant's own initiatives.

The implications of this finding are potentially consequential, given that the 'referential triangle' development (Tomasello 1999) in the 9–15-months age range critically depends on interaction patterns between infants and caregivers. Do Rossel infants display understanding of the referential triangle earlier than Tzeltal infants? To answer this, we need a second line of inquiry: analyses of the emergence of Rossel and Tzeltal infants initiating joint attention with another over an object/event, and an assessment of at what age this behavior begins.

Joint attention episodes in Rossel and Tzeltal

Joint attention episodes, where the infant is trying to get someone's attention or someone else is trying to get the infant's attention, were coded in the videotaped data for six types of attention-sharing behaviors,[11] which in laboratory studies have been found to be involved in the developmental trajectory to joint attention:

- Pointing: trying to get someone's attention or share attention through pointing at an object or event.
- Reaching: holding hand out towards object and signaling (vocalization, gaze) to interlocutor.
- Indicative gesturing: gesturing towards object and signaling to interlocutor.
- Showing: holding out an object to interlocutor.
- Vocalizing: attention-getting sounds or speech.
- Gazing: mutual gaze, versus infant–interlocutor gaze, at indicated object/ event.

Four questions guided the analysis of gaze-pointing attention management actions (Liszkowski and Brown 2007):

- Do caregivers point for 9–15-month-old infants in both societies?
- Does pointing have the canonical index-finger-extended form?
- Do 9–15-month-old infants follow others' points/gestures that aim to draw them into joint attention at this age in both societies?
- Do infants themselves initiate joint attention by pointing/gesturing at objects at this age in both societies?

The answer is 'yes' to all four questions! At least some Rossel and Tzeltal infants do point for joint attention, canonically with outstretched arm and extended index finger, some of the time. The following examples of index-finger pointing by adults and by infants illustrate how these interactions unfold in the two cultural settings.

Example 2.1:   Rossel [2003v10]

Participants: Dini (D, 14 months) and his Uncle (Unc), his aunt (Aun), and Maria (Mar, D's teenage caregiver), with various other children off camera. The adults are sitting around chewing betelnut and relaxing near the river.

D, standing right next to his uncle's back, squats and urinates on the ground. Maria (off camera) calls attention to D's action, laughing and calling out, as Uncle looks down at D:

Mar: *kââ vye pwo paa? hehehe*
       'Is urine out up going?' ((laughs))
Aun: ((turns and looks, then says excitedly))
       Ee Dinimgaa dê vy:oo !
       'Eh, Dinimgaa has peed!'

Unc: ((taps D on the shoulder and says 'huh' several times, until D gazes
      at him, then he (Unc) points at the puddle))
      Kê n:uu? (0.9) Kê n:uu?
      'This who (did it)? This who?' ((pointing at puddle))
D: ((squats and looks down at his puddle))
Unc: *N:uu dê yo?*
      'Who did that?' ((pointing))
      (0.9)
      kê n:uu? (1.3) kê n:uu?
      'This who? This who?' ((pointing))
D: ((turns and walks away))

Here several participants draw attention to the child's delict, and no further sanction ensues. Notice that there is more to joint attention than just pointing to an
object to identify it: the adult points to the result of an action (puddle), indirect
evidence of the child's delict (urinating on the ground next to his uncle). The
accusation is also indirect ('Who (did) this?'). Dini responds to his uncle's summons
by gazing at him, and then he gazes at the puddle. He does not point at it but
shares his uncle's attention and (potentially) the message that his uncle does not
approve (see Figure 2.2).

Figure 2.2 Dini, his uncle, and his puddle of urine.

Example 2.2 illustrates a Rossel child drawing others' attention and sharing
excitement over the jointly-attended-to referent.

Example 2.2: Rossel [2005v23]

Participants: N:iin:ii (N, 10 months) with his mother (Mo), the researcher
(PB), N's six-year-old brother (Br), and his uncle (Gh).
      Mother and N:iin:ii are sitting together on their house verandah, with
PB and Br standing at the foot of the steps about eight feet away. N:iin:ii's

attention turns to his uncle kicking a ball about 30 feet away. N:iin:ii squeals (nonsense syllables of excitement; he can't yet produce recognizable words):

(// indicates speech or behavior overlapping with prior turn; = indicates latched speech)

N: *gu ii! ikee!* ((turns gaze to PB, back to uncle/ball, and points)) *iye.*
    ee. EEEEEE! ((affect and gaze toward soccer ball))
Mo: ((gazes at N, then at ball)) *ii. ball! // ball! ii?=*
    'Ii. Ball! Ball! Ii?'[12]
N: *// ee.*
Mo: *= ii. ball ball. ball hii. . . . ii ball ball ball (ndêwe).=*
    'Ii. Ball ball. Ball. Hii . . . ii ball ball ball (ndêwe).'
N: *// ee ee ee ee*
Mo: *= ii!*
    'Ii!'
Gh: ((calling from afar))
    a nu a nu a nu!
    'To me to me to me!'[13]
Mo: *hii! =*
    'Hii!'
    = ((points)) soccer soccer soccer. soccer.
    'Soccer soccer soccer. Soccer.'
    soccer, ehe.h hii hii. hii hii hii hii.
    'Soccer., eheh, hii hii. hii hii hii hii.'
N: *// ((gaze turns to PB/Br, then back))*
Gh: *// (.. ...)*
    '[unintelligible]'
((Mo helps N to stand up, holding onto his hand))
N: *ee*
Gh: *// soccer! soccer!*
    'Soccer. Soccer!'
N: ((gazes at Gh/ball, struggles to climb down from porch, Mo restrains him))
Mo: *// he. he he he. He used to go down.*
    'Ehe. Hii. He used to go down.' ((to PB, referring to N's attempt to get off porch))
    hm. hm. hm. soccer.
    'Hm. Hm. Hm. Soccer.'
N: *ee* ((waving hand gesture towards Gh/ball)) *EEEEEEEE!*
Mo: *ehe. ii. ii. soccer.*
    'Ehe. Ii. Ii. Soccer.'
N: *ee ide. de de* ((pointing to Gh/ball))
Mo: *// Ide de de de de de de de* [nonsense syllables] ((pointing at uncle/ball, alternating gaze between N's face and Gh/ball))

Figure 2.3   N:iin:ii and mother, with uncle, ball, and bystanders.

The name of the game here is sharing attention and affect over an object/event in a proto-conversation, exchanging excited and largely meaningless cries about playing ball (see Figure 2.3). The mother labels the event (calling it 'soccer') as well as the 'ball,' and takes an encouraging, facilitating role in the child's expression of excitement. Others (PB, Gh) are drawn into the interaction via the child's gaze and vocalizations; the result is collaborative, often simultaneous expression of excitement during joint attention, culminating in N and Mo jointly pointing.

In both these Rossel examples, interlocutors widely dispersed in space (up to 30 feet away) coordinate to share attention with the infant. While Tzeltal interactions are much more spatially constrained, analogous instances of joint attention are enacted, as illustrated below. In Example 2.3, Lus points for her father to draw an object into joint attention.

Example 2.3:   Tzeltal [2005v5B]

Participants: Lus (12 months) and her father (Fa).
     The whole family (both parents, four children) is sitting around relaxing in the cooking hut. Here the father's gaze is on the infant, who has his attention.

Lus: ((looks up to clothesline, points at her pants hanging on the line))
       Eee.
       ((looks at Fa))
Fa: ((gazes to referent))
       ba'ay?
       'Where is it?'
Lus: *eee* ((gazes at Fa, while point is held out at referent))
Fa: *eh in nix yael a, a'pantalon.*
       'Oh just look there ((gesturing to referent)), your pants.'
((The episode ends as Lus's attention shifts to a toy car on the ground.))

Figure 2.4   Baby Lus, father, and pants.

This Tzeltal example is a particularly clear case of a 'referential triangle episode': index-finger pointing along with gaze-checking by the infant, and a response that turns attention to the referent and labels it for the child. Note, however, that the father's first response is not a label but the question *banti* ('where?'), a standard response to infant pointing in Tzeltal. And the episode is brief and self-contained, unconnected to what precedes and what follows it (see Figure 2.4).

Example 2.4 shows a more extended exchange over an object being jointly attended to.

Example 2.4:   Tzeltal [2006 v26]

Participants: Xmik (Xm, 12 months) and her mother (Mo).

Mother and infant are inside the house, Mother sitting on a chair, baby Xmik sitting on the floor facing away from Mo. Xmik initiates joint attention to a pet bird, and a proto-conversation ensues:

Xm: ((looking around, her attention comes to focus on the bird hopping across the floor))

  hm. ((pointing at bird))
Mo   *hm.*
  'Hm.'
Xm: ((looks at Mo))
  hm. ((gesturing at bird))
Mo: // *la' me uta.*
  'Come here, say to it'
  la' me uta.
  'Come here, say to it.'

Xm: *me* ((looking back at bird and gesturing toward it))
Mo: *hm. ila'wil.*
       'Hm. Look.'
Xm: *a' me* ((gesturing to bird))
Mo: *Hm.*
Xm: ((turns to look at Mo))
((a few moments later, Mother re-initiates attention to bird)):
Mo: *ile' ch'i .*
       'Here it is for sure.'
       ((points over her shoulder to bird))
Xm: ((turns and gazes at bird))
Mo: ((gazes at Xmik))
       wa'y.
       'You see.'
Xm: *hee* ((pointing to bird))
Mo: *in.*
       'This one.'
Xm: ((looks away))
Mo: *in te lumine.* ((points over her shoulder again, looks at bird, then
          back at Xmik))
Xm: ((gazes where Mo points, then shifts gaze and points to where bird
          has now gone))
       hee.
Mo: *in. li' bajt li'i.* ((pointing to floor, where bird has now hopped to))
       'Hm. Here it went here'.
Xm: *hm* ((pointing))
Mo: *hm*

Here Xmik calls her mother's attention to the bird and her mother responds noncommitally until Xmik looks around at her, then suggests what she (Xmik) should say to the bird ('Come here, say to it'). Twice Xmik partially repeats the instructed words ('me,' 'a me'), and Mo's response is minimal ('Hm.' 'Look'). For the most part, the infant's gaze tracks the object, not the interlocutor's attention; she is presuming (or possibly indifferent to) the mother's visual attentional focus. At no point is the name of the bird uttered, and the mother does not treat this as an opportunity to teach the child words (see Figure 2.5).

In general, Rossel and Tzeltal infants' pointing appears within the expected age range of 9 to 15 months, though it is not found in the sampled data for all the infants.[14] In both societies babies point at objects (a bird, a ball, a piece of clothing) and adults point both at static objects (toys, animals, people) and at events (Dini's urine on the ground, piglets coming across the field, the rain starting to fall). Joint-attention caregiver–infant episodes in Rossel are more frequent and they tend to

Figure 2.5   Baby Xmik, mother, and bird.

be longer and more affectively aroused than in the Tzeltal community; however, they are similar in this fundamental respect: joint attention is clearly achieved and the child displays a sense of the others' communicative intention to share attention over an object or event.[15]

These findings support developmentalists' claims (e.g. Butterworth 2003) that infant pointing appears around 11 months, suggesting a biological basis to pointing as a joint-attention behavior. However, at this age, spontaneous pointing by Tzeltal and Rossel infants is rare and not evidenced in the data samples for all infants, and the infants are not yet very competent at pointing: they often do not attend to others' points, often do not cue what they are pointing at with their gaze, and do not reliably gaze to check the affective response of the addressee. Pointing is just one of several ways – holding out an object, reaching or gesturing towards things, vocalizing, gazing – of bringing something into joint attention, and all the infants show evidence of achieving joint attention by one or more of these means. In both the Tzeltal and the Rossel data, these other forms of initiating joint attention predominate. In addition, pointing in Tzeltal and Rossel joint attention interactions with children does not have the canonical result observed in postindustrial societies, with the adult labelling the object pointed at. Indeed, in Tzeltal, caregivers' responses do not usually label the object but instead acknowledge it (e.g. 'where is it?') or attempt to get the child to interact with it ('tell it to come here'). Tzeltal infants' gaze patterns in these episodes reveal a presumption of (or indifference to) interlocutors' attention.

On the basis of these observations, it is hard to believe that indexical pointing *per se* is playing a critical role in the infants' understanding that others have minds and communicative intentions of their own. Other forms of drawing an interlocutor into joint attention do not seem to be sharply differentiated yet from pointing, and nonetheless both Rossel and Tzeltal infants clearly display attention to others' communicative intents, and in turn draw others' attention to a joint focus.

The research reported here is ongoing. Analysis has not yet determined whether there are demonstrable differences at this age between Tzeltal and Rossel infants' gaze behavior in joint-attention episodes, or in how these episodes sequentially unfold. What is clear is that, despite the differences in interactional style between Tzeltal and Rossel, there is no evidence so far that the highly active style of Rossel infant–caregiver interaction brings in the referential triangle earlier for Rossel than for Tzeltal infants.

Conclusions

The results from this study are compatible with the view of developmentalists that the cultural organization of attention operates on a preprogrammed biological base. Infants have proclivities to share attention and their abilities to do so blossom in the period of 9–15 months. Infants are not all little clones – there is considerable individual variation, and likely cultural variation in the interactional sequential details, if not of the developmental sequence, of joint-attention behavior. Tzeltal caregivers are much less interventionist and less affectively expressive in interacting with their infants than are Rossel Islanders, yet these differences do not seem to have a radical effect on the emergence of pointing. While the interactions are socially and culturally organized and reveal what caregivers take to be interesting objects for children's attention, the desire for interaction over objects between infants of this age and their caregivers is apparent in both locales.

An analogous conclusion was drawn by the infant specialist Barry Brazelton, who studied Zinacanteco Mayan babies. Despite dramatic differences in the amount of stimulation provided by Mayan mothers (in comparison with mothers in the United States), Brazelton (1977) found that Zinacanteco and American babies develop at a comparable rate. In the absence of contingent reinforcement for smiling, vocalizing, and motor development, Mayan infants walk, can be coaxed to smile and vocalize, and appear to speak on time. Brazelton (1977: 177) proposes that developmental milestones are not notably affected by these kinds of differential interactional treatment in infancy. A similar point is made by Schieffelin and Ochs (1983) with respect to the absence of Baby Talk. Yet this issue remains controversial: others have argued (for other populations) that there are clear differences in development linked to differential conditions in infancy (see e.g. Shweder et al. 2006).

Can we generalize to universals in interaction with infants? Many authors have argued for the universality of certain acoustic/prosodic features of child-directed speech (e.g. Fernald 1992a, 1992b; Kuhl et al. 1997; Monnot 1999). Harkness and Super (1996: 2) offer two-year-old tantrums as a candidate universal. Lancy (1996: 83) suggests a universal tendency for infants to observe and imitate elders. Playing with objects is another candidate (Lancy 2008: 159); where children lack toys they pick up random objects (sticks, stones, flowers) to play with. We propose index-finger pointing at around 12 months as a candidate universal, one that is currently being explored in the Communication before Language project at the Max Planck Institute for Psycholinguistics. Evidence for pointing as a universal is that a critical age for joint attention is found in pointing behavior, which appears within the same age range in widely varying cultures (Liszkowski et al. forthcoming). Universals are arguably more likely to be found in these fundamental underpinnings to communicative interaction – in attention management or turn-taking, for example – than in the details of language structure (Evans and Levinson 2009; Stivers et al. 2009).

What then are the implications of cultural differences in social interaction with prelinguistic infants? While the imputation of intentions to infants' behavior may be a universal, the disposition to do so varies radically across situations and social groups, and intentions imputed do not necessarily lead to social interaction. Kulick (1992: 100) reports that New Guinea Gapun caregivers impute intentions to infants, but these are most often aggression, anger, or dissatisfaction, and lead neither to labelling nor to positive interactions with the infant. In addition, the mere fact that infants point does not necessarily mean that pointing leads to joint attention and an understanding of others' communicative intents; the critical developmental modality may well be something more diffuse such as gestural indicating, not explicitly index-finger pointing. Social groups may also differ in the kinds of objects to which infants' attention is directed and the social ends of such acts. Gapun caregivers, for example, point for infants to focus their attention on something outside of themselves, but the thing pointed at is often not actually there! Until the child itself initiates these routines (Kulick 1992: 121),

> it must often be unclear what a prompt to look at actually refers to, since the referent will either be obscure (as when a mother points towards a mass of trees in the distance and tells her child . . . 'There a bird'), invisible (as when children are told to look at spirits whom caregivers claim are coming to get them), or something completely different from what is being pointed at.

Similarly, Tzeltal pointing for infants is frequently a matter of pointing at things that are not clearly discriminable. This practice, along with the absence of labelling, suggest that the link between joint attention, pointing, labelling, and the child's understanding of referential actions is not necessarily as straightforward as it would appear from studies of infant interactions in university laboratories elsewhere in the world. This raises the possibility that, in the cultural organization of attention, indexical pointing does not necessarily play a special role.

A comparative perspective on social practices in caregiver–infant interactions will allow us to refine our understanding of the role of joint attention in learning to become a communicative partner. Children are socialized through and into different interactional styles across different cultural settings, yet the evidence so far supports the view that there is a universal propensity for children to engage in episodes of joint attention over objects and events by around the age of 12 months.

NOTES

1   For overviews of the comparative infancy and early childhood literature from a variety of disciplinary perspectives, see, for example, Bullowa 1979; Eibl-Eibesfeld 1983; Field et al. 1981; Harkness and Super 1996; Jahoda and Lewis 1988; Lancy 2008; Leiderman, Tulkin, and Rosenfeld 1977; LeVine 2007; LeVine, Miller, and West 1988; Schwartzman 2001; Shweder et al. 2006; Super 1981; Werner 1988.

2   See, for example, Kendon 1997, 2004; Kita 2003, 2009; Kleinke 1986; Rossano, Brown, and Levinson 2009; Rutter 1984.

3   Kulick (1992: 195) claims that, when Gapun adults (mainland New Guinea) speak to infants and small children, they switch to Tok Pisin to secure and hold the child's attention. Gapun children learn Tok Pisin rather than the indigenous language, perhaps as an unintentional consequence of this caregiving practice.

4   For example, there are disagreements over the criteria for establishing that infants are indeed engaged in joint attention, and the integration of gaze with pointing (Franco and Butterworth 1996; Liskowski 2006; Masataka 2003b). There is also debate about the developmental sources of index-finger pointing. Vygotsky (1962) thought that it develops out of reaching and grasping movements. Masataka (2003a) argues that it develops from the three-to-four-month index-finger extensions of infants, and is shaped by interactants' responses to these behaviors.

5   We do not actually know whether pointing is universal; it certainly is subject to cultural variation (Kita 2003, 2009; Kendon 2004). If not, sharing of attention must be accomplished by other means. Even within developmentalist studies, there are individual differences in pointing that depend on interactional patterns. For example, pointing behavior is encouraged if mothers respond to early infant index-finger extensions by pointing themselves (Masataka 2003b).

6   This picture contrasts strongly with that described by Kulick (1992) for the Gapun of mainland New Guinea – the Gapun, like the Tzeltal Maya, hardly speak to infants under six months, indicating wide variation in interaction with infants even within geographical and cultural areas.

7   This research is part of an ongoing large comparative project on multimodal interaction at the Max Planck Institute for Psycholinguistics in the Netherlands, which explores universals in interactional organization and cultural differences in interactional style. Tzeltal and Rossel are also the focus of comparative study of adult interaction, which turns out to be quite different in some respects – for example, pace, feedback mechanisms, gaze behavior (Brown and Levinson 2005; Rossano, Brown, and Levinson 2009). Further research with Tzeltal and Rossel infants is being undertaken in collaboration with the Project Group on Communication before Language, headed by Ulf Liszkowski, at the Max Planck Institute.

8   'Primary focus of attention' was judged by gaze and other signals of attention focus; there were no cases of double coding (e.g. both SO and PwO).

9   There is variation across infants, depending on the time of day of individual samples and the activities involved. Yet it is still clear that the pattern of social orientation (SO) is much higher for Rossel than for Tzeltal infants: for only one of the Tzeltal infants was social orientation the predominant activity sampled, while social orientation prevailed for all but two of the Rossel infants.

10   The following were not considered to be new sequences: mere physical contact without vocalization and/or gaze, laughter, self-absorbed vocalizations (with no sign of intention to communicate), or immediate repeats of the same action.
11   The coding scheme was developed with the help of Suzanne Gaskins, to whom I am also indebted both for theoretical discussions and for advice about the logistics of studying infant interaction in field conditions. See also a related coding scheme in Bakeman and Adamson (1984).
12   *Ball* and *soccer* are English borrowings in Yélî Dnye. *Ii* and *hii* are attention-getters.
13   'To me' is a standard invitation to play ball together.
14   In the data analyzed so far, 11 of 20 Tzeltal infants (age range 11–15 months) and all nine Rossel infants (age range 10–15 months) pointed at least once during the periods of observation or were reported by their mothers to be pointing. A detailed quantitative comparison awaits the analysis of data from more controlled situations (Liskowski and Brown 2007).
15   A recent study of joint attention in a rural community in Nigeria (Childers, Vaughan, and Burquest 2007), comparable in some respects to the Tzeltal community, also found that by early in the second year the toddlers' joint attention behaviors did not differ from those of American toddlers, as reported, for example, in Bakeman and Adamson (1984).

REFERENCES

Bakeman, R. and Adamson, L. B. (1984) Coordinating attention to people and objects in mother–infant and peer–infant interactions. *Child Development* 55: 1278–89.

Bakeman, R., Adamson, L. B., Konner, M., and Barr, R. G. (1990) !Kung infancy: The social context of object exploration. *Child Development* 61: 794–809.

Bates, E., Benigni, L., Bretherton, I., Camaioni, L., and Volterra, V. (1979) *The Emergence of Symbols: Cognition and Communication in Infancy*. New York: Academic Press.

Bigelow, A. E. and Rochat, P. (2006) Two-month-old infants' sensitivity to social contingency in mother–infant and stranger–infant interaction. *Infancy* 9(3): 313–25.

Brazelton, T. B. (1977) Implications of infant development among the Mayan Indians of Mexico. In P. H. Leiderman, S. R. Tulkin, and A. H. Rosenfeld (eds.), *Culture and Infancy*. 151–87. New York: Academic Press.

Brooks, R. and Meltzoff, A. N. (2008) Infant gaze following and pointing predict accelerated vocabulary growth through two years of age: A longitudinal growth curve modeling study. *Journal of Child Language* 35: 207–20.

Brown, P. (2007) The integration of gaze and pointing in infant–caregiver interaction in two cultures. Paper delivered at the 106th annual meetings of the American Anthropological Association. San Francisco, CA.

Brown, P. and Levinson, S. C. (2005) Comparative response systems. Paper delivered at the 104th annual meetings of the American Anthropological Association. Washington, DC.

Bruner, J. (1975a) The ontogenesis of speech acts. *Journal of Child Language* 2(1): 1–19.

Bruner, J. (1975b) From communication to language – A psychological perspective. *Cognition* 3(3): 255–87.

Bruner, J. (1982) *Child's Talk*. New York: Norton.

Bruner, J. (1995) From joint attention to the meeting of minds: An introduction. In C. Moore and P. Dunham (eds.), *Joint Attention: Its Origins and Role in Development*. 1–14. Hillsdale, NJ: Lawrence Erlbaum.

Bullowa, M. (ed.) (1979) *Before Speech: The Beginning of Interpersonal Communication*. Cambridge: Cambridge University Press.

Butterworth, G. (2003) Pointing is the royal road to language for babies. In S. Kita (ed.), *Pointing: Where Language, Culture, and Cognition Meet*. 9–33. Mahwah, NJ: Lawrence Erlbaum.

Carpenter, M., Nagell, K., and Tomasello, M. (1998) Social cognition, joint attention, and communicative competence from 9 to 15 months of age. *Monographs of the Society for Research in Child Development* 63(4): Serial No. 255.

Chavajay, P. and Rogoff, B. (1999) Cultural variation in management of attention by children and their caregivers. *Developmental Psychology* 35: 1079–90.

Childers, J. B., Vaughan, J. and Burquest, D. A. (2007) Joint attention and word learning in Ngas-speaking toddlers in Nigeria. *Journal of Child Language* 33: 199–225.

Clark, E. V. (2001) Grounding and attention in language acquisition. In M. Andronis, C., Ball, H. Elston, and S. Neuvel (eds.), *Papers from the 37th meeting of the Chicago Linguistic Society, Vol. 1*. 95–116. Chicago, IL: Chicago Linguistic Society.

Clark, H. H. (1996) *Using Language*. Cambridge: Cambridge University Press.

de León, L. (1998) The emergent participant. *Journal of Linguistic Anthropology* 8(2): 131–61.

Eibl-Eibesfeld, I. (1983) Patterns of parent–child interaction in a cross-cultural perspective. In A. Oliverio (ed.), *The Behavior of Human Infants*. 177–217. New York: Plenum Press.

Elman, J. L., Bates, E. A., Johnson, M. H., Karmiloff-Smith, A., Parisi, D., and

Plunkett, K. (1996) *Rethinking Innateness: A Connectionist Perspective on Development*. Cambridge, MA: MIT Press/Bradford Books.

Estigarribia, B. and Clark, E. V. (2007) Getting and maintaining attention in talk to young children. *Journal of Child Language* 34: 799–814.

Evans, N. and Levinson, S. C. (2009) The myth of language universals: Language diversity and its importance for cognitive science. *Behavioral and Brain Sciences* 32(5): 429–92.

Farroni, T., Csibra, G., Simion, F. F., and Johnson, M. H. (2002) Eye contact detection in humans from birth. *Proceedings of the National Academy of Sciences of the United States of America* 99: 9602–5.

Fernald, A. (1992a) Meaningful melodies in mothers' speech to infants. In H. Papoušek, U. Jürgens, and M. Papoušek (eds.), *Nonverbal Vocal Communication: Comparative and Developmental Approaches*. 262–82. Cambridge: Cambridge University Press.

Fernald, A. (1992b) Human maternal vocalizations to infants as biologically relevant signals: An evolutionary perspective. In J. H. Barkow, L. Cosmides, and J. Tooby (eds.), *The Adapted Mind*. 391–428. New York: Oxford University Press.

Field, T. M., Sostek, A. M., Vietze, P., and Leiderman, P. H. (1981) *Culture and Early Interactions*. Hillsdale, NJ: Lawrence Erlbaum.

Franco, F. and Butterworth, G. (1996) Pointing and social awareness: Declaring and requesting in the second year. *Journal of Child Language* 23: 307–36.

Gratier, M. (2003) Expressive timing and interactional synchrony between mothers and infants: Cultural similarities, cultural differences, and the immigration experience. *Cognitive Development* 18: 533–54.

Gratier, M. and Trevarthen, C. (2008) Musical narrative and motives for culture in mother–infant vocal interaction. *Journal of Consciousness Studies* 15(10–11): 122–58.

Harkness, S. and Super, C. (eds.) (1996) *Parents' Cultural Belief Systems: Their Origins, Expressions, and Consequences*. New York: The Guilford Press.

Jahoda, G. and Lewis, I. M. (1988) *Acquiring Culture: Cross-Cultural Studies in Child Development*. London: Croom Helm.

Jones, S. and Zimmerman, D. (2003) A child's point and the achievement of intentionality. *Gesture* 3: 155–85.

Keenan, E. O. and Schieffelin, B. (1976) Topic as a discourse notion: A study of topic in the conversations of children and adults. In C. Li (ed.), *Subject and Topic*. 335–84. New York: Academic Press.

Kelly, S., Manning, S. M., and Rodak, S. (2008) Gesture gives a hand to language and learning: Perspectives from cognitive neuroscience, developmental psychology and education. *Language and Linguistics Compass* 2/4: 569–88.

Kendon, A. (1997) Gesture. *Annual Review of Anthropology* 26: 109–28.

Kendon, A. (2004) On pointing. In A. Kendon (ed.), *Gesture: Visible Action as Utterance*. 199–224. Cambridge: Cambridge University Press.

Kidwell, M. (2003) *'Looking to See if Someone is Looking at You': Gaze and the Organization of Observability in Very Young Children's Harassing Acts Toward a Peer*. Doctoral Dissertation. Santa Barbara, CA: University of California.

Kidwell, M. (2005) Gaze as social control: How very young children differentiate 'the look' from a 'mere look' by their adult caregivers. *Research on Language and Social Interaction* 38(4): 417–49.

Kidwell, M. (2009) Gaze shift as an interactional resource for very young children. *Discourse Processes* 46: 145–60.

Kidwell, M. and Zimmerman, D. (2006) 'Observability' in the interactions of very young children. *Communication Monographs* 73(1): 1–28.

Kidwell, M. and Zimmerman, D. (2007) Joint attention as action. *Journal of Pragmatics* 39: 592–611.

Kita, S. (ed.) (2003) *Pointing: Where Language, Culture, and Cognition Meet*. Mahwah, NJ: Lawrence Erlbaum.

Kita, S. (2009) Cross-cultural variation of speech-accompanying gesture: A review. *Language and Cognitive Processes* 24(2): 145–67.

Kleinke, C. L. (1986) Gaze and eye contact: A research review. *Psychological Bulletin* 100(1): 78–100.

Kuhl, P. K., Andruski, J., Chistovich, I., Chistovich, L., Kozhevnikova, E., Ryskina, V., Stolyarova, E., Sundberg, U., and Lacerda, F. (1997) Cross-language analysis of phonetic units in language addressed to infants. *Science* 277: 684–6.

Kulick, D. (1992) *Language Shift and Cultural Reproduction: Socialization, Self, and Syncretism in a Papua New Guinean Village*. Cambridge: Cambridge University Press.

Lancy, D. F. (1996) *Playing on the Mother-Ground: Cultural Routines for Children's Development*. New York: Guilford Press.

Lancy, D. F. (2008) *The Anthropology of Childhood: Cherubs, Chattels, Changelings*. Cambridge: Cambridge University Press.

Leiderman, H. P., Tulkin, S. R., and Rosenfeld, A. H. (eds.) (1977) *Culture and Infancy: Variations in the Human Experience*. New York: Academic Press.

LeVine, R. (2007) Ethnographic studies of childhood: A historical overview. *American Anthropologist* 109(2): 247–60.

LeVine, R. A., Miller, P. M., and West, M. M. (eds.) (1988) *Parental Behavior in Diverse Societies*. San Francisco, CA: Jossey-Bass Inc.

LeVine, R., Dixon, S. LeVine, S., Richman, A., Liederman, P. H., Keefer, C. H., and Brazelton, T. B. (1994) *Child Care and Culture: Lessons From Africa*. New York: Cambridge University Press.

Levinson, S. C. (2006) On the human 'interaction engine.' In N. Enfield and S. C. Levinson (eds.), *Roots of Sociality: Culture, Cognition, and Interaction*. 153–78. Oxford: Berg.

Liszkowski, U. (2005) Human twelve-month-olds point cooperatively to share interest with and helpfully provide information for a communicative partner. *Gesture* 5(1–2): 135–54.

Liszkowski, U. (2006) Infant pointing at twelve months: Communicative goals, motives, and social-cognitive abilities. In N. Enfield and S. C. Levinson (eds.), *Roots Of Sociality: Culture, Cognition, and Interaction*. 153–78. Oxford: Berg.

Liszkowski, U. and Brown, P. (2007) Infant pointing (9 to 15 months) in different cultures. In A. Majid (ed.), *Field Manual Volume 10*. 82–9. Nijmegen, The Netherlands: Max Planck Institute for Psycholinguistics.

Liszkowski, U., Brown, P., Callaghan, T., Takada, A., and de Voss, C. (forthcoming) A gestural prelinguistic universal of human communication.

Liszkowski, U., Carpenter, M., Henning, A., Striano, T., and Tomasello, M. (2004) Twelve-month-olds point to share attention and interest. *Developmental Science* 7(3): 297–307.

Liszkowski, U., Carpenter, M., and Tomasello, M. (2007) Pointing out new news, old news, and absent referents at 12 months of age. *Developmental Science* 10(2): F1–F7.

Liszkowski, U., Carpenter, M., and Tomasello, M. (2008) Twelve-month-olds communicate helpfully and appropriately for knowledgeable and ignorant partners. *Cognition* 108(3): 732–9.

Liszkowski, U., Schäfer, M., Carpenter, M., and Tomasello, M. (2009) Prelinguistic infants, but not chimpanzees, communicate about absent entities. *Psychological Science* 20: 654–60.

Masataka, N. (2003a) From index-finger extension to index-finger pointing:

Ontogenesis of pointing in preverbal infants. In Sotaro Kita (ed.), *Pointing: Where Language, Culture and Cognition Meet*. 68–84. Mahwah, NJ: Lawrence Erlbaum.

Masataka, N. (2003b) *The Onset of Language*. Cambridge: Cambridge University Press.

Meltzoff, A. N. and Moore, M. K. (1977) Imitation of facial and manual gestures by human neonates. *Science* 198(4312): 75–8.

Monnot, M. (1999) Function of infant-directed speech. *Human Nature* 10: 415–43.

Moore, C. and Dunham, P. J. (eds.) (1995) *Joint Attention: Its Origins and Role in Development*. Hillsdale, NJ: Lawrence Erlbaum.

Murray, L. and Trevarthen, C. (1985) Emotional regulation of interactions between two-month-olds and their mothers. In T. M. Field and N. A. Fox (eds.), *Social Perception in Infants*. 177–97. Norwood, NJ: Ablex.

Ninio, A. and Bruner, J. (1978) The achievement and antecedents of labelling. *Journal of Child Language* 5: 1–15.

Ochs, E. (1988) *Culture and Language Development*. Cambridge: Cambridge University Press.

Ochs, E. and Schieffelin, B. B. (1984) Language acquisition and socialization: Three developmental stories and their implications. In R. A. Shweder and R. LeVine (eds.), *Culture Theory: Essays on Mind, Self, and Emotion*. 276–320. New York: Cambridge University Press.

Paradise, R. and Rogoff, B. (2009) Side by side: Learning by observing and pitching in. *Ethos* 37(1): 102–38.

Rogoff, B., Mistry, J., Göncü, A., and Mosier, C. (1993) Guided participation in cultural activity by toddlers and caregivers. *Monographs of the Society for Research in Child Development* 58(8).

Rogoff, B., Paradise, R., Arauz, R. M., Correa-Chavez, M., and Angelillo, C.

(2003) Firsthand learning through intent participation. *Annual Review of Psychology* 54: 175–203.

Rossano, F. (2009) *Gaze Behavior in Face to Face Interactions*. Doctoral Dissertation. Nijmegen, The Netherlands: Radboud University.

Rossano, F., Brown, P., and Levinson, S. C. (2009) Gaze and questioning in three cultures. In J. Sidnell (ed.), *Comparative Studies in Conversation Analysis*. 187–249. Cambridge: Cambridge University Press.

Rutter, D. R. (1984) *Looking and Seeing: The Role of Visual Communication in Social Interaction*. Chichester, U. K. and New York: Wiley.

Schieffelin, B. B. (1990) *The Give and Take of Everyday Life: Language Socialization of Kaluli Children*. Cambridge: Cambridge University Press.

Schieffelin, B. B. and Ochs, E. (1983) A cultural perspective on the transition from prelingusitic to linguistic communication. In R. Golinkoff (ed.), *The Transition From Prelinguistic to Linguistic Communication*. 115–31. Hillsdale NJ: Lawrence Erlbaum.

Schieffelin, B. B. and Ochs, E. (1986) *Language Socialization Across Cultures*. Cambridge: Cambridge University Press.

Schwartzman, H. (2001) Children and anthropology: A century of studies. In H. Schwartzman (ed.), *Children and Anthropology: Perspectives for the 21st Century*. 15–37. Westport, CT: Bergin and Garvey.

Shweder, R. A., Goodnow, J. J., Hatano, G., LeVine, R. A., Marcus, H. R., and Miller, P. J. (2006) The cultural psychology of development: One mind, many mentalities. In W. Damon and R. M. Lerner (eds.), *Handbook of Child Psychology, Vol. 1*. 6th ed. 716–92. New York: John Wiley and Son.

Stivers, T., Enfield, N. J., Brown, P., Englert, C., Hayashi, M., Heinemann, T., Hoymann, G., Rossano, F., de Ruiter, J.-P., Yoon, K.-E., and Levinson, S. C. (2009) Universals and cultural variation in turn-taking in conversation. *Proceedings of the National Academy of Sciences of the United States of America* 106: 10587–10592.

Super, C. M. (1981) Cross-cultural research on infancy. In H. C. Triandis and A. Heron (eds.), *Handbook of Cross-Cultural Psychology, Vol. 4: Developmental Psychology*. 17–53. Boston, MA: Allyn and Bacon.

Tomasello, M. (1999) *The Cultural Origins of Human Cognition*. Cambridge, MA: Harvard University Press.

Tomasello, M. (2008) *Origins of Human Communication*. Cambridge, MA: MIT Press.

Tomasello, M., Carpenter, M., Call, J., Behne, T., and Moll, H. (2005) Understanding and sharing intentions: The origins of cultural cognition. *Behavioral and Brain Sciences* 28: 675–91.

Tomasello, M., Carpenter, M., and Liszkowski, U. (2007) A new look at infant pointing. *Child Development* 78(3): 705–22.

Tomasello, M. and Ferrar, M. J. (1986) Joint attention and early language. *Child Development* 57: 1454–63.

Tomasello, M. and Todd, J. (1983) Joint attention and lexical acquisition style. *First Language* 4: 197–211.

Trevarthen, C. (1988) Universal co-operative motives: How infants begin to know the language and culture of their parents. In G. Jahoda and I. Lewis (eds.), *Acquiring Culture: Cross-Cultural Studies in Child Development*. 37–90. London: Croon Helm.

Vygotsky, L. (1962) *Thought and Language*. Boston, MA: MIT Press.

Werner, E. E. (1988) A cross-cultural perspective on infancy. *Journal of Cross-Cultural Psychology* 19: 96–113.

Wootten, A. J. (1997) *Interaction and the Development of Mind*. Cambridge: Cambridge University Press.

3 Preverbal Infant–Caregiver Interaction

AKIRA TAKADA

Social Interactions in 'Babyscience'

It is fascinating to observe how a child grows. Seemingly helpless, a newborn infant soon starts interacting with parents and others, and about one year later starts to utter words. A number of researchers have attempted to understand the mechanisms by which this development occurs. The most heated discussions have concerned whether a newborn is capable of *mimicry*.[1] Meltzoff and Moore (1977) and Meltzoff (1985) argued that a just-born infant is able to mimic an adult's facial expressions, including protruding the tongue, opening the mouth, and pursing the lips. These innate competencies are a driving force in infant development. Yet, to nurture these innate competencies, those surrounding the infant must influence her.

On the basis of outstanding experiments, Sander and colleagues consider the infant and caregiver to comprise a single system and contend that it is necessary to analyze the relationship as a unit (e.g. Sander 1977). Similarly, Kaye and colleagues analyzed the mother–child interaction as a process in which a social system forms and discerned developmental transitions (e.g. Kaye 1982). The social system here has two prerequisites: (1) members must be able to anticipate the behavior of one another based on their experiences and (2) the members of the system need to share common aims.

Kaye (1982) claimed that the child gradually begins to share the same aims as its mother and, soon, interactions between the mother and child become a social system. This argument, inherited from Vygotsky (1962 [1934]), places importance on the 'outside-in' (interpersonal to intrapersonal) approach to development. In the following sections, some important achievements of relevant research will be introduced along with the time axis of the model developed by Kaye.

The Handbook of Language Socialization, First Edition. Edited by Alessandro Duranti, Elinor Ochs, and Bambi B. Schieffelin.

Shared rhythms and regulations (from birth)

From the moment of birth, the mother (or primary caregiver) and infant are reciprocally involved and create their own behavioral patterns by accommodating contingent behaviors and capitalizing on innate regularities. The first instance of 'turn-taking' and reciprocal contingent characteristics can be observed during feeding directly following birth (Kaye 1982). After the newborn has sucked for a certain period of time (4 to 10 seconds), it stops for a while (4 to 14 seconds). Such a pattern is innate in humans but not other mammals. During the pauses in sucking, all the mothers observed 'jiggled' the infant or breast. The cessation of jiggling encouraged the resumption of sucking. The pattern of sucking–stopping–jiggling–stopping gradually became more synchronized and rhythmically repeated.

The mother begins to slowly share her aims, and the infant relates sensations to a 'contingent detection game' and forms schema regarding body, object, and other people (Shimojo 1988). Rules regarding reciprocal interplay form the basis for turn-taking and morality at a later developmental stage (Emde et al. 1991).

Shared attention (from two months after birth)[2]

Accommodation capitalizing on innate regularities gradually becomes the communication of consciousness through the establishment of 'joint attention'; that is, 'to observe what others observe or instruct' (Butterworth and Jarrett 1991). Scaife and Bruner (1975) demonstrated that, when a mother changes her line of vision, even a two-month-old infant follows and changes its line of gaze accordingly. At this age, mother and child communicate with each other by coordinating not only lines of gaze but also facial expressions, phonation, and gestures (Stern 2000).

When a mother introduces an object for joint attention (Brown, this volume), she often accompanies it with language even though the child has no indication of understanding (Bruner 1983). The language used by mothers in the study is characterized by high voice pitch, exaggerated intonation, slow tempo, and long pauses between utterances. This infant-directed speech (Werker and McLeod 1989) consists of musical elements (Malloch 1999; Papoušek and Papoušek 1981) that capture the attention of the child (Fernald and Kuhl 1987; Werker and McLeod 1989). Around six months the infant becomes responsive to the unique sound of the native language and can control its phonation (Kuhl et al. 1992). By this time, the infant enjoys repeatedly hearing the caregiver's voice in a musical format.

Bruner (1983) notes that a child discovers 'what to observe' in a signal that indicates the object to which the mother pays attention. By making herself clear, the mother helps to redirect the child's attention and create a habitual approach to language.

Shared memory (from eight months after birth)

An infant who learns to specify an object of shared attention is able to devote herself to the particular object. Differentiation of ends and means and a combination of behaviors that Piaget (2001 [1967]) called coordination of secondary schema soon emerge, allowing the infant to be involved cooperatively with others over an object.

Children at this age further differentiate schema within the framework of activities provided by adults (Kaye 1982), allowing them to anticipate the behavior of others and understand their intent.

According to Tomasello and colleagues, a child's understanding of others' intentions becomes possible as important social-cognitive skills gradually appear at around the ninth month after birth (Tomasello 1999). Distinct from *mimicking* (exactly recreating the observed behavior) and *emulation* (recreating the outcomes of the behavior through trial and error on one's own), *imitation* recreates the intention of a behavior and is key to cultural learning. Through imitation an infant begins to learn about culture, including the historically formed aspects of language, practices, and skills.

Shared language (from 14 months after birth)

With the assistance of adults, children gradually adopt current forms of culture, including language, which is constantly in flux (Bruner 1983). Bruner (1990) claims that a form of communication and intention exists even before a child adopts an 'official language' and that acquisition of the mother tongue is highly context sensitive. Research based on the 'social pragmatic approach' (e.g. Tomasello 2003) likely empirically supports Bruner's (1990) argument mentioned above.

In essence, words acquire meaning in the same way as joint attention is achieved. Language is a means to elicit children's attention to a particular element in shared social conditions. Children gradually invent meanings and behaviors. At the same time, adults too change their speech content and practices. Language makes reciprocal communication more effective (Bruner 1983).

Yet, the relation between the particularity and universality that characterize interactional systems in which children participate have yet to be fully analyzed (Adamson 1995).[3] In this regard, research that places cultural practices at the center is fruitful. A key agenda of the language socialization framework is precisely to analyze how a community's habitus of communicative code, practices, and strategies is related to an array of sociocultural logics (Ochs, Solomon, and Sterponi 2005: 548). Researchers inquire into the reasons for an action to be executed at a particular point, in a particular way, and by a particular participant in the course of interactions in the society of interest (Duranti 1997; Ochs 1988; Ochs, Solomon, and Sterponi 2005). Therefore, this chapter examines preverbal child development from a language socialization viewpoint, which is summarized below through research on caregiver–child interactions among the San (also known as Bushmen), an indigenous people residing in southern Africa.

Language socialization before speech

Ochs, Solomon, and Sterponi (2005: 552–3) proposed a model of Child-Directed Communication as a theoretical tool for illuminating how members of social groups verbally or nonverbally interact with children (see also Solomon, this volume). That is, child-directed communication extends the range of communicative modalities beyond speech, as does my research. In this vein, an inquiry into language socialization 'before speech' merits particular attention. As suggested by much of the research on child development, gestures such as facial expression, gaze direction, back channel response, and pointing are effectively used in caregiver–child interactions long before children start speaking. Each gesture indexes its immediate context in the course of interaction and can be recognized as an action (Goodwin 2000) that is not only embedded in but also generative of context. To better understand the use of language, this approach emphasizes how caregivers and children construct actions through a range of appropriate semiotic resources (Goodwin 2000) other than language.

Positioning of participants in caregiver–child interactions

When two people talk face to face, regardless of the topic of discussion or gestures that they may perform, their physical occupancy of the social space is in play (Hanks 1996: 249). This point is particularly important in analyzing interactions between a caregiver and a young child, because young children can operate only a narrow variety of body usages. The approach put forward in this chapter pays special attention to how each participant's positioning contributes toward organizing caregiver–child interactions. The inquiry leads to consideration of 'micro-habitats,' in which participants in interactions dwell. Micro-habitats include both 'corporeal niches' (e.g. infant held upright, lying down in caregiver's arms, etc.) and 'material niches' (e.g. slings, blankets, etc.) (Ochs, Solomon, and Sterponi 2005: 554–5; see also de León, this volume). The body as part of the field of cultural practice is nested in the micro-habitats of a sociocultural group. At the same time, the formation of micro-habitats reflects the history of communication in the sociocultural group.

Multiple contexts of caregiving

Research on the development of social interaction, especially psychological studies, focuses on the mother (or primary caregiver)–child dyad. The use of experimental or relatively controlled situations has facilitated these trends. In contrast, my approach foregrounds how children are socialized in a particular speech community. That mothers are embedded in a given community is particularly important, considering that San mothers spend most of the daytime in the open space outside their huts, which are primarily used to stow their commodities (Tanaka 1980: 25–9).

'Context' entails intersubjective contracts, ongoing discourse, and a horizon of background experience (Hanks 1996: 86). The context of caregiver–child interactions is not monolithic, for caregivers are involved in complicated human relationships and as cultural practice caregiver–child interactions are embedded in multiple contexts, as well as generative of such contexts.

Caregiver–Child Interactions Among the San

The people generally referred to as the San consist of various groups distinguished by language, locale, and practice. This discussion uses mainly the data of my field research on two neighboring groups of San, the |Gui and ||Gana of central Botswana. Additionally I review the literature on other groups of San (Ju|'hoan and !Xun[4]) as needed. Kinship, language, rituals, and folk knowledge indicate a close relationship between the |Gui and ||Gana (Tanaka 1980).[5] As the |Gui and ||Gana are broadly similar in their caregiving practices, the analysis that follows considers the two groups as a unit.

The |Gui/||Gana lived a nomadic life within the central part of the Kalahari Desert. This lifestyle required the ability to range through a huge living space, now encompassed by the Central Kalahari Game Reserve. Since the 1970s, however, the Remote Area Development Program has affected most of the San living in Botswana. Local infrastructure, such as wells, schools, and clinics, has been developed at several settlement sites. *!Koi!kom* has become the largest |Gui and ||Gana settlement. In 1986, the national government decided to encourage residents of the Central Kalahari Game Reserve to resettle outside the reserve. Eleven years later, those who favored relocation began to move to *Kx'oēsakene*, a new settlement outside the Central Kalahari Game Reserve. Migration snowballed, and most *!Koi!kom* residents resettled in *Kx'oēsakene*.

Analysis here is based on archival and field research in southern Africa over a three-year period, beginning in 1997 with a focus on |Gui and ||Gana residing in *Kx'oēsakene* (I recognized 1002 |Gui/||Gana in April 2000). I periodically visited all of their houses (346 huts in April 2000), including houses with young children who were born after 1997 (24 boys and 36 girls), and sporadically video-recorded interactions between caregivers and young children (35 hours in total) and interviewed residents about caregiving behaviors.

To establish a theoretical perspective on the development and ethnographic particularities of San caregiver–child interaction, I focus on two aspects in the following discussion: (1) cultural formation of reciprocal accommodation to contingent behaviors, capitalizing on infant regularities, and (2) musicality in early vocal communication.

Cultural formation of reciprocal accommodation for contingent behaviors capitalizing on infant regularities

Across language/area-based groups, young children of the San have extremely close relationships with their mothers. The degree of mother–infant physical contact is much greater than that between their counterparts in Western societies.

Moreover, nursing occurs only for a few minutes at a time, about four times each hour. Konner and Worthman (1980) claimed that frequent nursing with short intervals occurs among a group of the San (Ju | 'hoan) because the constant physical contact sensitizes mothers to minute changes in their infants' state. I investigated the daily contexts of nursing of a group of the San (!Xun) and determined the following reasons for forming this kind of nursing pattern (Takada 2005b).

First, mothers could nurse their infants at any time, in any location. For example, mothers breastfed their infants while cooking, sewing, or smoking, not hesitating to nurse when others were present. Second, mothers nursed their infants to soothe them. Infants tended to stop fussing when their mothers started to nurse them. Third, sucking was negatively correlated with 'gymnastic' behavior (see below) in all infants. Fourth, sucking was negatively correlated with the caregivers' gaze. This could be because when mothers nursed, they became more relaxed than usual. Only when infants initiated a fretful movement did mothers take action. Fifth, the rate of jiggling after a break in sucking was almost the same as the base rate of jiggling in the whole data set among all infants. Kayes (1982) posit a contingent, turn-taking relationship between sucking and jiggling, which enables breastfeeding to be prolonged. Conversely, repeated jiggling–sucking 'turn-taking' hardly occurred among the !Xun San. The !Xun caregivers react not to the onset of a pause in sucking but to infant fretting or crying.

A similar pattern of nursing practices has been observed among the | Gui/ | | Gana, where mothers usually nurse a few minutes at a time about four times each hour, as illustrated in Table 3.1.[6] In this case, a woman, M, nursed her seven-week-old infant Ax in front of her hut. Inside the hut were two people, Gt, Ax's 39-month-old sister, and P, M's 10-year-old nephew. At the beginning of the video clip, Gt took up the cap from a bottle of ketchup and was licking it, P looked at the video camera, and Ax was sucking on M's left breast while moving her extremities slightly. Ax soon dropped the nipple from her mouth (line 1) then moved her extremities significantly and assumed a recurvate position (line 2). M then looked at Ax and made Ax mouth the nipple using her right hand (lines 3 and 4). Subsequently, Ax stopped moving her extremities and again started sucking (line 6). Slightly later, M averted her gaze from Ax and looked ahead (line 7).

During this unfussy practice of nursing, mothers were involved in a wider participation framework. In line 10, M talked to Gt about her grandfather and his colleague, who were seen at some distance, while nursing Ax. Ax may have sensed this shift of M's attention, for, although appearing drowsy (line 9), she opened her eyes immediately after M's utterance (line 11). Her attention was then probably attracted by the glint of the video camera (line 13). M noticed Ax's change of state, for she looked into her face while continuing to talk to Gt (line 15). In the meantime, Gt reacted to M's utterances mainly with nonlexical vocalization and laughter (e.g. lines 16, 17, and 21).

Approximately 55 seconds after the onset of sucking, Ax started moving her right arm (line 21). Although M looked into Ax's face twice (lines 22 and 25), as well as holding her in a blanket (line 23), she did not initiate jiggling to compel further sucking. Consequently, Ax took her mouth from the nipple and immediately started swinging her extremities widely (lines 26 and 27). M then looked into

Table 3.1 Nursing activity

Time of Footage	Line	Gt (3.3.8)		Ax (0:1.13)		M (Gt's and Ax's mother)		Author		Others	
		Nonverbal	Verbal	Nonverbal	Verbal	Nonverbal	Verbal	Nonverbal	Verbal	Nonverbal	Verbal
0:25:30	1	Gt was sitting inside the hut (not seen in the frame). She had picked up a bottle cap of ketchup and was licking it. The video camera was set on the tripod and placed between M and A. A dog, which appears drowsy, was lying to the left of M. The radio-cassette was playing some (audible) music in the distance throughout the excerpt.		Ax was sucking on M's left breast while moving her extremities slightly. Simultaneously, her eyes looked in the direction of the video camera. Ax drops the nipple from her mouth.		M was sitting in front of her hut. She had started nursing approximately four minutes ago. She looked to the front while nursing Ax at her left breast.		A was sitting to the right of M.			

Time	No.	Dog	Ax	M	Context
0:25:32	2		Ax flails her extremities and is in the recurvate position.		
0:25:33	3			M looks at Ax. Looking at Ax's face, M uses her right hand to make Ax mouth the nipple.	A youngster passes in front of M and Ax.
	4				
0:25:35	5	The dog lifts its head and follows the youngster with its gaze.			
0:25:38	6		Ax stops moving her extremities and starts sucking.		
0:25:44	7	The dog lowers its head and closes its eyes.		M looks away from Ax and looks ahead (first looks to the front and then immediately toward the left).	
0:25:48	8	A goat bleats.			

(Continued)

Table 3.1 (Continued)

Time of Footage	Line	Gt (3:3.8)		Ax (0:1.13)		M (Gt's and Ax's mother)		Author		Others	
		Nonverbal	Verbal	Nonverbal	Verbal	Nonverbal	Verbal	Nonverbal	Verbal	Nonverbal	Verbal
0:25:50	9			Ax appears drowsy, although she keeps sucking on the nipple.							
0:25:53	10						Xakitire-si ciа / / ko xa tsere / /naom xa / /naan ya ≠qx'oa (Xalitele, grandfather has come out of the hut) hhh ((M coughs))				
0:25:58	11			Ax's eyes open.							
0:26:00	12										
0:26:06	13			Ax's eyes appear to be looking in the direction of the video camera.		M looks further toward the left.					

(Continued)

Time	No.			
0:26:09	14	The dog lifts its head and scratches its shoulder with its left hind leg. The sound of wind becomes stronger.		M looks to the front.
0:26:15	15			M looks into Ax's face and then looks back toward Gt.	*Etsera koma xa ci sii /aotshaa-si va //om cia mee //goa ka ≠qx'oa* (They said they would arrive in /aotshaa and then sleep ((there)). However, they ((seem to)) leave ((here)) in the evening).
0:26:20	16		*a ha(h) a ha(h) a ha(h) a ha(h)*	Ax looks up at M's face.	M smiles at Gt.

Table 3.1 (Continued)

Time of Footage	Line	Gt (3:3.8) Nonverbal	Verbal	Ax (0:1.13) Nonverbal	Verbal	M (Gt's and Ax's mother) Nonverbal	Verbal	Author Nonverbal	Verbal	Others Nonverbal	Verbal
0:26:22	17		a [ha(h)] a ha(h)			M smiles at Gt.	[hh]				
0:26:24	18					M looks away from Gt and looks to the front.					
0:26:25	19								khuri (((ketchup in the bottle)) is finished)		
0:26:26	20					M looks back toward Gt.					
0:26:28	21		a ha(h) [ha(h)]	Ax moves her right arm.		M smiles at Gt.	[hh]		[hh]h hhh		
0:26:32	22			Ax moves her right arm.		M looks into Ax's face.					
0:26:34	23			Ax moves her right arm.		M looks back toward Gt, smiling. Simultaneously, M holds Ax under a blanket.					
0:26:35	24		e hhh [hh]	Ax moves her right arm.					[hhh]		
0:26:40	25		ʔhh	Ax moves her right arm.		M looks into Ax's face and then looks around in front of her.					

Time	#	Utterance	Ax's action	M's action
0:26:43	26	*hhh*	Ax takes her mouth off the nipple and then swings her extremities.	
0:26:47	27	*ʔhh*	Ax swings her extremities while looking in the direction of the camera.	M looks into Ax's face.
0:26:50	28	*aii(h)*		
0:26:52	29	*ayaa(hhhh)*	Ax attempts to suck her right hand but fails.	
0:26:54	30		Ax attempts to suck her right hand but fails.	M looks back toward Gt, smiling.
0:26:56	31	*hʔ]*	Ax attempts to suck her right hand but fails.	[hh]
0:26:57	32	*aii(h)*	Ax tries to mouth the nipple.	M looks into Ax's face.
	33		Ax tries to mouth the nipple.	M looks at the youngster.
				A youngster passes in front of M and Ax.

(*Continued*)

Table 3.1 (Continued)

Time of Footage	Line	Gt (3.3.8)		Ax (0:1.13)		M (Gt's and Ax's mother)		Author		Others	
		Nonverbal	Verbal	Nonverbal	Verbal	Nonverbal	Verbal	Nonverbal	Verbal	Nonverbal	Verbal
0:26:59	34	The dog lifts its head slightly and looks at the youngster.	*uuu(h)*	Ax tries to mouth the nipple.			*maaxo e xa cie cie saa ezi / / qx'aa* (Where is it ((the Sun)). I wash them ((clothes)) for long time).				
0:27:03	35			Ax tries to mouth the nipple.		M makes Ax mouth the nipple, using her right hand.					'()'
0:27:04	36			Ax tries to mouth the nipple.		M looks at Ax's face.	*[ae]*				['()'
0:27:06	37	The dog lowers its head and closes its eyes.		Ax starts sucking; the movement of her extremities slows.		M looks to the front.					

Ax's face twice (lines 27 and 32) but did not act to encourage sucking. Instead, M looked at Gt (line 30) and then talked to P (line 34). Subsequently, Ax tried to mouth the right hand (lines 29–31) and then the nipple (lines 32–36) by herself. Approximately 20 seconds after Ax took her mouth from the nipple, M finally made Ax mouth the nipple, using her right hand (line 35) while vocalizing (i.e. 'ae'), and looked at Ax's face again (line 36). Ax resumed sucking, and the movements of her extremities slowed (line 37). M immediately looked away from her and ahead (line 37), then asked P to fetch the basin (not shown in the excerpt).

A seven-week-old infant in a reclining position can perform only a narrow range of actions, such as sucking the nipple or her own hand, looking at a human face or glinting things, and moving her extremities. Using these actions, however, Ax apparently reacted to the given context. In the meantime, the mother was dealing with a much broader context while she sat and nursed the infant in front of their hut. Even within this short fragment of interactions, she looked in front of her, gossiped about her relatives with her older daughter, and asked an errand of her nephew, in addition to continuously holding the infant and caring for her. She was thus involved in a complicated participation framework. This is one of the reasons why the mother tended not to gaze at the infant while she was sucking, and reacted only after the infant started fretting.

Sucking correlated negatively with gymnastic behavior, and breastfeeding was sometimes terminated at the onset of this behavior (Takada 2005b). Across language/area-based groups, San caregivers frequently keep infants standing or jumping on their laps, beginning several weeks after birth (Konner 1973, 1976; Takada 2002, 2004, 2005b). |Gui/||Gana caregivers engage infants in these gymnastic exercises throughout the day at intervals of seven minutes (Takada 2004). !Xun San (Takada 2005b), as well as other caregivers in eastern and western Africa (Bril et al. 1989; Super 1976), also practice such behavior.

Gymnastic behavior induces the stepping reflex, also called the 'U-shaped' primitive reflex, which is present at birth but usually disappears within the first few months of life and a similar stepping movement reappears when the infant begins to stand and walk (Bly 1994; Cole and Cole 1993: 136–7, 152). Yet, among the |Gui/||Gana, gymnastic behavior induced the stepping reflex and prevented its disappearance in infants over two months of age. This finding supports the hypothesis that the stepping reflex is not innately programmed to disappear but is a flexible behavior that will persist in certain situations.

Gymnastic behavior occurred in a cheerful atmosphere. Caregivers often tried to soothe fussy infants by engaging them in gymnastic activity (Takada 2002, 2004, 2005b). An example is shown below.

Example 3.1

One minute after the interactions described in Table 3.1. Ax is a seven-week-old girl. M is Ax's mother.

M was sitting in front of the hut, nursing the infant Ax. After a short sucking period lasting for approximately 34 seconds, Ax dropped the nipple from her mouth and then started swinging her extremities. M immediately looked into Ax's face and tried to make Ax mouth the nipple, using her right hand. This attempt failed, however, and M voiced 'oʔo: oʔo:' to Ax to soothe her. Nonetheless, Ax kept swinging her extremities. M then put her in a sitting posture by holding Ax's body up by her hands. Ax's movement slowed. Furthermore, M picked her up and held her in a standing position, which immediately induced the continuous stepping movement of Ax's legs. M then grabbed Ax's body twice and tapped it repeatedly while engaging her in gymnastic behavior. She then reduced the pressure of her hands, which were holding up Ax's body. Ax shifted to a crouch posture, as she could not sustain her own bodyweight. M looked at Ax and once again put her into a sitting position.

In the above sequence, the mother's and infant's bodies in both breastfeeding and gymnastic behavior provided the infant with pleasure. On one hand, breast-feeding satisfies the infant's hunger and provides the infant with the simple rhythmical stimulus of sucking. On the other hand, a standing position is effective in soothing fretful infants (Korner and Thoman 1972; Zelazo 1976). It should be noted that the stepping movement of Ax (seven weeks old) gradually changed from a reflex to a voluntary action. Ax's mother thus created rhythms collabora-tively with the infant in the course of gymnastic activity and made the interaction pleasurable.

Moreover, the mother often changed the posture of the infant while in a sitting position or walking around the village, having folded the infant in a sling. With the infant close at hand, the mother easily shifts to breastfeeding or gymnastic behavior.

These uses of the body characterize the communication style between mothers and infants among the San. They communicate through their intercorporeality (Merleau-Ponty 2002 [1945]). This corporeal field, as the embodiment of values and the setting of cultural practices (Hanks 1996: 257, 265), works as the ground engendering their characteristic intersubjectivity (see following sections).

Musicality in early vocal communication

Speech to young children is organized in relation to a systematic set of historically rooted, sociocultural practices (Ochs, Solomon, and Sterponi 2005: 550). The |Gui/||Gana have several language genres that involve infants. First, the |Gui/|||Gana name a newborn after a conspicuous incident that occurred during pregnancy, which is sometimes modified when soothing the infant (Takada 2005a). Caregivers sometimes utter this modified name in a cheerful manner; this practice is called *sao kxʼam*, which literally means 'soothing way.'

Second, the |Gui/|||Gana have another genre of verse-like language activities called ǂxano, which literally means 'praising something,' characterized by repeti-tion of an appellation, playful banter, and monologue-like utterances (Nakagawa

1996b). While males engage in ‡*xano* more often than females, because it is usually performed when males are hunting, versification similar to the ‡*xano* is used in addressing infants. The verse-like expression constitutes a transitional form from appellation to verse.

Songs for infants were also observed among the |Gui/||Gana. Song is inseparable from dance for the |Gui/||Gana. A folk term, |*kii*, denotes both song and dance in |Gui/||Gana languages. |*kii* is used for various activities, including medical treatment, addressing a lover, and affording pleasure, in the life of the |Gui/||Gana. When people gather, particularly at night, they frequently perform |*kii*, often joining in a circle one after another.

The following example illustrates the short |*kii* of *tsando*. The meaning of *tsando* overlaps with that of gymnastic behavior. In the *tsando* excercises, the caregiver makes the infant jump to imitate walking behavior or leads the infant by the hands to help her walk. The |Gui/||Gana believe that *tsando* behavior promotes unaided walking and also improves the dance performance of the infant.[7] When engaging an infant in *tsando* activity, caregivers often set the following phrase to a particular melody: '*tsando, tsando,* |*koã-rì kú-kûa khúri.*' Here, |*koã* means 'child,' *rì* is a suffix that indicates common gender, plural and subjective, and *kú-kûa* is probably a compressed phonation of *kõwã kõwã. Kõwã* is the alternant form of the verb *kôõ,* which means 'go.' Its reduplication *kõwã kõwã* means 'keep going.' *khúri* is a lexical root that means 'finish.' A native speaker suggested that the word implies 'finish crawling.' Hence, the meaning of the phrase is as follows: '*tsando tsando,* children keep going and finish crawling.'

Figure 3.1 is a transcription of the actual performance of the |*kii* of *tsando* in terms of the lyrics and musical score, which illustrate several features of the |*kii*. First, as indicated by the pitch contour and musical score, the melody uses the tonal information of each word. Second, the dental click (|) of the word |*koã* effectively functions as the sound of percussion and helps tap out the rhythm. Third, although the phonations of the lyrics are constrained by the syllable structure of morphemes,[8] those of some words are modified according to the rhythm of the song. Prior to the first *tsando*, a lexically meaningless syllable (*a*) is inserted; the phonations of the third syllable (*do*) of the first *tsando* and the first syllable (*khu*) of the word *khúri* are prolonged; and the phonations of |*koã* and *kõwã kõwã* are shortened to match the rhythm of the song.

The |*kii* of *tsando* is incompatible with the practice of *tsando* exercises. Moreover, people around the *tsando* performer often act in unison, clapping their hands or singing the phrase together in a cheerful atmosphere. This is shown in Example 3.2.

Figure 3.1   The |*kii* of *tsando*.

Example 3.2

> Two adult females, Tk and Gp, visited a household used as a local bar. Tk and Gp were sitting on the ground with their infants, Mt (seven months, three weeks old) and B (six months, three weeks old), respectively. Several other people were also present, including Tt, brother-in-law of Tk; K, husband of Gp; |N, a friend of K; and A, the author.
>
> The gathering was discussing whether they should move back to the previous living area, where they used to get water from plant roots. Alongside this discussion, Tk began to engage Mt in gymnastic exercises, holding Mt's body by grasping her under the arms and picking her up. She held Mt in a standing position and then made her jump twice, which immediately elicited Mt's voluntary stepping movements. After placing Mt in a sitting position, Tk delightedly commented to Mt, saying [*ai:*] *ʔabe kua ǂnaa khoa ʔii* ('[Oh] he seems to make dance steps').

After the above event, A talked with Tt about whether Tk had engaged in *tsando* exercises with Mt. Almost simultaneously Gp also started engaging B in gymnastic exercises (Example 3.3).

Example 3.3

> Five seconds after the interactions described in Example 3.2. B is a girl aged 6 months, 3 weeks. Gp is B's mother.
>
> B moved her legs. Gp picked up B and put her in a standing position while looking at her. Subsequent to the gymnastic behavior given by Gp, B made walking movements on the ground, aided by Gp. Note that B could load her bodyweight onto her legs and move her body weight to each leg in turn, when supported by the caregiver. B then touched the water tank and gripped the handle.

Gp's gymnastic behavior was a prompt reaction to leg movements by B, who was lying down. At the same time, it is plausible that Gp was prompted to engage in the gymnastic behavior because she had seen the gymnastic exercises given by Tk (Example 3.2) and heard the subsequent utterances by A and Tt. After the verbal exchanges with A, Tt shifted to performing *tsando* practices by himself (Example 3.4).

Example 3.4

> Immediately after the interactions described in Example 3.3. Tt is Tk's brother-in-law. K is Gp's husband.

1   Tt: *kana cie ʔama, | |noori, TSANDO EE*
          So I do *TSANDO* to 'him,' my niece
2   Tt: *TSANDO, TSANDO, |koãde ku-kua khuri ta mee*

saying, *TSANDO, TSANDO*, children go and go, and finish
crawling
3   K: *ʔesa ciexo na* [*ʔesa*] *aa* | | *kae*
Put her ((in the standing position)) and teach that to [her].
4   Tt: [*aa*] *cie zi* | | *kam* | *xoa* | *neẽ tana xoo ciẽ*
[Those] who are sitting, while feeling, make them stand like this.

In line 1, Tt mentioned his kinship relationship to Mt. The mother of Tt married
the father of Tk after her spouse (Tt's father) passed away. Mt, the daughter of
Tk, was thus his niece and classified as | | *noori* in the | Gui/ | | Gana kinship
system.[9] From Mt's side, Tt is her uncle and classified as *cia* | | *ku*. *Cia* | | *ku* is
expected to take special care of his/her | | *noori*, which constitutes the joking class
(Takada 2005a).

Encouraged by verbal exchanges with A, Tt thus initiated a new sequence,
which enhanced musical performativity in their interactions, while locating
his position in the web of the group's kinship relationships. Tt then performed
a complete version of the | *kii* of *tsando* followed by a verb *ta mee* ('saying')
(line 2).

Then K mentioned *tsando* exercises. The utterance, which was enhanced by Tt's
prior utterance, provided an account of the *tsando* exercises. Tt also gave an
account of the *tsando* exercises while overlapping K's utterance (line 4). K's utterance in line 3 also worked as an instruction to his wife Gp, who was holding B's
left hand. Gp accordingly raised up the body of B, who had gradually dropped
into a crouching position. Gp then supported B in a standing position while
looking at her.

Like appellations for infants and verse-like utterances addressing infants
(Takada 2005a), songs for infants introduce communicative musicality (Malloch
1999; Trevarthen 1999)[10] in | Gui/ | | Gana caregiver–infant interactions. The | *kii*
of *tsando* is of particular interest because the chant of this song is often accompa-
nied by physical contact with the infant. In the above example, the | *kii* of *tsando*
chanted by Tt was accompanied by gymnastic behavior, which synchronized
nonverbal behavior, prosodic features, and segmental structures of verbal utterances into a cultural activity frame (*tsando*) for caregiver–infant interaction. The
!Xun San have also developed (but in a significantly different way from the
| Gui/ | | Gana) a frame that links the behavioral rhythm of gymnastic exercises
with the verbal rhythm of naming practices (Takada 2005b).

In adult conversation, one's typical focus of attention in talk is not on the poetic
function of language forms (Hanks 1996: 82; Jakobson 1960). In infant-directed
speech, in contrast, prosodic features and segmental structures are often used to
achieve mutual involvement between caregiver and infant. The | *kii* of *tsando*
particularly provides melody as a semiotic resource to help caregivers accommodate the narrow range of infant actions. For example, they can attune the melody

to the rhythm of infant stepping movements, which are recognized as walking or dancing.

Outside of *tsando* and similar musical genres, caregivers reward appropriate timing in turn-taking in rhythmic exchanges involving infants. For instance, Takada (2005a) reported an episode in which a 27-week-old infant gave nonverbal/verbal reactions exactly at the transition relevant point of a caregiver's utterances, and then the caregiver promptly replied with a delighted expression of admiration. Along with the increase in infant initiation of timely (re)actions, caregivers also vary their efforts to attract, manage, and reward the timing of infant attention. In this way, caregivers actively coordinate the timing of infant involvement in their communicative field.

This does not necessary mean, however, that the musicality of caregiver–infant interactions is confined to dyadic relationships. Indeed, involving infant(s) in multiparty interactions is characteristic of song. *Tsando* activity includes the subject (usually the infant), the performer of gymnastic behavior (including the infant), the performer of the |kii of *tsando*, the audience, and bystanders. These roles are not necessary played by different persons. Rather, interactants contingently adjust the ways in which they are involved in the activity.

Conclusion

The main objective of this chapter was to establish a theoretical perspective on the development of caregiver–child interactions, focusing on language socialization prior to speech development, the positioning of participants in caregiver–child interactions, and the multiple contexts of caregiving. To close, I refocus on the themes that underlie the preceding analyses.

Caregiver–child interaction as cultural practices

Research on child development and its recent companion, baby science, has focused on the universal aspects of early caregiving behaviors. In contrast, the approach proposed here inquires into how caregiver–infant interactions are organized in particular times and places. This perspective helps us to recognize caregiver–infant interactions as cultural practices.

'What might appear to be the transparent physicality of the body' may in fact have evolved through a history of practitioners' involvement with 'a complex, nuanced interplay of social and cultural forces' (Hanks 1996: 248). Kaye and his proponents have asserted that turn-taking between sucking and jiggling is a fundamental, universal feature of mother–infant interaction (Kaye 1982). Yet, this interaction pattern was rarely observed among groups of San. Instead, infant fretful behaviors induced culturally distinct caregiving behaviors such as brief nursing with short intervals and frequent gymnastic behavior. These findings suggest that jiggling after a break in sucking is a cultural practice that occurs in particular speech communities such as those in the United States and Japan.

To explain patterns in caregiver–infant interaction, we analyzed relations between the habitus (Bourdieu 1977 [1972]) of participants and the micro-habitats in which the participants in an interaction dwell (Ochs, Solomon, and Sterponi 2005: 547). In this regard, the present study demonstrates that both frequent breastfeeding and gymnastic behavior are profound cultural practices that provide the infant with pleasure. These cultural practices constitute the habitus of |Gui/| |Gana caregivers, which is developed through interplays among the sequence of |Gui/| |Gana mundane activities, their parental ideology, and the conditions that they encounter in the environment (Takada 2004). Moreover, at the same time they provide |Gui/| |Gana infants with the micro-habitat that engenders their social involvement.

Musicality and cultural learning of responsibility

Caregivers introduce communicative musicality in their bodily involvements with the infant. Among the |Gui/| |Gana, several forms of communicative musicality are institutionalized. Communicative musicality develops infants' propensities concerning what to do and what not to do in the course of interaction, and accordingly enhances desirable responses. As such, communicative musicality provides the infant with foundations to develop a sense of responsibility.

The view of responsibility here can be traced to the etymology of the word, namely 're' (back), 'spondere' (to engage oneself or promise), and 'ibilis' (ability). Facilitated by communicative musicality, even young infants sometimes produce responses according to the expectancy of the caregiver (but at other times do not). The early forms of responsibility pave the way for an infant to take part in the more complicated sequential organization of interaction in later life. In essence, an infant in its incipiency may respond to caregiving behaviors by what is called reflex. However, the responses gradually become voluntary. By the third month after birth, for example, infants generally become able to coordinate their emotional state with that of the caregiver. The infant then increases the range of responses and, accordingly, the caregiver increases his or her range of expectations. Consequently, the infant becomes involved in more complex structures of interaction.

Tomasello (1999) has contended that an infant becomes able to understand others' intentions and viewpoints at around the ninth month after birth. The infant then begins to imitate events in social interaction, which is the most important medium of cultural learning. The view of responsibility presented here allows the exploration of the continuity from reflex to reciprocal interaction in consciousness and thereby makes us reconsider the distinctions between *mimicking, emulation,* and *imitation* (Tomasello 1999) through locating temporality at the core of the analytical process. Temporality, like corporeality, is tacit in practices and constitutes a background aspect of interactional organization evident in timing, rhythm, sequence, anticipation, and memory (see Duranti and Black, this volume; Hanks 1996; Heidegger 2008 [1927]; Husserl 1999 [1950]; Merleau-Ponty 2002 [1945]; Schutz 1970). This chapter argues that the sequential structure of imitation activity has its precursors in earlier forms of temporally coordinated responsiveness as social practice. Hence, the development of timely interactional responsibilities is key to the formation of cultural learning.

Language socialization perspectives on the development of caregiver–child interaction

Kaye (1982) proposed that, for the caregiver and child to form a social system, each must share common aims. Tomasello and colleagues also promoted this view in studies of cultural learning (e.g. Tomasello 1999).

Language socialization research provides a broader perspective on caregiver–infant interactions. It inquires into the process by which 'children develop concepts of [a] socioculturally structured universe through their *participation* in language activities' (Ochs 1988: 14). Instead of considering only the state of the children's inner worlds (i.e. the mind), this line of research examines how children are apprenticed into the participation framework in a given speech community.

The San study indicates that caregivers involve children in the participation framework of socially and culturally organized practices long before children become able to understand others' intentions and viewpoints. At the same time, infants respond to proximal contexts with a narrow variety of actions, and their forms of participation change significantly as they age. This process constitutes an important facet of caregiver–infant interactions as emergent biological and cultural engagements. Moreover, most activities regarding caregiver–infant interactions involve multiple contexts. Accordingly, the infant attempts to engage in the broader contexts of interaction. In this process, the multiple contexts surrounding the infant provide him or her with rich resources for forming actions that maintain and create culture.

In sum, this chapter reconsiders how to locate culture in caregiver–infant interactions. Culture is not only a system constructed in the mind, thereby making a child a fully developed individual. It is also an ever-shifting accumulation of temporally coordinated actions by which children and other members of a particular speech community collaboratively realize social meanings. Imitation is just one milestone along a pathway infused with culturally rooted interactional practices. The practices draw infants from birth into forms of responsible corporeal engagement that promote and display cultural learning.

NOTES

1 Although much of the research uses the term *imitation* to indicate this behavior, this discussion uses the term *mimicry*, according to Tomasello's (1999) definition. *Imitation* strictly means 'recreating the intention of the behavior' (Tomasello 1999).

2 Kaye (1982: 66, 161) used 'shared intentions' to indicate this period. The phrase is modified referring to the usage of the term 'intention' in recent studies.

3   As an exception, Fogel et al. (2006) promote a relational-historical research approach to exploring this issue. Based on longitudinal observation of caregiver–child interactions in the United States, they demonstrate that infant skills are relational achievements as well as the product of a historical process of mutual regulation within the dyad.

4   San languages have traditionally been classified into northern, central, and southern families. While the |Gui and ||Gana languages are classified as two languages in the central family, the !Xun and Ju|'hoan languages are classified as different lects in the northern family. The Ju|'hoan adopted a nomadic lifestyle based on foraging activities in their semiarid environment. By contrast, the !Xun have had close associations with the neighboring Owambo agro-pastoral people and have learned a sedentary lifestyle (Takada 2005b).

5   Nakagawa (1996a) proposed a tentative practical orthography that enables a phonologically adequate documentation of |Gui material. I adopt that orthography here. According to Nakagawa (1996a), |Gui has clicks and nonclick consonants. Click consonants consist of 'click types' and 'click accompaniments.' |Gui has four click types – (|: (dental), ||: (lateral), ≠: (palatal), and !: (alveolar) – and thirteen click accompaniments: *g* (voiced velar plosive), *k* (voiceless velar plosive), *kh* (aspirated velar plosive), *G* (voiced uvular plosive), *q* (voiceless uvular plosive), *qh* (aspirated uvular plosive), *k'* (voiceless velar ejective), *q'* (voiceless uvular ejective), *x* (voiceless uvular affricate), *qx'* (affricated uvular ejective), *n* (voiced velar nasal), *nh* (aspirated velar nasal), and *ʔ*: (glottal stop). Combinations result in 52 'click consonants,' all of which are phonologically distinct. There are 36 phonologically distinct variations of nonclick consonants. As for vowels, there are six plain vowels (*i, e, a, o, u,* and *oa*), three nasal vowels (*ẽ, ã,* and *õ*), and three pharyngealized vowels ($a̰$, $o̰$, and $o̰a̰$). Additionally, |Gui is a tonal language with a complex tonal system. However, tonal information is omitted in the transcriptions when it is not necessary for discussion.

6   Table 3.1 shows the nonverbal and verbal behaviors of each interactant along a timeline. The following analyses are based on such systematic transcriptions of the video-recorded interactions. However, I simplify or omit those transcriptions for the remainder of this chapter, because of space constraints.

7   Each group of the San shows considerable differences in its interpretation of gymnastic behavior (Takada 2004, 2005b).

8   Limited patterns of consonant–vowel combinations form the morphemes of |Gui (see Nakagawa 1996a: 114–9). More than 90 percent of |Gui morphemes consist of two syllables, which have been roughly classified into two types (CVCV or CVN, where C is a consonant, V is a vowel, and N is a syllabic nasal, i.e. *m* or *n*). Most of the others are one-syllable morphemes, which have been roughly classified into two types (CV or N).

9   To designate Mt, Tt used the pronoun *ʔama*, which indicates third person, *male*, single, and objective case, even though Mt is a *female* infant. According to my informant, the gender of an infant does not always accord with the gender of the pronoun in |Gui/||Gana conversation.

10 According to Malloch (1999), 'pulse' is the regular succession of expressive events over time. 'Quality' consists of the melodic and timbral contours of the vocalizations (equivalent to the contour and speed of body gestures). 'Narrative,' which allows people to share a sense of passing time, is built from the units of pulse and quality found in the jointly created gestures of vocalizations and bodily movement.

REFERENCES

Adamson, L. B. (1995) *Communication Development During Infancy*. Madison, WI: Brown and Benchmark.

Bly, L. (1994) *Motor Skills Acquisition in the First Year: An Illustrated Guide to Normal Development*. Tucson, AZ: Therapy Skill Builders.

Bourdieu, P. (1977 [1972]) *Outline of a Theory of Practice*. R. Nice, transl. New York: Cambridge University Press.

Bril, B., Zack, M., and Nkounkou-Hombessa, E. (1989) Ethnotheories of development and education: A view from different cultures. *European Journal of Psychology of Education* 4: 307–18.

Bruner, J. (1983) *Child's Talk: Learning to Use Language*. Oxford: Oxford University Press.

Bruner, J. (1990) *Acts of Meaning*. Cambridge, MA: Harvard University Press.

Butterworth, G. and Jarrett, N. L. M. (1991) What minds have in common is space: Spatial mechanism serving joint visual attention in infancy. *British Journal of Developmental Psychology* 9: 55–72.

Cole, M. and Cole, S. R. (1993) *The Development of Children*. 2nd ed. New York: Scientific American Books.

Duranti, A. (1997) *Linguistic Anthropology*. Cambridge: Cambridge University Press.

Emde, R. N., Biringen, Z., Clyman, R. B., and Oppenheim, D. (1991) The moral self of infancy: Affective core and procedural knowledge. *Developmental Review* 11: 251–70.

Fernald, A. and Kuhl, P. K. (1987) Acoustic determinants of infant preference for motherese speech. *Infant Behavior and Development* 10: 279–93.

Fogel, A., A. Garvey, Hsu, H.-C. and West-Stroming, D. (2006) *Change Processes in Relationships: A Relational-Historical Research Approach*. New York: Cambridge University Press.

Goodwin, C. (2000) Action and embodiment within situated human interaction. *Journal of Pragmatics* 32: 1489–522.

Hanks, W. F. (1996) *Language and Communicative Practices*. Boulder, CO: Westview Press.

Heidegger, M. (2008 [1927]) *Being and Time*. J. Macquarrie and E. Robinson, transl. New York: Harper.

Husserl, E. (1999 [1950]) *The Idea of Phenomenology: A Translation of Die Idee Der Phänomenologie Husserliana II*. L. Hardy, transl. Dordrecht, The Netherlands: Kluwer Academic.

Jakobson, R. (1960) Linguistics and poetics. In T. A. Sebeok (ed.), *Style in Language*. 350–77. Cambridge, MA: MIT Press.

Kaye, K. (1982) *The Mental and Social Life of Babies: How Parents Create Persons*. Chicago, IL: University of Chicago Press.

Konner, M. J. (1973) Newborn walking: Additional data. *Science* 179: 307.

Konner, M. J. (1976) Maternal care, infant behavior and development among the !Kung. In R. B. Lee and I. DeVore (eds.), *Kalahari Hunter-Gatherers: Studies of the !Kung San and their Neighbors*. 218–45. Cambridge, MA: Harvard University Press.

Konner, M. J. and Worthman, C. (1980) Nursing frequency, gonadal function, and birth spacing among !Kung hunter-gatherers. *Science* 207: 788–91.

Korner, A. F. and Thoman, E. B. (1972) The relative efficacy of contact and vestibular-proprioceptive stimulation in soothing neonates. *Child Development* 43: 443–53.

Kuhl, P. K., Williams, K. A., Lacerda, F., Stevens, K. N., and Lindblom, B. (1992) Linguistic experience alters phonetic perception in infants by 6 months of age. *Science* 255: 606–8.

Malloch, S. N. (1999) Mothers and infants and communicative musicality. *Musicæ Scientiæ, Special Issue 1999–2000*: 29–57.

Meltzoff, A. N. (1985) The roots of social and cognitive development: Models of man's original nature. In T. M. Field and N. A. Fox (eds.), *Social Perception in Infants*. 1–30. Norwood, NJ: Ablex.

Meltzoff, A. N. and Moore, M. K. (1977) Imitation of facial and manual gestures by human neonates. *Science* 198: 75–8.

Merleau-Ponty, M. (2002 [1945]) *Phenomenology of Perception*. C. Smith, transl. London: Routledge.

Nakagawa, H. (1996a) An outline of |Gui phonology. *African Study Monographs, Supplementary Issue* 22: 101–24.

Nakagawa, H. (1996b) Literature and ethnography: Poetry of |Gui khoe = Bushman. In J. Tanaka, M. Kakeya, M. Ichikawa, and I. Ohta (eds.), *Anthropology of Nature and Society, Vol.2: Changing Africa*. 81–116. Kyoto: Academia Publisher (in Japanese).

Ochs, E. (1988) *Culture and Language Development: Language Acquisition and Language Socialization in a Samoan Village*. Cambridge: Cambridge University Press.

Ochs, E., Solomon, O., and Sterponi, L. (2005) Limitations and transformations of habitus in Child-Directed Communication. *Discourse Studies* 7(4–5): 547–83.

Papoušek, M. and Papoušek, H. (1981) Musical elements in the infant's vocalization: Their significance for communication, cognition, and creativity. In L. P. Lipsitt and C. K. Rovee-Collier (eds.), *Advances in Infancy Research* 1: 163–224.

Piaget, J. (2001 [1967]) *The Psychology of Intelligence*. M. Piercy and D. E. Berlyne, transl. London: Routledge.

Sander, L. W. (1977) The regulation of exchange in the infant–caretaker system and some aspects of the context–content relationship. In M. Lewis and L. A. Rosenblum (eds.), *Interaction, Conversation, and the Development of Language*. 133–56. New York: Wiley.

Scaife, M. and Bruner, J. (1975) The capacity for joint visual attention in the infant. *Nature* 253: 265–6.

Schutz, A. (1970) *On Phenomenology and Social Relations: Selected Writings*. Chicago, IL: University of Chicago Press.

Shimojo, S. (1988) *Birth of the Gaze: The Baby Science Revolution*. Tokyo: Shinyosha (in Japanese).

Stern, D. N. (2000) *The Interpersonal World of the Infant: A View From Psychoanalysis and Developmental Psychology*. 2nd ed. New York: Basic Books.

Super, C. M. (1976) Environmental effects on motor development: The case of African infant precocity. *Developmental Medicine and Child Neurology* 18: 561–7.

Takada, A. (2002) The meaning of caregiving behaviors among the San for child development. *The Japanese Journal of Developmental Psychology* 13(1): 63–77 (in Japanese).

Takada, A. (2004) Nomadic lifestyle and childrearing: Analysis of gymnastic behavior among the Central Kalahari San. In J. Tanaka, S. Sato, K. Sugawara, and I. Ohta (eds.), *Nomad: Life in the Wilderness of Africa*. 228–48. Kyoto: Showado (in Japanese).

Takada, A. (2005a) Early vocal communication and social institution: Appellation and infant verse addressing among the Central Kalahari San. *Crossroads of Language, Interaction, and Culture* 6: 80–108.

Takada, A. (2005b) Mother–infant interactions among the !Xun: Analysis of gymnastic and breastfeeding behaviors. In B. S. Hewlett and M. E. Lamb (eds.), *Hunter-Gatherer Childhoods: Evolutionary, Developmental, and Cultural Perspectives*. 289–308. New Brunswick, NJ: Transaction Publishers.

Tanaka, J. (1980) *The San: Hunter-Gatherers of the Kalahari, a Study in Ecological*

Anthropology. Tokyo: University of Tokyo Press.

Tomasello, M. (1999) *The Cultural Origins of Human Cognition*. Cambridge, MA: Harvard University Press.

Tomasello, M. (2003) *Constructing a Language: A Usage-Based Theory of Language Acquisition*. Cambridge, MA: Harvard University Press.

Trevarthen, C. (1999) Musicality and the intrinsic motive pulse: Evidence from human psychology and infant communication. *Musicæ Scientiæ, Special Issue* 1999–2000: 155–215.

Vygotsky, L. S. (1962 [1934]) *Thought and Language*. E. Hanfmann and G.

Vakar, transl. Cambridge, MA: MIT Press.

Werker, J. F. and McLeod, P. J. (1989) Infant preference for both male and female infant-directed talk: A developmental study of attentional and affective responsiveness. *Canadian Journal of Psychology* 43: 230–46.

Zelazo, P. R. (1976) Comments on genetic determinants of infant development: An overstated case. In L. Lipsitt (ed.), *Developmental Psychobiology: The Significance of Infancy*. Hillsdale, NJ: Lawrence Erlbaum.

4 Language Socialization and Multiparty Participation Frameworks

LOURDES DE LEÓN

Introduction

Language socialization studies have highlighted the relationship between participatory complexity and sociocentrism in children's communicative environments (Ochs 1988; Ochs and Schieffelin 1984; Schieffelin 1990). Along these lines, Chavajay and Rogoff assessed cross-cultural differences in the way children are socialized to interact with others. The Euro-American middle-class 'dyadic prototype interaction of one-partner-at-a-time' (2002: 144) contrasts with Guatemalan Mayan children's socialization, which routinely involves 'complex multidirectional shared arrangements' (Rogoff 2003: 145). This major cross-cultural contrast is also documented by Brown (this volume) for other societies. This chapter examines how communicative environments organized along dyadic or multiparty interactional arrangements are relevant to early language socialization as well as to children's organization of attention and participation in learning and apprenticeship situations.

Children are, in fact, able to learn language through participatory roles not only as addressees but also as active overhearers monitoring conversations (Akhtar 2005a, 2005b; Akhtar, Jipson, and Callanan 2001; Blum-Kulka and Snow 2002; Forrester 1992; Heath 1983). In other triadic (or multiparty) interactions, children may be embedded speakers through prompting (de León 1998, 2009; Demuth 1986; Eisenberg 1986; Sidnell 1997; Watson-Gegeo and Gegeo 1986) or may be animated by others (Paugh 2001; Schieffelin 1990).

Children may also be indirect participants in teasing, scolding, or polite interactions, among other participatory configurations (Burdelski 2006, 2010; de León 1998, 2008a, 2008b, in press a, in press b; Field 2001; Schieffelin 1986).

The Handbook of Language Socialization, First Edition. Edited by Alessandro Duranti, Elinor Ochs, and Bambi B. Schieffelin.
© 2014 John Wiley & Sons, Ltd. Published 2014 by John Wiley & Sons, Ltd.

This chapter advocates a language acquisition and socialization model based on the participation framework as the unit of analysis. The term 'participation' refers to 'actions demonstrating forms of involvement performed by parties within evolving structures of talk' (Goodwin and Goodwin 2004: 222). This concept highlights the interactive work in which *both* hearers as well as speakers and other participants engage. Analysis of language socialization and acquisition as processes lodged in participation frameworks reveals:

(1) The child as an active participant occupying different participatory roles in multiparty interactions.
(2) The central role of multimodal semiosis (e.g. gaze, gesture, body, and touch) beyond just vocal language in the language acquisition and socialization process.
(3) The primacy of action and activity as the locus of the socialization process.

The present discussion extends the analysis of the emerging participatory competence to Zinacantec Mayan infants in their first 18 months of life, integrating local theories of socialization and ethnographically informed micro-analysis of interactions in which children are embedded (de León 1998, 2005). The theoretical advantages of a participation framework analysis are outlined in relation to variation in participation configurations and corporeal niches, especially triadic participation frameworks as a locus of learning. Participation roles played by Mayan Zinacantec infants along the developmental timeline are examined for how they afford opportunities for infants to be active participants and co-constructors of meaning.

The study is rooted in over two decades of in-depth longitudinal linguistic and anthropological research in the Mayan hamlet of Nabenchauk, Zinacantan, Chiapas, Mexico (de León 1998, 1999, 2005, 2007, in press a, in press b). The data come from a focal family and six additional families.

Participation Frameworks and Language Learning

Cross-cultural variation in language socializing practices can be explained by the inter-relation of ideologies, habitats, participation frameworks, activities, and semiotic repertoires. These sociocultural dimensions are variably organized by a community's habitus in line with practice theory (Ochs, Solomon, and Sterponi 2005: 560).

This chapter focuses on how participation frameworks organize infants' communicative development. It embraces Goffman's (1974, 1981) critique of the speaker–hearer dyad and his participation framework model, with further elaborations by Goodwin (1984) and Goodwin and Goodwin (2004) (see also also Clark 1996; Goodwin 1990; Hanks 1996; Irvine 1996; Levinson 1988; Philips 1972). The notion of 'participation' 'provides one framework for investigating how multiple

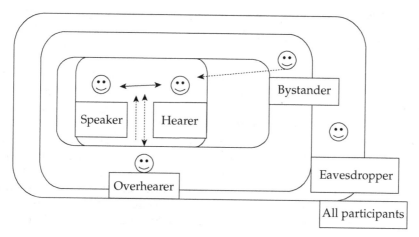

Figure 4.1 Diagramming participation. Adapted from Clark (1996). © Cambridge University Press.

parties build action together while both attending to and helping to construct relevant action and context' (Goodwin and Goodwin 2004: 239).

Clark's model of participation, represented in Figure 4.1, uses Goffman's (1974, 1981) participant roles of speaker, hearer, side participants, overhearers, bystanders, and others. The concentric spaces distinguish focal or explicitly ratified participants (speaker, hearer) from 'side participants and overhearers [who] may help shape how Speakers and Hearers act toward each other. They also represent different ways of listening and understanding' (Clark 1996: 15; see also Hindmarsh and Pilnick 2002).

The participation framework diagram provided by Clark illustrates participant roles and places. The diagram also illustrates with arrows reciprocal and nonreciprocal relations between participants. It should be clear, however, that participation frameworks unfold temporally and that participants have shifting roles.

Goffman's decomposition of the speaker into animator, author, principal, and figure ('the production format') allows one to trace the child's emergence as a 'speaker' long before (s)he produces speech. In the case of prompting routines, the child is embedded as animator of others' gestural actions or speech in triadic to multiparty interactions (de León 2009; Demuth 1986; Eisenberg 1986; Pfeiler 2007; Schieffelin 1990; Sidnell 1997; Watson-Gegeo and Gegeo 1986; see also Bruner 1978). She can also be embedded as a 'speaker' through the reported speech of the 'meaning' of his or her gestures or pointing actions (de León 1998; Haviland 1998).

Goffman's deconstruction of the hearer into ratified as opposed to unratified participants and intended versus nonintended addressees (overhearers) endows the recipient of child-directed speech (the so-called 'hearer' in the conventional acquisition model) with participatory agency.[1] One hearer participant status that has been understudied is the overhearer (see Clark 1996; Hindmarsh and Pilnick 2002). The import of this role was introduced decades ago in Mead's study of children and ritual in Bali: '[V]erbal directions are meager; children learn from the feel of other people's bodies and from watching, although this watching has a *kinesthetic* quality' (1955: 42, emphasis mine). More recently, Akhtar (2005a, 2005b) and Akhtar, Jipson, and Callanan (2001) have argued that young children are quite adept at monitoring third-party conversations and that the precondition of inter-subjectivity and joint attention between two focal participants in a dyadic format is not necessary in a language acquisition model (see also Forrester 1992; Oshima-Takane 1988). Learning through overhearing plays a particularly important role in communities in which children are not frequently directly addressed by adults (Lieven 1994) or where communication is not child centered. Studies with older children also highlight the role of multiparty discourse in developing complex communicational competences (Blum-Kulka and Snow 2002; Fung, Miller, and Lin 2004; Miller 1994).

In summary, cross-cultural overhearer participation configurations indicate:

(1) Infants may develop a participatory competence occupying different positions in the participation framework without necessarily being focal addressees.
(2) The participant status of 'overhearer' relativizes the putative centrality of the speaker (primary caregiver) and hearer (infant) dyadic interaction, with child-directed speech as the sole guiding force of language learning.
(3) Overhearing may play a more central role than acquisition theories recognize. It affords children with other learning skills such as observation, attention, inference, and participation long before they learn to speak.

Learning as a third party by keenly attending and listening to others' coordinated actions has been documented by Correa-Chávez and Rogoff (2009), Gaskins (1996: 352; 2000), Greenfield (1984, 2004), Rogoff (1990), and Rogoff et al. (2003) for other Mayan communities, and by Lancy (2010), López et al. (2010), and Paradise and Rogoff (2009), among other researchers, for other cultures.

Observers/overhearers keenly learn from the margins of the participation framework. As such, this participation status is central not only to children's interactions with others but also to the course of human development.

Overall, the value of the participation framework as an analytic dimension of socialization rests on the following benefits:

(1) Situated activities constitute the locus of the learning process rather than just child-directed speech, as stated by some psycholinguistic approaches.
(2) The deconstruction of speaker and hearer into different kinds of participation provides a more realistic analysis of what becoming a language user involves.
(3) Speaker and hearer are imbued with a rich cognitive life, 'reflexively orienting toward each other and the larger events in which they are engaged' (Goodwin and Goodwin 2004: 236). This important theoretical step opens up a space for the learner as an active co-participant.

(4) Speakers and hearers are joined together 'in a common course of action, one that encompasses not only linguistic structure in the stream of speech' but also gaze, gesture, orientation, and posture (Goodwin and Goodwin 2004: 227).

Corporeal Niches and Participant Configurations

Participation frameworks can refer to the 'corporeal configurations' of participants in relation to each other, and, on occasion, aspects of the environment such as artifacts and spaces. Such configurations are embedded in and organized by communicative practices and habitus across communities (Ochs, Solomon, and Sterponi 2005; see also Brown, this volume; Solomon, this volume; Takada, this volume). In their Child-Directed Communication model, Ochs, Solomon, and Sterponi (2005) schematize recurrent cross-cultural caregiver–child corporeal niches as face to face, nested (with the child on his/her back or on the lap of the caregiver, positioned facing outwards), and side by side, and provide schematic representations, as in Figure 4.2. Another very recurrent corporeal niche that I add here is the 'L spatial orientation' (Kendon 1990), where the baby is placed in relation to the caregiver in an L alignment, either on the caregiver's hip with or without a sling or on the caregiver's lap (see Figure 4.5).

One major difference between the different corporeal arrangements is that, with the exception of face-to-face alignment, other arrangements allow for multiparty interaction where the child shares with the caregiver a visual field of 30 to 180 degrees. Figure 4.3, Figure 4.4, and Figure 4.5 illustrate the most frequent corporeal configurations in Zinacantan.[2] They also show that the infant interacts with multiple caregivers in the extended family household (e.g. mother, siblings, grandfather, aunt, and grandmother).

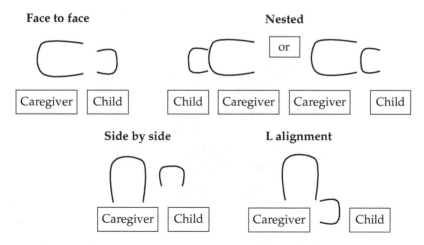

Figure 4.2 Corporeal arrangements in participation frameworks. After Ochs, Solomon, and Sterponi (2005).

Figure 4.3a   Nested (behind caregiver).

Figure 4.3b   Nested (behind caregivers).

Figure 4.4   Nested (in front of caregiver).

Figure 4.5a L alignment.

Figure 4.5b L alignment.

Figure 4.6 offers a quantitative profile of the number of interactions within various corporeal arrangements that two 12-month-old Tzotzil Mayan children engaged in over one hour of videotaped naturalistic observation. Face-to-face interactions are less frequent than nested and L corporeal arrangements. Side-to-side and face-to-face interactions are similar in frequency. Overall, the higher frequency of nested interactions and interactions in L arrangements influence, in important ways, the communicative habitats in which children develop, favoring, specifically, triadic and more complex multiparty interactions (de León and Martinez 2008).

Kendon has referred to certain 'spatial-orientational arrangements' (1985: 237) as 'facing formations' (F formations):

Whenever two or more individuals are placed close to each other, orienting their bodies in such a way that each of them has an easy, direct, and equal access to every other participant's transactional segment, and agree to maintain such an arrangement, they can be said to create an F formation. (Kendon 1990: 239)

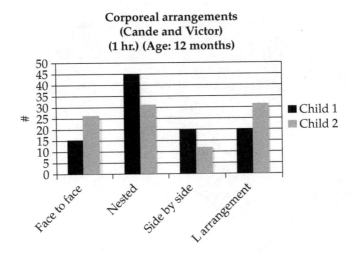

Figure 4.6   Corporeal arrangements in two Mayan Tzotzil infants' interactions.

Middle-class child-directed speech in the United States involves face-to-face F formations as the default participation framework, speech as the privileged semiotic medium, and a simplified register. However, language socialization studies have shown that this is just 'one kind of developmental story' (Ochs and Schieffelin 1984; see also Lieven 1994; Stoll 2009). In a comparative study, LeVine et al. (1996) demonstrated that dyadic vocal language is considerably less frequent among the Gusii from Western Kenya in comparison with Boston mothers and children. Gusii also engage in the practice of gaze aversion, in contrast to American mothers, who interact with their children with sustained mutual gaze (LeVine et al. 1996: 222; see also Quinn 2005). It is thus clear that the different corporeal arrangements privilege different F formations, semiotic mediums, and participation frameworks.

In cultures where face-to-face corporeal arrangements are not the default, babies occupy on many occasions the third party slot in the participation framework with obvious changes of footing as the interaction evolves. The low frequency of dyadic face-to-face interaction versus other corporeal arrangements illustrated in Figure 4.5 indicates that in Zinacantán and probably in other 'sling' baby communities, one 'preferred participant configuration' is triadic, involving three parties. Here the child may play different participatory roles, as 'speaker,' focal addressee, overhearer 1 (intended addressee), or overhearer 2 (nonintended addressee), as elaborated below:

(1) Triadic with child as 'speaker': The child enacts a participation framework through vocalization, gesture, gaze, or body motion that is interpreted as intentional by the caregiver who holds her; the latter glosses the child's utterance in a 'she said' frame to a third party (see Example 4.1 and Figure 4.18).

Figure 4.7   Mock offer: 'Take your lollipop.'

Figure 4.8   'Take this one away, take him!'

(2) Triadic with child as embedded speaker: As amply documented in language socialization studies, when performing prompting routines, the caregiver asks the child to perform a gesture or a vocalization that, in turn, embeds the child as a 'speaker' who directs the prompt to a third party (see Example 4.2).

(3) Triadic with child as addressee, as documented in teasing interactions. The child can be a focal addressee while other parties align with the teaser. Figure 4.7 shows how a teaser makes a mock offer of a lolly to a 10-month-old Zinacantec baby in a triadic participation framework (see de León 2005). The child can also be indirectly targeted as overhearer 1 (intended addressee): The caregiver embeds the child in interactions where she is the intended addressee, but does it through talk directed to a ratified hearer who, in turn, complies with the speaker. The child ratifies himself/herself as an overhearer by crying or showing distress (de León 2005). In Zinacantan this typically happens in teasing interactions with infants and in scolding or accusations with older children. Figure 4.8 shows Cande (10 years old) teasing her 20-month-old

brother, Jonas. She asks the filmmaker to 'take (Jonas) away, take him!' Jonas first looks distracted but then shows distress.

(4) Triadic with child as overhearer 2 (nonintended addressee): The child is at the margins of the participation framework but follows the ongoing interaction. This role has been analyzed as that of an overhearer (Akhtar 2005a, 2005b; Akhtar and Gernsbacher 2007; Akhtar, Jipson, and Callanan 2001; de León 2005; Loyd 2005) or 'keen observer' in studies of learning and apprenticeship (Gaskins 1996, 2000; Rogoff 2003; Rogoff et al. 2003) (see Example 4.3).

Triadic interactions are common in child-directed communication where face-to-face interaction is not the default. In prompting interactions involving Yucatec Mayan children, about 10 percent occur in a dyadic design versus 90 percent in a triadic design (Pfeiler 2007: 193). In Zinacantan, prompting interactions are also predominantly triadic. Research on attention and learning designs for autistic children also note that side-by-side interactions through mediated third objects are more effective than the face-to-face format (Akhtar and Gernsbacher 2007; Ochs, Solomon, and Sterponi 2005). Triadic interactional designs in language socialization have been documented (among others) for transferring caregiving responsibilities to older siblings in triadic dialogue among the Wolof (Rabain-Jamin 1998); for narrative socialization with Taiwanese children (Fung, Miller, and Lin 2004: 318);[3] for politeness with Japanese children (Burdelski 2006, 2010); for socializing respect through directives among the Navajo (Field 2001); and for scaring, scolding, shaming, and giving moral advice among Zinacantec Mayans (de León 2008a, 2008b, in press a, in press b).

Preferred triadic configurations provide children with a learning environment that enables them to actively engage and co-participate from the margins, ratifying themselves as the target of a mock threat or overhearing the glosses of their own actions as a quoted speaker. These configurations unfold amidst the flow of everyday life, where participation roles are in a constant flux.

The Emergent Participant: The Language Socialization of Zinacantec Mayan Infants

Along the lines of Ochs and Schieffelin's (1984) seminal work, Gaskins (2006: 281–3) analyzes patterns of social engagement in terms of how caregivers interpret (1) the child's expression of inner experience, (2) how the child influences other people, and (3) ways in which the child obtains and exchanges information about the world. She draws major cross-cultural differences between the levels of attention and feedback that caregivers give to infants, and how caregivers read infants' (communicative) intentions. The Euro-American child-centric interactive style stands out from other socializing styles, such as those of the Gusii (LeVine et al. 1996), the Kaluli (Schieffelin 1990), the Mayan (Brown 1998, this volume; de León 1998; Gaskins 2006), and rural Samoan communities (Ochs 1982, 1988) where caregivers tend not to engage in protoconversations with infants.

While Mayan Zinacantec caregivers do not engage in proto-conversations with infants, they attribute intention to the infant's expressions of inner experience as well as to acts influencing others. The infant's gestures and vocalizations are taken as requests, rejections, and, in general, attention-getting devices. These are glossed in triadic interactions as communicative utterances, often using explicit metapragmatic framing verbs (e.g. *ta jk'an ch'uch'u`*, *xi* ('"I want to nurse," **she says**'); or *peton, xi* ('"hold me," **she says**')), along with further commentaries such as *pukuj xa* ('she is already a demon') (e.g. when a baby gets upset as a result of a teasing action) or *ta xa'i xa* ('she understands, she discerns') (e.g. if a baby gives cues of ratifying herself as the target of a mock threat) (see also Haviland 1998). Around the first months of the infant's life, vocalizations or motions that indicate a desire for elimination are also quoted to a third party in a 's/he said' frame, as if the child were a virtual proto-speaker (de León 1998).[4]

As babies orient their gaze towards a target, stretch a hand to reach something, or express fear of a stranger or anger at someone who playfully separated him or her from her mother, the commentary *xtal xa xch'ulel* ('its soul is arriving') glosses the insight of expression of attention, intention, understanding, and participation. Local ideologies couched in such glosses play an important role in the socialization of the infant in her emergent participatory status.

Below is an analysis of how the infant comes to occupy different spaces in the participation framework – as a 'focal' proto-speaker, an addressee in interactional routines, or an overhearer in triadic interactions (see also de León 1998). Most of the data are micro-interactional sequences of naturally occurring behavior drawn from video recordings and supplemented by contextual and ethnographic note-taking.[5]

The child as a proto-speaker

In contrast to the local Euro-American notion of the baby as a proto-speaker who initiates and responds in dyadic interactions, in Zinacantan, the baby is normally embedded as a *quoted* proto-speaker in *triadic* interactions. As noted, evidence of this disposition lies in the prevalence of glosses for gestures and vocalizations; for example, *chivay xa, xi* ('"I want to go to sleep," **she says**,' said of a baby that yawns).

Zinacantan caregiver–infant dyadic interactions reflect semiotic attunement in the embodied dyad without a necessary face-to-face interaction. These interchanges basically involve nursing and body elimination. Around four months of age, we observe, for example, that caretakers systematically attune themselves to the infant's bodily functions. Given that infants are ordinarily carried wrapped in a shawl or cloth on the mother's back, the mother will sense any body movements that indicate whether the baby wants to urinate or defecate.[6] I have recorded semiotically mediated triadic interactions involving the routine alignment of caregiver and infants that are glossed to a third party as 'I want to pee, she says' (see de León 1998).

From about four months of age, caregivers also attribute intention to babies' gestures, as in Example 4.1:

Example 4.1:   *'Give it here (to me), she says' (Petu, four months)*

Situation: Aunt Lucia is holding Petu on her lap as she is looking towards the path. The baby makes eye contact with the filmmaker (LL), who is sitting on the ground facing them (Figure 4.9). Baby Petu starts raising her right arm in a reaching gesture (Figure 4.10), then raises her left arm and pushes herself forward towards the camera (Figure 4.11 and Figure 4.12). Aunt Lucia looks at the child and the filmmaker, quoting the gestural action as a request, *ak'o xi* ('give it here (to me), she says') (the baby, according to her, wanted the videocamera) (Figure 4.13). Baby Petu lowers her arms, smiling at the filmmaker as Aunt Petu 'talks for her' (Figure 4.14).

Figure 4.9   Baby Petu makes eye contact with LL.

Figure 4.10   Baby Petu raises one arm.

Figure 4.11 Baby Petu raises both arms.

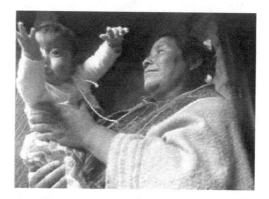

Figure 4.12 Baby Petu gestures towards LL.

Figure 4.13 Aunt Loxa reports the gesture as 'Give it here (to me), she says.'

Figure 4.14   Baby Petu smiles at LL. 'See? "Give it here," she says.'

The child's 'hands up' gesture is indexically grounded by the participation framework and activity. It initiates a participation framework of a triadic kind (Figure 4.13). The fluid communication between gesturer (who, through the reported speech frame, is actually the 'principal') and the 'quoter' ('animator/ author') arises from the embodied unity of caregiver and child in the specific activity. The caretaker is monitoring the child's actions and her field of attention, as if she is sharing it. The alignment of the three participants is keyed by a shared smile between infant and filmmaker and by Aunt Lucia's smile at the baby. This alignment 'through smiling' closes the interactional unit as a sort of indication of achievement.

The expression of the gestural action as participants align with each other nicely illustrates Goodwin's (2003: 15) observation that 'gestures are contextualized by participation frameworks constituted through the embodied mutual orientation of the participants within an interaction' and that 'actions are instantiated in semiotic fields that mutually elaborate each other.' In Example 4.1, the baby's evolving gesture initiates participant configurations and emerging shared semiotic fields.

Several scholars (Achtar and Tomasello 1998; Bates 1979; Trevarthen 1998) have argued that infants display primary intersubjectivity before six months of age but that their gestures are not symbolic (Bates 1979 in Achtar and Tomasello 1998: 327):

> Pre-linguistic infants use a number of intentional gestures that are often ritualized from non-communicative behaviours; for example, the 'hands-up' gesture as a request to be picked up may be a ritualization of the infant trying to pull its way up to the parent's arms. There is no evidence that pre-linguistic infants comprehend these early gestures when produced by another, so they cannot be viewed as true symbols. [...] These so-called pre-symbolic forms are often characterized as being simply a part of an activity, not a symbol standing for anything else in the activity.

Example 4.1 demonstrates that the child's gesture is indexical and iconic; in Bates' terms, however, it is not symbolic. Nevertheless, this 'nonsymbolic gesture' is treated by other participants as symbolic: it 'becomes' an *embedded* 'symbolic' gesture consequential to the emergent organization of participation and semiotic fields shared by participants in the unfolding activity. To this effect, the embodied dyad of caregiver and infant provides a basic ecological niche that facilitates the alignment between the triad of infant, caregiver, and researcher, elaborating on what Sinha (2001) calls 'the epigenesis of symbolization.' The caregiver's report of the child's action to the researcher in the form of a quoted request further meta-pragmatically embeds the child's initial alignment with the filmmaker in the temporally unfolding participation framework. Evidence of the unfolding align-ments lies in the progression from a dyadic to a triadic participation framework of infant, researcher, and caregiver with a desired object (the camera) crowned by the baby's smile at the end.

During the 'nine-month revolution,' children are reported to move from pre-dominantly dyadic interactions to those involving infants and others engaged in joint reference to objects, a configuration referred to as the 'referential triangle' (Tomasello 1999; see Trevarthen 1998). Four-month-old Baby Petu has not reached that developmental milestone; however, her gestural actions are metapragmati-cally glossed as a projection of a referential triangle due to the *consequentiality* of her gesture and to the unfolding semiotic fields treated as shared by the partici-pants. Here, Baby Petu is positioned as both author of the message and overhearer of the gloss to her gestural action. In a parallel way, the filmmaker is positioned as a double addressee: (1) addressed by the caregiver and (2) embedded as the addressee of the infant's presumed request. Participant status is not always as straightforward as a single occupied footing, but, rather, it may involve embed-dedness, laminations, or 'interlocking participation frames' (Sidnell 1997: 159).

The L spatial alignment of the caregiver and Baby Petu, along with the resulting triadic participation framework, allows for the overhearer learning ecology pro-posed for Zinacantan. The interaction unfolds in two stages: Figure 4.15 illustrates the dyadic alignment between infant and filmmaker in relation to the camera. Figure 4.16 displays how the triadic participation framework evoked through the quoted gloss projects the 'referential triangle.'

In sum, Zinacantec language socialization ideologies and practices, as well as the local ecologies provided by corporeal arrangements, F formations, and par-ticipation frameworks, position the child as an embedded proto-speaker whose footing shifts as complex interlocking frameworks unfold.

Socializing the addressee in interactional routines

Studies of Mayan language acquisition suggest that adults address minimal lan-guage to children until the children themselves can engage in conversation (Brown 1998; Gaskins 2006: 286; Pfeiler 2007; Pye 1992: 241–4; Vogt 1969: 185; Wagley 1949: 29–30 cited in Pye 1992: 241). Pye, however, reports a Baby Talk register for K'iche' (1986, 1992), and both de León (1998, 2005) and Martínez Perez (2008) document

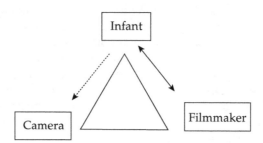

Figure 4.15 Dyadic interchange between infant and filmmaker.

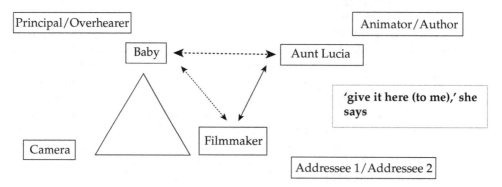

Figure 4.16 Projection of 'referential triangle' in triadic participation ('Give it here (to me), she says').

a special register to address infants in Tzotzil (Zinacantan and Huixtan). It is not used in the proto-conversational style of Euro-American mothers (Ferguson 1977, 1982; Fernald and Morikawa 1993; Snow 1994; Snow and Ferguson 1977); rather, it mainly consists of rhetorical questions and attention-getting expressions.

In Zinacantan, a frequent setting of the infant's socialization as an addressee occurs in interactional routines that start when the baby is around five months old and that continue through approximately the first 18 months of life. The routines are performed in both triadic and multiparty formats, with the child playing diverse participatory roles. Interactional routines socialize the child in situated activity systems that are 'the contingent and the co-constructed product of sequentially organized communicative acts, both verbal and nonverbal' (Garrett and Baquedano-López 2002: 343; see also Wooton 1997). As a social encounter, interactional routines present the child with a particular socializing niche that involves sequentiality, co-construction, shared attention, and relevance (Bruner 1983; Bruner and Sherwood 1976; Goodwin 2006). Central to this study is the notion that interactional routines are embodied in participation structures that specify who can say what to whom (Peters and Boggs 1986: 81). Interactional routines are

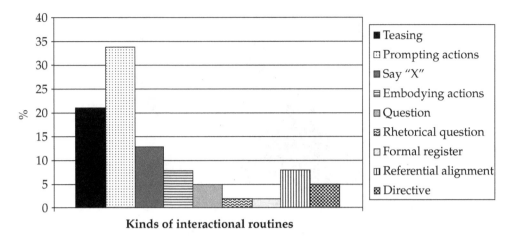

Figure 4.17   Percentage of interactional routines with Cande (11 months).

a perfect illustration of the child's emerging skills as a semiotic agent who cooperatively co-constructs action within a situated activity. Cooperative semiosis implies that meaning is co-constructed by the child and others who are engaged as semiotic agents (see Goodwin 2010).

The most frequent interactional routines documented in the present study are prompting actions (e.g. 'Close your eyes'), teasing (e.g. 'It is going to grab you!'), and prompting (e.g. 'Say "goodbye"'). Less frequent routines are directives to perform embodied actions (e.g. 'Walk,' accompanied with walking motion), directives for referential alignment (e.g. 'See Grandma chopping wood'), questions (e.g. 'Do you want more?'), rhetorical questions (e.g. 'What do you think?'), and formal register used to index third parties of higher status interacting with the infant (de León 1998).

Figure 4.17 indicates the frequency of interactional routines across three hours of video-recorded observations in the focal family of the study when the focal child, Cande, was 11 months old.

The most frequent interactional routine practiced by all the members of the family with Cande (and more generally with children over eight months of age in Zinacantan) is prompting gestural actions:

- *chabal xa*: 'No more' (child raises both hands and rotates them)
- *ti'o lavoke*: 'Bite your toe' (child puts toe in mouth)
- *atinan*: 'Wash your head' (child rubs her head with hand)
- *vayan*: 'Sleep' (child makes a snoring sound, reclines her head, and/or closes her eyes)
- *paso lajole*: 'Make your head (shake)' (child shakes head)
- *paso la-k'obe*: 'Make your hand (shake)' (child shakes hand)
- *mutz'o lasate*: 'Close (eye) your eye' (child blinks)

Figure 4.18   A prompting routine.

- *ak'o tzitzi* (Baby Talk): 'Give me a little toy (Baby Talk)' (the child extends hand with palm up).

At 11 months old, prompting actions are very popular activities across the household since the child is very gesturally expressive and engaging, as seen in Example 4.2 (Figure 4.18). These co-constructed actions evidence Zinacantec language socialization ideologies, wherein language is seen as emergent via several semiotic channels that are not strictly vocal and emerge in embodied action.

Example 4.2:   'Give me a little toy' (Cande, 11 months)

Grandpa is squatting as he holds Cande, who is standing in front of him facing the filmmaker. He says for the child *ak'bon tzitzi* ('Give me a little toy') as he extends the child's hand towards the filmmaker. Cande engages by extending her little hand with palm up in a requesting gesture. Grandpa then changes the frame by saying *kixtalan* ('Let's play') and goes on to prompt the child to say 'Goodbye Daddy, goodbye.' As the child is still holding her hand palm up in the requesting gesture, he turns her hand down and waves it for her.

This interaction is particularly interesting because of the unfolding responses of the child. The first prompt is followed by the child's gestural reply, revealing the flowing alignment between both participants. In contrast, the subsequent prompt, still embodied in the previous gesture, is not followed by the corresponding gestural action until Grandpa forms the gesture in the child's hand. The second unsuccessful response unveils the socialization of a new prompting routine through embodiment and scaffolding. In this triadic interaction, vocal and gestural action conjoin in the activity.

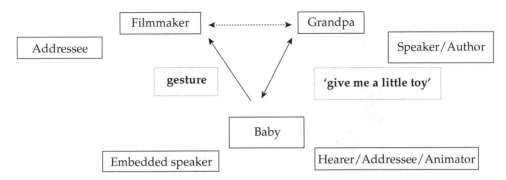

Figure 4.19 Participation frameworks in a prompting routine.

Prompting routines exemplify interlocking participation frameworks. The prompter is the speaker/author as the designer of the prompt; the child as a co-participant is an embedded author and animator. The conjoined action in the activity relies on the primary relation between the speaker (prompter) and the hearer (child), who ratifies herself as the intended addressee by redirecting the prompted action to a third participant who is, in fact, the addressee of the prompt. The child is, in this manner, socialized into three-party interaction through laminated participant statuses. Figure 4.19 illustrates the process.

Triadic teasing interactions produce other kinds of interactional effects in which the target child is positioned as the intended addressee through a third party that aligns with the teaser. The target child, sometimes not even in eye contact with the aligned teasers, typically ratifies himself as a participant through crying or showing discomfort (de León 2005). Similar triadic formats are used for shaming or scolding older children (de León 2008a, in press a, in press b) or between siblings to persuade a noncompliant toddler who is not paying attention or complying with a directive (de León 2008b, in press b).

Such interactional routines reveal the centrality of the activity, action, and participation framework as a child emerges as an addressee who changes footing and learns to co-participate in sequentially organized forms of turn-taking.

The overhearer: Finding a way from periphery to focality

The previous section, 'Corporeal Niches and Participant Configurations,' outlined possible participant statuses of addressees. Overhearers who are not intentionally addressed may remain at the periphery of the interaction or may show interest in finding their way into 'focality.' In this case, they may act as if they were intentionally addressed, displaying focused attention and keen observation. Zinancantec young children play this participant role throughout a good part of the day while they are wrapped in a sling and attached to their caregivers as the latter perform their everyday chores.

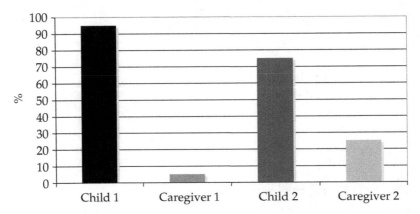

Figure 4.20   Pointing by caregiver and child (two dyads).

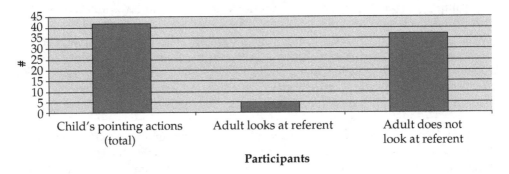

Figure 4.21   Adult's attention to referent in child's pointing actions (age: 12 months; one-hour sample).

Evidence of infants' intention to be focal participants can be traced through the analysis of multimodal moves occurring in situated activities. Pointing, reaching, gesturing, gaze, vocalizing, and changes in body orientation provide this source of evidence. In Example 4.3 below I provide an analysis of the multimodal actions of a 14-month-old child attempting to move from the periphery to focal participation. Figure 4.20 and Figure 4.21 show a quantitative profile of infant and caregiver pointing.

Figure 4.20 shows the mean number of pointing actions of two dyads of caregivers and infants (age 10–12 months) in the Tzotzil municipalities of Zinacantan and Huixtan in Chiapas (de León and Martinez 2008). In a three-hour sample of video-taped ethnographic observation, the caregivers' mean rate of pointing was below 25 percent in contrast to a 73 to 95 percent rate for pointing by children. This large asymmetry reveals that the children were trying to enact a participation framework to establish joint attention on the current course of action in contrast to the adults, who were attending other matters.

Figure 4.21 further shows that, out of 43 pointing actions by a child in a one-hour sample, the caregiver just looks five times at the pointed referent. Again, efforts to build joint attention largely come from the child, whose intention is to reorganize the participation framework and engage participants in the current course of action.

Example 4.3 provides a micro-analysis of the reaching and vocalization of Lol (14 months old), who is attempting to contribute to an ongoing activity as an engaged 'speaker' and actor.

Example 4.3

Situation: Lol is with his mother wrapped to her in an L corporeal arrangement. As Mother is in the little grocery shop owned by the family, a customer arrives and asks for one peso (*mil* in Tzotzil) that the family owed her from a previous transaction. Mother agrees and shifts her attention towards a little bag by the wall to take the coin out. As Lol hears the word *mil* he repeats it twice and shifts his body to reach the little coin bag in synchrony with his mother's line of sight and oriented motions. Mother keeps talking to customer, grabs the coin, keeping it away from Lol's hand, who reaches out to grab it. Lol says *mil* again, trying to enact a participation framework where he could be ratified as a participant and have access to the coin. Mother gives the coin to customer, aware of her child's actions, but excludes him from the interaction. The child demonstrates an intensive desire to pick the coin up himself and perhaps to hand it to the customer (or keep it!).

1	Customer:	ak'bon *mil*
		Yes, give me the one peso coin (you owed me)
2	Mother:	ah, *mil* chak'an=
		Oh, you want one peso
3	Baby:	=*mil, mil*
4	Mother:	((turns towards hanging bag))
5	Baby:	*mil, mil*
		coin, coin
		((focuses on the search area and reaches for coin))

6 Mother: ((moves towards Customer with coin in hand))
7 Baby: ((reaches out to grab the coin from Mother's hand))

8 Mother: ((extends arm and shows coin as baby looks at coin and
                reaches out))

 9 Mother: *ja` li'e*
                Here it is
10   ((hands in coin))
11 Baby: ((gazes at customer with extended hand))

12 Customer: *kolaval*
            Thanks

Although joint attention unfolds between the two focal adult participants, the child is actively participating from the periphery. The interaction neatly reveals how Lol extracts the word *mil* from the stream of speech as part of a larger sequence of actions in which he embeds his own. The baby shows understanding of the meaning of the extracted word as he becomes embodied in the routinized encounter. Several factors conjoin here in his active engagement as overhearer:

(1) The synchronized multimodal moves of the embodied caregiver–child dyad in the ecology of actions and objects within the shop (see Hindmarsh and Pilnick 2002).[7]
(2) The routinized face-to-face transaction of the focal participants, which involves sequentiality, co-construction, shared attention, and relevance.

Example 4.3 reveals that children show signs of learning the meaning of words not as mere vocal productions but as part of multimodal actions of co-participants in the specific activities in which they are involved. This generalization parallels Nelson's (1984, 1986) finding that children's lexical understanding is embedded in and structured through conventionalized social events with which they are associated. That such learning can happen from the periphery of the participation framework is consistent with experimental studies of overhearing and word learning (Akhtar, Jipson, and Callanan 2001; Forrester 1992). This participation framework also further specifies the context of observing and learning with keen attention, in line with the work of Rogoff et al. (2003) and Gaskins and Paradise (2009), and the mechanisms used by overhearers to find their way into focal participation.[8]

Conclusions

This chapter embraces the view that multimodal communication offers diverse ways in which novices coordinate with others in social interaction over the course of their development and socialization. Interactional coordination involves not only what one person ('the speaker,' typically the caregiver) says to another ('the hearer,' typically the child), but also how speaking and nonspeaking participants coordinate their actions. The source of language and sociocultural learning does not reduce to verbal input but rather extends to an array of semiotic resources displayed by participants in situated activities. From the perspective of practice theory (Bourdieu 1977), activities become practices when they recur in particular ecologies consisting of preferred environmental niches and participation frameworks. The corporeal arrangements documented across cultures reveal that the default face-to-face interaction in the Euro-American middle-class context of language acquisition and socialization is one among *many* other possibilities. A central focus of this chapter is the cross-cultural pervasiveness of multiparty socialization and its effect on infants' communicative development.

Participation framework is a basic analytic unit of socialization and learning. Language socialization studies have documented cultural differences in how infants are socialized into being proto-speakers, addressees, or peripheral participants. Typical proto-conversations of Euro-American middle-class mothers heighten the infant's contributions as proto-speakers and addressees in turn-taking exchanges. In Zinacantan, children are considered proto-speakers only when they initiate interaction through multimodal resources. Attribution of communicative intent is indicated through the glossing of infants' multimodal actions as reported speech to a third party. Infants are not socialized as addressees in proto-conversations but are immersed in interactional routines that reveal their semiotic agency as they co-construct meaningful actions with caregivers and third participants.

This chapter has problematized speaker and hearer roles by demonstrating how they may be embedded in interlocking participation frames. Analysis evidences the complexities of intersubjective processes in language socialization contexts. Infants develop participatory competence through different positions in the participation framework *without* necessarily being focal addressees. This approach gives theoretical space to triadicity in language acquisition and socialization. Examining corporeal arrangements, facing formations, and preferred participation frameworks, it demonstrates that the overhearer participant status affords children with observation, attention, inference, and participation long before they speak. In socializing the overhearer status the child can be positioned as an intended addressee or not. As intended addresees, children may be socialized to listen as they are constructed as the targets of mock threats or teasing. Of further interest is how children positioned as nonintended addressees find their way into focality.

In Zinacantan, directives addressed to older children within triadic formats in which adults align position the child as the intended overhearer of commentaries about tasks or evaluations of behaviours (de León 2008a). Younger caregivers use this format as well to encourage younger charges to comply (de León 2008b, in press a, in press b). Triadic directives in Zinacantec Tzotzil reveal the social organization of family life in a way that differs noticeably from the dyadic facing formations typical of middle-class American families (Goodwin 2006). In Zinacantan, directives rely upon indirection, affect, and triadic participation frameworks. Shaming and scaring children as a third party is a common resource to gain compliance.

In sum, participation frameworks and their interactional consequences account for the organization of language socialization, revealing how infants and older children become competent social and semiotic agents through an array of participant roles in an ongoing activity.

ACKNOWLEDGMENTS

I acknowledge Elinor Ochs for her generous comments and thoughtful editorial suggestions on a previous version of this chapter. I also thank Nameera Akhtar, Candy Goodwin, Chuck Goodwin, and Barbara Rogoff for inspiring ideas behind this chapter. Heartfelt thanks to CELF and CLIC of the Department of Anthropology at UCLA for hosting an extraordinary sabbatical year. Heather Loyd's stylistic suggestions and Lance Brunner's meticulous review of the bibliography were of invaluable help, too. Last, but not least, eternal thanks to my godchildren and their loving families in Nabenchauk, Zinacantan, Mexico. Any errors or misconceptions are my responsibility.

NOTES

1 For studies on the design of the audience see Bell (1984), Duranti and Brenneis (1986), Goodwin (1981a, 1981b), and Hindmarsh and Pilnick (2002).

2 Photos are frame grabs from the videotape archives of Lourdes de León. Photo 5b was taken by Margarita Martinez in Huixtan, Chiapas, another Mayan Tzotzil community of study (de León and Martinez 2008).

3 Fung, Miller, and Lin (1994) and Miller (1994) highlight the socialization of children as listeners of other stories in different participation roles (as intended recipients in dyadic or multiparty interactions). See also Ochs and Taylor (1995).

4 Scollon (1982) refers to parental 'gloss' to the interpretation of children's communicative intentions in early verbal productions. Here I extend this notion of 'gloss' to preverbal gestural language.

5 These procedures are representative of language socialization methodology (Schieffelin and Ochs 1996).

6 See Rogoff (1990: 120) for this practice among Mayan Guatemalan infants and infants in other cultures.

7 Hindmarsh and Pilnick's (2002) analysis of talk within a surgery room, with the patient as an overhearer, argues that bodily conduct and the *particular local contexts of action* can be used to infer a trajectory for collaborative involvement and of the practical ordering of activities.

8 With respect to focal participation, Goodwin's (2007) study of a tag-along girl in preadolescent girls' interactions analyzed how this particular participation framework can also be strategically used to intentionally exclude 'stigmatized' overhearers and block their way into focality.

REFERENCES

Akhtar, N. (2005a) The robustness of learning through overhearing. *Developmental Science* 8(2): 199–209.

Akhtar, N. (2005b) Is joint attention necessary for early language learning? In B. D. Homer and C. S. Tamis-

LeMonda (eds.), *The Development of Social Cognition and Communication.* 165–79. Mahwah, NJ: Lawrence Erlbaum.

Akhtar, N., Jipson, J., and Callanan, M. A. (2001) Learning words through overhearing. *Child Development* 72: 416–30.

Akhtar, N. and Gernsbacher, M. A. (2007) Joint attention and vocabulary development: A critical look. *Language and Linguistic Compass* 1(3): 195–207.

Akhtar, N. and Tomasello, M. (1998) Intersubjectivity in early language learning and use. In S. Bråten (ed.), *Intersubjective Communication and Emotion in Early Ontogeny.* 316–35. Cambridge: Cambridge University Press.

Bates, E. (1979) *The Emergence of Symbols.* New York: Academic Press.

Bell, A. (1984) Language style as audience design. *Language in Society* 13: 145–204.

Blum-Kulka, S. and Snow, C. (2002) Editors' introduction. In S. Blum-Kulka and C. Snow (eds.), *Talking to Adults: The Contribution of Multiparty Discourse to Language Acquisition.* 1–12. Mahwah, NJ: Lawrence Erlbaum.

Bourdieu, P. (1977) *Outline of a Theory of Practice.* R. Nice, transl. Cambridge: Cambridge University Press.

Brown, P. (1998) Conversational structure and language acquisition: The role of repetition in Tzeltal adult and child speech. *Journal of Linguistic Anthropology* 8(2): 197–221.

Bruner, J. S. (1978) The role of dialogue in language acquisition. In A. Sinclair, R. J. Jarvella, and W. J. M. Levelt (eds.), *The Child's Conception of Language.* 241–56. New York: Springer-Verlag.

Bruner, J. (1983) *Child Talk.* New York: Norton.

Bruner, J. and Sherwood, V. (1976) Peekaboo and the learning of rule structures. In J. Bruner, A. Jolly, and K. Silva (eds.), *Play: Its Role in Development and Evolution.* 227–85. New York: Basic Books.

Burdelski, M. J. (2006) *Language Socialization of Two-Year Old Children in Kanzai, Japan: The Family and Beyond.* Doctoral Dissertation. Los Angeles, CA: University of California, Los Angeles.

Burdelski, M. J. (2010) Socializing politeness routines: Multimodality and social action in a Japanese preschool. *Journal of Pragmatics* 42: 1606–21.

Chavajay, P. and Rogoff, B. (1999) Cultural variation in management of attention by children and their caregivers. *Developmental Psychology* 35: 1079–90.

Chavajay, P. and Rogoff, B. (2002) Schooling and traditional collaborative social organization of problem solving by Mayan mothers and children. *Developmental Psychology* 38: 55–66.

Clark, H. H. (1996) *Using Language.* Cambridge: Cambridge University Press.

Correa-Chávez, M. and Rogoff, B. (2009). Children's attention to interactions directed to others: Guatemalan Mayan and European American Patterns. *Developmental Psychology* 45(3): 630–41.

de León, L. (1998) The emergent participant: Interactive patterns of socialization of Tzotzil (Mayan) children. *Journal of Linguistic Anthropology* 8(2): 131–61.

de León, L. (1999) Verb roots and caregiver speech in Tzotzil Mayan acquisition. In L. Michaelis and B. Fox (eds.), *Language, Cognition, and Function.* 99–119. Palo Alto, CA: Stanford Center for Language and Information, Stanford University.

de León, L. (2005) *La Llegada del Alma: Lenguaje, Infancia y Socialización entre los Mayas de Zinacantán.* México: CIESAS-INAH-CONACULTA.

de León, L. (2007) Parallelism, metalinguistic play, and the interactive emergence of Tzotzil (Mayan) siblings' culture. *Research on Language and Social Interaction* 40(4): 405–36.

de León, L. (2008a) Directives and the socialization of attention in a Mayan family. *Seminar for the Center for the Study of the Everyday Lives of Families.* University of California, Los Angeles.

de León, L. (2008b) Authority, attention, and affect in directive/response sequences in Mayan Zinacantec siblings. Paper presented at the annual meetings of the American Anthropological Association. San Francisco, CA.

de León, L. (in press a) 'Calibrando' la Atención: Directivos, adiestramiento y responsabilidad en el trabajo doméstico de los niños Mayas Zinacantecos. In V. Zavala and F. Susana (eds.), *Aprendizaje, Cultura y Desarrollo.* Lima, Perú: Fondo Editorial de la Universidad Católica Pontificia.

de León, L. (in press b) 'The *j'ik'al* is coming!' Triadic directives and emotion in the socialization of Zinacantec Mayan children. In A. Breton and P. Nondédéo (eds), *Maya Daily Lives. Proceedings of the 13th European Maya Conference. Acta Mesoamericana 21.* Markt Schwaben: Verlag Anton Saurwein.

de León, L. and Martinez, M. (2008) Socializing attention to third referents: A look at Tzotzil (Mayan) caregiver–infant interactions in natural and created environments. Paper presented at the International Conference for the Study of Child Language. Edinburgh.

Demuth, K. (1986) Prompting routines in the language socialization of Basotho children. In B. B. Schieffelin and E. Ochs (eds.), *Language Socialization Across Cultures.* 51–79. Cambridge: Cambridge University Press.

Duranti, A. and Brenneis, D. (eds.) (1986) The audience as co-author. *Text* 6(3): 239–347.

Eisenberg, A. R. (1986) Teasing: Verbal play in two Mexican homes. In B. B. Schieffelin and E. Ochs (eds.), *Language Socialization across Cultures.* 182–99. Cambridge: Cambridge University Press.

Ferguson, C. A. (1977) Baby Talk as a simplified register. In C. E. Snow and C. A. Ferguson (eds.), *Talking to Children: Language Input and Acquisition.* 209–35.

Cambridge: Cambridge University Press.

Ferguson, C. A. (1982) Simplified registers and linguistic theory. In Loraine Obler (ed.), *Exceptional Language and Linguistics.* 49–66. New York: Academic Press.

Fernald, A. and Morikawa, H. (1993) Common themes and cultural variations in Japanese and American mothers' speech to infants. *Child Development* 64: 637–56.

Field, M. (2001) Triadic directives in Navajo language socialization. *Language in Society* 30: 249–63.

Fung, H., Miller, P. J., and Lin, L.-C. (2004) Listening is active: Lessons from the narrative practices of Taiwanese families. In M. W. Pratt and B. E. Fiese (eds.), *Family Stories and the Life Course: Across Time and Generations.* 302–22. Mahwah, NJ: Lawrence Erlbaum.

Forrester, M. A. (1992) *The Development of Young Children's Social-Cognitive Skills.* Hillsdale, NJ: Lawrence Erlbaum.

Garrett, P. B. and Baquedano-López, P. (2002) Language socialization: Reproduction, continuity, transformation, and change. *Annual Review of Anthropology* 31: 339–61.

Gaskins, S. (1996) How Mayan parental theories come into play. In S. Harkness and C. M. Super (eds.), *Parents' Cultural Belief Systems: Their Origins, Expressions, and Consequences.* 345–63. New York: The Guilford Press.

Gaskins, S. (2000) Children's daily activities in a Mayan village: A culturally grounded description. *Cross-Cultural Research* 34(4): 375–89.

Gaskins, S. (2006) Cultural perspectives on infant–caregiver interaction. In N. J. Enfield and S. C. Levinson (eds.), *Roots of Human Sociality: Culture, Cognition and Interaction.* 279–98. Oxford: Berg Publishers.

Gaskins, S. and Paradise, R. (2009) Learning through observation in daily life. In D. Lancy, J. Bock, and S. Gaskins (eds.), *The Anthropology of Learning in Childhood*. Walnut Creek, CA: Altamira Press.

Goffman, E. (1974) *Frame Analysis: An Essay on the Organization of Experience*. New York: Harper and Row.

Goffman, E. (1981) *Forms of Talk*. Philadelphia, PA: University of Pennsylvania Press.

Goodwin, C. (1981a) *Conversational Organization: Interaction between Speakers and Hearers*. New York: Academic Press.

Goodwin, C. (1981b) Designing talk for different types of recipients. In C. Goodwin (ed.), *Conversational Organization: Interaction between Speakers and Hearers*. 149–66. New York: Academic Press.

Goodwin, C. (1984) Notes on story structure and the organization of participation. In J. M. Atkinson and J. Heritage (eds.), *Structures of Social Action*. 225–46. Cambridge: Cambridge University Press.

Goodwin, C. (2003) The semiotic body in its environment. In J. Coupland and R. Gwyn (eds.), *Discourses of the Body*. 19–42. New York: Palgrave/Macmillan.

Goodwin, C. (2010) Constructing meaning through prosody in aphasia. In D. Barth-Weingarten, E. Reber, and M. Selting (eds.), *Prosody in Interaction*. 373–94. Amsterdam, the Netherlands: John Benjamins.

Goodwin, M. H. (1990) *He-Said-She-Said: Talk as Social Organization among Black Children*. Bloomington: Indiana University Press.

Goodwin, M. H. (2006) Participation, affect, and trajectory in family directive/response sequences. *Text & Talk* 26(4/5): 513–42.

Goodwin, M. H. (2007) Participation and embodied action in preadolescent girls' assessment activity. *Research on Language and Social Interaction* 40(4): 279–89.

Goodwin, M. H. and Goodwin, C. (2004) Participation. In A. Duranti (ed.), *A

Companion to Linguistic Anthropology*. 222–44. Malden, MA: Blackwell Publishers.

Greenfield, P. (1984) A study of the teacher in the activities of everyday life. In B. Rogoff and J. Lave (eds.), *Everyday Cognition*. 117–38. Cambridge, MA: Harvard University Press.

Greenfield, P. (2004) *Weaving Generations Together: Evolving Creativity in the Maya of Chiapas*. Santa Fe, NM: School of American Research.

Hanks, W. F. (1996) Exorcism and the description of participant roles. In M. Silverstein and G. Urban (eds.), *Natural Histories of Discourse*. 160–202. Chicago, IL: University of Chicago Press.

Haviland, J. B. (1998) Early pointing gestures in Zinacantán. *Journal of Linguistic Anthropology* 8(2): 162–96.

Heath, S. B. (1983) *Ways with Words: Language, Life, and Work in Communities and Classrooms*. New York: Cambridge University Press.

Hindmarsh, J. and Pilnick, A. (2002) The tacit order of teamwork: Collaboration and embodied conduct in anesthesia. *The Sociological Quarterly* 43(2): 139–64.

Irvine, J. T. (1996) Shadow conversations: The indeterminacy of participant roles. In M. Silverstein and G. Urban (eds.), *Natural Histories of Discourse*. 131–59. Chicago, IL: University of Chicago Press.

Kendon, A. (1985). Behavioural foundations for the process of frame attunement in face-to-face interaction. In G. Ginsberg (ed.), *Discovery Strategies in the Psychology of Action*. 229–53. London: Academic Press.

Kendon, A. (1990) Spatial organization in social encounters: The f-formation system. In A. Kendon (ed.), *Conducting Interaction: Patterns of Behavior in Focused Encounters*. 209–38. Cambridge: Cambridge University Press.

Lancy, D. (2010). The limited role of teaching in folk theories of children's development. *Childhood in the Past* 3: 79–106.

LeVine, R. A., Dixon, S., Levine, S., Richman, A., Liederman, P. H., Keefer, C. H., and Brazelton, T. B. (1996) *Child Care and Culture: Lessons from Africa*. Cambridge: Cambridge University Press.

Levinson, S. C. (1988) Putting linguistics in its proper footing: Explorations in Goffman's notion of participation. In P. Drew (ed.), *Erving Goffman: Exploring the Interaction Order*. 161–227. Boston, MA: Northeastern University Press.

Lieven, E. V. M. (1994) Crosslinguistic and crosscultural aspects of language addressed to children. In C. Gallaway and B. J. Richards (eds.), *Input and Interaction in Language Acquisition*. 56–73. Cambridge: Cambridge University Press.

López, A., Correa-Chávez, M., Rogoff B., and Gutiérrez, K. (2010). Attention to instruction directed to another by U.S. Mexican-heritage children of varying cultural backgrounds. *Developmental Psychology* 46(3): 593–601.

Loyd, H. (2005) *Language Socialization in Nicastro, Italy*. Masters Thesis. Los Angeles, CA: University of California.

Martínez Perez, M. (2008) *Socialización Lingüística Infantil en el Tzotzil Huixteco, Chiapas*. México: Maestría en Lingüística Indoamericana, CIESAS.

Mead, M. (1955) Children and ritual in Bali. In M. Mead and M. Wolfenstein (eds.), *Childhood in Contemporary Cultures*. 40–51. Chicago, IL: University of Chicago Press.

Miller P. J. (1994) Narrative practices: Their role in socialization and self-construction. In U. Neisser and R. Fivush (eds.), *The Remembering Self: Construction and Memory in the Self Narrative*. 158–79. New York: Cambridge University Press.

Nelson, K. (1984) Playing with scripts. In Inge Bretherton (ed.), *Symbolic Play: The Development of Social Understanding*. 45–71. Orlando, FL: Academic Press.

Nelson, K. (1986) *Event Knowledge: Structure and Function in Development*. Hillsdale, NJ: Lawrence Erlbaum.

Ochs, E. (1982) Talking to children in Western Samoa. *Language in Society* 11(1): 77–104.

Ochs, E. (1988) *Culture and Language Development. Language Acquisition and Language Socialization in a Samoan Village*. Cambridge: Cambridge University Press.

Ochs, E. and Schieffelin, B. B. (1984) Language acquisition and socialization: Three developmental stories and their implications. In R. A. Shweder and Robert A. LeVine (eds.), *Culture Theory: Essays on Mind, Self, and Emotion*. 276–322. Cambridge: Cambridge University Press.

Ochs, E., Solomon, O., and Sterponi, L. (2005) Limitations and transformations of habitus in child-directed communication. *Discourse Studies* 7(4): 547–83.

Ochs, E. and Taylor, C. (1995) The 'father knows best' dynamic in dinnertime narratives. In K. Hall and M. Bucholtz (eds.), *Gender Articulated: Language and the Socially Constructed Self*. 97–120. New York: Routledge.

Oshima-Takane, Y. (1988) Children learn from speech not addressed to them: The case of personal pronouns. *Journal of Child Language* 15: 94–108.

Paradise, R. and Rogoff, B. (2009). Side by side. Learning by observing and pitching in. *Ethos* 37(1): 102–38.

Paugh, A. (2001) *Creole Is Everyday: Language Socialization, Shift and Ideologies in Dominica, West Indies*. Doctoral Dissertation. New York: New York University.

Peters, A. M. and Boggs, S. T. (1986) Interactional routines as cultural influences upon language acquisition. In Schieffelin, B. B. and Ochs, E. (eds.), *Language Socialization across Cultures*. 80–96. Cambridge: Cambridge University Press.

Pfeiler, B. (2007) *Lo oye, lo repite y lo piensa: The contribution of prompting to the* socialization and language acquisition in Yukatek Maya toddlers. In B. Pfeiler (ed.), *Learning Indigenous Languages: Child Language Acquisition in Mesoamerica*. 183–202. Berlin: Walter de Gruyter.

Philips, S. U. (1972) *The Invisible Culture: Communication in Classroom and Community on the Warm Springs Indian Reservation*. Prospects Highs, IL: Waveland Press.

Pye, C. (1986) Quiché Mayan speech to children. *Journal of Child Language* 13: 85–100.

Pye, C. (1992) The acquisition of K'iche'. In D. I. Slobin (ed.), *The Crosslinguistic Study of Language Acquisition, Vol. 3*. 221–308. Hillsdale, NJ: Lawrence Erlbaum.

Quinn, N. (2005) Universals of child rearing. *Anthropological Theory* 5(4): 475–514.

Rabain-Jamin, J. (1998) Polyadic language socialization strategy: The case of toddlers in Senegal. *Discourse Processes* 26: 43–65.

Rogoff, B. (1990) *Apprenticeship in Thinking: Cognitive Development in a Social Context*. Oxford: Oxford University Press.

Rogoff, B. (2003) *The Cultural Nature of Human Development*. New York: Oxford University Press.

Rogoff, B., Paradise, R., Arauz, R. M., Correa-Chavez, M., and Angelillo, C. (2003) Firsthand learning through intent participation. *Annual Review of Psychology* 54: 175–203.

Schieffelin, B. B. (1986) Teasing and shaming in Kaluli children's interactions. In Schieffelin, B. B. and Ochs, E. (eds.), *Language Socialization across Cultures*. 165–81. Cambridge: Cambridge University Press.

Schieffelin, B. B. (1990) *The Give and Take of Everyday Life: Language Socialization of Kaluli Children*. Cambridge: Cambridge University Press.

Schieffelin, B. B. and Ochs, E. (eds.) (1986) *Language Socialization Across Cultures*. Cambridge: Cambridge University Press.

Schieffelin, B. B. and Ochs, E. (1996) The microgenesis of competence: Methodology in language socialization. In D. I. Slobin, J. Gerhardt, A. Kyratzis, and J. Guo (eds.), *Social Interaction, Social Context, and Language*. 251–64. Hillsdale, NJ: Lawrence Erlbaum.

Scollon, S. (1982) *Reality Set, Socialization, and Linguistic Convergence*. Doctoral Dissertation. University of Hawaii.

Sidnell, J. (1997) Organizing social and spatial location: Elicitation in Indo-Guyanese village talk. *Journal of Linguistic Anthropology* 7(2): 143–65.

Sinha, C. (2001) The epigenesis of symbolization. In C. Balkenius, J. Zlatev, H. Kozima, K. Dautenhahn, and C. Breazeal (eds.), *Proceedings of the First International Workshop on Epigenetic Robotics. Lund University Cognitive Studies*, 85.

Snow, C. E. and Ferguson, C. A. (eds.) (1977) *Talking to Children: Language Input and Acquisition*. Cambridge: Cambridge University Press.

Snow, C.E. (1994). Beginning from Baby Talk: Twenty years of research on input and interaction. In C. Galloway and B. Richards (eds.), *Input and Interaction in Language Acquisition*. 3–12. London: Cambridge University Press.

Stoll, S. (2009) Crosslinguistic approaches to language acquisition. In E. L. Bavin (ed.), *The Handbook of Child Language*. 89–104. Cambridge: Cambridge University Press.

Tomasello M. (1999) *The Cultural Origins of Human Cognition*. Cambridge, MA: Harvard University Press.

Trevarthen, C. (1998) The concept and foundations of infant intersubjectivity. In S. Bråten (ed.), *Intersubjective Communication and Emotion in Early Ontogeny*. 15–46. Cambridge: Cambridge University Press.

Vogt, E. Z. (1969) *Zinacantan: A Maya Community in the Highlands of Chiapas*. Cambridge, MA: Harvard University Press.

Wagley, C. (1949) *The Social and Religious Life of a Guatemalan Village. Memoirs of the American Anthropological Association, 71.* Arlington, VA: American Anthropological Association.

Watson-Gegeo, K. A. and Gegeo, D. W. (1986) Calling-out in Kwara'e children's language socialization. In Schieffelin, B. B. and Ochs, E. (eds.), *Language Socialization Across Cultures.* 17–50. Cambridge: Cambridge University Press.

Wooton, A. J. (1997) *Interaction and the Development of Mind.* Cambridge: Cambridge University Press.

Part II   Socialization Strategies

The ways in which members of speech communities think about how their young children acquire language and the appropriate ways of using it are deeply tied to culturally specific notions of how one becomes a competent person, and the role of language and interaction in that process. The chapters in Part II highlight the dynamic relation between local theories of social reproduction, cultural transmission, and knowledge acquisition, and the interactional strategies and preferential practices used in language socialization practices motivated by such theories. Whether intended or not, many of these strategies, deployed by more experienced members, help shape novices' identities, orientations, intuitions, and social knowledge more generally. Simultaneously, participation in such exchanges shapes the course of children's grammatical and pragmatic development.

Cultural orientations that are central throughout the life cycle to both novices and experts, or learners and teachers – such as autonomy and dependence, and ideas about and the expression of identity, morality, affect, and social control, to name but a few – are socialized through verbal routines such as shaming; the use of registers, styles, and genres, such as narrative; and interactional strategies including repetition. Child and adult speakers carefully select appropriate discursive techniques from their verbal and nonverbal repertoires to achieve their desires and interests, and to inform and conform others to particular stances and demeanors, whether speaking or engaged in literacy activities. These techniques, and how they are responded to and sequenced, provide invaluable information to learners about how they are to feel about what they say and who they are, whether at home, at school, or in any number of settings in which they find they have to speak for themselves. For researchers, understanding the strategies used in language socialization requires systematic investigation of socially and culturally embedded practices. As the chapters in Part II demonstrate, such systematic attention to details that might otherwise be deemed irrelevant reveals the subtle dynamics of agency, pattern, choice, preference, and transformation.

The Handbook of Language Socialization, First Edition. Edited by Alessandro Duranti, Elinor Ochs, and Bambi B. Schieffelin.
© 2014 John Wiley & Sons, Ltd. Published 2014 by John Wiley & Sons, Ltd.

The chapters in this section indicate ways in which language socialization strategies provide appropriate contexts for learning about persons and ways of knowing and being in the world. Moreover, in multilingual societies, these same language socialization strategies may also be crucial to the future of a language itself. Language socialization research in such settings sheds light on local conceptions of language(s) as object(s) and illuminates the complex interactions between linguistic and cultural continuity, transformation, and change more broadly.

No socialization strategy has been more controversial than the phenomenon of Baby Talk. As discussed in Solomon's chapter, 'Rethinking Baby Talk' (Chapter 5), interest in Baby Talk increased as debates surrounding innatism surfaced in linguistics and psychology in the latter decades of the last century. In the course of pursuing the question of whether or not input facilitates language acquisition, the cross-cultural prevalence and configuration of Baby Talk, a dedicated simplified register for talking to infants and young children, became a point of contention. Close scrutiny of the arguments surrounding Baby Talk indicated that (1) the register includes features beyond simplification, including clarification and heightened affective displays; (2) the scope of simplification (phonological, morpho-syntactic, discursive), clarification, and affective speech varied cross-culturally; and (3) evidence for the cross-cultural import of Baby Talk relies upon relatively few direct, systematic observations of Baby Talk *in situ* relative to reported use elicited in interviews. Baby Talk is widespread, but tends to involve prosodic modifications that garner attention and express affect, phonological simplifications, and special lexicon. Moreover, although the affordances of these features may be significant for language learning, societies differ in the extent to which infants are treated as addressees of Baby Talk as opposed to being positioned as overhearers of older members' conversations. Solomon notes that when and how Baby Talk is deployed is integrally tied to local notions of infants as persons with certain capacities and about the developmental path to language. Kaluli caregivers (Schieffelin 1990), for example, felt strongly that infants need exposure to fully formed adult language (e.g. as overhearers) to become good speakers. As such, Baby Talk is not only linguistic input; it is also a culturally configured social practice that requires ethnographic unpacking.

Solomon's chapter traces the potentially harmful consequences of using certain forms of Baby Talk with children with neurodevelopmental conditions such as autism. Exaggerated intonation, heightened praising, vowel lengthening, and slowed pace, for example, may be distressing to these children in that they often become overwhelmed by sensory stimuli and have difficulty sustaining attention, among other concerns. Especially in the case of children severely affected by autism, these register features may inhibit sociality, as may insistence that children look at their interlocutors in face-to-face alignment and converse through speech rather than pointing at letters or writing on a computer. Solomon's observations of alternative modes of interacting with children with these conditions make evident that different varieties of Baby Talk are necessary to render a child as socially, cognitively, and emotionally present.

Paugh's chapter, 'Local Theories of Child Rearing' (Chapter 6) offers insights from language socialization research into a continuing academic debate on the relation of nature and nurture in the process of becoming a competent member of a social group. Communities vary in terms of the extent to which they can, or even desire to, make explicit, rationalize, or explain the theoretical underpinnings of what they do with their young children. Local ideas of what is 'natural' and what must be socialized determine which attributes and behaviors must be encouraged or suppressed and which develop by themselves in the course of maturation. Paugh identifies patterns in social and communicative child-oriented practices: one is a continuum of child-centered to situation-centered orientations, which encourage ego- and sociocentric practices. Another concerns an attitude toward developmental pacing, wherein some communities value precocity while others believe children's abilities unfold in their own time. This orientation may be consistent or selective, encouraging some capacities over others. Local notions of infants' and children's natural dispositions also give rise to patterns of reward or punishment.

Paugh's chapter calls attention to the consequences of language preferences in language socialization for multilingual communities. Different languages and varieties with their predictably asymmetrical assignments of prestige constrain which varieties adults use in front of children and which varieties they want children to speak. In postcolonial societies engaged in nation-building, Creole languages are especially vulnerable to shift and change. Children may be socialized to lose or change their vernacular due to parental rationalizations and practices. Paugh draws on research in Dominica, West Indies to illustrate the relation between theories of child rearing and rapid language shift from Patwa to varieties of English. As in similar multilingual settings, the two languages have become indexically linked to local notions of personhood, status, and authority within the context of child–adult relationships. While Patwa is assumed to be natural and not require instruction, English must be taught. In addition, Patwa is 'rough,' 'vulgar,' or 'hard,' while English is 'soft, gentle' and associated with respect, education, and formality, qualities that children are expected to demonstrate. Adults emphasize the importance of children using Patwa and English in age- and place-related appropriate ways, a practice that young children are highly sensitive to. Emphasizing the broader temporal and historical dimensions of language socialization activities, Paugh's analyses evidence that transformations associated with colonialization and social contact may be instigated by young speakers.

In their chapter, 'Language Socialization and Shaming,' Lo and Fung (Chapter 7) examine the various forms and meanings of this critical and consequential activity, salient in language socialization practices across a range of societies. They place the shame/guilt binary within a broad sociohistorical perspective, pointing out the predominantly positive moral valence accorded to internalized guilt (adaptive, constructive, prosocial, mature) in opposition to public shame, which is negatively evaluated (maladaptive, antisocial, and primitive) in both anthropological and psychological studies. Lo and Fung view shame as culturally constructed and examine its use across cultures as a form of social control aimed at conforming and including, rather than excluding, the child in society. In Taiwanese, South Korean, and Korean American settings, shame is related to Confucian ideology, motivated by love and the desire to protect the child from future sanctions, and integral to moral education. In these communities, disgrace-shame leads to an internalized sense of discretion-shame, which is deemed central to prosocial behaviors.

Lo and Fung detail different types of shaming interactions in the communities they have investigated. In dyadic shaming episodes, caregivers offer strong negative assessments of children's behavior, aimed at giving the child moral guidance through different speech genres. Dramatic enactments include assessments, and use conventionalized nonverbal cues associated with shaming, which are intensified through repetition and paralinguistic cues. In multiparty shaming episodes, relevant onlookers were drawn into the event for affective intensification. Shaming has specific contextually dependent qualities, depending on age, setting, and social relationships. While South Korean children and youths were expected to be silent, look down, and act repentant, such stances were not observed to the same extent among Korean Americans. Taiwanese children are not discouraged from challenging the elder if they believe the shaming to be unjustified. The authors make the important point that shaming sequences have variable outcomes and meanings. Through culturally embedded sequential analyses one also appreciates the close attention children must pay to linguistic and emotional keyings when participating in these affectively intensive verbal exchanges.

Miller, Koven, and Lin's chapter, 'Language Socialization and Narrative' (Chapter 8), foregrounds cultural variation and difference in the use of narrative with children and the social and emotional consequences of these differences. The chapter is organized around four perspectives. The first is the heterogeneity of narrative socialization practices. The language socialization paradigm affords a view of narrative as an interactional occasion in which children across communities and settings take a variety of participant roles (e.g. narrators, overhearers) and experience a range of formats, topics, and meanings. The second area concerns how narratives are implicated in the formation of both social and private senses of self and identity. Reporting on their comparative work on Taiwanese and Euro-American children, the authors point out that the Taiwanese, with their orientation to strongly guided moral development, are more likely to narrate the child as transgressor and use narratives to instruct appropriate demeanors.

In the third perspective, Miller, Koven, and Lin use narrative differences to highlight the ways in which speech genres reflect hegemonic relations and suggest that early narrative socialization practices are yet another way to marginalize certain categories of persons. In home settings, for example, narrative participation frameworks lead to the socialization of gender inequalities. Similarly, educational contexts favor narrative practices of certain social groups over others. The authors underscore the importance of looking at patterns and frequency of narrative practices as part of socialization, and also investigating broader contexts (e.g. migration, gate-keeping, and other bureaucratic settings) in which narrative differences evaluated according to institutional values have differential outcomes. The authors call attention to competencies not valorized in mainstream settings as their fourth and final dimension of narrative socializations. Elaborating on their research on untold or devalued narratives of working-class and minority language speakers, they report that working-class urban Euro-American children are not only encouraged to become skilled co-narrators but do, and by the age of two and a half or three years produce two to three times more co-narrated stories compared to their middle-class age mates. Their narratives featured more emotional topics, dramatic language, and negative content, and were often challenged by caregivers, who expected them to defend their positions. Nonetheless, the personal stories recounted by their middle-class cohort at school were more accepted, even when misguided or inaccurate.

Moore's chapter, 'Language Socialization and Repetition' (Chapter 9), views repetition as a critical discursive resource that enables children's participation in social interaction. Careful ethnographic study demonstrates how repetition is central to the creative and transformative ways in which communication is accomplished. Moore details four patterns of repetition reported in the language socialization literature: revoicing, prompting, guided repetition, and language play. Revoicing refers to the speaker reproducing or ventriloquizing another's voice, and, depending on context and community, preferences vary in terms of the accuracy expected and the affective outcomes desired. Revoicings can be used to achieve authorial control as well as to mock or be playful. Caregivers in Japan and Korea revoice children's utterances to make them more socially appropriate. Prompting routines, found in a broad range of communities, also figure significantly in language socialization routines. They typically occur when more competent members of a community directly instruct a less competent one to say something to a third party, or, less commonly, back to the initial speaker. Linked to ideas about personhood, learning, and language ideologies, prompting socializes children into affective stances and verbal routines. In some communities, children's status as nonresponsible animators positions them to convey information between adults.

Guided repetition, used in verbal routines that do not stress comprehension of the literal meanings, is a way of reframing rote learning and recitation. These practices are not embedded in ongoing interaction but are the interactional routine, most commonly used for pedagogical purposes. Moore elaborates the components of these routines among the Fulbe (Cameroon) in religious and public schools. Qur'anic schooling socializes children into Fulbe and Muslim values of self-control, respect for religious authority and hierarchy, and proper recitations of the Arabic text, whereas public school aims to create Cameroonian citizens capable of carrying out their responsibilities in French.

Due to the repetitive and often scripted nature of language play, less competent speakers can join in, allowing the development of more complex discursive practices. Societies and settings vary in terms of the kinds of language play allowed, encouraged, or stopped. Among the Fulbe, mothers allowed verbal play with Qur'anic verse at home to enable children to learn it, whereas such behaviors would be punished in school. Moore offers observations about the ways in which repetition fosters a range of language practices found in every community – inter-textuality, production of canonical forms and meanings, and, of course, in appropriate settings, the skills required for improvisation and creative forms of language use supporting social participation, membership, and particular types of learning during first- and second language socialization.

Sterponi's chapter, 'Literacy Socialization' (Chapter 10), examines reading and writing practices within the paradigm of New Literacy Studies, an ethnographic and social theoretical framework that views literacy as a set of historically contingent, culturally organized, and ideologically shaped social practices. Scholars working in this paradigm have documented the heterogeneous ways in which people engage with text and the multiple meanings of reading and writing across contexts and within broader communicative repertoires. From the perspective of language socialization, processes of literacy socialization both within and outside of school contexts are viewed as shaping individual involvement with text and central to the acquisition of a literacy habitus.

After reviewing historical roots and ideological underpinnings of the debates about orality and literacy, then highlighting ethnographic work on literacy socialization, Sterponi outlines the tradition of essayist literacy, which treats written text as explicit and self-contained representation of meaning. This perspective, she argues, is the basis upon which instruction from kindergarten and early grades to higher education and academia is premised, one whose efficacy Sterponi challenges through her own and others' scholarship: what she calls 'alternative literacies'; that is, practices developed by communities to use literacy in culturally meaningful ways and unofficial literacy practices.

Based on her findings from ethnographic research on spontaneous reading activities in elementary-school classrooms in California, Sterponi sheds light on child-organized clandestine interactional reading a context that shows the mechanisms that bring about variations and transformations in literacy practices. In contrast to teacher-organized reading activities, students draw on more symmetrical participant roles and are engaged and verbally interactive, drawing from multiple books to create intertextual links across topics of interest and jointly interpreting dialogic texts in relation to each other. Such situated analyses show the interpenetration of reading and writing practices and how language socialization conceptualizes participation and apprenticeship into a literacy habitus that engages the person at the emotional, sensorimotor, and intellectual levels. Sterponi's chapter highlights the importance of child agency, oral/literacy connections, and the micro-analysis of literacy activities.

Departing from the two dominant contexts of language socialization research, everyday caregiver–child interactions, and more formal education settings, Stivers' chapter, 'Language Socialization in Children's Medical Encounters' (Chapter 11), focuses on healthcare settings. In so doing, she highlights socialization into a culturally salient role in a Euro-American setting, that of a patient. Patients need to display appropriate verbal skills and knowledge to inform healthcare professionals of their condition as well as to comprehend information from those professionals so as to benefit from it. Stivers asks how and when doctors involve child patients in routine care visits as part of socialization into the patient role. Complementing ethnographic research on language socialization, her research consists of a large, diverse, cross-sectional data set, which includes extensive videotaped recordings of primary-care interactions in California with English-speaking child patients aged between two and half and ten and their parents. Her research combines conversation analysis with quantitative analysis in order to analyze factors (race, age, class) to determine patterns of child patient/parent selection for answering health questions.

In pediatric encounters, a physician either does or does not include the child patient in the interaction. If given the opportunity, children will answer questions that are common in routine visits. Whether the physician directs a question to a child depends upon the child's age and the parent's gender. Compared to Latino, Asian American, and white families, physicians were less likely to ask questions of black children. Socioeconomic status, significant for children in many other institutional settings, is also critical here. Again, black children in general and Latino children whose parent has a low level of education are less likely to be involved as active participants than highly educated Latinos, Asian Americans, and whites, independent of child age. Stivers concludes that the two racial/ethnic groups most likely to suffer from chronic illness as adults (blacks and Latinos) are those least likely to receive adequate socialization in childhood to prepare them for medical encounters as patients.

REFERENCE

Schieffelin, B. B. (1990) *The Give and Take of Everyday Life: Language Socialization of* *Kaluli Children.* Cambridge: Cambridge University Press.

5 Rethinking Baby Talk

OLGA SOLOMON

Introduction

The development of children's linguistic and cultural competence and the role of caregivers in this process continue to be important areas of social science research. While both commonalities and differences in caregiver–child interactions exist within and across cultures (Gaskins 1999, 2006; Slobin 1967, 1985), the question of how and to what extent they organize children's social development remains open. The answer to this question has been elusive because, as Gaskins (2006) notes, most theories of human social development are based on three presumptions that may be uncontroversial on their own but that are at odds with one another. The first presumption is that there is a shared developmental trajectory and a universal developmental outcome that characterizes the human species as a whole, assured by the universal presence of learning-relevant experiences in all cultures. The second is that social development is experience-dependent and that there may be different outcomes by gender, socioeconomic status, or culture. Third, it is assumed that both the content of social learning and its everyday environments are culturally organized, and that social development is therefore culturally variable in both its processes and its outcomes. It is the first presumption that has been dominant in psychological research conducted in Western Europe and the United States claiming that, in spite of cultural variability, the universal outcome of human development is a result of infants' and young children's dyadic social interaction with caregivers (e.g. Tomasello 1999; Trevarthen 1987; cf. Gaskins 2006).[1] Thus, the question about the role of caregivers in human development goes to the core of the social-science debate about the sources of linguistic and cultural competence. This chapter considers the question from the

The Handbook of Language Socialization, First Edition. Edited by Alessandro Duranti, Elinor Ochs, and Bambi B. Schieffelin.
© 2014 John Wiley & Sons, Ltd. Published 2014 by John Wiley & Sons, Ltd.

language socialization perspective by examining a culturally distinct way of talking to infants and young children called 'Baby Talk' (BT).

Baby Talk is observed in many languages, including Arabic, Bengali, Comanche, American and British English, German, Mandarin Chinese, Marathi, Latvian, Russian, and Spanish (see e.g. Brown 1977; Chew 1969; Ferguson 1959, 1964, 1977; Snow and Ferguson 1977).[2] When using BT, caregivers modify their speech by increasing its pitch, exaggerating its positive affect, slowing down its tempo, and speaking in short, syntactically simple sentences. Through such modifications and an extensive use of repetition, specialized lexicon, and diminutives and kinship terms, adult speech is phonologically, lexically, and grammatically transformed into BT.

Baby Talk is a speech register, a way of speaking employed in different social situations (Biber and Finegan 1994). Register reflects different occasions for language use and the social positions and identities of the addressees: members speak differently when they address someone who is older or younger, or someone who is of higher or lower status (Ferguson 1994; Howard, this volume). Thus, speech register indexes a certain social position and identity of the addressee.

Baby Talk is associated with specific social practices of interacting with infants and young children across many communities and cultures. In some languages, however, such as American and British English, German, and Dutch, there is a secondary Baby-Talk register characterized by extended functions of prototypical BT (Ferguson 1977). Secondary BT is spoken to interlocutors other than infants and young children, including the elderly, the intellectually disabled, lovers, foreigners, family pets, and even plants.[3] A language socialization perspective on BT illuminates both tacit and explicit assumptions about cultural ontologies of personhood, child development, and communicative competence that exist across cultures and contexts. It also sheds light on culturally variable notions of intentionality, intersubjectivity, agency, and a preferred organization of attention.

Baby Talk is part of situated cultural activities where caregivers' actions are guided by their ontological understandings of self and others; that is, the infant or young child and other co-present members. Practices of self- and other-fashioning through language have been described as 'en-registering,' where a speaker uses a register from a culture's speech repertoire that performatively selects and authorizes certain identities with certain ontological properties for both speaker and addressee (Silverstein 2004). In this sense, a caregiver who addresses an infant in BT en-registers a kind of addressee who (1) is an 'always already there' (Derrida 1990; Merleau-Ponty 1945) social being capable of intentional acts immediately after birth (Bruner 1978); (2) is linguistically and cognitively immature; (3) contributes meaningful and intentional vocalizations and physical movements to the social interaction; and (4) is able to act contingently and participate in reciprocal turn-taking. The 'self- and other- fashioning,' the enregistering of identities, also projects culturally ratified subjectivities, a certain kind of organization of participation around a focal activity, and a culturally preferred organization of participants' *attention* to others.

Besides structuring attention and participation, BT also involves the expression of affection, tenderness, and intimacy in the context of a nurturing social interaction (Brown 1977; Ferguson 1964, 1977). Because of this affective component, BT is considered by many psychologists to be universal and necessary for the infant's attachment and emotional attunement with the caregiver (see Bowlby 1969; Fernald 1984; Miall and Dissanayake 2003; Stern et al. 1985; Trevarthen 1979). Psychological research on interactional dynamics of attachment in dyadic mother–infant interactions contributed an understanding of the link between responsivity, or sensitivity, of parental interactional behavior (Keller et al. 1999) and caregivers' and infants' psychological wellbeing. For example, caregiver responsivity may be hindered by maternal borderline personality disorder (Delavenne et al. 2008) or depression (Reissland, Shepherd, and Herrera 2002).

Interview- and survey-based research on the use of BT across different speech communities illuminates a wide diversity of values and ideologies in the use of language and attitudes towards language use. In communities where corporal punishment is practiced, for example, BT is reported to signal the imminence of physical punishment and the authority of an adult (Haynes and Cooper 1986). Far from straightforward, the use of BT across communities, cultures, and contexts is characterized by a complex interaction of beliefs, practices, and ideologies.

Simplifying their adult speech, caregivers may be accomplishing several tacit goals: communicating with the child, making salient specific grammatical features of the language, making themselves understood, or inferring what the child is intending by attending to what the child is doing and where the child is looking (Ochs and Schieffelin 1984). Caregivers using BT also *accommodate* to the child in systematic ways. They engage in proto-conversational exchanges even with newborns, interpreting infants' facial expressions, gestures, or vocalizations (Bates, Camaioni, and Volterra 1979; Bullowa 1979; Trevarthen 1979).

In such interactions, the caregiver assumes the roles of both speaker and addressee, providing meaning and interpretation of the behaviors of the participants and of the discourse itself. Moreover, caregivers' and infants' participation in sociocultural activities (see Rogoff et al. 1995) involving BT provides an interactional scaffold that helps the infant to develop culturally appropriate beliefs about her own and others' mental processes and intentions, and about the mind itself (Schieffelin 1985). Infant participation in social interaction may be scaffolded through a range of discursive strategies by the caregiver: posing yes/no and fill-in-the-blank questions, ventriloquating the infant's projected utterances, or offering candidate understandings of the infant's vocalizations or body movements. As Ochs, Solomon, and Sterponi (2005: 551, emphasis in original) write,

> The question of *whether or not*, and *how* linguistic modifications account for children's acquisition of linguistic competence remains an open one. Strict dichotomies between innatism and behaviorism, for example, have given way to approaches that attempt to analyze the interfaces between innate neurological and cognitive proclivities and facilitating faucets of communicative environments in which infants are immersed (Bates and Elman 2000; Cole and Cole 1996; Fernald 1992; Gratier 1999, 2001, 2003; Trevarthen 1988, 1998, 2003). That is, the contemporary issue is not so much nature

versus nurture as how the two together conspire to organize the development of human competence (Boyd and Richerson 2005).

To better illuminate the language socialization perspective on BT and the contemporary state of Baby-Talk research, the section below traces its historical development to the present time.

Historical Roots of Baby-Talk Research

The earliest known reference to BT, referred to by Otto Jespersen in his book *Language: Its Nature, Development and Origin* (1922), is found in the text of a Roman grammarian, Varro, in the first century BC (Ferguson 1977). The first known anthropological account of Baby-Talk lexicon, morphology, and phonology was given by Edward Sapir in an article 'Abnormal types of speech in Nootka' (1915) and in a later article 'Nootka baby words' (1929). Based upon interview data from two informants, Sapir (1915) provides a detailed account of Nootka language use addressed to and about children. Such speech is marked by consonant alteration, diminutive suffixes, and 'baby words' lexicon. The use of diminutives in Nootka is used to show affection to children and also occurs in lullabies (1915: 357–60).[4] These characteristics, first identified by Sapir over 50 years[5] before BT became a focus of linguistic inquiry, place Nootka among other languages where BT is used as described by Ferguson (1964) and others (see also Kess and Kess 1986).

The explosion of research on BT took place in response to the innateness theory of language acquisition that cast caregiver talk as irrelevant and insufficient to children's linguistic development (Chomsky 1965, 1986). The theory posited that a 'language acquisition device' is responsible for the extraction of rule-governed 'universal grammar' from the linguistic environment, a process that takes place in spite, not because, of the malformed speech that caregivers direct to infants and young children. The Chomskyan model both responded to and challenged the earlier Skinnerian stimulus-response model of language learning (Skinner 1957). Chomsky made a claim that caregivers' speech is 'degenerate' – poorly executed and formed – and thus presents an inadequate source for the child to inductively reconstruct a language (Chomsky 1968).

Responding to Chomsky's innateness hypothesis, Snow and Ferguson (1977) led the first debate about the nature/nurture issue in language development. Reviewing studies of speech addressed to children in different cultural settings, Snow presented a view opposite to the innateness theory, arguing that (1986: 71):

> such (caregiver) speech could be assumed to be universally available to language-learning children, and not just children growing up in middle-class North America and cared for by their mothers, but also children in other cultures who live in extended families, who are cared for by older siblings or cousins, and who may have little opportunity for dyadic interaction with their mothers; these children could also be assumed to have access to a modified speech register.

Rigorous analytic attention was directed to societies where caregivers directly addressed infants and young children, and specifically to child-rearing practices characterized by dyadic caregiver–child interactions and the use of BT. It was assumed from the beginning of the Baby-Talk research paradigm that BT exists in all societies as a stable conventionalized register (Ferguson 1964, 1978). From this early assumption, however empirically unsupported, it was deduced that in all human societies adults modify their speech when talking to infants and young children and that BT is necessary for children's language acquisition.

In a seminal article, 'Baby Talk in six languages,' Ferguson first described BT in Arabic, Comanche, American English, Gilyak, Marathi, and Spanish as 'any special form of a language which is regarded by the speech community as being primary appropriate for talking to young children and which is generally regarded by the adults as not the normal, adult use of language' (1964: 103). Ferguson's argument was based upon survey and interview data from six languages and a consequent analysis of linguistic accounts of 27 languages, rather than on ethnographic research of communicative practices. From the survey and interview data it was deduced that BT was a stable register characterized by 22 features. These features included prosody (high pitch, exaggerated intonation contours, slower rate), lexicon (kin terms and body parts, infant games), phonology (cluster reduction, reduplication, special sounds), syntax (shorter sentences, telegraphic style, repetition, parataxis) and discourse (questions, pronoun shifts) (Ferguson 1978).

A later survey study by Haynes and Cooper (1986) examined 34 languages of which 22 had not been surveyed by Ferguson.[6] Most of the characteristics suggested by Ferguson were found in at least half of these languages and language varieties, but eight of these characteristics were reported in 27 out of 34 of the languages. These characteristics included high pitch, exaggerated intonational contours, shorter sentences, repetitions, special terms for kin and body parts, reduplication, pronoun shifts, and the use of BT by older children (Haynes and Cooper 1986). Because most Baby-Talk research was based upon reported survey and interview data rather than ethnographic observations, it was more a study of cultural ideologies of caregiving and members' attitudes toward language use than of language use itself. It was assumed, also without empirical support, that BT is a beneficial practice that characterizes good caregiving and promotes language development.

Ethnographic studies of language development in communities where caregivers do not routinely simplify their speech in the presence of infants and young children suggest that language socialization practices are as varied and multifaceted as the societies in which they are embedded (Garrett and Baquedano-López 2002; Ochs 1982a; Ochs and Schieffelin 1984; Schieffelin 1990). Moreover, the relation between caregivers' cultural practices and children's communicative development has been viewed as neutral to positive in language socialization research. The neutral relation has been promoted by the culturally relative notion that each community's practices are guided by its own sociocultural logic and cannot be measured by external norms. The positive relation has been assumed based upon the developmental psychological notion of cultural amplifiers (Bruner 1966), where certain social groups selectively amplify certain intellectual, social, or emotional capabilities of its members in order to benefit their development (Ochs, Solomon, and Sterponi 2005). Used by caregivers as a practice assumed beneficial to infants, the Baby-Talk register presents a unique case that refracts these concerns in an important way.

Because BT is a speech register characterized by a constellation of features, it is possible to examine these features in relation to their bearing on different aspects of developing communicative abilities. Brown (1977) considered two opposing views regarding the integrity and unity of BT as a register. One view was that BT is a powerfully integral product of its component features; the other is that the register is composed of basic components that are used in addressing different requirements of addressees, as guided by the speaker's understanding of their linguistic and cognitive abilities. Two Baby-Talk components that Brown believed to be most significant were simplification-clarification and affective expression. Brown (1977) suggests that the two basic drives behind their use are (1) to be understood and (2) to express affection (cf. DePaulo and Coleman 1977). Ferguson's analysis (1977) of Baby-Talk register use, however, posited that simplification and clarification are separate components. He grouped under the clarification such features as redundancy, repetitiveness, a slower rate of speech, clear articulation, and louder speech. It has been suggested that simplification indexes perception of intellectual or linguistic inferiority of the addressee while clarification is a process that signals a respectful attitude of the speaker toward an interlocutor of an equal or superior status (Valdman 1981).

It is still an open question, however, to what degree the features of BT facilitate language learning of typically developing children. Three general explanations have been offered, articulating a potential motivation for adult use of Baby-Talk prosody and a potential benefit for the infant (Greiser and Kuhl 1988). First, the linguistic explanation suggests that Baby-Talk prosody parses speech in a way that makes syntactic boundaries more noticeable (Jusczyk 1997; Kooijman, Haqoort, and Cutler 2005); second, the attentional explanation argues that the dramatic expansions in pitch contours make BT acoustically salient and perceptually distinctive, attracting the infant's attention to the turn-taking with the caregiver. Third, BT's high prosody signals positive affect (Fernald 1985; Fernald and Kuhl 1987; Miall and Dissanayake 2003), which encourages the infant to recognize and respond to the caregivers in a culturally appropriate way.

Providing possible insight into this question, recent research on the relation between prosody, empathy, and the mirror neuron system (Aziz-Zadeh, Sheng, and Gheytanchi 2010) suggests that, under some circumstances, the acoustic signals from another person's prosodic speech are transformed into articulatory signals and that, to understand someone else's prosodic intonation, humans may utilize their own motor representations of how they would produce the prosodic contour. Besides suggesting a mechanism for language acquisition and the development of empathy, this research also suggests a link between low measures of empathy and poor prosodic ability in autism.

Culturally organized local ideologies of competence project a well-defined set of linguistic and interactional skills necessary for membership in a child's community and culture. In this sense, a child's future is not a generic temporal construct that evolves in its own time, but rather is influenced by culturally configured trajectories that are conveyed, enacted, and maintained through specific patterns of communication (Clancy 1986; Scollon 1982). Thus, language socialization practices envision children's sociocultural membership in their communities (see also Cole 2002).

The language socialization perspective made groundbreaking contributions to understanding the development of human sociality, demonstrating that human beings develop the ability to speak a language as a way of becoming competent members of society (Ochs 1988; Ochs and Schieffelin 1984, 2008; Schieffelin 1990; Schieffelin and Ochs 1986a). Furthermore, these studies showed that novices' social understandings are accomplished through attention to and participation in verbal activities (e.g. Clancy 1986, 1999; Crago 1988; Crago, Annahatak, and Ningiuruvik 1993; Demuth 1986; Eisenberg 1982, 1986). This theoretical premise captures the bidirectional relation between practices of language use and sociocultural dispositions, foregrounding their mutually constitutive nature.

Language socialization research also extends the analytic lens beyond dyadic mother–child interaction and shifts the focus to interaction within the social group, including siblings, other family members, and others present in the children's social worlds (see de León, this volume; Goodwin and Kyratzis, this volume). This reorientation has been a formidable task, as psychological scholarship on human development and learning has been historically based upon studies of dyadic, usually mother–child, interaction (Tomasello, Kruger, and Ratner 1999). While this interactional formation is universal, other interactional arrangements, especially multiparty interactions, prevail in certain communities.[7]

Sociocultural Ecologies of Early Development

The focus on cross-cultural diversity of communicative orientations towards infants and young children has been foundational to language socialization. Its systematic attention to the sociocultural nexus of children's communicative development was preceded by the 'ethnography of communication' perspective rooted in Gumperz's notion of speech community (Gumperz 1968) and Hymes' concept of communicative competence (Gumperz and Hymes 1964, 1972; Hymes 1972). Ethnography of communication posited that members of speech communities engage in socially recognized activities through the use of a culturally appropriate linguistic repertoire that indexes certain kinds of identities and other social meanings and requires certain kinds of interpretive practices.

Longitudinal studies have provided evidence that local beliefs, practices, and institutions organize the process of becoming a competent member of a social group (socialization through language) and that this process is constituted through language development (socialization to use language) (Ochs and Schieffelin 1984;

Schieffelin and Ochs 1986a). These studies demonstrated how young children had been apprenticed into particular kinds of childhood identities, social orientations, and ways of thinking and feeling, as well as into participating in particular kinds of sociocultural activities. These identities and activities were shown to be as diverse as the practices that organize them. A language socialization approach is consistent with an updated version of linguistic relativity, where the children's acquisition and understanding of grammatical forms and discursive preferences are linked to local views of how one is expected to conduct one's self – in terms of thinking, feeling, and interacting with others – and what it means to be a competent speaker in a particular society (Ochs 2002; Ochs and Schieffelin 1995; see also Duranti 1997, 2001a, 2001b, 2004).

Cultural attitudes to language learning itself are varied. Although children in all societies are expected to engage in interactions in socially appropriate ways, the degree to which caregivers intentionally use interactional routines to overtly promote language learning varies. Moreover, the kind of language learning emphasized may differ somewhat across communities. Heath's (1983) study of language socialization in three communities in the southeastern United States indicates that each community's differential engagement in literacy practices has consequences for how children succeed at school. In one of these communities, children learned to offer reason-based explanations and affective commentaries as a way of participating in book reading; in another, they were expected to sit and listen quietly. These practices either supported or hindered the formation of the children's mainstream-preferred academic identities surrounding literacy.[8] Moreover, within this region there was variation in expectations and practices surrounding how children learned to talk and the extent to which they were expected to participate in conversations with adults. For example, Trackton infants (1983: 75, emphasis in the original) are

> listeners and observers in a stream of communication that flows about them, but is not especially channeled or modified for them. Everyone talks *about* the baby, but rarely *to* the baby. [...] When infants begin to utter sounds which can be interpreted as referring to items or events in the environment, these sounds receive no special attention.

Roadville caregivers instead spoke in BT to infants, engaging them in a conversation such as 'Wha's a matter, Bobby, yo widdle tum-tum all empty?' In such an utterance, the adult asks a question, addresses the baby by name, and provides an answer to the question. She also drops the ending of some words, substitutes /l/ for /w/ and /d/ for /t/ in 'little,' and uses a special term, 'tum-tum,' for the stomach (1983: 119).

White middle-class caregivers in postindustrial societies frequently repeat children's utterances with an expansion that fills in the missing words, and model and comment on the semantic content of children's words (Brown and Bellugi 1964; Slobin 1968). These practices are embedded in assumptions that even infants have to be treated as persons with thoughts that warrant explicit interpretation and responses and that the use of these practices makes one a good caregiver. Schieffelin and Ochs (1986a) argued that interactions among white middle-class caregivers and their infants are organized in relation to a historically contextualized developmental story rather than a species-specific, universal model of caregiver–infant interaction. In this story, mother–infant interaction is the most common one in which children are involved. In this interactional arrangement, young infants are held in a face-to-face orientation and treated as communicative partners in social interaction. Their vocalizations and movements are interpreted as intentional and meaningful by the mother, yielding proto-conversations (Bates, Camaioni, and Volterra 1979) with a dyadic turn-taking organization.

These mothers simplify and affectively mark their utterances to express their own as well as their infants' feelings and intentions. They en-register a certain kind of infant, one who is intersubjectively oriented and reciprocally engaged. Mothers accommodate their social interaction to their infants' communicative abilities so that infants' vocalizations are expanded and interpreted as intentional responses. In such interactions, infants and young children are socialized into the assumption that it is possible and desirable to explicitly talk about others' intentions, beliefs, and feelings. More broadly, they are apprenticed into culturally specific modes of attending, acting, feeling, and speaking (Schieffelin and Ochs 1986b).

A doctrine of the opacity of others' minds, or the 'opacity doctrine' (Duranti 2008; Robbins and Rumsey 2008; Schieffelin 2008), prevails in many communities and is especially prominent in many Pacific societies, where it is dispreferred to publicly speculate on what others may be thinking because their intentions and mental states are assumed to be unknowable. Such orientations force social scientists to rethink the centrality of reading intentions as a prerequisite for social engagement.

Kaluli (Papua New Guinea) and Samoan caregivers' communication with young children indicates that many features of BT were not habitually used at the time of field observations (Schieffelin 1990; Ochs 1982a, 1988; Ochs and Schieffelin 1984; Schieffelin and Ochs 1986a), suggesting that certain features such as Baby-Talk lexicon, simplified grammar, and expansions are neither universal nor necessary for language acquisition (e.g. Blount 1972, 1995; Falk 2004; Kuhl 1998, 2000; Monnot 1999).[9] Kaluli mothers did not believe that infants understood language, yet engaged their infants in interactions by ventriloquating for infants' utterances in a high-pitched, nasalized voice that was directed to third parties, often siblings. In these ventriloquations, the mothers used well-formed language appropriate for an older child while moving the baby up and down and facing the interlocutor. During such interactions, infants learned to distinguish and pay attention to other members of their social group, while at the same time siblings were socialized into treating infants as persons.

Babbling and other vocalizations were treated as nonreferential and unrelated to speech development, and there was no interpretation of these vocalizations by adults. When small children attempted to gloss a babbling or uninterpretable utterance, the adults reproduced the unintelligible sound, thus disconfirming any verbal speculation. This may have been motivated by the Kaluli belief that it is both impossible to know and thus inappropriate to say what another person might be thinking and feeling (Schieffelin 1986, 2008).

In Ochs' study of child language in Western Samoa's highly stratified society, infants were cared for by many members besides the mother and the activity of care-giving was socially stratified. In the early months, infants were talked *about* but rarely treated as conversational partners. That is, caregivers directed songs, high-pitched rhythmic vocalizations, and occasionally utterances at infants but tended not to engage them in dyadic conversation. When children started to speak, multiparty interaction was the norm: they were often prompted to call out names of passersby and repeat phrases to them. By the time they reached three to four years of age they were expected to deliver messages for others and adjust levels of respect in relation to the status of the addressee. This practice requires close attention to others' speech and excellent auditory memory. The prevailing Samoan cultural model of childhood was that young children are by nature willful and mischievous and require external control from adults to learn respectful demeanor. Perhaps paradoxically, defiance and anger were treated as desirable qualities for children and youths to display on certain occasions when the honor of the extended family required defense. In addition, the Samoan cultural model of intentionality discouraged explicit conjecture of the motives behind others' actions. Consequently, caregivers usually tended not to provide an explicit gloss of unintelligible utterances of young children (Ochs 1982a, 1982b; Schieffelin and Ochs 1986a).

These developmental stories have important theoretical implications for understanding how caregivers' communication and social conduct en-register infants and young children as cultural beings. Communication is organized around local beliefs about intersubjectivity, intentionality, child rearing, and language learning. These beliefs generate local preferences for the organization of attention and coordination of social action with young children. The discussion will now turn to the contribution of language socialization research to understanding how communicative practices impact social potentialities of children and youths affected by atypical development.

Language Socialization and Developmental Difference

The language socialization paradigm has made an important contribution to research and clinical practice in the field of communication disorders. Crago (1992) provided a succinct and insightful review of language socialization scholarship, highlighting its relevance to understanding communicative difference and variation. Taking as a point of departure a continuum of communicative accommodation that spans child-centered to situation-centered cultures (Schieffelin and Eisenberg 1984; Schieffelin and Ochs 1986a), Crago (1992) illuminates how language socialization practices tacitly organize adult–child interaction in clinics and classrooms.

Another contribution of the language socialization perspective has been in the area of autism research. A lifelong neurodevelopmental condition that disrupts sociocommunicative development, autism currently affects 1 in 110 eight-year-old children and 1 in 70 eight-year-old boys in the United States (Centers for Disease Control and Prevention 2009; see Solomon 2010b). Autistic impairments include language delay, atypical use of gesture and eye gaze, diminished reciprocity and shared enjoyment of objects or events, and difficulties in forming age-appropriate friendships (Lord and Spence 2006).

Ochs and colleagues (2004) moved the scope of inquiry on autism and social interaction beyond the focus on interpersonal 'theory of mind' (Baron-Cohen 1995; Baron-Cohen, Leslie, and Frith 1985; Happe 2003) to a sociocultural one. Making a distinction between social interaction as *interpersonal* and social interaction as *sociocultural*, Ochs et al. (2004) argued that persons affected by autism display both abilities and difficulties. This distinction lead to systematic analysis of sociocultural perspective-taking as the understanding of other members' expected intentions, beliefs, knowledge, or feelings that are conventionally linked to socioculturally organized practices, roles, institution, and membership in a social group (Ochs 2002). Persons with autism are evaluated by others (and often by themselves) relative to socioculturally organized expectations of situational conduct. This reframing of autism provided a new approach to understanding social challenges faced by individuals with autism (see Solomon 2008 for a review).

Euro-American Habitus of Baby Talk and Autism

It appears that there may be a fourth developmental story to be considered besides the Kaluli, Samoan, and Euro-American white middle-class stories described by Ochs and Schieffelin (1984), a story of language socialization of children whose development does not proceed as expected. In describing this fourth developmental story, the concept of 'habitus' (Bourdieu 1977, 1990a) is helpful for understanding how caregivers and others engage with infants and young children, including those with atypical development, across communities and contexts. Habitus is a set of socially organized, historically rooted yet transformable dispositions that enable members to interpret and engage in the flow of social practices that exist in a given culture (Bourdieu 1977, 1990a, 1990b). Additionally, the fourth developmental story relies upon a notion of 'child-directed communication' that extends BT to include nonverbal dimensions of social interaction (see Ochs, Solomon, and Sterponi 2005).

In each community there is at least one habitus of child-directed communication, and this habitus is considered to be helpful and, indeed not harmful, to a child's development. The habitus of child-directed communication may, however,

Figure 5.1   Lev with a speech therapist (left) and aide. Reproduced from Ochs, Solomon, and Sterponi (2005).

hinder a child's potential when the child is affected by neurodevelopmental conditions that interfere with communication and social participation (Ochs, Solomon, and Sterponi 2005). As will be discussed below, in societies in which BT and face-to-face orientation prevail in child-directed communication, this habitus may indeed be unfavorable to enhancing the social and cognitive development of children with conditions such as autism.

Euro-American child-directed communication is characterized by three default features: a face-to-face orientation for caregiver and child, speech as a medium, and BT. Of particular consequence to children with autism are the Baby-Talk features of slowed speech, vowel lengthening, and heightened positive affect through exaggerated intonation and praise. Autism magnifies the developmental and interactional consequences of these default communicative practices, as observed when their deployment draws children with this condition and their interlocutors into a struggle to maintain social, emotional, and cognitive engagement. These features of Euro-American child-directed communication challenge children with severe autism, who are often uninterested in or avoidant of eye gaze and face-to-face orientation (Klin et al. 2002; Pelphrey, Morris, and McCarthy 2005), find articulating spoken words difficult, lose attention across slowed and lengthened stretches of talk, and become overwhelmed by heightened affect (Lord and Spence 2006).

Consider how these features are used by a speech therapist during a group session with children affected by different communication disorders (see Ochs, Solomon, and Sterponi 2005 for detailed analysis).[10] Nine-year-old Lev, who was diagnosed with autism at the age of two, is participating in a group activity in which the speech therapist asks children to pronounce the name 'Jamie,' which is written on a flashcard that she holds up in front of her, as shown in Figure 5.1. She begins by asking the children to pronounce the sound represented by the letter 'J':

Example 5.1: 'Jamie'[11]

Participant	Behavior	Selected Child-Directed-Communication Features
Therapist:	((facing children, holding up a flashcard with 'Jamie' written in cursive, covering all the letters but 'J' with fingers, smiles))	Face-to-face
Boy 1:	Juh! (('J'))	
Therapist:	GOO↑ :::: ↓D!	Slow, lengthened speech; profuse praise
Therapist:	((moves flashcard to face another child, Boy 2)) WHAT SOU:ND↑	
Boy 2:	Juh! (('J'))	
Therapist:	GOO :: D!	Slow, lengthened speech; profuse praise
	((turns to face Lev)) Your turn!	Face-to-face
Lev:	((looks down and to the right, away from the flashcard, pats right hand with left several times))	
Aide:	((holds Lev's head to face therapist and flashcard, and points to flashcard, then holds down Lev's hands)) Try Lev.	Face-to-face
Lev:	/ ɛ l / (('L'))	
Therapist:	Good TRY↑:::ING↓!	Slow, lengthened speech; profuse praise
Aide:	((nods several times)) ° Good boy °	Praise
Lev:	((pats right arm with left hand again))	
Therapist:	((faces group, opens mouth wide, slowly demonstrating how to articulate sound /e/ for letter 'A')) LOOK! ((keeps mouth wide open, turns to face Lev))	Face-to-face; slow tempo
Boy 1:	/ a I / (('I'))	
Therapist:	((turns to face Lev, holding flashcard))	Face-to-face

Participant	*Behavior*	*Selected Child-Directed-Communication Features*
Aide:	((holds Lev's head to face therapist and flashcard, points to flashcard))	Face-to-face
Lev:	/ I e /	
Therapist:	((softly articulates the sound with her mouth wide open)) / e:::/ (('A'))	Slow, lengthened speech
Boy 1:	/ e:::/ (('A'))	
Lev:	[/ I ε / (('A'))	
Aide:	[((*touches Lev's chin*))	
Therapist:	((looks at Lev, holding up flashcard, softly articulates the sound with her mouth wide open)) / e:::/ (('A'))	Face-to-face; slow, lengthened speech
Boy 2:	/ e:::/ (('A'))	
Therapist:	((eyes wide open, smiling, touches Lev, whispered, affectionate voice)) Very nice ↑try↓!	Face-to-face; praise

Lev faces multiple challenges in this interaction. First, he has difficulties maintaining face-to-face orientation with the therapist and attending to the flashcard that she is showing him. To help Lev with the face-to-face orientation, his aide stabilizes his body by holding his right hand down on his knee and fixing his head in position for maintaining eye gaze and body orientation with the therapist.

Second, because in this interaction *speech* is assumed to be the primary medium of communication for both therapist and child and the focus of the speech therapy intervention, Lev is asked to speak. At nine years of age, Lev has experienced lifelong difficulties and frustrations with verbal communication, including articulating sounds similar to the ones elicited by the therapist. His aide touches his chin to help him in this task.

Finally, the speech therapist slowly pronounces each of the sounds that compose the word 'Jamie' and lengthens her vowels in both her modeled and spontaneous utterances, for example '/ e:::/' , 'GOO :: D!' It is likely that the lengthening of individual sounds and the slowing down of their pronunciation interferes with Lev's understanding that the individual sounds compose the whole word 'Jamie.' In addition, the therapist's speech displays the BT characteristic of *heightened positive affect* conveyed through exaggerated intonation and effusive praising. This level of affective intensity may be overwhelming for children with autism, who are susceptible to sensory overload (Bogdashina 2004).

The impact of these features of child-directed communication on social potentialities of children with autism becomes especially visible when the example above is contrasted with Lev's interaction with Soma Mukhopadhyay, the founder of the Rapid Prompting Method (RPM), and with other interlocutors who use this communicative practice. RPM differs in fundamental ways from Euro-American child-directed communication (see Ochs, Solomon, and Sterponi 2005; Ochs and Solomon 2010) in that it presents a different kind of simplification that appears uniquely tailored to autistic impairments and challenges. Caregivers who use RPM systematically employ strategies that include (1) side-by-side, rather than face-to-face, orientation; (2) pointing to symbols, rather than speaking, as the primary medium of the child's communication while the adult interlocutor primarily uses speech in combination with gesture and touch; (3) use of a letter and number board (ABC or QWERTY, the layout of a computer keyboard), to which the child is expected to point; (4) caregiver speech that is rapid and accentuated, and characterized by frequent prompts that parse activities into manageable small parts; and (5) praise that is restrained and does not involve exaggerated positive affect.

Lev and other children with autism were more socially engaged when interlocutors communicated with them using the RPM approach. When Mrs. Mukhopadhyay communicated with Lev, only correct responses were praised, with emphatic stress placed on the word 'good,' produced rapidly and rhythmically to punctuate the end of a unit of action. The pitch contours of these praises were moderately rising and falling, while the amplitude of her voice moderately increased in loudness or remained the same (Engelke and Mangano 2007, 2008). A consistently rapid rhythm of interaction was maintained during delivery of information, questions, prompts to attend and proceed, and assessments. Such an organization of participation, along with other features of this situation, drew the children into active and orderly social engagement with others.

An Algorithm to Support Social Engagement in Autism

Based upon decade-long research on social interactions involving high-functioning and severely affected children with autism, Ochs and Solomon (2010) proposed an 'algorithm' of communicative conditions that enhance the domain of possibilities for social coordination with individuals affected by autism. Communication is enhanced when (1) corporeal alignment is non-face-to-face (e.g. side-by-side); (2) display of affect is restrained; (3) the tempo of speech is moderate to rapid (versus slowed); (4) writing, pointing, and music are favored as communicative media (versus speaking); (5) semiotic artifacts (e.g. computers, keyboards, letter boards) and/or specially trained therapy animals mediate communication (see Solomon 2010a); (6) social interaction focuses on brief (versus extended) conversational sequences; (7) objective knowledge (versus subjective states) is the topic of conversation; and (8) the child's home/first language (versus national language/ second language) is the privileged medium of communication within the family.

To illustrate what constitutes an algorithm-sensitive social interaction between an individual with autism and a caregiver, I offer Example 5.2, from a corpus

Figure 5.2   Jacob and his mother, Shannon.

collected for a language socialization study of 16 severely affected children and youths with autism and their family members. The interaction is provided in its entirety to convey the level of interactional work that individuals with autism and their family members engage in to participate in everyday discourse.

Jacob, an 18-year-old youth with autism from a Euro-American middle-class family is finishing breakfast in the kitchen. Jacob was diagnosed with autism at the age of three and is considered severely affected, having difficulty communicating verbally. He and his mother Shannon (see Figure 5.2) are planning their activities for the day. The interaction is accomplished through a side-by-side orientation: Shannon asks questions and Jacob points to letters to spell out the answers on a yellow QWERTY letter board that Shannon holds in front of him. The cardboard letter board has the layout of a computer keyboard. As Jacob points to the letters one at a time, Shannon often voices each letter and then pronounces the whole answer.

Example 5.2:   *'White Sox for Papa'*

Participant	Behavior	Selected Child-Directed Communication Features
Shannon:	Okay. I have a quick question for you?	Question; Politeness
Jacob:	((looks down at his bowl, does not look up)) (1.0)	
Shannon:	Do you think it would <u>distra</u>:ct you if we continued to do your schedule?	Question; Politeness
Jacob:	((continues eating, does not look up)) (0.5)	
Shannon:	While you were eating? (0.5)	Question

Participant	Behavior	*Selected Child-Directed Communication Features*
	[((puts the yellow QWERTY board in front of Jacob))	Placing a communication device to prompt
	[Will you be distracted (.) if we do your schedule while you are eating?	Question;
	No?	Repetition;
	Can we have conversation?	Expansion;
	While you are eating then?	Question;
	Is that <u>okay</u>?	Repetition; Clarification
Jacob:	[((points to letter 'Y' for 'Yes' on the board))	
	[((verbally says)) Yeah	
Shannon:	Ah. Okay very good.	Moderate positive affect;
	[All righty.	
	[((puts the letter board down on the table))	Rephrasing; Comment;
	That sounds like a plan.	Question;
	Ah – what do you want your to:pic to be?	Repetition
	While you are eating.	
Jacob:	((UI))	
Shannon:	What do you want your topic to be?	Repetition; Request for clarification
Jacob:	((begins pointing to the board))	
Shannon:	((voices the letters that Jacob is pointing to))	Voicing
	Es-	
Jacob:	[((continues pointing))	
Shannon:	[Ayh- Pee- Pee- Ai- En-	Voicing; Prompt/
	Okay. Last letter? Reach it plea:se.	Question; Prompt; Politeness
Jacob:	((points to letter 'G'))	
Shannon:	Shopping. Yeah. I agree. We need to talk about shopping. We have to get some- birthday gifts. Ehhhm =	Repetition; Agreement; Rephrasing; Expansion
Jacob:	((speaks)) = for <u>Papa</u>	

Participant	Behavior	Selected Child-Directed Communication Features
Shannon:	((places the board in front of Jacob)) Did you want to buy something for papa?	Placing the board for communication; Expansion; Question
Jacob:	((points to Y denoting 'Yes' on the board))	
Shannon:	Okay. They are coming in tonight? Great. Do you want to go to::- uhm- Bloomingdales? That's number one. Or (.) do you think- that you want to shop for Papa at Nordstrom? ((places the board in front of Jacob)) Number two. Which <u>one</u>?	Agreement; Question; Moderate positive affect; Offering a candidate answer
Jacob:	((places finger in the number line above 'one' and 'two' and hits down))	
Shannon:	Number <u>three</u>? Something <u>else</u>?	Offering a candidate answer
Jacob:	((points to 'Yes' on the board))	
Shannon:	Oh, all right! Oh then I don't know what you're thinking about, we have to figure that out. ((places the board in front of Jacob)) Do you have something in mind you want to buy for papa?	Agreement; Desire to determine Jacob's meaning; Placing communicative device to prompt communication; Question
Jacob:	[((UI)) [((points to 'Yes'))	
Jacob:	((Several turns later, points to letters that spell out 'Can we get him a shirt?'))	Request for clarification; Question
Shannon:	What kind of a shirt? Do you have the word for it?	

Participant	*Behavior*	*Selected Child-Directed Communication Features*
Jacob:	Points to the letter board	Request/offer of a candidate
Shannon:	Is it a sports shirt?	answer;
Jacob:	((points to 'Y' for 'Yes'))	Question;
	((looks up at Shannon))	Inferred mental
Shannon:	Does that help?	state;
Jacob:	((Smiles and embraces her))	Moderate positive
Shannon:	((kisses him)). Okay.	affect;
	Do you want to get him- what?	Fill-in-the-blank
	A special kind of shirt-	question;
	A sports shirt-	Offering a candidate answer
Jacob:	((points to the board))	
Shannon:	((exaggeratedly articulating every letter))	Voicing;
	Es – O - Ex- Es.	Exaggerated positive affect;
	((eyes wide open, smiling, exaggerated intonation))	Parsing words;
	YOU- ARE- the nicest person!	Increased voice volume;
	A 'WHITE SOX' shirt!	
	Absolutely! Okay.	Agreement;
	((writes it down on the yellow paper))	Using writing as medium of
	I'm gonna ask Dad if he's got an extra one for papa	communication;
	That was great Jake! Excellent.	Future plan of actions;
	((laughing, leaves the table))	Moderate positive affect
	((later that day Jacob's father Richard is in the kitchen with Jacob and Shannon))	
Shannon:	Number one, earlier this morning you had a goal about Papa. You can ask Dad. Can you read this?	Realizing a plan for action
Jacob:	((reads what his mother wrote in the morning on the yellow paper))	
	'White Sox shirt for papa'	

This interaction is heavily saturated with Shannon's autism-attuned discursive strategies. The social actions that the two participants carry out together are made possible by extensive accommodation to Jacob's communicative challenges: Shannon engages Jacob in question–candidate answer sequences and expands Jacob's projected meanings when he spells his answers on the letter board. She offers repetitions, shows mostly moderate positive affect, and parses words. However simplifying and accommodating Shannon's speech is and however it resembles Euro-American middle-class Baby-Talk register, she systematically avoids certain features of BT such as exaggerated positive affect and intonation. Shannon's discourse matches the algorithm for optimizing social participation as outlined above: the social orientation of Shannon and Jacob is side-to-side, together looking at the letter board; Jacob spells his answers by pointing to letters. The commonality with the Baby-Talk register is in Shannon simplifying her talk by asking yes/no and fill-in-the blank questions and breaking down information into small, discrete discourse units.

Shannon's discourse, however, is reaching far beyond the guessing of meaning seen in BT addressed to infants. In this interaction, Jacob is afforded (and he participates in enacting) an identity of a person whose thoughts are so important that they are worthy of the laborious, time-consuming work of pointing, guessing, and voicing (see Goodwin 1995, 2000, 2003). Although Jacob is addressed with deference and politeness, also a feature of child-centered Euro-American middle-class BT, his mother's polite speech does not have the semiserious quality reminiscent of BT directed to infants. Rather, Jacob is afforded the respect and admiration that is due to a young man of his age in his social group.

Jacob's mother also affords Jacob respect by knowing what kind of social interaction would be painful or frustrating. She carefully voices Jacob's pointing and offers him candidate answers that he might choose.[12] She shows respect by *not* using exaggerated intonation and heightened praise and by *not* insisting on speech and face-to-face orientation. The two participants are engaged in the laborious, painstaking work of accomplishing a shared meaning clouded by autism. The overarching sequential organization of this interaction is visible and hearable in Shannon's question, 'Do you have something in mind ....' What is at stake in this interaction is not only what is on Jacob's mind, but also that there is a mind for Jacob to have, a mind of a generous and thoughtful person, a son, a grandson, a White Sox fan, a young man who shares his passion for sports with his family.

This interaction demonstrates how Euro-American middle-class families share their life worlds through participation in sociocultural activities that make up the fabric of their everyday life: engaging with children in extracurricular activities; going to sports events; shopping in department stores; going to book stores, museums, restaurants, and coffee houses; using credit cards; and planning gifts of a certain kind for family members. In spite of autism and severe limitations in communication, Jacob is ontologically positioned as a person with interesting and valuable ideas, whose self-esteem and talents are to be cultivated, who is to be addressed with love and respect by his mother and his other family members.

What language socialization perspective contributes to analyses of such interactions is its ethnomethodological impulse. Rather than concentrating on how this young man's communication is hindered by his autism, we are given the analytic tools to look beyond the simplified register used by Jacob's mother in search of sociocultural methods that he and his mother orchestrate and enact to solve a very important question: what activities they will engage in with each other that day, and what he has 'in mind.' The focus of language socialization on 'doing together' (Schegloff 2006) as well as on knowing and speaking together allows for a very different ontological view on the subjectivities and identities of participants in social interaction, be they infants or individuals affected by autism.

Conclusion

This chapter examined the Baby-Talk register from a language socialization perspective as a common but culturally distinct practice of addressing infants, young children, and persons whose communicative abilities are perceived to be impaired, among other types of interlocutors. In the case of typically developing children, BT affords simplification, possibly to facilitate various aspects of infants' social development, from acquisition of syntax to developing attachments. It does not, however, afford simplification for a child with severe autism, as seen in the example of Lev during a speech-therapy session.

As illustrated by examples across communities and contexts, including an example of a social interaction involving a Euro-American middle-class mother and her 18-year-old son with autism, it may be that it is not the register of BT *per se* that has an impact on the social development of children with and without developmental disabilities. Rather, it is *certain kinds* of BT that have facilitating and supporting properties for the development of communication and sociality. The main argument of this chapter is that BT and other culturally organized practices of interaction with and around children are implicated in 'self - and other-fashioning' (Silverstein 2004) and enregister a kind of addressee with particular ontological properties including subjectivities, potentialities, entitlements, and restrictions concerning participation in social life. What counts in emergent self- and other-fashioning is participation in ongoing, recurrent, situated cultural activities, whose organization affords infants, young children, and individuals with developmental disabilities ecologies of apprenticeship into the use of language and enables them through language to be members of their families and communities.

ACKNOWLEDGMENTS

The author wishes to thank the *Handbook*'s editors, Alessandro Duranti, Elinor Ochs, and Bambi Schieffelin, for their careful and patient reading and for their useful comments and suggestions. The responsibility for any shortcomings that remain in this chapter belongs solely to the author. I also would like to thank Elinor Ochs, my mentor and colleague, for a shared commitment to the study of autism. Very deep gratitude goes to the families who have let the author into their and their children's lives, dreams, and challenges. Without you this work would have not been possible.

NOTES

1   See Arnett (2008) and Cole (2006) for recent critique of the neglect of culture in psychological research.
2   Caregiver register is also described in psycholinguistic research as 'motherese' (Snow 1977, 1984; Snow and Ferguson 1977).
3   In some languages such as Marathi, British and American English, German, Portuguese, and Spanish, the affect-conveying function of BT is a possible reason it is reported to be used among lovers as a hallmark of intimacy and attachment (Bombar and Littig 1996; Ferguson 1964, 1977; Haynes and Cooper 1986) or directed at a family dog in a secondary Baby-Talk register called 'doggerel' (Hirsh-Pasek and Treiman 1982; Mitchell 2004).
4   Besides children, other classes of people addressed in 'abnormal types of speech in Nootka' are 'unusually fat or heavy people, unusually short adults, those suffering from defect of the eye, hunchbacks, those that are lame, left-handed persons, and circumcised males' (Sapir 1915: 359). This may correspond to the secondary BT in English directed to addressees who are considered retarded and to the elderly.
5   Data for the 1915 article were obtained in 1910 and 1913–14.
6   These languages included Amharic; Anggor; Tunisian Arabic; Assamese; Betawi; Cantonese; Catalan; Dutch; Australian, British, Canadian, Guyanese, and Hawaiian English; German; Hebrew; Hokkien; Indonesian; Javanese; Korean; Palauan; Brazilian Portugese; Sindhi; Soddo; American, Castilian, and Cuban Spanish; Sundanese; Swahili; Tagalog; Tarascan; Tumbuka; Ukrainian; Ullogooli; and Yiddish. Arabic, Dutch, American English, German, Portuguese, and Spanish were common to both Ferguson's original study and Haynes and Cooper (1986).
7   While characteristic of many non-Euro-American cultures and across linguistic repertoires associated with different occasions for language use, depending on the social organization of caregiving, multiparty organization is also found in Euro-American societies.
8   Heath's (1986: 104) example from Scollon and Scollon (1979) demonstrates the nuances of organization of attention during language socialization interactions involving Scollons' daughter, a child from an academic family: 'She knew before age 2 how to focus on a book and not on herself. Even when she told a story about herself, she moved herself out of the text and saw herself as author, as someone different from the central character of her story. She learned to pay close attention to parts of objects, to name them and to provide a running commentary on features of her environment' (1986: 104).
9   See *A World of Babies: Imagined Childcare Guides for Seven Societies* (2000), edited by psychologist Judy DeLaoche and anthropologist Alma Gottlieb, a collection of imaginary guides for parents living in seven societies that describe strikingly different child-rearing practices shaped by each society's habitus.

10   The examples in this chapter are part of a data corpus of approximately 200 hours collected for a study of 16 children and youths with autism aged 3 to 18 and their families. The study participants were engaged in a communicative practice called the Rapid Prompting Method (RPM), introduced by South-Indian educator Soma Mukhopadhyay. The studies '"Rapid prompting" communication with severely autistic children,' and 'The "rapid prompting" method of communicating with severely autistic children: A language socialization study' were approved by the University of California Los Angeles Institutional Review Board. The study 'The "Rapid Prompting" method of communicating with severely autistic children: A language socialization study' was approved by the University of Southern California Institutional Review Board, Health Science Campus.

11   Originally published in *Discourse Studies* 7(4–5), p. 562. Reproduced here with the permission of Sage Publications. © Sage 2005.

12   One of the practices that families with severely impacted children develop is interactional shortcuts. Because pointing words letter by letter is such a laborious and slow process, the families assign numbers one and two to two choices and leave number three to indicate 'something else.' The 'something else' allows for the possibility that the parents do not know what is on their autistic child's mind and to enable a communicative practice that does not assign arbitrary meaning to the child.

REFERENCES

Arnett, J. J. (2008) The neglected 95%: Why American psychology needs to become less American. *American Psychologist* 63(7): 602–14.

Aziz-Zadeh, L., Sheng, T., and Gheytanchi, A. (2010) Common premotor regions for the perception and production of prosody and correlations with empathy and prosodic ability. *Public Library of Science* 5(1): 8759.

Baron-Cohen, S. (1995) *Mindblindness: An Essay on Autism and Theory of Mind*. Boston, MA: MIT Press.

Baron-Cohen, S., Leslie, A. M., and Frith, U. (1985) Does the autistic child have a 'theory of mind'? *Cognition* 21(1): 37–46.

Bates, E. and Elman, J. (2000) The ontogeny and phylogeny of language: A neural network perspective. In S. T. Parker, J. Langer, and M. L. McKinney (eds.), *Biology, Brains, and Behavior: The Evolution of Human Development*. 89–130. Santa Fe, NM: School of American Research Press.

Bates, E., Camaioni, L., and Volterra, V. (1979) The acquisition of performatives prior to speech. In E. Ochs and B. B. Schieffelin (eds.), *Developmental Pragmatics*. 111–31. New York: Academic Press.

Biber, D., and Finegan, E. (1994) *Sociolinguistic Perspectives on Register*. Oxford: Oxford University Press.

Blount, B. G. (1972) Parental speech and language acquisition. *Anthropological Linguistics* 14: 119–30.

Blount, B. G. (1995) *Language, Culture, and Society: A Book of Readings*. 2nd ed. Long Grove: Waveland Press.

Bogdashina, O. (2004) *Sensory Perceptual Issues in Autism and Asperger Syndrome*. London: Jessica Kingsley.

Bombar, M. L. and Littig Jr., L. W. (1996) BabyTalk as a communication of intimate attachment: An initial study in adult romances and friendships. *Personal Relationships* 3(2): 137–58.

Bourdieu, P. (1977) *Outline of a Theory of Practice*. Cambridge: Cambridge University Press

Bourdieu, P. (1990a) *In Other Words: Essays Towards a Reflexive Sociology*. Stanford, CA: Stanford University Press.

Bourdieu, P. (1990b) *The Logic of Practice*. Stanford, CA: Stanford University Press.

Bowlby, J. (1969) *Attachment*. New York: Basic Books.

Boyd, R. and Richerson, P. (1985) *Culture and the Evolutionary Process*. Chicago, IL: University of Chicago Press.

Boyd, R. and Richerson, P. J. (2005) *The Origin and Evolution of Cultures*. New York: Oxford University Press.

Brown, R. (1977) Introduction. In C. Snow and C. Ferguson (eds.), *Talking to Children*. 1–27. Cambridge: Cambridge University Press.

Brown, R. and Bellugi, U. (1964) Three processes in the child's acquisition of syntax. *Harvard Educational Review* 34: 133–51.

Bruner, J. S. (1966) *Studies in Cognitive Growth*. New York: Wiley.

Bruner, J. S. (1978) The role of dialogue in language acquisition. In A. Sinclair, R. J. Jarvella, and W. J. M. Levelt (eds.), *The Child's Conception of Language*. New York: Springer.

Bullowa, M. (1979) *Before Speech: The Beginning of Interpersonal Communication*. London: Cambridge University Press.

Caporael, L. R. (1981) The paralanguage of caregiving: Baby Talk to the institutionalized aged. *Journal of Personality and Social Psychology* 40(5): 876–84.

Centers for Disease Control and Prevention (2009) Prevalence of autism spectrum disorders – Autism and Developmental Disabilities Monitoring Network, United States, 2006. *Morbidity and Mortality Weekly Report, Surveillance Summaries* 58(SS10): 1–20.

Chew, J. J. (1969) The structure of Japanese Baby Talk. *Journal-Newsletter of the Association of Teachers of Japanese* 6(1): 4–17.

Chomsky, N. (1965) *Aspects of the Theory of Syntax*. Cambridge, MA: MIT Press.

Chomsky, N. (1968). *Language and Mind*. New York: Harcourt, Brace and World.

Chomsky, N. (1986) *Knowledge of Language: Its Nature, Origins and Use*. New York: Praeger.

Clancy, P. (1986) The acquisition of communicative style in Japanese. In B. B. Schieffelin and E. Ochs (eds.), *Language Socialization Across Cultures*. 213–50. New York: Cambridge University Press.

Clancy, P. (1999) The socialization of affect in Japanese mother–child conversation. *Journal of Pragmatics* 31(11): 1397–421.

Cole, M. (2002) Culture and development. In H. Keller, Y. H. Poortinga, and A. Scholmerich (eds), *Between Culture and Biology: Perspectives on Ontogenic Development*. 303–19. Cambridge: Cambridge University Press.

Cole, M. (2006) Internationalism in psychology: We need it now more than ever. *American Psychologist* 61: 904–17.

Cole, M. and Cole, S. (1996) *The Development of Children*. New York: W. H. Freeman.

Crago, M. B. (1988) *Cultural Context in Communicative Interaction of Inuit Children*. Montreal: McGill University Press.

Crago, M. B. (1992) The sociocultural interface of communicative interaction and L2 acquisition: An Inuit example. *TESOL Quarterly* 23(3): 487–506.

Crago, M. B., Annahatak, B., and Ningiuruvik, L. (1993) Changing patterns of language socialization in Inuit homes. *Anthropology and Education Quarterly* 24(3): 205–23.

DeLaoche, J. and Gottlieb, A. (2000) *A World of Babies: Imagined Childcare Guides for Seven Societies*. New York: Cambridge University Press.

Delavenne, A., Gratier, M., Devouche, E., and Apter, G. (2008) Phrasing and fragmented time in 'pathological' mother–infant vocal interaction. *European Society for the Cognitive Sciences of Music, Special Issue*: 47–70.

Demuth, K. (1986) Prompting routines in the language socialization of Basotho children. In B. E. Schieffelin and E. Ochs (eds.), *Language Socialization Across Cultures*. 51–79. Cambridge: Cambridge University Press.

DePaulo, B. M. and Coleman, L. M. (1977) Verbal and nonverbal communication of warmth to children, foreigners, and retarded adults. *Journal of Nonverbal Behavior*. 11(2): 75–88.

Derrida, J. (1990) Sending: On representation. In G. L. Ormiston and A. D. Schrift (eds.), *Transforming the Hermeneutic Context: From Nietzsche to Nancy Gayle*. 107–38. Albany, NY: State University of New York Press.

Duranti, A. (1997) *Linguistic Anthropology*. Cambridge: Cambridge University Press.

Duranti, A. (2001a) *Linguistic Anthropology: A Reader*. Malden, MA: Blackwell.

Duranti, A. (2001b) *Key Terms in Language and Culture*. Malden, MA: Blackwell.

Duranti, A. (2004) *A Companion to Linguistic Anthropology*. Malden, MA: Blackwell.

Duranti, A. (2008) Further reflections on reading other minds. *Anthropological Quarterly* 81(2): 483–95.

Eisenberg, A. R. (1982) *Language Acquisition in Cultural Perspective: Talk in Three Mexican Homes*. Doctoral Dissertation. Berkeley, CA: University of California.

Eisenberg, A. R. (1986) Teasing: Verbal play in two Mexican homes. In E. Ochs and B. B. Schieffelin (eds.), *Language Socialization across Cultures*. 182–98. Cambridge: Cambridge University Press.

Engelke, C. and Mangano, D. (2007) Meaningful looks: Temporality and intersubjectivity in interactions involving children with severe autism. Paper presented at the 106th annual meeting of the American Anthropological Association, Washington, DC.

Engelke, C. and Mangano, D. (2008) Temporal cues: What children with severe autism can teach us about intersubjectivity. Paper presented at the Symposium about Language and Society-Austin, TX (SALSA XVI).

Falk, D. (2004) Prelinguistic evolution in early hominins: Whence motherese? *Behavioral and Brain Sciences* 27: 491–503.

Ferguson, C. A. (1959) Arabic Baby Talk. In Morris Halle (ed.), *For Roman Jacobson*. 121–8. The Hague: Mouton.

Ferguson, C. A. (1964) Baby Talk in six languages. *American Anthropologist* 66(6): 103–14.

Ferguson, C. A. (1977) Baby Talk as a simplified register. In C. E. Snow and C. A. Ferguson (eds.), *Talking to Children: Language Input and Acquisition*. 209–35. Cambridge: Cambridge University Press.

Ferguson, C. A. (1978) Talking to children: In search of universals. In J. Greenberg, C. A. Ferguson, and E. A. Moravscik (eds.), *Universals of Human Language, Vol. 1*. 203–24. Stanford, CA: Stanford University Press.

Ferguson, C. A. (1994) Dialect, register, and genre: Working assumptions about conventionalization. In D. Biber and E. Finegan (eds.), *Sociolinguistic Perspectives on Register*. 15–30. Oxford: Oxford University Press.

Fernald, A. (1984) The perceptual and affective salience of mothers' speech to infants. In L. Feagans, C. Garvey, and R. Golinkoff (eds.), *The Origins and Growth of Communication*. 5–29. New York: Ablex.

Fernald, A. (1985) Four-month-old infants prefer to listen to motherese. *Infant Behavior and Development* 8(2): 181–95.

Fernald, A. (1992) Human maternal vocalizations to infants as biologically relevant signals: An evolutionary perspective. In J.H. Barkow, L. Cosmides, and J. Tooby (eds.), *The Adapted Mind: Evolutionary Psychology and the Generation of Culture.* 391–428. New York: Oxford University Press.

Fernald, A., and Kuhl, P. (1987) Acoustic determinants of infant preference for motherese speech. *Infant Behavior and Development* 10(3): 279–93.

Garrett, P. and Baquedano-López, P. (2002) Language socialization: Reproduction and continuity, transformation and change. *Annual Review of Anthropology* 31: 339–61.

Gaskins, S. (1999) Children's daily lives in a Mayan village: A case study of culturally constructed roles and activities. In A. Goncu (ed.), *Children's Engagement in the World: Socio-Cultural Perspectives.* 25–61. New York: Cambridge University Press.

Gaskins, S. (2006) Cultural perspectives on infant–caregiver interactions. In N. J. Enfield and S. C. Levinson (eds.), *Roots of Human Sociality: Culture, Cognition, and Interaction.* 279–98. New York: Berg.

Goodwin, C. (1995) Co-constructing meaning in conversations with an aphasic man. *Research on Language and Social Interaction* 28(3): 233–60.

Goodwin, C. (2000) Action and embodiment within situated human interaction. *Journal of Pragmatics* 32(10): 1489–522.

Goodwin, C. (2003) Pointing as situated practice. In S. Kito (ed.), *Pointing: Where Language, Culture and Cognition Meet.* 217–41. Mahwah, NJ: Lawrence Erlbaum.

Gratier, M. (1999) Expressions of belonging: The effect of acculturation on the rhythm and harmony of mother–infant vocal interaction, rhythms, musical narrative and the origins of human communication. *Musicae Scientiae, Special Issue: Current Trends in the Study of Music and Emotion, 1999–2000,* 93–122.

Gratier, M. (2001) *Rythmes et Appartenances Culturelles: Etude Acoustique des Échanges Vocaux Entre Mères et Bébés Autochtones et Migrants.* Doctoral Thesis. Université de Paris V – René-Descartes, Paris, France.

Gratier, M. (2003) Expressive timing and interactional synchrony between mothers and infants: Cultural similarities, cultural differences, and the immigration experience. *Cognitive Development* 3: 1–22.

Greiser, D. and Kuhl, P. (1988) Maternal speech to infants in a tonal language: Support for universal prosodic features in motherese. *Developmental Psychology* 24:14–20.

Gumperz, J. (1968) The speech community. In D. L. Sills (eds.), *International Encyclopedia of the Social Sciences.* 381–6. London: Macmillan.

Gumperz, J. and Hymes, D. (1964) The ethnography of communication. *American Anthropologist* 66(6): Part 2.

Gumperz, J. and Hymes, D. (1972) *Directions in Sociolinguistics: The Ethnography of Communication.* New York: Holt, Rinehart, and Winston.

Happe, F. (2003) Theory of mind and the self. *Annals of the New York Academy of Sciences* 1001: 134–44.

Haynes, L. M. and Cooper, R. L. (1986) A note on Ferguson's proposed Baby-Talk universals. In J. A. Fishman, A. Tabouret-Keller, M. Clyne, B. Krishnamurti, and M. Abdulazizz (eds.), *The Fergusonian Impact.* 127–34. Berlin: Mouton de Gruyter.

Heath, S. B. (1983) *Ways with Words: Language, Life and Work in Communities and Classrooms.* Cambridge: Cambridge University Press.

Heath, S. B. (1986) What no bedtime story means: Narrative skills at home and school. In B. B. Schieffelin and E. Ochs (eds.), *Language Socialization across Cultures.* 97–124. New York: Cambridge University Press.

Hirsh-Pasek, K. and Treiman, R. (1982) Doggerel: Motherese in a new context. *Journal of Child Language* 9: 229–37.

Hymes, D. (1972) On communicative competence. In J. B. Pride and J. Holmes (eds.), *Sociolinguistics*. 269–85. Harmondsworth: Penguin.

Jusczyk, P. W. (1997) Finding and remembering words: Some beginnings by English-learning infants. *Current Directions in Psychological Science* 6 (6):170–4.

Jespersen, O. (1922) *Language: Its Nature, Development and Origin*. London: G. Allen and Unwin.

Keller, H., Lohaus, A., Völker, S., Cappenberg, M., and Chasiotis, A. (1999) Temporal contingency as an independent component of parenting behavior. *Child Development* 70(2): 474–85.

Kess, J. F. and Kess, A. C. (1986) On Nootka Baby Talk. *International Journal of American Linguistics* 52(3): 201–11.

Klin, A., Jones, W., Schultz, R., Volkmar, F., and Cohen, D. (2002) Visual fixation patterns during viewing of naturalistic social situations as predictors of social competence in individuals with autism. *Archives of General Psychology* 59: 809–16.

Kooijman, V., Haqoort, P., and Cutler, A. (2005) Electrophysiological evidence for prelinguistic infants' word recognition in continuous speech. *Cognitive Brain Research* 24(1): 109–16.

Kuhl, P. K. (1998) Language, culture and intersubjectivity: The creation of shared perception. In S. Bråten (ed.), *Intersubjective Communication and Emotion in Early Ontogeny*. 297–315. Cambridge: Cambridge University Press.

Kuhl, P. K. (2000) A new view of language acquisition. *Proceedings of the National Academy of Science* 97(22): 11 850–7.

Lord, C. and Spence, S. (2006) Autism spectrum disorders: Phenotype and diagnosis. In S. O. Moldin and J. L. R. Rubenstein (eds.), *Understanding Autism: From Basic Neuroscience to Treatment*.

1–23. Boca Raton, FL: Taylor and Francis.

Merleau-Ponty, M. (1945) *Phenomenology of Perception*. C. Smith, transl. New York: Humanities Press.

Miall, D. S. and Dissanayake, E. (2003) The poetics of BabyTalk. *Human Nature* 14(4): 337–64.

Mitchell, R. W. (2004) Controlling the dog, pretending to have a conversation, or just being friendly? Influences of sex and familiarity on Americans' talk to dogs during play. *Interaction Studies* 5(1): 99–129.

Monnot, M. (1999) Function of infant-directed speech. *Human Nature* 10(4): 415–43.

Ochs, E. (1982a) Talking to children in Western Samoa. *Language in Society* 11: 77–104.

Ochs, E. (1982b) Ergativity and word order in Samoan child language. *Language* 58: 646–71.

Ochs, E. (1988) *Culture and Language Development: Language Acquisition and Language Socialization in a Samoan Village*. Cambridge: Cambridge University Press.

Ochs, E. (2002) Becoming a speaker of culture. In C. Kramsch (eds.), *Language Acquisition and Language Socialization*. 99–120. London: Continuum.

Ochs, E. and Schieffelin, B. B. (1984) Language acquisition and socialization: Three developmental stories. In R. Shweder and R. LeVine (eds.), *Culture Theory: Essays on Mind, Self, and Emotion*. 276–320. Cambridge: Cambridge University Press.

Ochs, E. and Schieffelin, B. B. (1995) The impact of language socialization on grammatical development. In P. Fletcher and B. MacWhinney (eds.), *The Handbook of Child Language*. 73–94. Oxford: Blackwell.

Ochs, E. and Schieffelin, B. B. (2008) Language socialization: An historical overview. In P. A. Duff and N. H. Hornberger (eds.), *Encyclopedia of Language Education, Vol. 8: Language Socialization*. 2nd ed. 3–15. New York: Springer.

Ochs, E. and Solomon, O. (2010) Autistic sociality. *Ethos, Special Issue: Autism: Rethinking the Possibilities* 38(1): 69–92.

Ochs, E., Solomon, O., and Sterponi, L. (2005) Limitations and transformations of habitus in child-directed communication. *Discourse Studies, Special Issue: Theories and Models of Language, Interaction and Culture* 7(4–5): 547–83.

Ochs, E., Kremer-Sadlik, T., Sirota, K. G., and Solomon, O. (2004) Autism and the social world: An anthropological perspective. *Discourse Studies* 6(2): 147–83.

Pelphrey, K. A., Morris, J. P., and McCarthy, G. (2005) Neural basis of eye gaze processing deficits in autism. *Brain* 128(5): 1038–48.

Reissland, N., Shepherd, J., and Herrera, E. (2002) The pitch of maternal voice: A comparison of mothers suffering from depressed mood and non-depressed mothers reading books to their infants. *Journal of Child Psychology and Psychiatry* 43(7): 1–7.

Robbins, J. and Rumsey, A. (2008) Introduction: Cultural and linguistic anthropology and the opacity of other minds. *Anthropology Quarterly* 81(2): 407–20.

Rogoff, B., Baker-Sennet, J., Lacasa, P., and Goldsmith, D. (1995) Development through participation in sociocultural activity. *New Directions for Child and Adolescent Development* 67: 45–65.

Sachweh, S. (1998) Granny darling's nappies: Secondary BabyTalk in German nursing homes for the aged. *Journal of Applied Communication Research* 26(1): 52–65.

Sapir, E. (1915) Abnormal types of speech in Nootka. Memoir 62, Anthropological Series 5, Geological Survey, Department of Mines, Ottawa, Canada. Reprinted in Golla, V. (ed.) (1991) *The Collected Works of Edward Sapir, Vol. 6: American Indian Languages*. Berlin: Mouton de Gruyter.

Sapir, E. (1929) Nootka baby words. *International Journal of American Linguistics* 5: 118–9.

Schegloff, E. (2006) *Sequence Organization in Interaction: A Primer in Conversation Analysis*. Cambridge: Cambridge University Press.

Schieffelin, B. B. (1985) The acquisition of Kaluli. In D. Slobin (ed.), *The Crosslinguistic Study of Language Acquisition*. 525–93. Hillsdale, NJ: Lawrence Erlbaum.

Schieffelin, B. B. (1986) Teasing and shaming in Kaluli children's interactions. In B. B. Schieffelin and E. Ochs (eds.), *Language Socialization Across Cultures*. 165–81. New York: Cambridge University Press.

Schieffelin, B. B. (1990) *The Give and Take of Everyday Life: Language Socialization of Kaluli Children*. Cambridge: Cambridge University Press.

Schieffelin, B. B. (2008) Speaking only your own mind: Reflections on talk, gossip and intentionality in Bosavi. *Anthropological Quarterly* 81(2): 431–44.

Schieffelin, B. B. and Eisenberg, A. R. (1984) Cultural variation in children's conversations. In R. L. Schiefelbusch and J. Pickar (eds.), *The Acquisition of Communicative Competence*. 379–420. Baltimore, MD: University Park Press.

Schieffelin, B. B. and Ochs, E. (1986a) Language socialization. *Annual Review of Anthropology* 15: 163–91.

Schieffelin, B. B. and Ochs, E. (eds.) (1986b) *Language Socialization Across Cultures*. Cambridge: Cambridge University Press.

Scollon, R. (1982) The rhythmic integration of ordinary talk. In D. Tannen (ed.), *Analyzing Discourse: Text and Talk*. 335–49. Washington, DC: Georgetown University Press.

Scollon, R. and Scollon, S. W. (1979) The literate two-year old: The fictionalization of self. *Working Papers in Sociolinguistics*. Austin, TX: Southwest Regional Laboratory.

Skinner, B. F. (1957) *Verbal Behavior*. New York: Appleton, Century, Crofts.

Silverstein, M. (2004) 'Cultural' concepts and the language-culture nexus. *Current Anthropology* 45(5): 621–45.

Slobin, D. I. (ed.) (1967) *A Field Manual for Cross-Cultural Study of the Acquisition of Communicative Competence*. Language Behavior Research Laboratory. University of California, Berkeley, CA.

Slobin, D. I. (ed.) (1968) Recall of full and truncated passive sentences in connected discourse. *Journal of Verbal Learning and Verbal Behavior* 7(5): 876–81.

Slobin, D. I. (ed.) (1985) *The Crosslinguistic Study of Language Acquisition, Vol. 5: Expanding the Contexts*. Mahwah, NJ: Lawrence Erlbaum.

Snow, C. (1977) Mother's speech research: From input to interaction. In C. E. Snow and C. A. Ferguson (eds.), *Talking to Children: Language Input and Acquisition*. 31–49. Cambridge: Cambridge University Press.

Snow, C. (1984) Parent–child interaction and the development of communicative ability. In R. L. Schiefelbusch and J. Pickar (eds.), *The Acquisition of Communicative Competence*. 69–108. Baltimore, MD: University Park Press.

Snow, C. E. (1986). Conversations with children. In P. Fletcher and M. Garman (eds.), *Language Acquisition: Studies in First Language Development*. 69–89. Cambridge: Cambridge University Press.

Snow, C. and Ferguson, C. (eds.) (1977) *Talking to Children*. Cambridge: Cambridge University Press.

Solomon, O. (2008) Language, autism, and childhood: An ethnographic perspective. *Annual Review of Applied Linguistics. Special Issue: Language and the Brain* 28: 1–20.

Solomon, O. (2010a) What a dog can do: Children with autism and therapy dogs in social interaction. *Ethos, Special Issue: Autism: Rethinking the Possibilities* 38(1): 143–66.

Solomon, O. (2010b) Sense and the senses: Anthropology and the study of autism. *Annual Review of Anthropology* 39: 241–59.

Stern, D., Hofer, L., Haft, W., and Dore, J. (1985) Affect attunement: The sharing of feeling states between mother and infant by means of inter-modal fluency. In T. Field and N. Fox (eds.), *Social Perception in Infants*. 249–68. Norwood, NJ: Ablex.

Tomasello, M., Kruger, A. C., and Ratner, H. H. (1999) Cultural learning. In P. Lloyd and C. Fernyhough (eds.), *Lev Vygotsky: Critical Assessments, Vol. 4*. 101–43. New York: Taylor and Francis.

Tomasello, M. (1999) *The Cultural Origins of Human Cognition*. Cambridge, MA: Harvard University Press.

Trevarthen, C. (1979) Communication and cooperation in early infancy. A description of primary intersubjectivity. In M. Bullowa (ed.), *Before Speech: The Beginning of Human Communication*. 321–47. London: Cambridge University Press.

Trevarthen, C. (1987) Sharing makes sense: Intersubjectivity and the making of an infant's meaning. In R. Steele and T. Threadgold (eds.), *Language Topics: Essays in Honour of Michael Halliday, Vol. 1*. 177–99. Amsterdam, The Netherlands: John Benjamins.

Trevarthen, C. (1988) Universal cooperative motives: How infants begin to know language and skills of culture. In G. Jahoda and I.M. Lewis (eds.), *Acquiring Culture: Ethnographic Perspectives on Cognitive Development*. 37–90. London: Croom Helm.

Trevarthen, C. (1998) The concept and foundations of infant intersubjectivity. In S. Braten (ed.), *Intersubjective Communication and Emotion in Early Ontogeny*. 15–46. Cambridge: Cambridge University Press.

Trevarthen, C. (2003) Conversations with a two-month-old. In J. Raphael-Leff (ed.), *Parent–Infant Psychodynamics: Wild Things, Mirrors, and Ghosts*. 25–34. London: Whurr Publishers.

Valdman, A. (1981) Sociolinguistic aspects of foreigner talk. *International Journal of the Sociology of Language* 28: 41–52.

6 Local Theories of Child Rearing

AMY PAUGH

Introduction

This chapter explores how local theories of child rearing influence language social-ization practices, patterns, and outcomes. Ways of speaking to children, or not speaking to them, are culturally organized, including when infants or children are considered to be conversational partners and persons (de León 1998; Ochs and Schieffelin 1984). Child language socialization patterns are linked to, organized by, and indicative of culturally specific understandings about children, childhood, and the role of adults and other caregivers, such as siblings, in the child-rearing process. The chapter begins by exploring how the study of local theories of child rearing is central to language socialization research. This is followed by a review of relevant cross-cultural literature that highlights how local theories of child rearing have an impact on and can be analyzed through language socialization activities. The third section provides a case study from my own research, examin-ing how local theories of child rearing influence language socialization practices and an ongoing language shift in Dominica, West Indies.

Caregivers everywhere have expectations for how their children should speak, behave, and comport themselves. Ochs and Schieffelin (1984) highlight the impor-tance of parental expectations of children in their seminal essay comparing Samoan, Kaluli, and American developmental stories. They detail a continuum of child-rearing orientations ranging in communicative accommodation from child-centered to situation-centered. At the more child-centered end of the continuum, for example among white middle-class Americans, caregivers tend to accommo-date children through child-centered topics, self-lowering strategies, use of a specialized child-directed register, and proto-conversations with preverbal infants.

The Handbook of Language Socialization, First Edition. Edited by Alessandro Duranti, Elinor Ochs, and Bambi B. Schieffelin.
© 2014 John Wiley & Sons, Ltd. Published 2014 by John Wiley & Sons, Ltd.

Situations are adapted to the child, including modifications to the environment such as baby-proofing in houses and provision of specialized clothing, furniture, and toys for infants (later tailored to other perceived stages of childhood). At the more situation-centered end of the continuum, for example among the Kaluli and Samoans, caregivers expect the child to accommodate to the situation and persons around them, and do not modify their speech when addressing children. The Kaluli, for example, do not view infants as conversational partners, but they do hold children facing others while speaking for them in a high-pitched voice, thus orienting infants outward to others in their social environment (see also Schieffelin 1990). Ochs and Schieffelin's research and subsequent language socialization studies show that perceptions of children and children's competence influence caregiver–child interaction, including how much adult accommodation, such as use of a Baby-Talk register, is considered possible, appropriate, and beneficial, or at least not harmful, to children's linguistic and social development. Further, cultural orientations toward children affect whether and when children are treated as ratified participants in interaction, the communicative roles that are available to or expected of them, and what language varieties they are permitted or encouraged to use (Ochs and Schieffelin 1995).

Across societies, caregivers and other adults employ relatively predictable routines that socialize children into culturally expected and acceptable ways of being a person and interacting with others (Garrett and Baquedano-López 2002; Schieffelin 1990; Schieffelin and Ochs 1986). Such routines are culturally constructed and are shaped by local theories of child rearing and what it means to be a child. Caregivers socialize culturally preferred ways of speaking that are appropriate to one's age and social status, including knowing how to greet others and use proper names and kin terms; knowing when, how, and with whom to share; knowing when and how to demonstrate politeness and accommodation versus assertiveness and control; knowing how to display appropriate and culturally intelligible affective stances; and knowing how much attention is to be paid to the affairs of others. Culturally specific understandings about how children develop, how language acquisition takes place, and how caregivers may facilitate or hinder these processes result in diverse child-rearing priorities that affect the saliency or frequency of particular linguistic and cultural practices during interactions with children. Local theories of childhood and child rearing thus may influence the types and order of acquisition (or not) of grammatical forms, speech acts, registers, styles, languages, and so on over developmental time and across the lifespan. Further, children themselves play a role in shaping child rearing theories and practices, as it has been well noted that children actively socialize others into and help constitute caregiving roles such as parent, grandparent, and sibling.

The methods utilized by language socialization researchers allow them to link micro-analysis of mundane social interactions involving children to more general ethnographic descriptions of the cultural beliefs, ideologies, and practices of their families and communities (Garrett and Baquedano-López 2002; Schieffelin and Ochs 1996). Through study of the social organization of caregiving and everyday interaction in home, school, and other community settings during longitudinal ethnographic fieldwork, researchers can investigate local child-rearing theories from multiple vantage points. Interviews with caregivers, teachers, and others provide opportunities for asking about expectations of children and how one raises a culturally and linguistically competent member of the social group. Participant observation in daily life and video/audio recording of actual social interaction across contexts allow direct investigation of how these goals and expectations play out in reality. Child-rearing theories become evident in the interactional fiber of everyday life; as Kulick (1992: 16) states, 'caregiver–child speech is an important source of data for locating and understanding salient local ideas about what society is, what people are, and how they should behave.' Local theories of child rearing also become visible as caregivers socialize children how *not* to behave and feel (Fader 2006; Kulick and Schieffelin 2004). Caregivers offer on-the-spot commentary about child behavior, parenting, or the nature of learning to others participating in or observing the interaction, including the researcher. Likewise, during transcription of video/audio recordings with family members, caregivers' spontaneous evaluations of children's speech, actions, and comportment provide a rich source of data on theories of child rearing and other cultural and linguistic ideologies.

The observation of everyday social interaction offers insights into local theories of child rearing; at the same time, local theories of child rearing inform our analyses of what it means to create culturally competent members, as well as 'bad subjects' (Kulick and Schieffelin 2004). However, it is important to note that people do not simply pass on static child-rearing ideologies across generations, nor are they uniform across all sectors of a population. Further, as language socialization studies have shown, ideologies do not always match actual practice (Kulick 1992; Schieffelin 1990). Local theories of child rearing are historically situated and may change over time in response to shifting political and social climates, socioeconomic conditions, and other factors, such as social conflict and warfare, immigration, novel technologies, social and religious movements, and new forms of labor (see Ariès 1962 for a history of changing Western ideologies about childhood and child rearing). But it is precisely through attention to local theories of child rearing in conjunction with everyday practice that we can investigate the tensions between 'real' and 'ideal,' tradition and transformation, for the insights they give us into a key goal of language socialization research and a central concern of anthropology: understanding processes of cultural and linguistic reproduction and change (Garrett and Baquedano-López 2002).

Local Theories

During early socialization activities, parents and other caregivers often make explicit for children's benefit cultural rules and knowledge that are usually tacit, offering researchers insights into local goals or priorities of child development. Local theories of child rearing become analyzable as caregivers repeat and/or paraphrase their speech and the speech of others, expand children's utterances to be grammatical and socially appropriate, correct children's errors or inappropriate speech, and model linguistic behavior, often explicitly prompting children to 'say,' 'tell,' 'ask,' or respond in particular ways (e.g. Clancy 1986; Demuth 1986; Miller 1982; Ochs 1988; Ochs and Schieffelin 1995; Schieffelin 1990). In middle-class American families, the negotiation of autonomy and responsibility often leads to extensive 'bargaining' with children (Goodwin 2006; Paugh 2008; Paugh and Izquierdo 2009; Sirota 2006; see also Kusserow 2004) that actually may foster a kind of co-dependency rather than independence (Ochs and Izquierdo 2009). Linguistic practices, such as code-switching, verbal play, teasing, praising, and reprimanding, display to children culturally salient values and appropriate linguistic and social behavior across a range of activities and contexts. Watson-Gegeo and Gegeo (1986), for example, found that a central child-rearing goal for the Kwara'ae of the Solomon Islands is to 'speed' the child toward adult communicative competence and norms of behavior. In line with this goal, the Kwara'ae engage in intensive instruction with children under five years of age on how to speak and behave, including frequent use of calling-out and repetition routines, imperatives, corrections and explanations of behavior, praise of adult-like behavior, and criticism of childish behavior (Watson-Gegeo and Gegeo 1986: 19). Less obvious, more implicit linguistic devices such as conversational turn-taking procedures, distribution of communicative roles, interactional sequencing, and the management of miscommunication similarly socialize children to understand social relationships and activities, and give insights into local theories of childhood, child rearing, and language acquisition that caregivers may be more or less able to explicitly articulate.

Schieffelin's (1990) ethnography of the Kaluli highlights how the exploration of local theories of child rearing and learning is essential for making sense of and contextualizing what people do and say during daily life. Kaluli caregivers conceive of child development as a process of 'hardening,' which consists of 'the production of well-formed individuals in control of themselves as well as able to control and influence others' (1990: 5). This central child-rearing goal intersects with local language acquisition theories and the socialization of two interactional strategies integral to the system of reciprocity underlying Kaluli social life: assertion and appeal. The Kaluli claim that infants and young children are *taiyo* ('soft') and that for them to become *halaido* ('hard') they must be 'shown' language by caregivers, a process that begins after children say their first words, conventionally interpreted as *no:* ('mother') and *bo* ('breast') (Schieffelin 1990: 74). To this end, caregivers do not grammatically simplify language to children and children's verbal play is discouraged, as these are thought to impede language acquisition. Further, caregivers focus on the socialization of assertive stances, largely through *ɛlɛma* ('say like this') routines, because they believe that children already know how appeal, as evidenced by their early use of begging and whining. As Kaluli children learn to speak, they demonstrate greater complexity in the construction of their requests based on *appeal* than their *assertive* requests. Schieffelin and Ochs (1996: 256–7) describe this progression as surprising from a developmental psycholinguistic perspective, but 'entirely compatible with Kaluli notions that children "naturally" beg, but must be explicitly socialized to request assertively using a different set of linguistic resources.' Despite the belief that direct instruction is required for children to develop communicative competence, Kaluli caregivers do not feel that children must be 'shown' how to do actions or tasks, as they will do such things when they are ready (Schieffelin 1990: 76).

In contrast to the Kaluli, caregivers in Western Samoa view children as naturally *assertive* and in need of explicit socialization to appropriately respectful behavior (Ochs 1988). Children are considered willful, cheeky, and hard to control and, according to caregivers, their first word, a curse, confirms this (Ochs 1988: 159). While aggressive behavior is viewed as natural and is generally tolerated during the first few years of life, children must be taught rank-appropriate conduct to become competent social actors in this hierarchical society. As Ochs states, 'Samoan caregivers feel that the single most important goal of child rearing is to teach children *fa'aaloalo* "respect" (1988: 161). Adult and sibling caregivers strive to teach respectful conduct through direct instruction of awareness of others, perspective taking, and accommodation. They do not employ a Baby-Talk register, as social accommodation and grammatical simplification is considered appropriate for high-ranking addressees but not for children. These local theories and strategies of child rearing produce a noteworthy result: as they are socialized into local notions of status and social role, Samoan children learn to use the cognitively more complex linguistic form 'give' before its relatively simpler counterpart 'come' due to social constraints on the use of this form by children (Platt 1986). By the age of four or five, children are expected to be competent in the display of respect to higher-ranking persons and in caring for younger siblings (Ochs 1988: 25).

While Kaluli prioritize assertiveness and Samoans prioritize respect, Japanese caregivers prioritize empathy and indirection in their child-rearing theories and practices (Burdelski, this volume; Clancy 1986). Japanese core values of social harmony, indirection in speech, and avoidance of imposing on others emerge in child-rearing practices as mothers engage in 'empathy training' and 'conformity training' of young children through a range of strategies including indirect and direct imperatives, indirection when saying no to children, attributing speech to others, and evoking imaginary *hito* ('other people') who are watching and evaluating the child's behavior (Clancy 1986). When reflecting on their child-rearing theories, Japanese caregivers say a primary goal is teaching children *aisatsu*, a category of 'polite formulas,' over any other verbal skill (Burdelski 2006). Children are prompted to use *aisatsu* well before adults actually expect them to use it, including during early socialization of embodiment, such as putting hands together during the mealtime *aisatsu* (Burdelski 2006: 104). In addition to such prompting, caregivers also explicitly praise older children's use of *aisatsu* in front of younger children. Socialization of distinct gender roles and patterns of interaction is also an important focus in Japanese child-rearing theories and practices (Burdelski 2006; Cook 2008).

Religious principles intertwine with local ideologies of child rearing and child morality among Hasidic Jews in Boro Park, Brooklyn, New York (Fader 2009, this volume). According to Hasidic beliefs, each Jew is born with an inclination for good, called *yaytser hatoyv*, which includes the traits of charity, modesty, and a propensity for good deeds. This inclination toward good, however, coexists with an inclination for evil, called *yaytser hure*. Hasidic caregivers take responsibility for bringing out the good inclination while teaching children to manage the evil one through the process of *khinekh*, the moral upbringing of children and young adults. Infants and young children are conceived of as innocent and purely concerned with physical needs, and thus require explicit socialization to become faithful Jews who can fulfill the Jewish commandments once they reach the age of *bar/bas mitsve* at 12 or 13 years of age. Language socialization practices revolve around a central tension in this process: children must be taught personal moral autonomy and responsibility while at the same time learning to reject individualism, which is considered secular and immoral. As part of this process, caregivers engage in elaborate praising routines to encourage children to do good deeds. When children ask culturally unacceptable questions or otherwise do not conform, caregivers utilize a range of tactics to reaffirm their authority or to shore up violated gender, generational, or religious boundaries, including responding with silence, reminders of responsibility, evocations of essentialized difference between Jews and Gentiles, or public shaming (Fader 2006: 206). Narratives about caregivers who have failed to socialize their children to control themselves circulate in the community, highlighting local theories of child rearing that attribute to caregivers the responsibility for children's moral development and require them to put children above their personal involvement in the material world (Fader 2000: 80–5).

Among the Zinacantecos of Chiapas, Mexico, local theories about infancy and the development of the *ch'ulel* ('soul'; also 'understanding') influence how caregivers interact with small children and guide their moral development (de León 2005). Adults distinguish distinct phases marked by whether the *ch'ulel* is absent or in the process of arriving, which is thought to occur between 4–24 months of age and is marked by the child showing signs of communicative ability. Before the soul has arrived, infants and young children require protection from dangers, such as the gaze of strangers or witchcraft. Between the ages of two and four years, after the soul has arrived, fears of soul loss shape caregivers' child-rearing strategies. To protect the newly emerged *ch'ulel*, adults refrain from discipline and scolding, allowing toddlers considerable autonomy while simultaneously trying to ensure their physical safety. At the same time, mothers and other caretakers utilize 'toughening' or teasing routines to intentionally encourage *k'ak'al* ('anger') in young children. This practice is thought to strengthen the delicate *ch'ulel*, but also models for children ways in which anger can be redirected in emotionally nonconfrontational ways. These routines help children develop the interactive skills needed for managing conflict, thus socializing a distinctly Zinacanteco moral consciousness. By the age of seven, it is believed that all children should 'have souls' and they are attributed greater social responsibility, given gender-differentiated chores, and expected to avoid socially inappropriate behavior.

Multilingual language socialization

Child-rearing goals and strategies can impact the future of a language, often inadvertently, as studies of multilingual language socialization illustrate (Garrett 2005; Howard 2003; Kulick 1992; Paugh 2005a, 2005b; Zentella 2004 [1997]). In Gapun,

Papua New Guinea, local theories of child rearing and changing conceptions of the self are contributing to a language shift from Taiap, the village vernacular, to Tok Pisin, a widespread lingua franca, among children (Kulick 1992). Parental ideology does not advocate this shift; rather, adult villagers blame language-learning children for willfully refusing to speak the vernacular. Kulick contextualizes the shift and related attribution of blame in local theories of personhood and conceptions of children. In Gapun, there are two basic conceptions of the self: *hed*, which is associated with selfishness, individualism, and personal autonomy, and *save*, which is associated with cooperation, sociability, and knowledge about appropriate behavior and speech. The expression of these dual aspects of personhood were formerly subsumed within one language (Taiap), but have now become separated along linguistic lines, with Taiap linked to the (negative) expression of one's *hed* and Tok Pisin to the (positive) expression of one's *save*. Everyone is born with both dimensions of personhood, but children are believed to be dominated by *hed* until their *save* 'breaks open,' which is indicated when they begin to use language in interaction with others at 20–30 months of age (Kulick 1992: 122). Until then, children are believed to be *bikhed* ('willful' or 'big-headed') and are not treated as conversational partners. The first word attributed to them reflects this perceived willfulness: *oki*, translatable as 'I'm getting out of here.' They are believed to utter this Taiap word as early as two months of age (1992: 101). However, once their *save* breaks open, adults interpret children's speech as Tok Pisin. To respect children's autonomy and show their own *save*, adults respond to children in Tok Pisin, which, combined with other practices (such as ignoring or criticizing their Taiap usage and leaving young children in the care of Tok-Pisin-speaking siblings) leads to an implicit devaluation of Taiap and heavily unbalanced input favoring Tok Pisin. Community adults sometimes complain that their children are 'Tok Pisin people' (1992: 223), but they generally are not concerned with the language shift. Like previous generations, children gradually come to display *save* and continue to structure their talk, regardless of language, in appropriate ways. Thus, local theories of child rearing and the self contribute to language socialization practices that speed up loss of Taiap but maintain other aspects of being a Gapuner, such as the ability to tell a properly structured and detailed *stori* ('narrative account') (Kulick 1992: 246–7).

Language continuity and change is tied to theories of child rearing and language socialization practices among working-class Puerto Ricans in El Barrio, East Harlem, New York (Zentella 2004 [1997]). Cultural continuity is evinced through the enduring centrality of *respeto* ('respect') to child-rearing theories in both Puerto Rico and the New York Puerto Rican immigrant community. *Respeto* includes shared cultural norms and expectations for strict age- and gender-appropriate roles, speech, and comportment, including children's obedience to and respect of their elders (Zentella 2004 [1997]: 10). Child-rearing ideologies and practices in El Barrio exhibit the persistence of a working-class Puerto Rican situation-centered orientation, with little accommodation to children; a focus on family relationships and ties; and the belief that children learn through observing and emulating adult models as 'future *mamis* [mothers] and *papis* [fathers] in training' (Zentella 2004

[1997]: 232). Yet, cultural contact with mainstream Anglo-American society is leading to changes in child-rearing practices among many families, including adoption of child-centered socialization practices and, significantly, an overall shift in the language of child rearing from Spanish to English. Second-generation New York Puerto Rican parents prioritize providing their children with English so that they can *defenderse* ('defend themselves') in dominant mainstream American society (Zentella 2004 [1997]: 244). Spanish is less necessary for child rearing, community membership, and New York Puerto Rican identity than acting with *respeto* and in age- and gender-appropriate ways, contributing to significant language loss by the third generation.

In the bilingual Muang community of Northern Thailand, child-rearing ideologies and practices are shaped not only by core cultural values concerning respect, accommodation, and hierarchy, but also by beliefs about the role of adults in the learning process (Howard 2003, this volume). Muang caregivers espouse a Buddhist philosophy of child rearing that advocates a noninterventionist approach and respects the individual development of the child. Reflecting an overarching ethos of accommodation, caregivers maintain that it is important to guide children but not to 'pressure' them or make them feel 'stressed' (Howard 2003: 287). Children will conform to expected norms of behavior only when they are ready, and telling young children not to do something is believed to provoke dangerously strong emotions. The responsibility for self-control is thus located in children themselves, and local strategies of child rearing focus on influencing rather than controlling the child (Howard 2003: 291–2).

Social hierarchy is a central organizing principle of Muang society, however, and socialization practices entail explicit instruction in the display of respect and deference. Children are routinely monitored, evaluated, and corrected in linguistic and embodied displays of respect by both adults and peers. For example, the bodies of infants are shaped into socially appropriate gestures such as bowing while parents voice respectful greetings for them (Howard 2003: 283–4). However, while caregivers take a strongly interventionist approach to ensuring that children learn to use appropriate linguistic markers of respect, they take a noninterventionist approach to other aspects of language use, such as children's mixing of Standard Thai with the local language, Kam Muang. Caregivers and teachers largely ignore children's hybrid linguistic practices because children are viewed as not yet ready to appropriately use Standard Thai. Yet, when children grow older, adults lament their syncretic language varieties as 'inauthentic' and associated with urban youth (Howard 2008: 195).

In other cases, local theories of child rearing include an explicit goal to transmit one linguistic variety at the risk of losing another in an effort to provide children with access to other socioeconomic and linguistic resources, opportunities, and identities. Even then, parental ideologies do not always match language use in practice, in which adults speak both languages with and around children. For example, in St. Lucia in the Eastern Caribbean, language socialization lies at the center of an ongoing language shift from Kwéyòl, a widespread French-based Creole, to varieties of English, the official language (Garrett 2005, this volume).

Adults widely believe that children must learn to speak English (or VESL, Vernacular English of St. Lucia) before speaking Kwéyòl, which is thought to have a detrimental effect on English acquisition. Despite this, there are times at which adults actively encourage children to use Kwéyòl; namely, to *jiwé* ('curse') (Garrett 2005). Kwéyòl is the preferred code for this genre and a means of socializing verbal assertiveness and related affective stances. Children must learn to 'be able to fend for oneself, to make known one's needs and wants, to stand up for one's rights, to demand respect, and to be prepared to give as good as one gets' (Garrett 2005: 348). Thus, while the ideal St. Lucian child speaks to an adult only when spoken to, is respectful, and speaks English (Garrett 1999: 289), self-assertion and autonomy are also necessary and are modeled for children through socialization to curse. Yet, while displaying willful stances is acceptable among young language-learning children, it is unacceptable for older children, who according to local theories of child rearing require strict discipline and regular monitoring of their English (Garrett 2005: 347). It remains to be seen whether and how the socialization of code-specific genres such as cursing will affect the language shift from Kwéyòl to English in St. Lucia.

Theories of Child-Rearing and Language Shift in Dominica, West Indies

As the above studies highlight, child-rearing ideologies and strategies may not always play out in expected ways. We now turn to a case study from my research in Dominica, a formerly British postcolonial island nation in the Eastern Caribbean (Paugh 2001, 2005a, 2005b). English is the official language of government, schools, and urban settings, while a French-lexicon Creole commonly called Patwa has been the oral language of rural residents since French colonization in the seventeenth century. Over the past few decades, however, there has been a rapid language shift from Patwa to varieties of English. Caregivers recognize this shift and actively promote it through their child-rearing strategies, claiming that Patwa 'interferes' with children's acquisition of English and threatens their educational and occupational success. Language socialization practices, and adults' reflections on them, however, indicate there is more to it than the future-oriented goal of providing children with English to succeed, as adults claim. As will be explored below, in the course of the shift, Patwa and English have become indexically linked to local notions of personhood, status, and authority within the context of the adult–child relationship. Bilingual adults may use both languages, but children are socialized to be English-dominant and are monitored by adults for any Patwa usage. In this way, children's Patwa usage has become threatening not only to their English, but also to adult authority and control at home and at school. The analysis draws on a year-long video-recorded language socialization study of six children aged two to four years and their families in one rural village (see Paugh 2001 for details).

From birth children are spoken to predominantly in English and are expected to do the same once they begin talking. Direct instruction is considered essential to learning English; this seems to be related to perceptions of it having to be 'brought in' to the village by the school system (Paugh 2001). Caregivers employ English for explicit instruction and socialization, such as calling out and greeting routines, teaching politeness, and routines directing children to 'look at' and name objects, as well as most other interactions concerning children's wants, needs, and feelings. Direct instruction in Patwa, however, is considered unnecessary and potentially harmful, as caregivers worry that children may not learn the English equivalents once they begin using Patwa. Many claim that Patwa is already *adan yo* or 'in them' and in need of being suppressed, at least until the children get older. A woman in her twenties expressed a common view of Patwa in reference to her three-year-old cousin Lewis: 'Patwa is not very hard once you get the hang of it. To me it's not even learned, it just comes naturally. When we speak Patwa to Lewis, he understands us. Amazing, isn't it?' Patwa is so 'natural' that many adults assume children will begin speaking it eventually, and most are adamantly against the idea of teaching it in schools, as suggested by urban cultural preservation activists (Paugh 2001).

Adults strive to speak 'good English' to children, but this does not always occur in practice. In local theories of child rearing, children are perceived as naturally messy, rude, and in need of control for them to *lévé* or 'raise up' to be good persons. Children are constantly scolded for 'dirtying up the place,' disturbing people's things, soiling their clothes, and generally disrupting the orderliness of the home and yard. A mother of three explained: 'When you have children in a home? The place doesn't stay how you want it. You have to satisfy with that.' Caregivers spend much of their day trying to keep children under control and their homes clean. In line with this goal, speech to children frequently consists of imperatives (e.g. 'Come here!' 'Don't do that!' 'Put it back!'), assessments of their actions and comportment, and questions about why they do the things they do. Under calm circumstances, and when it only has to be said once, this is usually in English. Adults frequently 'resort' to Patwa for scolding, directing, and negatively evaluating children's behavior, however, claiming in their metapragmatic reflections that it is more 'commanding' than English. Despite local language ideologies that devalue Patwa as a 'broken' language that has 'held back' the community, adults commonly describe English as *two mòl*, meaning too 'soft' or 'gentle,' while Patwa is 'rough,' 'vulgar,' and *pli wèd*, or 'harder,' than English. Code-switching from English to Patwa systematically draws on the contrast between the languages to intensify negative affect and indicate an escalation in seriousness when children have not complied after being told in English to do or not do something. When adults code-switch to Patwa, they say their patience has run out and they are just 'fed up.' Children are extremely sensitive to such switches, and typically do what they are told immediately or risk corporal punishment.

Thus, in the course of the language shift, Patwa has become a potent resource for adults to assert their rights as more mature, culturally knowledgeable members to control children's lives and actions, particularly within the adult-controlled settings of home, yard, and school. When children are judged to be overstepping the boundaries of appropriate childhood behavior, adults reaffirm the status hierarchy through their language choice, as Example 6.1 illustrates. Alisia (2;9), her mother, and her brother (1;1) are having lunch at home, when Alisia begins asking for juice. Her mother, following her usual strategy of withholding drinks until Alisia has eaten enough, attempts to delay it as Alisia becomes increasingly impatient and demanding:

Example 6.1:   Who are you calling girl?[1]

1	Alisia:	Mommy I want juice.
2	Mother:	((continues eating))
3	Alisia:	I want juice. ((begins to whimper and whine))
4	Mother:	Let me feed you *kòk* [**Patwa term of endearment**]. I'll give you juice.
5	Alisia:	((whining and turning away)) I don't want it [re: food]. ((xxx))

((*five-second pause as Alisia looks around and then watches her mother eat*))

6	Alisia:	((whining)) Mo::mmy::
7	Alisia:	[((whining)) Mo:mmy
8	Mother:	[((speaking fast)) I will give you juice Alisia!
9	Alisia:	((cries)) ((whining)) I want juice. I want juice girl. ((loudly)) Girl I want juice! ((cries))
10	Mother:	((speaking fast)) *Kilè ou ka kwiyé* girl *la* Alisia? [**'Who are you calling** girl **there Alisia?'**]
11	Alisia:	((whining)) I want juice girl.
12	Mother:	Who you calling girl?
13	Alisia:	I want juice girl.
	(0.5)	
14	Mother:	Who? Who is the girl?
15	Alisia:	You.
16	Mother:	((shakes head)) Well if I'm a girl you have to go and make juice for me *non* [**Patwa sentence final tag**].
17	Alisia:	((whining softly)) Make juice for me::. ((continues to cry sporadically until her mother goes to the kitchen to make juice))

When Alisia's initial request for juice is ignored (lines 1 and 2), she begins to whine and cry in what adults consider a baby-like manner. At first, her mother calmly assures her that she will get juice but offers to feed her more first, using the Patwa term of endearment *kòk* that signifies positive affect (line 4). When Alisia refuses to eat (line 5) and continues to beg for juice (lines 6 and 7), her mother's quick and emphatic assertion, 'I will give you juice Alisia!' (line 8), suggests that she is starting to lose her patience. Alisia continues to whine then shifts to a more assertive stance on line 9 by utilizing a common form of address among children with their peers, 'girl' ('boy' is similarly used). Use of this form implies that Alisia's mother is of the same or lower status as her, and her mother swiftly responds to this breech with a code-switch to Patwa: '*Kilè ou ka kwiyé* girl *la Alisia?*' (line 10). This was not the first time she had uttered this exact reprimand when Alisia called her 'girl,' and it was usually successful in squelching her inappropriate speech. This time, however, it does not work; Alisia ignores the question and again calls her 'girl' (line 11). Her mother then translates her question into English (line 12). Alisia nevertheless repeats her demand again (line 13), to which her mother responds by paraphrasing her question: 'Who? Who is the girl?' (line 14). When Alisia boldly responds, 'You' (line 15), her mother retorts by explicitly highlighting adult/child role and status differences: 'Well if I'm a girl you have to go and make juice for me *non*' (line 16). She then leaves Alisia to cry for just a bit longer before making the juice. In the end, the lesson serves multiple functions, including re-establishing the status hierarchy, highlighting children's dependence on adults, correcting inappropriate language use ('girl'), and, importantly, linking use of Patwa to adult authority and the right to control children's actions and comportment.

Though seemingly contradictory, in that adults forbid children from speaking Patwa but continue to speak it to them for particular functions, these language ideologies and language socialization practices are consistent with local ideologies of child rearing, childhood behavior, and personhood. As in other Caribbean societies, children are expected to be obedient, respectful, and deferent to their elders, and to do as they are told. Sociality and politeness are considered to need direct socialization by caregivers, for example how children must be taught English. Adults frequently praise children for sharing, displaying good manners, and knowing the correct English names for things. A child who disobeys or talks in a manner that is considered too 'grown up' is criticized for acting *two nonm* ('too mannish') or *two fanm* ('too womanish'), explained to me by one parent as '*ni mannyé gwo moun*' ('to act like a grownup'). Local expectations about childhood behavior have become linked to village language ideologies that associate English with education, politeness, accommodation, and formality – all qualities that children are expected to demonstrate – and Patwa with individual will, autonomy, assertiveness, and informality – qualities that adults are expected to demonstrate.

Being polite and only speaking English does not make an entire person, however. To attain the highly valued qualities of personal autonomy and self-sufficiency, one must become *bon pou kò'w* or 'good for yourself.' A child who is viewed as too assertive will not tolerated by an adult, but there are certain times when it is better to be 'mannish' or 'womanish.' A fundamental tension is thus to socialize children into obedience and respect while simultaneously encouraging them to become independent and 'bold,' as part of a larger constellation of sociability. This endeavor is largely accomplished through the division of labor between

Patwa and English. Children are directly socialized important aspects of sociality and politeness through English but are both explicitly and implicitly socialized, whatever the degree of intention by adults, through both languages to learn to stand up for themselves. Adults do not want their children to be *kapon* ('cowardly') and encourage them to verbally defend themselves and to use language for expressive purposes such as joking and teasing. Not surprisingly then, some speaking of Patwa is expected if not encouraged in children's speech in particular contexts, and, other than Baby Talk, its use for this function is one of the only acceptable reasons for children to speak it around adults.

Adults frequently tease and joke with children, purposefully inciting them to respond by calling them derogatory names, accusing them of doing something bad or wrong, using rhetorical questions, or lying about something the child would know to be untrue. Children are often then told by their caregivers how to respond to this teasing, such as with an emphatic, 'leave me alone' or a curse such as *tèt papa'w* or its English equivalent, 'your father('s) head'. This response is acceptable among very young children and in interactions with peers, but school-age children are negatively sanctioned for cursing at an adult outside of a playful teasing session. Teasing routines socialize this culturally valued skill but also help to build children's confidence and teach them to assert themselves (see also Miller 1986). In Example 6.2, Jonah (2;11) stands up for himself when he is teased by his aunt, who has come to his house to visit and is sitting about five feet away on his verandah with his mother and her friend, Clarice. He is aided by his cousin Claudette (13 years), who is playing with him in the yard.

Example 6.2:   You are talking too much!

1	Jonah:	((calling out)) Auntie!
2	Aunt:	What?
3	Jonah:	Where Franklin? [re: Jonah's cousin]
4	Aunt:	Franklin go to school.
		(.5)
5	Jonah:	And you yourself not going to school?
6	Aunt:	((speaking fast)) Why you yourself not going? You don't see I too big to go to school?
7	Clarice:	((laughs))
8	Aunt:	Uh?
9	Claudette:	((to Jonah)) Say you too small. Say I too small.
10	Jonah:	((repeating Claudette)) I too small.
11	Clarice:	((laughs))
12	Aunt:	You not too small. You talking so much, you too small?!
13	Jonah:	No boy.
14	Aunt:	When people talking like that they not too small to go to school.

((two-second pause as Jonah and Claudette look at a doll))

15	Aunt:	Because you talking TOO MUCH.
		(1)

16	Aunt:	Uh? Jonah?
17	Jonah:	((in deep, low tone of voice)) Wha:t?
18	Claudette:	((laughs quietly))
19	Aunt:	You not talking too much?
20	Jonah:	No: boy.
21	Aunt:	Of course yes.
22	Jonah:	((in a raspy voice)) No boy.
23	Aunt:	I never see a boy talking like you.
24	Jonah:	Me *menm*?! Me?!
		[half-code-switched emphatic first person reflexive
		pronoun, from Patwa *mwen menm*, '**myself**'; translated by
		Jonah's mother as 'Me **self**?!']
25	Aunt:	((looks at Jonah and shakes her head))
26	Jonah:	((continues playing with Claudette))

The interaction begins with Jonah calling out to his aunt and asking her a polite, appropriate question about her son's whereabouts (lines 1 and 3). After her response, however, Jonah asks this woman in her late thirties the odd if not inappropriate question, 'And you yourself not going to school?' (line 5). This could indicate his social incompetence or could be viewed as an attempt to initiate a teasing session. Either way, his aunt seizes the opportunity for a teasing session and prefaces her reply that she is too big to go to school with a challenge to Jonah: 'Why you yourself not going?' (line 6). Clarice's laugh (line 7) and Claudette's prompt for Jonah to respond that he is too small to go to school (line 9) help to co-construct the teasing frame. Jonah follows Claudette's prompt (line 10) but is again challenged by his aunt when she asserts that he should go to school because he talks so much (lines 12 and 14). These assessments of his language ability teeter between complementing and criticizing Jonah. While early loquaciousness generally is considered a positive sign of a child's future educational success, a child that talks *too* much runs the risk of violating local expectations that children should be 'seen but not heard.' Again, Jonah stands up for himself, this time without prompting. His bold response of 'Wha:t?' (line 17) triggers laughter from Claudette (line 18). He then responds to his aunt's teasing with an emphatic 'no boy,' a common phrase used to emphatically deny something (lines 20 and 22). He successfully ends the teasing session with a rhetorical question using a brief Patwa code-switch: 'Me *menm*?! Me?!' (line 24). 'Me *menm*' is a half-English, half-Patwa version of *mwen menm* ('myself,' like French *moi-même*) used by adults as a reflexive pronoun, but also for the same function that Jonah uses it for here: as an emphatic, rhetorical response to an accusation or assessment of oneself that one wants to challenge as unfounded, untrue, or otherwise ridiculous. Though the code-switch creates an awkward construction that adults do not use, it is consistent with children's usage, as Claudette and Jonah's siblings commonly tacked *menm* onto their English pronouns for added emphasis. Further, it is an adept response in a teasing session, and the three adults that are present do not correct it. Later, during transcription, Jonah's mother said proudly: 'That boy good for himself yeah!' Adults often implicitly praise bold actions and speech with such comments, even when in the process of telling children *not* to do something. This is typically accompanied by a laugh or shake of the head, as Jonah's aunt does on line 25. Young children are scolded only if they are viewed as trying to 'rule' themselves; in other words, a balance between being confident and being respectful must be maintained.

As children get older, their English is believed to get 'stronger' or 'harder' and to not be so vulnerable to Patwa 'interference.' Yet, they are expected to continue speaking English in the presence of adults, and are more overtly monitored and sanctioned for speaking Patwa than younger children. These rebukes often are accompanied with age- or place-related admonishments that suggest it may be permissible for them to speak Patwa in some other context or at another point in their developmental cycle. Teachers remind their pupils that they are to speak only English while they are 'in school,' and caregivers tell their children not to speak Patwa 'in the house' or 'in the yard' (see examples in Paugh 2001, 2005b). For example, 13-year-old Claudette was in her aunt's (Jonah's mother) kitchen with her cousins Jonah (two years) and his sister (five years) watching a hen that had laid an egg. Though they had been speaking in English, Claudette spontaneously made the following comment in Patwa: '*An patjé zé i ni an bonda'y* man' ('**It has lots of eggs its bottom** man'). Her aunt did not tell her to stop speaking Patwa. Instead, she quietly posed a scolding rhetorical question: '*Ou déwò?!*' ('**Are you outside?!**'). Claudette did not respond, and did not speak Patwa in her presence after that (see Paugh 2005b for the full example). The implication of the short but potent Patwa scold is that Claudette has crossed a context-related boundary by using Patwa within the home, suggesting that such usage is acceptable somewhere else – that is, 'outside.' But, at another level, Claudette has crossed the boundaries of acceptable childhood behavior. This key point emerged during my transcription with her aunt. She commented that Claudette was 'feeling so big to use that word there.' I asked what she meant by 'big' and she explained that, by using Patwa, Claudette was trying to act 'too womanish'; in other words, too much like an adult. Further, there were younger children present to overhear and potentially imitate her, thus increasing the inappropriateness of her language choice. While Claudette's use of Patwa could potentially enhance her status among the children, it is a transgression of unspoken age- and place-related boundaries for appropriate speech and behavior when an adult is present.

Similarly, 11-year-old Marcel was scolded by his grandmother for speaking Patwa when role-playing farmers with his three male cousins aged three to nine. The children had been playing behind the house, out of their grandmother's hearing range. Upon nearing the house, however, Marcel continued speaking Patwa to narrate the role-play activity. As soon as his grandmother heard him, she quickly scolded: 'Stop the Patwa in the yard *mouché Marcel*' (see Paugh 2005a for the full example). Significantly, she included a place-related qualifier, 'in the yard,' in her prohibition against speaking Patwa. Further, she used a Patwa address term, '*mouché Marcel*' ('**mister Marcel**'). Caregivers frequently use *mouché* when scolding children, and it implies that a child is acting too adult-like. Hence, when children use Patwa, they come across as acting too grown up for their age, thus challenging pervasive cultural ideologies about adult–child status differences. Adults swiftly sanction this by evoking ideas about place, context, or age as reasons for prohibiting its use.

Conclusion

Local ideologies of child rearing thus play a key role in the process of language shift in Dominica, but also contribute to the maintenance of Patwa, at least for particular functions. Rural children are exposed to a great deal of Patwa in their everyday verbal environments, and they learn early on that Patwa is associated with affective stances that complement or intensify those expressed through English. Children then creatively draw on the indexical links between Patwa and adult status, authority, and assertiveness to structure their play frames, direct and evaluate one another's actions and character, curse at each other, intensify their speech, and enact adult roles during imaginary play (see Paugh 2001, 2005a). Though such uses are restricted and usually occur within their *English* speech, they afford children practice in this otherwise forbidden language. Thus, children's sensitivities to the indexical associations of the languages of their communities and to adult expectations of children can lead to sometimes surprising transformations of local ideologies and patterns of language use (see also Meek 2007).

As this and the other studies described above illustrate, local beliefs about how to raise children to become appropriate social, moral, and communicatively competent beings emerge in language socialization practices and may affect cultural and linguistic reproduction and change. All normally developing human children have the capacity to learn language; however, local theories of child rearing manifest in language socialization practices that may affect when, how, and what language(s) children learn to speak, and how they become communicatively competent in their social group. Language socialization practices and linguistic ideologies are historically situated and shaped by local and global power dynamics, political economies, population movements, and other forms of sociocultural contact and change. Investigation of local theories of child rearing thus can inform our understandings of why caregivers interact with children in particular ways, why children are encouraged to behave in some ways and not others, and why unexpected outcomes might occur, such as children learning more complex linguistic forms earlier than their less complex counterparts, or not being able to speak a language of their community. It is therefore critical for language socialization researchers to contextualize their studies of verbal and embodied practices within the ideologies of child rearing that inform and render those practices meaningful.

NOTE

1   Transcription conventions: *italic*, Patwa speech; **bold**, English glosses of Patwa speech;
    (1), pause between utterances (in seconds); ((action)), nonverbal action; (xxx), unintel-
    ligible speech; :, elongated speech; period indicates falling, final contour; ?, rising
    intonation, question; !, exclamation; ?!, rhetorical question; CAPITALS, emphasis;
    [, overlapping speech.

REFERENCES

Ariès, P. (1962) *Centuries of Childhood: A Social History of Family Life*. R. Baldick, trans. New York: Vintage.

Burdelski, M. (2006) *Language Socialization of Two-Year-Old Children in Kansai, Japan: The Family and Beyond*. Doctoral Dissertation. Los Angeles, CA: University of California.

Clancy, P. M. (1986) The acquisition of communicative style in Japanese. In B. B. Schieffelin and E. Ochs (eds.), *Language Socialization Across Cultures*. 213–50. New York: Cambridge University Press.

Cook, H. M. (2008) Language socialization in Japanese. In P. Duff and N. Hornberger (eds.), *Encyclopedia of Language and Education, Vol. 8: Language Socialization*. 2nd ed. 313–26. New York: Springer.

de León, L. (1998) The emergent participant: Interactive patterns in the socialization of Tzotzil (Mayan) infants. *Journal of Linguistic Anthropology* 8(2): 131–61.

de León, L. (2005) *La Llegada del Alma: Lenguaje, Infancia y Socializacion entre los Mayas de Zinacantan (The Advent of the Soul: Language, Childhood and Socialization among the Mayans of Zinacantan)*. Mexico: CIESAS, INAH.

Demuth, K. (1986) Prompting routines in the language socialization of Basotho children. In B. B. Schieffelin and E. Ochs (eds.), *Language Socialization Across Cultures*. 51–79. New York: Cambridge University Press.

Fader, A. (2000) *Gender, Morality, and Language: Socialization Practices in a Hasidic Community*. Doctoral Dissertation. New York: New York University.

Fader, A. (2006) Learning faith: Language socialization in a community of Hasidic Jews. *Language in Society* 35(2): 205–29.

Fader, A. (2009) *Mitzvah Girls: Bringing Up the Next Generation of Hasidic Jews in Brooklyn*. Princeton, NJ: Princeton University Press.

Garrett, P. B. (1999) *Language Socialization, Convergence, and Shift in St. Lucia, West Indies*. Doctoral Dissertation. New York: New York University.

Garrett, P. B. (2005) What a language is good for: Language socialization, language shift, and the persistence of code-specific genres in St. Lucia. *Language in Society* 34(3): 327–61.

Garrett, P. B. and Baquedano-López, P. (2002) Language socialization: Reproduction and continuity, transformation and change. *Annual Review of Anthropology* 31: 339–61.

Goodwin, M. (2006) Participation, affect, and trajectory in family directive/response sequences. *Text & Talk* 26(4/5): 515–44.

Howard, K. M. (2003) *Language Socialization in a Northern Thai Bilingual Community*. Doctoral Dissertation. Los Angeles, CA: University of California.

Howard, K. M. (2008) Language socialization and language shift among school-aged children. In P. Duff and N. Hornberger (eds.), *Encyclopedia of Language and Education, Vol. 8: Language Socialization*. 2nd ed. 187–99. New York: Springer.

Kulick, D. (1992) *Language Shift and Cultural Reproduction: Socialization, Self, and Syncretism in a Papua New Guinean Village*. Cambridge: Cambridge University Press.

Kulick, D. and Schieffelin, B. B. (2004) Language socialization. In A. Duranti (ed.), *A Companion to Linguistic Anthropology*. 349–68. Malden, MA: Blackwell.

Kusserow, A. (2004) *American Individualisms: Child Rearing and Social Class in Three Neighborhoods*. New York: Palgrave Macmillan.

Meek, B. A. (2007) Respecting the language of elders: Ideological shift and linguistic discontinuity in a Northern Athapascan community. *Journal of Linguistic Anthropology* 17(1): 23–43.

Miller, P. (1982) *Amy, Wendy, and Beth: Learning Language in South Baltimore*. Austin, TX: University of Texas Press.

Miller, P. (1986) Teasing as language socialization and verbal play in a white working class community. In B. B. Schieffelin and E. Ochs (eds.), *Language Socialization Across Cultures*. 199–212. New York: Cambridge University Press.

Ochs, E. (1988) *Culture and Language Development: Language Acquisition and Language Socialization in a Samoan Village*. New York: Cambridge University Press.

Ochs, E. and Izquierdo, C. (2009) Responsibility in childhood: Three developmental trajectories. *Ethos* 37(4): 391–413.

Ochs, E. and Schieffelin, B. B. (1984) Language acquisition and socialization: Three developmental stories and their implications. In R. Shweder and R. LeVine (eds.), *Culture Theory: Essays on Mind, Self, and Emotion*. 276–320. Cambridge: Cambridge University Press.

Ochs, E. and Schieffelin, B. B. (1995) The impact of language socialization on grammatical development. In P. Fletcher and B. MacWhinney (eds.), *The Handbook of Child Language*. 73–94. Cambridge, MA: Blackwell.

Paugh, A. (2001) *'Creole Day Is Every Day': Language Socialization, Shift, and Ideologies in Dominica, West Indies*. Doctoral Dissertation. New York: New York University.

Paugh, A. (2005a) Multilingual play: Children's code-switching, role play, and agency in Dominica, West Indies. *Language in Society* 34(1): 63–86.

Paugh, A. (2005b) Acting adult: Language socialization, shift, and ideologies in Dominica. In J. Cohen, K. McAlister, K. Rolstad, and J. MacSwan (eds.), *ISB4: Proceedings of the 4th International Symposium on Bilingualism*. 1807–20. Somerville, MA: Cascadilla Press.

Paugh, A. (2008) Language socialization in working families. In P. A. Duff and N. H. Hornberger (eds.), *Encyclopedia of Language and Education, Vol. 8: Language Socialization*. 2nd ed. 101–13. New York: Springer.

Paugh, A., and Izquierdo, C. (2009) Why is this a battle every night? Negotiating food and eating in American dinnertime interaction. *Journal of Linguistic Anthropology* 19(2): 185–204.

Platt, M. (1986) Social norms and lexical acquisition: A study of deictic verbs in Samoan child language. In B. B. Schieffelin and E. Ochs (eds.), *Language Socialization Across Cultures*. 127–52. New York: Cambridge University Press.

Schieffelin, B. B. (1990) *The Give and Take of Everyday Life: Language Socialization of Kaluli Children*. New York: Cambridge University Press.

Schieffelin, B. B. and Ochs, E. (1986) Language socialization. *Annual Review of Anthropology* 15: 163–91.

Schieffelin, B. B. and Ochs, E. (1996) The microgenesis of competence: Methodology in language socialization. In D. Slobin, J. Gerhardt, A. Kyratzis, and J. Guo (eds.), *Social Interaction, Social Context, and Language: Essays in Honor of Susan Ervin-Tripp*. 251–63. Mahwah, NJ: Lawrence Erlbaum.

Sirota, K. (2006) Habits of the hearth: Children's bedtime routines as relational work. *Text & Talk* 26(4/5): 493–514.

Watson-Gegeo, K. A. and Gegeo, D. W. (1986) Calling-out and repeating routines in Kwara'ae children's language socialization. In B. B. Schieffelin and E. Ochs (eds.), *Language Socialization Across Cultures*. 17–50. New York: Cambridge University Press.

Zentella, A. C. (2004 [1997]) *Growing Up Bilingual: Puerto Rican Children in New York*. Malden, MA: Blackwell.

7 Language Socialization and Shaming

ADRIENNE LO AND HEIDI FUNG

Shame, which has been called 'the master emotion of everyday life' (Scheff 2003: 239), is a topic that has been of great interest across several fields. Psychologists have debated whether it is a 'healthy' emotion or not (Probyn 2005), sociologists have noted its central importance for managing one's social conduct (e.g. Goffman 1963; Lynd 1958), and anthropologists have looked at how shame-like emotions work in different cultures (e.g. Rosaldo 1983; Shweder 2003). Philosophers have examined the role that shame plays in creating a sense of morality (e.g. Taylor 1985; Williams 1993), while social critics have debated its appropriateness as a form of punishment (e.g. Etzioni 2001; Nussbaum 2004). Scholars of language socialization have had an abiding interesting in shaming practices since the earliest days of the field (Ochs 1988; Schieffelin 1990). Through shaming, caregivers bring to bear the weight of other individuals' disapproving regard, with the hope of stimulating a heightened awareness of the individual's connectedness to others in the social fabric and the capacity for self-reflection and self-examination. As children participate in shaming routines, they learn how specific actions become identified as displays of attitudes and stance (Cook, this volume) towards others, and what kinds of linguistic utterances and bodily demeanors can bring about shaming. These verbal routines, which link affect, morality, and linguistic practices, instantiate a language ideology in which words spoken by others can have a powerful and immediate impact on one's sense of self (see also Fader, this volume).

Work on shaming in the language socialization tradition has documented the verbal routines through which it is enacted, its cultural salience and local meanings, and the ways that young children learn the social and moral norms of a community through shaming (Fader 2006; Han 2004; Reynolds 2008; Schieffelin

The Handbook of Language Socialization, First Edition. Edited by Alessandro Duranti, Elinor Ochs, and Bambi B. Schieffelin.
© 2014 John Wiley & Sons, Ltd. Published 2014 by John Wiley & Sons, Ltd.

and Ochs 1986). In this chapter, we review how shame has been contrasted against guilt and associated with more 'primitive' stages of children's emotional development and with 'less advanced' cultures. We then review work on shaming in language socialization, and sketch some of the discursive features of shaming episodes with examples from our own research in Taiwanese, South Korean, and Korean American settings. We hope to demonstrate how a language socialization approach can shed greater light on how the cultural meaning of shame is revealed during discursive interactions.

Critical Perspectives on Shame

In the psychoanalytic literature, shame and guilt are often treated as two distinct emotions, although studies have shown that many people have difficulty differentiating the two and use both terms interchangeably (Gilbert, Pehl, and Allan 1994; Tangney 2005). Shame is seen as a response to the external judgment of others, as opposed to guilt, where the individual's internalized sense of wrongdoing is more paramount. Guilt is often portrayed as adaptive, constructive, prosocial, and mature, whereas shame is described as maladaptive, counterproductive, antisocial, primitive, and even pathological (Benson and Lyons 1991; Nathanson 1987, 1992). Although some work has attempted to reclaim the value of shame as a positive force for embedding individuals within a social and moral world (e.g. Etzioni 2001; Scheff 2003; Taylor 1985; Williams 1993), it is not difficult to find shame being evaluated negatively while guilt is lauded as a morally and culturally superior emotion.[1]

Such a distinction was expressed in Margaret Mead's (1937) comparative analysis of 13 different societies that applied the psychoanalytic formulation of shame and guilt to the cultural level (Creighton 1990). In some societies, Mead argued, the individual 'internalizes the standards of his society and obeys them in the absence of force exerted upon him from the outside' (Mead 1937: 493). In others, however, the individual 'is not so delicately impressed with his society's standards, and has merely developed a responsiveness to forces which must be set in motion by others' (Mead 1937: 493). Similar attitudes were expressed in Leighton and Kluckhohn's (1947: 170) work on Navaho children, who were characterized as reacting only to the 'surface sensation' of shame whereas white North American children oriented to 'abstract standards of behavior' through 'deep, internalized feeling[s]' of guilt.

This moral ranking of shame as inferior to guilt was perhaps disseminated most widely through Ruth Benedict's ethnography of Japan, *The Chrysanthemum and the Sword*, which drew a sharp distinction between 'shame cultures' and 'guilt cultures' (1946: 223):

> True shame cultures rely on external sanctions for good behavior, not, as true guilt cultures do, on an internalized conviction of sin. Shame is a reaction to other people's criticism. A man is shamed either by being openly ridiculed and rejected or

by fantasying to himself that he has been made ridiculous. In either case it is a potent sanction. But it requires an audience or at least a man's fantasy of an audience. Guilt does not. In a nation where honor means living up to one's own picture of oneself, a man may suffer from guilt though no man knows of his misdeeds and a man's feeling of guilt may actually be relieved by confessing his sin.

In this description of guilt cultures as superior because they 'inculcat[e] absolute standards of morality and rel[y] on man's developing a conscience' (1946: 222), Benedict set the stage for subsequent analyses. Although researchers have since questioned her dichotomization of guilt and shame and her claim that guilt does not rely upon an audience (e.g. Doi 1973; Levy and Rosaldo 1983; Rosaldo 1984; Piers and Singer 1953), Benedict's work was seminal in promulgating a view of the superiority of internalized guilt over public shame. As the excerpt makes clear, Benedict's description of guilt as cognitively superior and morally cleansing was centered in a Christian understanding of sin and the redemption of confession, two concepts that may not necessarily be relevant elsewhere.

Other scholars of Benedict's era echoed her association of shame with less developed individuals and cultures. The classicist E. R. Dodds (1951), for example, argued that the culture of ancient Greece evolved from a reliance on the public sanction of shame to the more developed principles of guilt and universal principles of justice. Shame is still associated with less advanced cultures, as in psychologists June Tangney and Ronda Dearing's characterization of shame 'as a primitive emotion that likely served a more adaptive function in the distant past, among ancestors whose cognitive processes were less sophisticated in the context of a much simpler human society,' whereas guilt is 'the moral emotion of the new millennium' (Tangney and Dearing 2002: 126–7). In sum, in various psychological and anthropological models of development, shame is often seen as a more 'primitive' emotion than guilt, because guilt supposedly requires more advanced reasoning powers and an understanding of 'abstract' laws whereas shame is simply an emotional reaction to another person (Hoffman 2000; Kohlberg 1984). Shame is seen as unhealthy because it targets the entire person and is irreversible. In contrast, guilt is seen as less painful because it deals with a specific act. In the next section of this chapter, we discuss how this evaluation of shame is not necessarily shared across cultures.

Shame Re-examined

What are we to make of these harsh evaluations of shame and its association with less advanced, less enlightened societies and earlier stages of emotional development? First, such a view seems at odds with ethnographic depictions of societies in which a sense of shame may be highly valued (e.g. Geertz 1983; Levy 1973; Rosaldo 1983; Shweder 2003). Second, descriptions of the ennobling virtues of guilt as an emotion that is temporary and linked only to actions, not selves, are rooted in a Christian understanding of forgiveness, sin, and the redemptive powers of confession. Much of the privileging of guilt over shame, we argue, should be understood as relevant to a Christian worldview rather than as a psychological universal. Third, this perspective seems predicated on a particular view of morality, in which adherence to 'universal laws' is seen as superior to one's emotional connectedness to others. As philosopher Bernard Williams (1993: 220) points out, this Kantian vision of morality rests on a 'false conception of total moral autonomy.' It thus privileges a Western idea of the virtues of the autonomous individual, we argue, just as the descriptions of shame as less advanced than guilt give short shrift to the complex forms of emotional and logical reasoning that it requires (Rosaldo 1984).

Lastly, this framing of constructive guilt versus destructive shame relates to a culturally specific understanding of a strict distinction between one's self and one's actions and the idea of the vulnerable self, as understood through the construct of self-esteem (Miller et al. 2002). Many negative evaluations of shame argue that it is damaging because of its effects on self-esteem (e.g. Lewis 1992; Nathanson 1987; Tangney and Dearing 2002). As Peggy Miller has noted, the idea that one's self-esteem is highly susceptible to damage from others is part of an ethnopsychological theory popular among middle-class white Americans (Miller et al. 2002). While the idea that social interaction may damage the self may be found across cultures (Goffman 1982 [1967]), in the American theory, children's self-esteem is thought to be especially fragile and easily harmed by the negative opinions of others. As Miller (Miller et al. 2002) describes, however, this theory is a recent development; it is not necessarily shared either by older Americans or by members of other cultures.[2] The portrayal of shame as a destructive, unhealthy emotion, we argue, thus represents a historically and culturally situated understanding of shame. We now turn to work on shaming and teasing in language socialization, which has examined how shaming can have different valences in other parts of the world.

Socializing Shame Across Cultures

Studies of the socialization of shame include anthropologist Hildred Geertz's (1959) seminal paper on emotions in Java, which highlighted how caregivers socialize children into when and how to feel shame. In the language socialization tradition, shaming has been studied since the earliest days of the field. Schieffelin (1986), for example, discussed dyadic and triadic teasing and shaming routines in Kaluli society. These routines, which require explicit teaching, include name-calling, negative imperatives, mock offerings, rhetorical questions, sarcastic statements, and third-party threats. They occur 'when an adult is angered or frustrated by the actions of a child who is expected to know better' (1986: 169) and also among children. These practices, Schieffelin argues, 'are used to teach children how to be part of Kaluli society, to include them rather than set them apart' (1986: 179). Patricia Clancy's (1986: 234) research likewise examined how Japanese mothers socialized their children to be aware of the regard of others through statements such as 'Older sister is saying "I'm surprised. I'm surprised at Maho."' When mothers explicitly label a child's actions as 'shameful,' this 'conveys both the mother's own feeling and the strong implication that the child should feel the same way' (Clancy 1986: 239).

Other work in language socialization on shaming includes Kulick's (1998) work on verbal conflict among the Gapun, which illustrated how the public shaming of one woman by another was linked to ideologies about gender and the expression of anger. Fung's (1999) observations of preschool-aged children in Taipei, Taiwan offer extensive examples of how shaming took place in the home setting. She argues that, through participation in recurring shaming events, novices come to acquire the communicative and cultural competence necessary for being full-fledged members of society. Recent work on shaming includes Han's (2004) investigations of verbal routines of discipline and shaming at a preschool program for Korean American children in Los Angeles; Fader (2006)'s examination of shaming of children in a Hasidic school in Brooklyn; and Bartlett's (2007) research on narratives of 'speech and literacy shame' in two Brazilian cities. Reynolds (2008) has also investigated the role of teasing/shaming routines in socializing respect and responsibility among child peers in a Guatemala Maya town.

The Discursive Practices of Shaming

We now turn to an analysis of the practices of shaming, which we define as the activity through which one person attempts to instill a sense of shame in another. We are interested here in how novices acquire this sense of shame in particular cultural contexts. In this part of the chapter, we draw on our own research on shaming among urban Taiwanese families with young children (Fung) and among South Koreans and Korean Americans (Lo). In Taiwan and South Korea, shaming is quite common. It is a routine, everyday occurrence in the lives of children and continues in different forms throughout the lifespan. A sense of shame is seen as an essential component of an individual's moral outlook. According to Confucian ideology, knowing shame (Ch. *zhi chi*) enables a person to humbly examine and reflect upon their behavior; after experiencing shame, you become courageous enough to admit your inadequacies and to amend them. Shaming events are designed to instill the active internalization of moral principles through the intertwining of the moral message with a moderate amount of emotion, turning shame into 'a hot moral cognition' (Hoffman 1983, 1994). Thus, episodes of disgrace-shame (Ch. *xiu*) in a child's early years, where the child is actively shamed by others, lead to an internalized sense of discretion-shame (Ch. *chi*), which helps the child to engage in appropriate, prosocial behavior in the future. Shaming of young children is thus understood as a form of love, discipline, and moral teaching that aims to protect the child from future external sanctions.

Shaming as social practice can have different emotional valences, ranging from light-hearted teasing to somber moral lessons. We believe that these emotionally charged and value-laden practices have to be understood as situated events that arise from multiple layers of context (ranging from the immediate interactional situation to broad institutional processes) and various timescales (ranging from proximate to remote historical circumstances). Shaming episodes may also be contextualized within a specific genre of talk such as scolding or nagging. While power, capital, and resources are not equally distributed among all participants, these interactions are nevertheless joint efforts accomplished by all parties involved, including the young novice. Through these routinely occurring practices, the novice comes to acquire not only the linguistic skills but also the cultural meanings and moral messages embedded in these affective experiences.

Dyadic shaming: Children as targets

In both Taiwan and South Korea, the idea that one's conduct is susceptible to being evaluated by others is at the root of shaming. Shaming episodes rest on the premise that words are highly powerful and that, by speaking certain words, you can cause others to feel certain kinds of emotions. That is, the act of labeling something as shameful will then cause the child to experience the feeling of shame. While it is common to think of emotions as interior and individual experiences, shaming episodes illustrate how emotions are socially constructed through interaction. In these contexts, shaming is also linked to an ideology of moral personhood that derives from Confucianism. Children are not seen as naturally moral but as needing careful moral guidance and instruction from their elders. Since a child's character is malleable but also perfectible, caregivers see themselves as having tremendous potential influence over a child's moral development. While moral education may continue throughout the lifespan, early childhood is seen as a particularly critical period in which one's moral character is formed by the efforts of one's caregivers. Ethical lapses in one's later years may be attributed, for example, to indifferent or lazy parenting rather than to any inherent flaw in one's character.

By conducting shaming episodes in which they perform strong negative assessments of a child's behavior, elders thus uphold their moral duty to enforce societal norms. These evaluations can occur in relation to events in the past (in narrative retellings), present (for an immediately precipitating transgression), or future (in hypothetical or imagined events) and caregivers often moved fluidly between different time frames within a single shaming episode (Fung 1999; Fung and Chen 2001). In addition, the negative evaluations of the transgressing individual could be attributed to the speaker, a co-present participant, absent third parties, or generic or hypothetical others.

By performing direct, unmitigated, and affectively intensified negative assessments, speakers sought to arouse children's sense of shame through a dramatic enactment of the severity of the transgression. Examples include (1) ones that explicitly predicate shame of the child or the situation, for example 'shame on you,' 'how shameful,' 'shame shame shame'; (2) gestures conventionally associated with shame, such as sliding one's index finger down the cheek in Taiwan or sliding one index finger across another in the United States; and (3) negative assessments, for example 'such a disobedient child,' 'you're terrifying,' '[you] bandit.' Affective intensity was communicated through features such as repetition, tone of voice, and paralinguistic gestures such as sighs or pursed lips. In these encounters, children are recurrently situated as targets of negative assessment while caregivers and siblings are situated as those who have the right and the power to evaluate a child's conduct.

In Example 7.1, a Korean American seventh grader is the target of an extended shaming sequence performed in English by his Korean American teacher at a private after-school program in California. The student had been claiming that school had been going well for several months; on this day, his mother had shown the teacher his report card, which indicated that he was in danger of failing several classes. Before she began the shaming, the teacher took the student to a separate area of the classroom, although the rest of his classmates were still overhearers to this dyadic interaction:

Example 7.1

1	Teacher:	You have to think about what you're doing that is right.
2		And what you're doing that is not right at all.
3		You have to think.
4		This is the way you solve your problems.
5		If it's hard, you don't want to try.
6		You don't like it, you don't want to try.
7		Don't tell anybody, don't ask for help.
8		And this is the reason. Don't let people know.
9		It's not the first time you've done this.
10		It's when we started to do this planner.
11		Seems to have worked for a little bit.
12		And then it got better
13		But then you're giving up.
14		Remember?
15		You wanted to stop doing things
16		And I said we can't because it's not part of your calendar.
17		Well, I guess maybe we should have stopped.
18		Cause your attitude was not up.
19		You cannot care whether you do it or not, huh?
20		That's what it seems.

In this example, the child's conduct and behavior are repeatedly negatively assessed in ways that seek to arouse his sense of shame over his poor academic results. Here, the role of shame as a moral emotion that attempts to trigger the child's own reflections about his moral shortcomings is apparent in the teacher's injunctions to 'think about what you're doing that is right and what you're doing that is not right at all.' Over the course of the following 22 minutes, the teacher performs an extended sequence of direct negative assessments of the child. Her narrative casts this latest transgression as symptomatic of an enduring, recurrent, and persistent character flaw that can only be solved through the child's own admission of his problem and resolve to fix it.

Native South Korean informants who listened to this episode characterized it as *honnayki*, a genre of scolding in which a younger person is justifiably shamed for her past conduct by an older one in a repetitive, affectively intensified way. South Koreans identified several genres of shaming depending upon the relationship between the participants; whether the shaming was justified or not; the institutional context; the emotional impact upon the person being shamed; and the severity of the infraction. The child is supposed to acknowledge wrongdoing by agreeing with the caregiver's negative assessments of her past conduct, but should be able to distinguish between questions that demand a verbal answer and rhetorical questions. In this case, the child responded with brief affirmative answers to questions that assigned him moral responsibility for his poor grades and that demanded a change in future behavior.

Multiparty shaming

While shaming could involve only two people, configurations that drew other people into the shaming event were also quite common. Other parties were presented as figures in narratives who aligned with the adult conducting the shaming. By animating the voices of nonpresent others as co-shamers (e.g. 'Uncle hasn't visited for a long time because he's scared of you,' 'Other kids won't play with you'), caregivers emphasized the importance of others' regard (Clancy 1986). In the contexts that we studied, shaming was also linked to the idea that one's actions did not merely bring shame upon oneself but also upon one's family, teacher, classmates, people, or nation as a whole. Through statements such as 'You made your mother lose face' (Fung) or 'Even though you are just one student, all Korean people will be blamed [for your wayward actions]' (Lo), mothers and teachers inculcated the idea that shameful acts on the part of the child spread shame upon others that the child was connected to, and that shame that parents experienced as a result of their children's actions was a serious matter (Clancy 1986).

In the Korean American classrooms that Lo studied, co-present students were drawn into shaming episodes as witnesses whose gaze intensified selected students' shame. In Fung's data, co-present adults were recruited into the shaming, either as co-shamers or as defenders of the child (e.g. *heilian* ('black face') versus *bailian* ('white face')). Siblings could also take on roles as co-shamers. In Example 7.2, both the researcher and the five-year-old elder sister, TingTing, participate in the shaming event. While the adults were talking, Didi (age three) approached the unattended camcorder. When his mother found out, she immediately upbraided him. This event lasted nearly four and a half minutes and consisted of nearly 90 turns-at-talk.

Example 7.2

1	Mother:	*Ei, Didi, mama jiang hua ni dou shi . . .*

Hey, Didi, whenever Mom tells you something, you
    always . . .
((walks up to Didi))

2	Didi:	*Kan dao le.*

I saw it.
((pretending to peek through the lens))

3	Mother:	((spanks Didi))

Bu keyi, wo lai da pigu. Bu shou guiju de xiao haizi
You are not allowed. I'm gonna spank you. You're a
    child who doesn't obey rules.

4   *Bu shou guiju de xiao haizi, bu keyi zhe yangzi, mama gen
    ni jiang guo bu keyi dao zhe bian lai a.*
A child who doesn't obey rules. You are not allowed to
    act like this. Mom has told you before that you are
    not allowed to come to this side.
((dragging Didi away from the camcorder))

5   *Women bu yao ni, ni fa zhan.*
We don't want you. You are being punished. Stand here.

6	Didi:	((sits down on the floor and starts to cry loudly))
7	Mother:	*Ta jiu shi ai ku.*

He's such a crybaby.

8	Researcher:	*Zao gao, zao gao.*

Oh no, oh no.

9	Mother:	*Mei guan xi. Rang ta ku yixia.*

It doesn't matter. Let him cry for a while.

10   *Bu guai de xiao haizi, wo jiang guo hua le. Mama
    hen sheng qi! Ni kan, zhao ni ku de yang zi, duo
    chou a!*
Such a disobedient child. I've told you before. Mom is
    really mad! Look, they're filming you crying, how
    ugly that is!

11	Researcher:	*Hao bu hao?*

Are you okay/Is it okay [to tape your crying]?

12	Didi:	((cries more loudly))
13	Sister:	*Chou ba guai, chou ba guai, xiu xiu lian!*

Ugly monster, ugly monster, shame on you!
((displays shaming gesture by sliding her index finger
    down her cheek))

14   ((to M)) *Ni shuo ta xiu xiu lian a.*
You say to him 'shame on you.'

15	Mother:	*Rang ta ku, mei guan xi, rang ta ku yixia. Ta zhe ge ren,
laba yi kai jiu bu ting.*

Let him cry. It doesn't matter. Let him cry for a while.
Once his trumpet goes off, it's hard to make it
stop. ((i.e. once he starts to cry, you can't make him
stop))

((sits down on sofa and extends her arm to Didi))

16   *Lai, wo gen ni jiang hua. Qi lai, qi lai!*

Come here, let me talk to you. Get up, get up!

17 Didi: ((turns to M, continues crying))

18 Sister: *Zai ayi mian qian jiu da yi dun.*

Give him a good spanking in front of Auntie ((referring
to R))

19 Mother: *Ta bu guai a. Mama jiang hua shuo na bian bu ke yi
qu a.*

He is not behaving. Mom said no one is allowed to go
there. ((points to the camcorder))

((picks Didi up from the floor; Didi stands next to M
and leans his head into M's lap))

20   ((holding Didi's chin)) *Zuiba bi qilai. Mama jiang hua.
Mama jiang hua. Ni yao wo bao, wo yao jiang yi ju. Zuiba
bi qilai.*

Close your mouth. Mom wants to say something. Mom
wants to say something. You want to be held, but I
want to say one thing first. Close your mouth.

21 Didi: ((stops crying))

22 Mother: ((points to the camcorder)) *Ni shi bushi bu guai, shi
bushi? You meiyou? You meiyou? Ni bu shuo, wo
sheng qi.*

You didn't behave, did you? Did you? Did you? If you
don't answer me, I'm gonna be mad at you.

23 Didi: ((looks at R and S, who are talking to each other))

24 Researcher: ((laughs)) *Xiao le ye; Didi dou xiao le.*

He's smiling; Didi is smiling.

25 Didi: ((starts to cry))

26 Sister: *Hei, aiyo, hao a, Ni gan jia zhuang ku a! Da ni yixia!*

Hey, what! Alright. How dare you fake crying! I'm
coming to spank you!

((spanks Didi and walks away))

27 Mother: *Ei ei ei! TingTing, guo lai! TingTing!*

Hey hey hey! TingTing, come here! TingTing!

((smacks the coffee table with her hand, shakes her
head and smiles))

28 Sister: ((laughs))

29 Researcher: *Chen huo da jie.*

'To loot when the house is on fire.' ((e.g. 'to take
advantage of someone when he is in crisis'))

In this excerpt, Didi's mother accused him of interfering with the researcher's equipment. Although Didi responded to the initial reprimand quickly by moving away from the camcorder, his subsequent response, crying, was interpreted as another transgression and resulted in more shaming. Didi's mother employed various shaming techniques, including public reprimand (spanking Didi in front of the researcher), disparaging comments (e.g. 'A child who doesn't obey rules,' 'Such a disobedient child,' 'How ugly'), and threats of abandonment (e.g. 'We don't want you,' 'It doesn't matter; let him cry'). Didi's sister also displayed her knowledge of shaming by calling him names (e.g. 'Ugly monster'), employing shame labels (e.g. 'Shame on you'), using shaming gestures, urging her mother to further shame Didi ('You say to him "shame on you,"' 'Give him a good spanking in front of Auntie'), and spanking Didi herself.

In this interaction, Didi's mother played multiple roles, not only as a discipliner and a shamer but also as a mitigator. Didi's sister attempted to take on the role of shamer as well, but she was allowed to do so only to a certain degree and was reprimanded for going too far and spanking Didi. The researcher was also recruited into the shaming event, as a witness whose presence intensified the shaming (e.g. 'Give him a good spanking in front of Auntie,' 'Look, they're filming you crying, how ugly that is'). Her interjections helped to affectively frame the shaming event, first by keying Didi's crying as a problem (e.g. 'Oh no, oh no,' 'Are you ok/Is it ok [to tape your crying]'), then by intervening to help him stop crying ('He's smiling. Didi is smiling'), and lastly by chiding his sister by portraying her spanking of her brother as inappropriate. As Mother explained to TingTing, shaming was intended to discipline Didi for repeatedly not listening to his mother, not to shame him merely for the sake of shaming him. Following this excerpt, Didi's mother spent a lengthy period of time holding him and reasoning with him about why he was punished. Indeed, most disciplinary shaming episodes included an extended reasoning period following the initial shaming.

Embodied Practices of Shaming

This exposure to the regard of others was not only enacted discursively but also through physical practices through which the child was made into an object of shame. Such practices include the dunce cap of American classrooms of yore or the South Korean practice of *son tulko seisski* (lit. to stand with one's hands raised). In this practice, the child who is being shamed holds her arms straight up in the air over her head while standing. This practice usually takes place from kindergarten through early adolescence, in accordance with local ideologies that see school-aged children as old enough to know how to conduct themselves appropriately. Children who are being shamed in this way in a classroom setting in South Korea might be asked to go to a location that is visible to others, like the front or back of the classroom, the teacher's lounge, or a hallway, and to kneel, face the wall, or raise a chair above their heads. In these cases, the regard of others is an integral part of the shaming practice.

Lo witnessed a use of this practice in a Korean American tae kwon do class, where a teacher told a child who had disobeyed his commands to stand on top of a bench at the front of the class with his hands held high. Other embodied practices of shaming found in South Korea include *ephtulye ppetchye*, where a person who has misbehaved placed her hands and feet on the floor and backside in the air in a V-shape, and *oli kelum*, 'to walk like a duck,' a punishment often meted out for school infractions. A child who is late for school might be ordered to walk in an area visible to everyone while squatting and holding her ears (e.g. like a duck). In all of these cases, shame is enacted physically as well as discursively, in ways that bring the gaze of others to bear upon the child.

Keying Shaming

While shaming can be associated with discipline, it can also be keyed as fun. Just as much of the fun in American bridal showers can involve lighthearted shaming of the bride-to-be, so too shaming in both Taiwan and Korea can be keyed as fun and akin to teasing. For example, when children play group games in South Korea, one common punishment meted out to the losing group is *engdengilo ilumssuki* (lit. 'writing your name with your butt'). In this practice, which typically takes place from elementary school through college, the losers 'write' their names in the air with their butts while standing with their backsides facing the winners. These acts of writing usually occasion much good-natured laughter from the winning team.[3] Similarly, friendly contests between children in South Korea may conclude with the losers being asked to sing a song in front of the whole group. In such contexts, shaming is associated with play, fun, and close friendships.

Understanding the emotional import of shaming also requires attention to local ideologies about what shaming means. In South Korea, shaming can be understood as a way to display affection and intimacy. In Example 7.3, Kyunghee, a South Korean graduate student in her thirties who had spent a year in the United States, explains how sibling closeness can be constituted through direct and unmitigated shaming:

Example 7.3

> If you have a relationship where you can scold the other person,
> then you are really close.
> If it's not close, then you can't scold them.
>
> If I'm not at all close to someone [in this case, a school friend],
> Even if they did horrible on their test, [I would say]
> 'Oh, it's okay, you can do better next time'
> I would say something like that.
> That would be understood as *indifference* in Korea.

But if we were siblings and were very close,
especially within a sibling relationship,
Then [I would say] 'See, you didn't study. Geez, you dummy!

How disappointed Mom and Dad are going to be. . . . Geez, you dummy!'
I would say something like that.
[translated from Korean; English in italics]

In this excerpt, bland encouragement is seen as a marker of emotional distance, while unmitigated, affectively intensified dyadic shaming is understood as a demonstration of warmth and affection. Informants' metapragmatic ideologies – beliefs about the force of their utterances – linked genres of shaming and scolding to gendered intimate kinship relations, like the scoldings a new bride receives from her mother-in-law, the nagging that a wife directs towards her husband or children, or the affectionate scolding that 'aunt' types direct towards younger customers.

The way in which shaming events could shift from serious to fun was evident in Fung's observations, where over 60 percent of the spontaneously occurring shaming events at home were keyed playfully. In Example 7.4, two-and-a-half-year-old Didi is shamed by his mother and older sister, TingTing (aged four and a half), for his inappropriate behavior in his sister's music class a few days earlier.

Example 7.4

1	Mother:	((looks at Didi and gently pats his back))
		Ei, ei, ni na tian gen ma, gen mei, gen jiejie qu shang yinyue ke, hao bu hao wan?
		Um um, the other day, when you went to the music class with Mom, with younger, with older sister, was it fun?
2	Didi:	*Hao wan a.*
		It was fun.
3	Mother:	*Laoshi dou meiyou gei ni shenme dongxi?*
		Didn't the teacher give you anything?
4	Didi:	*Mei, meiyou gei wo tiezhi.*
		No, she didn't give me a sticker.
5	Mother:	*Meiyou gei ni tiezhi, ranhou ni jiu, ni jiu zenme la?*
		She didn't give you a sticker. Then you, then what did you do?
6	Didi:	*Jiu ku le.*
		I cried.
7	Sister:	*Da sheng ku. 'Waah, waah, waah!'*
		You cried real loud. 'Waah, waah, waah!'
8	Mother:	*O, ni jiu ku la. Jiu yizhi: 'Waah! Meiyou, weishenme meiyou gei wo tiezhi! Weishenme meiyou gei wo tiezhi?!' Dui bu dui?*

		Oh, you cried. You just kept going: 'Waah! Why didn't you give me a sticker? Why didn't you give me a sticker!' Isn't that right? (((mimics C's crying and wipes her eyes; makes staccato gesture of fists away from body then back and whines))
9	Didi:	((looks up from a book, smiles, and looks down at the book again))
10	Sister:	*Dui a. 'Weishenme meiyou gei wo tiezhi?'* Yes. 'Why didn't you give me a sticker?' ((claps hands))
11	Mother:	*Tiezhi. A ya, hai de mama hao meiyou mianzi. Nage, nage tou dou yao wang di shang zuan le, dui bu dui?* A sticker. Boy, didn't you make your mom really lose face? Well, I really wanted to bury my head in the ground, isn't that right? ((smiles, shakes head, and smiles again))
12	Didi:	[unintelligible] ((points to the book))
13	Sister:	*Dou yao hun dao le. Mama yao kaishi hun dao le.* We were all gonna faint. Mom was gonna faint.
14	Mother:	*Hun dao, zhen yao hun dao le.* I was gonna faint. I really wanted to faint. ((tilts head back))
15	Didi:	*Kan wo hun, kan wo hun dao le.* Look, I faint, look, I'm fainting. ((dramatically throwing head and body back against sofa))
16	Mother:	*Hun dao. O, hun dao, zhen shi hun dao.* Fainted. Wow, I fainted. I really fainted. ((leans head and body back)).
17	Didi:	*Wo hun dao luo!* I am fainting! ((points to his cheek, emphasizing that HE fainted))
18	Mother:	*Wo cai hun dao le. Laoshi mei gei ni . . .* I'm the one who fainted. The teacher didn't give you . . . ((points to her cheek, emphasizing that SHE fainted))
19	Didi:	*Ni kan, ni kan, wo hun.* Look, look, I'm fainting. ((dramatically throwing head and body back against sofa))
20	Mother:	*Laoshi de nage tiezhi shi gei jiejie de. Zhi you yi zhang de, ni yi zhi yao: 'Laoshi meiyou gei wo tiezhi. Laoshi meiyou gei wo tiezhi.' Dui bu dui?* The teacher gave the sticker to your sister. There was only one. But you really wanted it: 'Teacher didn't give me a sticker! Teacher didn't give me a sticker!' Isn't that right?
21	Sister:	*Jiejie yao . . .* Sister was going to [faint] . . .
22	Mother:	*Shang xue cai you a.* You could only get one if you were in class

In this two-minute-long shaming event, both Didi's mother and his sister employed explicit emotional descriptors that pointed to the seriousness of Didi's offense (e.g. 'Didn't you make your mom really lose face?', 'I really wanted to bury my head in the ground'). They reenacted Didi's transgressions, thereby illustrating for the child the specific nature of his inappropriate responses to the shaming, by mimicking his crying, whining, wiping his eyes, and moving his fists. Nevertheless, Didi's mother invited him to relate his transgression with a light-hearted tone: 'Was it fun?' Didi appropriated, exaggerated, and repeatedly played with his sister's use of the word 'faint.' His mother joined him by mimicking his gestures and movements. The event was filled with smiles, laughter, and dramatic body movements, which all indexed a playful key.

After shaming the child directly, Didi's mother related the events of that day to the researcher. In this retelling, where Didi was an overhearer, she told the story much more sympathetically from the child's point of view. Referring to Didi in the third person, she admitted that it was a mistake to take him along that day; in fact, he was very well-behaved until he realized that he was the only one who did not get a sticker from the teacher. His crying was portrayed as an understandable reaction due to his feelings of exclusion from the group. The emotional import of shaming events thus unfolds over time, as children heard multiple versions of narratives about shaming episodes.

Responses to Verbal Shaming

While the analysis thus far has focused primarily on the actions of the person performing the shaming, the person being shamed was also expected to act in certain ways. In South Korean contexts, the person who is being shamed in a serious way is expected to display a repentant attitude by bowing her head, casting her eyes down, and maintaining a silent and composed demeanor during the shaming. Any attempt to speak while being shamed or any display of emotion (e.g. crying) can be understood as insolence and can result in intensification of the shaming. Korean American children, however, did not always conform to this expectation. They would agree with rhetorical questions during shaming episodes when they should have been silent, for example, or contest the teacher's version of events (see Lo 2009 for an example).

In Fung's study, as children grew older they were able to take on more active roles in shaming episodes. Whereas younger children simply confessed or acceded to their caregiver's shaming, by age four, several children were able to resist their caregivers' shaming or to actively shame younger siblings. In cases where caregivers appeared to violate expectations of 'balanced shaming,' novices could challenge what they saw as unfair shaming. Example 7.5 illustrates how a four-year-old child accuses her aunt of inappropriately shaming her. Angu's aunt, her primary caregiver, had repeatedly upbraided Angu for a series of past misdeeds, including knocking over a pile of dishes when rushing into the living room and spilling food. Frustrated and angry, Angu waited for an auspicious moment. After two hours had passed and her aunt had relaxed somewhat, Angu seized the floor.

Example 7.5

1   Angu: *Mama, wo wen ni yi ge wenti. Weishenme wo yong jiao ti panzi ti hen yuan, ni jiu bu jiangli, gen wo jiang! Hm!*

Mom ((Angu's normal address term for her aunt)), I want to ask you a question. When I used my feet to kick the dishes and kicked them far away, why were you unreasonable with me? Tell me why! Hm!

((finger pointed towards Aunt, holding up her chin with a scornful expression))

2   Aunt: *Wo zenme bu jiangli? Ni ba wo de panzi pilipala di, cong name yuan, ni jiu gei wo yizhi ti, ti dao pinglang da dao nali qu le, ni zuo shenme?*

In what way was I unreasonable? You knocked over my dishes, 'ping ping pang,' from all the way over there. You just kept kicking and kicked them all the way, kicked 'ping pang' all the way over there. What were you doing?

3   *Yi da zao, ni ti panzi, cong name [yuan], fei yao haohao de lu bu zou, yi, yi xia zi chong guo lai, jiu quanbu kuanglang yi da dui de panzi dou gei ni ti po.*

Early in the morning, you kicked the dishes, from all the way over there. How come you chose not to walk the right way and just ran on over here, into all those dishes, and you broke all of them?

4   Angu: *Wo die dao ma!* ((very loudly))
Because I fell!

5   Aunt: *Ni weishenme yao die dao? Ni lu buhui zou a?*
Why did you fall? You don't know how to walk?

6   *Ni mei, ni jiejie zai chaojia le. Ta hao qi a.*
Your younger sister, your older sister is arguing with me. Boy, isn't she mad.

((looking down at Angu's five-month-old sister, who is drinking from a bottle))

7   *Ni weishenme, ni gen wo jiang daoli a.*
Why did you [fall]; tell me the reason why
((looks up at Angu))

8   Angu: *Tao yan!* ((loudly))
Stop it!

9   Aunt: *Ha? Dui bu dui? Weishenme ni mei tian . . .*
Huh? Right? How come everyday you . . .

10   Angu: *Bu dui!* ((very loudly))
That's not right!

11	Aunt:	*Weishenme ni mei yiyang dongxi dou bu haohao di zuo zhe lai chi.*
		Why can't you ever sit properly when you eat?
12		*Ran hou na, chi shenme sa shenme, chi shenme sa shenme.*
		And, then, whenever you eat, you spill, whenever you eat, you spill.
13	Angu:	*Na ni weishenme bu gen wo haohao jiangli? Ni you bushi mei baba mama de! Ni yiqian you baba mama. Ni you mei you da sa guo?*
		But why didn't you reason with me nicely? It's not like you didn't have a daddy or a mommy. You had a daddy and a mommy before. Haven't you ever spilled anything? ((e.g. Since you were young once, you must have also spilled things before; you should be more sympathetic towards me.))
14	Aunt:	((laughs)) *Wo a? Wo hen guai de, wo bu hui da sa dongxi.*
		Me? I was very well-behaved. I never spilled anything.
15	Angu:	*Zhen de?*
		Really?
16	Aunt:	*Dui.*
		Yes.
17	Angu:	*Dui a?*
		Really?
18	Aunt:	*Ni wen ni mama, kan wo shi bushi, wo dongxi dou bu hui da sa.*
		You go ask your mom ((Aunt's youngest sister)), ask her if this is true, cause I never spilled anything.
19	Angu:	*Wo wen ni waipo la.*
		I'm gonna ask your grandma.
20	Aunt:	*Dui a, ni yao wen wo waipo a? Bu, ni yao wen wo mama, wen ni wai po a?*
		Right. You want to ask my grandma? No, you ask my mom, your grandma.
21	Angu:	*Hao, wo xianzai jiu qu.*
		Ok. I'm gonna ask her right now.
		((Angu phones her grandmother, but no one answers))

In this excerpt, Angu demonstrated a remarkable level of moral autonomy by forcefully challenging her aunt's moral reasoning. She berated her aunt for having shamed her inappropriately and for having been 'unreasonable' when she scolded her for having broken some dishes and spilling food when eating. Angu used sophisticated moral reasoning as she pointed out that she had broken the dishes accidentally, not intentionally, and that her aunt should be sympathetic to Angu's clumsiness because she herself was young once too. The fact that Angu waited nearly two hours to register her protest, until her aunt was in a sufficiently good mood, demonstrated her emotional attentiveness. Although Angu's aunt did not necessarily ratify her point of view, she nevertheless validated the strong emotions Angu was expressing ('[She] is arguing with me. Boy, isn't she mad!'). Angu's onslaught on her aunt was indulged, and she was not silenced for speaking her mind. By age four, Angu already understood that shaming was intended to instill moral lessons, not to randomly inflict emotional damage.

Shaming Over the Lifespan

Shaming takes different forms over the lifespan, as certain shaming practices are contextualized as age-specific and also linked to particular institutions. Shaming gestures such as sliding the finger on the cheek, for example, were common in the interactions Fung observed with young children but not with adolescents. The South Korean embodied practice of standing with one's hands and feet on the ground in a V-shape and backside in the air (*eptulye pechye*) was associated with school discipline and a variant (*elcharye*) was linked to the military, but neither practice would be expected in a college setting or in a workplace. Likewise, threats of corporal punishment or being called a 'stupid egg' were not used in the families Fung revisited when their children were adolescents.

However, some forms of shaming did persist well into adulthood. Informants noted that one would expect to be shamed by one's boss in South Korea and, in fact, the managers' manual at the South Korean conglomerate studied by Janelli (1993: 162) contained a section entitled 'When you intend to give a scolding.' Similarly, accounts of shaming by elderly strangers figure prominently in narratives collected by Lo from Korean Americans in their twenties and thirties about their visits to South Korea. The fun shaming of *endengilo ilumssuki* ('writing your name with your butt') was also practiced by some South Koreans living in the United States well into their twenties.

Conclusion

As we hope to have demonstrated, shaming is a complex verbal practice whose meaning and import can only be discussed in relation to a specific cultural and historical context and local ideologies about what shaming means. In both Taiwan and South Korea, shaming is seen as a necessary and integral part of moral education that helps to guide the child to reflect upon her own deeds and to develop a sense of right and wrong. Shaming practices are linked to beliefs about children as creatures who are in need of firm guidance in the crucial years of childhood, when moral character is formed. As children grow older, they learn how to participate as shamers of younger siblings and how to defend themselves against inappropriate moments of shaming. Shaming also relies upon a belief in the power of language and the idea that, simply by labeling something as shameful, caregivers can cause children to feel the corresponding emotion. Shaming episodes were not always serious and were sometimes associated with affection, play, or intimacy. Close attention to shaming as an interactive phenomenon can give us a greater understanding of how novices come to acquire the cultural, emotional, and moral skills necessary to become competent members of society.

NOTES

1   As sociologist Thomas Scheff (2003) notes, whereas many other languages have words that distinguish 'everyday shame' from 'disgrace shame' (e.g. German *scham* versus *schande*; French *pudeur* versus *honte*), English does not:

> Everyday shame usually carries no offense; we treat a tacit understanding of everyday shame (a sense of shame) as a necessary part of our equipment as proper persons. Since English has no word for everyday shame, we cannot discuss shame in English without risking offense. (Scheff 2003: 241)

This linking of shame in English to disgrace and humiliation might account, in part, for the negative portrayal of shame by contemporary American scholars.

2   As Twitchell (1997) notes, in Shakespeare's plays, shame was regarded as good, necessary, and even progressive. Victorian scholars considered those who did not demonstrate the ability to blush as shameless or subhuman. Until the 1950s shame and honor were considered effective tools in regulating individual behavior in the United States (Twitchell 1997).

3   The practice of *endengilo ilumssuki* can undergo various transformations in Korean American contexts. A Korean American student in her mid-twenties living in Los Angeles' Koreatown reported that she and her friends would play *engdengilo ilumssuki* as charades, where others would have to guess what word was being spelled. The Korean American children in the heritage language school Lo studied would suggest either *engdengilo ilumssuki* or having to sing a song in front of the class as punishments for the losing side in class contests (though the teacher she observed never actually enacted either of these). *Engdengilo ilumssuki* could also be sexualized, as Lo once observed in an Asian American fraternity/sorority mixer in Los Angeles, where newly inducted sorority girls were asked to go up on a stage by fraternity brothers and write their names with their butts.

REFERENCES

Bartlett, L. (2007) Literacy, speech, and shame: The cultural politics of literacy and language in Brazil. *International Journal of Qualitative Studies in Education* 20(6): 1–17.

Benedict, R. (1946) *The Chrysanthemum and the Sword: Patterns of Japanese Culture.* Boston, MA: Houghton Mifflin.

Benson, J., and Lyons, D. (1991) *Strutting and Fretting: Standards for Self-Esteem.*

Niwot, CO: University Press of Colorado.

Clancy, P. M. (1986) The acquisition of communicative style in Japanese. In B. B. Schieffelin and E. Ochs (eds.), *Language Socialization Across Cultures*. 213–50. New York: Cambridge University Press.

Creighton, M. R. (1990) Revisiting shame and guilt cultures: A forty-year pilgrimage. *Ethos* 18(3): 279–307.

Dodds, E. R. (1951) *The Greeks and the Irrational*. Berkeley, CA: University of California Press.

Doi, T. (1973) *The Anatomy of Dependence*. Tokyo: Kodansha International.

Etzioni, A. (2001) *The Monochrome Society*. Princeton, NJ: Princeton University Press.

Fader, A. (2006) Learning faith: Language socialization in a community of Hasidic Jews. *Language in Society* 35(2): 205–29.

Fung, H. (1999) Becoming a moral child: The socialization of shame among young Chinese children. *Ethos* 27(2): 180–209.

Fung, H. and Chen, E. C.-H. (2001) Across time and beyond skin: Self and transgression in the everyday socialization of shame among Taiwanese preschool children. *Social Development* 10(3): 419–37.

Geertz, C. (1983) *Local Knowledge: Further Essays in Interpretive Anthropology*. New York: Basic Books.

Geertz, H. (1959) The vocabulary of emotion: A study of Javanese socialization practices. *Psychiatry* 22: 225–37.

Gilbert, P., Pehl, J., and Allan, S. (1994) The phenomenology of shame and guilt: An empirical investigation. *British Journal of Medical Psychology* 67(1): 23–6.

Goffman, E. (1963) *Stigma: Notes on the Management of Spoiled Identity*. New York: Simon and Schuster.

Goffman, E. (1982 [1967]) On face-work. In *Interaction Ritual: Essays on Face-to-Face Behavior*. 5–46. Garden City, NY: Anchor Books.

Han, N. (2004) *Language Socialization of Korean-American Preschoolers: Becoming a Member of a Community Beyond the Family*. Doctoral Dissertation. Los Angeles, CA: University of California, Los Angeles.

Hoffman, M. L. (1983) Affective and cognitive processes in moral internalization. In E. T. Higgins, D. N. Ruble, and W. W. Hartup (eds.), *Social Cognition and Social Development: A Sociocultural Perspective*. 236–74. New York: Cambridge University Press.

Hoffman, M. L. (1994) Discipline and internalization. *Developmental Psychology* 30: 26–8.

Hoffman, M. L. (2000) *Empathy and Moral Development: Implications for Caring and Justice*. New York: Cambridge University Press.

Janelli, R. L. (1993) *Making Capitalism: The Social and Cultural Construction of a South Korean Conglomerate*. Stanford, CA: Stanford University Press.

Kohlberg, L. (1984) *The Psychology of Moral Development: The Nature and Validity of Moral Stages*. San Francisco, CA: Harper and Row.

Kulick, D. (1998) Anger, gender, language shift, and the politics of revelation in a Papua New Guinean village. In B. B. Schieffelin, K. A. Woolard, and P. V. Kroskrity (eds.), *Language Ideologies: Practice and Theory*. 87–102. New York: Oxford University Press.

Leighton, D. C. and Kluckhohn, C. (1947) *Children of the People: The Navaho Individual and His Development*. Cambridge, MA: Harvard University Press.

Levy, R. I. (1973) *Tahitians: Mind and Experience in the Society Islands*. Chicago, IL: University of Chicago Press.

Levy, R. I. and Rosaldo, M. Z. (eds.) (1983) Self and Emotion. *Ethos: Special Issue* 11(3).

Lewis, M. (1992) *Shame: The Exposed Self*. New York: Free Press.

Lo, A. (2009) Respect and affect in a Korean American heritage language classroom. *Linguistics and Education* 20(3): 217–34.

Lynd, H. M. (1958) *On Shame and the Search for Identity*. New York: Harcourt.

Mead, M. (1937) *Cooperation and Competition among Primitive Peoples*. New York: McGraw-Hill.

Miller, P. J., Wang, S.-H., Sandel, T., and Cho, G. E. (2002) Self-esteem as folk theory: A comparison of European American and Taiwanese mothers' beliefs. *Parenting: Science and Practice* 2(3): 209–39.

Nathanson, D. L. (1987) *The Many Faces of Shame*. New York: Guilford Press.

Nathanson, D. L. (1992) *Shame and Pride: Affect, Sex, and the Birth of the Self*. New York: W. W. Norton.

Nussbaum, M. C. (2004) *Hiding from Humanity: Disgust, Shame, and the Law*. Princeton, NJ: Princeton University Press.

Ochs, E. (1988) *Culture and Language Development: Language Acquisition and Language Socialization in a Samoan Village*. New York: Cambridge University Press.

Piers, G. and Singer, M. B. (1953) *Shame and Guilt: A Psychoanalytic and a Cultural Study*. Springfield, IL: Thomas.

Probyn, E. (2005) *Blush: Faces of Shame*. Minneapolis, MN: University of Minnesota Press.

Reynolds, J. (2008) Socializing *puros pericos* (little parrots): The negotiation of respect and responsibility in Antonero Mayan sibling and peer networks. *Journal of Linguistic Anthropology* 18(1): 82–107.

Rosaldo, M. Z. (1983) The shame of headhunters and the autonomy of self. *Ethos* 11(3): 135–51.

Rosaldo, M. Z. (1984) Toward an anthropology of self and feeling. In R. A. Shweder and Robert A. LeVine (eds.), *Culture Theory: Essays on Mind, Self, and Emotion*. 137–57. Cambridge: Cambridge University Press.

Scheff, T. (2003) Shame in self and society. *Symbolic Interaction* 26(2): 239–62.

Schieffelin, B. B. (1986) Teasing and shaming in Kaluli children's interactions. In B. B. Schieffelin and E. Ochs (eds.), *Language Socialization across Cultures*. 165–81. New York: Cambridge University Press.

Schieffelin, B. B. and Ochs, E. (eds.) (1986) *Language Socialization across Cultures*. New York: Cambridge University Press.

Schieffelin, B. B. (1990) *The Give and Take of Everyday Life: Language Socialization of Kaluli Children*. New York: Cambridge University Press.

Shweder, R. A. (2003) Toward a deep cultural psychology of shame. *Social Research* 70(4): 1109–29.

Tangney, J. P. (2005) Self-relevant emotions. In M. R. Leary and J. P. Tangney (eds.), *Handbook of Self and Identity*. 384–400. New York: The Guilford Press.

Tangney, J. P. and Dearing, R. L. (2002) *Shame and Guilt*. New York: Guilford Press.

Taylor, G. (1985) *Pride, Shame, and Guilt: Emotions of Self-Assessment*. New York: Oxford University Press.

Twitchell, J. B. (1997) *For Shame: The Loss of Common Decency in American Culture*. New York: St Martin's Press.

Williams, B. A. O. (1993) *Shame and Necessity*. Berkeley, CA: University of California Press.

8 Language Socialization and Narrative

PEGGY J. MILLER, MICHELE KOVEN, AND SHUMIN LIN

As a tool and outcome of socialization, narrative has interested scholars of language socialization from the field's inception (Heath 1982; Miller and Sperry 1987; Scollon and Scollon 1981; Watson-Gegeo and Boggs 1977). This is hardly surprising, since narrative has long been assumed to be a powerful, universal strategy for transmitting valued ways of acting and being to the next generation; one can easily imagine a parent reading a fairy tale to a child or an elder intoning a sacred story to a circle of attentive youths.

Over the past 25 years, however, research on language socialization has revealed that narrative socialization occurs in a wide range of circumstances that transcend these iconic scenes, with different types of narrative, different ways of participating in narrative practices, and different understandings of the function of narrative beyond the didactic (see reviews by Miller and Moore 1989; Ochs and Capps 1996, 2001; Shweder et al. 2006). Like all research in the language socialization tradition, this work has several features that distinguish it from other approaches to socialization. The overarching contribution has been to illuminate how narrative socialization works 'on the ground.' Researchers study socialization in real time, privileging routine practices. Most importantly, researchers in this paradigm have focused attention on local narrative practices – in all their complexity and variability – as both the prism through which to study socialization and the mechanism through which socialization transpires.

This chapter will address this fundamental achievement in relation to four areas: (1) the heterogeneity of narrative practices, especially in the early years of life; (2) the construction of selves and identities through narrative; (3) narrative practices as sites for (re)producing social inequality; and (4) untold and devalued narratives. We use our own work to illustrate narrative socialization, especially in

The Handbook of Language Socialization, First Edition. Edited by Alessandro Duranti, Elinor Ochs, and Bambi B. Schieffelin.

the fourth section. Throughout, we indicate fruitful problems for future research, including potentially beneficial convergences between language socialization research and adjacent fields of study.

Heterogeneity of Narrative Practices

A specific contribution of research on narrative socialization is detailed documentation of how narrative varies within and across socializing venues. Heterogeneity is evident not only in the multiplicity of narrative genres available to novices (e.g. Dyson 2003; Preece 1987; Sperry and Sperry 1996) but also in the variety of forms that particular genres assume within and across communities (Miller and Moore 1989). While stories of personal experience are universal and 'primary' in the Bakhtinian (1986) sense, socialization into and through personal storytelling is culturally differentiated, starting from infancy (e.g. Eisenberg 1985; Engel 1995; Miller, Fung, and Mintz 1996; Miller and Sperry 1988; Scollon and Scollon 1981; Watson-Gegeo and Gegeo 1990).

Locally hued versions of personal storytelling are constituted partly through norms of reportability. For example, mothers in the working-class community of South Baltimore treated childbirth, romantic misfortunes, and events of anger, aggression, and self-assertion as highly reportable and did not censor these topics in deference to child bystanders (Miller 1994; Miller and Sperry 1987). Hell-raising stories about youthful misdeeds and antics were told by middle-class parents and relished by children in Chicago but not in Taipei (Miller et al. 2001). Youngsters in a working-class Euro-American community in the Piedmont Carolinas learned to denigrate themselves as narrated characters, whereas their counterparts in a nearby working-class African American community aggrandized themselves as narrated characters; these communities also enacted different norms along the continuum of literal truth/fictional embellishment (Heath 1983). African American children in rural Alabama incorporated fantasy creatures into their stories, but girls received less encouragement than boys for telling fantasy stories (Sperry and Sperry 1996).

Because language socialization researchers study stories in context, as part of novices' everyday lives, they can identify variation in participant frameworks (Goffman 1979). They ask the basic question, 'What kinds of participation pathways are available to children in storytelling events?' This question distinguishes language socialization research from developmental studies that rely entirely on elicited stories or stories lifted out of context. An important insight that has emerged from inquiry into participant roles is that children participate not just as (co)narrators but also as overhearers. For example, Kwara'ae children (Solomon Islands) were present as quiet overhearers at 'shaping the mind' events in which adults told stories to resolve family conflict (Watson-Gegeo and Gegeo 1990). In dinner-table narrations in middle-class American families, children were routinely overhearers of their own experiences (Ochs and Taylor 1992). In Taiwanese families, adults explicitly invoked events in which the child committed a misdeed, positioning him or her in the narrative activity alternately as an overhearer/transgressive protagonist and as a co-narrating confessor, sometimes shifting within moments of one another (Fung and Chen 2001). In contrast, Western Apache handled misconduct indirectly (Basso 1996). These studies illustrate that not only the content of stories but also the participant roles available to children convey socializing messages.

Ochs and Capps (2001) highlight other dimensions of narrative variability. They argue that personal narrative oscillates between narrators' desire for coherence and their desire for authenticity, but that research on children's storytelling has focused on the former as an ideal of narrative competence. The privileged 'default' storytelling situation involves one active teller, crafting a relatively linearly sequenced, coherent account of a highly tellable event; further, the story tends to be framed by a constant moral stance and is easily detached from surrounding discourse. Children, however, also learn to tell stories that question and express doubts, make sense of puzzling events, grapple with moral dilemmas, and explore alternative or hypothetical versions of events. An important insight is that variation occurs across levels of analysis within and across individuals as well as within and across communities.

Narrative and Self-Construction

Vygotskian sociocultural theory, with its emphasis on semiotically mediated activity (Cole 1996; Scribner and Cole 1981; Wertsch 1991), has influenced how scholars think about narrative socialization (e.g. Fivush 1998; Miller 1994; Miller et al. 1990; Miller and Goodnow 1995; Nelson 1989; Ochs and Capps 2001; Sperry and Sperry 2000).When children or other novices routinely participate in storytelling, lasting social and psychological consequences can occur, including the development of self and identity. However, in this chapter, inspired by Goffman (1959), we do not posit self/identity as a purely internal or psychological entity; rather we adopt a notion of self/identity as images of self and others and patterns of interactional engagement that are situated in, emergent from, and under certain conditions, transportable across social interactions.

Narrative has important features that make it apt for examining socialization of self. Narratives do far more than depict the past; they have the power to perform identities. With the perspective of narrative as communicative practice, one can see self and social identity as emergent in interaction, rather than as an internal psychological essence or substratum.[1] Storytelling is multifunctional, involving complex relations between the referential and the pragmatic, or talk that 'describes' there-and-then events and talk that performs actions in the 'here and now.'

Connected to this multifunctionality, participants often present selves and others by straddling narrating and narrated events (Bauman 1986; Jakobson 1957; Silverstein 1993). In this way, narratives of self are interdiscursive, involving indexical and iconic linkages across more than one communicative event (Agha 2005; Silverstein 2005). Rather than conveying a unified, monolithic identity, storytellers speak through multiple roles within particular utterances and throughout a narrative. How speakers manage their roles as narrator, narrated character, and performed character is precisely what has been called 'footing' (Goffman 1979) or 'voicing' (Bakhtin 1981; Hill 1995; Koven 2002, 2007; Wortham 2001). A sense of a speaker's identity lies in the coordination of multiple identities of here-and-now, there-and-then selves and others. (See also Ochs and Capps' (1996) review paper, where the idea of multiple protean selves in narrative is presented.)

For example, as elaborated in Koven (2007: 92), a storyteller can simultaneously perform and comment upon perspectives of narrated selves and others. One can recount important life events from a more distant perspective, or alternatively seem to relive those events, fusing current and past selves (Wortham 2001). Koven (2002) showed how one woman recounted the same event in one instance as an adult and in another instance as her past 13-year-old self.

With its focus on singular events, this general perspective on narrative and identity is useful. However, to fulfill the criterion that studies of language socialization attend to the effects of *recurrent* discursive practices (Kulick and Schieffelin 2004), analysis needs to link specific narratives to routinized narrative practices (Bourdieu 1977, 1984; Goffman 1959).[2] One approach is to study the same narrator across settings (Koven 2007, 2011) or over time (e.g. Fung 2003; Miller et al. 1993; Wolf and Heath 1992; Wortham 2005, 2006). Indeed, it is precisely language socialization's longstanding focus on social actors' recurrent participation that makes it valuable for studying self-construction.

Effects of recurrent participation

Although the effects of recurring narrative practices on local constructions of self are important across the lifespan, most research has focused on early childhood. A comparative study of narrative socialization practices and their impacts on development of self in middle-class Taiwanese families in Taipei and middle-class Euro-American families in Chicago found that telling stories of personal experience was a frequent practice in both sites at two and a half years and continued apace at three, three and a half, and four years (Miller, Fung, and Mintz 1996; Miller et al. 1997; Miller et al. 2001; Miller et al. in press). In counterpoint to this similarity, the Taipei and Chicago families differed dramatically in how they narrated events in which the child was a key figure. Taiwanese families were much more likely than their Euro-American counterparts to tell stories that cast the child protagonist as a transgressor. In keeping with local beliefs that parents should take every opportunity to correct young children (Fung 1999), many stories occurred immediately after the child had committed a misdeed. Families repeatedly invoked moral and social rules, structured their stories to establish the child's misdeed as the point of the story, and concluded with didactic codas. In contrast, the Chicago families enacted a child-favorability bias, erasing or downplaying children's misdeeds. Although personal storytelling was a rich purveyor of values in these families, the Taipei families practiced a more didactic version of personal storytelling, reflecting and reinforcing larger systems of meaning that prioritize moral education and self-perfection (see Li 2002). Confucian discourses that valorize teaching, listening, and self-improvement continue to circulate in the complex mix of local and global influences that are reshaping child rearing and education in contemporary Taiwan (Fung, Miller, and Lin 2004).

Both the Taipei and Chicago children participated more actively in personal storytelling as they got older (Miller et al. in press), routinely carving out different versions of personal experience and self. Evaluative frameworks linked to larger currents of cultural meaning infused narrators' creative responses to here-and-now social contingencies. In these practices we catch a glimpse of how culturally hued selves might originate. A need for positive self-regard may be rooted, in part, in storytelling that systematically constructs the child's self in favorable terms, whereas an inclination to self-improvement may be rooted, in part, in the narration of misdeeds and the explicit invocation of moral standards (Miller, Fung, and Koven 2007). More generally, recurring narrative practices reveal how self-construction is both dynamic and rife with redundancies that anchor and stabilize versions of self across contexts.

Directions for future research

More scholarship is needed to bridge studies of identity performance in individual narratives and habitual or stable practices of narrative identity socialization (Agha 2005; Wortham 2005).[3] It would be useful to examine how events involving children as tellers and/or protagonists are recast and re-embedded across storytelling contexts for different audiences (Bauman 1986; Bauman and Briggs 1990; Koven 2007, 2011; Norrick 1998). How family members create interdiscursive links across storytelling situations may influence their experience of self as more or less durable beyond a given interaction (Agha 2005, 2007). Narratives' repeatability, in content and form, may be vital to personal or autobiographical continuity.

Socialization and Narrative Inequality

Narrative inequality refers to the systematic privileging of some ways of narrating experience over others (Blommaert 2005; Hymes 1996 [1980]; Ochs and Capps 1996). Differential access to more or less socially valued or more or less legitimate resources for narrating may be one site where inequalities of status, power, or prestige on both micro- and macro-social levels are accomplished and experienced. (See, for example, Mehan's (1996) cogent analysis of the construction of a child as learned disabled through the privileging of the school psychologist's narrative over the accounts of the mother and the classroom teacher.)

Narrative inequality at home

From its inception, the field of language socialization has examined the family as the universal site where childhood socialization begins. In many communities, children participate verbally in narrative from the second year of life; however, their access is restricted not only by their limited communicative competence but also by their locally defined role as young children and novice speakers (Ochs and Capps 1996; Taylor 1995). Although young children in some communities are allowed and even encouraged to tell stories of their own experiences, their story-telling rights are limited relative to those of adults. Children may be subject to repeated parental interventions, reflecting local norms: adults may correct children's accounts for accuracy (Wiley et al. 1998), direct them toward some topics and away from others (Miller et al. 1990; Miller et al. 1997), deny them equal access to the floor (Heath 1983), tell stories about them in their presence in a manner that would be demeaning to adults (Miller et al. 1990), or dismiss their legitimate concerns about parental misbehavior (Taylor 1995). By participating routinely in such interactions, children are socialized into age-related asymmetric relationships in which caregivers have more power than children.

Narrative socialization may also be a site where children are socialized into gender inequalities. In dinnertime narratives in middle-class, Euro-American families, narrative roles were systematically differentiated, reproducing gender-relevant power relations (Ochs and Taylor 1992, 1995). Mothers were repeatedly positioned as introducers of stories, fathers as problematizers and critics. Children were 'overhearers, recipients, and active contributors to gender-implicative, asymmetrical exchanges dozens of times in the course of sharing a single meal together' (Ochs and Taylor 1995: 98). Narrative participation creates socializing pathways for instantiating gender hierarchies, with potentially lasting implications in and beyond the home.

Social contexts beyond the home

Children's early socialization into narrative practices in their families may be more or less in synch with those practices expected and valued in school and other contexts. Non-narrative discourse is favored over narrative discourse at all levels of the American educational system, and children socialized to communicate via personal narratives in homes and peer groups may find their stories excluded or suppressed in the classroom (Cazden and Hymes 1996 [1978]). Labov's ground-breaking book, *Language in the Inner City* (1972), presents a devastating critique of the argument that preschool 'language deprivation' at home explains educational underachievement. Instead, he favorably contrasts the virtuoso narrative performances of low-income children growing up speaking African American English with the less vivid performances of children raised to speak Standard English. The error at the heart of the language deprivation position is misrecognizing these differences as deficits by educational and scholarly authority (Labov 1972; see also Bernstein 1972; Bourdieu 1991; Corsaro 1994; Miller 1982).

Bourdieu's (1991) notions of misrecognition and symbolic domination are particularly useful for understanding the narrative socialization of inequality. Misrecognition is the process through which both mainstream and minority speakers come to view those ways of speaking commanded by dominant groups as inherently more desirable. Systematic misrecognition essentializes the authority of dominant modes of speaking and the lesser legitimacy of other ways of speaking, becoming a key mechanism through which 'symbolic domination' of minority speakers is achieved. Despite critiques of Bourdieu's vision as overly totalizing (Gal 1989; Woolard 1985), misrecognition and symbolic domination remain valuable notions for understanding how macro-level 'dominant' political and economic orders are (re)produced in institutions such as schools (see Baquedano-López and Mangual Figueroa, this volume; García-Sánchez, this volume; Riley, this volume) on the micro level. Mastering the dominant ways of narrating at school may be a key way in which children acquire the symbolic capital that ultimately provides access to later professional and socioeconomic success.

More recent scholarship demonstrates the disproportionate social, psychological, and educational costs of misrecognition in classrooms for nonmainstream children. In 'show and tell' or 'sharing time' in a first-grade US classroom, for example, a subtle but powerful mismatch between the teacher's middle-class narrative style and African American children's narrative style recurred day by day, effectively denying these children equal access to oral preparation for literacy (Michaels 1981; Michaels and Cazden 1986). By following one child (Deena) over time, Michaels (1991) documented the 'dismantling' of Deena's narrative development through the teacher's well-meaning but undermining responses. Although the teacher effectively collaborated with the middle-class children, whose narrative style more closely resembled her own, she was not able to do so with Deena and her working-class African American peers, who used a topic-associating style. The teacher's repeated interventions demonstrated her misrecognition of the child's narratives as incoherent and pointless rather than discursively different. As this pattern continued, Deena became increasingly frustrated and annoyed at the teacher, and the teacher began to see Deena as less capable of producing organized texts.

A similar pattern emerged in Corsaro, Molinari, and Rosier's (2002) study of the educational transitions of Zena, a low-income African American child. Zena flourished academically and socially in Head Start, where most of her peers and teachers followed African American norms of speaking. Her teachers judged her academic performance favorably, and Zena's skill with oppositional and narrative speech allowed her to interact effectively with her peers and take a leadership role in dramatic play. While Zena continued to excel in kindergarten, in first grade the same verbal strengths stigmatized her in the eyes of her white middle-class teacher and peers. Her verbal style was judged to be offensive and she was perceived as bossy and moody; conflict with peers had an impact on her academic achievement.

Bourdieu's notion of misrecognition implies that the systematic underestimation of the verbal competence of children like Deena and Zena goes hand in hand with the misattribution of exceptional ability to children who use the middle-class discursive styles valorized in the educational market. Studies of the latter type of misjudgment are strikingly rare. Michaels and Sohmer's (2000) analysis of fourth-grade science lessons in US schools is an important exception.

While none of the children correctly understood the phenomenon in question – that is, seasonal change – the middle-class children sounded 'smarter' and more 'scientific' in their explanations compared with their working-class counterparts, who used narrative accounts to interpret seasonal change. Reflecting on these results, Michaels noted, 'Nathaniel was considered a brilliant student, but he never understood how the inscriptions he spouted related to his phenomenal experience; Christopher, in contrast, struggled to do just that by recruiting his embodied experience via narrative accounts but he was rarely thought of by his teacher as a thoughtful, capable learner' (Michaels 2005: 142).

In sum, the classroom is a context where the narrative practices that children carry with them from home may be differentially supported and evaluated. As such, some children experience a smooth extension of the home socializing trajectory, whereas others experience a discontinuity, resulting in a progressive curtailment in the classroom. By exposing the discursive clashes or meshings that occur routinely at the micro level, these studies help to explain how broader patterns of unequal school achievement and alienation are established. Because these micro-level interpretive processes occur largely out of participants' awareness, they promote misrecognition of self and other in terms of social stereotypes (Bourdieu 1990; Gumperz 1982). Such misrecognitions may become reinforced over time as children move through the educational system and eventually into adult-oriented institutions.

Directions for future research

A remaining challenge is to go beyond documenting the fact that minority speakers possess complex narrative competencies that are eclipsed in mainstream school settings. Scholars should also analyze precisely how micro-level narrative practices are connected to larger political and economic contexts of sociolinguistic prejudice and symbolic domination. Research outside narrative socialization has examined the relations between language and political economy (Blommaert 2005; Gal 1987; Irvine 1985; Lippi-Green 1997; Silverstein and Urban 1996). Such research on language and inequality takes issue with scholarship that only seeks to revalorize the practices of nonmainstream speakers without also attending to the institutional dynamics that present ways of speaking of socioeconomically dominant groups as inherently superior. One direction for future work is precisely a tighter integration of micro- and macro-social perspectives on the socialization of narrative inequality.

Scholars should resist seeing all instances of social interaction as sites of socialization (Kulick and Schieffelin 2004). One dimension in the determination of the socializing potency of an interaction is its frequency. At what level of frequency does a type of encounter become a site of socialization of narrative inequality? One might argue that beyond the daily interaction between child and caregiver are less frequent but highly consequential adult–adult language socializing exchanges in bureaucratic settings, such as those between patients and doctors (Ainsworth-Vaughn 1988) or job seekers and interviewers (Roberts and Campbell

2005). Narrative socialization in such contexts becomes another opportunity to better link specific practices and lifespan apprenticeship into the broader institutions with which they articulate.

A related direction for linking micro- and macro-narrative socialization of inequality addresses situations in which participants encounter inequality as a result of transnational migration. Those who travel beyond their communities of origin, where local ways of narrating have garnered legitimacy or even prestige, may suddenly find themselves delegitimized, particularly in bureaucratic settings (Blommaert 2005; Philips 2004). For example, asylum seekers may offer narratives that are not 'heard' by European bureaucrats who have the authority to ratify those narratives and grant asylum status (Blommaert 2005; Jacquemet 2005; Maryns 2005). In such sites of narrative inequality, participants find themselves socialized into socially devalued identities and denied asylum. Asymmetries of access to differently valued narrative resources are thereby linked to differential access to particular institutional rights. Command of narrative genres is inextricably tied to questions of institutional legitimacy, inequality, and transnational mobility. Future research on the socialization of narrative inequality might analyze the extent to which participants' narrative performances in bureaucratic settings over time converge on or diverge from institutionally valued practices.

Listening to Untold and Devalued Narratives

When participants find no place for their stories or when their efforts to tell stories go awry again and again, they may respond with silence (Labov 1972). One should be cautious, however, before equating silence with powerlessness and speaking with empowerment (Gal 1991), given the numerous ethnographic examples where power may be exercised or resisted through silence. However, when participants cannot transfer narrative skills from one context to another, and their narratives are misrecognized and perhaps prevented from even being told, narrative inequality may be particularly pronounced. Untold or censored narratives, with their associated methodological challenges, have been of keen abiding interest to the authors of this chapter. This final section highlights strands of our own work that bear on this phenomenon.

Entering the world of working-class children's narratives

Scholarly response to misrecognized or untold narratives may take several forms. The researcher may turn to other contexts in order to 'hear' those voices and their virtuosity according to local norms. Language socialization scholars have used this strategy to document working-class and minority children's narrative participation in the contexts of home, peer group, community, and church, where interlocutors comprehend, legitimize, and encourage the contributions of nonmainstream children (Goodwin 1990; Haight 2002; Heath 1983; Miller 1994; Miller and Sperry

1987, 1988; Scollon and Scollon 1981; Shuman 1986; Sperry and Sperry 1996; Watson-Gegeo and Gegeo 1990). The goal of such scholarship is to demonstrate participants' range of narrative skills across contexts, enabling one to grasp participants' competencies in settings where they may display less self-censorship and/or find themselves in interaction with others who share or appreciate their ways of speaking.

Miller, Cho, and Bracey (2005) synthesized several decades of ethnographic research by Miller and her colleagues in two working-class Euro-American communities, South Baltimore and Daly Park in Chicago (Burger and Miller 1999; Cho and Miller 2004; Miller 1994; Miller and Sperry 1987, 1988). They concluded that adults participated prolifically, avidly, and artfully in personal storytelling in the family context and brought children into this valued activity from an early age. These youngsters experienced home environments saturated with stories: adults and older children co-narrated stories with young children and cast young children as bystanders and listeners to stories of their own and others' experiences. By the time the children were three years of age, they had learned to co-narrate their own past experiences with considerable skill, providing temporal ordering and using evaluative devices to convey the point of the story. Moreover, when compared with youngsters from Longwood, a middle-class neighborhood in Chicago, Daly Park children's narrative advantage became apparent: they produced two to three times more co-narrated stories in the home context at two and a half and three years.

Two other features distinguished working-class children's narratives (Miller, Cho, and Bracey 2005). First, these stories privileged dramatic language and negative story content. This is best illustrated by the children from South Baltimore, who told many stories of physical harm, including stories of anger and aggression, casting them in a dramatic language that favored verbs of aggression and pejorative names (Miller and Sperry 1987, 1988; see also Bauman 1986, 2004; Labov and Waletzky 1967). This disposition toward dramatizing negative experience mirrored the stories that the children heard from adults as well as their mothers' socializing goal of 'toughening' children for the harshness of life in a poor community. The Daly Park children's stories were also skewed negatively, reflecting their mothers' belief in openness and honesty with children about the hard realities of life (Burger and Miller 1999; Cho and Miller 2004). Although the negative slant was less pronounced in the more economically secure Daly Park families, compared with the South Baltimore families, both working-class groups differed from the middle-class families, where children's stories were skewed positively and favored a psychological language of emotion-state words. This narrative differentiation within working-class families, on the one hand, and between working-class and middle-class families, on the other, helps to constitute what Kusserow (2004) has called 'hard' and 'soft' forms of American individualism.

The second feature of working-class children's narratives is also relevant to these different versions of individualism. In South Baltimore and Daly Park, young children's stories were hybridized (Bakhtin 1986) with genres of dispute, challenge, and self-defense, a pattern discernible in stories by older working-class children and adolescents (Corsaro, Molinari, and Rosier 2002; Goodwin 1990; Shuman 1986). For example, Daly Park mothers tended to contradict the children in a matter-of-fact manner; they did not soften their opposition or give in quickly, making children defend their claims in the face of resolute opposition. Thus, these working-class children had to earn and defend the right to express their views, a lesson in 'hard' individualism. Alternatively, the middle-class Longwood children were granted a great deal of latitude to express their views, even when those views were factually inaccurate or misguided. They were learning that the right to express one's views could be taken for granted, a lesson in 'soft' individualism.

In sum, when poor and working-class American children are studied in settings where interlocutors find their talk intelligible and meaningful, it becomes possible to 'hear' their narrative voices and to discern the storytelling pathways on which they embark. These pathways are marked by dramatic self-narration, engagement with and comic relief from life's harsh realities, and early immersion in 'hard' individualism (Kusserow 2004). By three years of age, telling and listening to stories of personal experience is second nature. Although middle-class US children also learn to tell stories of personal experience in family contexts, working-class children have a distinct advantage and may well be more developmentally advanced in this arena. It is thus all the more poignant that their narrative strengths may not be recognized or cultivated in school. When Miller and Mehler (1994) observed three kindergartens in Daly Park, they found that opportunities to engage in oral narrative were extremely limited. Although show-and-tell occurred daily in one classroom, it was not defined as a narrative event. Miller and Mehler concluded that very few personal stories either by teachers or children were as complex as those told in homes in Daly Park (see also Wells 1986).

Making room for elders' previously untold life stories

The preceding section cited work in which ethnographers deliberately studied children in contexts likely to display values and competencies bequeathed to them in the process of their primary language socialization. The ethnographic challenge in that work was the same challenge that all ethnographers face: to discern and adapt to participants' practices and meanings. (See Briggs, 1986, for a discussion of the importance of not imposing the researcher's notion of 'interviewing' on ethnographic encounters with people for whom this may be a foreign type of communicative event.) In this section we focus on a strategy that places even more of a premium on the ethnographer's unusual status as an open-minded and sympathetic participant observer. At times a community member may take advantage of the unusual relationship with the ethnographer to tell previously untold stories. Good ethnographers remain flexible when events diverge from what they had thought would take place. Indeed, ethnography depends upon moments where someone uses the encounter to confide in the participant observer and tell stories about subjects in ways that may differ from what would emerge in the more habitual contexts of daily life. The ethnographer's status as a knowledgeable outsider affords a novel opportunity to try out new kinds of narratives that would be sanctioned or ignored if told to more familiar interlocutors.

After studying narrative socialization in Taiwanese families with young children and working with one family for several years, Fung asked to interview a grandmother who lived in the parents' household about her beliefs concerning child rearing and language learning (Fung 2003; Miller, Fung, and Koven 2007). The grandmother, Mrs. Lin, had a more urgent priority, however: she wanted to tell Fung the emotionally powerful story of her two marriages. Widowed in her twenties, Mrs. Lin remarried when her oldest child was about to enter college. In this interview and in four subsequent conversations over the course of a decade, Mrs. Lin revealed that she had never before told these stories to anyone, including to her grown children, in deference to their moral sensibilities and to protect her reputation. Yet, this does not mean that these stories were absent. Rather, Mrs. Lin kept these stories alive by telling them to herself as part of a process of private self-socialization that spanned 40 years (Miller, Fung, and Koven 2007). The ethnographic encounter became a safe place to share and vocally reflect upon these secret stories.

Similarly, in Lin's (2009) ethnographic study of her grandmother, the grandmother used the encounter to tell her life stories and experiences of linguistic marginalization for the first time to her ethnographer-granddaughter. A-ma was a Taiwanese monolingual illiterate elder who was routinely misrecognized as quiet and inarticulate by her family members and herself. Lin documents narrative inequality among adult family members with different educational backgrounds and language repertoires. Due to class and gender inequality and political changes, A-ma was 'left behind' – uneducated, illiterate, and monolingual in Hoklo, a language systematically suppressed in Taiwan (Sandel 2003). Conversely, A-ma's younger family members became literate (in Japanese, the former colonial language, or in Mandarin) and spoke Mandarin, the dominant language.

Over time, A-ma became socialized into the role of 'nonspeaker' in family conversations. This role was co-constructed: compared with other adult family members, most of whom were virtuoso storytellers, A-ma was considered inarticulate when she attempted to tell her personal stories. Her narratives were often ignored, or others took the floor from her. Gradually, A-ma lost confidence in speaking and rarely, if ever, initiated or told stories. Narrative inequality at home was reinforced and complicated by the intersections between television-viewing and family conversations. Given the dominance of Mandarin programming, A-ma had limited access to the content of shows and had little to say when family members discussed them, even when they used her own language, Hoklo. A-ma had equal access to watch and hear television but unequal access to listen and comprehend.

With her ethnographer-granddaughter listening creatively, A-ma gradually came to find a narrative voice. Various methodological challenges had to be recognized and overcome to support this new relationship. Recording life stories in long stretches would not have worked with A-ma. Instead, in her ethnographer role, Lin learned to wait patiently during long silences for another laboriously produced utterance from A-ma. Lin learned that A-ma would not speak much during family interviews because others would answer for or take the floor from her. When others' presence was unavoidable, Lin sustained the floor for A-ma, violating family communication norms, to prevent A-ma's younger sister from speaking for A-ma. In these ways, Lin gave A-ma control over the direction of her narratives. Although such an approach may seem to go against that advocated by Briggs (1986), in which the researcher adapts to local communicative norms, Lin learned how those norms themselves may sometimes constrain some participants more than others.

In sum, ethnographic methodology offers a solution to the problem of how to study habitually untold or self-censored stories. Just as baseline socialization processes inhibiting certain topics or ways of narrating are co-constructed, ethnography-induced 'resocialization' processes are also a joint accomplishment. A sense of trust between the ethnographer and others cultivated across time in the course of extended interactions also helps to make room for previously untold stories. Unlike children who straddle two contexts (e.g. home and school) where their storytelling is evaluated in strikingly different ways, these elders' life stories had found *no* safe context before the ethnographic encounter. A methodological implication is that ethnographic flexibility and self-reflexivity about the impact of one's presence is required for socially or personally sanctioned stories to be told.

Conclusion

This chapter has addressed important concerns that cross-cut the heterogeneity of narrative practices, narrative socialization of self, narrative socialization of inequality, and untold and devalued narratives. The pervasiveness of narrative renders it a potent medium of socialization across the lifespan and sociocultural contexts. Attention to the effects of recurrent participation in narrative practices furthers the goals of discourse-oriented research to demonstrate the real-time, interactive (re) production of a range of social and psychological phenomena. Narrative socialization offers insight into the recurring communicative events and speech chains (Agha 2007) through which selves and inequality come to be understood and experienced by novice and expert members of families, by institutions and communities, and by analysts as at once situational, perduring, and transformable.

NOTES

1   For further discussion, see Bamberg (1997a, 1997b); De Fina, Schiffrin, and Bamberg (2006); Goffman (1959, 1979); Hill (1995); Johnstone (1997); Keller-Cohen and Dyer (1997); Koven (1998, 2002, 2007); Miller et al. (1990); Miller, Fung, and Koven (2007); Miller, Fung, and Mintz (1996); Ochs and Capps (1996, 2001); Schiffrin (1996); and Wortham (1999, 2000, 2001).

2   One occasion when a narrator alternated between assertive and vulnerable performance of here-and-now and there-and-then identities does not afford speculation about more stable patterns of self-enactment and description.
3   Note, however, Wortham's (2005) critique of language socialization's focus on the recurrent and the generic. Wortham argues that scholars should attend to unique and indeterminate trajectories of socialization for the same social actors.

REFERENCES

Agha, A. (2005) Introduction: Semiosis across encounters. *Journal of Linguistic Anthropology* 15(1): 1–5.

Agha, A. (2007) *Language and Social Relations*. New York: Cambridge University Press.

Ainsworth-Vaughn, N. (1988) *Claiming Power in Doctor–Patient Talk*. New York: Oxford University Press.

Bakhtin, M. (1981) *The Dialogic Imagination*. Austin, TX: University of Texas Press.

Bakhtin, M. (1986) *Speech Genres and Other Late Essays*. Austin, TX: University of Texas Press.

Bamberg, M. (1997a) Positioning between structure and performance. *Journal of Narrative and Life History* 7(1–4): 335–42.

Bamberg, M. (1997b) *Oral Versions of Personal Experience: Three Decades of Narrative Analysis*. Mahwah, NJ: Lawrence Erlbaum.

Basso, K. (1996) *Wisdom Sits in Places: Landscape and Language Among the Western Apache*. Albuquerque, NM: University of New Mexico Press.

Bauman, R. (1986) *Story, Performance, and Event: Contextual Studies of Oral Narrative*. New York: Cambridge University Press.

Bauman, R. (2004) *A World of Others' Words: Cross-Cultural Perspectives on Intertextuality*. Malden, MA: Blackwell Publishing.

Bauman, R. and Briggs, C. L. (1990) Poetics and performance as critical perspectives on language and social life. *Annual Review of Anthropology* 19: 59–88.

Bernstein, B. B. (1972) A critique of the concept 'compensatory education.' In C. Cazden, V. P. John, and D. Hymes (eds.), *Functions of Language in the Classroom*. 135–51. New York: Teachers College Press.

Blommaert, J. (2005) *Discourse*. New York: Cambridge University Press.

Bourdieu, P. (1977) *Outline of a Theory of Practice*. New York: Cambridge University Press.

Bourdieu, P. (1984) *Distinction*. Cambridge, MA: Harvard University Press.

Bourdieu, P. (1990) *The Logic of Practice*. Cambridge: Polity.

Bourdieu, P. (1991) *Language and Symbolic Power*. Cambridge, MA: Harvard University Press.

Briggs, C. (1986) *Learning How to Ask*. New York: Cambridge University Press.

Burger, L. K. and Miller, P. J. (1999) Early talk about the past revisited: A comparison of working-class and middle-class families. *Journal of Child Language* 26(1): 133–62.

Cazden, C. and Hymes, D. (1996 [1978]) Narrative thinking and storytelling rights: A folklorist's clue to a critique of education. *Keystone Folklore* 22(1–2): 21–35.

Cho, G. E. and Miller, P. J. (2004) Personal storytelling: Working-class and middle-class mothers in comparative perspective. In M. Farr (ed.), *Ethnolinguistic Chicago: Language and Literacy in Chicago's Neighborhoods*. 79–101. Mahwah, NJ: Lawrence Erlbaum.

Cole, M. (1996) *Cultural Psychology: A Once and Future Discipline*. Cambridge, MA: Harvard University Press.

Corsaro, W. A. (1994) Discussion, debate and friendship: Peer discourse in nursery schools in the United States and Italy. *Sociology of Education* 67: 1–26.

Corsaro, W. A., Molinari, L., and Rosier, K. B. (2002) Zena and Carlotta: Transition narratives and early education in the United States and Italy. *Human Development* 45: 323–48.

De Fina, A., Schiffrin, D., and Bamberg, M. (2006) *Discourse and Identity*. New York: Cambridge University Press.

Dyson, A. H. (2003) *The Brothers and Sisters Learn to Write: Popular Literacies in Childhood and School Cultures*. New York: Teachers College Press.

Eisenberg, A. R. (1985) Learning to describe past experiences in conversation. *Discourse Processes* 8(2): 177–204.

Engel, S. (1995) *The Stories Children Tell: Making Sense of the Narrative of Childhood*. New York: W. H. Freeman.

Fivush, R. (1998) Gendered narratives: Elaboration, structure, and emotion in parent–child reminiscing across the preschool years. In C. P. Thompson, D. J. Herrmann, D. Bruce, J. D. Read, D. G. Payne, and M. P. Toglia (eds.), *Autobiographical Memory: Theoretical and Applied Perspectives*. 79–103. Mahwah, NJ: Lawrence Erlbaum.

Fung, H. (1999) Becoming a moral child: The socialization of shame among young Chinese children. *Ethos* 27(2): 180–209.

Fung, H. (2003) When culture meets psyche: Understanding the contextualized self through the life and dreams of an elderly Taiwanese woman. *Taiwan Journal of Anthropology* 1(2): 149–75.

Fung, H. and Chen, E. C.-H. (2001) Across time and beyond skin: Self and transgression in the everyday socialization of shame among Taiwanese preschool children. *Social Development: Special Issue* 10: 419–36.

Fung, H., Miller, P. J., and Lin, L.-C. (2004) Listening is active: Lessons from the narrative practices of Taiwanese families. In M. W. Pratt and B. H. Fiese (eds.), *Family Stories and the Life Course: Across Time and Generations*. 303–23. Mahwah, NJ: Lawrence Erlbaum.

Gal, S. (1987) Codeswitching and consciousness in the European periphery. *American Ethnologist* 14(4): 636–53.

Gal, S. (1989) Language and political economy. *Annual Review of Anthropology* 18: 145–67.

Gal, S. (1991) Between speech and silence: The problematics of research on language and gender. In M. di Leonardo (ed.), *Gender at the Crossroads of Knowledge: Feminist Anthropology in the Postmodern Era*. 175–203. Berkeley, CA: University of California Press.

Goffman, E. (1959) *The Presentation of Self in Everyday Life*. New York: Doubleday.

Goffman, E. (1979) Footing. *Semiotica* 25: 1–29.

Goodwin, M. H. (1990) *He-Said-She-Said: Talk as Social Organization Among Black Children*. Bloomington, IN: Indiana University Press.

Gumperz, J. J. (1982) *Discourse Strategies*. New York: Cambridge University Press.

Haight, W. (2002) *The Socialization of African-American Children at Church: A Sociocultural Perspective*. New York: Cambridge University Press.

Heath, S. B. (1982) What no bedtime story means. *Language in Society* 11(1): 49–76.

Heath, S. B. (1983) *Ways with Words*. Cambridge: Cambridge University Press.

Hill, J. (1995) The voices of Don Gabriel: Responsibility and self in a modern Mexicano narrative. In D. Tedlock and B. Mannheim (eds.), *The Dialogic Emergence of Culture*. 97–147. Chicago, IL: University of Illinois Press.

Hymes, D. (1996 [1980]) *Ethnography, Linguistics, Narrative Inequality: Toward an*

Understanding of Voice. London: Taylor and Francis.

Irvine, J. T. (1985) When talk isn't cheap: Language and political economy. *American Ethnologist* 16(2): 248–67.

Jacquemet, M. (2005) The registration interview: Restricting refugees' narrative performances. In M. Baynham and A. de Fina (eds.), *Dislocations/Relocations: Narratives of Displacement*. 197–220. Manchester, UK: St. Jerome Publishing.

Jakobson, R. (1957) *Shifters, Verbal Categories, and the Russian Verb*. Cambridge, MA: Department of Slavic Languages and Literatures, Harvard University.

Johnstone, B. (1997) Social characteristics and self-expression in narrative. *Journal of Narrative and Life History* 7(1–4): 315–20.

Keller-Cohen, D. and Dyer, J. (1997) Intertextualtiy and the narrative of personal experience. *Journal of Narrative and Life History* 7(1–4): 147–53.

Koven, M. (1998) Two languages in the self/the self in two languages: French-Portuguese bilinguals' verbal enactments and experiences of self in narrative discourse. *Ethos* 26(4): 410–55.

Koven, M. (2002) An analysis of speaker role inhabitance in narratives of personal experience. *Journal of Pragmatics* 34(2): 167–217.

Koven, M. (2007) *Selves in Two Languages: Bilingual Verbal Enactments of Identity in French and Portuguese*. Amsterdam, The Netherlands: John Benjamins.

Koven, M. (2011) Comparing stories told in sociolinguistic interviews and spontaneous conversation. *Language in Society* 40: 75–89.

Kulick, D. and Schieffelin, B. B. (2004) Language socialization. In A. Duranti (ed.), *A Companion to Linguistic Anthropology*. 349–68. Malden, MA: Blackwell.

Kusserow, A. (2004) *American Individualisms: Child Rearing and Social Class in Three Neighborhoods*. New York: Palgrave.

Labov, W. (1972) *Language in the Inner City: Studies in the Black English Vernacular*. Philadelphia, PA: University of Pennsylvania Press.

Labov, W. and Waletzky, J. (1967) Narrative analysis: Oral versions of personal experience. *Journal of Narrative and Life History* 7(1–4): 3–38.

Li, J. (2002) A cultural model of learning: Chinese 'heart and mind for wanting to learn.' *Journal of Cross-Cultural Psychology* 33: 248–69.

Lin, S. (2009) How listening is silenced: A monolingual Taiwanese elder constructs identity through television viewing. *Language in Society* 38(3): 311–37.

Lippi-Green, R. (1997) *English with an Accent: Language, Ideology, and Discrimination in the United States*. New York: Routledge.

Maryns, K. (2005) Displacement in asylum seekers' narratives. In M. Baynham and A. de Fina (eds.), *Dislocations/Relocations: Narratives of Displacement*. 174–96. Manchester, UK: St. Jerome Publishing.

Mehan, H. (1996) The construction of an LD student: A case study in the politics of representation. In M. Silverstein and G. Urban (eds.), *Natural Histories of Discourse*. 253–76. Chicago, IL: University of Chicago Press.

Michaels, S. (1981) 'Sharing time': Children's narrative styles and differential access to literacy. *Language in Society* 10: 423–42.

Michaels, S. (1991) The dismantling of narrative. In A. McCabe and C. Peterson (eds.), *Developing Narrative Structure*. 303–51. Hillsdale, NJ: Lawrence Erlbaum.

Michaels, S. (2005) Can the intellectual affordances of working-class storytelling be leveraged in school? *Human Development* 48: 136–45.

Michaels, S. and Cazden, C. (1986) Child collaboration as oral preparation for literacy. In B. B. Schieffelin and P.

Gilmore (eds.), *The Acquisition of Literacy*. 132–54. Norwood, NJ: Ablex.

Michaels, S. and Sohmer, R. (2000) Narratives and inscriptions: Cultural tools, power, and powerful sensemaking. In M. Kalantzis and B. Cope (eds.), *Multiliteracies: Literacy, Learning, and the Design of Social Futures*. 267–88. New York: Routledge.

Miller, P. J. (1982) *Amy, Wendy, and Beth: Learning Language in South Baltimore*. Austin, TX: University of Texas Press.

Miller, P. J. (1994) Narrative practices: Their role in socialization and self-construction. In U. Neisser and R. Fivush (eds.), *The Remembering Self: Construction and Accuracy in the Self-Narrative*. 158–79. New York: Cambridge University Press.

Miller, P. J., Cho, G. E., and Bracey, J. (2005) Working-class children's experience through the prism of personal storytelling. *Human Development* 48(3): 115–35.

Miller, P. J., Fung, H., and Koven, M. (2007) Narrative reverberations: How participation in narrative practices co-creates persons and cultures. In S. Kitayama and D. Cohen (eds.), *The Handbook of Cultural Psychology*. 595–614. New York: Guildford University Press.

Miller, P. J., Fung, H., Lin, S., Chen, E., and Boldt, B. (in press) *Personal Storytelling as a Medium of Socialization in Taiwanese and European-American Families: A Longitudinal Study of Alternate Developmental Pathways*. Monographs of the Society for Research in Child Development.

Miller, P. J., Fung, H., and Mintz, J. (1996) Self-construction through narrative practices: A Chinese and American comparison of early socialization. *Ethos* 24: 1–44.

Miller, P. J. and Goodnow, J. J. (1995) Cultural practices: Toward an integration of culture and development. In J. J. Goodnow, P. J. Miller, and F.

Kessel (eds.), *Cultural Practices as Contexts for Development: New Directions for Child and Adolescent Development, Vol. 67*. 5–16. San Francisco, CA: Jossey-Bass.

Miller, P. J., Hoogstra, L., Mintz, J., Fung, H., and Williams, K. (1993) Troubles in the garden and how they get resolved: A young child's transformation of his favorite story. In C. A. Nelson (ed.), *Memory and Affect in Development: The Minnesota Symposia on Child Psychology, Vol. 26*. 87–114. Hillsdale, NJ: Lawrence Erlbaum.

Miller, P. J. and Mehler, R. A. (1994) The power of personal storytelling in families and kindergartens. In A. H. Dyson and C. Genishi (eds.), *The Need for Story: Cultural Diversity in Classroom and Community*. 38–54. Urbana, IL, National Council of Teachers of English.

Miller, P. J. and Moore, B. B. (1989) Narrative conjunctions of caregiver and child: A comparative perspective on socialization through stories. *Ethos* 17(4): 428–49.

Miller, P. J., Potts, R., Fung, H., Hoogstra, L., and Mintz, J. (1990) Narrative practices and the social construction of self in childhood. *American Ethnologist* 17: 292–311.

Miller, P. J., Sandel, T. L., Liang, C.-H. and Fung, H. (2001) Narrating transgressions in Longwood: The discourses, meanings, and paradoxes of an American socializing practice. *Ethos* 29(2): 159–86.

Miller, P. J. and Sperry, L. L. (1987) The socialization of anger and aggression. *Merrill-Palmer Quarterly* 33(1): 1–31.

Miller, P. J. and Sperry, L. L. (1988) Early talk about the past: The origins of conversational stories of personal experience. *Journal of Child Language* 15: 293–315.

Miller, P. J., Wiley, A. R., Fung, H., and Liang, C.-H. (1997) Personal storytelling as a medium of socialization in Chinese and American families. *Child Development* 68: 1557–68.

Nelson, K. (ed.) (1989) *Narratives From the Crib*. Cambridge, MA: Harvard University Press.

Norrick, N. (1998) Retelling stories in spontaneous conversation. *Discourse Processes* 25(1): 75–97.

Ochs, E. and Capps, L. (1996) Narrating the self. *Annual Review of Anthropology* 25: 19–43.

Ochs, E. and Capps, L. (2001) (eds.) *Living Narrative: Creating Lives in Everyday Storytelling*. Cambridge, MA: Harvard University Press.

Ochs, E. and Taylor, C. E. (1992) Family narrative as political activity. *Discourse & Society* 3: 301–40.

Ochs, E. and Taylor, C. E. (1995) The 'father knows best' dynamic in dinnertime conversation. In K. Hall and M. Bucholtz (eds.), *Gender Articulated*. 97–120. New York: Routledge.

Philips, S. (2004) Language and social inequality. In A. Duranti (ed.), *A Companion to Linguistic Anthropology*. 474–95. Malden, MA: Blackwell.

Preece, A. (1987) The range of narrative forms conversationally produced by young children. *Journal of Child Language* 14: 353–73.

Roberts, C. and Campbell, S. (2005) Fitting stories into boxes: Rhetorical and textual constraints on candidates' performances in British job interviews. *Journal of Applied Linguistics* 2(1): 45–73.

Sandel, T. L. (2003) Linguistic capital in Taiwan: The KMT's Mandarin language policy and its perceived impact on language practices of bilingual Mandarin and Tai-gi speakers. *Language in Society* 32: 523–51.

Schiffrin, D. (1996) Narrative as self-portrait: Sociolinguistic constructions of identity. *Language in Society* 25: 167–203.

Scollon, R. and Scollon, S. B. K. (1981) *Narrative, Literacy, and Face in Interethnic Communication*. Norwood, NJ: Ablex.

Scribner, S. and Cole, M. (1981) *The Psychology of Literacy*. Cambridge, MA: Harvard University Press.

Shuman, A. (1986) *Storytelling Rights: The Uses of Oral and Written Texts by Urban Adolescents*. New York: Cambridge University Press.

Shweder, R. A., Goodnow, J. J., Hatano, G., LeVine, R. A., Markus, H., and Miller, P. J. (2006) The cultural psychology of development: One mind, many mentalities. In W. Damon and R. M. Lerner (eds.), *Handbook of Cultural Psychology: Vol. 1: Theoretical Models of Human Development*. 6th ed. 716–92. New York: Wiley.

Silverstein, M. (1993) Metapragmatic discourse and metapragmatic function. In J. Lucy (ed.), *Reflexive Language: Reported Speech and Metapragmatics*. 33–58. New York: Cambridge University Press.

Silverstein, M. (2005) Axes of evals. *Journal of Linguistic Anthropology* 15(1): 6–22.

Silverstein, M. and Urban, G. (eds.) (1996) *Natural Histories of Discourse*. Chicago, IL: University of Chicago Press.

Sperry, L. L. and Sperry, D. E. (1996) Early development of narrative skills. *Cognitive Development* 11: 443–65.

Sperry, L. L. and Sperry, D. E. (2000) Verbal and nonverbal contributions to early representation: Evidence from African American toddlers. In N. Budwig, I. C. Uzgiris, and J. V. Wertsch (eds.), *Communication: An Arena of Development*. 143–65. Norwood, NJ: Ablex.

Taylor, C. E. (1995) 'You think it was a fight?' Co-constructing (the struggle for) meaning, face, and family in everyday narrative activity. *Research on Language and Social Intersection* 28: 283–317.

Watson-Gegeo, K. A. and Boggs, S. T. (1977) From verbal play to talk story: The role of routines in speech events among Hawaiian children. In S. Ervin-Tripp and C. Mitchell-Kernan (eds.), *Child Discourse*. 67–90. New York: Academic Press.

Watson-Gegeo, K. A. and Gegeo, D. W. (1990) Shaping the mind and straightening out conflicts: The discourse of Kwara'ae family counseling. In K. A. Watson-Gegeo and G. M. White (eds.), *Disentangling: Conflict Discourse in Pacific Societies*. 161–213. Stanford, CA: Stanford University Press.

Wells, G. (1986) The language experience of five-year-old children at home and at school. In J. Cook-Gumperz (ed.), *The Social Construction of Literacy*. 69–93. Cambridge: Cambridge University Press.

Wertsch, J. V. (1991) *Voices of the Mind: A Sociocultural Approach to Mediated Action*. Cambridge, MA: Harvard University Press.

Wiley, A. R., Rose, A. J., Bruner, L. K., and Miller, P. J. (1998) Constructing autonomous selves through narrative practices: A comparative study of working-class and middle-class families. *Child Development* 69: 833–47.

Wolf, S. A. and Heath, S. B. (1992) *The Braid of Literature: Children's Worlds of Reading*. Cambridge, MA: Harvard University Press.

Woolard, K. A. (1985) Language variation and cultural hegemony: Toward an integration of sociolinguistic and social theory. *American Ethnologist* 12: 738–48.

Wortham, S. (1999) The heterogeneously distributed self. *Journal of Constructivist Psychology* 12(2): 153–72.

Wortham, S. (2000) Interactional positioning and narrative self-construction. *Narrative Inquiry* 10: 1-27.

Wortham, S. (2001) *Narratives in Action: A Strategy for Research and Analysis*. New York: Teachers' College Press.

Wortham, S. (2005) Socialization beyond the speech event: Intertextuality and interdiscursivity in social life. *Journal of Linguistic Anthropology* 15(1): 95–112.

Wortham, S. (2006) *Learning Identity: The Joint Emergence of Social Identification and Academic Learning*. New York: Cambridge University Press.

9 Language Socialization and Repetition

LESLIE C. MOORE

Introduction

Repetition plays a major role in the development of linguistic and sociocultural competence and in the transmission and transformation of cultural and linguistic practices. Thus, language socialization scholars have always been interested in repetition and several have made it an analytic focus, examining its organization and meaning in a wide range of communities, codes, and activity settings. This chapter discusses patterns in and insights from this work. Four practices of repetition that have been studied by language socialization scholars are examined – revoicing, prompting, guided repetition, and language play – followed by a discussion of repetition-related findings from studies conducted in contexts of second language socialization and religious socialization. The chapter concludes with a discussion of how attention to repetition in socializing interactions expands and enriches our understanding of the nature of communicative competence, its development over time and across texts and contexts, and the active and sometimes transformative role of the novice in socialization processes.

In the past 30 years, repetition in discourse has received considerable attention from anthropologists, linguists, and education and language development scholars (Bauman 2004; Becker 1995; Johnstone 1994; Tannen 2007). This work has demonstrated the centrality of repetition to language, learning, and the (re)production of culture and social organization. As Brown (2001: 223) observes, repetition is

> fundamental to the definition of all cultural objects: of the phoneme, of particular kinds of act, of chunks of ritual, art, music, and performance, all of which involve meaningful re-enactments in some sense. Repetition is a prerequisite for learning,

The Handbook of Language Socialization, First Edition. Edited by Alessandro Duranti, Elinor Ochs, and Bambi B. Schieffelin.
© 2014 John Wiley & Sons, Ltd. Published 2014 by John Wiley & Sons, Ltd.

providing the possibility of assimilating experience, committing it to memory, and thus also the basis for prediction. Repetition is pervasive in social life.

Research on repetition has made clear that no two productions of the 'same' language are in fact the same because each new production recontextualizes the language and thus changes the meaning (Bakhtin 1981; Tannen 2007). Speakers and writers reshape prior texts to fit new contexts using a variety of strategies, such as expansion, embedding, and rearrangement (Becker 1995). Thus, while repetition often contributes to the reproduction of linguistic and cultural practices, it can also be(come) transformative (Deleuze 1994).

Repetition is a resource that is always available and can be used to do many different things (Merritt 1994, 1998), and this affordance is significant for language socialization. Even before the research paradigm was formulated, Keenan (1977) shed light on children's use of repetition to accomplish a wide range of social acts and thereby progress in their pragmatic competence. Analysis of talk between two white middle-class siblings made visible the complex, creative, and strategic ways in which children used repetition to shape interactions despite limited linguistic resources. Keenan's findings challenged the then widely held view that very young children's repetitions of adult speech were mere 'imitations,' a view that reflected researchers' underestimation of children as communicators and repetition as a communicative resource.

The work of language socialization scholars is distinct from other socially and linguistically oriented research on repetition in that it combines a holistic, ethnographic perspective with longitudinal case study design and field-based collection and analysis of a substantial corpus of audio- or video-recorded naturalistic discourse (Garrett 2006). This methodology makes it possible to (1) document the role of repetition in the acquisition (or not) of particular cultural and linguistic practices and (2) understand the meanings of practices of repetition, the ideologies that inform them, and their relationship to other practices in the community (cf. Schieffelin and Ochs 1996). Language socialization scholars are concerned not only with how repetition supports language development but also with its role in the novice be(com)ing a culturally intelligible subject, if not always one who conforms completely to expectations (cf. Kulick and Schieffelin 2004).

The first language socialization studies showed that repetition was a significant feature of speech to and by young children in many different societies (Heath 1983; Ochs and Schieffelin 1984; Schieffelin and Ochs 1986). Moreover, these studies documented variation in the use and meaning of repetition across communities and over developmental time. Repetition figured prominently in Ochs and Schieffelin's (1984) comparison of caregiver behaviors in Kaluli, Samoan, and white middle-class American communities. White middle-class American caregivers often repeated and expanded the utterances of young children, accommodating their limited linguistic competence to treat them as conversational partners. In contrast, Kaluli and Samoan caregivers prompted young children to repeat to a third party unsimplified utterances produced by the caregiver, thereby obliging children to reproduce adult-like speech and to attend to the people and situation around them. Ochs and Schieffelin also contrasted the use of repetition in instances when a child produced unintelligible speech. White middle-class American caregivers were willing to guess at the child's meaning by offering expanded repetitions of their speech, a strategy that was consistent with larger cultural patterns of minimizing differences in competence by adapting the situation to the child. Samoan adults preferred to deal with unintelligible speech by a child by eliciting a repeat performance, which is consistent with the cultural norm that higher-ranking individuals do not accommodate lower-ranking ones. Ochs (1988: 137) also saw in the Samoan clarification strategy a reflection of local epistemology, the belief that 'the path to knowledge is through repeated exposure, i.e. listening and watching over and over.'

Practices of Repetition

Repetition gives rise to routines, and language socialization research 'places a premium on the study of routine' (Baquedano-López 2008: 596). Recurring and thus predictable patterns of linguistic and other behaviors provide novices with multiple opportunities to observe and engage in language use in socioculturally defined situations (Peters and Boggs 1986). Moreover, routines allow more competent members to adjust over time the scaffolding they provide for novices, who may assume increasingly active and self-regulating roles as they develop familiarity and facility with different aspects of the routine. These shifts in participation in routines over time provide language socialization researchers with insights into developmental trajectories, both actual and expected. Moreover, routines are of interest to researchers because they 'instantiate, in more or less explicit ways, important cultural categories, identities, ideologies, norms and values' (Howard 2009b: 342).

Some language socialization scholars have examined not only routine interactions but also 'practices of repetition.' That is, they have studied patterns in the use of repetition that are widely shared by members of the group and carry normative expectations about the way things should be done. This work seeks to understand how repetition is used in socializing interactions in particular communities, how these uses are socially organized, and how this organization shapes and is shaped by community members' beliefs, values, and ideologies (cf. Schieffelin and Ochs 1996). Here I discuss four practices of repetition – revoicing, prompting, guided repetition, and language play. These practices are used in a wide range of communities to socialize children and other novices into language and other forms of sociocultural knowledge, while novices may use practices of repetition for their own purposes as well.

Revoicing

Several language socialization researchers have examined revoicing, in which a speaker reproduces the voice of another (sometimes referred to as 'ventriloquizing') (Bakhtin 1981).[1] Revoicing may be grammatically or prosodically marked as a repetition of another's speech or it may not be marked, instead merging with the speaker's own voice. In revoicing, a speaker does not necessarily repeat another's speech accurately, and they may animate, rephrase, or invent speech in ways that express a particular stance toward the talk and/or the person who (is presented as having) produced it (Maybin 2006).

Several studies have examined revoicing in formal educational contexts, and most of this work examines teachers' revoicing of students' speech. In Japanese and Inuit elementary classrooms, Cook (1999) and Eriks-Brophy and Crago (2003) found that teachers revoiced students' utterances to provide affective support and to socialize children into cultural values of cooperation with and respect for others. He (2003) describes a less benevolent use of revoicing. She found that a Chinese heritage language teacher revoiced student contributions not to ratify but to appropriate them in order to maintain control of classroom interaction. The teacher's revoicings obscured the students' roles as authors and thereby ensured 'that interaction remains between two parties: the teacher and the class' (2003: 136). Baquedano-López, Solis, and Kattan (2005) use a Goffmanian framework (1981) to analyze revoicing in an elementary school science lesson. In this study the teacher used revoicing as a strategy to neutralize breaches in classroom discourse, reauthorizing and rekeying student utterances to mark them as relevant to the ongoing official classroom talk.

Some studies have looked at revoicing by children and adolescents. Heath (1998) found that adolescent members of a youth organization used revoicing to mock co-present peers and adults and that adult leaders accepted this practice. The leaders viewed such practice as an effective and creative (and physically nonviolent) means for resolving tensions, building collegiality, and developing communication skills, and thus consistent with the goals of the organization. Cekaite and Aronsson (2004) analyzed immigrant children's 'playful recyclings' of teachers' utterances as evidence of the children's developing metapragmatic awareness in a second language and their sensitivity to the social order in the classroom. Gordon (2007, 2009) interpreted a toddler's revoicings of her mother's words as the 'trying on of maternal identities.'

Revoicing has been examined as a strategy used by caregivers for showing children the 'right' way to speak. Clancy (1999) and Song (2009) describe Japanese and Korean mothers changing children's utterances in ways that make the speech socially and culturally more appropriate and position the child in relation to others in culturally preferred ways (see also Burdelski, this volume). Kaluli mothers did not permit older children to revoice young children's speech in ways that distorted it because they believed this would interfere with the child's language development (Schieffelin 1990). More analytic attention to the 'rules' of revoicing in different communities and settings will help us tease apart the universal and the culturally particular in this practice (cf. Schieffelin and Ochs 1996).

Prompting

Prompting is another pervasive practice of repetition and one that has been studied extensively by language socialization scholars. In prompting routines, community members give direct instruction in speech behavior by modeling utterances for children to repeat. The ways in which more competent members tell children exactly what to say have been examined in various cultural and linguistic communities, including Basotho (Demuth 1986), Kaluli (Schieffelin 1990), Samoan (Ochs 1988), Kwara'ae (Watson-Gegeo and Gegeo 1986), Inuit (Crago, Allen, and Pesco 1998), Marquesan (Riley 2001), Mayan (de León 1998, 2007; Reynolds 2008), Samoan (Ochs 1988), Wolof (Wills 1977), and English- and Spanish-speaking Americans (Bhimji 2001; Eisenberg 1986; Iwamura 1980; Miller 1982). These studies examine what kinds of speech are prompted, for what social purposes, and within what kinds of discursive and interactional structures. Researchers situate prompting routines in relation to other community practices, ideologies about child development, and larger cultural patterns in order to show how prompting routines socialize children into linguistic and sociocultural competencies valued by their communities (see Burdelski, this volume; de León, this volume).

Prompting routines are usually embedded in ongoing interaction rather than staged for purely pedagogical purposes (Schieffelin 1990). The speech that is to be repeated may be marked by intonation contour, an imperative verb of saying (such as 'say' in English), a pro-adverb (such as '*uri* ('in this manner') in Kwara'ae), or a contracted verb phrase (*dile* ('say it') in Spanish or ɛlema from ɛle sama ('like this say') in Kaluli). Prompting routines appear to be more often triadic than dyadic, with the modeled speech being designed as much if not more for the intended recipient of the prompted speech as for the novice (Ochs and Schieffelin 1984). Prompting practices provide insights into ideologies about the acquisition of linguistic resources because they highlight which kinds of speech community members believe are important and must be taught as opposed to being learned without explicit instruction. For example, Kaluli mothers used the ɛlema prompting routine to teach their toddlers assertive speech but not appeal. Both kinds of speech were important in Kaluli social life, but it was believed that appeal came naturally to children while assertiveness needed to be taught.

Prompting is an example of a widespread language socialization practice with multiple functions both within and across communities. Like the Kaluli, the Basotho (Demuth 1986) and white middle-class Midwestern mothers (Miller 1982) used prompting to teach children to be assertive. However, they also used prompting to teach politeness and to talk through children to a third person, often to deal with an awkward situation. Kwara'ae use prompting routines to distract the child, put the child to sleep, and to teach polite conversational style (Watson-Gegeo and Gegeo 1986). Mexicano adults used prompting to involve young children in teasing and the behaviors and social relationships that teasing sequences were meant to enforce and reinforce (Eisenberg 1986). Prompting routines prepared Kaluli and Samoan children for their eventual role as messenger, in which they are expected to deliver verbatim messages (Ochs and Schieffelin 1984), a role played by children in many communities (cf. de León 2007; Moore 1999, 2004b; Rabain-Jamin 1998; Reynolds 2008).

In many cases, prompting routines provide children with models of and practice in appropriate speech, and children reproduced the speech as expected. This is not always the case, however. Marquesan caregivers used prompting to elicit speech from children that would amuse others either because it was socially inappropriate or because the speech was likely to be phonologically ill-formed (Riley 2001). Prompting routines by Kaqchikel Mayan peer caregivers delivered inappropriate messages and conflict talk through younger children, cast as 'little parrots' who were seen as not competent enough to be held accountable for speech they repeated (Reynolds 2008). The little parrots sometimes resisted their assigned role and at other times exploited it to 'laugh at, challenge, and undermine different relations of power from a relative position of powerlessness' (Reynolds 2008: 100). In the Tzotzil Mayan community, young children used repetition to manipulate footing when conveying messages to adults, reframing and rekeying the speech of the message-sender to their own playful ends (de León 2007).

Guided repetition

Many researchers have documented teaching and learning practices that are highly routinized and characterized by repetitive language use that often does not entail much or any attention to or comprehension of the literal meaning (Ausberger 2004; Chick 1996; Fader 2008; Hornberger and Chick 2001; Kulick 1992; Moore 1999; Needham 2003; Watson-Gegeo 1992). Commonly referred to as rote learning or recitation, such practice was examined in detail by Moore (2004a) in her study of the language socialization of Fulbe children in Qur'anic and public schools in Maroua, Cameroon.

Out of this study came the concept of guided repetition, a reframing of rote learning as social practice (Moore 2006b, Rogoff et al. 2007). Guided repetition is similar to prompting in that more expert members explicitly model linguistic forms for imitation by less expert members. Guided repetition activities, however, are not embedded in ongoing interaction. Rather, they *are* the ongoing interaction, staged for pedagogical purposes, often spanning several encounters. Guided repetition activities have four phases – modeling, imitation, rehearsal, and performance – each of which entails particular rights and obligations for both expert and novice. In each phase the expert supervises the novice and may provide assistance, evaluation, and/or correction as the novice works toward mastery of the new skill.

Among the Fulbe, guided repetition may be dyadic or multiparty and was used to socialize novices into multiple modalities. Dyads were preferred in Qur'anic schools to ensure the accurate transmission of Qur'anic texts, while multiparty structures dominated in the public school, where collective instruction in French was believed to build community and provide children with useful models of what and what not to do with language. In both schooling traditions, guided repetition was used first to develop oral language skills on which literacy skills were later built. Teachers paid close, corrective attention to children's bodies at they reproduced French and Arabic texts because pointing, eye gaze, body positioning, and other forms of embodiment were believed to be both signs of and means for developing the desired skills, knowledge, and orientations that were associated with the two languages. In both schooling traditions, participants believed that guided repetition was the appropriate, effective, and right way to teach. This commitment to the practice was rooted in the shared belief that children in early and middle childhood were excellent and eager imitators and memorizers and that skills and knowledge (or bad habits and incorrect understandings) acquired in this period were more likely to take root and endure than those introduced at a later age.

Children were expected – or at least hoped – to learn very different ways of being in the world through Qur'anic and public schooling, and guided repetition was accomplished in culturally specific ways. Qur'anic schooling was meant to socialize children into reproductive competence in Arabic and into Fulbe and Muslim values of self-control, respect for religious authority and hierarchy, and submission to the word of God. The practice of guided repetition in Qur'anic schools emphasized strict discipline, the authority of the teacher, and reverent renderings of the text. Public schooling was supposed to create Cameroonian citizens, individuals who could speak and write and think in French as was required in the social, civic, and economic activities of a modern, democratic nation state. Guided repetition as practiced in the classroom was characterized by more peer interaction, liberal manipulation of the text, and greater fluidity in the roles of expert and novice.

Guided repetition recently emerged as a new practice for socializing Fulbe children into the telling of folktales, an innovation that was contemporaneous with the Fulbe's increased participation in schooling (Moore 2006a). Traditionally, children learned folktales by observing multiple performances by experts, but expert tellers had begun explicitly teaching folktales to children through guided repetition, and children were using the practice amongst themselves to teach and learn folktales. Fulbe women, concerned that children were no longer immersed in folktales as in the past, may have appropriated a contemporary and effective institutional practice for teaching other kinds of oral texts to prevent the loss of the folktale tradition. The innovative use of guided repetition for teaching and learning folktales may have also reflected shifting beliefs and expectations among adults and children regarding the role of children in language-centered activities. In guided repetition interactions with adults and with their peers, younger children took more vocal, active roles in an activity in which formerly they had played a more passive role as recipient until puberty or later. Thus, the folktale tradition was being both sustained and transformed by guided repetition, as children assumed new roles and created new narratives.

Language play

Language play is the use of rhyme, rhythm, alliteration, and other repeating patterns in language to amuse, delight, dispute, and confound. The role of repetition in children's exploration, practice, and manipulation of language in verbal play has been studied by scholars in a wide range of communities, including African American (Goodwin 1990), Caribbean (Garrett 2005; Paugh 2005), Euro-American (Keenan 1977; Ochs and Schieffelin 1983), Italian (Fasulo, Liberati, and Pontecorvo

2002), Kaluli (Schieffelin 1990), Mayan (de León 2007; Reynolds 2007), Northern Thai (Howard 2009b), Polynesian (Riley 2001), and immigrants to Sweden (Aronsson, this volume; Cekaite and Aronsson 2006). This work illuminates language play as a resource for the development of communicative competence and for the negotiation of the social order in families and peer groups.

Several of these studies illustrate the ways in which language play supports language development by making particular linguistic features salient for the novice and by providing opportunities for practice of patterns of phonology, morphology, syntax, discourse, and pragmatics. Thus, children's practices of language play can be understood as an occasion to develop and display metalinguistic awareness and, more particularly, awareness of the repeating patterns that constitute various genres and types of talk. Children's play with language forms found in the adult world is not just about acquisition of these forms, however, but also children's appropriation and transformation of them for their own purposes (Goodwin and Kyratzis 2007). Thus, language play is examined as a site where children can engage with the cultural and linguistic practices of their community in ways that are creative and sometimes subversive.

In rural Mexico, young Tzotzil Mayan siblings in family settings play with the repetitive structures characteristic of Mayan conversation (de León 2007). This observation builds on Brown's (1998) study of the impact of the Mayan conversational pattern known as dialogic repetition on the early language development of Tzeltal Mayan children. Even very young Mayan children displayed competence in this conversational structure, in which each speaker repeats all or much of the prior speaker's turn.[2] Tzotzil toddlers' playful engagement with this pattern of parallelism reflected and contributed to their metalinguistic awareness (de León 2007). Analysis of two siblings' greeting games and their playful disruption of the preferred structure of conversation indicates that even very young children were able to manipulate the repetitive structures of their language community for their own ends.

Language play in Kam Muang (Thailand) mixed-age peer groups demonstrates how the repetitive, scripted, and predictable nature of children's language play enables a younger child to join in the activities of older and more competent children (Howard 2009b). Moreover, Kam Muang children were able to use the activity as a 'jumping-off point,' tweaking the repetitive structure to achieve a humorous breach of expectations to the delight of all. Such creative violations of the genre demonstrate the child's awareness of and emergent skill in the improvisational aesthetic so highly valued in the peer group.

Mixed-age peer groups in an African American community made skilled and creative use of repetition in talk, called 'format tying' (Goodwin 1990). Boys and girls used repetition to challenge, argue with, and negatively assess others, findings that challenged the widely held view that repetition was primarily a linguistic resource for doing alignment and agreement. Children use repetition not only in talk but also in gesture to construct assessments – and thus norms, identities, and relationships – within peer-group interactions (Goodwin 2007).

There is variation across communities, codes, and settings with respect to which kinds of language play are allowed. Kaluli mothers forbade language play that had bird-like qualities such as high pitch and melodic descent because such 'bird talk' interfered with language development and created a dangerous association between children and birds (Schieffelin 1990). Fulbe children studying at home with their mothers were allowed to play with Qur'anic verses by stretching sounds and exaggerating rhythms, whereas such behaviors would have been punished by the teacher at Qur'anic school (Moore 2004a). Mothers affirmed the teacher's obligation and right to punish such behavior, but they also asserted that, in playing with the sounds of the Qur'an, children made it their own. Language play often entails violation of the 'rules' of linguistic and sociocultural behavior, and language socialization research illuminates how language play is organized and constrained by ideologies about language, learning, and childhood.

Repetition in Context

Recent work on repetition has focused on language socialization in second language settings and religious communities. Not surprisingly, there is overlap, for religious education often entails socialization into a second language. The following section discusses insights into socialization in these contexts that attention to repetition has yielded.

Second language socialization

Researchers have examined repetition in second language socialization in many countries, including Cameroon (Moore 1999, 2004a, 2006b, 2008b), Canada (Duff, Wong, and Early 2002), Hungary (Duff 1995), Japan (Cook 2006; Meacham 2007), Mexico (Ausberger 2004), Papua New Guinea (Kulick and Stroud 1993), Thailand (Howard 2003, 2009a), the Solomon Islands (Watson-Gegeo and Gegeo 1992), and the United States (Fader 2001; Kanagy 1999; Ohta 1999). Repetition plays an important role in second language learning, learning in a second language, and the development of second language learning communities and learner identities.

Several scholars have discussed the importance of repetition for learners with limited linguistic resources in the second language, as it provides opportunities to observe and practice second language forms (Cekaite and Aronsson 2004, 2006; Pallotti 2002; Rydland and Aukrust 2005). Moreover, children learning a second language use repetition of themselves and others to gain access to and participate in play, conversation, and second language learning activities. Repetition within a lesson helped to build cohesion across a stretch of whole-class talk in an English-immersion class in Hungary (Duff 2000). Repetition across lessons also helped to build community, as class members refer back to talk and text from previous sessions. In Sweden, immigrant children's alliteration, sound repetitions, and other parallelisms in second language play at school extended play and created opportunities for collaborative repetitions and variations on a pattern, what the authors called 'peer-run language lessons' (Cekaite and Aronsson 2006: 187).

Repetition is not always a good thing in second language contexts. Duff (2000) demonstrates that too much repetition of a linguistic form undermines community building in an American foreign language classroom. Many researchers have documented the use of highly repetitive language and interactional structures in under-resourced second language classrooms, and they have examined how such practices hinder children's development of second language competence by providing few opportunities for children to use the language for their own expressive purposes (Howard 2008). Poole (1992) found that American English-as-a-second-language teachers used many of the same practices of repetition that characterize Baby Talk in speaking with their adult students, and such practices were not always well received.

A language socialization perspective on repetition in the second language classroom reveals that practices of repetition often reflect larger discourses and create particular kinds of second language users. Meacham (2007) compared the 'replaying practices' (repetitions of lexical items and syntactic formats) of teachers and students in English-as-a-foreign-language classrooms in two Japanese high schools. She found that students at the technical high school were positioned as 'defensive receivers' of English through simple, repetitive, highly routinized patterns in which English forms were produced with Japanese phonology. In contrast, students at the highly ranked liberal arts high school were positioned as 'active tellers' who were trained to use English to explain Japanese culture to native English speakers, a participant framework that required them to approximate the pronunciation of their imagined audience. Meacham argues that repetition practices in these two schools were linked to broader discourses about the role of English in Japanese society and the communicative roles of different kinds of Japanese citizens.

Local and national language practices and identities are in contact and sometimes in conflict in the second language classroom, and repetition can be used to mediate differences (Howard 2009a). In a first-grade classroom in Northern Thailand, where children who speak Kam Muang must learn (in) Standard Thai, children were socialized into the linguistic and bodily practices for displaying respect through repetitive correction sequences (Howard, this volume). The teacher and children created in these ritual exchanges a local version of polite and respectful Thai citizenship. Children were allowed to speak their first language so long as they used Standard Thai politeness particles, which the correction routines had made into emblematic markers of speaking the official language of the classroom and the nation.

Religious socialization

Johnstone (1987) notes that repetition is particularly prevalent in two kinds of language: child-directed speech and ritual speech. And, indeed, practices of repetition figure prominently in the socialization of children and other novices into religious texts and their associated activities, identities, and ideologies, as shown by work among Latino Catholics (Baquedano-López 1998, 2008), Spanish Gitano

Evangelicals (Poveda, Cano, and Palomares-Valera 2005), Hasidic Jews (Fader 2006, 2008, 2009), American Muslims (Aminy 2004), Fulbe Muslims (Moore 2004a, 2008a), and Samoan American Protestants (Duranti, Ochs, and Ta'ase 1995; Duranti and Reynolds 2000).

In her study of *doctrina* classes in a Latino community, Baquedano-López (2008) explored the different processes through which the Act of Contrition was constructed as a text that was sacred, shared, and relevant to the children's lives. Choral readings led by the teacher in both small groups and as a whole class required children to focus their attention and synchronize their actions as they committed the text to memory, creating a collective ritual of remembering. *Doctrina* lessons also included small-group work that was intended to promote children's understanding of the text. In these activities the teacher recited the Act of Contrition with the children, stopping after each line to reframe it grammatically, prosodically, and conceptually in ways that made the text more comprehensible for the children, more clearly relevant to their lives, and thus a text that 'matters to them in the present moment and as a blueprint for future action' (2008: 597).

Multiple patterns in the use of repetition also characterized language and literacy socialization practices in a girls' school for Hasidic Jews in Brooklyn (Fader 2008, 2009, this volume). Lessons on *loshn koydesh* or 'holy language' texts (a mixture of Ancient Hebrew and Aramaic that is the language of the Torah, its commentaries, and prayer) emphasized accurate and fluent reproduction of the text, while no explanation of the literal meaning of texts was provided. Literacy instruction in Yiddish and English had a 'rote, embodied aspect' similar to the holy language lessons. Lessons were highly repetitive, and writing instruction emphasized Hasidic values of femininity: neatness, following directions, and disciplining the body. In this community, where literacy is seen as transformative, secular English literacy had been transformed to serve Hasidic Jewish socialization goals.

Oral recitation lessons in these classrooms differed from literacy lessons in that they stressed 'the performance of earnest intention,' manifested primarily through loud and clear articulation in the choral recitation of prayers (Fader 2008: 626). Such performance was believed in this community to be not a reflection of proper religious feeling but rather a means for developing it. Such repetitive ritual practice was a crucial part of training the bodies and minds of children not only to conform to God's commandments but also to commit to them.

A similar pattern of practice and belief also characterized the Maroua Fulbe (Moore 2006b, 2008a). Guided repetition was used to teach children to recite, memorize, read, and write the Qur'an. The schooling experience was intended to teach the child not only to respect God's Word and those knowledgeable therein but also to develop in him good moral character and a deep and enduring emotional response to the sounds of the Qur'an. A child did not need to comprehend the literal meaning of the text, for the accurate and fluent reproduction of its sounds and signs constituted the fundamental layer of understanding of and commitment to the text, the foundation on which all further moral, spiritual, and intellectual development should be built.

All three of these studies note that highly repetitive educational activities prepared children intellectually, emotionally, and corporally for participation in other religious practices that were important in the community. *Doctrina* classes were considered direct preparation for a child's first confession and first communion, and teachers trained children in the textual knowledge and bodily comportment they needed to partake of these two sacraments for the first time and for a lifetime. Qur'anic schooling trained children in ways of producing and relating to Arabic texts that were essential to competent participation in prayer, sermons, religious ceremonies, and healing practices. Lessons in *loshn koydesh* oral recitation and literacy prepared girls to be pious Jewish women who prayed loudly and clearly. In all three communities, the mastery of sacred texts was essential to religious competence and community membership. The process of learning these texts was one of ritualization that fostered a sense of connection with the text and with co-religionists. Once a text was mastered, children were expected to recontextualize it many times and in many ways, thereby infusing faith and morality into their daily lives.

Conclusions

As Tannen (2007: 56) states, 'repetition is at the heart of language,' and much of what we do with language entails recycling language we have heard or read before. Thus, it is no surprise that repetition is at the heart of language socialization, too. Language socialization research that gives analytic attention to repetition has made clear that repetition is central to the formation and the performance of the competent and creative speaker/member. Practices of repetition such as revoicing, prompting, guided repetition, and language play are part of socializing interactions all over the world. Such practices facilitate 'accurate acquisition of canonical linguistic and cultural practices by children and novices' (Howard 2009b: 341), as well as the development of skill in adapting these practices that is crucial to functioning and being recognizable as competent community members.

Repetition is an important resource for accomplishing social action, and thus attention to repetition helps us to appreciate the active role played by the novice in his or her own socialization. Each repetition is something new (Deleuze 1994), and the act of repeating can be transformative. Several of the studies discussed here use a Goffmanian framework to decompose speaker roles, and this work shows that even young children are able to use repetition in complex ways to accomplish their own social aims in talk with peers, siblings, parents, and teachers. Having acquired canonical, traditional, or authoritative language forms, novices are able to diverge from them in creative and possibly innovative ways. An important part of becoming communicatively competent is learning how to manipulate the repetitive patterns of language in ways that are both original and intelligible, as well as when and where one may do so, to what benefit, and at what risk.

Several of the studies discussed here demonstrate the intertextuality of language socialization, and further exploration of this dimension will enrich the field (cf. Poveda, Cano, and Palomares-Valera 2005; Wortham 2005). In religious socialization, children participate in the repetition of sacred texts not only in school contexts but also in many other kinds of speech event. Language play in peer groups gives rise to language forms that children bring into play in later encounters and other contexts. The challenge for language socialization researchers is to illuminate this interconnectedness by linking events, texts, and language forms across settings and over time to see how they shape the developmental trajectories of individuals and the social groups to which they belong. More attention to repetition is essential to expand and deepen our understanding of the intertextual nature of communicative competence and the processes through which it is developed.

Looking at repetition through the lens of language socialization increases our understanding of the complexity and rich variation in how repetition is used in discourse and what it means across different cultures, communities, codes, and activities. As the work on revoicing, prompting, and guided repetition shows, attention to repetition in caregivers' speech to and for children gives us insights into the culture because such speech highlights (implicitly or explicitly) identities, acts, texts, stances, and/or relationships that are valued in the community. Language socialization research shows how the use of repetition with and by children and other novices varies across communities and is shaped by cultural values and beliefs about children, language, learning, and the social order. The paradigm will benefit from more attention to how practices of repetition are organized and how these practices shift over time as individuals develop and communities change. We may find that patterns of repetition vary across time and communities in systematic ways, with particular practices regularly co-occurring with each other and with particular goals, values, identities, and social-ecological conditions. Through rich ethnographic accounts and comparisons across individuals, communities, time, and space, language socialization research has and will continue to illuminate the role of repetition in the construction of meaning, selfhood, and social groups.

NOTES

1 I use the term revoicing to refer to reproductions of others' speech that are not required by the interactional structure (as in prompting and guided repetition, as well as in the phenomenon often referred to as language brokering) and do not make use of rhythm, alliteration, or other forms of parallelism (as in language play).

2 Brown (1998) also found that the productive vocabulary of young Mayan children consisted predominantly of verb roots (in contrast to the noun-dominated vocabularies of children learning European languages). She attributed this developmental trend to dialogic repetition in adult conversation, which gave rise to utterances in which the verb was highlighted.

REFERENCES

Aminy, M. (2004) *Constructing the Moral Identity: Literacy Practices and Language Socialization in a Muslim Community.* Doctoral Dissertation. Berkeley, CA: University of California, Berkeley.

Ausberger, D. (2004) *Language Socialization and Shift in an Isthmus Zapotec Community of Mexico.* Doctoral dissertation. Philadelphia, PA: University of Pennsylvania.

Bakhtin, M. M. (1981) *The Dialogic Imagination: Four Essays.* Austin, TX: University of Texas Press.

Baquedano-López, P., Solís, J., and Kattan, S. (2005) Adaptation: The language of classroom learning. *Linguistics and Education* 6: 1–26.

Baquedano-López, P. (1998) *Language Socialization of Mexican Children in a Los Angeles Catholic Parish.* Doctoral Dissertation. Los Angeles, CA: University of California, Los Angeles.

Baquedano-López, P. (2008) The pragmatics of reading prayers: Learning the Act of Contrition in Spanish-based religious education classes (doctrina). *Text & Talk* 28(5): 582–602.

Bauman, R. (2004) *A World of Others' Words: Cross-Cultural Perspectives on Intertextuality.* Malden, MA: Wiley.

Becker, A. L. (1995) *Beyond Translation: Essays Toward a Modern Philology.* Ann Arbor, MI: University of Michigan Press.

Bhimji, F. (2001) *'Dile Family': Socializing language skills with directives in three Mexican families.* Doctoral Dissertation. Los Angeles, CA: University of California, Los Angeles.

Brown, P. (1998) Conversational structure and language acquisition: The role of repetition in Tzeltal. *Journal of Linguistic Anthropology* 8: 197–221.

Brown, P. (2001) Repetition. In A. Duranti (ed.), *Key Terms in Language and Culture.* 219–22. Oxford: Blackwell.

Cekaite, A. and Aronsson, K. (2004) Repetition and joking in children's second language conversations: Playful recyclings in an immersion classroom. *Discourse Studies* 6: 373–92.

Cekaite, A. and Aronsson, K. (2006) Language play, a collaborative resource in children's L2 learning. *Applied Linguistics* 26: 169–91.

Chick, J. K. (1996) Safe-talk: Collusion in apartheid education. In H. Coleman (ed.), *Society and the Language Classroom.* 21–39. Cambridge: Cambridge University Press.

Clancy, P. M. (1999) The socialization of affect in Japanese mother–child conversation. *Journal of Pragmatics* 31: 1397–421.

Cook, H. M. (1999) Language socialization in Japanese elementary schools: Attentive listening and reaction turns. *Journal of Pragmatics* 31: 1443–65.

Cook, H. M. (2006) Joint construction of folk beliefs by JFL learners and Japanese host families. In M. A. DuFon and E. Churchill (eds.), *Language Learners in Study Abroad Contexts.* 120–50. Clevedon, UK: Multilingual Matters.

Crago, M., Allen, S. E. M., and Pesco, D. (1998) Issues of complexity in Inuktitut and English child-directed speech. Paper presented at the Twenty-ninth Annual Child Language Research Forum. Stanford University, Palo Alto, CA.

de León, L. (1998) The emergent participant: Interactive patterns in the socialization of Tzotzil (Mayan) infants. *Journal of Linguistic Anthropology* 8: 131–61.

de León, L. (2007) Parallelism, metalinguistic play, and the interactive emergence of Zinacantec Mayan siblings' culture. *Research on Language and Social Interaction* 40: 405–36.

Deleuze, G. (1994) *Difference and Repetition*. New York: Columbia University Press.

Demuth, K. (1986) Prompting routines in the language socialization of Basotho children. In B. B. Schieffelin and E. Ochs (eds.), *Language Socialization Across Cultures*. 51–79. New York: Cambridge University Press.

Duff, P. (1995) An ethnography of communication in immersion classrooms in Hungary. *TESOL Quarterly* 29: 505–37.

Duff, P. (2000) Repetition in foreign language classroom interaction. In J. K. Hall and L. S. Verplaetse (eds.), *Second and Foreign Language Learning Through Classroom Interaction*. 139–59. Mahwah, NJ: Lawrence Erlbaum.

Duff, P., Wong, P., and Early, M. (2002) Learning language for work and life: The linguistic socialization of immigrant Canadians seeking careers in health care. *The Modern Language Journal* 86: 397–422.

Duranti, A., Ochs, E., and Ta`ase, Elia K. (1995) Change and tradition in literacy instruction in a Samoan American community. *Educational Foundations* 9: 57–74.

Duranti, A. and Reynolds, J. F. (2000) Phonological and cultural innovations in the speech of Samoans in Southern California. *Estudios de Sociolingüística* 1: 93–110.

Eisenberg, A. R. (1986) Teasing: Verbal play in two Mexicano homes. In B. B. Schieffelin and E. Ochs (eds.), *Language Socialization Across Cultures*. 182–98. New York: Cambridge University Press.

Eriks-Brophy, A. and Crago, M. (2003) Variation in instructional discourse features: Cultural or linguistic? Evidence from Inuit and non-Inuit teachers of Nunavik. *Anthropology and Education Quarterly* 34: 396–419.

Fader, A. (2001) Literacy, bilingualism, and gender in a Hasidic community. *Linguistics and Education* 12: 261–83.

Fader, A. (2006) Learning faith: Language socialization in a Hasidic community. *Language in Society* 35: 207–29.

Fader, A. (2008) Reading Jewish signs: Multilingual literacy socialization with Hasidic women and girls in New York. *Text & Talk* 28(5): 621–41.

Fader, A. (2009) *Mitzvah Girls: Bringing Up the Next Generation of Hasidic Jews in Brooklyn*. Princeton, NJ: Princeton University Press.

Fasulo, A., Liberati, V., and Pontecorvo, C. (2002) Language games in the strict sense of the term. Children's poetics and conversation. In S. Blum-Kulka and C. Snow (eds.), *Talking to Adults*. 209–37. Hillsdale, NJ: Lawrence Erlbaum.

Garrett, P. B. (2005) What a language is good for: Language socialization, language shift, and the persistence of code-specific genres in St. Lucia. *Language in Society* 34: 327–61.

Garrett, P. B. (2006) Language socialization. In *Encyclopedia of Language and Linguistics*. 2nd ed. 604–13. Oxford: Elsevier.

Goffman, E. (1981) *Forms of Talk*. Philadelphia, PA: University of Pennsylvania Press.

Goodwin, M. H. (1990) *He-Said-She-Said: Talk as Social Organization among Black Children*. Bloomington, IN: Indiana University Press.

Goodwin, M. H. (2007) Participation and embodied action in preadolescent girls' assessment activity. *Research on Language and Social Interaction* 40: 353–73.

Goodwin, M. H. and Kyratzis, A. (2007) Children socializing children: Practices for negotiating the social order among peers. *Research on Language and Social Interaction* 40: 279–89.

Gordon, C. (2007) Repetition and identity experimentation: One child's use of repetition as a resource for 'trying on' maternal identities. In M. Bamberg, A. de Fina, and D. Schiffrin (eds.), *Selves and Identities in Narrative and Discourse*. 133–58. Amsterdam, The Netherlands: John Benjamins.

Gordon, C. (2009) *Making Meanings, Creating Family: Intertextuality and*

Framing in Family Interaction. Oxford: Oxford University Press.

He, A. W. (2003) Novices and their speech roles in Chinese heritage language classes. In R. Bayley and S. R. Schecter (eds.), *Language Socialization in Bilingual and Multilingual Societies* 128–46. Clevedon, UK: Multilingual Matters.

Heath, S. B. (1983) *Ways with Words: Language, Life, and Work in Communities and Classrooms*. New York: Cambridge University Press.

Heath, S. B. (1998) Working through language. In S. M. Hoyle and C. T. Adger (eds.), *Kids Talk: Strategic Language Use in Later Childhood*. 217–40. New York: Oxford University Press.

Hornberger, N. and Chick, J. K. (2001) Co-constructing safetime in Peruvian and South African classrooms. In M. Heller and M. Martin-Jones (eds.), *Voices of Authority: Education and Linguistic Difference*. 31–55. Westport, CT: Ablex.

Howard, K. (2003) *Language Socialization in a Northern Thai Bilingual Community*. Doctoral Dissertation. Los Angeles, CA: University of California, Los Angeles.

Howard, K. (2008) Language socialization and language shift among school-aged children. In P. A. Duff and N. H. Hornberger (eds.), *Encyclopedia of Language and Education, Vol. 8: Language Socialization*. 2nd ed. 187–200. New York: Kluwer Academic Publishers.

Howard, K. (2009a) 'When meeting Mrs. Teacher each time we should show respect': Standardizing respect in a Northern Thai classroom. *Linguistics and Education* 20: 254–72.

Howard, K. (2009b) Breaking in and spinning out: Repetition and de-calibration in Thai children's play genres. *Language in Society* 38: 339–63.

Iwamura, S. G. (1980) *The Verbal Games of Pre-School Children*. New York: St. Martin's Press.

Johnstone, B. (1987) An introduction. *Perspectives on Repetition. Text* 7: 205–14.

Johnstone, B. (1994) *Repetition in Discourse: Interdisciplinary Perspectives*. Norwood, NJ: Ablex.

Kanagy, R. (1999) Interactional routines as mechanisms for L2 acquisition and socialization in an immersion context. *Journal of Pragmatics* 31: 1467–92.

Keenan, E. O. (1977) Making it last: Repetition in children's discourse. In S. Ervin-Tripp and C. Mitchell-Kernan (eds.), *Child Discourse*. 125–38. New York: Academic Press.

Kulick, D. (1992) *Language Shift and Cultural Reproduction: Socialization, Self, and Syncretism in a Papua New Guinean Village*. New York: Cambridge University Press.

Kulick, D. and Stroud, C. (1993) Conceptions and uses of literacy in a Papua New Guinea village. In Brian Street (ed.), *Cross-Cultural Approaches to Literacy*. 30–61. Cambridge, MA: Cambridge University Press.

Kulick, D. and Schieffelin, B. (2004) Language socialization. In A. Duranti (ed.), *A Companion to Linguistic Anthropology*. 349–68. Oxford: Blackwell.

Maybin, J. (2006) *Children's Voices: Talk, Knowledge, and Identity*. New York: Palgrave MacMillan.

Meacham, S. (2007) The educational soundscape: Participation and perception in Japanese high school English lessons *Mind, Culture, and Activity* 14: 196–215.

Merritt, M. (1994) Repetition in situated discourse: Exploring its forms and functions. In B. Johnstone (ed.), *Repetition in Discourse: Interdisciplinary Perspectives*. 23–36. Norwood, NJ: Ablex.

Merritt, M. (1998) Of ritual matters to master: Structure and improvisation in language development at primary school. In S. M. Hoyle and C. T. Adger (eds.), *Kids Talk: Strategic Language Use in Later Childhood*. 134–50. New York: Oxford University Press.

Miller, P. J. (1982) *Amy, Wendy, and Beth: Learning Language in South Baltimore*. Austin, TX: University of Texas Press.

Moore, L. C. (1999) Language socialization research and French language education in Africa: A Cameroonian case study. *The Canadian Modern Language Review* 52: 329–50.

Moore, L. C. (2004a) *Learning languages by heart: Language socialization in a Fulbe community (Maroua, Cameroon)*. Doctoral Dissertation. Los Angeles, CA: University of California, Los Angeles.

Moore, L. C. (2004b) Second language acquisition and use in the Mandara Mountains. In G. Echu and S. G. Obeng (eds.), *Africa Meets Europe: Language Contact in West Africa*. 131–48. New York: Nova Science.

Moore, L. C. (2006a) Changes in folktale socialization in a Fulbe community. *Studies in African Linguistics, Supplement* 11: 176–87.

Moore, L. C. (2006b) Learning by heart in Qur'anic and public schools in northern Cameroon. *Social Analysis: The International Journal of Cultural and Social Practice* 50: 109–26.

Moore, L. C. (2008a) Body, text, and talk in Maroua Fulbe Qur'anic schooling. *Text & Talk, Special Issue: The Spirit of Reading: Practices of Reading Sacred Texts* 28: 643–65.

Moore, L. C. (2008b) Language socialization and second/foreign language and multilingual education in non-Western settings. In P. A. Duff and N. H. Hornberger (eds.), *Encyclopedia of Language and Education, Vol. 8: Language Socialization*. 175–85. Norwell, MA: Kluwer Academic Publishers.

Needham, S. (2003) 'This is active learning': Theories of language, learning, and social relations in the transmission of Khmer literacy. *Anthropology and Education Quarterly* 34: 27–49.

Ochs, E. and Schieffelin, B. B. (1983) *Acquiring Conversational Competence*. Boston, MA: Routledge and Kegan Paul.

Ochs, E. and Schieffelin, B. B. (1984) Language acquisition and socialization: Three developmental stories and their implications. In R. A. Shweder and Robert A. LeVine (eds.), *Culture Theory: Essays on Mind, Self, and Emotion*. 276–313. Cambridge: Cambridge University Press.

Ochs, E. (1988) *Culture and Language Development: Language Acquisition and Language Socialization in a Samoan Village*. New York: Cambridge University Press.

Ohta, A. (1999) Interactional routines and the socialization of interactional style in adult learners of Japanese. *Journal of Pragmatics* 31: 1493–512.

Pallotti, G. (2002) Borrowing words: Appropriations in child second-language discourse. In J. Leather and J. van Dam (eds.), *The Ecology of Language Acquisition*. 183–203. Amsterdam, The Netherlands: Kluwer Academic Publishers.

Paugh, A. (2005) Multilingual play: Children's code-switching, role play, and agency in Dominica, West Indies. *Language in Society* 34: 63–86.

Peters, A. M. and Boggs, S. T. (1986) Interactional routines as cultural influences on language acquisition. In B. B. Schieffelin and E. Ochs (eds.), *Language Socialization Across Cultures*. 80–96. New York: Cambridge University Press.

Poole, D. (1992) Language socialization in the second language classroom. *Language Learning* 42: 593–616.

Poveda, D., Cano, A., and Palomares-Valera, M. (2005) Religious genres, entextualization and literacy in Gitano children. *Language in Society* 34: 87–115.

Rabain-Jamin, J. (1998) Polyadic language socialization: The case of toddlers in Senegal. *Discourse Processes* 26: 43–65.

Reynolds, J. (2007) 'Buenos días/((military salute))': The natural history of a coined insult. *Research on Language and Social Interaction* 40: 437–65.

Reynolds, J. (2008) Socializing *puros pericos* (little parrots): The negotiation of respect and responsibility in Antonero Mayan sibling and peer networks. *Journal of Linguistic Anthropology* 18: 82–107.

Riley, K. C. (2001) *The Emergence of Dialogic Identities: Transforming Heteroglossia in the Marquesas.* Doctoral Dissertation. New York: City University of New York.

Rogoff, B., Moore, L. C., Najafi, B., Dexter, A., Correa-Chávez, M., and Solís, J. (2007) Children's development of cultural repertoires through participation in everyday routines and practices. In J. Grusec and P. Hastings (eds.), *Handbook of Socialization.* 490–515. New York: Guilford Press.

Rydland, V. and Aukrust, V. G. (2005) Lexical repetition in second language learners' peer play interaction. *Language Learning* 55: 229–74.

Schieffelin, B. B. and Ochs, E. (1986) *Language Socialization Across Cultures.* New York: Cambridge University Press.

Schieffelin, B. B. and Ochs, E. (1996) The microgenesis of competence: Methodology in language socialization. In D. I. Slobin, J. Gerhardt, A. Kyratzis, and J. Guo (eds.), *Social Interaction, Social Context, and Language.* 251–64. Mahwah, NJ: Lawrence Erlbaum.

Schieffelin, B. B. (1990) *The Give and Take of Everyday Life: Language Socialization of Kaluli Children.* New York: Cambridge University Press.

Song, J. (2009) Bilingual creativity and self-negotiation: Korean American children's language socialization into Korean address terms. In A. Reyes and A. Lo (eds.), *Beyond Yellow English: Toward a Linguistic Anthropology of Asian Pacific America.* 213–32. New York: Oxford University Press.

Tannen, D. (2007 [1989]) *Talking Voices: Repetition, Dialogue, and Imagery in Conversational Discourse.* New York: Cambridge University Press.

Watson-Gegeo, K. (1992) Thick explanation in the ethnographic study of child socialization and development: A longitudinal study of the problem of schooling for Kwara'ae (Solomon Islands) children. *New Directions in Child Development* 58: 51–66.

Watson-Gegeo, K. and Gegeo, D. W. (1992) Schooling, knowledge, and power: Social transformation in the Solomon Islands. *Anthropology and Education Quarterly* 23: 10–29.

Watson-Gegeo, K. A. and Gegeo, D. W. (1986) Calling out and repeating routines in Kwara'ae children's language socialization. In B. B. Schieffelin and E. Ochs (eds.), *Language Socialization Across Cultures.* 17–50. New York: Cambridge University Press.

Wills, D. D. (1977) *Culture's Cradle: Social, Structural and Interactional Aspects of Senegalese Socialization.* Doctoral Dissertation. Austin, TX: University of Texas.

Wortham, S. (2005) Socialization beyond the speech event. *Journal of Linguistic Anthropology* 15: 95–112.

10   Literacy Socialization

LAURA STERPONI

Introduction

The presence and influence of written signs in contemporary Western cultures is widespread, and in fact so pervasive that it often passes unnoticed (Todorov 1990 [1978]). While living in environments saturated with written signs that require multiple forms of engagement with text, we tend to perceive reading and writing as simple and straightforward decoding and encoding processes. This perspective on literacy permeates the popular media. It also bears witness to a scholarly conceptualization of reading and writing as decontextualized tools that was only recently criticized and debunked.

This chapter engages with reading and writing research in the language socialization tradition to illuminate the multifarious ways in which literacy is implicated in broader sociocultural processes. The paradigm of language socialization posits that learning to read and write implies not only the acquisition of a set of cognitive and motor skills but also cultural apprenticeship into a community's values, social positions, and identities, which are associated with locally shaped literacy practices (Garrett and Baquedano-López 2002; Schieffelin and Ochs 1986). Bourdieu's notion of habitus is employed in the language socialization tradition to highlight the historical and cultural nature of literacy practices (Kulick and Schieffelin 2004; Sterponi 2007a). Thus, rather than conceiving of reading and writing as decoding and encoding skills, we are compelled to think of a literacy habitus, a set of historically contingent and culturally situated organizing principles that shape individual involvement with text.

In this chapter, I trace the shift from theorizing literacy as a decontextualized technology to situated accounts of reading and writing practices. In addition, I examine the historical roots and ideological underpinnings of literacy instruction, from kindergarten and early grades to higher education and academia. In the last

The Handbook of Language Socialization, First Edition. Edited by Alessandro Duranti, Elinor Ochs, and Bambi B. Schieffelin.

section of the chapter, I present an ethnographic study of spontaneous reading activities in two elementary-school classrooms to shed light on the surreptitious mechanisms that bring about variations and transformations in literacy practices.

Shifting Notions of Literacy: From 'Great Divide' Theories to Situated Perspectives on Reading and Writing

Reflections on the impact of forms of inscription on individuals and societies can be traced back to antiquity. Plato formulated his perspective in *Phaedrus*, expressing it via the pharaoh Thamus when Theut, the alleged inventor of writing, presents his creation to him. After a brief preface that praises the supposed advantages of Theut's invention, which would allow storage of a great amount of information, Thamus expresses his deep concern (Plato 2005: 275a–b):

> If men learn this, it will implant forgetfulness in their souls; they will cease to exercise memory because they rely on that which is written, calling things to remembrance no longer from within themselves, but by means of external marks. What you have discovered is a recipe not for memory, but for reminder. And it is no true wisdom that you offer your disciples, but only its semblance, for by telling them of many things without teaching them you will make them seem to know much, while for the most part they know nothing, and as men filled, not with wisdom, but with the conceit of wisdom, they will be a burden to their fellows.

The pharaoh/Plato is concerned that writing will decrease the capacities of the human mind and change the practices of knowledge acquisition, removing novices from the key relationship with their teacher.

In the eighteenth century, modes of textual transmission and forms of writing came to be linked to major changes in the development of the human mind and to the progress of nations and peoples. For example, Vico in his *Scienza Nuova* (1999 [1725]) identified three stages in the evolution of all societies and linked each period with a particular type of language and writing system. The third and most advanced epoch, the age of men, is characterized by the introduction of alphabetic writing, which in turn makes possible abstract thinking. Furthermore, according to Vico, the replacement of a great number of signs (in logographic systems) with a few letters representing the various linguistic sounds breaks the clergy's and aristocrats' monopoly on knowledge to increase individual freedom and to promote equal access to information and the law.

In the twentieth century, scholars from different disciplines reconsidered and further articulated arguments about the impact of literacy on human cognition and cultural tradition. In 1963, anthropologist Jack Goody and literary critic Ian Watt published a now classic essay, 'The consequences of literacy' (1963). Therein the two scholars put forth a conception of literacy as an intellectual tool that, by creating a distance between the word and its referent, yields abstract thinking. More broadly, Goody and Watt argued that the invention of the alphabet brought about basic transformations in the approach to and transmission of knowledge. In particular, they contended that the inception of alphabetic literacy afforded distinctions between (1) myth and history, (2) opinion and truth, and (3) group cohesiveness and individuality. This chapter will not review these assumed key changes in detail, but it is important to note that literacy is taken as the organizing principle of large-scale periodizations in human history and of fundamental distinctions between literate and nonliterate societies.

Goody and Watt's literacy thesis was echoed by classic, historical, and psychological scholarship. Walter Ong (1982) concerned himself with communicative modalities and proposed a set of distinctive characteristics of oral and written cultures. Oral culture, according to Ong, is conservative and traditionalist: it centers on the figures of wise old men, who have the privilege and responsibility of holding (mnemonically) and transmitting (orally) the cultural patrimony of the community. In addition, orality fosters not only activities but also personality structures that are oriented toward communal and participatory experience. With writing, Ong claimed, human consciousness is enhanced to an unprecedented and unsurpassed extent. Writing restructures thought, fosters reflection, heightens accuracy in the treatment of information, and favors greater individuality. While attributing major and straightforward consequences of (alphabetic) literacy to thinking and social dynamics, Ong's theorization also highlights interaction and mutual influences between orality and literacy. For instance, Ong pointed out that the inception of writing did not reduce orality but enhanced it, making possible the development and systematization of the principles of oratory and the art of rhetoric.[1]

Some theorists have argued for a fundamental divide between literate and nonliterate societies, emphasizing the cognitive and conceptual implications of reading and writing. Notably, psychologist David Olson (1977) linked abstraction, metacognitive awareness, and logical and ideational thinking to alphabetic literacy (see also Greenfield 1972; Luria 1976). In fact, Olson contended that literate culture did not attain its full potential until well after the invention of the alphabet: the transition 'from utterance to text' (Olson 1977) – which makes it possible for language to be used unambiguously, separately from the circumstances of production and independent from context – was achieved only in the seventeenth century, when the Protestant Reformation's orientation toward the scriptures as autonomous text extended to a wider range of written materials and genres.[2] At the same time in England the Royal Society formulated a set of norms for the production of writing that included employment of definitions, explicit premises, and formal rules of logic enabling sentences 'to have only one interpretation' (Olson 1977: 270).

While the belief that literacy brought about individual and societal advancement is still widespread in the popular media, 'great divide' theories have been a target of critiques since the 1970s. Scholars in a variety of fields, including anthropologists, folklorists, historians, linguists, and psychologists, have rejected the conception of literacy as a technology and the idea of a big divide between spoken and written language practices.[3] They have challenged on numerous grounds the claimed consequences of the invention of the alphabet: historical material from ancient India and China offers counter-evidence of a causal link between alphabetic literacy and historiography, and between alphabetic literacy and discernment regarding beliefs and empirical corroboration (Gough 1968). Contemporary research on nonliterate peoples shows that they have richly developed philosophies of language and metalinguistic discourse (Finnegan 1988a, 1988b) and that they practice introspection and individual critical reflection (Akinnaso 1992; Finnegan 1988b).

One of the most compelling and influential critiques of the great divide perspective comes from cultural psychologists Sylvia Scribner and Michael Cole. They found among the Vai people of Liberia the ideal context in which to assess whether cognitive consequences can be ascribed to literacy, and in particular to test the idea that only alphabetic literacy enables abstraction and analytic thinking (Scribner and Cole 1981). In the Vai community three literacy traditions coexisted, each related to a different language and script (Arabic, English, and Vai – the first two having alphabetic writing systems and the Vai script being a syllabary), distinct social activities, and separate institutions. Because different Vai subgroups were differently acquainted with the three languages and scripts, Scribner and Cole were able to evaluate the effects of different literacy experiences on people's cognitive skills. They found no generalizable consequences of alphabetic literacy for cognition, and only literacy-specific effects on distinct task-specific skills. For example, individuals a few years into Qur'anic schooling obtained high scores on incremental recall tests.

In lieu of examining the technology of writing systems or literacy as a monological phenomenon, Scribner and Cole proposed a *situated account* that conceives of literacy as 'a set of socially organized practices' (Scribner and Cole 1981: 236). Practices of literacy are various and highly differentiated, and to be literate means not only knowing how to read and write a particular script but also how to employ this ability for specific purposes in specific contexts.

Such a situated perspective on literacy has been further developed by anthropologist Brian Street, who posed an 'ideological model' of reading and writing that foregrounded the sociocultural matrix and the political and economic conditions that shape any literacy practice (Street 1984, 1993) (in contrast to the traditional view of reading and writing referred to as the 'autonomous model' of literacy). Street tested the analytic purchase of his model by considering the literacy landscape of the Mashad area in northeastern Iran, where he conducted fieldwork in the 1970s. Among the people who inhabited the area, Street witnessed the co-presence and interaction of different literacies, each inextricably associated with distinct social institutions, power relationships, and practical and ideological goals. Reading and writing in the *maktabs*, or religious schools, differed from the commercial language used by the traders in managing transactions and exchanges of goods with other villages or the city of Mashad. Yet another set of practices and meanings developed with the introduction of state-school literacy. Further, Street noticed that those who had been educated at the *maktab* and then engaged in commerce were able to adapt the literacy skills they had acquired in the religious context to the needs of their profession. In contrast, newly literate youths trained in state schools did not transfer their literacy skills to trading. Street employed notions of ideology and social relations to explain this opposite outcome, ultimately arguing that political and ideological forces are inherent in all literacy practices (Street 1984: 8).

The idea that literacy is a social practice, historically contingent, culturally organized, and ideologically shaped, is the grounding assumption and motivation of the trend of ethnographic studies of literacy known as New Literacy Studies. Since its emergence in the early 1980s, this school of thought has produced detailed descriptions of particular literacy events (e.g. Messick 1993; Sarroub 2002; Shuman 1986) and more comprehensive examinations of literacy practices in focal communities (e.g. Barton and Hamilton 1998; Besnier 1995; Reder and Green 1983). Both types of analysis have contributed to our understanding of the heterogeneous ways in which people engage with text and the multiple meanings of reading and writing in different contexts. In addition, New Literacy Studies has shed light on the embedding of these activities in broader communicative repertoires, on the role of literacy in identity formation and group dynamics, and on the relationship between power and the ability to access and produce written texts. The following section discusses these issues in the process of literacy socialization in school and out-of-school contexts.

Learning to Read and Write

Shirley Brice Heath's (1983) classic ethnographic study in the Piedmont Carolinas documented the ways in which young children are apprenticed to make meaning with words in three communities. Heath found that the white working-class community of Roadville, the black working-class community of Trackton, and the mixed-race middle-class community of Maintown differed in their assumptions about and expectations of young children, in patterns of language use among children and adults, and in the ways adults were oriented toward written texts and children were introduced to literacy.

Heath's study analyzed how children from the three communities experienced school and performed on academic tasks. Heath observed that, for Maintown children, school activities were remarkably similar to those they had practiced at home since they were infants. The questions teachers asked students were similar in kind to those frequently heard in Maintown households. The narrative style nurtured and legitimized in school showed overlapping characteristics with that employed in recounting everyday experiences at dinnertime or in bedtime storytelling. Furthermore, she found that Maintown adults used books and other literacy materials in their interactions with children as young as six months of age. As a result, Maintown children thrived in school, excelling in classroom activities and ranking consistently highly on reading tests.

In contrast, when Trackton children entered school they experienced many unfamiliar activities and communication styles: teachers asked rhetorical questions or 'what-explanation' questions, which were rarely heard in Trackton's households. At home, Trackton's children were most frequently asked analogical questions, which prompted them to draw comparisons between a focal object/person/event and something/someone else. In the classroom, Trackton children were required to listen silently while books were read to them, and the comprehension questions related to the text did not allow them to draw parallels or metaphorical links as they were used to doing in oral storytelling and everyday conversation. In recounting what they had read, Trackton children were not encouraged to employ their ability to embellish tales with original fictionalized elements; nor were they allowed to proceed nonlinearly in the presentation of chains of events. Thus, for Trackton children school presented multiple challenges. Teachers were often unaware of these challenges, misunderstanding the children's different communication style and approach to literacy as resistance or cognitive weakness. In most cases, therefore, Trackton children lagged behind and dropped out of school or became disengaged well before their analogical and creative skills could be fruitfully used in text-related school activities.

Roadville children experienced easy entry to school, where they were asked to perform tasks their caregivers had already been apprenticing them in. Roadville children were used to sitting still and being read to aloud, as this classroom activity paralleled the reading of Bible stories at home. They were also prepared to answer 'what-explanation' questions, which were very similar to the factual questions adults in Roadville asked children, both in the context of moral narratives and in Bible reading. When, however, the teacher presented extra-credit activities – tasks requiring a more creative take on texts, personal commentary, or exploring a imaginary realm – the Roadville children's performance declined. Such activities were indeed not practiced or approved in Roadville households. As a consequence, these children experienced increasing difficulties after the early primary grades, and by fourth grade they were most often found in the low-achieving group.

Heath's study played a pivotal role in revealing how language and literacy learning is embedded in the broader process of becoming a competent member of a community. It also showed that tensions may result from the encounter between certain ideological orientations toward oral and written language and contrasting literacy habituses.

Ethnographic studies carried out in newly literate communities have further illuminated frictions and transformations brought about by the introduction of literacy (see e.g. Dyer and Chksi 2001; Kulick and Stroud 1990; Schieffelin 2000). Duranti and Ochs (1986) examined literacy instruction in a traditional village in (Western) Samoa, showing how, through learning to read and write, Samoan children were also socialized to expectations and dynamics of adult–child relationships and task accomplishment that differed from those typical of their native community. Thus, literacy acquisition for Samoan children had far more encompassing effects than mastering a script receptively and productively: it engendered transformations in social identity and relationships. Briefly, in the village of Falefa, children as young as three or four were introduced to formal instruction when they began attending the pastor's school. There they learn the alphabet and basic decoding in order to recite passages from the Bible. (Older children were also instructed on how to interpret those passages.) Literacy materials (e.g. the alphabet table) were filled with 'Western' images and indexes of an orientation rather distant from the traditional Samoan lifestyle. Further, the pedagogical procedures employed by the pastor/instructor differed from those used by Samoan caregivers. Whereas at school children were exposed to simplifying actions and partitioning of the task to reduce the cognitive load, at home, simplification and other forms of accommodation to children were rare as Samoan caregivers assigned greater responsibility for learning to the child. Moreover, in literacy instruction children were often praised individually for succeeding in a task. The effort and support of the instructor, arguably key to the child's success on the task, were not acknowledged. The emphasis on individual achievement was remarkably different from the traditional Samoan orientation that foregrounded the social and collaborative nature of most everyday pursuits. Thus, in the course of becoming literate, young Samoan children were socialized to attitudes toward themselves and others that were typical among the Western missionaries. Beyond the acquisition of decoding and comprehension skills needed to read the Bible and cultivate their Christian faith, Samoan children were socialized into worldviews and interactional patterns that prepared them to enter and contribute to a Western economy and labor market.

Literacy is also often deeply implicated in gender socialization. Linguistic anthropologist Ayala Fader has described the markedly different paths of literacy acquisition for boys and girls in a Hasidic community in Brooklyn in the mid-1990s (Fader 2001). While boys spent their entire school day acquiring literacy in liturgical Hebrew and Yiddish and studying religious texts, girls were from first grade introduced to English language and literacy and to secular subjects. In this way, literacy instruction contributed to socializing boys and girls to distinct roles and activities within and across the community boundaries. There was not, however, a simple one-to-one differentiation: while girls' fluency in English was strongly associated with their role as mediator between the community and the secular world – a role that girls considered to be important and proudly took on to allow their brothers and fathers to focus exclusively on Torah study – they were also pressed to maintain their fluency in Yiddish. Literacy materials and activities contributed to mitigating this tension and shifting the ideology of English from a gentile language to a language that could convey Hasidic values too: in the school library and neighborhood bookstores, new books for Hasidic children and young adolescents were available. These books had been written in English and had orthodox Jewish peers as protagonists. The narratives promoted an orthodox Jewish lifestyle and worldview. In this way, on the one hand literacy activities played an important role in an early gender socialization that inculcated essentialized differences between girls and boys; on the other, they deflected the tension that using a secular language could bring to an orthodox community.

Ideologies of Text and Literacy Instruction

The theoretical concepts outlined above enable us to critically examine school-based literacy practices, from kindergarten and early grades to higher education and academia. They allow us to identify the ideological and institutional underpinnings that shape literacy instruction and inform schooled reading and writing activities. In other words, we can analyze the modes of production and reception of the written word that dominate educational institutions as products of a historically evolved textual ideology, one that began to emerge at the inception of the modern age (Chartier 1994; Foucault 1977; Trimbur 1990).

In the field of literacy studies, such orientation toward the production and reception of text is usually referred to as 'essayist literacy.' Essayist literacy treats written text as explicit and self-contained representation of meaning. Such a textual orientation is in turn grounded in the assumption that written language is transparent – eminently literal and referential (Collins 1996; Cook-Gumperz 1986; de Castell and Luke 1983; Olson 1977; Scollon and Scollon 1981).

This perspective has implications for our understanding of current pedagogic practices as well as ideals of academic literacy: reading and writing are treated as distinct, decomposable, and quantifiable skills. In the early grades they are taught as a uniform, generalizable, and context-independent set of technical abilities (Gee 1996; Luke and Baker 1991). Students are invited to think of their reading activity as decoding words and sentences, or in the most difficult cases as deciphering the hidden meaning that is there on the page waiting to be apprehended. Writing in turn consists of rendering the intended (singular) meaning through unambiguous, self-contained language (Luke 1992).[4]

Deborah Poole's (2008) study of fifth-grade reading groups offers convincing evidence of the dominance of essayist literacy as orientation to text explicitly taught or implicitly legitimized in the classroom. Poole focuses on two central characteristics of essayist literacy, decontextualization and componentiability,[5] and delineates linguistic and interactional patterns that instantiate such an orientation to text: (1) the students' turns at reading aloud, which are orchestrated by the teacher and render the text as a collection of distinct segments; (2) the question-and-answer sequences following reading-aloud cycles, which are mostly centered on the text so that the student is expected to respond by identifying text segments that match the wording used in the teacher's question; and (3) the teacher's favoring of short and self-contained responses over longer and more complex ones.

A similar orientation to text and instructional strategies has been found by James Collins (1996) in third-grade reading lessons. The extensive teacher focus on dialect correction during reading-aloud cycles attests to the fact that 'the text is treated as an object of faithful utterance' (1996: 208). In addition, the most frequent teacher comprehension queries and student answers illustrate a concentration on factual knowledge of the text rather than possible multiple meanings and interpretations.[6]

Focusing on reading literature rather than essays, and on higher education rather than early school grades, Michael Warner (2004) has highlighted comparable ideological underpinnings of the modes of engagement with text that are cultivated and legitimized in academia. In particular, Warner considers the chief pedagogical goal of English departments across the United States to be 'critical reading,' framing it as one (but not the only) mode of engagement with text and placing it in a history of textual practices. In literature classes, however, critical reading is taught as the appropriate mode for apprehending texts; alternative reading habits are discouraged (2004: 13). Warner provocatively asks whether there are any other kinds of engagement with text, besides critical reading, that can or should be taught in college classes (2004: 16):

> But what if it isn't true, as we suppose, that critical reading is the only way to suture textual practice with reflection, reason, and normative discipline of subjectivity? If we begin to understand critical reading not simply as the coming-into-reflexivity of reading, but as a very special set of form relationships, then it might be easier to recognize rival modes of reading and reflections on reading as something other than pretheoretically uncritical.

One of Warner's main points is that critical reading is 'the folk ideology of a learned profession, so close to us that we seldom feel the need to explain it' (2004: 14). He also points out that, despite strict censoring and meticulous inculcation practices, college readers do in fact engage with texts in ways other than those included in the official curriculum.

Similarly, Poole (2008) observed that fifth-grade students also related to text in ways that departed from the teacher-imparted and -orchestrated essayist mode: especially when they focused on text illustrations, students employed 'a more situationally contextualized and personal form of language' (2008: 400). Poole's analysis showed that this alternative approach to the text 'afforded opportunities for more complex expression and extensive interactional involvement with the curricular topic' (2008: 401). The illustration-oriented sequences were longer and included more student initiations and fewer teacher-led IRE[7] exchanges than text-oriented sequences. In general, the talk students produced in the illustration-oriented sequences was also more nuanced and less scripted: for instance, hypothetical constructions and metacognitive expressions were more frequently produced when children were focusing on images.

Alternative Literacies

A number of studies of reading and writing activities in educational contexts attest to the existence of unofficial literacy practices – that is, modes of engagement with texts that diverge from the scripted curriculum or flout the rules of cultural orthodoxy (Dyson 1993; Gutierrez, Rymes, and Larson 1995).

In newly literate communities, the ways in which individuals actively and creatively adapt reading and writing to their own goals is sometimes particularly noticeable (Besnier 1995). Don Kulick and Christopher Stroud (1990), for instance, observed that the villagers of Gapun, Papua New Guinea, perceived and used literacy according to their own cultural concerns, primarily linked to a 'cargo-oriented' worldview: as soon as Gapuners acquired rudimentary literacy skills from the Catholic missionaries, they most often used them to compose letters to obtain cargo or worldly goods. Even when Gapun children began attending a government-run grammar school – where the language of instruction was English and the texts were not religious – the newly available language and reading materials were interpreted within a millenarian framework as powerful resources to connect with spiritual beings and obtain an abundance of material possessions. Thus, the aims of the agencies that introduced literacy to Gapuners remained largely marginal to them.

In the classroom, researchers have witnessed the tension between the literacy curriculum and children's spontaneous reading and writing activities (Dyson 2001; Gilmore 1986). Children's appropriation of literacy materials and use of newly acquired coding and decoding skills often depart from those prescribed in the curriculum and promoted by the teacher.[8] An ethnographic and analytic discourse study of children's clandestine interactional reading is used in what follows to shed light on the interface between the acquisition of a normative reading habitus and the tactical operations that produce its clandestine transformations (see also Sterponi 2007a).

Reading habitus and clandestine reading

In the early 2000s I conducted a study of children's reading activities in two classrooms, one second grade and one third grade, in an elementary school in southern California, for the duration of an academic year. Approximately 45 hours of video recordings document the reading activities practiced in the two classrooms. I integrated the video-recorded data with daily fieldnotes, which provide additional information about the classrooms' micro-culture, implementation of curricular goals, and daily decision-making by the teachers.

The reading pedagogy in the classrooms I observed promoted individual silent reading as the preferred mode of engagement with text and the ultimate goal of reading instruction. Twenty minutes of independent silent reading followed the children's lunch break every day. In addition, the children visited the library once a week and were invited to circulate independently in order to select books to borrow and bring to class or take home (for individual reading). Teacher-led group story time also occurred regularly in the classrooms, although less frequently than individual silent reading. The official reading practices in the classrooms mirrored a reading ideology dominant in the popular media and education campaigns, one that frames reading as an individual, invariable, and often decontextualized activity. In my observations, however, children displayed a preference for collaborative involvement with text and organized complex interactive reading events, usually surreptitiously. When they were brought to the library, children took time from the official task of book selection to gather in small groups and engage in collective reading. Even in the classroom, children used peripheral areas, corners, or the space under the desks to elude the teacher's surveillance, share and compare books, and read them together.

The structure and organization of children's interactional reading episodes were remarkably different from other reading or instructional activities orchestrated by the teacher. The participant roles assigned by the teacher to different students during group story time (e.g. primary reader, audience, commentator) were not explicitly taken up by the children engaged in interactional reading, nor did they remain the same throughout the joint-reading episode. Most frequently, the children created a symmetric arena and all participants treated each other as readers and audience. Moreover, peers' interactional reading often involved more than one book at a time. Children usually selected texts that shared themes or broad topics with the ones the other classmates had chosen. In this way they created a rich textual platform to explore together. Example 10.1 illustrates the establishment of a joint reading episode:

Example 10.1[9]

Upon entering the library with the class, Paul follows Jeremy to the bookshelves that have books about animals. Jeremy proposes to find out if there are owls in the desert. The two boys reach the bookshelf and pull out a few books about owls.

Then they take a seat at a desk and begin reading together:

1	Paul:	there are all kinds of owls here. ((leafing through a book titled *About Owls*))
2	Jeremy:	is there one that lives in the desert?
3	Paul:	I'm not sure. Let me see.

Paul continues to leaf through the book, examining pictures and reading segments of the text. Jeremy begins silently reading another book titled *Owl Moon* (a storybook with pictures):

4	Jeremy:	look how owls make their nest. ((pointing at page))
5	Paul:	but that's a story.
6	Jeremy:	I know but you can learn a lot from stories.
7	Paul:	then we have to find a story about an owl in the desert.

In Example 10.1, Jeremy and Paul's reading activity is motivated by a specific inquiry: to learn whether there are owls in the desert. To this aim, they examine different books, primarily science texts but a book of fiction as well. Paul raises some doubts about the usefulness of consulting a storybook to address their inquiry (turn 5). Jeremy's answer indicates that he is aware of the genre distinction (turn 6). However, he argues that some trustworthy information can be gained from reading stories, not only nonfiction books.

In interactional reading, the simultaneous engagement of multiple texts both fostered and was fostered by the weaving of intertextual links. In other words, texts were not merely juxtaposed but were interpreted in light of one another. Consider Example 10.2:

Example 10.2

Anthony (A), Jeremy (J), Sharon (S), and Wendy (W) have arrived one by one at a desk in the library. Each of them has chosen a book and has begun reading independently. Soon Anthony attracts the others' attention through a verbal summons accompanied by a pointing gesture. It will become clear in the unfolding of the exchange (examined in the next section) that Anthony is reading a book about dogs because his family is planning to buy one:

1   A: ehi look. ((pointing on the page))
2   (2.8) ((Jeremy and Sharon move closer to Anthony; Wendy turns head toward Anthony's book))
3   A: I am not going to buy this.
4   J: let me see.
5   S: ugly ((looking at the page)) these are poodles=
6   J: =poodles. ((reading from the page))
7   S: [they're just so-
8   A: [I know, I- I- I read from the book that there are some ((turning to following page))
      that are nice [(and)
9   S: [nn- ((making a grimace and shaking head))
      ((Jeremy sits back and resumes reading his book))
10 A: but the poodles that have that- those little furry things
      right [there in the legs.

11 S: [`nd then they- ((mimicking with right hand scissors cutting))
      and then they get shaved ((facial expression of disgust))
12 A: e:nn. ((of disgust; flipping his hands))
13 J: how about this kind of dog? ((pointing at page))

14 (1.0) ((Anthony, Sharon, and Wendy look at the image Jeremy is
     pointing *to*))
15 J: golden retriever.
16 A: mhm, I'm not sure.
17 J: ((starts reading from his book)) These are lovable, well-mannered,
           intelligent dogs with a great charm. (0.2) they are easily trained,
           and always patient and gentle with children.
18 S: yes, they're nice.
19 J: ((turns the page and points to text and then looks toward
           Anthony)) and they also love swimming.
20 W: wow, swimming?
21 J: ((turns to Wendy)) yeah.
           ((resumes reading pointing to text)) these dogs also love to swim.
[…]

Anthony's book, left flat open on the desk, offers the other participants space in which to maneuver: Jeremy and Sharon can access the text directly to see the breed of dog indicated by their classmate (turns 5–6). Then, through talk and iconic gestures, Anthony and Sharon 'sketch' an additional picture, juxtaposing it to the one offered in the text (turns 8–12). Drawing from the text and their previous knowledge, they co-construct, through language, prosody, gestures, and facial expressions, a negative evaluation of the target of attention. In this way, Anthony and Sharon jointly create a multivocal text in which the authorial voice is animated and put into dialogue with their own voices as readers. At this point, Jeremy intervenes again (turn 13), inviting the others' gaze to the book he has been reading. Jeremy's verbal accompaniment to the pointing gesture provides an interpretive frame for the action that he is soliciting gesturally: the participants are not merely invited to look at a picture, but also to look at it in relation to Anthony's book and as an illustration of a possible alternative to the object previously examined and assessed. In other words, Jeremy's contribution outlines an intertextual link, thereby expanding Anthony and Sharon's analysis and inviting further reading and commentary. In order to convince Anthony that golden retrievers are good dogs, Jeremy proceeds to read an excerpt from his book, which gives a very positive description of the breed.

This sequence brings to light some of the ways in which the children I observed engaged with texts and made sense of them. The co-construction of intertextual links as well as the engagement of prior knowledge and personal experience were among the most frequent and effective comprehension strategies the children employed.

The active readership exercised by children in clandestine interactional reading emerged also in the form of interpretive double-voicing or double-voiced reading: the young readers actively engaged in dialogue with the text and produced a reading/interpretation that was internally dialogized – that is, one that acknowledged the authorial voice while actively and creatively accentuating or refracting it with their own intention (Bakhtin 1981).

In Example 10.3 we observe Jason, Luca, and Nate engaged in reading together a book on the solar system (while also leafing through another text on the Earth and planetary geology). Jason reads aloud portions of the text, specifically a section on Galileo. His reading is punctuated by pauses that allow Luca and Nate, but also Jason himself, to offer commentaries on the text. These commentaries often both animate the authorial voice and challenge it:

Example 10.3

1	J:	((reading from the page)) Galileo's father, who let him stay up late to look at the sky (0.8) filled with (1.0) thousands of stars, couldn't answer all the boy's questions.
2	N:	let me see. ((getting closer to the open book)) what questions?
3	J:	((reading)) what are they made of? Galileo cried. where did they come from? His father (1.0) laughed. Always asking questions aren't you?
4		(2.0) ((the boys laugh))
5	J:	((reading)) Galileo was a very good student in school
6	L:	he was a troublemaker. ((smiling voice)) (0.2) always asking questions ((giggles))
7	J:	((giggles)) always looking at the sky

In this segment of the interactional reading episode, the boys first display an understanding of and alignment with the authorial voice, when they laugh together (line 4). In a sense the boys are laughing with Galileo's father, thereby ratifying the authorial stance. However, after Jason's reading of the author's assessment of Galileo's success as a student (turn 5), Luca juxtaposes a different interpretation of Galileo's behavior at school, one that challenges the authorial stance (turn 6). Jason promptly aligns with Luca's perspective using a parallel construction but proposing a different image of Galileo the student, one of a day-dreamer with his head always in the clouds. This excerpt illustrates the multivocal character of peers' interactional reading: the textual voices were animated in different ways, interwoven with one another, and punctuated by the readers' own voices.

In summary, this study shows that, as children are being socialized into a particular reading habitus, they concurrently and surreptitiously cultivate unofficial variants of the prescribed praxis. As clandestine practitioners of interactional reading, children are like de Certeau's consumers; that is, they are 'unrecognized producers, poets of their own affairs, trailblazers in the jungles of functionalist rationality' (de Certeau 1984: 34). Within the territory of a foreign power, young readers clandestinely produce their own signifying practices. Creative manipulation of the habitus is thus intermingled with the habitus' transmission and reproduction (Bourdieu 1977).

Conclusions

In this chapter I have discussed pivotal theoretical issues that have long framed and still strongly influence our thinking about texts, and about reading and writing, broadly conceived. The 'great divide' theorists revisited previously articulated perspectives and established the terms of debate about the nature of written language, as well as about the relationship between orality and literacy and between literacy and social and cognitive development. Situated perspectives on literacy tempered grand claims about the consequences of literacy and pluralized the term, documenting a multiplicity of reading and writing practices shaped by historical, sociocultural, ideological, and institutional circumstances and conditions. Learning to read and write is no longer seen as a matter of acquiring a set of cognitive skills afforded by neurophysiological maturation; the acquisition of coding and decoding abilities has been shown to be part of a wider process of socialization through which children come to participate in recognized practices and take on sanctioned social identities.

A language socialization perspective on literacy thus conceptualizes the acquisition of reading and writing abilities through apprenticeship in a literacy habitus, namely as a set of organizing principles that regulates individuals' engagement with texts at the sensorimotor and the intellectual and emotional levels (Luke 1992; Sterponi 2007b). At the same time, the language socialization paradigm conceives of apprentices as agents in the social world and investigates how their actions contribute to variations in and transformations of prescribed practices.

Ethnographic research on literacy activities in school contexts has shown that, as children are socialized into a particular literacy habitus, they concurrently and surreptitiously, playfully and seriously, cultivate unofficial variants of the dominant praxis. Young apprentices in literacy operate in liminal spaces, both within and outside institutionally defined contexts. For instance, the children's clandestine reading practice that I described in the previous section engages an institutionally valued activity while subverting its official format. In other words, while transcending the normative praxis, peer interactional reading rests on resources, both material and intellectual, made available by the institutional context and through the official literacy curriculum. A deeper understanding of how literacy is concurrently implicated in empowering and limiting practices in sociocultural reproduction and transformation remains a central aim of literacy socialization research.

NOTES

1   Furthermore, Ong (1982) makes a distinction between primary oral culture, which is foreign to writing, and secondary orality, which coexists with writing and is linked to the emergence of electronic media such as telephone, radio, and television. Much like primary orality, according to Ong, secondary orality is aggregative and communal. Secondary orality, however, is a more deliberate and self-conscious practice than primary orality.

2   Luther's contention that the meaning of the scriptures did not depend on dogmas promoted an approach to text that no longer required the mediation of clerics or masters to supply the necessary context for interpretation. A more independent engagement with text was also made possible by the invention of printing, which in producing multiple copies of any work allowed a more direct and widespread access to written texts.

3   Noteworthy are Gough's (1968), Heath's (1980, 1983), and Street's (1984) contributions in anthropology; Finnegan's (1973, 1988a, 1988b) in folklore; Clanchy's (1979), Eisenstein's (1979), Graff's (1979), and Kaestle's (1985) in history; Biber's (1986), Chafe's (1982), and Tannen's (1982, 1987) in linguistics; and Scribner and Cole's (1981) in psychology.

4   This orientation is particularly salient when the reading materials are textbooks and the written text is expository (Luke, de Castell, and Luke 1983; Trimbur 1990).

5   'Componentiability' is a (re)presentation of knowledge as constituted of discrete information units (Poole 2008).

6   In contrasting high- and low-ranked reading groups, Collins found that prescriptivism pervaded the reading activities of low-ranked children to a much greater degree than it did of high-achieving students. On the other hand, the teacher prompted and supported an interpretivist orientation with high-ranked students more frequently and systematically than with poor readers (Collins 1996).

7   A prototypical pattern of classroom interaction, an IRE sequence involves the teacher opening the exchange by asking the student a question (initiation), the student who is called on producing an answer (response), which the teacher then evaluates (evaluation) (Cazden 1988).

8   In fact, research on emergent literacy has shown that young children actively and autonomously construct their notions of how written language works long before entering school (Ferreiro and Teberosky 1982; Hiebert 1978; Pontecorvo et al. 1996).

9   All images in this chapter are reproduced from Sterponi (2007).

REFERENCES

Akinnaso, N. F. (1992) Schooling, language, and knowledge in literate and nonliterate societies. *Comparative Studies in Society and History* 34(1): 68–109.

Bakhtin, M. (1981) Discourse in the novel. In M. Holquist (ed.), *The Dialogic Imagination*. 259–422. Austin, TX: University of Texas Press.

Barton, D. and Hamilton, M. (1998) *Local Literacies: Reading and Writing in One Community*. New York: Routledge.

Besnier, N. (1995) *Literacy, Emotion, and Authority: Reading and Writing on a Polynesian Atoll*. New York: Cambridge University Press.

Biber, D. (1986) Spoken and written textual dimensions in English: Resolving the contradictory findings. *Language* 62(2): 384–414.

Bourdieu, P. (1977) *Outline of a Theory of Practice*. R. Nice, transl. Cambridge: Cambridge University Press.

Cazden, C. B. (1988) *Classroom Discourse: The Language of Teaching and Learning*. Portsmouth, NH: Heinemann.

Chafe, W. (1982) Integration and involvement in speaking, writing, and oral literature. In D. Tannen (ed.), *Spoken and Written Language: Exploring Orality and Literacy*. 35–53. Norwood, NJ: Ablex.

Chartier, R. (1994) *The Order of Books*. Stanford, CA: Stanford University Press.

Clanchy, M. T. (1979) *From Memory to Written Record 1066–1307*. London: Edward Arnold.

Collins, J. (1996) Socialization to text: Structure and contradiction in schooled literacy. In M. Silverstein and G. Urban (eds.), *Natural Histories of Discourse*. 203–28. Chicago, IL: The University of Chicago Press.

Cook-Gumperz, J. (1986) Literacy and schooling: An unchanging equation? In *The Social Construction of Literacy*. 16–44. Cambridge: Cambridge University Press.

de Castell, S. and Luke, A. (1983) Defining 'literacy' in North American schools. *Journal of Curriculum Studies* 15: 373–89.

de Certeau, M. (1984) *The Practice of Everyday Life*. Berkeley, CA: University of California Press.

Duranti, A. and Ochs, E. (1986) Literacy instruction in a Samoan village. In B. B. Schieffelin and P. Gilmore (eds.), *The Acquisition of Literacy: Ethnographic Perspectives*. 213–32. Norwood, NJ: Ablex.

Dyer, C. and Chksi, A. (2001) Literacy, schooling and development: Views of Rabari nomads, India. In B. Street (ed.), *Literacy and Development*. 27–39. London and New York: Routledge.

Dyson, A. H. (2001) Coach Bombay's kids learn to write: Children's appropriation of media material for school literacy. In E. Cushman, E. R. Kintgen, B. M. Kroll, and M. Rose (eds.), *Literacy: A Critical Sourcebook*. 325–57. Boston, MA: Bedford/St. Martin's.

Dyson, A. H. (1993) *Social Worlds of Children Learning to Write in an Urban Primary School*. New York and London: Teachers College Press.

Eisenstein, E. L. (1979) *The Printing Press as an Agent of Change*. New York: Cambridge University Press.

Fader, A. (2001) Literacy, bilingualism, and gender in a Hasidic community. *Linguistics and Education* 12(3): 261–83.

Ferreiro, E. and Teberosky, A. (1982) *Literacy Before Schooling*. Exeter, NH: Heinemann.

Finnegan, R. (1973) Literacy versus non-literacy: The great divide. In R. Finnegan and R. Horton (eds.), *Modes of Thought*. 112–44. London: Faber.

Finnegan, R. (1988a) *Literacy and Orality*. Oxford: Blackwell.

Finnegan, R. (1988b) Literacy versus non-literacy: The significance of 'literature' in non literate cultures. In *Literacy and Orality: Studies in the Technology of Communication*. 59–85. New York: Blackwell.

Foucault, M. (1977) *Language, Counter-Memory, Practice: Selected Essays and Interviews*. D. F. Bouchard (ed.). Ithaca, NY: Cornell University Press.

Garrett, P. B. and Baquedano-López, P. (2002) Language socialization: Reproduction and continuity, transformation and change. *Annual Review of Anthropology* 31: 339–61.

Gee, J. P. (1996) *Social Linguistics and Literacies: Ideology in Discourses*. London: Routledge/Falmer.

Gilmore, P. (1986) Sub-rosa literacy: Peers, play and ownership in literacy acquisition. In B. B. Schieffelin and P. Gilmore (eds.), *The Acquisition of Literacy: Ethnographic Perspectives*. 155–68. Norwood, NJ: Ablex.

Goody, J. and Watt, I. (1963) The consequences of literacy. *Comparative Studies in Society and History* 5(3): 304–45.

Gough, K. (1968) Implications of literacy in traditional China and India. In J. Goody (ed.), *Literacy in Traditional Societies*. 69–84. Cambridge: Cambridge University Press.

Graff, H. (1979) *The Literacy Myth: Literacy and Social Structure in the 19th Century*. New York: Academic Press.

Greenfield, P. (1972) Oral and written language: The consequences for cognitive development in Africa, the United States, and England. *Language and Speech* 15: 169–78.

Gutierrez, K., Rymes, B. R., and Larson, J. (1995) Script, counterscript, and underlife in the classroom: James Brown versus Brown v. Board of Education. *Harvard Educational Review* 65(3): 445–71.

Heath, S. B. (1980) The functions and uses of literacy. *Journal of Communication* 30(1): 123–33.

Heath, S. B. (1983) *Ways with Words*. Cambridge: Cambridge University Press.

Hiebert, E. H. (1978) Preschool children's understanding of written language. *Child Development* 49: 1231–4.

Kaestle, C. F. (1985) The history of literacy and the history of readers. *Review of Research in Education* 12: 11–54.

Kulick, D. and Schieffelin, B. B. (2004) Language socialization. In A. Duranti (ed.), *A Companion to Linguistic Anthropology*. 349–68. Malden, MA: Blackwell.

Kulick, D. and Stroud, C. (1990) Christianity, cargo and ideas of self: Patterns of literacy in a Papua New Guinea village. *Man (New Series)* 25: 286–304.

Luke, A. (1992) The body literate: Discourse and inscription in early literacy training. *Linguistics and Education* 4: 107–29.

Luke, A. and Baker, C. D. (1991) Towards a critical sociology of reading pedagogy: An introduction. In C. D. Baker and A. Luke (eds.), *Towards a Critical Sociology of Reading Pedagogy*. xi–xxi. Amsterdam, The Netherlands and Philadelphia, PA: John Benjamins.

Luke, C., de Castell, S., and Luke, A. (1983) Beyond criticism: The authority of the school text. *Curriculum Inquiry* 13(2): 111–27.

Luria, A. R. (1976) *Cognitive Development: Its Cultural and Social Foundations*. Cambridge, MA: Harvard University Press.

Messick, B. M. (1993) *The Calligraphic State: Textual Domination and History in a Muslim Society*. New York: Cambridge University Press.

Olson, D. (1977) From utterance to text: The bias of language in speech and writing. *Harvard Education Review* 47: 257–81.

Ong, W. (1982) *Orality and Literacy: The Technologizing of the Word*. London and New York: Methuen.

Plato (2005) *Phaedrus*. London: Penguin Classics.

Pontecorvo, C., Orsolini, M., Burge, B., and Resnick, L. B. (1996) *Children's Early Text Construction*. Mahwah, NJ: Lawrence Erlbaum.

Poole, D. (2008) The messiness of language socialization in reading groups: Participation in and resistance to the values of essayist literacy. *Linguistics and Education* 19: 378–403.

Reder, S. and Green, K. R. (1983) Contrasting patterns of literacy in an Alaskan fishing village. *International Journal of the Sociology of Language* 42: 9–39.

Sarroub, L. K. (2002) In-betweenness: Religion and conflicting visions of literacy. *Reading Research Quarterly* 37(2): 130–48.

Schieffelin, B. B. (2000) Introducing Kaluli literacy: A chronology of influences. In P. Kroskrity (ed.), *Regimes of Language*. 293–327. Santa Fe, NM: School of America Research Press.

Schieffelin, B. B. and Ochs, E. (1986) Language socialization. *Annual Review of Anthropology* 15: 163–91.

Scollon, R. and Scollon, S. (1981) *Narrative, Literacy, and Face in Interethnic Communication*. Norwood, NJ: Ablex.

Scribner, S. and Cole, M. (1981) *The Psychology of Literacy*. Cambridge, MA: Harvard University Press.

Shuman, A. (1986) *Storytelling Rights: The Uses of Oral and Written Texts by Urban Adolescents*. Cambridge: Cambridge University Press.

Sterponi, L. (2007a) Clandestine interactional reading: Intertextuality and double-voicing under the desk. *Linguistics and Education* 18: 1–23.

Sterponi, L. (2007b) Reading as involvement with text: Insights from a study of high-functioning children with autism. *Rivista di Psicolinguistica Applicata* VII(3): 87–114.

Street, B. V. (1984) *Literacy in Theory and Practice*. Cambridge: Cambridge University Press.

Street, B. V. (ed.) (1993) *Cross-Cultural Approaches to Literacy*. Cambridge: Cambridge University Press

Tannen, D. (1982) The myth of orality and literacy. In William Frawley (ed.), *Linguistics and Literacy. Proceedings of the Delaware Symposium and Language Studies.* 37–50. New York: Plenum.

Tannen, D. (1987) The orality of literature and literary conversation. In J. A. Langer (ed.), *Language, Literacy and Culture: Issues of Society and Schooling.* 67–88. Norwood, NJ: Ablex.

Todorov, T. (1990 [1978]) Reading as construction. In *Genres in Discourse*. 39–49. Cambridge: Cambridge University Press.

Trimbur, J. (1990) Essayist literacy and the rhetoric of deproduction. *Rhetoric Review* 9(1): 72–86.

Vico, G. (1999 [1725]) *The New Science*. London: Penguin Classics.

Warner, M. (2004) Uncritical reading. In J. Gallop (ed.), *Polemic: Critical or Uncritical.* 13–38. New York: Routledge.

11 Language Socialization in Children's Medical Encounters

TANYA STIVERS

Research on child language socialization has its roots in understanding the ways that adults and other caregivers interact with children in mundane social life and how these practices might enculturate the child into local communicative norms and ways of thinking (Brown 1998; Clancy 1999; Danziger 1971; de León 1998; Garrett and Baquedano-López 2002; Heath 1983; Ochs and Schieffelin 1983, 1984). A second primary area of interest has been the effect of different socialization practices on more formal educational settings (Heath 1983; Howard 2004; Michaels 1981; Moore 2006, this volume; Philips 1983; Rogoff et al. 2003). However, as discussed in other contributions to this volume, language socialization extends into many other facets of life. Just as being a member of a cultural group or being a student requires socialization into the associated rights and obligations, so too does the role of medical patient or client.[1] For instance, patients must understand how to explain their problems (Halkowski 2006; Heritage and Robinson 2006); what information they should know about their bodies, their treatment, their life, and their medical history; and where to look during examinations (Heath 1986), to name but a few of the norm-governed aspects of medical interaction. Physicians play an important role in a child's socialization into the patient role by providing child patients with opportunities to adopt the social role of patient and allowing them to learn what they are accountable for in this particular role (e.g. Mead 1934).[2]

The healthcare context is of particular concern from a language socialization perspective for a couple of key reasons. First, this is an institutional context where outcomes can be affected by the ways that patients interact with physicians. Patient participation (usually understood to mean indicating preferences and giving opinions on treatment and diagnostic test options) has been promoted in the world of modern American medicine on the basis that patients fare better

The Handbook of Language Socialization, First Edition. Edited by Alessandro Duranti, Elinor Ochs, and Bambi B. Schieffelin.
© 2014 John Wiley & Sons, Ltd. Published 2014 by John Wiley & Sons, Ltd.

(Brody 1980; Frosch and Kaplan 1999; Greenfield et al. 1988; Guadagnoli and Ward 1998; Kaplan, Greenfield, and Ware 1989; Pozo et al. 1992; Schulman 1979) and are more satisfied (Evans et al. 1987; Mandelblatt et al. 2006; Pozo et al. 1992; Xu 2004) when they take a proactive role in their medical visits. Moreover, a range of healthcare organizations assert that patients should participate, implying a moral and ethical obligation to do so. In fact, an increasing number of states in the United States require physicians to inform patients about treatment options (Nayfield et al. 1994). According to Healthy People 2010, patients who participate actively in decisions about their healthcare can positively impact national health (US Department of Health and Human Services, Public Health Service 2000). The World Health Organization has stated that patient involvement in healthcare is a social, economic, and technical necessity (Waterworth and Luker 1990).

If being a proactive patient is important to successful healthcare in the United States, how children are socialized into this role – how they learn what they are accountable for knowing and what they should do in interaction with a physician – is critical. This chapter draws on a corpus of 322 video-taped primary-care interactions in English between community-based pediatricians and child patients (aged between two and a half and ten) accompanied by a caregiver, usually their mother. In terms of race and education, the parents broadly reflected the population of the greater Los Angeles area, from which these data came during 2000–2001 (see Stivers and Majid, 2007, for a more detailed description of the data). These children were being seen for routine illness symptoms such as stuffy/runny noses, sore throats, fevers, coughs, and/or ear pain. This chapter investigates when and how American physicians involve child patients in visits to the doctor for routine illnesses.

The work discussed here differs in methodology from much of the work represented in this volume, and in language socialization more generally, in several key ways. First, in contrast to the more common longitudinal designs employed in studies of language socialization, the work discussed here is cross-sectional, allowing us a snapshot of but a few minutes in the lives of many children of different ages visiting the doctor. From this we do not learn how any individual child changes and we must be cautious about generalizing about development since we see how children behave at different ages but not the *same* children at different points in time (for a longitudinal study of child participation see Clemente 2005). However, we gain insight into whether physicians interact with children of different ages and racial and/or socioeconomic backgrounds patterns similarly or differently. Second, in contrast to the more common ethnographic approach to language socialization, this chapter combines conversation analysis (with its focus on *structures* of social interaction) with quantitative analyses. This combination allows us to examine the relationships between factors such as race, class, and age on the one hand and interactional practices such as those for selecting between the parent and child to answer the question on the other. This chapter therefore complements the other chapters of this volume and suggests that language socialization can be investigated from different methodological perspectives and relyies on physician–parent–child interaction as a case study.

Background

An initial problem with the study of child involvement in the medical encounter is that children, even adolescents, participate very little in medical encounters (Aronsson and Rundström 1988; Freemon et al. 1971; Tates and Meeuwesen 2001; van Dulmen 1998; Wassmer et al. 2004). Moreover, primary-care pediatricians in both US and European contexts direct relatively little talk to their child patients and instead direct most of their communication to parents (Aronsson and Rundström 1988; Pantell et al. 1982; Stivers 2001; Stivers and Majid 2007; Tates and Meeuwesen 2001; van Dulmen 1998). The primary opportunity in which children have to be involved in the healthcare encounter is when doctors ask them questions (Wassmer et al. 2004). Physicians begin to direct questions to children relatively consistently from the age of two and a half. Still, most of the time, even as children approach 10 years of age, physicians direct their questions to parents. This is illustrated in Example 11.1. Here the physician makes no effort to involve the child in her verbal investigation of the problem. Indeed, she begins her questioning with her back to both the mother and daughter (see Figure 11.1) and refers to the girl using the third-person pronoun 'she.'

Example 11.1: 100106 – seven-year-old girl

```
 1  DOC:   Now she's been having some co:ld
 2          and some chest congestion?
 3  MOM:   Yes:.
 4  DOC:   [And how long has this been going on now?
 5          [((Figure 11.1 image taken from here))
 6  MOM:   S::i:nce probably the beginning (.) of:
 7          thuh weekend.
 8  MOM:   ((gesture with left hand back))/(0.5)
 9  DOC:   ((n[ods))
10  MOM:      [Last week.
11  DOC:   Okay so it's [all (started) it's been=
12  MOM:                [( comin' down) we=
13  DOC:   =[just about one week now,
14  MOM:   =[started on thuh medication
```

Even when the physician later turns around towards the mother and daughter, she looks past the girl and continues conversation solely with the mother (e.g. line 11/13).

Example 11.2, however, illustrates a very different approach. Here, as can be seen in Figure 11.2, the physician moves across the examining room to the boy and sits next to him. The first few questions are kept simple 'what's 'uh m^atter,' which is not generally true of questions directed to parents.

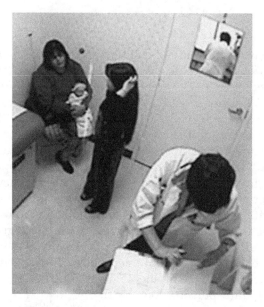

Figure 11.1   Physician selecting the mother to answer.

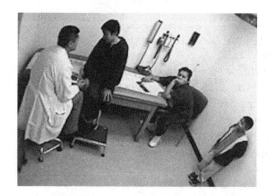

Figure 11.2   Physician selecting the boy to answer.

Example 11.2:   *140511 – nine-year-old boy*

```
1   DOC:   Renaldo what's 'uh ma^tter.
2          (0.5)/((DOC gazing at records))
3          (0.2)/[((DOC brings gaze to BOY))
4               [((Figure 11.2 image taken from here))
5   BOY:   Mmm y=I got a cough:.
6   DOC:   Ya got a cou:gh?,
7   DOC:   An' what else d'you have.
```

8		(1.0)
9	BOY:	Kind of uh:: hh cold.
10	DOC:	Kind of a co:ld.
11		(.)
12	DOC:	An' why do you say thaˆt.
13		(0.8)
14	BOY:	Because I snee:ze, a little bit.
15	DOC:	Uh huh?

One of the most obvious disincentives for directing questions to children is how parents and children respond. All of the questions asked of the mother in Example 11.1 are answered and are done so without delay. Even the last question, which is asked in overlap with the mother's completion of something else, is answered without delay with a head nod at turn completion. By contrast, the boy delays each of his responses. For instance, his answer to line 1 is delayed by 0.7 seconds; his answer to line 7 is delayed by 1.0 second; and his answer to line 12 is delayed by 0.8 seconds. These observations appear to generalize across doctor–patient encounters in these data – adults are more likely both to respond and to do so more quickly than children (Stivers under review).

Despite these disincentives, physicians do ask children questions. Children of all ages are more erratic than their parents in responding both in terms of speed and quality of response, but children, even at two and a half years, can and do competently answer substantive questions a fair amount of the time. In these data physicians ask an average of 21 questions per visit, and 37 percent of these questions were addressed to children (Stivers and Majid 2007). Children respond 65 percent of the time (Stivers, under review).[3] For instance, in Example 11.2 the boy does provide his illness history. Example 11.3 also shows a girl answering questions competently. She not only answers social questions but provides a description of her primary problem: a sore throat and a blister in her mouth.

Example 11.3:   *0308 – seven-year-old girl*

1	DOC:	.hh Uhm: how <u>o</u>ld are you Ariana?
2	PAT:	Seven?
3	DOC:	S:<u>even</u>:?, ((very dramatically)) (Well that) pretty
4		goˆo:d.
5		(0.2)
6	DOC:	Didju do that all by yours<u>e</u>lf?
7		(.)
8	DOC:	Get to sev (h)en all by yourself?
9	PAT:	Mm hm,
10	DOC:	(W(h)o[(h):w (h):)
11	MOM:	[(Heh:: hmh hmh hmh hmh hmh [hmh)
12	DOC:	[.hhh O:kay. What

```
13               can we do for you today (.)/(,)
14               (3.0)
15   DOC:        [Oh! we're- you're fine t'day huh?
16   PAT:        [(Uhm:,)
17               (0.2)
18   PAT:        I- have uh- my throat [is hurtin[g?
19   DOC:                               [.hhhh [O:h No^:.
20   PAT:        And I have s:- uh blister? in my mouth?
```

Thus, although children in these data do exhibit less interactional competence than their parents generally (erratic responses and delays), we also see that children can answer questions competently and can do so without delay.[4]

Giving children the opportunity to answer questions is important from a language socialization perspective. Questions are *a* – if not *the* – central interactional mechanism physicians have for socializing children into the patient role. With a question, the physician shows the child what sort of information s/he should have at hand in a medical visit. For instance, when a physician asks about the quality of a cough ('Is it a wet cough?'; 'Are you coughing up phlegm?') the child is socialized into an aspect of their illness that they should (1) pay attention to and (2) be prepared to answer questions about. Children are, through questions, indirectly *instructed* on the sorts of information that they are responsible for knowing as a patient. If asking children questions is important for socialization into the patient role and if physicians sometimes ask children questions, what influences doctors to ask a child a particular question?

When Physicians Ask Children Questions

Question content

One important consideration for physicians in whether or not a question is directed to the parent or to the child is what the question is about. Questions in medical visits tend to fall into one of the nine content areas shown in Table 11.1.

These question areas indicate the range of information that any patient is accountable for knowing when they arrive at the clinic. Thus, patients (and parents) should be able to answer questions about why they are visiting; what their symptoms are; the quality of those symptoms; the frequency, severity and duration of the symptoms; their general health; their background and social situation; whether they are ready for a given examination or procedure; and how something feels. Physicians consistently ask questions in all of these content areas and thus treat patients (and parents) as accountable for knowing this information. Children who are asked questions in more content areas are held accountable for a wider range of information than those who are asked questions in a more narrow

Table 11.1   Content Areas of Questioning

Content Area	Examples
Opening the visit	'How can I help you? 'Are you sick?'
Identifying symptoms	'Does she have a fever?' 'Do you have a runny nose?'
Quality of symptoms	'Is it a wet cough?' 'Does the cough keep you awake?'
Quantity/duration of symptoms	'How long has he had the cough?' 'How many times did you throw up last night?'
Medication/treatment	'Have you given her any Robitussin?' 'Did you take some medicine?'
General health	'Does he have asthma?' 'Do you have any allergies?'
Social/background	'What grade's she in?' 'Did you get any presents from Santa Claus?'
Examination preparation	'Which ear should I look at first?' 'Are you ready?'
Illness experience	'Does this hurt?' 'Is it hard to breathe?'

range of content areas. In this way they are treated as more knowledgeable and more competent.

Perhaps surprisingly, doctors do address all of these types of questions to children, though they do so to varying degrees. Very few questions about quantity and duration, for instance, were addressed to children, whereas children received a lot of social/background questions. In particular, children were most likely to be asked social/background questions, examination preparation questions, and illness experience questions; other question types were more likely to be directed to parents (Stivers and Majid 2007).

Questioning in the latter two content domains – examination preparation and illness experience – may be driven by the fact that parents may simply be unable to say how something feels to the child or whether the child is ready. The former content domain – social/background – may reflect an effort to build rapport with children in the most innocuous content domain possible or may reflect a sense that in this domain children are in fact at least as competent as their parents to answer. Nonetheless, physicians do ask children other questions and whether physicians address these other questions to children is affected by four other factors that will be discussed in the sections that follow.

Child age

How old the child is also affects whether the physician directs a question to the child or not and thus whether they hold the child as accountable for knowing particular information. For instance, seven-to-nine-year-old children were asked questions about quantity and duration in 65 percent of visits (n = 22) whereas two-to-four-year-old children in these data almost never were (6 percent; n = 2). No matter what the question is about, older children are more likely to be asked questions than younger children (Stivers and Majid 2007). This suggests that physicians treat older children as more broadly knowledgeable than their younger counterparts.

Participant sex

Whether the physician is male or female and whether the child is a girl or a boy does not seem to affect whether the physician directs a question to the child. However, the sex of the parent does matter. Mothers usually bring children to the doctor (84 percent of the time), but fathers are present 20 percent of the time (sometimes along with mothers). Although one would not necessarily expect the presence of the father or mother to matter for whether a child is asked a question, this does in fact condition physicians' selection patterns. If the father is present, doctors are more likely to ask children questions, independently of the age of the child. The most plausible interpretation of this is that physicians treat fathers as less knowledgeable of health information about their children than mothers. Thus, if the father is present, the child is more likely to be treated as knowledgeable than if the mother is present (in which case she is oriented to as more knowledgeable most of the time). Although it is often the case that fathers are in a position to answer questions about their children, we can observe in Example 11.4 what may underlie this unexpected association: here, the physician directs her question to the father (line 1). In response he first claims to not know and then requests confirmation from his daughter that they have new soap at home (line 8; see also line 16).

Example 11.4:   SG517 ± eight-year-old girl

```
 1   DOC:   Any new soaps, new detergents,
 2   DAD:   Uh::, (1.0) I don' know. Could be new soap.
 3   DOC:   Mm:.
 4          (.)
 5   DOC:   That could be thuh rea[son.
 6   DAD:                          [That could be it?,
 7          (2.0)
 8   DAD:   Du- We have new bottle of soap right Caroline?
 9   PAT:   ((head nod))
10   DAD:   Yeah.
```

```
11              (2.0)
12   DAD:       Do you think [that's it?
13   DOC:                    ([) (That it.)
14   DAD:       (That's allergic [to it,)
15   DOC:                       [Any idea what kinda soap?
16   DAD:       I have no idea.
17   DOC:       huhhh ((laugh??))
18   PAT:       Prob'ly thuh uh:m#:
19   DAD:       Which one thuh o:ne,=
20   PAT:       =It's not thuh bar soap I think,
21   DAD:       [Oh:.
22   PAT:       [Because I use that all thuh ti:me.
23   DAD:       Okay which one do you (u[se to )
24   PAT:                              [I think it's that s:queeze one,
25   DAD:       Thuh squeeze one that you use to rub your body?
26              (0.2)
27   PAT:       Uh: it's kinda like that pink lo:ng bottle one?
28   DAD:       Okay:,
```

In pediatric visits fathers are commonly treated as less knowledgeable and, as exemplified here, sometimes *show* themselves to be less knowledgeable. One unexpected consequence of this is that children gain opportunities to contribute to the medical interaction when visiting with their fathers. In Example 11.4 the child, perhaps somewhat empowered by her father's uncertainty, goes on to suggest a possible source of her allergic reaction (lines 18/20/22/24). This is unusually proactive behavior for a child in these data.

Participant race/ethnicity

Adult patients seem to differ in their level of proactivity. Although patients rarely provide insight into their opinions and preferences, some patients assert diagnostic theories about their illnesses (Gill 1999; Stivers 2002b); some exploit response opportunities for their own agendas (Stivers 2007; Stivers and Heritage 2001); and some resist physicians' treatment recommendations, including not only passive forms of resistance such as silence but active forms such as questioning the treatment recommendation (Stivers 2002a; Stivers 2005; Stivers and Heritage 2001). Populations may differ systematically in their level of proactivity as adults. In previous studies non-white patients appeared to be less proactive than white patients (Gordon et al. 2006; Street et al. 2005). Moreover, Street et al. (2005) suggest not only that non-white patients are more likely to be passive but that physicians use less 'supportive talk' with them, which could perpetuate a more passive communication pattern (Makoul 1998). Similarly, in a different analysis of the present data, black parents never resisted or quarreled with a non-antibiotic treatment for an upper-respiratory-tract infection whereas whites, Asians, and Latinos did, at times, resist (Mangione-Smith et al. 2006).

In these data physicians were less likely to direct questions to children in African American families than they were to direct questions to children in Latino, Asian, or white families (Stivers and Majid 2007). This finding suggests that, although children of all racial and ethnic backgrounds are receiving 'passive socialization' into the patient role simply by attending the medical visit, black children are receiving less 'active socialization' by being held accountable for information about their health less frequently than other children. There is substantial evidence that the level of participation matters for the type of socialization children receive (e.g. Schieffelin and Ochs 1986). As a silent participant in an interaction, a child can, to the extent that they attend to the ongoing interaction, certainly learn and benefit (Bandura 1977; Rogoff et al. 2003). However, as an active interactant, the learning process (here, learning what one's responsibilities are in the patient role) is enhanced (Garton 1992). Thus, a child who passively observes her mother being held accountable for knowing how deep the child's cough is receives less socialization into the patient role than she would if she were asked herself and thus *herself* held accountable for a response. Through direct questioning, physicians can also subsequently treat a response as more or less acceptable, giving children feedback on the adequacy of their response and potentially on their knowledge level.

Socioeconomic status

In the United States, inequalities rooted in race and those rooted in class are frequently intertwined. However, in her ethnography *Unequal Childhoods* (2003), Annette Lareau offers a compelling account of differences between American middle-class and working-class child-rearing practices. In particular, relying on observational data she argues that both white and black middle-class parents engage in 'concerted cultivation' that instills a 'robust sense of entitlement' (Lareau 2003: 2). She argues further that this sense of entitlement plays an especially important role in institutional settings, where 'middle-class children learn to question adults and address them as relative equals' (2003: 2). Lareau suggests that the different philosophies that middle-class and working-class parents follow in raising (and talking with) children lead to 'the transmission of differential advantages to children' (2003: 5). She cites, for instance, the way that both black and white middle-class children learn to shake hands and sustain mutual eye gaze with adults, a form of interaction that working-class children learn specifically *not* to do. Since studies of job interviews suggest that the use of eye contact and firm handshakes are important to outcomes (Burgoon et al. 1985; Stewart et al. 2008), Lareau argues that this kind of simple interactional skill can make a significant difference later in the lives of these children.

Lareau observes parents in some of their routine medical visits as well and suggests that in these interactions, as in other interactions with professionals, middle-class parents are typically relaxed and communicative and that their children exhibit 'emerging signs of entitlement' in these encounters (2003: 124). Lareau operationalizes 'signs of entitlement' as a child's willingness to, for instance, initiate repair on an opaque term used by a physician[5] – an action that, she suggests, working-class children do not appear to carry out with the same degree of entitlement. Such differences in behavior are likely attributable to different socialization patterns in interaction. In particular, Lareau discusses the way in which one middle-class African American parent coached her nine-year-old son to participate in his medical visit (Lareau 2003) and contrasts this with a working-class African American family's visit to the doctor where neither mother nor son exhibited signs of proactivity, answering questions minimally and softly. Lareau asserts that working-class families are frequently distrustful of people in positions of authority in major institutions such as medical clinics (on variations in beliefs about authority, see Kohn and Schooler 1983).

In pediatric visits in these data, socioeconomic status also matters for socialization, although it interacts with race in different ways. Black children in general, and Latino children whose accompanying parent has a low level of education, are less likely to be asked questions than their white, Asian, or highly educated Latino counterparts. In Southern California, the Latino parent population typically attained the lowest education of all racial/ethnic groups, and black parents were also, on average, less educated than white and Asian parents (Stivers and Majid 2007). Thus, most children from a Latino or black background are questioned less than their white and Asian counterparts, independently of child age.

It is widely acknowledged that socioeconomic and ethnic disparities exist in healthcare; the basic patterns are well known (for relevant reviews see Robert and House 2000; Schnittker and McLeod 2005; Smedley, Stith, and Nelson 2003; Williams and Collins 1995). Socioeconomic status is inversely associated with mortality (House and Williams 2000; Rogot 1992) and morbidity (House and Williams 2000), and ethnic/racial groups systematically vary in terms of rates of chronic illnesses. For instance, blacks are at greater risk than whites of morbidity and mortality resulting from asthma, heart disease, and diabetes (Smedley, Stith, and Nelson 2003). There is substantial and consistent evidence of both racial/ethnic and socioeconomic disparities in healthcare across a range of illnesses and healthcare services even after accounting for the effects of language ability and access to care (e.g. Weinick and Krauss 2000).

The results discussed in this section are summarized in Table 11.2. They show one way in which health disparities might manifest in interaction. They further suggest that the two racial/ethnic groups most likely to suffer from chronic illness as adults (Latinos and blacks) and thus most likely to need skills in how to be a proactive patient are the least likely to receive childhood socialization into that role.

Accounting for Physician Behavior

The findings reviewed here document one way in which physicians treat children differently based on socioeconomic status and race/ethnicity. However, they do

Table 11.2   Overview of Factors Associated with Physicians Selecting Children

Factors	Effect – Increase in Odds that Doctor will Select the Child

Question content:
  Social/background
  Examination preparation
  Illness experience
	5.58× more likely (p < .001)

Child age	1.22× more likely for each additional year (p < .001)
Father present at visit	1.63× more likely (p < .01)
Parent is black	.22× (i.e. decrease by 78 percent) p < .05
Parent is working-class Latino	1.56× more likely (p < .05)

Data from Stivers and Majid (2007).

not provide a clear account of why. One possible explanation is interactional – there may be something about the way physicians, parents, and children interact when the parents are black and/or working-class Latino that differs from the way in which physicians interact when parents are white or Asian that is independent of the ethncity of the physician.[6]

It could be that black parents are less facilitating of questions being directed to their children – they may view their children's participation as less desirable than their white and Asian counterparts.[7] If this were the case, we might expect black parents to display their preference for questions to be directed to them by *answering* questions directed to their children either in place of their children or after the child had answered. However, there is no indication of this in these visits. Black parents were no more likely to answer questions for their children or after their children than white parents (Stivers and Majid 2007). Rather, like their white and Asian counterparts, black parents typically respect their child's right to answer a question if the physician has selected them (Stivers 2001).

Another interactional possibility is that black physicians might understand cultural differences in the behavior of black parents and children better than physicians of other racial/ethnic backgrounds and thus the disparity in selecting black children, if it were the result of a misunderstanding of behavioral cues, should be less among black physicians. However, neither in these data nor in at least one other study investigating race effects and physician–patient communication (Gordon et al. 2006) is there an effect of racial concordance on these types of communication behaviors.

A final interactional explanation might be that children growing up in households where they are not expected or even not allowed to participate in professional interactions might not be as good at it (see, for instance, Kohn and Schooler

1983; Lareau 2003). Were this true of black families or of working-class Latino families in general, we would expect children from these backgrounds to be less responsive than children of other backgrounds. We can thus investigate what conditions a child to respond to a question s/he has been selected to answer. Does the racial/ethnic and education background of the parent matter? I address this question in the following section.

Predictors of child response

Two factors that predict when physicians will ask a child a question also predict whether a child will answer it: how old the child is and what the question is about. Children are more likely to answer all sorts of questions as they get older, and they are more likely to answer social questions, questions about their readiness for examination, and questions about their illness experience independent of age. In addition, girls are more likely than boys to answer questions asked of them (but recall that physicians are no more likely to ask questions of girls than boys). This suggests that a physician who holds an older child or a girl accountable for answering a question will be most successful in securing an answer. Similarly, physicians are more successful in getting an answer when they hold children accountable for social background information (something they are likely used to being held accountable for in school and other social contexts), how their illness makes them feel, and whether they are ready for an examination or procedure.

Certain other factors about the way in which the physician delivers the question also affect the child's likelihood of answering: (1) If a question is a polar question (yes/no), the child is more likely to answer; (2) if the physician looks at the child while asking the question, the child is also more likely to answer the question; (3) certain physicians are more likely to get a child to answer a question, and if they get one answer they are likely to get more answers to subsequent questions. These factors are summarized in Table 11.3.

What is striking is that neither parent race/ethnicity nor parent education is predictive of actual child responsiveness – children are equally likely to answer questions when their parent has only an eighth-grade education or when their parents are Latino or black. If the underlying account for physicians asking children of these backgrounds fewer questions is that these children consistently have trouble answering or that their parents discourage them from doing so, there should have been support for this in these analyses, and we see none.

Returning to the issue of what accounts for the differences in physician questioning patterns by race/ethnicity and education (as a proxy for socioeconomic status), an alternative possibility to the interactionally endogenous explanations discussed above is that the disparity in physician questioning patterns is driven by exogenous attitudes towards the participants as more or less competent to answer the questions. Specifically, when someone asks an individual a question, s/he treats that person as competent and willing to answer the question. There was no difference in the number of questions that physicians asked of families from different racial/ethnic backgrounds ($F(3321) = 1.79$, $p = .15$) or different

Table 11.3   Factors that Predict whether a Child will Answer a Physician's Question

Factor	Effect – Increase in Odds that Child will Answer the Question

Question content:
  Social/background
  Examination preparation
  Illness experience
	1.28× more likely (p ≤ .01)

Child age	1.19× more likely for each additional year (p ≤ .001)
Physician gazing at child during question	1.27× more likely (p ≤ .05)
Polar question	2× more likely (p ≤ .001)
Parent is black	Nonsignificant
Parent is working-class Latino	Nonsignificant

education levels (F(4321) = 1.85, p = .12) (Stivers and Majid 2007). However, physicians treat children with black or less-educated Latino parents as less able to answer their questions, as evidenced by the fact that physicians are more likely to ask parents rather than children in these contexts. This judgment appears not to be the result of overt racism insofar as physicians do not appear to be less willing to interact with these families nor are they less willing to ask them questions.

Nonetheless, this behavior may be a form of implicit racism in the sense that physicians appear to judge certain children as less able to answer questions than other children (Balsa and McGuire 2003). Research on implicit racism suggests that many white Americans hold implicit negative stereotypes about black Americans (Blair 2001; Dasgupta 2004; Greenwald, McGhee, and Schwartz 1998) and Latinos (Uhlmann et al. 2002), even if they do not have explicitly racist attitudes. Moreover, a range of studies show that interactions with black experimenters are more likely to be uncomfortable or negative if the individual scored high on an implicit prejudice scale (Dovidio et al. 1997; Fazio and Olson 2003; McConnell and Leibold 2001).

Relatedly, van Ryn and Burke show that physicians tend to perceive black individuals and people of low to middle socioeconomic groups more negatively than white individuals and members of higher socioeconomic groups (van Ryn 2002). Perhaps even more relevant were physicians' perceptions that black individuals are less intelligent and less educated (even when socioeconomic status was held constant): 'Blacks are only half as likely as whites to be considered "very intelligent" and less than two-thirds as likely as whites to be considered "very" or "somewhat" educated' (van Ryn and Burke 2000: 819). Further, members of lower socioeconomic groups are also more likely to be perceived as less intelligent (van Ryn and Burke 2000).

The findings discussed here, though not conclusive, are consistent with this work. In addition to physicians asking the children of black and working-class Latino families fewer questions, they also gazed significantly less at black children than at white children (though not less at Latino children). Physicians gazed at children when the child was being selected more often than they gazed at their parents when the parent was being selected (83 percent versus 55 percent of the time, respectively). However, whereas physicians gazed during 87 percent of questions asked of white children, they gazed during only 80 percent of questions selecting black children [χ^2 (1, $N = 1009$) = 7.41, $p < .001$]. Race-specific gaze aversion has previously been associated with implicit bias (Dovidio et al. 1997). Physician gaze to the child significantly predicted child responsiveness, so, in spite of reduced gaze, black children were nonetheless responding at the same rate as their white counterparts. Still, the lack of gaze suggests less engagement with black children and is, again, consistent with the hypothesis that physicians are behaving in an implicitly biased way towards black and working-class Latino children. It remains possible that physicians were very good at predicting, from their very first question, whether a child would answer a question across the ethnic/racial groups and that this predicting ability is the reason for this null result. This seems unlikely, though further exploration would be necessary.

Discussion

Pediatric visits help to shape child patients' views of and orientations to the role they are *able*, *allowed*, and, in the future, *obliged* to play in their own healthcare. Parents, physicians, and children each participate in the child's socialization into this role. As Lareau (2003) has documented, some parents actively prepare children to participate in medical visits while others do not. Although there is no systematic study of the effect of parent preparation on child participation, Lareau observed that children who were socialized to behave in more entitled ways participated more in their medical visits. In turn, children who participate more in medical visits contribute to the socialization process themselves by placing themselves in a position to be held accountable for information and as orienting to themselves as knowledgeable and accountable participants in their own right (see e.g. Corsaro (1997) and James and James (2004) for discussions of the role of the child in socialization processes).

However, even the children from upper-middle-class highly educated white families did not participate much in these medical visits. For this reason, physicians play a critical role in involving children (or not) through their questioning and thus in socializing them into their future roles as autonomous patients. This socialization may encourage children to respond passively and with a minimal sense of entitlement or it may encourage them to respond actively and to view themselves as both entitled to and accountable for participating in their own healthcare. It may teach them that they are simply receivers of information or that they bring significant information and knowledge to the medical visit. Finally, from these interactions, children may be socialized to believe that they must merely receive providers' decisions and that they have little efficacy over those decisions; or, alternatively, that they can learn to play an effective role with respect to their healthcare decisions. When physicians ask their child patients questions, they treat the child as a competent individual, first and foremost. They treat him/her as an individual with rights and responsibilities to know about his/her own health. With different types of questions, physicians treat children as experts about their social lives, bodies, symptoms, health history, and self-management.

There are at least two reasons why the differential socialization that minority children receive by virtue of physicians' differential involvement of them in the visit is an important problem. First, as has been suggested in this chapter, there is no evidence that such a pattern is motivated by doctors finding that black and Latino child patient populations are less responsive than their Asian and white counterparts. Second, all children stand to benefit from such socialization with professionals. As Lareau has suggested (2003), children learn a lot about how to interact with institutional professionals from these experiences. Certainly, routine medical visits do not happen every week, but visits with institutional professionals, of which physicians are one type, do happen routinely in the everyday lives of American families. If the physician behavior discussed here is similar to the behavior of other institutional professionals (and it likely is) then children are receiving different messages about their levels of entitlement and accountability through these interactions. Specifically, black and lower-socioeconomic-status Latino children are being held accountable for fewer types of information overall.

Moreover, as discussed earlier, the modern American medical system is increasingly set up in ways that ensure that proactive patients receive better healthcare than their more passive counterparts. If children of particular racial and socioeconomic backgrounds receive less socialization into the active patient role and are generally socialized to be less proactive and less direct with institutional authorities, then the individuals who stand to be at greatest risk for chronic health problems (minority and lower-socioeconomic-status individuals), and therefore most in need of resources to be proactive in their healthcare, are disempowered through this process as they grow to adulthood.

When physicians do not involve these minority children in their healthcare, they run the risk of bringing less competence as medical patients into being, as famously demonstrated by Rosenthal and Jacobsen (1992 [1968]) in the education context. When physicians ask parents, rather than children, questions about the child's health, they show the child that they view the parent as more competent to answer and by implication that they view the child as less competent. Because this applies differentially across racial and socioeconomic groups, the very children who are likely being perceived as less competent are having that (lack of) competence reinforced (see also Makoul 1998).

More generally, these studies are part of a long list showing that it is not only minority children who are being excluded from such interactions; children are more generally marginalized across these interactions and perhaps much more generally in daily social life (e.g. see James and James 2004). This chapter helps to elucidate how interactional marginalization occurs with institutional professionals. Such exclusion, while at times necessary and arguably appropriate, is nonetheless a mechanism for disempowering children (Lareau 2003). By not selecting them to answer questions about their own illnesses, doctors are treating children as neither accountable for nor knowledgeable about their own health status. It is certainly the case that by attending medical visits children are learning a substantial amount about the patient role, but I suggest that they learn more when they are asked and held accountable for responding to doctors' questions.

The studies discussed here open the door for new investigations into how practitioner–patient interactions both reflect and contribute to the structural factors that reproduce racial and socioeconomic health disparities through child language socialization. Future research using longitudinal data should investigate the hypothesis offered by these studies that how children are socialized into the patient role by physicians will affect future medical interactions when they are acting as autonomous adult patients or at least as older children or adolescents.

ACKNOWLEDGMENTS

This chapter is partially based on two journal articles, 'Questioning children: Interactional evidence of implicit bias in medical interviews' published in *Social Psychology Quarterly* 70, 424–41 in 2007 and 'Physician–child interaction: When children respond to physicians' questions in routine medical encounters,' currently under review. Thank you to Penny Brown for comments on an earlier draft and to participants of the CLIC workshop on socialization for comments on a previous presentation.

NOTES

1 In fact, learning to seek medical help at all may be seen as an important part of the sick role that must be learned within a culture (Parsons 1951).
2 But see also Bruner (1975).
3 Due to the context, it is possible that children are less responsive because they are ill. The illnesses the children in these data are suffering from are all similar – upper respiratory tract infections. However, some children may have felt more sick than others. We have no measure of this in the analyses that follow.
4 Although children of younger ages may have more problems of this kind, these data suggest that there is a qualitative difference between children (across the age spectrum represented here) and adults.
5 On different orientations to health providers and patient entitlement see Lutfey and Freese (2005).

6   The difference is clearly not as simple as being a native speaker of the language since Asians and Latinos would be expected to be grouped together if that were the underlying explanation.
7   Note that the sample is not large enough and has insufficient numbers of people of high and low socioeconomic status across the racial groups to definitively separate socioeconomic status and race, but at this point the results seem to generalize across race.

REFERENCES

Aronsson, K. and Rundström, B. (1988) Child discourse and parental control in pediatric consultations. *Text* 8(3): 159–89.

Balsa, A. I. and McGuire, T. G. (2003) Prejudice, clinical uncertainty, and stereotyping as sources of health disparities. *Journal of Health Economics* 22: 89–116.

Bandura, A. (1977) *Social Learning Theory*. Englewood Cliffs, NJ: Prentice Hall.

Blair, I. (2001) Implicit stereotypes and prejudice. In G. Moskowitz (ed.), *Cognitive Social Psychology: On the Tenure and Future of Social Cognition*. 359–74. Mahwah, NJ: Lawrence Erlbaum.

Brody, D. S. (1980) The patient's role in clinical decision-making. *Annals of Internal Medicine* 93: 718–22.

Brown, P. (1998) Conversational structure and language acquisition: The role of repetition in Tzeltal adult and child speech. *Journal of Linguistic Anthropology* 8(2): 197–221.

Bruner, J. (1975) The ontogenesis of speech acts. *Journal of Child Language* 2: 1–19.

Burgoon, J. K., Manusov, V., Mineo, P., and Hale, J. L. (1985) Effects of gaze on hiring, credibility, attraction and relational message interpretation. *Journal of Nonverbal Behavior* 9(3): 133–46.

Clancy, P. M. (1999) The socialization of affect in Japanese mother–child conversation. *Journal of Pragmatics* 31: 1397–421.

Clemente, I. (2005) *Negotiating the Limits of Uncertainty and Non-Disclosure: Communication and Culture in the Management of Pediatric Cancer Treatment in Barcelona*. Doctoral Dissertation. University of California, Los Angeles.

Corsaro, W. A. (1997) *The Sociology of Childhood*. Thousand Oaks, CA: Pine Forge Press.

Danziger, K. (ed.) (1971) *Readings in Child Socialization*. Oxford: Pergamon.

Dasgupta, N. (2004) Implicit ingroup favoritism, outgroup favoritism, and their behavioral manifestations. *Social Justice Research* 17(2): 143–69.

de León, L. (1998) The emergent participant: Interactive patterns in the socialization of Tzotzil (Mayan) infants. *Journal of Linguistic Anthropology* 8: 131–61.

Dovidio, J. F., Kawakami, K., Johnson, C., Johnson, B., and Howard, A. (1997) On the nature of prejudice: Automatic and controlled processes. *Journal of Experimental Social Psychology* 33: 510–40.

Evans, B. J., Kiellerup, F. D., Stanley, R. O., Burrows, G. D., and Sweet, B. (1987) A communications skills programme for increasing patients' satisfaction with general practice consultations. *British Journal of Medical Psychology* 60: 373–8.

Fazio, R. H. and Olson, M. A. (2003) Implicit measures in social cognition research: Their meaning and uses. *Annual Review of Psychology* 54: 297–327.

Freemon, B., Negrete, V., Davis, M., and Korsch, B. (1971) Gaps in doctor–patient communication: Doctor-patient interaction analysis. *Pediatric Research* 5: 298–311.

Frosch, D. L. and Kaplan, R. M. (1999) Shared decision making in clinical medicine: Past research and future directions. *American Journal of Preventive Medicine* 27(11): 1139–45.

Garrett, P. B. and Baquedano-López, P. (2002) Language socialization: Reproduction and continuity, transformation and change. *Annual Review of Anthropology* 31: 339–61.

Garton, A. F. (1992) *Social Interaction and the Development of Language and Cognition.* Hove, UK: Lawrence Erlbaum.

Gill, V. (1999) Doing attributions in medical interaction: Patients' explanations for illness and doctors' responses. *Social Psychology Quarterly* 61(4): 342–60.

Gordon, H. S., Street, R. L., Sharf, B. F., and Souchek, J. (2006) Racial differences in doctors' information-giving and patients' participation. *Cancer* 107: 1313–20.

Greenfield, S., Kaplan, S. H., Ware, J. E., Yano, E. M., and Frank, H. J. L. (1988) Patients' participation in medical care: Effects on blood sugar control and quality of life in diabetes. *Journal of General Internal Medicine* 3: 448–57.

Greenwald, A. G., McGhee, D. E., and Schwartz, J. L. K. (1998) Measuring individual differences in implicit cognition: The implicit association test. *Journal of Personality and Social Psychology* 74(6): 1464–80.

Guadagnoli, E. and Ward, P. (1998) Patient participation in decision making. *Social Science and Medicine* 47(3): 329–39.

Halkowski, T. (2006) Realizing the illness: Patients' narratives of symptom discovery. In J. Heritage and D. Maynard (eds.), *Communication in Medical Care: Interactions Between Primary Care Physicians and Patients.* 86–114. Cambridge: Cambridge University Press.

Heath, C. (1986) *Body Movement and Speech in Medical Interaction.* Cambridge: Cambridge University Press.

Heath, S. B. (1983) *Ways with Words: Language, Life and Work in Communities and Classrooms.* Cambridge: Cambridge University Press.

Heritage, J. and Robinson, J. (2006) Accounting for the visit: Giving reasons for seeking medical care. In J. Heritage and D. Maynard (eds.), *Communication in Medical Care: Interactions Between Primary Care Physicians and Patients.* 48–85. Cambridge: Cambridge University Press.

House, J. S. and Williams, D. R. (2000) Understanding and reducing socioeconomic and racial/ethnic disparities in health. In B. D. Smedley and S. L. Syme (eds.), *Promoting Health: Intervention Strategies From Social and Behavior Research.* 81–124. Washington, DC: National Academy Press.

Howard, K. (2004) Socializing respect at school in Northern Thailand. *Working Papers in Educational Linguistics* 21(1): 1–30.

James, A. and James, A. L. (2004) *Constructing Childhood.* New York, NY: Palgrave Macmillan.

Kaplan, S. H., Greenfield, S., and Ware, J. E. (1989) Assessing the effects of physician–patient interactions on the outcomes of chronic disease. *Medical Care* 27: S110–26.

Kohn, M. and Schooler, C. (eds.) (1983) *Work and Personality: An Inquiry Into the Impact of Social Stratification.* Norwood, NJ: Ablex.

Lareau, A. (2003) *Unequal Childhoods: Class, Race, and Family Life.* Berkeley, CA: University of California Press.

Lutfey, K. and Freese, J. (2005) Toward some fundamentals of fundamental causality: Socioeconomic status and health in the routine clinic visit for diabetes. *American Journal of Sociology* 110: 1326–72.

Makoul, G. (1998) Perpetuating passivity: Reliance and reciprocal determinism in physician–patient interaction. *Journal of Health Communication* 3: 233–59.

Mandelblatt, J., Kreling, B., Figeuriedo, M., and Feng, S. (2006) What is the impact of shared decision making on treatment and outcomes for older women with breast cancer? *Journal of Clinical Oncology* 24(30): 4908–13.

Mangione-Smith, R., Elliott, M. N., Stivers, T., McDonald, L. L., and Heritage, J. (2006) Ruling out the need for antibiotics: Are we sending the right message? *Archives of Pediatric and Adolescent Medicine, A.* 160: 945–52.

McConnell, A. R. and Leibold, J. M. (2001) Relations among the implicit association test, discriminatory behavior, and explicit measures of racial attitudes. *Journal of Experimental Social Psychology* 37: 435–42.

Mead, G. H. (1934) *Mind, Self, and Society.* Chicago, IL: University of Chicago Press.

Michaels, S. (1981) 'Sharing time': Children's narrative styles and differential access to literacy. *Language in Society* 10: 423–42.

Moore, L. C. (2006) Learning by heart in Qur'anic and public schools in northern Cameroon. *Social Analysis: The International Journal of Cultural and Social Practice* 50(3): 109–26.

Nayfield, S. G., Bongiovanni, G. C., Alciati, M. H., Fischer, R. A., and Bergner, L. (1994) Review of statutory requirements for disclosure of breast cancer treatment alternatives. *Journal of the National Cancer Institute* 86(16): 1202–8.

Ochs, E. and Schieffelin, B. B. (1983) *Acquiring Conversational Competence.* Boston, MA: Routledge and Kegan Paul.

Ochs, E. and Schieffelin, B. B. (1984) Language acquisition and socialization: Three developmental stories and their implications. In R. Shweder and R. LeVine (eds.), *Culture Theory: Essays on Mind, Self and Emotion.* 276–320. New York: Cambridge University Press.

Pantell, R. H., Steward, T. J., Dias, J. K., Wells, P., and Ross, A. W. (1982) Physician communication with children and parents. *Pediatrics* 70(3): 396–402.

Parsons, T. (1951) *The Social System.* New York: Free Press.

Philips, S. (1983) *The Invisible Culture: Communication in Classroom and Community on the Warm Springs Indian Reservation.* New York: Longman.

Pozo, C., Carver, C. S., Noriega, V., Harris, S. D., Robinson, D. S., Ketcham, A. S., Legaspi, A., Moffat Jr., F. L., and Clark, K. C. (1992) Effects of mastectomy vs lumpectomy on emotional adjustment to breast cancer: A prospective study of the first year postsurgery. *Journal of Clinical Oncology* 10: 1292–8.

Robert, S. A. and House, J. S. (2000) Socioeconomic inequalities in health: An enduring sociological problem. In C. E. Bird, P. Conrad, and A. M. Feremond (eds.), *Handbook of Medical Sociology.* 79–97. Upper Saddle River, NJ: Prentice Hall.

Rogoff, B., Paradise, R., Arauz, R. M., Correa-Chávez, M., and Angelillo, C. (2003) Firsthand learning through intent participation. *Annual Review of Psychology* 54: 175–203.

Rogot, E. (1992) *A Mortality Study of 1.3 Million Persons by Demographic, Social and Economic Factors: 1979–1985 Follow-Up.* Bethseda, MD: National Institutes of Health, National Heart, Lung, Blood Institute.

Rosenthal, R. and Jacobsen, L. (1992 [1968]) *Pygmalion in the Classroom.* New York: Irvington Publishers.

Schieffelin, B. B. and Ochs, E. (eds.) (1986) *Language Socialization Across Cultures.* Cambridge: Cambridge University Press.

Schnittker, J. and McLeod, J. D. (2005) The social psychology of health disparities. *Annual Review of Sociology* 31: 75–103.

Schulman, B. A. (1979) Active patient orientation and outcomes in hypertensive treatment. *Medical Care* 17: 267–80.

Smedley, B. D., Stith, A. Y., and Nelson, A. R. (eds.) (2003) *Unequal Treatment: Confronting Racial and Ethnic Disparities in Health Care.* Washington, DC: The National Academies Press.

Stewart, G. L., Dustin, S. L., Barrick, M. R., and Darnold, T. C. (2008) Exploring the handshake in employment interviews. *Journal of Applied Psychology* 93(5): 1139–46.

Stivers, T. (2001) Negotiating who presents the problem: Next speaker selection in pediatric encounters. *Journal of Communication* 51(2): 1–31.

Stivers, T. (2002a) Participating in decisions about treatment: Overt parent pressure for antibiotic medication in pediatric encounters. *Social Science and Medicine* 54(7): 1111–30.

Stivers, T. (2002b) 'Symptoms only' versus 'candidate diagnoses': Presenting the problem in pediatric encounters. *Health Communication* 14(3): 299–338.

Stivers, T. (2005) Parent resistance to physicians' treatment recommendations: One resource for initiating a negotiation of the treatment decision. *Health Communication* 18(1): 41–74.

Stivers, T. (2007) *Prescribing Under Pressure: Parent–Physician Conversations and Antibiotics.* New York: Oxford University Press.

Stivers, T. (under review) Physician–child interaction: When children answer physicians' questions in routine medical encounters. *Patient Education and Counseling.*

Stivers, T. and Heritage, J. (2001) Breaking the sequential mould: Answering 'more than the question' during comprehensive history taking. *Text* 21(1): 151–85.

Stivers, T. and Majid, A. (2007) Questioning children: Interactional evidence of implicit bias in medical interviews. *Social Psychology Quarterly* 70: 424–41.

Street, R. L., Gordon, H. S., Ward, M. M., Krupat, E., and Kravtiz, R. L. (2005) Patient participation in medical consultations: Why some patients are more involved than others. *Medical Care* 43(10): 960–9.

Tates, K. and Meeuwesen, L. (2001) Doctor–parent–child communication. A

(re)view of the literature. *Social Science and Medicine* 52: 839–51.

US Department of Health and Human Services, Public Health Service. (2000) *Healthy People 2010: Understanding and Improving Health.* Washington, DC: U. S. Government Printing Office.

Uhlmann, E., Dasgupta, N., Elgueta, A., Greenwald, A. G., and Swanson, J. (2002) Subgroup prejudice based on skin color among Hispanics in the United States and Latin America. *Social Cognition* 20: 198–225.

van Dulmen, A. M. (1998) Children's contributions to pediatric outpatient encounters. *Pediatrics* 102(3 Pt 1): 563–8.

van Ryn, M. (2002) Research on the provider contribution to race/ethnicity disparities in medical care. *Medical Care* 40: I140–51.

van Ryn, M. and Burke, J. (2000) The effect of patient race and socio-economic status on physicians' perceptions of patients. *Social Science and Medicine* 50(6): 813–28.

Wassmer, E., Minnaar, G., Aal, N. A., Atkinson, M., Gupta, E., Yuen, S., and Rylance, G. (2004) How do paediatricians communicate with children and parents. *Acta Paediatrica* 93: 1501–6.

Waterworth, S. and Luker, K. A. (1990) Do patients want to be involved in decisions concerning care? *Journal of Advanced Nursing* 15(8): 970–6.

Weinick, R. M. and Krauss, N. A. (2000) Racial/ethnic differences in children's access to care. *American Journal of Public Health* 90(11): 1771–4.

Williams, D. R. and Collins, C. (1995) U. S. socioeconomic and racial differences in health: Patterns and explanations. *Annual Review of Sociology* 21: 349–86.

Xu, K. T. (2004) The combined effects of participatory styles of elderly patients and their physicians on satisfaction. *Health Services Research* 39(2): 377–92.

Part III   Social Orientations

'Social orientations' refers to the subjectivities, demeanors, statuses, roles, stances, and other ways in which interlocutors, either by obligation or by choice, verbally and nonverbally position themselves vis-à-vis each other in interactions. These are incorporated in cultural systems of social hierarchy and of inclusion and exclusion, theories of personhood, and moral and religious practices such as modesty, respect, politeness, and deference. The chapters in Part III examine the verbal resources that typically draw on all levels of language, from phonology to pragmatics, and the language socialization practices that assist novices in using them so that they can appropriately participate in social interactions.

The chapters complement others in the volume with their careful attention to embodied, situated practices; multimodal perspectives on how attention, empathy, and intersubjectivity are achieved; the ways in which theory of mind is socialized across various communities; and the role that language and verbal routines play in how theory of mind is expressed. While usually thought to be the domain of small children during first language acquisition, we also see the implications of language socialization routines for multilingual and for older second language learners as part of 'getting into' a particular view of and set of actions organized around sociality. This requires sensitivity to participation frameworks, sequential organization of talk, topics of talk, and careful attention to the cultural meanings linked to social practices, as well as ethnographic data for identifying how talk-in-interaction constitutes and facilitates contextually nuanced, appropriate pedagogical opportunities.

The chapters in Part III also link to others in the volume by calling attention to the affective functions and uses of language for assessing and evaluating, but here the focus is on social categories, identities, and social stereotypes. Thus, this work on language socialization integrates earlier concerns in pragmatic development, paying attention to particular speech acts (e.g. requests/directives and tattling)

The Handbook of Language Socialization, First Edition. Edited by Alessandro Duranti,
Elinor Ochs, and Bambi B. Schieffelin.
© 2014 John Wiley & Sons, Ltd. Published 2014 by John Wiley & Sons, Ltd.

and genres (e.g. teasing and narrative) and the roles they play in creating social worlds.

In 'Language Socialization and Politeness Routines,' Burdelski (Chapter 12) focuses on the pervasive use of routines by more competent speakers to model particular stances associated with politeness, respect, or deference. Politeness, which he describes as ways of maintaining social and communicative concord and avoiding social discord, is often socialized in multimodal routines, embodied practices that display culturally relevant features (e.g. age, kinship, gender) and other forms of social hierarchy in addition to preferences for sociality. Burdelski highlights the salience of politeness routines throughout Japanese society. These are marked by specific linguistic resources – for example, honorifics, politeness formulas, pragmatic particles, and particular types of adjacency pairs – as well as empathy training and the use of indirection, forms that are used throughout the life cycle.

Because of early and consistent socialization and scaffolding by caregivers, by the age of two, children have acquired basic politeness practices. Based on micro-analyses of video-taped data in families and preschool settings in Japan, Burdelski details how Japanese caregivers effect this: they enact politeness routines on behalf of their preverbal children before they are capable of performing them, thus offering a model, and also perform appropriate demeanors with other adults (see Howard, this volume). Burdelski identifies three main politeness routine strategies: speaking for the child, directives and prompting, and reported speech, which can co-occur in a given sequence. One sees a type of intersubjectivity attempted when the caregiver speaks for the child that is associated with the close caregiver–child bond and 'speaking as one.' Directives and prompting are common, and overwhelmingly occur in triadic arrangements, where the caregiver tells the child to say something to a third party to encourage social relationships (see Moore, this volume). The chapter details four types of prompting: empty slot (a type of scaffolding that helps the child to complete a partial utterance); leading questions (use of a *wh* question); performative (using an explicit verb such as apologize); and elicited imitation, which provides the model utterance with the verb 'say,' this being the most frequent type in the data. Burdelski links this preference to broader cultural theories of learning that stress the importance of demonstration and modeling followed by imitation of form, such as is evidenced in later apprentice-ship in learning rituals and arts practices. Thus, these discursive and embodied strategies found in early language socialization routines are foundational to learn-ing how to learn in Japanese society. Caregivers are concerned that even small children publicly present appropriate social demeanors, and will correct their behavior toward persons, animals, and inanimate objects. Examining interactions in homes and preschools, Burdelski shows a consistency of practices, including attention to others' needs and wants, and social hierarchy.

Cook's 'Language Socialization and Stance-Taking Practices' (Chapter 13) shows the importance of the dialogic process of stance-taking for establishing a sense of shared understanding. While drawing on comparative data from other Asian languages, Cook focuses on the rich linguistic resources of Japanese for marking a range of affective stances used by parents and children to index particular identities and adherence to social norms at home and at school. Learning nonreferential indexes occurs as part of first language socialization but is more difficult for older, second language learners, especially in classroom settings where teachers' talk uses few pragmatic particles. Cook elaborates on a Japanese linguistic preference for establishing subjectivity and intersubjectivity by pragmatically marking the shared domains of knowledge/affect and authority of knowledge with evidential stance markers. The psychological state of the speaker is linguistically distinguished from that of second and third persons, which involves demonstrating how one has come to have the knowledge of others' internal states. The particle *deshoo*, for example, indexes two different knowledge domains: subjectivity (authority of knowledge) and intersubjectivity (shared knowledge). Unless speaker and addressee have access to the same shared knowledge, *deshoo* is not used. Given that certain domains of knowledge, such as cooking, are gendered, *deshoo* can also index social identities. Similarly, in intercultural situations, *deshoo* can also index Japanese cultural identity as it indexes a particular authority or 'territory' of knowledge. For Japanese foreign language learners to become competent users of the epistemic stance marker, they must become sensitive to participation frameworks, sequential organization of talk, topics of talk, and Japanese cultural practices, which elude the objectifying discourse of second language classroom instruction. Adult learners' informal settings become sensitive to these pragmatic markings and relatively early use this form appropriately. Cook's analyses underscore the importance of looking at stance-rich, naturally occurring settings, which aid in the establishment of subtle nuances of pragmatic meanings and provides evidence of the contextual dimensions that need to be taken into account to mark stance appropriately.

Fader's 'Language Socialization and Morality' (Chapter 14) theoretically links the politics of modernity, agency, and moral discourse as central to the formation and socialization of subjectivities, or concepts and practices of identity. Treating morality as culturally constructed embodied practices, Fader details how they are displayed in social interaction. But, to achieve a more political and historicized perspective, Fader argues for attention to immigration, colonialism, and religious and political movements as they afford contexts for transformation and change rather than social reproduction. She points out some limitations of Bourdieu's notions of the body and fields of power, suggesting that Foucault's ideas about power and embodiment are more relevant to socialization into religious beliefs and practices. Fader extends the idea of ethical practices that compose a genealogy of ethics and 'technologies of the self' – a term that integrates language and embodiment, including the sensory dimensions – to language socialization studies of morality.

Fader's research on demeanor, stance, affect, gender, and personhood among nonliberal Hasidic Jewish women and girls in Brooklyn, New York illustrates this framework. Contemporary Hasidic engagement with and critique of secular modernity highlights religious authorizing discourses that cultivate technologies of the self: praising, shaming, and using syncretic language practices, in addition to nonverbal behaviors. Modesty, a critical gendered technology of the self, which entails this set of moral practices, is socialized throughout the life cycle. Fader's chapter also signals the importance of socialization into and through practical and discursive moral consciousness to the anthropology of religion. Hasidic language socialization reveals at least two distinct orders of moral consciousness: rote habituation of the body (through prompting without explanation for certain religious practices) and aesthetics (rituals of prayer). The chapter evidences the widespread reliance on rote-guided repetition for moral education (see Moore, this volume). Participation in these rote interactions apprentices young children into practical consciousness that at a later time can be articulated as discursive consciousness, central to senses of identity in this community. Discursive consciousness is also enhanced through praising personal qualities and ethical ideals of gendered, moral subjects; carefully monitoring and disciplining desires; and discussing 'bad subjects,' where the intended outcome of parental or community socialization is not achieved. Fader persuasively argues that language socialization approaches open new insights into morality in the context of power, consciousness, and agency, and are thus relevant to current concerns in cultural and linguistic anthropology more broadly.

Howard's 'Language Socialization and Hierarchy' (Chapter 15) analyzes the discursive practices and processes through which children come to verbally express relative status asymmetries in relationships central to their social worlds. Linguistic anthropological studies emphasize the emergent dimensions and semiotic resources for marking identities that are relational and positional, including respect. Howard underscores the importance of paying attention to semiotic resources that are indexically associated with particular social relationships through regular patterns of use, acknowledging that issues of agency and heterogeneity of understanding and interests create opportunities for speakers to resist or transform, as well as conform, to existing social structures. In families, schools, and other institutional settings, hierarchy and power are intertwined and expressed in a variety of ways.

Howard details practices used to sensitize children to the meanings, social organization, and contextualized dimensions of social hierarchy. Particular speech styles display associated demeanors appropriate to specific phases of the life cycle, particular cultural settings, and broader sociohistorical frameworks. Language socialization research from several hierarchical societies – Western Samoa, Japan, Korea, and China – foregrounds how different types of social hierarchies are connected to local notions of personhood and social relationships, and how different linguistic resources are used to express them. Caregivers' active interventions in shaping children's appropriate language use for marking their relationship to addressees and referents is critical to children's acquisition of greeting and politeness routines, registers, honorifics, code choice, and reported speech. In addition to enabling children's participation in social worlds, these interventions also suggest how language and speech practices are locally conceptualized, as inappropriate uses are often the topic of metadiscursive elaboration. Such commentaries are found in monolingual communities but are especially salient in multilingual and diasporic communities, where, in the context of multiple social and linguistic hierarchies, selection may index other aspects of identity such as gender, class, or ethnicity.

Based on her fieldwork in Northern Thailand among Kam Muang villagers and more urban, middle-class speakers, Howard illuminates discursive processes through which children are socialized into highly salient status asymmetries associated with relative age, gender, social status, and role in this multilingual speech community (Kam Muang and Standard Thai). She focuses on the range of expressions used for speech event participants, marking person reference for degrees of hierarchy and examining variation in terms of speaker–addressee relationships. Village children used Kam Muang with each other (home/school) in contrast with middle-class children, who used Standard Thai almost exclusively. Given the higher prestige awarded to Standard Thai, socialization into respect at school leads children to adopt Standard Thai, marginalizing their vernacular (see Garrett, this volume; Paugh, this volume; Riley, this volume). Thus, issues of local language ideologies intersect with broader cultural practices regarding the verbal expression of hierarchy. In everyday face-to-face situations, as also reinforced in media representations, young children are initially prompted and corrected and are then expected to use correct forms (see Burdelski, this volume; Moore, this volume). Adults held particular stereotypes and values about children's speech choices, indexing their informal playgroups (as egalitarian). By kindergarten, children had learned to inhabit multiple social hierarchies across contexts, displaying more variation and subtle uses of interactional strategies for different outcomes than adults recognized or valorized.

Goodwin and Kyratzis (Chapter 16) turn our attention from the roles played by adults to the importance of other children in 'Peer Language Socialization.' Their focus on the talk-in-interaction of child participants reminds us that multiage groups are critical sites for learning in communities. Children's agency in relation to local peer and sibling organization is a central consideration when analyzing children's use of cultural and linguistic resources in constituting social worlds. Methodologically, the chapter highlights ethnographically contextualized, micro-analytic approaches that underscore the dynamics of sequencing in social activities, documenting a range of embodied language practices that children use in activities of social control and evaluation across a broad sociocultural spectrum. These include code-switching and appropriating verbal formulas to frame disputes, assert authority, and subvert established hierarchies and norms in playful and serious activities.

Goodwin and Kyratzis argue that discernment (Bourdieu 1984) is socialized through assessments, which are central to the establishment of boundaries and categories of value and difference. Peers use compliments, critiques, and name-calling as insults and mock insults to frame their comments as evaluative and to categorize social distinctions in terms of physical, social, and class orientations. In multiethnic settings, character and ethnicity figure prominently, and pejorative and negative labels index local cultural values. Practices used for membership categorization (following Sacks 1972) are also prominent in peer games and pretend play, showing the interactional dynamics of exclusion and insults. Pretend play in particular demonstrates children's understandings of stereotyped cultural and verbal practices. In multilingual communities, children's code choice in pretend play indexes their knowledge of how authority is displayed through particular codes, with the appropriate pragmatic particles, discourse markers, and nonverbal behaviors (see Aronsson, this volume; Paugh, this volume).

In 'Language Socialization and Exclusion,' García-Sánchez (Chapter 17) details peer language socialization practices that result in the production of social and ethnic inequalities. She offers this micro-genetic approach to language use in interaction as a corrective to previous research that views language as a means of symbolic domination that reproduces hegemonic ideologies. Set within Spain's current debates on immigration, politics, and educational policies of inclusion and exclusion, she offers a close examination of the systematic social and linguistic practices in an ethnically diverse rural fourth-grade classroom between Spanish peers and the targets of their prejudice, Moroccan immigrant children.

She identifies three interrelated verbal practices that justify, rationalize, or normalize social exclusion but that also, in and of themselves, constitute practices of exclusion and 'othering': tattling, peer directives (commands and corrections that shame) (see also Lo and Fung, this volume), and 'fueling the fire,' which generates inflammatory remarks toward the target child. In contrast to explicit racist behaviors, exclusionary practices are subtle and complex and are achieved through interactional alignments of Spanish peers and teachers, highlighting the importance of attention to participation frameworks in making these practices visible. She details Moroccan immigrant children's responses to these acts of marginalization – silence, embodied displays of shame, denials, and, occasionally, verbal confrontation – and takes them as evidence of the children's consciousness and alienation. García-Sánchez also points out that children initiating these negative identity acts have sophisticated understandings of local sociopolitical power asymmetries and verbally sustain them at the social interactional level.

REFERENCES

Bourdieu, P. (1984) *Distinction: A Social Critique of the Judgment of Taste.* Cambridge, MA: Harvard University Press.

Sacks, H. (1972) On the analyzability of stories by children. In J. J. Gumperz and D. Hymes (eds.), *Directions in Sociolinguistics: The Ethnography of Communication.* 325–45. New York: Holt, Rinehart and Winston.

12 Language Socialization and Politeness Routines

MATTHEW BURDELSKI

Introduction

In communities across the globe, politeness is a foundation of social interaction that can be broadly defined as a set of practices deployed to 'avoid communicative discord or offence, and maintain communicative concord' (Leech 2006: 173). While competent speakers of a language can identify speech and behavior that is normatively polite or impolite, in interaction politeness is often subtle and complex, conveyed through verbal and other semiotic channels that vary across situations and communities. As the appropriate use (or nonuse) of politeness can have an impact on the ways in which people are viewed by others and get along in the social world, politeness is a central aspect of socialization for many children. Politeness has attracted attention across a range of fields, such as linguistics and anthropology, and subfields, such as language acquisition and gender studies. Studies across fields have examined, in particular, the use of certain speech acts (e.g. requests, apologies), indirectness, honorifics, and politeness formulas. Studies have also examined socialization practices, shedding light on the ways in which children learn to convey norms of politeness in their community. While much of the research focuses on English speakers, a growing body of research in various communities contributes to a cross-cultural perspective.

This chapter discusses socialization into politeness with a focus on children in Japan. Japanese is a good case in which to examine the socialization of politeness because politeness is encoded in both linguistic resources such as honorifics and nonlinguistic resources such as the body. Thus, analyzing the ways in which children in Japan are socialized into acting in accordance with local conventions of politeness can help to raise issues regarding socialization practices into politeness in other communities. The chapter first reviews previous research on politeness from a

The Handbook of Language Socialization, First Edition. Edited by Alessandro Duranti, Elinor Ochs, and Bambi B. Schieffelin.
© 2014 John Wiley & Sons, Ltd. Published 2014 by John Wiley & Sons, Ltd.

cross-cultural perspective. It then draws upon linguistic fieldwork in urban Japanese households, neighborhoods, and a preschool to examine socialization into politeness routines.

Previous Research

Over the past few decades, several frameworks of politeness have been proposed (e.g. Brown and Levinson 1978, 1987; Lakoff 1973; Leech 1983). That of Brown and Levinson is among the most widely discussed. Following Goffman (1974 [1955]), Brown and Levinson propose that individuals have 'face' wants, including a desire to be unimpeded in action (negative face want) and a desire to be appreciated by others (positive face want). Politeness is motivated by a desire for the mutual maintenance of face; that is, to satisfy the face wants of others and in turn to have one's own face wants satisfied. According to Brown and Levinson, in managing face wants, speakers use two types of politeness: 'positive politeness' to build solidarity and 'negative politeness' to show restraint. Positive politeness includes asserting common ground and displaying interest, whereas negative politeness includes being indirect and minimizing imposition.

The Brown and Levinson framework has been challenged for its claims of cultural universality in regard to the expression of politeness, particularly in non-Western languages such as Japanese, which has an elaborate system of honorifics (Ide 1989; Matsumoto 1989). In particular, Matsumoto (1989) asserts that politeness in Japanese is motivated by the need to conform to social hierarchy and maintain group harmony. From this perspective, Japanese speakers use practices of politeness based upon their understandings of social position and broader understandings about the person in society.

Although Japan is described as a negative politeness culture (Brown and Levinson 1987: 245) in which people tend to be indirect and avoid imposing on others, Japanese speakers frequently use both positive and negative politeness practices in everyday communication. For this, they draw upon linguistic resources such as honorifics (e.g. Ide 2005; Okamoto 1999), politeness formulas, pragmatic particles, pitch, and repetition, and embodied resources such as bowing (Mizutani and Mizutani 1987). In particular, prior research has examined routine expressions and other politeness formulas (e.g. Ohashi 2003; Takekuro 2005), which have also been examined in English in relation to 'politeness routines' (Gleason, Perlmann, and Grief 1984) and 'politeness formulas' (Ferguson 1976). Verbal routines in general play an important role in language and cultural acquisition because they provide children with a relatively predictable structure in which to participate in interaction (Peters and Boggs 1986). As conversation analysis shows, a degree of predictability structures all conversation (Atkinson and Heritage 1984; Sacks, Schegloff, and Jefferson 1974). In particular, minimal sequences of conversation are composed of 'adjacency pairs' – social actions typically produced by separate speakers in succession, such as request–compliance (Schegloff and Sacks 1973). Cultural differences exist regarding the preference for more or less formulaic language within adjacency pairs, resulting in different scales of predictability. For instance, in examining the choices Japanese and American English speakers make in requesting a pen in relation to degree of social distance to an addressee, Hill et al. (1986) found that Japanese speakers were more likely than English speakers to agree on the linguistic expressions used. They posit that Japanese speakers choose expressions based on their *wakimae* ('discernment') of the social situation, particularly the relative social status between speaker and addressee.

While visitors to Japan often notice that people are generally polite, particularly in public settings, this does not mean they are polite all the time. In particular, scholars note the lack of politeness in some situations, such as the absence of verbal apologies to strangers for pushing or bumping on crowded trains (Lebra 1976). This suggests that communicative competence in politeness entails knowing when and how to use or not to use politeness practices across a range of situations.

Socialization into politeness

Competence in displaying polite demeanors including appreciation, respect, and deference is socialized in Japan and other communities from a young age. In particular, caregivers provide input to children through modeling and instruction. For instance, in North American white middle-class households, parents may address children using politeness formulas, such as 'please' and 'thank you,' and instruct children to say such formulas to family members and others, for example when making a request (e.g. Gleason 1980; Snow et al. 1990). Moreover, when making requests to children, US parents may use mitigation devices such as endearments, impersonal pronouns, passive voice, and inclusive constructions (e.g. 'Let's sit down' = 'You sit down') (Blum-Kulka 1997: 147).

Research within other communities also reveals that caregivers model and instruct children in politeness. For instance, among the Basotho of South Africa, mothers and older siblings prompt children in politeness, which includes, 'thank you's, greetings, respect to elders, and proper terms of address' (Demuth 1986: 62–3). Among the Kwara're in the Solomon Islands, caregivers instruct children to ask and answer questions, make requests, say greetings and leave-takings, and respond when food is offered (Watson-Gegeo and Gegeo 1986: 34). In a Guadeloupian community, children are encouraged to nod and verbally greet adults outside the home (Tessonneau 2005). In a Navajo community, teachers and parents engage children in triadic directive-giving exchanges, which socializes children into the practice of making requests through a third party as a form of indirectness (Field 2001). Finally, in some Asian communities, children are socialized to use honorifics to index respect and hierarchy related to age. For instance, in a Khmer American community, caregivers model greetings and polite requests that children are expected to say to elderly family members, socializing children to politeness in relation to deference and respect (Smith-Hefner 1999: 84–5). Further, in a Korean American community, mothers instruct children to address grandparents with honorific greetings and requests, which socializes them to display respect and deference to elders (Park 2006). This suggests that children in Asian-language-speaking communities are socialized into politeness and respect as systems relating to social hierarchy and other forms of sociality. This can be compared with politeness among the Basotho of South Africa, which, according to Demuth (1986: 63), 'is not highly stratified,' though 'there is a definite organization toward the respect of elders, and children are taught to indicate this deference verbally.'

In Japan, politeness is central to Japanese caregiver expectations of children's development in the home (Kobayashi 2001: 116) and preschool (Peak 1991: 72–3). Socialization into politeness begins well before children are able to speak. For instance, mothers address infants and toddlers using polite words and honorifics (Nakamura 2002) and use politeness formulas to speak for them (Okamoto 2001). In addition, when making requests to children, mothers often use mitigating devices such as pragmatic particles (Cook 1992), diminutives (e.g. Name [Ken] + –*chan* [Ken-*chan* = Kenny]), and polite words (e.g. X *kudasai* ('Please X')). They also instruct children in politeness formulas within ordinary interaction and role-play activities (Clancy 1986). In preschools, teachers encourage children to use greetings and formulaic responses (Peak 1991). In addition to politeness formulas and honorifics, children in Japan are socialized into indirectness. In particular, in addressing infants (Morikawa, Shand, and Kosawa 1988) and two-year-olds (Clancy 1986), mothers use indirect utterances such as hints, questions, and suggestions more often than direct utterances such as imperatives (Kobayashi 2001). Clancy (1986) also shows that, when a third party addresses a child with an indirect utterance, the mother may translate the indirect utterance (e.g. a refusal such as 'I'm good') into a more direct utterance (e.g. a refusal such as 'She said, "No"'), which may help children understand indirect polite speech. Mothers also socialize children to attend to the needs and desires of others by telling children what third parties may be thinking or feeling even when they have not spoken, as a form of empathy training (Clancy 1986: 233).

A result of Japanese socialization is that children typically acquire basic politeness practices fairly early. In particular, two-year-old children use politeness formulas (Clancy 1985; Yokoyama 1980) and somewhat older children (above two and a half years) use addressee honorifics, particularly in role-play activities to mark social distance (Fukuda 2005; Nakamura 1996). Many aspects of politeness, such as honorific forms including *sonkeigo* ('respect language') and *kenjoogo* ('humble language'), however, are not acquired until much later in life. For instance, Dunn (2009) shows that young adults in the business world undergo training in honorifics to display respect and deference, and in *kusshon kotoba* ('cushion words'), which can be used to preface an inquiry to a customer (e.g. *Shitsuree desu ga* [*onamae wa?*] . . . ('Excuse my rudeness, but [what is your name?]')). Indeed, socialization into politeness in many societies such as Japan seems to be a lifelong process.

While previous research provides critical insight into the socialization of politeness in various communities, our understanding of the process of acquisition is still quite limited. In particular, in relation to children in Japan, much of what we do know is based on dyadic mother–child verbal interaction in the home. What is needed is an analysis of various settings, activities, and participants, and a look at how caregiver verbal and nonverbal strategies shape children's participation in practices of politeness. More information is also needed on how learners of Japanese as a second language learn how to be polite (Kanagy 1999) in Japan. The following sections attempt to address these issues through an analysis of children's socialization into politeness routines, drawing upon audiovisual recordings made during two projects in Japan. The first was conducted from 2004 to 2005 in seven Japanese households and neighborhoods in the cities of Kyoto, Kobe, and Osaka (132 hours) (Burdelski 2006) and the second was conducted from 2006 to 2007 in a Japanese preschool near Tokyo in which approximately half the children are non-native speakers of Japanese (48 hours).

Politeness Routines: Linguistic and Embodied Practice

As do caregivers in some other communities, such as in Northern Thailand (Howard 2009, this volume), Japanese caregivers encourage children's embodied performance of politeness before children are able to speak. In particular, they provide modeling, verbal instruction, and tactile guidance. For instance, caregivers model how to bow the head during greetings and expressions of appreciation, and to put the hands together when saying appreciative mealtime expressions such as *Itadakimasu* ('I partake') and *Gochisoosamadeshita* ('Thank you for the meal'). They also give verbal instruction on how to use the body, for example Mom ((at end of meal, putting palms of hands together)): *Otete awasete* ('Put your hands together') → Male child (1;11): ((puts hands together)). Finally, they also provide tactile guidance, such as pressing a hand on a child's back to get him or her to bow (Hendry 1986: 75–6). Socializing the body may co-occur with instruction on what to do or say, which also begins before children are expected to say the expressions. For instance, in Example 12.1, a mother and focal child (Haru) (on the left of the frame grab) are in a sandbox where a father and his son have come up to them. When the boy tries to take one of Haru's sand toys (a small pail), Haru's mother encourages her to offer it to him.

Example 12.1:   Family neighborhood park[1]

Haru (2;1), Haru's mom, boy (1;11), and boy's dad.

1   Mom-H: *Kashite agete.*
              'Lend it (to him).'
2   Haru: ((handing toy to boy))
3   Mom-H: *Doo* [*zo tte.*]
              'Say, "Here you are."'

Figure 12.1   A girl (left) hands a sand toy to a boy (right).

4 →	Dad-B:	[*Ariga*]*to tte* ( ).
		'Say, "Thank you" ( ).'
5	Dad-B:	[((pressing hand on boy's back))]
6	Boy:	[((bows while reaching for sand toy))]
7	Mom:	*Doo::zo.*
		'Here you are.'

In Example 12.1, Haru's mother directs her to lend the toy to the boy (line 1) and tells her to say *doozo*, a common politeness formula meaning 'Here you are' (or 'Go ahead,' 'Please X') (line 3). In response, the father tells his son, 'Say "Thank you"' (line 4) while pressing his hand on the boy's back to encourage him to bow (line 5). Although neither child repeats the expressions, they nevertheless participate in the routine – in this case an offer–appreciation exchange – through embodied means.

Three socialization strategies

As suggested above, children's early participation in politeness routines in Japan is guided by various caregiver strategies. This section discusses three that are central in the home, neighborhood, and preschool: (1) speaking for a child, (2) directives and prompting, and (3) reported speech. Several of these appeared in Example 12.1: directive (line 1), prompting (lines 3 and 4), and speaking for a child (line 7). While these strategies will be examined separately below, one or more may be used across a sequence.

Daiben ('speaking for another')   In Japan, *daiben* ('speaking for another') occurs in a range of contexts and is an important aspect of interaction with preverbal children (e.g. Okamoto 2001).

Japanese caregivers, and on occasion older siblings, speak for children in dyadic and multiparty frameworks. Example 12.2 illustrates dyadic *daiben* from the preschool. Here a child (Sinh, from India, who has been in Japan for less than six months) has just finished eating lunch.

Example 12.2: Preschool lunch table

Sinh (male, India, 2;5) and the teacher.

1		Teacher:	((wipes Sinh's mouth with washcloth))
2		Sinh:	((stands up out of chair))
3	→	Teacher:	*Hai gochisoosamadeshi<u>ta</u>.*= ((bowing head))
			'Okay, "Thank you for the meal."'
4		Sinh:	=*ta:*. ((bows head))
			'ta:'
5		Teacher:	*Hai, orikoosan desu.*
			'Yes, (you)'re a good child.'

After wiping Sinh's mouth, while bowing her head the teacher says, *Gochisoodamadeshi<u>ta</u>* ('Thanks for the meal') (line 3), ending with emphatic stress on the last syllable (*ta*). Here, the teacher not only speaks for the child but also more generally performs a politeness routine through talk and embodied action. Sinh participates in the routine by repeating part of the expression – the final syllable (*ta*) (line 4) – while bowing his head. This response suggests that children attend not only to verbal aspects of these routines – such as the ends of words (cf. Slobin 1973) – but also to the crucial nonverbal aspects. The teacher acknowledges this participation by praising Sinh as a 'good child' (line 5).

Similarly to a strategy observed among Tzotzil (de León 1998, this volume), Kaluli (Schieffelin 1979), and Wolof caregivers (Rabain-Jamin 1998), Japanese caregivers also use *daiben* within multiparty frameworks to speak for a child who has not actually spoken *to a third party*. In the Japanese case, triadic *daiben* is often used to convey polite social actions such as offers and apologies. For instance, in Example 12.3, from the preschool, two children (Galina and Nalini, both non-native speakers of Japanese) have bumped heads while taking off their shoes. When Galina begins to cry, a teacher comes over to them.

Example 12.3: Preschool entrance

Teacher, Galina (female, Ukraine, 3;10), and Nalini (female, Bangladesh, 3;3).

1	Galina:	*Butsuka*[*cchatta:.*] ((crying, gazes at teacher and points towards Nalini))
		'(She) bumped into (me).'
2	Teacher:	[*Butsukacchatta*] *no?*
		'(She) bumped into (you)?'
3	Galina:	*Itai* [(*no ko*[*re*]).
		'It hurts (this).'
4	Teacher:	[*A.*
		'Ah.'
5	Nalini:	[*Ko*]*re.* ((puts arms out))
		'This.'

6	Teacher:	*Un.*
		'Mm.'
7	Nalini:	*Koo yatte.* ((puts arms out))
		'Like this.'
8	Teacher:	*A: soo yatte butsukacchatta no ka?*
		'Ah that's how (you) bumped?'
9	Nalini:	*Un.* ((nods three times))
		'Mm.'
10 →	Teacher:	*Gomen ne.* ((to Galina, bows head slightly))
		'(I) am sorry.'
11	Teacher:	((goes to put away children's shoes))

When the children convey what happened through verbalization and gesture (lines 1–9), the teacher apologizes to the crying child (Galina) (line 10). This apology is also embodied, as the teacher slightly bows her head. Triadic *daiben* often does double duty in that it functions as speaking for both the child and caregiver. This dual function is related to the notion *ittaikan* ('feeling of oneness') (Lebra 1976: 361), the strong bond between caregiver and child that frames thinking, feeling, and speaking as one. Moreover, here, by apologizing, the caregiver also takes on (partial) responsibility for the situation that allowed the accident to occur (i.e. the teacher was attending to something else at the time). While *daiben* is predominantly used with children under two years and non-native speakers, as children gain more competence, caregivers gradually use more directives, prompting, and reported speech, as discussed in the following sections.

Directives and prompting   A second strategy in socializing politeness routines is directives and prompting. Caregivers use directives on what to do (and not do), which take various forms, such as an imperative, suggestion, or hint (Clancy 1986; Ervin-Tripp 1976). A central type of directive is prompting, involving instruction in what to say and how to speak (or what not to say and how not to speak). Prompting is an explicit strategy in, '*socialization through the use of language* and *socialization to use language*' (Schieffelin and Ochs 1986: 163, italics in original). Previous research in various communities reveals that prompting pervades caregiver–child interaction, has many functions, and can be organized in different ways, and thus is a central strategy in socializing children into politeness routines (e.g. Becker 1994; Demuth 1986) and language more generally (e.g. Demuth 1986; Moore, this volume; Schieffelin 1990).

Japanese prompting typically involves a caregiver, and occasionally an older sibling or peer, directing a child to speak. Similarly to the Kaluli of Papua New Guinea (Schieffelin 1990), in these data, caregiver prompting predominantly occurs in triadic arrangements (98 percent in families; 99 percent in the preschool) in which a child is directed to say an utterance to one or more third parties (rather than back to the caregiver). Thus, prompting primarily functions in encouraging other-orientation and in establishing social relationships beyond the caregiver–

Table 12.1 Prompting of Social Actions (Number of Tokens and Percentage)

Social Actions	Families	Preschool
1. Offer–appreciation	326 (30.8 percent)	50 (10.4 percent)
2. Request–compliance	319 (30.2 percent)	216 (45.0 percent)
3. Greeting and leave-taking	296 (28.0 percent)	125 (26.0 percent)
4. Apology–acknowledgment	63 (6.0 percent)	23 (4.8 percent)
5. Question–answer	24 (2.4 percent)	16 (4.0 percent)
6. Other (e.g. congratulate, pray)	29 (2.7 percent)	48 (10 percent)
Total	**1058 (100 percent)**	**480 (100 percent)**

child dyad. However, when the prompter is a sibling or peer, prompting frequently occurs in dyadic frameworks in which a child is directed to say an utterance back to the child prompter (e.g. 'Say sorry [to me]'). The types of social actions prompted in the families and preschool are shown in Table 12.1.

In addition to the social actions listed as 1 through 5 in Table 12.1, question–answer pairs are also included in which there is an attention to the addressee's needs or concerns (e.g. *Daijoobu*? ('Are you okay?') in response to a crying child), which is a central aspect of positive politeness in the Brown and Levinson model. These data reveal similarities in the frequency of the types of social actions prompted across the home/neighborhood (family) and preschool. A notable difference is the frequency of offer–appreciation pairs, which occur nearly three times as often in the family (30.8 percent) as in the preschool (10.4 percent). Among families there is a preference to prompt children to offer their toys to playmates (non-family members) who want to use them (as in Example 12.1), whereas in the preschool, when a child wants to play with a toy that another child is playing with, there is a preference to prompt the child who wants it to make a request for it.

Caregivers around the world use various types of prompting. In these data, there are four types: (1) empty slot (Peters and Boggs 1986: 82), (2) performative (Austin 1962), (3) leading question (Ochs 1986: 6), and (4) elicited imitation (Hood and Schieffelin 1978). These are illustrated in Example 12.4, Example 12.5, Example 12.6, and Example 12.7, from family interactions. First, an empty slot entails providing part of an expression for the child to produce the rest. For instance, in Example 12.4, Naoki is about to start eating.

Example 12.4: Family dining table

Mom and Naoki (male, 1;11).

1 →   Mom: *Ita:::da:ki:?*
                    'I par-?'
2   Naoki: *m:::ma::su.* ((puts hands together))
                    '-ta:::ke::.'

When his mother says *Ita:::da:ki?* (line 1), the first part of the appreciative mealtime expression *Itadakimasu* ('I partake') followed by rising intonation, Naoki responds by saying the last part of the expression, *–masu* (line 2), an addressee honorific marker.

Second, a leading question employs a question word such as 'what' (e.g. 'What do you say?'), or a conditional phrase such as, 'If (I/someone) says X,' as in Example 12.5. Here, a father and son (Takahiro) are playing with toy blocks.

Example 12.5: Family living room

Takahiro (male, 2;5) and Dad.

1	Dad:	*Hai* (0.9) *doozo.* ((holds out block))
		'Yes (0.9), here you are.'
2	Takahiro:	((reaches for block, but Dad does not let go))
3 →	Dad:	*Doozo tte yuttara?*
		'If (I/someone) says, "Here you are" (what do you say)?'
4		(0.7)
5	Takahiro:	*Arigatoo.* ((receives block))
		'Thank you.'
6	Dad:	*Hai.*
		'Yes.'

As he hands one of the blocks to Takahiro saying the polite expression *doozo* ('Here you are') and Takahiro reaches out to take it, the father pauses and, while refusing to let go, prompts him using a leading question (line 3). In response, Takahiro says the expected expression, 'Thank you.'

Third, a performative utilizes a verb of speaking such as 'apologize,' 'greet,' or 'ask.' In Example 12.6, when a child (Takahiro) bangs his spoon on the side of his bowl like a drum and his mother scolds him by saying *Ogyoogi warui* ('It's bad manner'), his father responds by prompting the child to apologize.

Example 12.6: Family dining table

Dad, Mom, and Takahiro (male, 2;4).

1 →	Dad:	*Chanto ayamari*[*nasai.*] ((stern voice))
		'Properly apologize.'
2 →	Mom:	[°*Ayamari*]*nasai.*°
		'°Apologize.°'
3		(0.4)
4	Takahiro:	°*Gomennasai.*°
		'°I'm sorry.°'

Here, after the father and mother prompt Takahiro to apologize for his 'bad manner,' Takahiro responds by saying the expected expression, 'I'm sorry.'

Fourth, in elicited imitation, a speaker provides a model utterance followed by a directive to repeat it. Similarly to the use of *elema* ('say') among Kaluli caregivers (Schieffelin 1990), in Japanese (a subject-object-verb language) the directive follows the expression to be repeated (e.g. ' "Thank you," say'). In Example 12.7, a mother (Mom-M) and child (Masa) are being visited by a mother (Mom-B) and son (boy). The excerpt begins after the boy has lent Masa one of his toys.

Example 12.7:   Family living room

Masa's mom, Masa (male, 2;1), boy (3;0), and boy's mom.

1 → Mom-M: *Doozo shite kurehatta, arigato tte iwanna.*
              'He gave it to you, (so) you have to say, "Thank you."'
2   Masa: *Ari<u>ga</u>to.*
              'Thank you.'
3   Mom-M: *Hai.*
              'Yes.'
4 → Mom-B: *Hai, iie doo ita[shimashite tte.]*
              'Yes, say, "You're welcome."'
5   Boy: [*Iie, doo]itashimashite.* ((bows))
                             'You're welcome.'

Here Masa's mother prompts Masa to say 'Thank you' to the boy (line 1). When Masa repeats the expression, the boy's mother (Mom-B) prompts her son to say 'You're welcome' (line 4), which he immediately repeats in partial overlap while bowing (line 5).

Caregivers in various other communities also use the above types of prompting, for example elicited imitation among Tzotzil caregivers (de León 1998) and leading questions (e.g. 'What's the magic word?') in US households (Gleason, Perlmann, and Grief 1984). In examining socialization in US households, Becker (1994) categorizes two types of prompt: direct and indirect. Direct prompts, such as elicited imitation (Example 12.7), provide the child with an expression and a directive to repeat it, whereas indirect prompts, such as leading questions (Example 12.5) and performatives (Example 12.6), are open-ended, requiring the child to come up with the expression on his or her own. Prompting is not the same in every community, as the types of prompt used, their frequency, and their contexts are linked to local theories of language learning that help constitute a unique cultural profile.

In these data, elicited imitation is by far the most frequent type of prompting (96 percent in families and 97 percent in preschool). Although the frequency of caregiver prompting decreases with the child's age, caregivers also predominantly use elicited imitation when prompting older siblings (four to nine years) (98 percent). That is, Japanese caregivers prefer elicited imitation to other types of prompting, even with children who would likely come up with the expected expression on their own if given an indirect prompt such as, 'What do you say?'

The preference for elicited imitation across early childhood in Japan is rooted within practices of teaching and learning across the lifespan. For instance, apprenticeship in the traditional arts (e.g. Noh drama, tea ceremony) often relies on modeling and imitation of a *kata* ('form') (Rohlen and LeTendre 1996; Singleton 1998). In the arts, is it believed that the body learns first and then the 'heart' and 'spirit' come to understand (Hare 1996: 340). Further, in relation to child rearing, Japanese developmental psychologists assert that modeling and imitation constitute a crucial aspect of learning (Kojima 1986: 42). Anthropologists have observed that Japanese caregivers engage in 'ceaseless, patient demonstration for children to imitate' (Hendry 1986: 101). Similarly to caregivers in other communities, such as Papua New Guinea (Schieffelin 1990), Japanese caregivers not only use themselves as models but also guide children to observe and imitate others, particularly older siblings and peers. In particular, caregivers may praise the (polite) language use and behavior of older children to younger children, conveying the notion, 'be like that model child' (Lebra 1976: 152). Elicited imitation may prepare children for learning across the lifespan. That is, elicited imitation socializes children to attend to and imitate form (in this case, linguistic and embodied form), which is a highly valued learning strategy across a range of contexts in Japan.

The contexts of prompting are also socioculturally variable (Ochs 1986). In Japan, while prompting frequently occurs in play and at meal times, it also occurs in public settings such as stores and libraries. For instance, parents may prompt children in what to say before arriving at a service counter; for example, Mom ((while handing books to child in the hallway that leads up to the library counter)): *Oneesan doozo tte* ('Say to the older sister [=library clerk], "Here you are"'). Research in other communities also reveals that caregivers prompt children in what to say before coming into interaction with a third party, such as during trick-or-treating in the United States (Gleason and Weintraub 1976) or when delivering a message to someone in another household in Samoa (Ochs 1988). In Japan, prompting can encourage children to present a polite public persona.

As observed in other communities, such as the Basotho (Demuth 1986), Japanese caregivers also use prompting as correction. In the Japanese case, a caregiver may respond to a child's 'impolite' language towards another person or an animal; for example, Child: *Poi* ((throwing food towards a stray cat to feed it)) → Dad: *Poi janakute, doozo tte* ('It's not *poi*, say, "Here you are"'). Here, the father corrects the child's use of *poi* (an onomatopoetic sound of throwing away) and replaces it with *doozo*, a politeness formula for offering.

Also, similarly to a pattern observed in communities such as the Navajo (Field 2001), Japanese caregivers on occasion use prompting to speak *through* a child to a third party. For example, while visiting the home of a child's paternal grandparents, his mother prompted him (2;5) to ask his grandmother to relocate her activity (reading the newspaper) from the kitchen to the living room, where the child would shortly be playing, by saying, *Baaba mukoo de mite kudasai tte* ('Say "Granny please look at it [the newspaper] over there"'). The function of this prompt may be aimed less at getting the child to repeat the utterance (which he did not do) and more at being indirect in order to mitigate a face-threatening act – in this case, a request from the child's mother to her mother-in-law.

While children in Japan are prompted to speak to family members, peers, other adults and children, and animals, they are also on occasion prompted to say some of the same politeness formulas to inanimate objects, including toys and religious and natural objects. The social actions include greeting, offering, and apologizing; for example, Boy ((had taken a stone out of his mouth and thrown it on the sidewalk)) → Mom: *Ishi ni gomen nasai tte dekiru?* ('Can you say "I'm sorry" to the stone?'). Here, the mother prompts the child to apologize to a stone in response to his having done something socially inappropriate (and even dangerous).

In addition to variation across societies, the subtleties of prompting vary within a society, including in institutions, activities, and families. For instance, in relation to the families observed, some two-year-old children are prompted more frequently than other children (in some cases two to three times as often). This may be due to the greater weight that some families place on children's acquisition of politeness routines. There are also shades of difference in the types of strategy used. For instance, while all families frequently use elicited imitation, only some use empty slots and leading questions. The subtleties of prompting, and the strategies for socializing politeness in general, may also be affected by a variety of factors such as the age and gender of the child. In these data, while age is significant, as mentioned above, gender is not, as boys and girls are prompted with similar frequency to say polite expressions by their families and at the preschool.

Reported speech   A third strategy in socializing children into politeness routines is reported speech. Soviet scholars pointed out that reported speech or quotation (e.g. he said X) is a double-voiced utterance, in which a speaker transmits another's speech and simultaneously takes a stance towards it (e.g. Vološinov 1971). Previous studies have examined the role of reported speech in socialization (e.g. Ely, Gleason, and McCabe 1996; Rabain-Jamin 1998).

Japanese caregivers use reported speech in relation to politeness routines in two central ways: (1) to repeat or reformulate what a third party has just said and (2) to 'voice' what a third party has just enacted, mainly through nonverbal means. Example 12.8, from the preschool, contains an example of (1): when an older boy (Kazu) sees a younger boy (Sinh) taking a toy train car off its track that the older boy had been playing with, he grabs it out of the younger boy's hands. In response, the younger boy cries out *Dame* ('No') while pointing towards the toy in the older boy's hands and gazing towards the teacher. The teacher comes over to intervene.

Example 12.8:   Preschool classroom

Teacher, Kazu (male, Japan, 5;0), and Sinh (male, India, 2;6).

1	Kazu:	*Kore hosh:i*[*i*::::. ((to teacher))
		'(I) want this (=train car).'
2	Teacher:	[*Hoshiin dattara .h Shin ni chant*[*o kiite kara.*
		'If (you) want it, then properly ask Sinh.'

3		Teacher:	((takes toy from Kazu and gives it back to Sinh))
4		Kazu:	[*Shin kashite.* 'Sinh, lend it.'
5		Sinh:	((playing with train))
6		Teacher:	*Hora ko- kore koko ni mottekuru kara okashikunaru n da yo::.* 'Look, since (you) (=Kazu) connected it (=the track) here it (=train) goes off track::.''
7		Kazu:	[*Shin ka:shi:te::.* 'Sinh, lend it.'
8		Sinh:	[((looking down))
9	→	Teacher:	*Kashite da tte.* ((gazing towards Sinh)) '(He) says, "Lend it."'
10			(0.2)
11		Teacher:	*i-* ((turns towards Sinh))
12		Teacher:	((points towards train in Sinh's hands))
13		Sinh:	*Ha:i doo::zo:* ((setting train down in front of Kazu)) 'Yes, here you are.'
14		Kazu:	*A:riga:to::.* 'Thank you.'

After taking the train from Kazu, the teacher prompts him to ask Sinh if he may borrow it (line 2). Kazu responds by making two requests to Sinh (lines 4 and 7), who does not respond. Following the second request, the teacher repeats it as reported speech to Sinh (line 9). A similar kind of reported speech has been observed in Japanese mother–child interaction. In particular, Clancy (1986: 220–1) shows that, when an adult addresses a child with a request and the child does not respond, the mother repeats the request as reported speech. Also, similarly to a pattern observed among caregivers in the United States (Stivers 2001), here the teacher verbally intervenes in a child's interaction in order to deal with a 'problem' in the unfolding interaction, namely the absence of a response from the addressed child. Reported speech following a child's nonresponse may get the child to orient to making the next response without telling him or her what to do. In this way, similarly to leading questions and performatives, as discussed earlier, reported speech is a type of prompt that requires the child to come up with a response on his or her own. Here, while relevant responses to the teacher's reported speech include refusing, delaying, or granting the request, the child (Sinh) immediately complies with the embedded request using the polite expression *doozo* ('Here you are') (line 13). While *doozo* is used here as a compliance, in many other cases it is used as an offer (as in Example 12.5, line 1). In either case, children learn to use the expression *doozo* for object transfer.

In addition to repetition, caregivers also use reported speech to 'voice' or put into words an immediately prior or ongoing social action of another child who

Figure 12.2 A girl (left) holds out a sand toy towards a boy (right).

has performed a social action with little or no verbalization. For instance, in Example 12.9, at a playground, a boy (Masa) and his mother (on the right in Figure 12.2) are with a female playmate and her mother (on the left). At the beginning of the excerpt, the girl is holding out a plastic toy cup towards Masa while making minimal verbalizations.

Example 12.9: Family neighborhood park

Masa (male, 2;5), Masa's mom (Mom-M), girl (1;11), girl's mom.

1	Girl:	*n* (0.8) *n* ((holds out plastic toy towards Masa))
2 →	Mom-M:	*A* (0.5) *doozo tte yuttekureteharu Masa.*
		'Ah (0.5) (She)'s saying, "Here you are," Masa.'
3	Masa:	((walks towards girl, 0.2))
4 →	Mom-M:	*Doozo tte.*
		'(She) says, "Here you are."'
5	Girl:	((hands toy to Masa))
6	Masa:	((taking toy))
7	Mom-M:	*Arig (h)at (h)o h h .hh.*
		'Th (h)ank y (h)ou h h .hh.'

When Masa does not respond to the girl, Masa's mother responds by voicing the girl as making a polite offer: *doozo* ('Here you are') (lines 2 and 4). While saying this, the mother also attempts to draw Masa's attention towards the girl with a hand gesture (as in Figure 12.2). Masa responds by going towards the girl and accepting the toy. In addition to voicing young children, caregivers also voice pets as speaking politely; for example, Dog ((whimpers while looking at child's snack)) → Dad: *Gohan choodai tte yutteru* ('[The dog] says, "May I have some."') These examples suggest that Japanese caregivers use reported speech to 'ventriloquize' (Tannen 2010) a third party's (e.g. children, pets) minimal verbalizations and nonverbal actions. Notably, rather than describing a third party's actions (e.g.

'She's trying to give it to you'), in Example 12.9 the mother uses reported speech to provide a socioculturally appropriate 'gloss' (Schieffelin and Ochs 1986; Scollon 1982) of these actions as *doing politeness*. In concert with other strategies examined here, reported speech is an important means through which children learn to interpret their social world in terms of politeness.

Conclusion

This chapter has provided a review of research on politeness and how it is socialized in various communities, and has examined Japanese caregivers' and preschool teachers' socialization of children to speak and act politely. While politeness routines are a key aspect of interaction and socialization in many communities, they are highly amplified in Japanese interaction and socialization, involving a range of settings, activities, and participants. Moreover, politeness routines and their socialization are multimodal, involving talk and embodied actions. In any community, politeness routines socialize deeper cultural values. In the Japanese case, these values may include respect and responsibility. For instance, through (implicit) instruction to make offers (Example 12.1) and grant requests (Example 12.8), children may learn to respect others' negative face wants, or 'freedom of action' (Brown and Levinson 1987: 65). Attending to others' wants and needs is a central aspect of 'empathy' (*omoiyari*), which is socialized in Japan from a young age (Clancy 1986). Further, through instruction to apologize (Example 12.6), children may learn to take responsibility for their actions; moreover, when a caregiver apologizes on behalf of a child (Example 12.3), children may also learn that responsibility can be 'diffused' or distributed among members of a social group (Hill and Irvine 1993: 3). These findings suggest that, in Japan, deeper cultural values associated with politeness are linked to both the individual and the group, particularly in the pursuit of achieving interpersonal harmony.

Through participation in social interaction, children immersed in Japanese-speaking communities gradually 'emerge' (de León 1998, this volume) as participants in politeness routines. Most children rapidly acquire the ability to engage in basic politeness routines within ordinary interaction and role-plays, such as giving and receiving toys and expressing appreciation. While many of the frequent politeness routines are learned in early childhood, as children grow they will engage in interaction using the same and new formulas, including expressions using honorifics and indirectness, within a wide range of settings and activities. They will also learn to calibrate their use of politeness routines in relation to a range of contextual variables such as the difference in status between themselves and the addressee. In a society such as Japan in which hierarchy is an important organizing feature of social relationships, early socialization into politeness routines lays the groundwork for the acquisition of a range of politeness practices across the lifespan. This process involves acquiring not only these practices but also the strategies for socializing others into them, contributing to reproduction within and across the generations.

ACKNOWLEDGMENTS

I am grateful to the children, families, teachers, and principal who invited me into their homes and school and allowed me to observe their lives. The family research was made possible with the support of a Fulbright-Hays Doctoral Dissertation Research Abroad Grant, a Japan Society for the Promotion of Science Grant, and a Sasakawa Fellowship.

The preschool research was supported with a Ministry of Internal Affairs and Communications SCOPE grant and a Saitama University Collaborative Research with the Community grant (Keiichi Yamazaki, primary investigator). I am also grateful to the editors of this volume for organizing the CLIC Symposium on Language Socialization, Interaction, and Culture (February 23–24, 2007), where an earlier version of this paper was presented. Finally, I thank Haruko Cook, Merav Shohet, and Bambi Schieffelin for their feedback, and Heather Loyd for editing assistance.

NOTES

1   Transcription conventions: [, overlapping talk; :, lengthening (0.1 seconds each); -, cut-off sound; ° °, reduced volume; <u>word</u>, emphatic stress; (( )), nonverbal action; =, sound latching; (1.0), silence, measured in second and tenths of a second; (.), silence of less than 0.2 seconds; period indicates falling intonation; comma indicates continuing intonation; ?, rising intonation; ( ), transcriber uncertain about hearing of word within.

REFERENCES

Atkinson, J. M. and Heritage, J. (eds.) (1984) *Structures of Social Action.* Cambridge: Cambridge University Press.

Austin, J. L. (1962) *How to Do Things with Words.* 2nd ed. Oxford: Oxford University Press.

Becker, J. A. (1994) Pragmatic socialization: Parental input to preschoolers. *Discourse Processes* 17: 131–48.

Blum-Kulka, S. (1997) *Dinner Talk: Cultural Patterns of Sociability and Socialization in Family Discourse.* Mahwah, NJ: Lawrence Erlbaum.

Brown, P. and Levinson, S. C. (1978) Universals of language usage: Politeness phenomenon. In E. N. Goody (ed.), *Questions and Politeness: Strategies in Social Interaction.* 56–310. Cambridge: Cambridge University Press.

Brown, P. and Levinson, S. C. (1987) *Politeness: Some Universals in Language Usage.* Cambridge: Cambridge University Press.

Burdelski, M. J. (2006) *Language Socialization of Two-Year Old Children in Kansai, Japan: The Family and Beyond.* Doctoral Dissertation. Los Angeles, CA: University of California, Los Angeles.

Clancy, P. M. (1985) The acquisition of Japanese. In D. I. Slobin (ed.), *The Crosslinguistic Study of Language*

Acquisition: The Data, Vol. 1. 373–524. Hillsdale, NJ: Lawrence Erlbaum.

Clancy, P. M. (1986) The acquisition of communicative style in Japanese. In B. B. Schieffelin and E. Ochs (eds.), *Language Socialization Across Cultures.* 213–50. Cambridge: Cambridge University Press.

Cook, H. M. (1992) Meanings of non-referential indexes: A case study of the Japanese sentence-final particle *ne. Text* 12: 507–39.

de León, L. (1998) The emergent participant: Interactive patterns in the socialization of Tzotzil (Mayan) infants. *Journal of Linguistic Anthropology* 8(2): 131–61.

Demuth, K. (1986) Prompting routines in the language socialization of Basotho children. In B. B. Schieffelin and E. Ochs (eds.), *Language Socialization Across Cultures.* 51–79. Cambridge: Cambridge University Press.

Dunn, C. D. (2009) Language socialization in the workplace: Japanese 'business manners' training. Paper presented at the 11th International Pragmatics Conference. Melbourne, Australia.

Ely, R., Gleason, J. B., and McCabe, A. (1996) 'Why didn't you talk to your mommy, honey?': Parents and children's talk about talk. *Research on Language and Social Interaction* 29(1): 7–25.

Ervin-Tripp, S. (1976) 'Is Sybil there?': The structure of some American English directives. *Language in Society* 5: 25–67.

Ferguson, C. A. (1976) The structure and use of politeness formulas. *Language in Society* 5: 137–51.

Field, M. (2001) Triadic directives in Navajo language socialization. *Language in Society* 30: 249–63.

Fukuda, C. (2005) Children's use of the *masu* form in play. *Journal of Pragmatics* 37(7): 1037–58.

Gleason, J. B. (1980) The acquisition of social speech: Routines and politeness formulas. In H. Giles, W. P. Robinson, and P. M. Smith (eds.), *Language: Social Psychological Perspectives.* 21–7. Oxford: Pergamon Press.

Gleason, J. B., Perlmann, R. Y., and Grief, E. B. (1984) What's the magic word?: Learning language through politeness routines. *Discourse Processes* 7: 493–502.

Gleason, J. B. and Weintraub, S. (1976) The acquisition of routines in child speech. *Language in Society* 5: 129–36.

Goffman, E. (1974 [1955]) On face-work: An analysis of ritual elements in social interaction. In B. G. Blount (ed.), *Language, Culture and Society: A Book of Readings.* 224–49. Cambridge, MA: Winthrop Publishers, Inc.

Hare, T. (1996) Try, try again: Training in Noh drama. In T. Rohlen and G. LeTendre (eds.), *Teaching and Learning in Japan.* 323–44. Cambridge: Cambridge University Press.

Hendry, J. (1986) *Becoming Japanese: The World of the Pre-School Child.* Honolulu, HI: University of Hawaii Press.

Hill, B., Ide, S., Ikuta, S., Kawasaki, A., and Ogino, T. (1986) Universals of linguistic politeness: Quantitative evidence from Japanese and American English. *Journal of Pragmatics* 10(3): 347–71.

Hill, J. H. and Irvine, J. T. (eds.) (1993) *Responsibility and Evidence in Oral Discourse.* Cambridge: Cambridge University Press.

Hood, L. and Schieffelin, B. B. (1978) Elicited imitation in two cultural contexts. *Quarterly Newsletter of the Institute for Comparative Human Development* 2(1): 4–12.

Howard, K. M. (2009) 'When meeting Khun teacher, each time we should pay respect': Standardizing respect in a northern Thai classroom. *Linguistics and Education* 20(3): 254–72.

Ide, S. (1989) Formal forms and discernment: Neglected aspects of linguistic politeness. *Multilingua* 8(2): 223–48.

Ide, S. (2005) How and why honorifics can signify dignity and elegance. In R.

Lakoff and S. Ide (eds.), *Broadening the Horizon of Linguistic Politeness*. 47–64. Amsterdam, The Netherlands: John Benjamins.

Kanagy, R. (1999) The socialization of Japanese immersion children through interactional routines. *Journal of Pragmatics* 31(11): 1467–92

Kobayashi, S. (2001) Japanese mother–child relationships: Skill acquisition before the preschool years. In H. Shimizu and R. A. Levine (eds.), *Japanese Frames of Mind: Cultural Perspectives on Human Development*. 111–40. Cambridge: Cambridge University Press.

Kojima, H. (1986) Child rearing concepts as a belief-value system of the society and the individual. In H. Stevenson, H. Azuma, and K. Hakuta (eds.), *Child Development and Education in Japan*. 39–54. New York: W. H. Freeman and Company.

Lakoff, R. T. (1973) The logic of politeness; or, minding your p's and q's. In C. Corum, T. C. Smith-Stark and A. Weisner (eds.), *Papers from the Ninth Regional Meeting of the Chicago Linguistic Society* 292–305. Chicago, IL: Chicago Linguistic Society.

Lebra, T. S. (1976) *Japanese patterns of behavior*. Honolulu, HI: University of Hawaii Press.

Leech, G. N. (1983) *Principles of Pragmatics*. London: Longman.

Leech, G. (2006) Politeness: Is there an East–West divide? *Journal of Politeness Research* 3: 167–206.

Matsumoto, Y. (1989) Politeness and conversational universals. *Multilingua (Special Issue: Linguistic Politeness II)* 8(2/3): 207–21.

Mizutani, O. and Mizutani, N. (1987) *How to be Polite in Japanese*. Tokyo: The Japan Times Ltd.

Morikawa, H., Shand, N., and Kosawa, Y. (1988) Maternal speech to prelingual infants in Japan and the United States: Relationships among functions, forms

and referents. *Journal of Child Language* 15: 237–56.

Nakamura, K. (1996) The use of polite language by Japanese preschool children. In D. I. Slobin, J. Gerhardt, A. Kyratzis, and J. Guo (eds.), *Social Interaction, Social Context, and Language: Essays in Honor of Susan Ervin-Tripp*. 235–50. Mahwah, NJ: Lawrence Erlbaum.

Nakamura, K. (2002) Polite language usage in mother–infant interactions: A look at language socialization. In Y. Shirai, H. Kobayashi, S. Miyata, K. Nakamura, T. Ogura, and H. Sirai (eds.), *Studies in Language Sciences* 2: 175–91.

Ochs, E. (1986) Introduction. In B. B. Schieffelin and E. Ochs (eds.), *Language Socialization Across Cultures*. 1–13. Cambridge: Cambridge University Press.

Ochs, E. (1988) *Culture and Language Development: Language Acquisition and Language Socialization in a Samoan Village*. Cambridge: Cambridge University Press.

Ohashi, J. (2003) Japanese culture specific face and politeness orientation: A pragmatic investigation of yoroshiku onegaishimasu. *Multilingua* 22(3): 257–74.

Okamoto, S. (1999) Situated politeness: Manipulating honorific and non-honorific expressions in Japanese conversations. *Pragmatics* 8(2): 51–74.

Okamoto, Y. (2001) Boshi komyunikeeshon ni okeru hahaoya no daiben: 1saiji e no daiben no jookyoo to hatsuwa keitai no kanten (Mother speaking for the child in mother–child communication: Conditions and utterances to one-year-olds). *Boshi Kenkyuu (Mother–child Research)* 21: 46–55.

Park, E. (2006) Grandparents, grandchildren, and heritage language use in Korean. In K. Kondo-Brown (ed.), *Heritage Language Development: Focus on East Asian Immigrants*. 57–86.

Amsterdam, The Netherlands: John Benjamins.

Peak, L. (1991) *Learning to Go to School in Japan: The Transition from Home to Preschool Life*. Berkeley, CA: University of California Press.

Peters, A. M. and Boggs, S. T. (1986) Interactional routines as cultural influences upon language acquisition. In B. B. Schieffelin and E. Ochs (eds.), *Language Socialization Across Cultures*. 80–96. Cambridge: Cambridge University Press.

Rabain-Jamin, J. (1998) Polyadic language socialization strategy: The case of toddlers in Senegal. *Discourse Processes* 26(1): 43–65.

Rohlen, T. P. and LeTendre, G. (1996) Introduction: Japanese theories of learning. In T. P. Rohlen and G. LeTendre (eds.), *Teaching and Learning in Japan*. 1–15. Cambridge: Cambridge University Press.

Sacks, H., Schegloff, E. A. and Jefferson, G. (1974) A simplest systematics for the organization of turn-taking for conversation. *Language* 50: 696–735.

Schegloff, E. A. and Sacks, H. (1973) Opening up closings. *Semiotica* 8: 289–327.

Schieffelin, B. B. (1979) Getting it together: An ethnographic approach to the study of the development of communicative competence. In E. Ochs and B. B. Schieffelin (eds.), *Developmental Pragmatics*. 73–110. New York: Academic Press.

Schieffelin, B. B. (1990) *The Give and Take of Everyday Life: Language Socialization of Kaluli Children*. Cambridge: Cambridge University Press.

Schieffelin, B. and Ochs, E. (1986) Language socialization. *Annual Review of Anthropology* 15: 163–246.

Scollon, S. (1982) *Reality Set, Socialization, and Linguistic Convergence*. Dissertation. Honolulu, HI: University of Hawaii.

Singleton, J. (1998) Situated learning in Japan: An educational analysis. In J. Singleton (ed.), *Learning in Likely*

Places: Varieties of Apprenticeship in Japan. 3–19. New York: Cambridge University Press.

Slobin, D. (1973) Cognitive prerequisites for the development of grammar. In C. A. Ferguson and D. I. Slobin (eds.), *Studies in Child Language Development*. 175–208. New York: Holt, Rinehart and Winston.

Smith-Hefner, N. J. (1999) *Khmer American: Identity and Moral Education in a Diasporic Community*. Berkeley, CA: University of California Press.

Snow, C. E., Perlmann, R. Y., Gleason, J. B., and Hooshyar, N. (1990) Developmental perspectives on politeness: Sources of children's knowledge. *Journal of Pragmatics* 14(2): 289–305.

Stivers, T. (2001) Negotiating who presents the problem: Next speaker selection in pediatric encounters. *Journal of Communication* 51(2): 252–82.

Takekuro, M. (2005) Yoroshiku onegaishimasu: Routine practice of the routine formula in Japan. In R. T. Lakoff and S. Ide (eds.), *Broadening the Horizon of Linguistic Politeness*. 89–97. Amsterdam, The Netherlands and Philadelphia, PA: John Benjamins.

Tannen, D. (2010) Abduction and identity in family interaction: Ventriloquizing as indirectness. *Journal of Pragmatics* 42(2): 307–16.

Tessonneau, A.-L. (2005) Learning respect in Guadeloupe: Greetings and politeness rituals. In S. Mühleisen and B. Migge (eds.), *Politeness and Face in Caribbean Creoles*. 255–82. Amsterdam, The Netherlands: John Benjamins.

Vološinov, V. N. (1971) Reported speech. In L. Matejka and K. Pomorska (eds.), *Readings in Russian Poetics: Formalist and Structuralist Views*. 149–75. Cambridge, MA: MIT Press.

Watson-Gegeo, K. and Gegeo, D. (1986) Calling out and repeating routines in Kwara'ae children's language socialization. In B. B. Schieffelin and E. Ochs (eds.), *Language Socialization Across*

Cultures. 17–50. Cambridge: Cambridge University Press.

Yokoyama, M. (1980) Jidoo no aisatsu kotoba no shuutoku (Children's acquisition of *aisatsu* expressions).

Fukuoka Kyooiku Daigaku Kiyoo (*Annals of Fukuoka University of Education*) 30(4): 189–94.

13 Language Socialization and Stance-Taking Practices

HARUKO MINEGISHI COOK

Introduction

This chapter examines socialization into stance-taking practices with a focus on the linguistic construction of identities through stance by closely analyzing the Japanese epistemic stance marker *deshoo* in the assessment of food in Japanese homestay settings.

Following Stubbs (1986), du Bois (2007), and others, the chapter begins with the premise that social interaction cannot be carried out without signaling and relying on stance, and that stance-taking is thus fundamental to and ubiquitous in social life. As argued by du Bois (2007: 173), 'stance always invokes, explicitly or implicitly, presupposed systems of sociocultural value, while at the same time contributing to enactment and reproduction of those values.' In other words, stance-taking is a vehicle by which sociocultural values and ideologies are validated, maintained, and negotiated in local communities. When assessing people, objects, or events being addressed, the speaker takes a stance (see Kärkkäinen 2006), which simultaneously involves his or her self-positioning. In addition, since stance-taking acts are dialogic in nature, they align the interlocutors turn-by-turn, creating intersubjectivity, here defined as mutual understanding, between them.

In a broad sense, language socialization is socialization into stance-taking practices, showing how language provides phonological, morphological, and syntactical structures as resources to index epistemic and affective stance. Synthesizing the literature on stance and its relation to epistemic and affective dispositions (Besnier 1992; Clift 2006; Haviland 1989; Heritage and Raymond 2005; Ochs 1990, 1996), Ochs argues that such dispositions are recurrently employed to index a variety of social categories, and provides the following definitions (1996: 410):

The Handbook of Language Socialization, First Edition. Edited by Alessandro Duranti, Elinor Ochs, and Bambi B. Schieffelin.
© 2014 John Wiley & Sons, Ltd. Published 2014 by John Wiley & Sons, Ltd.

Epistemic stance refers to knowledge or belief vis-à-vis some focus of concern, including degrees of certainty of knowledge, degrees of commitment to truth of propositions, and sources of knowledge, among other epistemic qualities (Chafe and Nichols 1986).

Affective stance refers to a mood, attitude, feeling, and disposition, as well as degrees of emotional intensity vis-à-vis some focus of concern (Ochs and Schieffelin 1984; Labov 1984; Levy 1984).

Cross-linguistically, epistemic stance is directly indexed by evidentials, which are linguistic markers that indicate to what extent the speaker is personally committing to his or her assertion (Aksu-Koc and Alici 2000; Chafe and Nichols 1986; Field 1997; Givón 1982; Mushin 2001). A variety of linguistic categories can function as evidentials: verbs (Fox 2001; Kärkkäinen 2003, 2006; Rauniomaa 2007), adverbs (Biber and Finegan 1988), sentence-final particles (Cook 1990; Haviland 1989; He 2001; Ohta 1991; Wu 2004), conditionals (Akatsuka 1985), and clitics (Kockelman 2004), among others. Affective stance is indexed through a wide range of linguistic structures and other semiotic signs (Besnier 1990; Ochs and Schieffelin 1989), which include phonological properties (Kiesling 2005; Ochs 1996), pronouns and address terms (Brown and Levinson 1987; Ochs 1986), adjectives and verbs (Burdelski and Mitsuhashi 2010; Clancy 1999; Suzuki 1999), conditionals (Clancy, Akatsuka, and Strauss 1998), particles (Cook 1992; Ochs 1996; Ohta 1994), honorifics (Cook 1998), and written signs (Kataoka 1997). The distinction between epistemic and affective stance is not static but fluid, in the sense that epistemic stance can index affective stance (Cook 1992; Haviland 1989; Ohta 1991) and vice versa. For example, the Japanese particle *no* is an evidential marker that indexes the shared information status and simultaneously marks positive politeness (Cook 1990; McGloin 1984). The Chinese final particle *a* marks an utterance as news and at the same time indexes the speaker's affect toward the addressee or the topic addressed (Wu 2004).

Since social identities are constituted and encoded by linguistic structures, stance-taking practices serve as primary semiotic resources for identity and activity construction (Bucholtz 2009; Cook 1996a; Kiesling 2005; Ochs 1993, 1996, 2002). For example, in an urban high school in California, the identity of popular white girls is indexed by the epistemic stance marker, the 'be all' quotative (Bucholtz 2009). The English evidential marker 'I see' can distance the speaker from the proposition, indexing, for example, a visitor to the family who is not responsible for the care of the child (Fox 2001). In Japanese elementary schools, the students' classroom activity of *happyoo* ('presentation') is indexed by students' use of the affective stance marker; that is, the addressee honorific *masu* form (Cook 1996b). What is complex is that a stance and identity or activity do not usually hold a one-to-one relationship but a one-to-many relationship. A type of stance may index a range of social meanings depending on co-occurring linguistic and/or nonlinguistic features and may be mediated by the ideology of the local community. For example, an evidential marker that indexes the speaker as the source of information may further index the social identity of an authority or a knowledgeable person. Novices' socialization into stance involves the understanding of an unmarked (normative) link between a particular stance and a particular identity or activity as well as marked ones. Through socialization into stance, novices come to understand indexical links between linguistic forms and social identities and activities as well as sociocultural values indexed through the evaluation of people, objects, and events.

Previous Studies on Socialization into Epistemic and Affective Stances

The literature on socialization into stance discusses how caregivers' uses of evidential markers or affect vocabulary socialize young children, and provides important insight into how sense-making is accomplished in each community. Languages rich in morphology such as Japanese are particularly suitable for this type of research, since they provide abundant linguistic resources for language socialization and make the sense-making process more transparent. Thus, this chapter focuses on Japanese and related areal language socialization practices, while noting that many socialization studies cross-culturally indicate that caregivers often use reported speech in multiparty interaction and that in many communities elicitation routines, which involve the formula 'say X,' teach young children what to say to the co-present third party (Burdelski 2006, this volume; Clancy 1986; de León 1998, this volume; Dumuth 1986; Rabain-Jamin 1998; Schieffelin 1990; Sidnell 1997; Watson-Gegeo and Gegeo 1986). The formula 'say X' can not only instruct young children what to say and how to say it but also teach appropriate sequential organization in conversation. For instance, when the child does not respond to the co-present participant's first pair part (e.g. question), the caregiver prompts the child to produce the second pair part (e.g. answer) by using 'say X.' In this way, elicitation routines position young children as competent speakers in social interaction. In some communities, even prelinguistic children are treated by caregivers as 'speaking' participants. Zinacantec Mayan mothers quote prelinguistic children's intentional communicative movement using the 'she said' frame and report it to the co-present participants (de León 1998, this volume).[1] Similar examples have also been reported in the Wolof community (Rabain-Jamin 1998). In some communities, children are also positioned as the addressees by the caregivers' use of reported speech. For example, Japanese mothers quote voices of the third party (e.g. doctors, media, animals, and toys) to discipline children or provide 'empathy training' (Clancy 1986).[2]

Culturally appropriate positioning toward the addressee, events, and objects being addressed can be achieved by a social action of assessment. Assessment is an activity that evaluates 'in some fashion persons and events being described within their talk' (Goodwin and Goodwin 1987: 6). The literature on language socialization in Japanese documents that assessments by parents and teachers socialize children into appropriate positive and negative affective displays and sociocultural values associated with 'assessables' (i.e. people, objects, and events that are assessed) (Burdelski and Mitsuhashi 2010; Clancy 1999; Suzuki 1999). For example, Burdelski and Mitsuhashi (2010) illustrate how preschool children learn to show positive affect toward small and cute objects and animals through teachers' use of the adjective *kawaii* ('cute'). In contrast, Clancy (1999) and Suzuki (1999) discuss socialization of negative affect. Clancy (1999), who studied three pairs of Japanese mothers and two-year-olds, found that the mothers' use of *kowai* ('be scary/be afraid (of)') helps children to see themselves as the objects of others' evaluative affect. Suzuki (1999) also found that Japanese mothers teach children appropriate behavior through the use of the aspectual suffix *–chau* (or the past tense *–chatta*), which indexes the speaker's negative affect concerning the event or action soon to be completed (or just completed). American children are socialized into empathy with other people and animals when caregivers use affect lexicon such as 'happy' and 'sad,' terms of endearment, and verbs of emotion among others (Hérot 2002). Through the act of assessment performed by caregivers and teachers, children learn culturally appropriate displays of positive and negative affective stance toward people, objects, and events in their social world.

In the process of language socialization, novices learn the indexical associations between particular linguistic forms and particular social categories (Ochs 1996). Ochs (1996: 414) states, 'Indexical knowledge is at the core of linguistic and cultural competence and is the locus where language acquisition and socialization interface.' Although these associations are not static, in every community, particular affective or epistemic stance directly indexed by a linguistic form is normatively linked to a particular social identity or identities in a given context. Cook (1996a, 1996b, 1997, 2008), who discusses socialization into appropriate social identity through affective stance, analyzed the addressee honorific *masu* form as an affective stance marker (affective stance of self-presentation). Her studies demonstrate that this affective stance marker constitutes a variety of identities in different social contexts. For example, in the family setting, the *masu* form indexes the identity of a mother or a father when they use the *masu* form as they engage in acts associated with parental responsibilities (e.g. serving food), whereas it indexes a 'good child' when children speak in the *masu* form displaying their good behavior to their parents. In the elementary school classroom, the students' use of the *masu* form indexes the performer of the *happyoo* ('presentation') activity among other social identities. Japanese children first learn the indexical links between the self-presentational stance and the types of identity and activity through interaction with caregivers at home and later learn to display this stance in new social settings (e.g. at school) to index the appropriate identities that embody the self-presentational stance in a variety of social situations (Cook 1997).

Additionally, studies find that epistemic stance indexed by evidential markers is used to control novices' behavior at home and school. For example, Japanese mothers' use of the sentence-final particle *no* helps to de-emphasize the mother's personal will and appeals to the social norm in order to control children's behavior (Cook 1990). In contrast, the evidential markers *kath* ('seem') in Korean and *deshoo* in Japanese can position the teacher and caregiver as an authority figure (Lo 2004; Johanning 1982). While in a Korean heritage school the teacher employs the evidential marker *kath* as a resource for making a moral judgment, a Japanese mother and a teacher control their children's thoughts and feelings through the marker *deshoo*.[3]

A large number of linguistic structures that index affective or epistemic stance such as sentence-final particles are what Silverstein (1976) refers to as 'non-referential indexes.' Since much of sociocultural information is keyed implicitly through nonreferential indexes (Ochs 1990), studies on nonreferential indexes are essential for understanding the construction of the social world. In contrast to novices learning their first language, second language learners have difficulty in learning such indexes through classroom instruction alone (cf. Gumperz 1996). It is reported that adult learners of Japanese do not easily acquire appropriate uses of these markers in the second language classroom (Wade 2003; Yoshimi 1999). The studies on the uses of sentence-final particles in the second language classroom (Ohta 1994; Yoshimi 1999) suggest that difficulties may stem from the paucity of sentence-final particles in the teacher's talk as well as a difference in grammatical and pragmatic constraints between first language and second language. Ohta (1994) investigated types and frequencies of the pragmatic particles in first-year Japanese classrooms and compared them with those in ordinary Japanese conversations. The study revealed that fewer types and lower frequencies of particles were used in the classroom and that the teacher's philosophy had an impact on the use of particle. Yoshimi (1999), who analyzed Japanese as a foreign language (JFL) learners' incorrect uses of the sentence-final particle *ne*, argued that a difference in Japanese and English epistemic constraints led to improper uses. Even advanced learners may have difficulty in using nonreferential indexes appropriately. Siegal (1996) discusses a case of an advanced learner of Japanese who threatens her professor's face due to her inappropriate way of using the epistemic stance marker *deshoo*. She demonstrates that the learner in her study knows only one of the meanings of *deshoo*, as will be further discussed below. The rest of this chapter expands the investigation of *deshoo* by examining how its multiple meanings and appropriate use in context are taught to adult second language learners in Japanese homestay settings.

The Role of *Deshoo* in Japanese as a Foreign Language Learners' Language Socialization

As discussed above, a way in which second language learners learn to use non-referential indexes is 'through primary socialization in family or friendship circles or intensive communicative cooperation in a finite range of institutionalized environments' (Gumperz 1996: 383). Staying with a host family, then, is an ideal context for second language learners to acquire appropriate uses of affective and epistemic stance markers. This section examines how Japanese host family members use the epistemic stance marker *deshoo* in an assessment activity in interaction with JFL learners, and attempts to unravel how interaction with their host family members may help JFL learners to understand the complex web of indexical associations between *deshoo* and its social meanings.

Data

The data come from 25 video-taped dinner table conversations of nine JFL learners and their Japanese host families. The nine learners consisted of four female and five male learners whose Japanese proficiency level ranged from novice to advanced on the Oral Proficiency Interview (OPI) scale.[4] Alice, Tom, and Kate were novice-level learners according to the OPI scale; Rick and Greg were intermediate-level learners; and Skip, Pete, Mary, and Ellen were advanced-level learners. All learners were native speakers of English. They were college students who had studied Japanese as a foreign language at a university in their home country for two to four years prior to going to Japan. Both Mary and Ellen had a mother who was a native speaker of Japanese. They were enrolled in a year-in-Japan program for foreign students at a Japanese university in the Tokyo area, studying the Japanese language. The host families were typical middle-class Japanese families in the Tokyo area. They were speakers of Tokyo standard Japanese with one exception.[5] Almost all conversations in the data were carried out in Japanese. The entire corpus of conversations was transcribed and subjected to micro-analysis.

The Japanese theory of mind and evidential markers

This section briefly discusses the Japanese theory of mind, in which the use of *deshoo* is framed, and the next section will explore the socializing functions of *deshoo* in detail. The Japanese language has a preference for pragmatic specificity and sensitivity to the shared domain of knowledge/affect and the domain of authority of knowledge. These pragmatic distinctions are encoded by a large number of evidential markers. Shared knowledge/affect is indexed through the sentence-final particles *ne* and *no*, among others. In particular, *ne* occurs frequently in conversation. The fact that normal conversation cannot be carried out without *ne* indicates that shared affect is an essential component of Japanese conversation (Cook 1992). In addition, a high sensitivity to who authorizes knowledge manifests in many ways in Japanese grammar. In particular, the domain of knowledge related to one's psychological state is not equally accessible to all concerned parties in Japanese (Kamio 1994, 1998; Kuroda 1973).[6] Typically, the speaker does not have direct access to other people's psychological states. The bare forms of verbs and adjectives that express psychological states (i.e. desire, want, emotion, ability, feeling, thought, and perception, etc.) normally indicate the speaker's own state of mind. To describe the second or third person's state of mind, an evidential marker, which indicates how the knowledge is acquired, is suffixed to the bare form. For example, the bare adjective *sabishii* ('lonely') expresses the speaker's own psychological state. To say that the second or third party is lonely, an evidential marker such as *gatte iru* ('shows a sign of'), *yoo* ('looks'), or *soo* ('seems') is added to the bare form, as in *sabishi-gatte iru*, *sabishii yoo*, and *sabishi-soo*. However, if the speaker is an omniscient being (e.g. the narrator in a novel) who has a direct access to others' minds, he or she can use psychological verbs or adjectives without an evidential marker (cf. Kuroda 1973).[7] Furthermore, the second or third party's psychological state disclosed in the speech context is treated as shared information. Because Japanese is a pro-drop language, typically the subject noun phrase is omitted in spoken discourse. Often the presence or absence of evidential marking indicates who the sentential subject is. Consider the following examples.

Example 13.1a[8]

> A: *sabishii.*
>   '(I am) lonely'
> B: *sabishii no.* ((falling intonation))
>   '(You are) lonely.'

Example 13.1b

> A: *sabishii.*
>   '(I am) lonely'
> B: *sabishii.* ((falling intonation))
>   '(I am) lonely.'

In Example 13.1a, after speaker A expresses that she is lonely (*sabishii*), speaker B acknowledges speaker A's utterance by saying *sabishii no*. The particle *no* here indicates that speaker A's psychological state is now shared knowledge (i.e. a fact) in the context. Thus, *sabishii no* in this conversational sequence means 'You are lonely.' On the other hand, if speaker B simply repeats speaker A's utterance (i.e. *sabishii*) without any evidential marker as in (Example 13.1b), B's bare-form utterance indicates B's own psychological state, meaning that B herself is lonely. Thus, whenever they speak, Japanese speakers must pay close attention to epistemic stance. In other words, they calculate how subjectivity (the speaker's knowledge versus the second/third party's knowledge) and intersubjectivity (shared domain of knowledge and affect) are appropriately expressed along with the referential content of the utterance.

Kamio's (1994, 1998) theory of 'territory of information,' which attempts to capture the Japanese sensitivity to authority of knowledge, divides information status into two categories, namely the speaker's and hearer's territories of information. The information that falls into the speaker's territory (i.e. the information that the speaker authorizes) is encoded by the direct (i.e. bare) form of verbs and adjectives while the information that falls in the hearer's territory (i.e. the information that the addressee authorizes) is encoded by the indirect form (i.e. bare form + evidential marker). Kamio bases his theory of territory of information on made-up sentences. In practice, however, evidential markers are used much more fluidly and creatively than Kamio proposes.

In sum, Japanese is highly sensitive to the shared domain of knowledge and the domain of authority of knowledge. These domains are resources for constructing various identities as well as social control.

Deshoo: *An epistemic stance marker*

Deshoo has at least two distinct pragmatic functions (see Siegal 1996). It is often referred to as a 'tentative form of the copula' (e.g. Jorden and Noda 1987; Kamio 1994; Siegal 1996) that marks probability or lack of certainty, of which most native speakers have a 'limited awareness' (Silverstein 2001). Only a few scholars have suggested pragmatic meanings of *deshoo* other than that of probability (Kamio 1994; McGloin 2002). Noting that the function of *deshoo* is not limited to simple inference, McGloin (2002), has proposed that *deshoo* is a marker of shared knowledge (i.e. the speaker's assumption of knowledge on the part of the addressee). As discussed below, McGloin's proposal, however, does not clearly distinguish *deshoo* from another marker of shared knowledge, the sentence-final particle *ne*. In contrast, Kamio's (1994) proposal pertains to *deshoo* as a marker of authority of knowledge in that *deshoo* indexes that the information falls in the speaker's territory 'to the fullest degree' as well as in the addressee's territory 'to a lesser degree.' The difficulty of Kamio's proposal is that it is not possible to determine to what extent the information falls in the addressee's territory. I propose that *deshoo* indexes two different domains of knowledge: an intersection of subjectivity (authority of knowledge) and intersubjectivity (shared knowledge). In other words, *deshoo* indexes the speaker's 'territory of information' (Kamio 1994) as well as the shared status of the information. In this function, *deshoo* is often pronounced with a rising intonation and a short [o], as in *desho*.[9] The remainder of this chapter discusses this second function because in the present data *deshoo* is most often used in this manner.

Some scholars note that *deshoo* and the sentence-final particles *ne* and *yo* have similar functions (e.g. Johanning 1982; Jorden and Noda 1987). For example, both *deshoo* and *ne* serve as tag questions (e.g. Jorden and Noda 1987) and both index that the speaker assumes that the addressee's knowledge or feeling is the same as that of the speaker. As shown in Example 13.2, *deshoo* and *ne* are different in that *deshoo* indexes an intersection of the domain of authority of knowledge (the speaker's territory of information) and the domain of shared information/affect while *ne* only indexes shared information/affect. Here the host mother performs an assessment of the food she has cooked, using *deshoo*.

Example 13.2:   Kate[10]

Host mother (HM) and Kate (K).
((Kate and her host mother have just started to eat dinner))

```
1 →  HM.:   kore oishii desho?
            this delicious Cop
            'This is delicious desho?'
2    K:     oishii
            delicious
            'It's delicious.'
```

In this example, the deictic term *kore* ('this') refers to the food the host mother has cooked. The host mother's *deshoo* indexes (1) that the assessable (i.e. the food being talked about in this case) falls into her territory of information (Kamio 1994) and (2) that the speaker is asking the addressee (via rising intonation) if her assumption that the addressee shares the same position with respect to the assessable is correct. The speaker could use *ne* with a rising intonation (i.e. *kore oishii ne?* ('This is delicious *ne?*')), which may imply that the food was not cooked by the speaker (cf. Kamio 1994). The host mothers in the present data use *oishii deshoo* and do not use *oishii ne* when the assessable is the food they themselves prepared. These facts indicate that *deshoo* and *ne* index different epistemic stances. Morita (2005), in her study on Japanese sentence-final particles, analyzes *ne* as an alignment marker that displays the participants' mutual understanding achieved in interaction. A marked difference between *deshoo* and *ne* in assessment is that, while a *ne*-marked first assessment prefers a *ne*-marked second, a *deshoo*-marked first assessment disprefers a *deshoo*-marked second if *deshoo* is not used in the sense of probability.[11] This difference derives from the fact that *deshoo* indexes the speaker's territory of information while *ne* does not. The indexical meaning of *deshoo* marks asymmetry in information status between the speaker and addressee because the information in question is in the speaker's territory. Thus, it can position the speaker as an authority figure or a knowledgeable person.[12] Due to its asymmetry of information, *deshoo* in the second assessment made by a different speaker from that of the first assessment sounds too competitive. In contrast, because *ne* does not implicate asymmetry in information status, it is appropriate to mark both the first and the second assessment with *ne*.

Deshoo is also similar to the sentence-final particle *yo* in its function but indexes a different epistemic stance as well. Unlike *deshoo*, *yo* only prompts the addressee to pay attention to the speaker's assertion. Thus, the utterance *kono osushi oishii yo* ('This sushi is delicious *yo*') indexes neither that the *sushi* falls into the speaker's territory (e.g. the speaker prepared the *sushi*, or bought it because of his or her familiarity with *this sushi*) nor that the speaker assumes the addressee's shared knowledge.

The characterizations of the epistemic stance markers *ne*, *yo*, and *deshoo* are summarized in Table 13.1.

In sum, *deshoo* in Example 13.2 indexes that the information falls into the speaker's territory and that the speaker simultaneously assumes that the addressee shares the information. Like the particle *ne*, it aligns the addressee with the speaker and thus creates intersubjectivity between them. It is also similar to the English discourse marker 'you know,' which indexes the speaker's metacognition about the addressee's knowledge (Schiffrin 1987).

Studies on *deshoo* in the socialization of novices are scarce. Johanning (1982), who examined the use of *deshoo* by a Japanese mother and a teacher, found that *deshoo* teaches novices how to feel and act and is used to control their behavior and thoughts. She notes that most instances of *deshoo* index rationales of the mother and the teacher aimed at altering novices' behavior or thoughts. For example, when the child, who has a cracker in his hand, wants to grab another,

Table 13.1 *Ne, Yo,* **and** *Deshoo*

Epistemic marker	Authority of knowledge (S's territory of information)	Shared knowledge (S assumes A's knowledge)
Ne	−	+[a]
Yo	−	−
Deshoo	+	+

[a]The sentence particle *ne* can occur without a proposition. This fact indicates that *ne* does not always predicate on the information that the speaker assumes on the part of the addressee. It can index shared affect between the speaker and addressee (see Cook 1992).

the mother says, *anata hitotsu aru deshoo* ('You have one already, *deshoo'*). Johanning concludes that, through the use of *deshoo*, Japanese mothers express what they expect their children to understand. As discussed earlier, Siegal's study (1996) illustrates a novice's inappropriate use of *deshoo*. In that case, an advanced learner of Japanese tries to politely talk with her Japanese professor by means of *deshoo*, but sounds impolite to the professor because her use of *deshoo* positions her as an authority figure. Apparently, the learner only knows one of the meanings of *deshoo* (i.e. probability) and is not aware that the way in which she uses *deshoo* (an index of authority) is inappropriate for the occasion.

Deshoo in the Assessment of Food[13]

This section closely examines how the Japanese host family members perform an assessment of food by using *deshoo* and other sentence-final forms. Ways in which family members talk about food at dinnertime differ from culture to culture (cf. Ochs, Pontecorvo, and Fasulo 1996). During dinnertime, Japanese families often engage in talking about tastes of different kinds of food and express their enjoyment of eating them by means of the assessment adjective *oishii* ('delicious'). Accordingly, in the present data, during dinnertime all nine host families talk about the food they are eating as well as the food they often eat at home and in restaurants. In Japanese society, preparing and providing food for family members is one of the most important responsibilities of the housewife/mother. In all nine host families, the host mother is the sole preparer of food for the family. As the learner starts eating dinner, the host mother often utters *oishii deshoo* to makes sure that the food the learner is eating tastes good by eliciting the learner's affective reaction to it. The assessment adjective *oishii* ('delicious') often co-occurs with a variety of epistemic stance markers (e.g. *oishii deshoo, oishii ne, oishii yo,* and *oishii yo ne*). Each of these expressions positions the speaker, the addressee, and the co-present participants in different ways. Because these expressions are not randomly used and because they are recurrent in dinnertime conversation, routine participation in dinnertime conversation may help JFL learners acquire linguistic and cultural competence with respect to these markers. Focusing on *deshoo*, below I discuss how the host family members position themselves and others in the assessment of food.

'I know you have tasted the food'

Recall that *deshoo* presupposes that the speaker assumes that the addressee shares the knowledge of the assessable. Thus, the host family's assessment turn with *deshoo* is either preceded by the addressee's act of tasting the food or by a turn that indicates that he or she has tasted the food.

Consider Example 13.3. Here Pete and his host mother, host father, and host grandmother are eating beef for dinner.

Example 13.3: Pete

Host mother (HM), host father (HF), and Pete (P).

1→   HM: *tabete goran oishii kara   oishii kara*
                    eat try delicious because   delicious because
                    'Have some because it's delicious, delicious.'
              ((several turns are omitted)) (1.0)

2→   HM: *sungoi yawarakakute oishii*
                    very tender delicious
                    'It's very tender and delicious.'
              ((P is eating the beef)) (3.0)

3   P: *o:: ishii=*
                    delicious
                    'Delicious'

4   HF: *(chotto) onaka suku n da yo na=*
                    little stomach empty Cop SP SP
                    'I'm a little hungry *yo na*.'

5   HM: =((laugh)) (2.0)

6 →   HM: [*oishii desho? niowanai desho?*
                    delicious Cop smell Neg Cop
                    'It's delicious *desho*. It does not smell *desho*'

7   P: [*oishii*
                    delicious
                    'delicious'

8   P: *un*
                    uh huh
                    'uh huh'

Note the contrast between the host mother's assessments before and after Pete tastes the food.[14] Before Pete starts to eat, she performs an assessment by saying the beef is very tender and delicious without any epistemic stance marker in lines 1 and 2. In contrast, once Pete has tasted the beef and displays heightened affect toward the assessable by producing *o::ishii* ('delicious') in an emphatic manner with a prolonged [o], the host mother performs two assessments with *deshoo* (i.e. *oishii desho* ('delicious *desho*') and *niowanai desho* ('does not smell *desho*') in line 6). Pete aligns himself with the host mother by producing *un* 'uh huh.' This example shows that the host mother does not assess the taste of her food with *deshoo* until the addressee tastes the food.

Example 13.4 also shows the host mother's use of *oishii deshoo*, reflecting her knowledge of the learner's first-hand experience of the assessable. Here Ellen and her host mother are enjoying small pastries for dessert.

Example 13.4: Ellen

Host mother (HM) and Ellen (E).

1	E:	*okaasan tabeta?=*
		mom ate
		'Have you eaten it, Mom?'
2	HM:	=*tabeta moo mittsu tabechatta* [((laugh))
		ate already three ate
		'I already ate three'
3	E:	[((laugh)) *oishii*= ((eating the
		pastries))
		delicious
		'It's delicious.'
4	HM:	=*kore mo aru yo mittsu tabeta no* [*yo moo*
		this also exist SP three ate SP SP already
		'Here is this one. I already ate three of them *yo*.'
5	E:	[*nn oishi oishi* ((eating the
		pastries))
		uh huh delicious delicious
		'Uh huh, it's delicious,
		delicious.'
6 →	HM:	*oishii deshoo*
		delicious *deshoo*
		'It's delicious *deshoo*.'

After Ellen repeats her assessment of the pastries, saying *oishii* three times as she eats the sweets, the host mother solicits Ellen's reaction by proffering her assessment, *oishii deshoo*. Clearly, in this case, the host mother knows that Ellen finds the dessert tasty. Often pastries are not prepared by the housewife in a Japanese household but bought in a pastry shop. In this set of data, it is not clear whether the host mother herself made or bought the sweets. In either case, because she was responsible for the pastries appearing on the dinner table, the host mother treats them as something that falls in her territory by the use of *deshoo*.

Deshoo presupposes the speaker's assumption that both the speaker and the addressee have shared knowledge about the person(s), object(s), or event(s) being discussed or to be introduced. Example 13.5 and Example 13.6 demonstrate the dispreference for *deshoo* when not all parties have access to the same shared knowledge and the speaker does not treat the assessable as in her territory. Example 13.5 demonstrates the learner's lack of shared knowledge. It begins when the host mother, the host father, and Ellen are about to start dinner, and shows how the host mother does *not* use *deshoo* in her assessment of the food because Ellen has not started to eat yet. The host mother cooked duck for dinner and, because in Japanese the word *tori* means both 'bird' and 'chicken,' the use of *tori* in this excerpt is ambiguous.

Example 13.5: Ellen

Host mother (HM), host father (HF), and Ellen (E).

```
1 →   HM:   tori yo [oishii yo=
             bird yo delicious yo
             'It's a bird yo. It's delicious yo.'
2     E:            [kamo
                    duck
                    'duck'
3     E:    =tori?=
             bird/chicken
             'bird/chicken?'
4     HM:   =un
             'Yeah'
5     HF:   demo niwatori ja nai yo
             but chicken Neg SP
             'But it's not chicken yo.'
6     E:    aa soo=
             oh so
             'Oh, is that so?'
7     HM:   =demo tori no isshu da yo        [kamo tte
             but bird Lk one kind Cop SP     duck QT
             'But ducks are a type of fowl yo.'
8     HF:                                    [un kamo
                                             yeah duck
                                             'Yeah, it's duck.'
```

Ellen's utterance, *kamo* ('duck') in line 2 is overlapped with the host mother's assessment of the food in line 1. The host mother's assessment here does not co-occur with *deshoo* but with the particle *yo* because Ellen has not eaten the food yet. *Yo* prompts the addressee to pay attention to the speaker's utterance but does not assume the addressee's shared knowledge. Because her turn in line 2 receives no uptake, Ellen asks for clarification by repeating the word *tori*, which was uttered by the host mother in line 1. The host parents are trying to resolve the ambiguity of the word *tori* by explaining that the food on the table is not chicken but duck. In line 5, using the word *niwatori*, which specifically means 'chicken,' the host father repairs Ellen's ambiguous utterance *tori*.

In general, host mothers utter *oishii desho* after the learner has tasted the food that falls in their territory whereas they may use *oishii yo* when they know that the learner has not yet tasted the food in question. Furthermore, it is usually host mothers who use *oishii deshoo* in the assessment of the food they have cooked and the other members of the host family are unlikely to use it, even when they are aware that the learner has tasted the food. Such a contrast may teach learners the different social meanings of *oishii deshoo* and the other expressions such as *oishii*, *oishii ne*, and *oishii yo*.

In sum, the expression *oishii deshoo* in the assessment of food (1) indexes the assessable falls in the speaker's territory and (2) denotes that the speaker assumes the addressee's experience or knowledge of the assessable. The host mother's *oishii deshoo* creates intersubjectivity between herself and the learner and it teaches the learner the cultural practice of explicit appreciation of the food during the mealtime.

Gender roles

The presence or absence of *deshoo* in the assessment of food may index gender roles in Japanese society because cooking is the responsibility of the housewife/ mother in a family. As shown in Example 13.2 and Example 13.3, in the present data the host mother typically indexes her identity as housewife and mother by treating the food she cooks as something that falls into her territory with *oishii deshoo* ('delicious *deshoo*').[15] In contrast, in the present data, assessments made by the other members of the host family (e.g. the host father) about the food the host mother prepared do not co-occur with *deshoo* unless a frame that shifts the perspective is invoked (see next section). The absence of *deshoo* in this case can be linked to the identity of the husband or father in contrast to that of the housewife or mother. Example 13.6 demonstrates that Mary's host father does not use *deshoo* in the assessment of the food that the host mother has cooked. Instead, he uses *yo ne* and *yo na* (a variant of *yo ne*). Here the participants are eating *buri* ('yellowtail') for dinner. This conversation was recorded in January and the host father's comment on the fish in line 2 refers to the fact that yellowtail tastes the best in winter because it has more fatty meat.

Example 13.6: Mary

Host mother (HM), host Father (HF), and Mary (M).

1   M: *buri ga oishii*
                 yellowtail S delicious
                 'The yellowtail is delicious.'
2 →   HF: *oishii yo ne. choodo abura ga nottete=*
                 delicious SP SP just fat S attach
                 'It's delicious *yo ne*. It has fatty meat.'

3   HM: =*un*=
                uh huh
                'uh huh'
4 →   HF: =*ichiban oishii yo na*
                most delicious SP SP
                'It's most delicious (at this time) *yo na*.'

In line 1, Mary proffers an assessment of the fish cooked by the host mother. In line 2, the host father aligns himself with Mary by saying *oishii yo ne* ('delicious *yo ne*') and in line 4 he repeats his assessment with *yo na* (a variant of *yo ne*). In the collocation of the sentence-final particles *yo* and *ne*, *yo* prompts the addressee to pay attention to the speaker's utterance and *ne* seeks shared understanding of the information, act, and affect. The host father's assessment occupies the second and third positions. Here his *yo ne* indexes his independent assertion concerning the food (*yo*) and his acknowledgment of the shared understanding of the assessable (*ne/na*). The participants, assessable, and sequence in Example 13.7 are similar to those of Example 13.3, as summarized in Table 13.2.

In both Example 13.3 and Example 13.6, the learner and the host parents are participants and the assessable is the food cooked by the host mother. The first assessment position is occupied by the learner's *oishii* ('delicious'). The second assessment position is occupied by the host mother's *oishii deshoo* in Example 13.3 and by the host father's *oishii yo ne* in Example 13.6. By the use of *deshoo*, the host mother in Example 13.3 treats the food she herself cooked as something that falls into her territory. Thus, her use of *deshoo* positions her as a housewife or mother who is responsible for food preparation in the family. In contrast, by not using *deshoo*, the host father in Example 13.6 treats the food as being outside of his territory. Thus, the absence of *deshoo* in the host father's assessment positions him as someone who is not responsible for cooking for the family in the household, which could imply men's role in the family.

Example 13.7 also shows gender identities constituted by the presence or absence of *deshoo*. Here Pete's host parents are eating *namasu* salad that the host mother prepared. *Namasu* salad is a dish that families prepare for the celebration of New Year.

Table 13.2   Participants and Sequence of Assessment in Example 13.3 and Example 13.6

Participants	Assessable	Sequence
Learner, host mother, host father	Food cooked by host mother	1. Learner eats the food 2. First assessment by learner 3. Second assessment by host parent

Example 13.7: *Pete*

Host mother (HM) and host father (HF).

1 HM: ( ) *kotoshi no namasu wa demo amai (.) amai tte yuu ka (.)*
         this year Lk salad Top but sweet sweet QT say Q
         'But this year's *namasu* salad is sweet (.) rather than sweet (.)'
2 HF: *oishii yo*
         delicious SP
         'It's delicious *yo.*'
3 HM: *oishii desho?*
         delicious Cop
         'It's delicious *desho*'

In line 1 the host mother talks about the taste of the *namasu* salad that she prepared for this year. While she pauses to search for an appropriate word for the taste of the salad rather than the word 'sweet,' the host father takes the floor. Note the contrast between the host father's assessment and that of the host mother. The host father, who did not make the salad, proffers an assessment with *yo*, which draws the host mother's attention to the host father's utterance. The host father's identity is constituted by the absence of *deshoo*, for the assessable is not in his territory. In contrast, the host mother's assessment with *desho* indexes that the assessable is in her territory. The association of the person responsible for food preparation at home and the presence of *deshoo* as well as that of the person who is not responsible for cooking at home and the absence of *deshoo* in assessment of the food could teach learners not only the social meaning of *deshoo* but also the gender roles in a Japanese household.

In sum, the analysis has shown that the occurrence of *deshoo* in the assessment of food is in part linked to gender roles in Japanese society. The host mother's use of *deshoo* in the assessment of the food she prepared invokes the responsibility and territory of the housewife and mother in the family. Further, the absence of *deshoo* in the host father's assessment of food prepared by the host mother can position him as a husband and father.

Construction of the identity of 'Japanese'

Talk about the cultural differences between Japan and the JFL learner's home country typically positions the participants as representatives of their own culture (Mori 2003). The Japanese host family members treat Japanese food or food produced in Japan as something that falls into their territory (Japan) and the food from the home country of the learner as an object outside their territory.[16] When talking about food from the perspective of 'interculturality' (Mori 2003), not only the host mother but also the other members of the host family make an assessment with *deshoo* to index that the assessable is in their territory.

In Example 13.8, just prior to this segment, Skip, the host sister, and the host mother were talking about American food. Then, in line 1, the host sister brings up the topic of Japanese food by asking Skip whether Japanese food tastes very good. The contrast between the prior topic (American food) and the current topic (Japanese food) evokes an intercultural frame.

Example 13.8:   Skip

Host mother (HM), host sister (HS), and Skip (S).

1	HS:	*nihon no nihon no ryoori sugoi oishiku nai?*
		Japanese Japanese cuisine very delicious Neg
		'Isn't Japanese, Japanese cuisine very delicious ?'
2	S:	*oishii.*
		delicious
		'It's delicious'
3 →	HS:	*oishii deshoo.*
		delicious Cop
		'It's delicious *deshoo*'
4	S:	*oishii oishii tama ni hen dakedo, daitai oishii.*
		delicious delicious sometimes strange but usually delicious
		'It's delicious, delicious. Sometimes it's strange but usually delicious.'
5	HM:	[((laugh))
6	HS:	[((laugh))

After Skip responds positively to the host sister's question by saying that Japanese food is delicious (*oishii*), his host sister repeats *oishii* followed by *deshoo*, which indexes that the assessable (Japanese food) falls into her territory. Because of the intercultural frame in the current talk, the act of claiming that Japanese food falls into her own territory foregrounds the host sister's identity as Japanese.

While in Example 13.8 the assessable is Japanese food in general, in Example 13.9, the assessable is a specific Japanese food item (i.e. the apples that the participants are eating). In Example 13.9, Mary, the host mother, and host father are eating Japanese apples for dessert. Mary sets up an intercultural frame in lines 1 and 4.

Example 13.9:   Mary

Host mother (HM), host father (HF), and Mary (M).
((all the participants are eating (Japanese) apples))

1	M:	*tottemo nihon no ringo tte mezurashii no yo ne ookikutte=*
		very Japanese apple QT unusual Nom SP SP big
		'Japanese apples are very unusual *yo ne* because they are big.'

2   HF: = [*aa*
                aa
                'aa'

3   HM: =[*aa soo* [*e::*
                Aa so yeah
                'aa that's right yeah'

4   M: [*mukoo no ringo wa sugoi chiisai kara*=
                            over there Lk apple Top very small so
                            'Apples over there (in England) are very small so.'

5   HM: =*huun*
                uhm
                'uhm'

6 →   HF: *oishii deshoo ringo*=
                delicious Cop apple
                'It's delicious *deshoo,* the apple'

7   M: =*oishii*
                delicious
                'delicious'

Mary, a student from England, compares Japanese and English apples. The comparison between the apples from the two countries creates an intercultural frame. Once the intercultural frame has been evoked, the host father proffers an assessment *oishii deshoo* (line 6), referring to the Japanese apples they are eating. Here the host father treats the Japanese apples they are eating as objects that belong to his territory (Japan) by the use of *deshoo*. Because *deshoo* indexes that Japanese apples fall in the host father's territory within the intercultural frame, his assessment with *deshoo* highlights his identity as Japanese.

Japanese as a Foreign Language Learners' Understanding of *Deshoo*

The foregoing discussion indicates that, in order for JFL learners to become competent users of the epistemic stance marker *deshoo*, they have to learn the indexical associations between *deshoo* and the identities that emerge in the ongoing talk. To do so, they need to understand the pragmatic meaning of *deshoo* and how *deshoo* is used in relation to participation frameworks, sequential organization of talk, topics of talk, and cultural practices in Japanese society. Learners have to cognitively and socially orient themselves to the participants' experiences and actions both retrospectively and in the current talk. For example, they need to closely observe whether the assessment *oishii deshoo* is uttered after the recipient of *oishii deshoo* has already tasted the food or indicated if the food is tasty in the prior turn. They also need knowledge of cultural practice in Japanese society, for example gender roles. In addition, they have to orient to the frame of the current talk.

Because of these complexities, direct instruction in these details in the second language classroom is difficult if not impossible.

The present study, however, suggests that learners learn to use *deshoo* appropriately in routine participation in conversation with their host family members.

How does this occur? In the present data, all the learners including novice-level learners such as Kate and Alice do not simply repeat the host family members' *oishii deshoo*. When the food is prepared by the host mother, it is not appropriate for the learners to give an assessment of the food by saying *oishii deshoo*. As shown in Example 13.2, Example 13.3, Example 13.8, and Example 13.9, when the host family member's first assessment is *oishii deshoo*, the learners' second assessment is *oishii* without *deshoo*. Even in the speech of the learners with low proficiency in Japanese, such as Kate in Example 13.2, the absence of *oishii deshoo* in the second assessment position after the host mother's *oishii deshoo* in the first assessment position was observed. This fact suggests that the learners did not simply imitate the host family members' utterances. Furthermore, the intermediate and advanced learners in the present study used *deshoo* appropriately.[17] They tended to use *deshoo* to display what they knew or their newly acquired knowledge about Japanese culture and language, as shown in Example 13.10.

Just before this segment, Skip (an intermediate-level learner) and his host mother and host sister were talking about polite expressions in English. Then, in line 1, Skip changes the topic to Japanese polite expressions, prefacing *nihon wa* ('in Japan'), and then appropriately uses *deshoo* to display his knowledge about Japanese polite expressions.

Example 13.10:   Skip

Host mother (HM), host sister (HS), and Skip (S).

1	S:	*nihon wa kore ga*
		Japan Top this Sub
		'In Japan, this is'
2	HS:	*un*
		uh huh
		'uh huh'
3	S:	[*soo soo soo*
		so so so
		'yeah, yeah, yeah'
4	HM:	[*soo soo soo*
		so so so
		'yeah, yeah, yeah'
5 →	S:	'*itashimasu*,' '*shimasu*,' '*nasaimasu*' *aru* [*desho?*
		'*itashimasu*' '*shimasu*' '*nasaimasu*' exist Cop
		'there are (honorific expressions) '*itasimasu*,' '*shimasu*,' and '*nasaimasu*' desho?'
		((S moves hands vertically to indicate hierarchical structure of society))

6   HM: [*o: sugoi sugoi* ((laugh))
                                              oh terrific terrific
                                              'Oh, that's terrific, terrific.'

In line 5, by using *deshoo*, Skip lists examples of Japanese verbal expressions with different degrees of politeness (i.e. *itashimasu* ('to do – humble'), *shimasu* ('to do – neutral'), and *nasaimasu* ('to do – respect')). By the use of *deshoo*, he indexes that his knowledge about Japanese polite expressions is in his territory (i.e. he has mastered them) and assumes that the host family members will agree with him. To respond to his expectation, the host mother praises him in line 6. Interactions such as that in Example 13.10 suggest that learners are active agents who pay close attention to the ongoing contextual features in talk and link them to the linguistic form. In other words, they tacitly understand the social meaning of *deshoo*.

The ways in which the host family members respond to a particular use of *deshoo* by the learner can also be informative. In Example 13.11, Skip uses *deshoo* in the second assessment position. Recall that, when the first assessment occurs with *deshoo*, the *deshoo* in the second assessment position said by a speaker different from the one who uttered the first assessment makes it sound like the speaker has a competitive attitude. Here Skip, his host sister, and host mother are eating dinner. Prior to this segment, they have been talking about Japanese and American food. Skip's host sister, who spent some time in the United States as an exchange student, starts to talk about the taste of American peanut butter.

Example 13.11:   *Skip*

Host mother (HM), host sister (HS), and Skip (S).

1   HS: *mukoo de piinatsu battaa o tabeta* ((gazes at HM))
                over there in peanut butter Obj ate
                'I ate peanut butter over there (United States).'
2 →   *piinatsu no aji shika shinai deshoo?*
                peanut Lk taste only do Neg Cop
                'It only had the taste of peanuts *deshoo*?'
3 →   S: *oishii deshoo? sore ga=*
                delicious Cop that S
                'That's what is delicious (about American peanut butter)
                    deshoo?'
4   HS: *=OISHIKU NAI YO*
                delicious Neg SP
                'It's not delicious *yo*.'
5   HM: ((laugh))
6   HS: *piinatsu da yo. tada no* ((laugh))
                peanut Co SP mere Lk
                'It's merely peanuts *yo*.'

With *deshoo*, the host sister produces the first assessment stating that American peanut butter only has the taste of peanuts. It is somewhat ambiguous whether this is a positive or negative evaluation of American peanut butter. Skip produces the second assessment with *deshoo*, providing a positive evaluation of American peanut butter. Because the participants have been talking about Japanese and American food, an intercultural frame is evoked in the current talk. Thus, his *deshoo* indexes that American peanut butter falls in his territory and that he as an American is rightfully an authority on American peanut butter. In addition, Skip's assessment with *deshoo* in the second assessment position indexes his forceful and competitive attitude (i.e. 'As an American, I tell you that's what is delicious about American peanut butter'). In line 4, the host sister squarely opposes Skip by clearly stating her negative evaluation of American peanut butter with the sentence-final particle *yo* and using a loud voice, which indexes her strongly argumentative attitude. It could be that the host sister's strongly argumentative utterance is triggered by Skip's *deshoo* in the second assessment position. The host sister's strong reaction to Skip's *oishii deshoo* may teach him the social meaning of *deshoo* in the second assessment position when the first assessment is marked with *deshoo*.

Conclusion

This chapter has discussed functions of stance markers in language socialization. A wide range of linguistic structures serve as affective and epistemic stance markers. In particular, languages with rich morphology such as Japanese have a variety of linguistic features referred to as 'non-referential indexes' (Silverstein 1976). These features often mark subtle but different stances. Stance markers further index dimensions of social contexts including social identity. How stance markers are indexically associated with social dimensions is complex, for social dimensions do not statically lie outside of social interaction but are constantly emerging in interaction. Children learning their native language are socialized into expressing stance quite early by participating in routine activities with their caregivers. In contrast, second language learners have difficulty in learning appropriate uses of stance markers, in particular in the second language classroom. This chapter has examined in detail ways in which Japanese host family members use the epistemic stance marker *deshoo* in the assessment of food. It has illustrated that ways in which particular identities are indexed through *deshoo* depend on contextual features that surround the talk, such as participation framework, sequential organization, frames evoked in context, and cultural practice in society, among others. The findings of this study provide some evidence that learners become competent users of *deshoo* by paying attention to the details of the emerging context of talk. This chapter has focused only on the use of *deshoo* in the assessment of food, a routine activity in Japanese families. It is for future research to explore how novices are socialized into different kinds of affective and epistemic stance in other social activities that routinely take place at home and at school.

ACKNOWLEDGMENTS

This research was supported by a University of Hawaii Japan Studies Endowment Special Project Award and a grant from the US Department of Education, which established the National Foreign Language Resource Center at the University of Hawaii at Manoa. However, the contents do not necessarily represent the policy of the Department of Education, and one should not assume endorsement by the federal government.

NOTES

1 It is not clear whether the 'she said' frame is a direct or indirect quotation.
2 This practice does not happen in Kaluli (Schieffelin, personal communication).
3 To date, not much research has been done on language socialization through Korean epistemic and affective stance markers except for Lo's study (2004).
4 Yumiko Enyo, who was trained to be an OPI evaluator, assisted me in evaluating the learners' Japanese proficiency levels.
5 Pete's host father is a speaker of the Osaka dialect.
6 It is also reported that the speaker does not have a direct access to others' psychological states in Korean (Lee 1993; Lo 2004) and American indigenous languages (Aikhenvald 2003; McLendon 2003).
7 As discussed above, Lo (2004) shows that the Korean teacher in her study has direct access to the 'bad' students' minds.
8 Transcription conventions: [, overlapped speech; =, latching; (0.5), the length of a pause in seconds; (.), unmeasured micro-pause; ( ), unclear utterance; (( )), commentary; ::, sound stretch; CAPITALS, emphasis signaled by pitch or volume; ° °, portions that are delivered in a quieter voice; -, cut-off speech; ?, rising intonation; ., falling intonation.
9 In the examples, when *deshoo* is pronounced a with short [o], it is spelled *desho*, reflecting the pronunciation.
10 Abbreviations used in word-for-word translations: Cop, various forms of the copula verb 'be'; Lk, linking nominal; Neg, negative morpheme; Nom, nominalizer; O, object marker; S, subject marker; Q, question marker; QT, quotative marker; SP, sententce-final particle; Top, topic marker.
11 It is possible to mark the second assessment with *deshoo* if *deshoo* means 'probably':
    A: *ashita wa ame deshoo.*
        'It will probably rain tomorrow.'
    B: *ee ame deshoo.*
        'Yeah, it will probably rain.'
12 Since *ne* does not index the speaker's territory of information, it does not position the speaker as an authority figure.
13 The occurrence of *deshoo* is not limited to the act of assessment of food. But, because *deshoo* in assessment of food occurs frequently in the data, it provides a good context for language socialization.

14   *Kara* in *oishii kara* is a connective particle meaning 'because' and forms a subordinate clause. In a subordinate clause, the meaning of *deshoo* is limited to probability. Thus, the expression *oishii deshoo kara* means 'Because it is probably tasty.'

15   In the present study, there are some instances in which the host mother says *oishii?* ('delicious?') without *deshoo* when she talks about the food she herself cooked.

16   When the Japanese host family members believe that the information is correct, they often treat the assessable that concerns the custom of the learner's country as their own information. For example, Greg's host mother mentions to Greg, *amerikajin wa anmari sakana wa tabenai desho* ('Americans do not eat much fish *deshoo*').

17   The novice-level learners in the present study never used *deshoo*.

REFERENCES

Aikhenvald, A. (2003) Evidentiality in Tariana. In A. Aikhenvald and R. Dixon (eds.), *Studies in Evidentiality*. 131–64. Amsterdam, The Netherlands: John Benjamins.

Akatsuka, N. (1985) Conditionals and the epistemic scale. *Language* 61(3): 1–16.

Aksu-Koc, A., and Alici, D. (2000) Understanding sources of beliefs and marking of uncertainty: The child's theory of evidentiality. In E. Clark (ed.), *Proceedings of the Thirtieth Child Language Research Forum*. 123–30. Stanford, CA: Center for the Study of Language and Information.

Besnier, N. (1990) Language and affect. *Annual Review of Anthropology* 19: 419–51.

Besnier, N. (1992) Reported speech and affect in Nukulaelae. In J. Irvine and J. Hill (eds.), *Responsibility and Evidence in Oral Discourse*. 161–81. Cambridge: Cambridge University Press.

Biber, D., and Finegan, E. (1988) Adverbial stance types in English. *Discourse Processes* 11: 1–34.

Brown, P., and Levinson, S. (1987) *Politeness: Some Universals in Language Usage*. Cambridge: Cambridge University Press.

Bucholtz, M. (2009) From stance to style: Gender, interaction, and indexicality in Mexican immigrant youth slang. In A. Jaffe (ed.), *Sociolinguistic Perspectives on Stance*. 146–70. New York: Oxford University Press.

Burdelski, M. (2006) *Language Socialization of Two-Year Old Children in Kansai, Japan: The Family and Beyond*. Doctoral Dissertation. Los Angeles, CA: University of California, Los Angeles.

Burdelski, M., and Mitsuhashi, K. (2010) 'She says you're *kawaii*': Socializing affect, gender, and relationship in a Japanese preschool. *Language in Society* 39(1): 65–93.

Chafe, W. and Nichols, J. (eds.) (1986) *Evidentiality: The Linguistic Coding of Epistemology*. Norwood, NJ: Ablex.

Clancy, P. (1986) The acquisition of communicative style in Japanese. In B. B. Schieffelin and E. Ochs (eds.), *Language Socialization across Cultures*. 213–50. Cambridge: Cambridge University Press.

Clancy, P. (1999) The socialization of affect in Japanese mother–child conversation. *Journal of Pragmatics* 31: 1397–421.

Clancy, P., Akatsuka, N., and Strauss, S. (1998) Deontic modality and conditionality in discourse: A cross-linguistic study of adult speech to young children. In A. Kamio (ed.), *Directions in Functional Linguistics*. 19–57. Amsterdam, The Netherlands: John Benjamins.

Clift, R. (2006) Indexing stance: Reported speech as an interactional evidential. *Journal of Sociolinguistics* 10: 569–95.

Cook, H. M. (1990) The role of the Japanese sentence-final particle *no* in the socialization of children. *Multilingua* 9: 377–95.

Cook, H. M. (1992) Meanings of non-referential indexes: A case of the Japanese particle *ne*. *Text* 12: 507–39.

Cook, H. M. (1996a) Japanese language socialization: Indexing the modes of self. *Discourse Processes* 22: 171–97.

Cook, H. M. (1996b) The use of addressee honorifics in Japanese elementary school classrooms. In N. Akatsuka, S. Iwasaki, and S. Strauss (eds.), *Japanese/Korean Linguistics Vol. 5*. 67–81. Stanford, CA: Center for the Study of Language and Information.

Cook, H. M. (1997) The role of the Japanese *masu* form in caregiver–child conversation. *Journal of Pragmatics* 28: 695–718.

Cook, H. M. (1998) Situational meaning of the Japanese social deixis: The mixed use of the *masu* and plain form. *Journal of Linguistic Anthropology* 8(1): 87–110.

Cook, H. M. (2008) *Socializing Identities Through Speech Style: Learners of Japanese as a Foreign Language*. Bristol, UK: Multilingual Matters.

de León, L. (1998) The emergent participant: Interaction patterns in the socialization of Tzotzil (Mayan) infants. *Journal of Linguistic Anthropology* 8(2): 131–61.

du Bois, J. (2007) The stance triangle. In R. Englebretson (ed.), *Stancetaking in Discourse: Subjectivity, Evaluation, Interaction*. 139–82. Amsterdam, The Netherlands: John Benjamins.

Demuth, K. (1986) Prompting routines in the language socialization of Basotho children. In B. B. Schieffelin and E. Ochs (eds.), *Language Socialization Across Cultures*. 51–79. Cambridge: Cambridge University Press.

Field, M. (1997) The role of factive predicates in the indexicalization of stance: A discourse perspective. *Journal of Pragmatics* 27(6): 799–814.

Fox, B. (2001) Evidentiality: Authority, responsibility, and entitlement in English conversation. *Journal of Linguistic Anthropology* 11(2): 167–92.

Givón, T. (1982) Evidentiality and epistemic space. *Studies in Language* 6(1): 23–49.

Goodwin, C. and Goodwin, M. H. (1987) Concurrent operation on talk: Notes on the interactive organization of assessments. *Papers in Pragmatics* 1(1): 1–55.

Gumperz, J. (1996) The linguistic and cultural relativity of inference. In J. Gumperz and S. Levinson (eds.), *Rethinking Linguistic Relativity*. 374–406. Cambridge: Cambridge University Press.

Haviland, J. (1989) 'Sure, sure': Evidence and affect. *Text* 9(1): 27–68.

He, A. (2001) The language of ambiguity: Practices in Chinese heritage language classes. *Discourse Studies* 3(1): 75–96.

Heritage, J. and Raymond, G. (2005) The terms of agreement: Indexing epistemic authority and subordination in talk-in-interaction. *Social Psychology Quarterly* 68: 15–38.

Hérot, C. (2002) Socialization of affect during mealtime interactions In S. Blum-Kulka and C. Snow (eds.), *Talking to Adults: The Contribution of Multiparty Discourse to Language Acquisition*. 155–80. Hillsdale, NJ: Lawrence Erlbaum.

Johanning, Y. (1982) The role of the sentential copula 'deshoo' in Japanese socialization. Unpublished manuscript.

Jorden, E. and Noda, M. (1987) *Japanese: The Spoken Language*. New Haven, CT: Yale University Press.

Kamio, A. (1994) The theory of territory of information: The case of Japanese. *Journal of Pragmatics* 21: 67–100.

Kamio, A. (1998) *Territory of Information*. Amsterdam, The Netherlands: John Benjamins.

Kärkkäinen, E. (2003) *Epistemic Stance in English Conversation.* Amsterdam, The Netherlands: John Benjamins.

Kärkkäinen, E. (2006) Stance taking in conversation: From subjectivity to intersubjectivity. *Text & Talk* 26(6): 699–731.

Kataoka, K. (1997) Affect and letter-writing: Unconventional conventions in casual writing by young Japanese women. *Language in Society* 26: 103–36.

Kiesling, S. (2005) Variation, stance and style: Word-final, high rising tone and ethnicity in Australian English. *English World-Wide* 26(1): 1–42.

Kockelman, P. (2004) Stance and subjectivity. *Journal of Linguistic Anthropology* 14(2): 127–50.

Kuroda, S.-Y. (1973) Where epistemology, style and grammar meet: A case study from Japanese. In S. R. Anderson and P. Kiparsky (eds.), *A Festschrift for Morris Halle.* 337–91. New York: Holt, Rinehart and Winston.

Labov, W. (1984) Intensity. In D. Schiffrin (ed.), *Meaning, Form, and Use in Context: Linguistic Applications. Georgetown University Round Table on Language and Linguistics.* 43–70. Washington DC: Georgetown University Press.

Lee, H. S. (1993) Cognitive constraints on expressing newly perceived information with reference to epistemic modal suffixes in Korean. *Cognitive Linguistics* 4(2): 135–67.

Levy, R. (1984) Emotion, knowing and culture. In R. Shweder and R. LeVine (eds.), *Culture Theory: Essays on Mind, Self, and Emotion.* 214–37. Cambridge: Cambridge University Press.

Lo, A. (2004) Evidentiality and morality in a Korean heritage language school. *Pragmatics* 14(2/3): 235–56.

McGloin, N. (1984) Some politeness strategies in Japanese. In S. Miyagawa and C. Kitagawa (eds.), *Studies in Japanese Language Use.* 127–45. Carbondale, IL: Linguistic Research Inc.

McGloin, N. (2002) Markers of epistemic vs. affective stances: *Desyoo* vs. *zyanai.* In N. Akatsuka and S. Strauss (eds.), *Japanese/Korean Linguistics, Vol. 10.* 137–49. Stanford, CA: CSLI Publications.

McLendon, S. (2003) Evidentiality in eastern Pomo with a comparative survey of the category in other Pomoan languages. In A. Aikhenvald and R. Dixon (eds.), *Studies in Evidentiality.* 101–29. Amsterdam, The Netherlands: John Benjamins.

Mori, J. (2003) Construction of interculturality: A study of initial encounters between Japanese and American students. *Research on Language and Social Interaction* 36(2): 143–84.

Morita, E. (2005) *Negotiation of Contingent Talk.* Amsterdam, The Netherlands: John Benjamins.

Mushin, I. (2001) *Evidentiality and Epistemological Stance: Narrative Retelling.* Amsterdam, The Netherlands: John Benjamins.

Ochs, E. (1986) From feelings to grammar: A Samoan case study. In B. B. Schieffelin and E. Ochs (eds.), *Language Socialization Across Cultures.* 251–72. Cambridge: Cambridge University Press.

Ochs, E. (1990) Indexicality and socialization. In J. Stigler, R. Shweder, and G. Herdt (eds.), *Cultural Psychology: Essays on Comparative Human Development.* 287–307. Cambridge: Cambridge University Press.

Ochs, E. (1993) Constructing social identity: A language socialization perspective. *Research on Language and Social Interaction* 26(3): 287–306.

Ochs, E. (1996) Linguistic resources for socializing humanity. In J. Gumperz and S. Levinson (eds.), *Rethinking Linguistic Relativity.* 407–37. Cambridge: Cambridge University Press.

Ochs, E. (2002) Becoming a speaker of culture. In C. Kramsch (ed.), *Language Socialization and Language Acquisition: Ecological Perspectives.* 99–120. London and New York: Continuum Press.

Ochs, E., Pontecorvo, C., and Fasulo, A. (1996) Socializing taste. *Ethnos* 61(1–2): 7–46.

Ochs, E. and Schieffelin, B. B. (1984) Language acquisition and socialization: Three developmental stories. In R. Shweder and R. LeVine (eds.), *Culture Theory: Essays in Mind, Self, and Emotion.* 276–320. Cambridge: Cambridge University Press.

Ochs, E. and Schieffelin, B. B. (1989) Language has a heart. *Text* 9(1): 7–25.

Ohta, A. (1991) Evidentiality and politeness in Japanese. *Issues in Applied Linguistics* 2(2): 211–38.

Ohta, A. (1994) Socializing the expression of affect: An overview of affective particle use in the Japanese as a foreign language classroom. *Issues in Applied Linguistics* 5: 303–25.

Rabain-Jamin, J. (1998) Polydiadic language socialization strategy: The case of toddlers in Senegal. *Discourse Processes* 26(1): 34–65.

Rauniomaa, M. (2007) Stance markers in spoken Finnish. In R. Englebretson (ed.), *Stancetaking in Discourse: Subjectivity, Evaluation, Interaction.* 221–52. Amsterdam, The Netherlands: John Benjamins.

Schieffelin, B. B. (1990) *The Give and Take of Everyday Life: Language Socialization of Kaluli Children.* Cambridge: Cambridge University Press.

Schiffrin, D. (1987) *Discourse Markers.* Cambridge: Cambridge University Press.

Silverstein, M. (1976) Shifters, linguistic categories and cultural description. In K. Basso and H. Selby (eds.), *Meaning in Anthropology.* 11–55. Albuquerque, NM: University of New Mexico.

Silverstein, M. (2001) The limits of awareness. In A. Duranti (ed.), *Linguistic Anthropology: A Reader.* 328–401. Malden, MA: Blackwell.

Sidnell, J. (1997) Organizing social and spatial location: Elicitation in Indo-Guayanese village talk. *Journal of Linguistic Anthropology* 7(2): 143–65.

Siegal, M. (1996) The role of learner subjectivity in second language sociolinguistic competency: Western women learning Japanese. *Applied Linguistics* 17: 356–82.

Stubbs, M. (1986) A matter of prolonged fieldwork: Notes towards a modal grammar in English. *Applied Linguistics* 7: 1–25.

Suzuki, R. (1999) Language socialization through morphology: The affective suffix -CHAU in Japanese. *Journal of Pragmatics* 31: 1423–41.

Wade, J. (2003) *Searching for 'Pace' in the Japanese Language Classroom: Linguistic Realizations of Social Identity in Discourse and the Acquisition of Sociopragmatics.* Doctoral Dissertation. Berkeley, CA: University of California, Berkeley.

Watson-Gegeo, K. and Gegeo, D. (1986) Calling-out and repeating routines in Kwara'ae children's language socialization. In B. B. Schieffelin and E. Ochs (eds.), *Language Socialization Across Cultures.* 17–50. Cambridge: Cambridge University Press.

Wu, R.-J. (2004) *Stance in Talk: A Conversation Analysis of Mandarin Final Particles.* Philadelphia, PA: John Benjamins.

Yoshimi, D. (1999) L1 Language socialization as a variable in the use of *ne* by L2 learners of Japanese. *Journal of Pragmatics* 31: 1513–25.

14 Language Socialization and Morality

AYALA FADER

Introduction

Language socialization studies of morality face an ongoing methodological and theoretical challenge: to capture multiple levels of social life and then engage our analyses with social theory on morality, which emerges predominantly from the discipline of philosophy. Such an account requires the integration of three distinct bodies of research data: everyday interactions among children and between children and caregivers; the sociohistorical dynamics that shape local relationships of power; and broader theorizing that engages the politics of modernity, notions of agency, and the formation of subjectivities, among other issues. This chapter develops an approach to language socialization and morality in order to meet this challenge, showing that a language socialization approach and recent work on morality in the anthropology of religion have much to offer each other.

Studies of morality and language socialization have provided a rich focus on how micro-level interactions between adults and children prepare children to participate in local social structures, dynamics, and processes. Sterponi (2003: 80) notes that morality from this perspective can be defined as a situated practice enacted in social interaction (see e.g. Baquedano-López 1997; Capps and Ochs 1995; Duranti 1993; Goodwin 2002). This scholarship has less often embedded these local practices within broader sociohistorically specific forms of power and knowledge (except see Kulick 1992). Further, the language socialization approach has tended to limit attention to language rather than integrating language with embodiment and/or material culture.

Recent work in the anthropology of religion, especially that with nonliberal religious movements (e.g. evangelical Christianity and Islamism), elaborates a

The Handbook of Language Socialization, First Edition. Edited by Alessandro Duranti, Elinor Ochs, and Bambi B. Schieffelin.
© 2014 John Wiley & Sons, Ltd. Published 2014 by John Wiley & Sons, Ltd.

different perspective on morality. Influenced by Foucault's work (1997), this body of research focuses on the moral discourses and ethical practices that produce religious subjectivities, suggesting that they are inherently political. That is, they create culturally and historically specific forms of sociability (Mahmood 2005). Much of this work focuses exclusively on religious practices such as prayer, ritual, or study (e.g. Hirshkind 2006; Mahmood 2005; Robbins 2004), too often reproducing the social scientific categories of the religious and the secular as discrete. Further, there has been little attention devoted to children in studies of morality in nonliberal communities, though children are clearly critical to broader processes of social reproduction and change as the potential next generation of believers.

The formulation of a new approach to moral discourse in language socialization taken in this chapter builds on the work of Kulick and Schieffelin (2004), who demonstrate that language socialization has the potential to make important contributions to theories of becoming by, for example, showing how habitus and the performative power of language are acquired through everyday interactions. Their focus on affect, particularly desire and fear, in the processes by which subjectivities are produced or changed engages French poststructural theorists with a focus on psychoanalytic theory and discursive psychology. This theoretical bent provides new insights. While most studies of language socialization have focused on social reproduction, they can also show how subjectivities are fashioned differently from what was intended, suggesting that language socialization can contribute to theories of social change in addition to its obvious contributions to processes of social reproduction.

Similarly, this chapter on socialization into morality engages issues of affect, the production of subjectivities, social reproduction, and change. In contrast to Kulick and Schieffelin's discussion of work, which takes a psychoanalytic bent, though, Foucault's perspective on morality and ethics (1997) offers a more political, historicized framework, one that accounts for the discursive and embodied practices through which children come to participate in, reject, and/or transform particular ways of being in their worlds. After a brief review of language socialization studies of morality to date, Foucault's schema is introduced and then applied to my own research with nonliberal Hasidic Jews, particularly women and girls in Brooklyn, New York. A discussion of what a language socialization approach can provide to broader anthropological theorizing on morality in the anthropology of religion will follow. With its emphasis on interaction between caregivers and children as well as its focus on the everyday, a language socialization approach to morality problematizes assumptions about what constitutes the religious, the secular, and the political.

By reaching across subdisciplines, the language socialization research paradigm can contribute to new ways of thinking about contemporary religious movements and gender, language and embodiment, consciousness and agency, power and change. Broader conversations in language socialization, engaged with social theory, will continue to enrich the paradigm and make it ever more relevant for key concerns in cultural and linguistic anthropology.

Language Socialization Studies of Morality

Since its formulation (Ochs and Schieffelin 1984; Schieffelin and Ochs 1986), the language socialization research paradigm has aimed at bridging micro-level interactions with macro-level cultural processes. Those who have studied morality in language socialization do just that, by considering everyday interactions in the context of broader cultural topics of emotions, gender, knowledge, and the body (e.g. Briggs 1999; Clancy 1986; Fung 1999; Ochs 1988; Ochs and Kremer-Sadlik 2007; Rydstrom 2003; Smith-Hefner 1999). What constitutes the 'macro,' however, can be variable. In language socialization studies thus far, the 'macro' has predominantly been conceptualized as local relationships of power in a community. Local morality has less often been embedded in broader sociohistorical processes such as immigration, colonialism, and religious and political movements. This means that morality has been conceptualized as adult cultural norms for behavior without necessarily locating those norms in changing sociohistorical contexts.

Perhaps this partially accounts for why much of the scholarship on moral socialization has focused on social reproduction rather than change. For example, Clancy (1986) describes the way that hospitality and sharing, enacted in interactions between Japanese mothers and their toddlers, provide the moral training ground for broader expectations about cooperation and conformity in Japanese adult life. Similarly, Briggs (1999) shows how particular dramas or playful instances between a little girl and her caregivers lay the groundwork for participation in adult interpersonal dynamics and subjectivities. Briggs approaches morality as a psychosocial process that unfolds in a particular cultural and historical moment, although she does not address broader political, religious, or historical dynamics and change.

Attention to religious practice and language socialization is a productive avenue for conceptualizing morality in the context of sociohistorical political processes. With a few exceptions, religious practice has been given little elaboration in studies of moral socialization (see e.g. Zinsser 1986). In Baquedano-López's (1997, 2000) work on catechism classes (*doctrina*) in a church in Los Angeles with a large Mexican immigrant population, we see the centrality of sociohistorical dynamics between ethnic, religious, and racialized difference in moral education for children. Baquedano-López (2000), for example, analyzes the ways in which a narrative account of the apparition of the Virgin of Guadalupe in Mexico in the year 1531 told by a teacher in *doctrina* class invokes the hierarchies of Mexico's colonial regime as a framework for expressing Mexicans' contemporary experiences as immigrants (see also Baquedano-López and Mangual Figueroa, this volume). We might ask, further, whether these historical religious narratives are invoked in other, less explicitly religious contexts? Do children themselves engage with these narratives in play in order to engage with changing ideas of citizenship in the United States?

In diverse urban contexts, such as Los Angeles or New York, competing moral systems within, for example, immigrant communities or religious enclaves highlight relationships between religion, ethnicity, and citizenship. This is especially important in processes of language socialization, where children and teens are often at the forefront of social change as they straddle generations. Smith-Hefner (1999), for example, in her study of moral education among Khmer parents and children who had immigrated to Philadelphia, includes a discussion of how moral systems change in an urban diaspora. Smith-Hefner approaches morality as Khmer 'tradition,' something that the next generation either accepts or rejects. There are other questions we might explore, however. For example, how is Khmer morality, which is rooted in ethnic/religious practice and knowledge, in tension with the North American Judeo-Christian morality of the modern nation state, a state that has its own tangled history in Southeast Asian politics? How has Khmer 'tradition' been reinvented in the transition in the United States?

More recently, following an interest in gendered embodiment in cultural anthropology, Helle Rydstrom (2003) studied moral socialization between Vietnamese children and caregivers, using the work of Bourdieu (1977) and Butler (1993) to inject power into studies of language socialization.[1] The embodiment of gendered social norms – Rydstrom's perspective on morality – allows Vietnamese girls to gain social capital in fields of power (2004: 29). Rydstrom has been critiqued for neither adequately theorizing morality nor addressing the legacy of French colonial education in Vietnam, especially as it relates to neo-Confucian values in socialization (Schlecker 2006). Nevertheless, her elaboration of the body as the site of moral gendered socialization is important for expanding the object of study and experimenting with broader conversations in social theory. In my own work with language, embodiment, and morality in a nonliberal religious community of Hasidic Jews, Bourdieu's approach to the body and fields of power is less helpful. Bourdieu treats the body as a signifier of a deeper reality of social structures and cultural logics rather than the very basis by which moral sociability is produced (Mahmood 2005: 26–7). Further, Bourdieu's discussion of fields of power does not account for certain forms of religious and ethical practices (Lambek 2000). For example, how should we understand Hasidic women's notions of power that include the agency to transcend the materiality of the individual body through sanctification, for example reciting prayers after bodily functions such as eating or sleeping? What about the transformative power and divine rewards a woman can achieve if she dresses, comports herself, and speaks modestly?

Recent efforts in the anthropology of religion to understand religion as inextricably linked to political life, particularly drawing on Foucault's work, are promising. This body of scholarship suggests that, rather than norms or beliefs, religious practice can be framed as embodied modes of perception that train aesthetics and feelings (Asad 1993; Hirshkind 2006; but cf. Lambek 2000). This shift from privatized belief to power and embodiment[2] can make an important contribution to studies of children's moral socialization.

Foucault's Approach to Morality and Ethics

Foucault's writings more generally have been critiqued for being 'without women and without Jews, Africans, children, babies, poor people, and slaves' (Richlin

1997: 138). Nevertheless, Foucault's tracing of regimes of power and political constructions of knowledge can provide an important frame to the experiences of the marginalized or those without power. In his writings on morality and ethics, Foucault develops an approach that was inspired by Aristotelian ethics. His approach offers a theoretical framework for attending to how 'embodied attachments to historically specific forms of truth come to be forged' (Mahmood 2005: 34).

First, Foucault makes a distinction between moral discourse and ethical practice. Moral discourse includes the norms that establish certain forms of power and knowledge.[3] In contrast, ethics, according to Foucault, are a 'set of practical activities that are germane to a certain way of life [...] Ethics are a modality of power which allows people to transform themselves by their own means or with the help of others to become willing subjects of a particular moral discourse' (1997: 262). The distinction between morality and ethics, then, can account for both the specific norms of a particular historical and cultural moment and everyday practices.

Foucault describes four aspects of ethical practice that must be considered to capture what he calls the genealogy of ethics:

(1) The ethical substance or that which must be 'worked on' in order to 'constitute ourselves as subjects of knowledge' (1997: 262). Examples of the ethical substance might be sexuality or emotions.
(2) The mode of subjectivation that is the way people are 'incited or invited' to realize their moral obligations (1997: 264). This concerns the nature of moral authority.
(3) Techniques or technologies of the self: The operations one performs on oneself in order to become an ethical subject. Foucault calls these self-forming activities.
(4) Telos: The kind of being we aspire to when we behave in a moral way (1997: 265).

As noted above, while Foucault's work on ethics does not specifically address children, his focus on how people become willing subjects of a moral discourse resonates with a language socialization approach, with its practice-based attitude and attention to the lifecycle. Foucault's framework adds a more theoretical dimension to the language socialization paradigm by requiring that everyday interactions that socialize children to become ethical subjects always be in conversation with broader historical and cultural forms of modernity (and its multiple forms), agency, and power.

At the same time, focusing on socialization between children and caregivers raises some interesting complications for Foucault's genealogy of ethics. For example, how children come to participate in technologies of the self offers unique opportunities for rethinking our ideas about autonomy and agency. Children's autonomy is constrained in unique and temporary ways by adults. Their agency includes their capacity to reject or subvert the dominant moral discourse critical to the reproduction of their moral communities. Adults use affect and attempt to create the desire within children to become adherents to a moral discourse; this can be a form of social control (Ochs 1988). Further, children's autonomy and agency change over the course of the lifecycle, making it critical to consider how technologies of the self (and responsibilities for them) change over time as well, something a language socialization approach addresses. Below I consider what a Foucauldian approach to moral socialization might look like, drawing on my own research with Hasidic women and girls in Brooklyn.[4]

The Hasidic Example: A Nonliberal Religious Diaspora in Brooklyn

In the eighteenth century, European Jews (Ashkenazic Jews) wrestled with modernity and the rapid social changes it brought. One of the traditionalist responses to these changes was the Hasidic movement. Radical for its time, the Hasidic movement (Hebrew, *hasid* 'pious one,' *hasidim* 'pious ones') offered a transformed and transformative Judaism. The movement originated in Eastern Europe in the mid-eighteenth century, sparked by the teachings of Israel Ben Eliezer, known as the *Baal-Shem-Tov* ('Master of the Good Name,' a reference to his reputation as a worker of miracles). Hasidism spread quickly throughout much of Eastern and Central Europe, where pogroms against Jews were common and many, especially in Eastern Europe, lived in poverty (Hundert 1991; Rosman 1996).

The Hasidic movement was distinct from other forms of orthodoxy in its emphasis on Jewish mysticism, the creation of a new style of worship, and a unique social organization. In particular, Hasidic teachings asserted that the divine could be reached through an individual's joyous expression of faith, including singing, dancing, and ecstatic prayer. This was in contrast to the existing rabbinic structure, which was based on ascetic study of the Torah, primarily the domain of the elite (Hundert 1991; Rosman 1996). Hasidic Jews hope that, by fulfilling their religious obligations, they will bring the *geulah* ('redemption'), which includes an end to Jewish exile and a rebuilding of the temple in Jerusalem by God. The Messiah has been delayed, many believe, because of impieties committed by Jews and others (Mintz 1992).

By the close of World War II, the vast majority of Hasidic Jews in Europe had been killed. Those who arrived in the United States after the Holocaust claimed to be the bearers of authentic Jewish religion and, defying all predictions, they have flourished by growing religiously stringent. One of the effects of this heightened religiosity has been increasingly explicit elaboration of how Hasidic Jews are morally distinct from other peoples. This includes Gentiles, secular North Americans, and more 'modern' Jews – those who are less distinct from Gentiles according to lifestyle. Hasidic Jews today live in urban neighborhoods transnationally with the largest populations living in Israel and North America.

My research was conducted in Brooklyn, primarily with Hasidic women, girls, and very young boys, because of gender segregation in the community. The community's spoken vernaculars are Yiddish and Hasidic English and they read in liturgical Hebrew.[5] In this community it is women who mediate the secular world for men, whose religious obligation is to study the Torah. Women often work outside the home (at least until they have children) and, even when their husbands go out to work, it is women who take care of many of the mundane aspects of life in New York City, such as going to the doctor, shopping, and dealing with utilities or housing.

Applying Foucault's framework highlights the contemporary Hasidic engagement with, and critique of, secular modernity. Hasidic Jews elaborate a competing set of moral norms from Gentiles and what they call 'the secular.' For example, Hasidic women in my study, like many other New Yorkers, talk about the self as a project. Unlike other citizens whose goal is happiness or satisfaction, however, Hasidic women talk about developing the self-discipline to realize fulfillment through the acceptance of authority, both divine and embodied in communal hierarchies. The ethical substance for Hasidic Jews is to make the material world sacred, what one Hasidic woman described to me in Hebrew as *moyakh shalet halev*, the mind over the heart or mind over matter. The mode of subjectivation is the Torah (and its codified interpretations) as the inviolate words of God, although, as I have discussed elsewhere, for Hasidic children the abstract covenant between Jews and God is made explicit by investing hierarchies of communal authority with divine legitimation (Fader 2006).

For Hasidic children, religious authorizing discourses play out in a wide range of technologies of the self, such as praising or shaming, syncretic language practices, and aesthetics and embodiment. The telos for Hasidic women and girls is the inverse of what Keane calls 'the moral narrative of modernity,' which is told as a progressive move toward autonomy, among other things (2007: 6). Instead, for the Hasidic women I worked with, the aim is to emulate a more moral, past generation of women, both biblical and from pre-War Eastern Europe. When girls and women are able to accomplish this emulation of a more moral generation of Jewish women, they play their part in protecting their families; bring God's rewards to themselves and the Jewish people; assure themselves a place in the afterlife, the Garden of Eden; and even, perhaps, hasten the coming of the Messiah. This is a modality of agency with transformative (and divine) power.

Hasidic Gendered Modesty: A Technology of the Self

For language socialization studies of morality, the notion of technologies of the self, in particular, has the potential for engaging not only language and interaction but also the body, including the senses and affect. I suggest that we adopt the term 'technologies of the self' rather than the more common 'verbal routines' in order to integrate language and embodiment, creating a common vocabulary with anthropologists of religion, who are investigating shared processes. Some ethnographic snapshots from my research will demonstrate what such an approach can accomplish.

For the Hasidic women and girls in my study, modesty (Yiddish *tsnies*) is a gendered technology of the self, an embodied set of practices – including language but also clothing, comportment, and access to knowledge – by which Hasidic girls learn to engage with the secular world around them in order to collapse distinctions between the religious and the secular. In this way, girls come to imagine an alternative religious modernity, one where discipline, piety, and authority are the aims rather than freedom, secularism, and autonomy (Fader 2009).

The examples below concern materialism, comportment, and adornment. Hasidic women's modesty is taught through a variety of socialization practices across the lifecycle. In some socialization practices, the notion of sacralizing the material body through modest comportment is rote and mundane. With very young children, for example, women caregivers physically adjust girls' bodies and clothing, pulling down skirts, closing collars, or requiring girls to sit up straight. Older sisters, teachers, mothers, camp counselors, and relatives are vigilant over girls' bodies and behavior, frequently reminding or scolding girls simply by saying, *Tsnies!* ('modesty'). In other contexts, with older girls, caregivers are explicit about the ways in which modesty practices help girls to be more like biblical Jewish women or their own great-grandmothers, who are conceptualized as being at a 'higher' level than are girls today because they were less materialistic. For example, young Hasidic brides attend classes before their marriage in order to learn the laws of family purity. These laws regulate intimacy between husbands and wives. The brides' teacher told the girls on the first day that, by obeying these laws, they were crossing the sands of time, emulating their Jewish foremothers (*emosayni*), and making their bodies holy.

On another level, socialization into gendered modesty entails an ethical struggle to change the meaning of secular materiality and consumption, a task that is the special responsibility of women. Their efforts to collapse distinctions between materiality and spirituality through the disciplines of modesty contrast with a modern (and underlyingly Protestant) semiotic ideology that Keane describes, where spirituality is achieved through a denial of materiality (2007: 6). The aim for Hasidic women and girls in my study is to be able to discipline their bodies and desires, to use their moral autonomy to both participate in and transform the material world. Vanity and adornment, consumption and materialism are not denied; they have to be 'channeled,' as one woman suggested to me, and made to serve Hasidic goals of adhering to God's commandments. The girls I worked with learn in socialization practices that they can be attractive, intelligent, and fashionable; however, by also remaining modest, Hasidic women and girls provide visible and audible moral proof in diaspora that they are more disciplined, more beautiful, and even 'more civilized' than Gentiles, secular North Americans, or other kinds of Jews.

From an early age, mothers, teachers, and relatives teach girls how to transform secular objects and forms of consumption for Hasidic goals of modesty. For example, in most clothing stores sell, in addition to the clothing, attachable collars ('dickeys') that turn an immodest neckline into a modest one or extra yards of matching material in order to lengthen a hemline. Similarly, in a lecture for brides, the teacher told girls it was their obligation to dress 'regally.' The speaker reminded the audience that Jewish women's bodies are holy. She compared the girls' bodies to Torahs, the scrolls of sacred texts that, when not being used for prayer, are 'dressed' in velvet and ornamented with silver and jewels. 'When you are disrobed with your husbands,' the speaker said, 'you are fulfilling your holy God-given purpose of procreation.' In other situations, like a Torah, a Jewish girl should be adorned in a way that befits her holy, royal Jewish nature.

In contrast, some teachers told their students that Jewish women need no adornment because the beauty of their souls shines out and makes their bodies and faces beautiful naturally. Hasidic mothers and teachers try to counter the embourgeoisement that has come to define the neighborhood of Boro Park by elaborating a distinction between the simple, authentic beauty of Jewish women and the superficial materialism of Gentile femininity (see also Kranzler 1995; Rubin 1997). For example, when a first-grade teacher, Mrs. Silver, told the story of Purim, the carnivalesque spring holiday, to her class, she provided an allegory for feminine beauty, materialism, and the embodied differences between Jews and Gentiles. In a description of a beauty contest the King of Persia held to choose a new queen, Mrs. Silver ascribed the negative qualities of vanity, materialism, and greed to Gentile girls. The Jewish Esther, who had been forced to participate in the contest, was presented as a paragon of modesty, obedience, and simplicity. Mrs. Silver emphasized that Esther refused to wear fancy clothing, jewelry, or makeup, asking only that she be allowed to keep the Sabbath. Esther's authentic beauty eclipsed all the 'fancy' Gentile girls. The king had eyes only for Esther, and made her his queen. Note, however, that during the Purim celebrations that I attended I never saw a little girl dressed up as a 'simple' Queen Esther. Girls consistently wore makeup, sparkling costume jewelry, and high heels.

By transforming adornment from a form of vanity into a culturally and religiously appropriate set of signs for Jewish distinction, modesty channels the material world and sustains a workable tension between the material and the spiritual. A woman once laughingly told me that, with their modest wigs and hats, Hasidic women today look even more elegant than women in Manhattan. She meant that, though Hasidic women wear wigs and hats to fulfill God's commandments, they end up actually looking even better than sophisticated Manhattanites.

Finally, technologies of modesty, the technologies by which Hasidic girls become ethical Jewish women, are a modality of gendered agency that has the potential to transform the world. In a first-grade classroom for Hasidic girls, for example, the teacher, Mrs. Silver, told the girls that a woman's modesty can actually save her family from death. The example she gave was of a biblical woman who never let a strand of hair show, even in front of her family at home. Her vigilance in modesty (married women must cover their hair) was rewarded when God saved her family from death because she had been such a righteous woman. The technology of modesty is an aspect of the mode of subjectivation; that is, Jewish women's modesty legitimates the Jews as God's chosen people and in a patriarchal religion like Hasidic Judaism is also a site for women's disciplined piety to be a powerful force.

A Practice-Based Approach to Morality: Contributions from Language Socialization to the Anthropology of Religion

I have suggested that Foucault's approach to moral discourse and ethics might reframe how language socialization studies approach morality. By the same token, a language socialization approach can offer a practice-based approach to the study of morality, something currently lacking in the anthropology of religion (Lambek 2000). Lambek has recently (2010) suggested that a practice-based approach to morality and ethics, one that draws on both philosophy and linguistic anthropology, has the potential to go beyond the dialectics inherent in much of Western social theory, especially structure and action. A focus on everyday language between adults and children has the potential to challenge artificial distinctions between the religious, the social, and the political. Talal Asad (1993) has persuasively shown that the theoretical categories of the religious and the secular themselves are a sociohistorical product of European modernity and have surely shaped the anthropology of religion. Contemporary nonliberal religious communities provide evidence of the sociohistorical specificity of these categories through their rejection of a religiosity that is limited to a private, discrete part of one's national identity. Even more importantly, language socialization requires consideration of how multiple technologies of the self, rather than only prayer or ritual or the power of the nation state, produce pious, ethical persons. This is because a language socialization approach illuminates the processes by which embodied morality is learned or not over the lifecycle in social interaction, bringing everyday language into the study of religion, something that has rarely been attended to.

Hasidic children are trained in interactions from a very young age to make moral choices in everyday life that require embodied discipline. One day, for example, during a visit to one Hasidic family, two of the children, aged six and three, found some candy in the back of a kitchen cupboard. They had received the candy as a gift during a holiday celebration. They brought the candy to their mother who checked the *hekhsher*, a stamp on a food item by which a rabbi certifies the item is kosher. The certification, however, was unfamiliar to her. She told her children, 'You'll have to wait until *totty* [Daddy] comes home and checks it.' The children did not protest at all. They simply agreed and put the candy away. This small moment sheds light on the ways in which socialization into embodied discipline blurs the boundary between the religious and the secular. Eating candy is not often conceptualized as a religious practice and, yet, the moral discipline needed to wait until a male authority could make sure something was reputably kosher, for a small child, is an everyday practice where a Hasidic gendered subjectivity is socialized. Adults teach children that, when they see something from the secular world that they want, they must ask an adult authority figure, their mother, and, for the final word, their father.

This orientation to authority has implications for socialization along the lifespan as well. Hasidic brides learn in their classes that, when there is any question about how to observe the laws of family purity, they are to ask their husbands, the authority in their homes. If the husband is unsure, he in turn will ask his rabbi. An important aspect to Hasidic socialization is that embodied desires, for candy or for conjugal intimacy, for example, must be approved by the appropriate gendered authorities, be they a rabbi, a husband, or a father. This nonliberal notion of morality is based on the individual discipline to accept the authority of those with the greatest ability to understand God's intentions. Hasidic mothers and teachers tell girls that their own cultivation of the discipline to accept authority will lead to fulfillment and rewards from God. Such acceptance contrasts with liberal notions of self-realization that, Mahmood notes (2005: 14), is 'linked to individual autonomy, wherein the process of realizing oneself is equated with the ability to realize the desires of one's "true will."'

A language socialization perspective can also contribute to conversations on the role of consciousness in morality. Robbins' (2004: 14) study of morality, colonialism, missionization, and social change among the Urapmin in Papua New Guinea draws on recent anthropological work on ethical thinking to suggest that morality is a conscious domain. Community members are aware of moral choices and contradictions as they 'struggle to live caught between two cultures [...] trying to live as good people' (2004: 314). Robbins claims that, to make a moral choice, there must be some consciousness of the issues involved (2004: 316). This important study, as well as others touching on similar issues of consciousness in morality (see also, for example, Faubion 2001; Laidlaw 2002), only considers adults and morality. How do children come to understand these moral choices through their interactions with adults and each other over time? Are children, like adults, in contexts of cultural change always conscious of competing and contradictory moral systems and ethical practices?

With its grounded theorizing about consciousness, language socialization studies can provide an approach to exploring the relationship between morality and consciousness across the lifecycle. This has implications for understanding how children become (un)willing (conscious or unconscious) adherents to a moral discourse, with broader implications for processes of social reproduction and change.

Schieffelin (1990), in her ethnography of Kaluli children and caregivers in Papua New Guinea, engages Giddens' (1979) distinction between practical and discursive consciousness. Practical consciousness is the tacit stocks of knowledge that actors draw upon in the constitution of social activity. Giddens suggests that practical consciousness is nondiscursive but not unconscious knowledge (1979: 24). Discursive consciousness is knowledge that actors are able to express on the level of discourse (Giddens 1979: 5). Schieffelin critiques Giddens' definition of discourse, which treats language exclusively as content. Instead, she suggests that language be conceptualized as a set of discourse practices that bridge practical and discursive consciousness. Socialization of children, Schieffelin shows, often involves the discursive expression of practical consciousness (1990: 18). Building on Schieffelin's work, a language socialization approach to morality requires examination of a range of interactions where consciousness may take multiple forms.

Hasidic language socialization with women and girls reveals at least two distinct orders of moral consciousness enacted in technologies of the self between children and caregivers. The first, which includes rote habituation of the body to certain religious practices and aesthetics, emphasizes practical consciousness of morality. The second, such as praising routines, draws on discursive consciousness to explicitly instruct what defines gendered ethical subjectivity. Both technologies of the self focus on moral embodiment through interaction. For children under the age of three, caregivers prompt and demand participation in ritual behavior without explicit explanation or a concern that the child understands or even wishes to participate. Hasidic caregivers socialize young children to participate in ritual activities that bracket bodily functions. According to Orthodox Jewish law, different Hebrew blessings must be made before eating, after eating, upon waking, after going to the bathroom, before going to sleep, and so on. Children are technically not responsible for fulfilling all of the ritual requirements until they are *bar/bas mitsve* (aged 13 and 12, respectively, for boys and girls). Nevertheless, caregivers train preverbal children to make blessings by routinely prompting and repeating during mealtimes where they feed children.

In Example 14.1, a Hasidic mother prompted her twins, Aaron and Leye (1 year, 7 months) to recite or attempt to recite a prayer before eating. The mother repeats only the first word of any blessing, *burikh* ('blessed'), not completing the entire prayer. The twins were sitting in their high-chairs as their mother alternated giving each of them bites of the hot cereal she had prepared. The twins were only producing one-word utterances at this age.

Example 14.1

Mother: ((feeding the children)) Say *burikh. Burikh? Burikh?*
((Neither child responds. They babble.))
        Burikh. Burikh.
((Mother continues to feed each child giving alternating spoonfuls.))
        Burikh.

The mother continues to prompt, regardless of the children's responses, which is to simply continue babbling. She also does not attempt to say the blessing before giving food, which is customary with older children. At this point, caregivers' constant repetition seems designed to naturalize for children the associations between eating and Hebrew prayer, indexed in this case by only one word. From the time a Hasidic child is eating solid food, eating and prayer go hand in hand. Parents and teachers often stressed, implicitly and explicitly, the importance of rote repetition for moral education. In a very different context, Moore (2006, this volume), has described how Fulbe-speaking Muslim children in Cameroon acquire both French and Arabic in public and religious school respectively through what she calls 'guided repetition.' In Moore's work, guided repetition can have different underlying ideologies and simultaneously socialize both 'modern' and 'traditional' subjectivities (2006).

Ritual practice, not reasons or explanations, eventually evoke the appropriate feelings and desires of a pious Jew (Fader 2006, 2009). These kinds of rote interactions with little explanation socialize practical consciousness that can be later drawn on and articulated as a form of discursive consciousness once children are older. Indeed, in first grade, Hasidic girls learn from their teachers that prayer expresses Jews' gratitude to God for making the food they are about to eat. The socialization of embodied morality, as Schieffelin suggests, creates a bridge between practical and discursive consciousness.

The socialization of embodied morality through prayer before eating takes on an even greater moral resonance when children learn from their caregivers (who are citing an interpretation of a religious text) that Gentiles cannot control their appetites and so just 'dig in' without sanctifying the act of eating. This form of self-control builds on and creates a practical consciousness that legitimizes certain embodied practices as morally just. Socialization into this kind of practical, embodied moral consciousness can be helpfully thought of as socialization into an embodied sensory aesthetic. With very young children, socialization into certain forms of religious discipline occurs through rote repetition, which creates embodied, affective relationships between, in this case, prayer and eating. Hirshkind (2006) in his study of listening to audiocassette sermons among Muslims in Egypt suggests that studies of religion focus on the body and the senses as a site of moral learning and ethics. Embodied moral learning, however, he suggests, is often out of the realm of consciousness. In comparison, a language socialization approach to embodied morality and ethical learning shows that tacit knowledge is a resource for children and their caregivers over time, as Hasidic children must increasingly be able to articulate how Jews are different from Gentiles, the secular world, and other less observant Jews. When, for example, in a school cafeteria a Hasidic girl refuses to drink from a paper cup with a Christmas tree on it because it disgusts her, we begin to see the political implications of the socialization of embodied religious affect and aesthetics.

There are, in contrast, aspects of Hasidic children's moral socialization that draw on discursive consciousness, what Giddens describes as 'the giving of reasons in day to day activity which is closely associated with moral accountability of action' (1979: 58). For example, in praising, a gendered technology of the self, gender, affect, and adherence to a moral discourse are conflated, performed, and reproduced. The monthly assembly in the Bobover Hasidic school is a forum where girls (from first grade through high school) hear explicitly the kinds of girls they should be, as well as the very real potential for them to reach their goal if they can only use their autonomy for others and for God. At each assembly and for each class, a 'girl of the month' is chosen. These girls' mothers, grandmothers, and extended families are invited to attend. Each teacher chooses a girl who has been 'super' or 'excellent' that month and gives her name to the principal. At the end of the assembly, after speeches, dances, and singing, the principal announces the names of the girls chosen and the qualities that make them so special. As her name is called, each girl walks to the front of the auditorium and climbs onto the stage. The whole school applauds them. When they return to their seats, their teacher hugs and kisses them and tells them that they are so proud of them. If their mothers have come, they usually take pictures and give small toys, balloons, and treats.

One day before she announced the girls of the month, the principal told the girls in Yiddish that there are three important characteristics that give insight into a girl's 'nature': how much effort she makes (*vi azoy zi flast zikh*), how she prays (*vi azoy zi davnt*), and respectful behavior (*derekh-eyrets*). These three qualities are about a girl's relationship with herself, God, and other Jews. These are a litmus test for a girl's nature, the criteria for being an ethical Jewish girl. Other categories that the principal rewarded regularly over the course of a year included good in learning, always ready with a smile, prays sincerely, nicely behaved at lunch, always ready to help another, satisfied with everything, and speaks with refinement. More explicitly, these qualities stress that girls must be respectful and satisfied with what they are given. They must be helpful to others, and always have a smile on their face. They should have good manners and speak in a refined way. They also must do their work, pray with intent, and try hard to do their best. The principal ended assemblies by noting that the girls of the month were an example of beautiful character traits. However, each girl as a Jew, she said, had the capacity within herself to achieve this ethical ideal by working on her own character traits.

When I asked first-graders what a girl had to do to be best of the month, some seemed baffled and shrugged. Others, however, told me that 'you have to be excellent in everything,' while another told me that you have to *folgn* ('obey') the teacher and do your work. While first-graders' sense of the standards of excellence might be vague, as they go through the grades continuously hearing who gets elected girl of the month and why, the message they repeatedly hear is that those who accept what they are told and follow the rules are rewarded publicly at school and by their families, as well as by God. This explicit moral instruction is also embodied, affective, and sensory. Girls who can discipline themselves to, for example, be 'girl of the month' or who always know and remember the correct blessings to make before eating receive love, honor, and rewards from their families and perhaps God. In socialization practices, discursive and practical moral consciousness contribute to the production of nonliberal Hasidic gendered subjectivities. The desire to become certain kinds of women is cultivated through technologies of the self that may be embodied, discursive, sensory, and affective.

The socialization into Hasidic morality does not preclude children and young adults from making conscious moral choices. In the example above, girls of the month successfully use their personal autonomy to discipline desires that are not morally acceptable. They are aided in their individualized efforts by their embodied moral socialization, which makes certain activities just 'feel' wrong, as well as the physical and emotional rewards they receive from their communities when they succeed. There are also young Hasidic girls and boys and adults who cannot or will not become Hasidic moral subjects. Again, consciousness is an area for exploration in these cases, rather than a given. For a Hasidic young adult to leave his/her community is difficult and painful. Often this includes cutting off relationships, at least for a while, with family and friends, leaving their communities, and going to live in a community that has been framed to them since birth as unethical, immature, and selfish. Kulick and Schieffelin (2004) have noted that those who become what they call, following Althusser, 'bad subjects' are often the inverse of what defines a person as a 'good subject.' Indeed, I have heard stories of young adults who left only to become addicted to drugs or unable to function in secular society.

However, there is another group of young adults who leave their ways of life because they make a moral, conscious choice either to pursue, for example, higher education or because they are gay. These narratives of 'falling off the path' or leaving the Hasidic fold seem to support Robbins' claim that, at moments of social change, people make conscious moral choices. For example, over coffee a young woman, Chani, who grew up in an especially stringent Hasidic community in Boro Park told me of the moral test she set for God when she was only nine years old. Chani's parents had a troubled marriage and her mother was in the process of leaving the community, something that had led Chani to question her own faith. One day, she decided to test the power of God. Privately, she broke one of the Sabbath prohibitions, waiting with bated breath to see whether God would 'strike her down.' When nothing happened, Chani felt her faith in God crumble. Once she reached adolescence, she felt she could no longer continue to live in her community. She left and went on to eventually become a filmmaker and writer. For these disbelievers, technologies of the self do not produce ethical persons. On the contrary, these young adults through other technologies of the self embrace truths and socialities that oppose Hasidic ones.

Conclusions

Hasidic moral socialization is political in that it produces subjectivities whose very existence critiques the so-called secular nation state. Those who can become ethical Hasidic subjects participate in imagining an alternative religious modernity, where the shared goal is not citizenship in a nation or even global citizenship but membership in a global diaspora that awaits the coming of the final redemption. In contrast to Bourdieu's interest in the ways that people come to inhabit a habitus in a class structure, the Hasidic example shows that an alternative habitus can form part of a critique of secular modernity.

When language socialization studies theorize morality in broader cultural and political terms, new ideas in the anthropology of religion and morality become part of the conversation. This means that the classic topics in language socialization into morality, such as authority, praising, shaming, and embodiment, must be considered in the context of historical and political change of these same topics over time and space. Such an approach includes consideration of how children do or do not come to participate in adult moral norms but also considers these same adult moral norms in historical and political context.

My own investigation of Hasidic moral socialization required me to consider how, for example, the praising and incentives that are so common today among

Hasidic Jews is both Hasidic and North American; that is, part of a wider set of beliefs and practices popular in North American psychology and education, yet also informed by Jewish beliefs about the moral person. Examining both strands of influence clarified that Hasidic child-rearing practices had changed from child-rearing practices in pre-War Eastern Europe, or at least that Hasidic women's perceptions were that it had changed; North American Hasidic child rearing today has become more 'Americanized' and, simultaneously, more stringently Hasidic. The formation of ethical subjects, then, on a micro-level of the everyday takes place through an ongoing engagement with and critique of one narrative of modernity, which includes particular elaborations of the individual, autonomy, and freedom.

Further, opening a dialogue between language socialization and the anthropology of religion requires that scholars take a broad comparative perspective that can bring together theoretical concerns in linguistic anthropology and cultural anthropology. For example, my research with Hasidic women and girls' language socialization took on a new dimension when I considered how nonliberal post-War religious communities more generally – from evangelical Christianity to Islamists – think about gender or modernity. A language socialization approach read alongside scholarship in the anthropology of religion led to a rethinking of moral socialization as it relates to nonliberal women's agency in patriarchal power structures and nonliberal critiques of secular modernity.

Using Foucault's theoretical framework and reading across subdisciplines can encourage new ways of thinking about morality and socialization in the context of power, consciousness, agency, and change. Further discussions could compare, for example, adult socialization of Jewish returnees to the faith or born-again Christians with the socialization of children born within these communities, especially in terms of practical versus discursive consciousness and how these relate to choosing to participate in a form of religion as an adult. Luhrmann (2004), in her study of an evangelical church, has shown that there are specific embodied and verbal practices by which those who are born again renarrate their pasts and display their new identities. How do these kinds of practices, which may be seen as developing new forms of practical and discursive consciousness, compare to the consciousness socialized in children born into these kinds of communities? Broader conversations in language socialization with the anthropology of religion will continue to enrich the paradigm and make it ever more relevant for themes and theories in cultural anthropology more generally.

NOTES

1   Norma Gonzalez (2001) in her work on borderlands and Mexican mothers and children similarly critiques the language socialization paradigm for being apolitical and not addressing issues of power and hegemony. See, however, García-Sánchez's (2009, this volume) language socialization study of Moroccan immigrant children in Spain, in

which she investigates how these children are able to navigate (and are impacted by) both local and macro politics of inclusion/exclusion in the wake of the 2004 Madrid bombings and the increased levels of tension and surveillance directed towards Muslim and North African immigrants.

2   This reflects Asad's (1993) critique of Geertz's efforts to develop a universal definition of religion. Asad claims that Geertz's definition is actually a modern Protestant conception of religion, one that separates religion from politics. As such it is inadequate for accounting for other forms of religious life.

3   Asad notes that the Aristotelian concept of virtue is different from the current use of morality today. Today's morality is aligned with duty, obligation, and the 'moral sense of "ought,"' an inheritance from the Stoics, which came to inform Christianity (whose ethical notions in turn come from the Torah) (1993: 139).

4   The project from which the data in this chapter are drawn is fully elaborated in Fader (2009). For a more in-depth discussion of Hasidic Yiddish–English bilingualism see Fader (2007a) and for Hasidic children's literacy see Fader (2008). For a discussion on ethics and research methodology among Hasidic Jews as a liberal Jewish anthropologist see Fader (2007b).

5   For a more in-depth discussion of the social organization of the different Hasidic sects and the permeability of sects' boundaries, especially for women, see Fader (2009).

REFERENCES

Asad, T. (1993) *Genealogies of Religion*. Baltimore, MD: Johns Hopkins University Press.

Baquedano-López, P. (1997) Creating social identities through *doctrina* narratives. *Issues in Applied Linguistics* 8(1): 27–45.

Baquedano-López, P. (2000) Narrating community in *doctrina* classes. *Narrative Inquiry* 10(2): 1–24.

Bourdieu, P. (1977) *Outline of a Theory of Practice*. Cambridge: Cambridge University Press.

Briggs, J. (1999) *Inuit Morality Play: The Emotional Education of a Three Year Old*. New Haven, CT: Yale University Press.

Butler, J. (1999) *Gender Trouble: Feminism and the Subversion of Identity*. New York: Routledge.

Capps, L. and Ochs, E. (1995) *Constructing Panic: The Discourse of Agoraphobia*. Cambridge, MA: Harvard University Press.

Clancy, P. (1986) The acquisition of communicative style in Japanese. In B. B. Schieffelin and E. Ochs (eds.), *Language Socialization Across Cultures*. 213–50. Cambridge: Cambridge University Press.

Duranti, A. (1993) Intentions, self and responsibility: An essay in Samoan ethnopragmatics. In J. Hill and J. Irvine (eds.), *Responsibility and Evidence in Oral Discourse*. 24–47. Cambridge: Cambridge University Press.

Fader, A. (2006) Learning faith: Language socialization in a Hasidic community. *Language in Society* 35(2): 205–28.

Fader, A. (2007a) Reclaiming sacred sparks: Syncretism and gendered language shift among Hasidic Jews in New York. *Journal of Linguistic Anthropology* 17(1): 1–23.

Fader, A. (2007b) Reflections on Queen Esther: The politics of Jewish ethnography. *Contemporary Jewry* 27:112–36.

Fader, A. (2008) Reading Jewish signs: Multilingual literacy socialization with Hasidic women and girls in New York. *Text & Talk* 28(5): 621–41.

Fader, A. (2009) *Mitzvah Girls: Bringing up the Next Generation of Hasidic Jews in Brooklyn.* Princeton, NJ: Princeton University Press.

Faubion, J. D. (2001) *The Shadows and Lights of Waco: Millenialism Today.* Princeton, NJ: Princeton University Press.

Foucault, M. (1997) On the genealogy of ethics: An overview of work in progress. In P. Rabinow (ed.), *Essential Works of Foucault 1954–1984, Vol. 1: Ethics: Subjectivity and Truth.* R. Hurley et al., transl. 281–301. New York: New Press.

Fung, H. (1999) Becoming a moral child: The socialization of shame among young Chinese children. *Ethnos* 27(2): 180–209.

García-Sánchez, I. M. (2009) *Moroccan Immigrant Children in a Time of Surveillance: Navigating Sameness and Difference in Contemporary Spain.* Doctoral Dissertation. Los Angeles, CA: University of California, Los Angeles.

Giddens, A. (1979) *Central Problems in Social Theory.* Berkeley, CA: University of California Press.

Gonzalez, N. (2001) *I Am My Language: Discourses of Women and Children in the Borderlands.* Tucson, AZ: University of Arizona Press.

Goodwin, M. H. (2002) Exclusion in girls' peer groups: Ethnographic analysis of language practices on the playground. *Human Development* 45: 392–415.

Hirshkind, C. (2006) *The Ethical Soundscape: Cassette Sermons and Islamic Counterpublics.* New York: Columbia University Press.

Hundert, G. (ed.) (1991) *Essential Papers on Hasidism: Origins to Present.* New York: New York University Press.

Keane, W. (2007) *Christian Moderns: Freedom and Fetish in the Mission Encounter.* Berkeley, CA: University of California Press.

Kranzler, G. (1995) The economic revitalization of the Hasidic community of Williamsburg. In J. Belcove-Shalin (ed.), *New World Hasidim: Ethnographic*

Studies of Jews in America. 181–204. Albany, NY: State University of New York Press.

Kulick, D. (1992) *Language Change and Social Reproduction: Socialization, Self and Syncretism in a Papua New Guinean Village.* Cambridge: Cambridge University Press.

Kulick, D. and Schieffelin, B. B., (2004) Language socialization. In A. Duranti (ed.), *A Companion to Linguistic Anthropology.* 349–68. Malden, MA: Blackwell.

Laidlaw, J. (2002) For an anthropology of ethics and freedom (the Malinowski Memorial Lecture, 2001) *Journal of the Royal Anthropological Institute* 8(2): 311–32.

Lambek, M. (2000) The anthropology of religion and the quarrel between poetry and philosophy. *Current Anthropology* 41(3): 309–20.

Lambek, M. (2010) Introduction. In M. Lambek (ed.), *Ordinary Ethics.* 1–36. New York: Fordham University Press.

Luhrmann, T. (2004) Metakinesis: How God becomes intimate in contemporary US Christianity. *American Anthropologist* 106(3):518–28.

Mintz, J. (1992) *Hasidic People: A Place in the New World.* Cambridge, MA: Harvard University Press.

Mahmood, S. (2005) *Politics of Piety: The Islamic Revival and the Feminist Subject.* Princeton, NJ: Princeton University Press.

Moore, L. C. (2006) Learning by heart in Qur'anic and public schools in northern Cameroon. *Social Analysis* 50(3): 109–26.

Ochs, E. (1988) *Culture and Language Development: Language Acquisition and Socialization in a Samoan Village.* New York: Cambridge University Press.

Ochs, E. and Kremer-Sadlik, T. (2007) Introduction: Morality as family practice. *Discourse Studies* 18(1): 5–10.

Ochs, E. and Schieffelin, B. B. (1984) Language acquisition and socialization: Three developmental stories. In

R. Shweder and R. Levine (eds.), *Culture Theory: Essays in Mind, Self, and Culture*. 276–320. Cambridge: Cambridge University Press.

Richlin, A. (1997) Foucault's history of sexuality: A useful theory for women? In D. H. J. Larmour, P. A. Miller, and C. Platter (eds.), *Rethinking Sexuality: Foucault and Classical Antiquity*. 138–70. Princeton, NJ: Princeton University Press.

Robbins, J. (2004) *Becoming Sinners: Christianity and Moral Torment in a Papua New Guinea Society*. Berkeley, CA: University of California Press.

Rosman, M. (1996) *Founder of Hasidism: A Quest for the Historical Ba'al Shem Tov*. Berkeley, CA: University of California Press.

Rubin, I. (1997) *Satmar: Two Generations of an Urban Island*. New York: Peter Lang.

Rydstrom, H. (2003) *Embodied Morality: Growing up in Rural Vietnam*. Honolulu, HI: University of Hawaii Press.

Schieffelin, B. B. (1990) *The Give and Take of Everyday Life*. New York: Cambridge University Press.

Schieffelin, B. B. and Ochs, E. (1986) Language socialization. *Annual Review of Anthropology* 15:163–91.

Schlecker, M. (2006) Book review of *Embodied Morality: Growing up in Rural Vietnam*. *Journal of the Royal Anthropological Institute* 12(3): 721–2.

Smith-Hefner, N. (1999) *Khmer-American: Identity and Moral Education in a Diaspora Community*. Berkeley, CA: University of California Press.

Sterponi, L. (2003) Account episodes in family discourse. *Discourse Studies* 5(1):79–101.

Zinsser, C. (1986) For the Bible tells me so: Teaching children in a fundamentalist church. In B. B. Schieffelin and P. Gilmore (eds.), *The Acquisition of Literacy: Ethnographic Perspectives*. 55–71. Norwood, NJ: Ablex.

15 Language Socialization and Hierarchy

KATHRYN M. HOWARD

Culture is not only what we live by. It is also, in great measure, what we live for. Affection, relationship, memory, kinship, place, community, emotional fulfillment, intellectual enjoyment, a sense of ultimate meaning: these are closer to most of us than charters of human rights or trade treaties.

(Eagleton 2000: 131)

Social relationships are fundamental facets of the human quest for belonging, connectedness, and affirmation in family, community, and society. For children and other novices, participation in their social worlds involves knowing how to deploy a range of communicative resources to inhabit these social relations in cultural activities. Many human relationships are organized by asymmetries of rights and responsibilities, even in societies or institutions that seemingly orient primarily to equality and autonomy: as Dumont pointed out, 'to adopt a value is to introduce hierarchy, and a certain consensus on values, a certain hierarchy of ideas, things and people, is indispensable to social life' (1969: 87). This chapter examines the discourses, processes, and practices by which children are socialized into hierarchical social relationships. An infinite range of status hierarchies fit within the rubric of 'social hierarchy,' which refers to any differential value that is assigned to people, their roles and identities, or even their linguistic resources. For this chapter, however, the focus is primarily on how children come to recognize and enact relative status asymmetries within social relationships. Learning about hierarchy and how it is marked is a critical aspect of both language acquisition and social development throughout life. Furthermore, the practices of hierarchy are central to the production and/or contestation of social inequality in social fields and institutions such as peer groups, families, schools, workplaces, professions, and even nations or societies.

The Handbook of Language Socialization, First Edition. Edited by Alessandro Duranti, Elinor Ochs, and Bambi B. Schieffelin.
© 2014 John Wiley & Sons, Ltd. Published 2014 by John Wiley & Sons, Ltd.

Linton (1936) and Parsons (1951) defined 'status' as the set of cultural rights and duties linked to particular social positions and 'roles' as referring to the expected or normative forms of conduct linked to a status. Within this structural-functionalist paradigm, social stratification was viewed as arising from relations of inequality among status roles within a unified social system. To capture the dynamic and heterogeneous roles that any individual may inhabit, however, ethnomethodologists treated status hierarchies as emergent within the interactional and semiotic processes that produce them (Cicourel 1972; Giddens 1979; Goffman 1967). Goffman, for example, conceptualized *face* – the positively valued self-image managed within social encounters – as 'diffusely located in the flow of events in the encounter [that] becomes manifest only when these events are read and interpreted for the appraisals expressed in them' (1967: 7). Status asymmetries within social relationships, however, may at times also precede and condition such encounters. Some roles inhabited by social actors are dynamic, socially constructed categories that are produced in 'discourses of identity [...] by particular actors' (Blommaert 2005: 210) and indexically presupposed or entailed through the semiotic activities of participants in an interaction (Silverstein 1985a). Because individuals may inhabit multiple roles and identities in any given interaction, speakers indicate which identities are relevant through contextualization cues (Gumperz 1982; Hymes 1972) that point to 'which "side" of the referent's social persona or which particular relationship is relevant in the ongoing interaction' (Duranti 1992: 88). As with any identity, such roles within social relationships are understood in contrast with and in relation to other available positions and identities (Harré 1993; Mühlhäusler and Harré 1990), contributing to an understanding of hierarchical relations.

Status asymmetries within social relationships are marked through innumerable semiotic resources across communities, especially those resources that are implicated in the display of respect. Whether expressed as deference toward a relatively higher-status interlocutor or as the more general recognition of others' value, respect entails the affirmation of fellow human beings' sacredness and dignity. Goffman pointed out that 'societies everywhere [...] must mobilize their members as self-regulating participants in social encounters' (1967: 44) who sustain a viable interaction order through the embodiment of highly conventionalized interaction rituals that 'celebrate and confirm (one's) relationship to a recipient' (Goffman 1967: 57). Displays of deferential respect include linguistic and extra-linguistic communicative resources, such as the performance of particular genres and interaction rituals, forms of participation, speech acts, linguistic repertoires (languages, spoken and written registers, styles of speaking, honorifics, person reference and address, and social and interactive particles), embodied comportment, dress, and hygiene. Within particular social domains or social groups, these semiotic resources become indexically associated, either directly or indirectly, with particular social relationships and identities through their regular and recurrent patterns of use and through metapragmatic discourses that tie language and conduct to social life (Agha 2003, 2004; Ochs 1992; Schieffelin 1990).

Given that asymmetrical relationships are often marked differently by speakers in subordinate versus higher-status positions, adults' child-directed speech would not seemingly model the status-linked forms that children are expected to use. It must be the case, therefore, that children come to master these communicative practices in a range of socializing practices other than modeling. After outlining a semiotic approach to social hierarchy and reviewing previous research on language socialization research into hierarchy, this chapter examines Northern Thai (Muang) children's socialization into the practices of person reference that index hierarchical versus egalitarian social relationships.

Social Hierarchy as Semiotic Practice

The scope of inquiry into social hierarchy should extend beyond static models of ideal role conduct to include socioculturally informed *understandings* of hierarchy that members develop over the life course, including their understandings of how conduct reflects and creates particular schemes of social evaluation. Individuals within any social grouping will have diverse perspectives on the hierarchies at play in a given situation, and these perspectives arise from their individual experiences, identifications, desires, aspirations, and commitments. Speakers' perspectives on social hierarchy, then, include their understandings of the social nature of conduct, their evaluations of persons and their relative status, and their understandings of the meanings, effects, and consequences of particular types of social conduct.

The continuity and transformation of social hierarchies across generations involves, then, not only socially distinctive understandings across social groups but also emergent qualities arising from human agency within a particular group. Most crucially, the structures themselves are 'never either total or exclusive' (Williams 1977: 113). Rather, the heterogeneous social understandings of practical social actors constitute perceived affordances and constraints upon their tactical action within a field of activity, and that action, in turn, transforms the field of activity itself (Bourdieu 1990; de Certeau 1984; Giddens 1979). In the case of language socialization, multiple, competing, and dynamic social structures are variably oriented to and made relevant within fields of activity by expert and novice social actors, who (re)create, resist, or transform them (Ahearn 2001; Kulick and Schieffelin 2004; Rogoff 1990). Through their tactical activity, actors align with or resist particular social roles, statuses, and identities. The process of language socialization into social hierarchies involves becoming able to recognize the social meanings of behavior and to conduct oneself in recognizably social ways, whether these ways are normative, innovative, or defiant.

Children's socialization into hierarchy has profound implications for their learning, education, and participation in society. Children and other novices, through participation in social practices with more experienced members of their community, find themselves situated in asymmetrical social arrangements that allow them to imagine a life trajectory toward full membership in a social group

(Gee 2004). While entire societies may sometimes be characterized as collective or hierarchical, it is also the case that hierarchies may characterize certain institutions across societies with very different political and economic organizations. Schools, for example, may create hierarchies not only between teachers and students but also among children according to performance and abilities. These hierarchies, in turn, may be an effect of a more subtle and profound institutional validation of a certain socioculturally preferred habitus of communicating, thinking, and acting that may be more or less familiar to a child (Bernstein 1972; Bourdieu 1984). Finding one's way into institutional fields of power such as schools may involve an easy continuity or a painful distantiation from early childhood lifeworlds (see García-Sánchez, this volume).

Socialization into Hierarchy

To master ways of speaking and acting within hierarchical social relationships, children or novices must become acquainted with role-linked models of conduct and personhood (Agha 2003, 2004). Knowing how to speak to a superior at work, how to address one's teacher, or how to request a favor from a senior student all require knowledge of these models of conduct. Metapragmatic discourses (discourse about the social meanings of language) are produced in speakers' *uses*, *representations*, and *discourses about* language that link ways of speaking, feeling, and acting to hierarchical social positions and identities. Everyday talk is littered with such reflexive activity, both explicit and implicit, including powerful institutionalized practices in which models of respectful and hierarchically appropriate behavior are produced.

Crucially, such reflexive activity is often not about asymmetrical role behavior alone but simultaneously gestures toward additional parameters of social differentiation, such as situation, gender, age/generation, ethnicity, and social class. That is, speech styles and behaviors that mark hierarchy in a given society may be used differently by members of different social groups, leading distinctive styles of respectful conduct to become secondarily associated with other dimensions of identity and sociality (Silverstein 1985b). Furthermore, the social hierarchies operating in any given situation can be multiple (gender, age, education status, class status, role, expertise, etc.) and negotiated moment by moment as an interaction unfolds (Jacoby and Gonzalez 1991; Ochs 1988). As they are socialized into the practices for inhabiting asymmetrical social relationships, then, children are socialized into ways of speaking, feeling, and acting that index multiple and complex social identities.

The socialization of hierarchy involves making children aware of the meanings of social hierarchy in their communities as well as the communicative resources for inhabiting it. Language socialization research examines *which* particular semiotic resources are implicated in the enactment of social hierarchy, *how* socializing encounters target children's/novices' behavior (explicitly versus implicitly; creating versus presupposing hierarchy), *by/to whom* these socializing strategies are carried out, and what *types of novice participation* (repetition, alignment, or uptake) are involved. To excavate the multiplicity and complexity of social hierarchy, language socialization research must also delineate the interactional, developmental, and historical moments in which socializing activities take place: *when* socializing practices and discourses occur sequentially within an interaction, developmentally within the child's or novice's trajectory of changing participation over time, and historically over longer durations, generations, and eras. Because the speech styles implicated in hierarchy often vary across multiple social dimensions, it is important to examine for whom – which social domains of speakers – the practices of social hierarchy are recognizable, and to what degree reflexive activities involving hierarchy are frequent, institutionalized, and/or authoritative. Widespread or institutionalized practices are likely to generate meanings related to social stereotypes, while other meanings may be emergent and ephemeral in the particulars of an interaction (Agha 2007). This section reviews a selection of research into the socializing practices and reflexive activities employed in the socialization of hierarchy before turning to a discussion of my own research on the socialization of hierarchy Northern Thailand.

Ochs' (1988) early work on language socialization in a Samoan village documented the variability in children's simultaneous socialization into the social hierarchies operating in their everyday social worlds and the linguistic means of inhabiting them. Samoan society was organized according to multiple hierarchies of rank, gender, and age that underlie expectations about how individuals attended to and noticed others, to what extent they took others' perspectives, and to what extent they served or accommodated to others. Respect of and deference to those of higher status were marked by lower-ranking individuals in culturally significant demeanors such as greater degrees of physical movement, greater involvement in caregiving tasks, the use of polite speech registers, fewer directives and requests for clarification, fewer deictic verbs, and calling out or greeting others by name. Ochs noted that respectful conduct, viewed as a learned quality rather than a natural characteristic of children, was socialized primarily through direct instruction in Samoan households. More subtle linguistic indicators of social hierarchy, such as the use of deictic verbs, the use of directives, and requests for clarification, were also learned through children's exposure to the speech of others in everyday interactions. Ochs' account emphasizes the fact that social hierarchies are complex and flexible depending on situational particulars, such as the configurations of participants that change from moment to moment: 'Samoan children are socialized from birth into the notion of "person" as having a number of social "sides" [...], which emerge and subside (from one moment to the next) in the flow of social activity at any one time and place' (1988: 71)

In earlier work, I argued that caregivers' explicit interventions in children's communicative practices address the situational contingencies informing language use, while representations of speech and discourses about language tend to typify both social life and speech behavior (Howard 2009b). Caregivers often guide children to mark hierarchy within the flow of social activities, such as when they prompt a child to produce a particular hierarchically organized communicative practice (Burdelski 2009, this volume; Clancy 1986; Demuth 1986; Morita 2003; Song 2009; Watson-Gegeo and Gegeo 1986). The form and/or the social meanings of the form are not always made explicit for children in prompting routines (Garrett and Baquedano-López 2002), but may rather be hinted at or presupposed. For example, Clancy (1986) reported that, when Japanese mothers prompt children to repeat politeness formulas, either the sociocultural situation calling for these communicative practices was not made explicit or they 'did not specify clearly what the child was supposed to do' (Clancy 1986: 223). Still, such guidance draws children's attention to the communicative practices for marking and inhabiting social hierarchy.

Behavior that is explicitly prompted by adults often involves easily objectifiable communicative practices – greeting routines, politeness routines, person reference, and politeness markers – whereas more subtle linguistic resources and communicative resources for marking hierarchy may be only tacitly grasped by adults and children alike. To acquire these more subtle practices, children must infer cultural expectations, ideologies, and cultural values regarding social relations 'from performances of conventional, socially coordinated activities and interpretive practices' (Ochs 2002: 103), as has been reported for directives (Ochs 1988), honorific verb forms and pragmatic particles (Cook 1990, 1996a, 1996b, 1999, 2008), silence and listening (Meek 2007), and person reference and address (Morita 2003; Song 2009), among others. Both Cook (1990) and Morita (2005), for example, argue that first- and second language learners must acquire the nuanced social-interactional uses of Japanese pragmatic particles through participation in social interaction rather than direct instruction; that is, 'through experiencing the ways and procedures in which such social concerns are publicly displayed in interaction' (Morita 2005: 4; see also Cook 1996a, 1997, 2008). Furthermore, studies of children's acquisition of person reference practices marking complex social hierarchies in Japanese (Morita 2003) and Korean (Song 2009), for example, indicate that adults produced a specialized child-directed register in the presence of children in which they used the person reference terms that *children* would be expected to use with others (*allocentric reference*) in a practice termed 'empathetic identification' (Suzuki 1973 cited in Morita 2003), rather than the unmarked forms that they would use to refer to themselves and others in adult-directed speech. In both unmarked patterns of language use to which children are exposed and in specialized Baby-Talk registers, adults model for children the communicative practices for marking hierarchy in their community.

Patterns of language use by young children themselves provide evidence that children's developing sense of social hierarchy has a deep impact on their use and acquisition of language, including speech registers (Andersen 1986), deictic verbs (Ochs 1988; Platt 1986), communicative speech styles (Clancy 1986), and code choice (Garrett 2005, this volume; Paugh 2005, this volume). Children acquire language forms appropriate to their social position before acquiring forms they are not expected to use, even when the former are less frequent, more difficult, and more complex than the latter (Ochs 1988). Samoan children, for example, acquire the verb 'give' prior to the verb 'come' because the latter is an action that can only be requested by a person of higher status (Platt 1986), and Japanese children consistently use the request form appropriate to their status (*-te*) rather than the form they hear their superiors use toward them (*-nasai*) (Clancy 1986).

Representations of language use, such as reporting or depicting others' speech, implicitly tie ways of speaking to particular social roles and relationships. Reported speech and literary or mass-mediated representations of respectful or deferential demeanors often embed characterizations, evaluations, and assessments of that conduct. In Japan, for example, mothers literally re-present others' respectful speech in a positive light by repeating, for the child, third parties' politely formulated utterances (Clancy 1986). Young children also represent and convey stances to each other about hierarchical speech in their play, such as when they parody the language use of teachers (Rampton 2002, 2006) or dramatize characters in pretend play, representing the speech registers of mothers, teachers, and children (Andersen 1986; Gordon 2002). These representations are often stylized – they idealize and implicitly evaluate status-linked language use by conveying a stance on the speech being reported (Volosinov 1973). Recasts and embedded corrections of children's status-inappropriate language use also represent and implicitly evaluate children's speech (Song 2009), opening a space for children to take up or ignore the models of social life they represent.

Suitable ways of speaking within hierarchical social relationships are highlighted for children in *discourses about* language use, such as when interlocutors provide explicit accounts for the display of respect. Accounts are statements that explain the reasons or justifications for behavior (Scott and Lyman 1968), and they frequently define problematic aspects of behavior and suggest remedies for breaches (Sterponi 2003). Morita (2003) and Song (2009) show that mothers engaging in 'empathetic identification' of third parties sometimes provided accounts for their formulation of reference to third parties that pointed to aspects of the child's social relationship with that person. For example, Song shows how a Korean American mother provided an explicit account to her child for calling the researcher *nwuna* ('elder sister') rather than *imo* ('aunt'): 'because she's not married yet' (2009: 219). Accounts may also invite children to notice the moral, social, or affective consequences of their conduct. For example, adults may highlight the negative feelings that children's disrespectful behavior caused in adults (Clancy 1986; Lo 2009; Lo and Fung, this volume). Chinese-born teachers in a Chinese heritage language school socialized their Chinese American students into the cultural significance of filial responsibility and gratitude by prefacing their disciplinary directives with an account of the moral and practical consequences of displaying disrespect to teachers (He 2000).

Representations of and discourses about hierarchical language use in many communities simultaneously tie such communicative styles to other aspects of identity, such as ethnicity (He 2000; Lo 2009), social class or caste (Errington 1998; Howard 2010; Irvine 1990), or gender (Burdelski and Mitsuhashi 2010). Furthermore, it is important to note that 'politeness' and 'respect' come to be recognized differently across social domains. Language socialization research in diasporic settings has shown how competing models of social hierarchy butt up against one another in immigrant children's language socialization, resulting in children's minimal uptake or overt confrontation of the polite or respectful practices expected by adults (He 2003; Lo 2009; Morita 2009). He (2003), for example, explored tensions between cultural models of respect toward a teacher's authority that Chinese American students brought to heritage language classes in contrast to those of their Chinese teachers, and illustrated how children's responses varied as they took up, ignored, resisted, or rejected the teacher's model of respectful conduct. In the next section, I present my research on Northern Thai children's language socialization into person reference as they acquire two distinct varieties of Thai.

Socialization into Hierarchy in Northern Thailand

My ethnographic research on children's socialization into hierarchy has centered around the Muang (also known as Yuan, Lanna, and Northern Thai) community of Northern Thailand, located in the northwestern arm of the country. Although Thailand is characterized by great ethnolinguistic diversity (hosting approximately 74 distinct living languages), most of Thailand's people (93.5 percent) are Buddhist and speak one of 24 distinct Tai-Kadai (Daic) dialects and languages (Lewis 2009). Kam Muang (the Muang vernacular), Central Thai (Siamese), Isan (or Lao), and Southern Thai (or Paktay) are the major regional dialects of Tai-Kadai in Thailand. Of Thailand's population of 60 million, 11.5 million (18.8 percent) reside in the Northern Region, of which Muang people constitute the vast majority (probably about 75 to 80 percent of the region's residents).[1] Kam Muang and its written form, Lanna Thai, served as the official language of the Lanna Kingdom for centuries before the region was annexed by the Siamese-dominated Thai nation (Simpson 2007). While Kam Muang is still widely spoken across the region, Standard Thai (Thai) – a distinct variety based on the Siamese (Central Thai) vernacular – is the official language of government, education, and media across Thailand. While speakers of all Thailand's major regional languages perceive their vernacular as a mutually intelligible 'dialect' of Thai, the Muang vernacular constitutes a distinct code – including major differences in lexicon (~40 percent is non-shared), some grammatical morphemes, and phonology – that many Muang children encounter for the first time in school. The primary use for Standard Thai in rural villages was traditionally to communicate with Thai government officials, a task that was usually performed by a village headman (Moerman 1969). Villagers' need for this language has increased dramatically over past decades along with changes in the economy, increases in compulsory education, and increased state-internal migration (see Howard 2009b, 2010 for more detailed information). The varieties of language consequential to children's educational and social trajectories, then, are located in hierarchies of linguistic evaluation that extend beyond the village, the school, or the home: children's language use is the subject of metapragmatic discourses associating ways of speaking with multiple and complex hierarchies of identity, location, activity, and social relationship (Howard 2003, 2004, 2007, 2009a, 2009b, 2010). These schemes of evaluation are, in turn, socially positioned and only partially shared in a community undergoing rapid historical change, which involves increasing incorporation into the Thai nation and the global community, the spread of urban environments into surrounding country-side, and changing dynamics of class differentiation and political affiliation. In previous work, I have shown how the children's socialization into styles of respect-ful speech at Pong Noi village school simultaneously socialized them into a standardizing ideology that privileges Standard Thai over the children's vernacu-lar (Howard 2009b). I have also examined how this socialization varied across social domains, as teachers in more privileged urban schools regimented chil-dren's use of the Standard much more tightly than at the village school, down to even the standardized pronunciation of certain consonant clusters (Howard 2010).

In this section, I report findings from two studies of young Muang children's language at school, at home, and in peer groups. In the first study, I examined language socialization in a village on the outskirts of Chiang Mai, among young Muang children whose families were of modest means and who attended the local village school. In the second study, I investigated the language socialization at school of middle-class Muang children from around the Chiang Mai region who were attending the more privileged municipal school in the city. In both settings, Muang children negotiated multiple and competing social relationships in ways that were both conventional and novel. Yet, this research also shows that chil-dren's socialization into hierarchy varied across age groups and class-based social domains. In this paper, I explore children's socialization into the use of person reference for marking degrees of hierarchy in social relationships. While kindergarten-aged children appropriately used person reference terms[2] to display deference and respect to adults at home and school, they also inhabited multiple identities with other children, including egalitarian friendships, age-based hierar-chy within 'sibling' relationships, and gendered personae. Furthermore, social distinctions in peer language use emerged between village children, who prima-rily used Kam Muang with each other at home and school, and middle-class Muang children, who used Standard Thai almost exclusively. For village children, their socialization into respect at school motivated and led to their socialization into Standard Thai and the institutional discourses that marginalize their vernacu-lar language practices.

The ethnographic research in Northern Thailand

Over a 10-month period in 2000 and 2001, I conducted fieldwork in a peri-urban community outside of Chiang Mai, Thailand. I shadowed four Muang five-to-six-year-olds and their elder (seven-to-nine-year-old) siblings at home and the village school, regularly observing and video-recording their interactions in these set-tings. While the Muang children in my study spoke Kam Muang at home, in their village, and with their peers, they were taught and academically evaluated through Standard Thai upon entering school. This sample of Pong Noi families included less privileged villagers (e.g. laborers and those employed in an informal urban economy) because middle-class Muang families in the village invariably sent their children to more privileged schools (public and private). These families also frequently forbade their children's use of Kam Muang at home in favor of Standard Thai (Howard 2003, 2010) and restricted their children's social interactions with less privileged villagers. In the summer of 2004, I returned for a shorter-term study at the more privileged Municipal school in Chiang Mai City, conducting participant observations over six weeks and intensively videotaping the daily activities of one kindergarten and one second-grade class over two weeks. For both of these studies, ethnographic interviews were conducted with families, teachers, school administrators, and community members.

Registering social hierarchy in the Muang community

Status asymmetries associated with relative age and institutional roles of interlocutors are highly salient to Muang speakers. Like other Tai-Kadai groups, Muang social structure is deeply organized according to hierarchies of age, gender social status, rank, and role. Little social action is *not* guided by hierarchical relationships: 'The Thai have no way to interact except in hierarchical terms' (Kirsch 1973: 195). These hierarchies underlie the asymmetrical flow of authority and obedience between higher-ranking and lower-ranking individuals, but they also guide the provision of protection by the higher-ranking person and service from the lower ranking person. Hierarchies are systematically marked through a range of communicative practices, and some of these practices are the subject of explicit, widespread, and institutionalized metapragmatic discourses associating the appropriate display of respect with moral personhood and desirable social relations. From forming a baby's hands into a prayer gesture of greeting to commenting *maj suphaap* ('not polite') upon a child's breach of politeness norms, Muang adults routinely highlight for children what constitutes polite and respectful conduct, for example formulaic politeness rituals, deferential speech registers (lexical speech levels, honorific particles, and person reference terms), code choice (Standard Thai or Kam Muang), and embodied displays of respect (such as the prayer gesture).

In both Kam Muang and Standard Thai, reference to speech-event participants (speakers and hearers) is accomplished through a range of personal pronouns, titles, kin terms, occupational nouns, noun classifiers, and personal names or nicknames. Both languages boast sizable sets of first-person and second-person personal pronouns: the choice from among these alternatives indexes the relative status of the interlocutors and (sometimes) the gender of the speaker. That is, they mark differing qualities of formality, politeness, and relationship between the speaker and hearer.[3] An important distinction must be emphasized here about Thai person reference. In many languages, as in English, speakers may only use *pronouns* to refer to the speaker (I) and the addressee (you). That is, only classic pronoun 'shifters' (Jakobson 1957; Jespersen 1922) – pronouns that rely on the speech context to establish reference – are used for speech event participants in many languages. In fact, based on English, linguists such as van Valin even claim that 'first and second person pronouns' differ from third-person pronouns in that they 'refer to or index the speaker and addressee in a speech event and *do not replace or stand for a noun'* (2001: 6). When substantive nouns such as 'mommy' or 'daddy' are used by English-speaking adults to refer to themselves, this usage is interpreted as constituting a specialized register such as Baby Talk. The use of such nouns to refer to self and addressee in Thai, however, is emphatically *not* Baby Talk, but rather is quite ordinary. Unlike English, the actual use of pronouns in Thai speech is very limited for two reasons: (1) because overt reference to sentence subjects and objects is not grammatically obligatory (Iwasaki and Ingkaphirom 2005) and (2) speakers may (and often do) use proper and substantive nouns (personal names and nicknames, titles, kin terms, or occupational nouns) to refer to self and addressee.[4] So, while English-speakers normally associate substantive nouns only with third-person reference, nouns in Thai are also used to refer to speech event participants.[5] Furthermore, these terms carry differing social meanings and mark the relative social positions of interlocutors. Personal names are more formal and institutional than nicknames and are often used by teachers and officials to lower-status interlocutors; nicknames are usually reciprocated among peers or used to refer to a lower-status interlocutor. Titles (such as *khun* ('Mr./Mrs.')) and role terms (such as *ajarn* ('professor'), *khruu* ('teacher'), or *mɔɔ* ('doctor')) referentially describe the elevated social role of their referent, so they mark deference when used as address terms. Kin terms, too, are used for both self-reference and address to mark aspects of the relationship between interlocutors, including both actual and metaphorical kinship.

Like the person reference systems of other hierarchically organized societies, such as Vietnam (Luong 1990) and Laos (Enfield 2007), it is nearly impossible to avoid linguistically marking the social relationship between interlocutors in Muang speech events. Enfield notes that such 'ordinary' practices of person reference, however, 'do more than just refer. They instantiate and stabilize culture-specific views of the person' (2007: 97). Because any given pair of people may stand in multiple relationships to each other, the choice of person reference either marks some aspect of social hierarchy already in play or invokes a relevant hierarchy. Pronouns do this by indexing the relative status of speech participants, while the denotational semantics of nouns, kin terms, and occupational terms (e.g. 'teacher') literally describe their referent's social role vis-à-vis the other. Personal names carry social information through their paradigmatic contrast with these other terms and through the kinds of communicative practices in which they have come to be used. The choice of person reference may also convey something about the speaker's demeanor, personhood, or identity: social and personal distinctions are reflected in the demeanors that certain types of people adopt through their use of particular person referring registers within social relationships, as when the use of informal, intimate pronouns (such as Thai *kuu* ('I') and *mʉŋ* ('you')) are alternatively read as vulgar, low-class, or appropriately masculine. Muang children's linguistic repertoires include person reference terms from both Standard Thai and Kam Muang, so the choice of terms may also implicate broader sociolinguistic hierarchies and distinctions relevant to relations between the Muang and the Siamese. By focusing on children's use, acquisition, and socialization into the practices of person reference, my research contributes a unique perspective on the ways in which 'doing being ordinary' vary across different social domains of speakers and the ways in which the social registers of language come to index broader identities and commitments. Language socialization research also provides a rich source of metapragmatic discourses about language use that inform the ways that speakers tie language to social life.

Socializing the practices of person reference

Through participation in everyday activities, children are exposed to routine language use, representations of language use, and discourses about language use that tie person reference to social relationships and identities, providing cultural models that children must come to flexibly deploy in everyday activities. In highly asymmetrical social situations, such as children's interactions with familiar adults at home and at school, person reference was highly regimented and reciprocal. In these situations, children were exposed to adults' ordinary language use that modeled the same terms that children were expected to use to refer to that person. For example, teachers referred to themselves as *khruu* ('teacher') and adults at home referred to themselves with the appropriate kin term (e.g. 'mother,' 'aunt,' 'elder sister'), explicitly marking their specific relationship and higher status vis-à-vis the child.[6]

Example 15.1:   School: teacher self-reference

Teacher to students: *diaw* **khun khruu** *ca hâj sŏŋ nám phá ŋaj*
'Mrs. Teacher (=I) am going to have you anoint the Buddha.'

Example 15.2:   Home: adult self-reference

Adult to child: *kɔ̀ɔn tîi nɔ́-(.)ńɔɔŋ cun cà pík bāan* (0.4) **pîi cà hɯ̌ɯ ʔan níi**
'before litt- (.) little sister June (=you) go home (0.4) **elder sister (=I)** will give (you) this.'

As mentioned above, this practice is not an unusual or 'marked' child-directed register: speakers of all ages in any situation self-refer with nouns that describe their role or relationship, a practice that explicitly invokes the well-defined roles and asymmetrical social relations between interlocutors.

Second-person reference terms used by adults to refer to children also frequently modeled the terms that children could use to refer to themselves. Teachers used children's nicknames, *nɔ́ɔŋ* ('junior sibling') plus their nicknames, or the diminutive noun *nǔu* ('mouse'), as in Example 15.3.

Example 15.3:   *School: teacher's reference to addressee*

Teacher to a student: *ʔa* ***nɔ́ɔŋ*** *páam*
                              'ah **little brother Palm**'
Teacher to a student: *khɔ̌ɔŋ* ***nǔu*** *ʔàlaj lûuk tìt lɔɔŋtháaw ʔà*
                              'What is **mouse's (=yours)**, kid? (That is) stuck on
                              (your) shoes.'

Children sometimes mirrored this usage to self-refer when addressing adults (e.g. Example 15.4a–b), although they overwhelmingly used their bare nicknames (e.g. Example 15.4c).

Example 15.4:   *Child self-reference*

Student to teacher: *diaw* ***nɔ́ɔŋ*** *mâj hěn*
                              'Wait. **Little brother (=I)** can't see'
Student to teacher: *khruu kha krapɔ̌ɔŋ* ((unintelligible)) ***nǔu*** *cam dâj ná*
                              khá
                              'Teacher (honorific)? A container ((unintelligible))
                              mouse (=I) remembered it (honorific).'
Child to adult (home):   *ʔâaj ʔaam tǔa ñàj lǔa* ***nɔ́ɔm*** *ʔà*
                              'Big brother Arm (=he) is bigger than **Noam (=I)**.'

This use of nouns to refer to speech-act participants allows children to mirror the adult's person reference, in the sense that their nonreciprocal person reference constituted a mirror image of the adult's usage. Empathetic identification – child-directed speech that refers to a third person with the term that the child should use, rather than the one that the adult speaker should use – was another means by which adults modeled person reference for children. In Example 15.5, for example, the teacher's adult daughter has joined a class field trip for the day to assist her mother, and she identifies her mother as 'Mrs. Teacher' (rather than, for example, 'my mother') when addressing the students.

Example 15.5:   *School: adult to student*

Teacher's daughter to a student: *ʔâa fàak* ***khun khruu*** *wáj kɔ̀ɔn*
                                             'Ah, submit it to **Mrs. Teacher** first.'

Nonreciprocal practices of person reference were modeled not only by adults but also by other children. At home, as at school, children were frequently in the presence of many other children (siblings, neighbors, cousins) who routinely marked adults' higher status through kin and role terms and self-referred with nicknames, *nɔ́ɔŋ* ('junior sibling') or *nǔu* ('I/you/mouse'), as seen in Example

15.4. Furthermore, children encountered mass-mediated representations of respectful and deferential person reference in television, movies, songs, radio programs, books, internet sites, video games, and curricular texts and materials: even gangsters and outlaws are represented as showing deference to teachers, kin, and officials through respectful person reference.

In situations where status and role hierarchies were less clear, such as in children's peer groups, person reference was more variable and complex. In this case, children flexibly inhabited and invoked multiple social relationships and identities, revealing the complexity of children's socialization into hierarchy, including their age, life stage, and membership in a range of social domains. Socialization practices, too, were differentiated by age: young children's displays of deference and respect were explicitly prompted, ventriloquated, and corrected by adults (Howard 2003), while the socialization of older children was often more subtle. In Example 15.6, a three-year-old girl, Mai, referred to an older male cousin, Art, with a disrespectful title (*ʔìi*) usually used by adults (especially parents) to refer to small girls (like herself) or to refer to animals.

Example 15.6:   Correcting disrespectful person reference

Mai (three years old), Jen (six years old), and Pae (five years old).

1	Mai to Art:	*té ʔì iʔaam*
		'True, **little Art**.'
2		(1.5)
3	Jen:	*té ʔìiʔaam wãa*
		'She said "True, **little Art**."'
4	Mai:	*ʔìiʔaam paj lẽn*
		'**Little Art**, go play.'
5	Mai's aunt:	*hee heh heh heh heh*
		'hee heh heh heh heh'
6	Mai's mom:	*ʔìiʔaam*
		'**Little Art**'
7	?	*ʔúuj*
		'ouuu'
8		(1.0)
9	Pae:	*ʔìiʔaam paj lẽn*
		'**Little Art** go play'
10	Jen:	*nɔ́ɔŋ màaj pàak bɔ̀ɔ dii wâa ʔìiʔaam wâa:*
		'Little sister Mai (your) mouth is not good, (you) said "**little Art**"!'
11		(1.5)
12	Pae:	*bɔ̀ɔ câj (0.4) ʔìiʔaam bɔ̀ɔ câj*
		'it's not (0.4) "**little Art**." it's not.'

In this interaction, Mai's (mis)use of a disrespectful term is greeted with parody (lines 3, 6, 9), laughter (line 5), and exclamations of shock (line 7), evaluating her words as laughable and shocking and implying a problem with the respect level of her language. Yet she is also explicitly told that *Ɂii Ɂaam* is not good (line 10, 'your mouth is not good') and corrected (line 11, 'it's not "little Art."'). With older children, who were already expected to know socially appropriate behavior, adults' interventions, for example commenting on the child's conduct ('your mouth'), evaluating their speech in general ('your mouth is not good'), or displaying a stance toward it (laughter, parody, 'I don't want that'), were less likely to specify the problematic conduct. Certain person reference terms, such as low speech-level pronouns – Kam Muang *haa* ('I') and *khiŋ* ('you') or their Standard Thai equivalents *kuu* ('I') and *mɯŋ* ('you') – were subject to particularly negative evaluation, perhaps due to a widely circulating metapragmatic discourse that characterized them as 'improper,' 'vulgar,' and 'low class.' For example, the mother of two boys in the study called out 'hey, your mouth!' and 'your mouth is not good' from the next room when she heard one of them use *mɯŋ* ('you').

Example 15.7: Metapragmatic evaluation

1 Eck to younger   *Hŭa phɔ̂ɔ **mɯŋ** hnnh hnnh hnnh hnnh*
   brother: '**your** father's head hnnh hnnh hnnh hnnh'
2 Mother to Eck   *Ɂèek (.) Ɂèek (.) Ɂèek (.) pàak nɔ̂ɔ*
   (from next room):   'Eck (.) Eck (.) Eck (.) (your) mouth, hunh!'

In addition to developmental stage, life stages also affected socialization across the life course, as children and adults inhabited different forms of social relationships within the social activities typical of their life stage, in which they modeled for each other complex, age- (or stage-) appropriate practices of person reference. Young Muang children in my study constructed primarily egalitarian social spaces in their multiage friendship groups, while adolescents and adults marked age-based hierarchies more systematically in their social relationships with friends. As reported in Howard (2007), young Muang children normally reciprocated status-neutral terms, such as mid-speech-level pronouns and nicknames, to refer to themselves (125 out of 157 tokens) and to their addressee (145 out of 200 tokens). When older adults in the village engaged in multiaged, intimate interactions with friends or family members, however, they systematically used nonreciprocal, asymmetrical person reference terms: the elders routinely addressed and referred to their juniors using the Kam Muang term '*ii* (intimate classifier) + nickname,' while the juniors used Kam Muang terms for 'elder sibling + nickname for the elder.' Simpson (1997) reported that Muang university students in Chiang Mai also used nonreciprocal, asymmetrical person reference (primarily in Standard Thai) in their peer groups: for both self-reference and address, the elder students were referred to as 'elder sibling + nickname,' while nicknames were used for their juniors.

Indeed, Muang adults' widely held stereotypes about children's language use reflected these common patterns. Adults would typify children's play groups as highly egalitarian, especially in their pervasive use of Kam Muang mid-formality pronouns *pǝn* ('I') and *tua* ('you'). Muang speakers often commented that 'Muang kids always use *pǝn* and *tua* when they play together.' The patterns of usage observed among children in my study, however, diverged from this adult stereotype. First, while children self-referred most frequently with *pǝn* ('I') in their play groups, their use of *tua* ('you') was relatively rare; instead, they most commonly used nicknames to address their friends. Second, children not infrequently used a wide range of other person-referring terms. When out of adults' earshot, they sometimes used the informal, intimate pronouns *haa* ('I') and *khiŋ* ('you'), mentioned above, which are considered by adults to be 'vulgar.' These pronouns had a somewhat gendered patterning, as they occurred more frequently (though not exclusively) in all-boy play groups than in mixed or all-girl play groups. For example, during a small group task in the village school's second-grade classroom, one male student, James, was observed using *pǝn* ('I,' mid-level) when speaking to the girls or the whole group but *haa* ('I,' low-level) when addressing his talk to other boys:

Example 15.8:   Gendered pronoun use; language: Kam Muang

| James to whole group: | *khǐan cûʉ **pǝn** kɔ phɔ́ɔwâa **pǝn** cà pík paj lɛ́ɛw*
'Write **my** (*pǝn*) name? Because **I** (*pǝn*) am going home now.' |
| James to one boy: | *diaw **haa** khǐan hʉ̃ʉ*
'Here, I'll (*haa*) write it for you.' |

In contrast to the adult stereotype of children's egalitarian pronoun usage, children occasionally marked age-based hierarchies with peers when they sought beneficence or compliance from each other by using sibling terms ('elder brother/ sister' or 'younger sibling') in offers, requests, and directives (Howard 2007). This pattern implicitly forged indexical ties to the types of acts (directives and offers) and stances (generosity and compliance) commensurate with cultural models of hierarchical sibling relationships. In Example 15.9 (which also appears in Howard 2007), five-and-a-half-year-old Pae is attempting to force her younger cousin Mai out of her place in a coveted chair. Mai whines loudly, provoking her mother's intervention from the next room. Pae then switches to a more generous and inviting stance to coax the younger child out of the chair, and marks their relationship with sibling terms.

Example 15.9:   Inhabiting the generous elder sibling role

| 1 | Mai: | ((loudly whining)) *enh enh* |
| 2 | Mai's mom:
((from outside)) | *khǎj ñá **nɔ́ɔŋ***
'Who is bugging **little sister**?'
((after some intervening talk)) |

3 Pae to Mai: ((inviting))	*nɔ́ɔŋ nâŋ tãk pîi bɔ̌ɔ* 'Would **little sister (=you)** like to sit on **big sister's (=my)** lap?' ((after more intervening talk))
4 Pae to Mai: ((offering))	*ʔɔɔ nɔ́ɔŋ **maj** lo:ŋ maa nâŋ tãk pîi* 'Here! **little sister Mai (=you)** come do:wn and sit on **big sister's (=my)** lap.'

In lines 3 and 4 of this excerpt, Pae uses the Kam Muang terms for elder sibling (*pii*) and junior sibling (*nɔ́ɔŋ*) to refer to herself and her younger cousin as she pursues Mai's compliance. Her directive is designed as an invitation in line 3 (marked by the invitation particle *bɔ̌ɔ*) and as a generous offer in line 4 (marked by the offer particle *ʔɔɔ*). She invokes the younger child's role as compliant younger sibling and her own role as an elder sibling who has the right to direct Mai's behavior, but also instantiates a model of generosity by superiors that is significant in Thai models of superior–junior relations. This example also illustrates how adults' interventions into children's activities, though infrequent, sometimes highlighted the social expectations surrounding these hierarchical relationships. In this example, the aunt's intervention in response to Mai's whining (line 2, 'who is bugging little sister?'), explicitly invokes Pae's hierarchical sibling relationship with Mai through her empathetic identification of the younger child (her daughter) as 'little sister,' suggesting that some inappropriate conduct is being directed toward the younger child. Within this life stage, young children practiced the linguistic means of inhabiting egalitarian friendships, hierarchical 'sibling' relationships, and gender-differentiated friendships through their use of person reference. In adolescent and adult usage, though, multiage friendships were more explicitly and systematically marked as being hierarchically ranked by age and, to a lesser extent, gender.

Children's socialization into and through the multilingual repertoires of person reference in the Muang community were also differentiated by social class: the registers used by children at the village school, and the means of socializing these registers, were distinct from the more privileged children at the municipal school. Middle-class children attending the municipal school in the city spoke primarily Standard Thai at home, at school, and with each other. At home and school, many of these children were forbidden to use Kam Muang, and teachers systematically corrected their Kam Muang speech (Howard 2003, 2010). Commensurate with this prescriptivist language ideology oriented to the national language, at school these children referred to each other with either the Standard Thai mid-formality pronouns *chan* (first person, mid-level, intimate) and *thəə* (second person, mid-level, intimate) or with nicknames.

In institutionalized discourses such as curricular materials, textbooks, and mass-mediated discourses across Thailand, school students were frequently *re-presented* as using these Thai mid-speech-level pronouns with each other. Thus, while stereotypes about Muang children's use of the Kam Muang pronouns *pɑ̀n* ('I') and *tua* ('you') circulate in local and regional metapragmatic discourses about children's language use, the Standard Thai equivalent circulates more widely in authoritative, institutionalized, and mass-mediated texts and discourses. Even among Thai speakers, however, these Standard Thai pronouns are highly marked: they are typically used only with one's same-age schoolmates or with intimate romantic partners, as in the popular rock love song titled *chan rak thɔ̀ɔ* ('I love you!').

At the village school, where most students had learned Kam Muang at home, students were expected to use the Standard Thai registers of person reference for the first time. In fact, children were explicitly instructed to use *chan* ('I') and *thɔ̀ɔ* ('you') with each other at school. Early in the school year, for example, kindergarten children regularly sang a song that instructed them to greet each other in Standard Thai. The song's words, *thɔ̀ɔ kap chan, sawat dii* ('you and me, hello'), were accompanied by a well-executed *waj* (the prayer gesture used to greet others). Recorded on an instructional audiotape for teachers' use, this song promoted a particular model of classroom comportment between peers with Standard Thai as its medium. As she sang along with the students, the teacher prosodically highlighted these Thai pronouns and corrected children's performance of the *waj* when it was not perceived as 'beautiful.' Outside of these teacher-fronted instructional contexts, children rarely used use *chan* and *thɔ̀ɔ* – for the most part, they continued to use Muang pronouns that indexed solidarity and friendship (as seen, for instance, in Example 15.8).

Conclusion

While hierarchy is a central aspect of human relationships in many communities, social relations are marked in more or less explicit ways, and there are a variety of means by which children are socialized to display an orientation to hierarchy. Children in Northern Thailand encountered unwavering commentary on and evaluation of their conduct within hierarchical social relationships. When I first arrived in Thailand, a local linguist asserted that Muang children acquire the practices of respect and politeness with very little intervention from adults. For him, the asymmetrical positioning of social actors in relation to each other was experienced not only as vital to human relations but also as perfectly natural to them – that is, he understood respect to be a natural stance toward superiors and the means of displaying it to be acquired implicitly. Yet, all around me I observed persistent prompting and guidance of children's practices of respect, and I noticed that social life in Northern Thailand was imbued with commentary on (dis)respectful, (im)polite, or status-(in)appropriate comportment. The routine use of the languages of respect in children's everyday lives also exposes them to multiple models of social relationships and the linguistic means of inhabiting them. Given that deference flows upward to higher-status parties, it would seem that children would rarely be exposed, in the child-directed speech of adults, to the forms of respectful practice expected of them. There are many alternative ways, however, in which the practices for inhabiting their positions within social hierarchies are modeled for children. Muang adults' use of role and kin terms rather than first- or second-person pronouns, for example, explicitly refers to their social relationships with children and simultaneously models, in a mirror-like fashion, how particular individuals, including themselves, should be referred to. Such 'ordinary' usage may not be possible in other languages, so one might expect the practice of empathetic identification in Baby Talk to play a more central role in modeling person reference for children in those languages. Furthermore, the social meanings of these practices are conveyed not only in child-directed speech but also through representations of language use in conversation, play, curricular materials, the media, and various kinds of talk about language use that children see and hear in their everyday lives.

Of the many types of communicative practices indexing social hierarchy, the practices of person reference sketch a particularly detailed social landscape within culturally significant activities, position children within it, and invite them to take up, ignore, or resist those positions. By kindergarten, children in my studies had learned to inhabit multiple social hierarchies across settings and institutions, but they had yet to become aware of more nuanced social distinctions occurring on broader scales such as age-differentiated, gendered, and class-inflected ways of inhabiting hierarchical social relations. The social domain across which a given practice is (at least partially) shared and recognizable cannot be overlooked in the study of language socialization, for children are apprenticed into multiple, competing, and sometimes overlapping communities of practice to which they are accountable for inhabiting recognizable social identities. The nuanced, gendered use of *haa* ('I,' low-formality, intimate pronoun) in James' speech to his group-mates, for example, is not grasped by the adults, who scold or negatively evaluate such usage and characterize it as simply inappropriate for *children* to use. Nor is the model of identity presented in James' use of these pronouns encountered in explicit discourses *about* these person reference forms. In flexibly deploying the communicative practices of (dis)respect to inhabit their social relationships with others, children likely draw upon both kinds of model: the idealized and bounded categories such as 'vulgar' and 'low-class' embodied in explicit discourses, and the shadowy figure of masculinity embodied in actual use. As children expand their activities and social networks, the shadowy figures of class status evoked by standard versus vernacular linguistic repertoires may also begin to take shape for this new generation of Muang children. These ways of engaging in social relationships, these shadowy (and not so shadowy) figures that we embody in our symbolic practices, are centrally implicated in our understandings of who we are and what we aspire to become.

ACKNOWLEDGMENTS

I am indebted to the children and adults of Pong Noi village and Chiang Mai Municipal School, who invited me into their classrooms and homes and shared their perspectives with me. I am also grateful to Ajarn Aroonrut Wichienkeow and the Lanna Art and Culture Center at the Rajabhat Institute of Chiang Mai for sponsoring me during my fieldwork. Research in Pong Noi village was supported by a Fulbright Grant from the Fulbright Institute for International Education/ Thailand–United States Educational Foundation, a Doctoral Dissertation Improvement Grant from the National Science Foundation, and doctoral disserta- tion year fellowship from the Spencer Foundation, and the University of California Graduate Division. Research at the Municipal School in 2004 was funded by a grant from the University of Pennsylvania's University Research Foundation. The chapter was improved a great deal by feedback from Elinor Ochs, Merav Shohat, Bambi B. Schieffelin, and Adrienne Lo. I must also thank Khun Wanida Naloka, Khun Thosaporn Laonapensaeng, and Khun Sichon Koowuttayakorn, who assisted with transcription and translation on these projects.

NOTES

1   The 2000 Thai Census Bureau does not report this directly. Rather, it reports that approximately 15 percent of the population of the North Region migrated there from other regions and that 6 percent of the region's population 'speak hill tribe languages.' The largest non-Daic (Tai Kadai, or 'Thai') ethnic groups in this region are the Karen (approximately 250,000) and the Hmong (approximately 100,000).

2   Throughout this chapter I use the term 'person reference' to encompass reference to self, addressee, and third parties.

3   In general, high-speech-level pronouns mark politeness, formality, and self-lowering/ other-raising; mid-speech-level pronouns mark symmetrical but polite relations; and low-speech-level pronouns mark intimacy, informality, and other-lowering (see Howard 2007 for a detailed description). As Enfield (2007) notes for another Tai-Kadai language, Lao, the etymology of pronouns reveals the provenance of their function in self-lowering and other-raising: for example, the other-raising Lao second-person pronoun *caw* was derived from the substantive noun 'lord' and the self-lowering first-person pronoun *khooj* was derived from the substantive noun 'slave.'

4   This characteristic of Thai 'person' leads linguists to assert that some nouns (kinship terms, role terms) may be used 'pronominally' or that they function 'as' or 'instead of' pronouns (e.g. Smyth 2002), for example when a speaker uses her nickname to refer to herself or to her addressee.

5   Varenne (1984), in fact, reminds us that Jespersen's (1922: 222) original formulation of 'shifters' included

> a large set of nominal forms [...] kinship terms, words like enemy or friend, and probably all words and linguistic forms that map social relations. With some exceptions, a word like 'mother' – particularly when used in address and in direct speech – does not refer to the substantive quality of the addressee, it refers to the (social) relationship of the speaker to the addressee.

For this reason, one might wish to claim that substantive nouns that are used to refer to speech event participants by indicating that the relations between them are also shifters of a sort: their reference is established by mapping the social relations they denote onto speaker and addressee.

It should also be noted that the category of 'person' (first-, second-, or third-person reference) operates only weakly, if at all, in Thai language: there is no grammatical marking of person agreement, and certain pronouns are used for both first- and second-person reference or both second- and third-person reference.

6 Phonetic transcription of Thai speech roughly follows Haas (1955). Tone is marked as a diacritic over the first vowel of the relevant syllable. Chiang Mai Kam Muang's additional tone 'high with glottal closure' is marked with a ˜. Transcription conventions and notations for segments include **bold**: analyst's emphasis; single parentheses in both Thai and translation lines: uncertain hearings; single parentheses occurring only in translation line: constituents required in English – usually noun constituents – that are not realized in the Thai utterance; double parentheses: extralinguistic information; square brackets: overlapping speech; =: latched talk; bracketed numbers: pause length to tenths of a second.

REFERENCES

Agha, A. (2003) The social life of cultural value. *Language & Communication* 23(3): 231–73.

Agha, A. (2004) Registers of language. In A. Duranti (ed.), *A Companion to Linguistic Anthropology*. 23–45. Oxford: Blackwell.

Agha, A. (2007) *Language and Social Relations*. Cambridge: Cambridge University Press.

Ahearn, L. M. (2001) Language and agency. *Annual Review of Anthropology* 30: 109–37.

Andersen, E. (1986) Register variation among Anglo-American children. In B. B. Schieffelin and E. Ochs (eds.), *Language Socialization Across Cultures*. 153–64. Cambridge: Cambridge University Press.

Bernstein, B. B. (1972) A sociolinguistic approach to socialization: With some reference to educability. In J. Gumperz and D. Hymes (eds.), *Directions in Sociolinguistics: The Ethnography of Communication*. 465–97. New York: Holt, Rinehart and Winston.

Blommaert, J. (2005) *Discourse*. Cambridge: Cambridge University Press.

Bourdieu, P. (1984) *Distinction*. Cambridge, MA: Harvard University Press.

Bourdieu, P. (1990) *The Logic of Practice*. Stanford, CA: Stanford University Press.

Burdelski, M. (2009) Prompting Japanese children. In L. Y. Takubo, T. Kinuhata, S. Grzelak, and K. Nagai (eds.), *Japanese/Korean, Vol. 16*. 235–49. Stanford, CA: CSLI Publications.

Burdelski, M. and Mitsuhashi, K. (2010) 'She thinks you're kawaii': Socializing affect, gender and relationships in a Japanese preschool. *Language in Society* 39(1): 65–93.

Cicourel, A. (1972) Basic and nonbasic rules in negotiation of status and role. In H. P. Dreitzel (ed.), *Recent Sociology No. 2: Patterns of Communicative Behavior*. 4–45. New York: Macmillan.

Clancy, P. (1986) The acquisition of communicative style in Japanese. In B. B. Schieffelin and E. Ochs (eds.), *Language Socialization Across Cultures*. 213–50. Cambridge: Cambridge University Press.

Cook, H. M. (1990) The role of the Japanese sentence-final particle *no* in the socialization of children. *Multilingua* 9(4): 377–95.

Cook, H. M. (1996a) Japanese language socialization: Indexing the modes of self. *Discourse Processes* 22(2): 171-97.

Cook, H. M. (1996b) The use of addressee honorifics in Japanese elementary school classroom. In *Japanese/Korean Linguistics Vol. 5.* N. Akatsuka, S. Iwasaki, and S. Strauss (eds.), 67–81. Stanford, CA: Center for the Study of Language and Information.

Cook, H. M. (1997) The role of the Japanese *masu* form in caregiver–child conversation. *Journal of Pragmatics* 28(6): 695.

Cook, H. M. (1999) Situational meanings of Japanese social deixis: The mixed use of the *masu* and plain forms. *Journal of Linguistic Anthropology* 8(1): 87–110.

Cook, H. M. (2008) *Socializing Identities Through Speech Style: Learners of Japanese as a Foreign Language.* Clevedon, UK: Multilingual Matters.

de Certeau, M. (1984) *The practice of everyday life.* Berkeley, CA: University of California Press.

Demuth, K. (1986) Prompting routines in the language socialization of Basotho children. In B. B. Schieffelin and E. Ochs (eds.), *Language Socialization Across Cultures.* 51–79. Cambridge: Cambridge University Press.

Duranti, A. (1992) Language in context and language as context: The Samoan respect vocabulary. In A. Duranti and C. Goodwin (eds.), *Rethinking Context: Language as an Interactive Phenomenon.* 77–101. Cambridge: Cambridge University Press.

Dumont, L. (1969) Homo hierarchicus. *Social Science Information* 8(2): 69–87.

Eagleton, T. (2000) *The Idea of Culture.* Oxford: Blackwell Publishers.

Enfield, N. J. (2007) Meanings of the unmarked: How 'default' person reference does more than just refer. In N. J. Enfield and T. Stivers (eds.), *Person Reference in Interaction: Linguistic, Cultural and Social Perspectives.* 97–120. Cambridge: Cambridge University Press.

Errington, J. (1998) *Shifting Languages: Interaction and Identity in Javanese Indonesia.* Cambridge: Cambridge University Press.

Garrett, P. B. (2005) What a language is good for: Language socialization, language shift and the persistence of code-specific genres in St. Lucia. *Language in Society* 34(3): 327–61.

Garrett, P. B. and Baquedano-López, P. (2002) Language socialization: Reproduction and continuity, transformation and change. *Annual Review of Anthropology* 31: 339–61.

Gee, J. P. (2004) *Situated Language and Learning: A Critique of Traditional Schooling.* New York: Routledge.

Giddens, A. (1979) *Central Problems in Social Theory.* Berkeley, CA: University of California Press.

Goffman, E. (1967) *Interaction Ritual: Essays on Face-to-Face Behavior.* Garden City, NY: Anchor Books.

Gordon, C. (2002) 'I'm mommy and you're Natalie': Role-reversal and embedded frames in mother–child discourse. *Language in Society* 31: 679–720.

Gumperz, J. (1982) *Discourse Strategies.* Cambridge: Cambridge University Press.

Haas, M. (1955) *The Thai System of Writing.* Washington, DC: American Council of Learned Societies.

Harré, R. (1993) *Social Being.* Oxford: Blackwell.

He, A. W. (2000) Sequential and grammatical organization of teachers' directives. *Linguistics and Education* 11(2): 119–40.

He, A. W. (2003) Linguistic anthropology and language education: A comparative look at language socialization. In S. Wortham and B. Rymes (eds.), *Linguistic Anthropology of Education.* 93–121. Westport, CT: Praeger.

Howard, K. M. (2003) *Language Socialization in a Northern Thai Bilingual Community.* Doctoral Dissertation. Los Angeles, CA: University of California, Los Angeles.

Howard, K. M. (2004) Socializing respect at school in Northern Thailand. *Working Papers in Educational Linguistics* 20(1): 1–30.

Howard, K. M. (2007) Kinterm usage and hierarchy in Thai children's peer groups. *Journal of Linguistic Anthropology* 17(2): 204–30.

Howard, K. M. (2009a) Breaking in and spinning out: Repetition and de-calibration in Thai children's play genres. *Language in Society* 38(3): 339–63.

Howard, K. M. (2009b) 'When meeting Mrs. Teacher, each time we should show respect': Standardizing respect and politeness in a northern Thai classroom. *Linguistics and Education* 20(3): 254–72.

Howard, K. M. (2010) Social relationships and shifting languages in northern Thailand. *Journal of Sociolinguistics* 14: 313–40.

Hymes, D. (1972) Models of the interaction of language and social life. In J. J. Gumperz and D. Hymes (eds.), *Directions in Sociolinguistics: Ethnography of Communication*. 35–71. New York: Holt, Rinehart and Winston.

Irvine, J. T. (1990) Registering affect: Heteroglossia in the linguistic expression of emotion. In C. Lutz and L. Abu-Lughod (eds.), *Language and the Politics of Emotion*. 126–61. Cambridge: Cambridge University Press.

Iwasaki, S. and Ingkaphirom, P. (2005) *A Reference Grammar of Thai*. Cambridge: Cambridge University Press.

Jacoby, S. and Gonzalez, P. (1991) The constitution of expert–novice in scientific discourse. *Issues in Applied Linguistics* 2: 149–81.

Jakobson, R. (1957) Shifters and verbal categories. In *Selected Writings of Roman Jakobson: Vol. 2*. 130–47. The Hague: Mouton.

Jespersen, O. (1922) *Language: Its Nature, Development, and Origin*. London: George Allen and Unwin Ltd.

Kirsch, A. T. (1973) The Thai Buddhist quest for merit. In J. T. McAlister (ed.), *Southeast Asia: The Politics of National Integration*. 188–201. New York: Random House.

Kulick, D. and Schieffelin, B. B. (2004) Language socialization. In A. Duranti (ed.), *A Companion to Linguistic Anthropology*. 349–68. Oxford: Blackwell Publishing.

Lewis, M. P. (ed.) (2009) *Ethnologue: Languages of the World*. Dallas, TX: SIL International.

Linton, R. (1936) *The Study of Man*. New York: Appleton-Century Company.

Lo, A. (2009) Lessons about respect in a Korean heritage language school. *Linguistics and Education* 20(3): 217–34.

Luong, H. V. (1990) *Discursive Practices and Linguistic Meanings*. Amsterdam, The Netherlands: John Benjamins.

Meek, B. A. (2007) Respecting the language of elders: Ideological shift and linguistic discontinuity in a Northern Athapascan community. *Journal of Linguistic Anthropology* 17(1): 23–43.

Moerman, M. (1969) A Thai village headman as a synaptic leader. *Journal of Asian Studies* 28: 535–49.

Morita, E. (2003) Children's use of address and reference terms: Language socialization in a Japanese–English bilingual environment. *Multilingua* 22: 367–95.

Morita, E. (2005) *Negotiation of Contingent Talk*. Amsterdam, The Netherlands: John Benjamins.

Morita, E. (2009) Arbitrating community norms: The use of English *me* in Japanese discourse. In A. Reyes and A. Lo (eds.), *Beyond Yellow English: Toward a Linguistic Anthropology of Asian Pacific America*. Oxford: Oxford University Press.

Mühlhäusler, P. and Harré, R. (1990) *Pronouns and People: The Linguistic Construction of Social and Personal Identity*. Oxford: Blackwell.

Ochs, E. (1988) *Culture and Language Development*. Cambridge: Cambridge University Press.

Ochs, E. (1992) Indexing gender. In A. Duranti and C. Goodwin (eds.), *Rethinking Context: Language as an Interactive Phenomenon*. 335–58. Cambridge: Cambridge University Press.

Ochs, E. (2002) Becoming a speaker of culture. In C. Kramsch (ed.), *Language Acquisition and Language Socialization*. 101–20. New York: Continuum.

Parsons, T. (1951) *The Social System*. Glencoe, IL: Free Press.

Paugh, A. L. (2005) Multilingual play: Children's code-switching, role play, and agency in Dominica, West Indies. *Language in Society* 34: 63–86.

Platt, M. (1986) Social norms and lexical acquisition: A study of deictic verbs in Samoan child language. In B. B. Schieffelin and E. Ochs (eds.), *Language Socialization Across Cultures*. 127–52. New York: Cambridge University Press.

Rampton, B. (2002) Ritual and foreign language practices at school. *Language in Society* 31: 491–525.

Rampton, B. (2006) *Language in Late Modernity*. Cambridge: Cambridge University Press.

Rogoff, B. (1990) *Apprenticeship in Thinking: Cognitive Development in Social Context*. New York: Oxford University Press.

Schieffelin, B. B. (1990) *The Give and Take of Everyday Life: Language Socialization of Kaluli Children*. Cambridge: Cambridge University Press.

Scott, M. B. and Lyman, S. M. (1968) Accounts. *American Sociological Review* 33(1): 46–62.

Silverstein, M. (1985a) The functional stratification of language and ontogenesis. In J. V. Wertsch (ed.), *Culture, Communication, and Cognition*. 205–35. Cambridge: Cambridge University Press.

Silverstein, M. (1985b) Language and the culture of gender. In E. Mertz and R. J. Parmentier (eds.), *Semiotic Mediation*.

219–59. New York: Academic Press.

Simpson, A. (ed.) (2007) *Language and National Identity in Asia*. Oxford: Oxford University Press.

Simpson, R. C. (2007) Metapragmatic discourse and the ideology of impolite pronouns in Thai. *Journal of Linguistic Anthropology* 7(1): 38–62.

Smyth, D. (2002) *Thai: An Essential Grammar*. London and New York: Routledge.

Song, J. (2009) Bilingual creativity and self-negotiation: Korean American children's language socialization into Korean address terms. In A. Reyes and A. Lo (eds.), *Beyond Yellow English: Toward a Linguistic Anthropology of Asian Pacific America*. 213–32. New York: Oxford University Press.

Sterponi, L. (2003) Account episodes in family discourse: The making of morality in everyday interaction. *Discourse Studies* 5(1): 79–100.

Suzuki, T. (1973) *Kotoba to Bunka* (*Language and Culture*). Tokyo: Iwanami Shoten.

van Valin Jr., R. D. (2001) *An Introduction to Syntax*. Cambridge: Cambridge University Press.

Varenne, H. (1984) The interpretation of pronominal paradigms: Speech situation, pragmatic meaning and cultural structure. *Semiotica* 50: 221–48.

Volosinov, V. N. (1973) *Marxism and the Philosophy of Language*. L. Matejka and I. R. Titunik, transl. Cambridge, MA: Harvard University Press.

Watson-Gegeo, K. A. and Gegeo, D. W. (1986) Calling out and repeating routines in Kwara'ae children's language socialization. In B. B. Schieffelin and E. Ochs (eds.), *Language Socialization Across Cultures*. 17–50. Cambridge: Cambridge University Press.

Williams, R. (1977) *Marxism and Literature*. Oxford: Oxford University Press.

16 Peer Language Socialization

MARJORIE H. GOODWIN AND AMY KYRATZIS

Introduction

An essential feature of work in the language socialization paradigm is examining how in becoming competent participants of their social group children (or other members) are socialized through language and to use language (Kulick and Schieffelin 2004: 350). Learning appropriate affective stances is an important dimension of becoming a competent social group member, as studies of language socialization are fundamentally concerned with how it is that novices acquire a habitus or ways of being in the world (Kulick and Schieffelin 2004: 249); rather than asking how societies vary cross-culturally, the focus in language socialization studies is on how specific affective alignments or positions come into being and are negotiated (Kulick and Schieffelin 2004: 351; see also Cook, this volume). Analysis of the acquisition of particular practices over time is based on extensive longitudinal ethnographic study of specific embodied language resources. Participants in the process of language socialization mutually shape one another; thus, in the family, children as well as parents are 'mutual apprentices' (Pontecorvo, Fasulo, and Sterponi 2001) to one another.

Seminal studies in language socialization (Kulick 1992; Ochs and Schieffelin 1984; Schieffelin and Ochs 1986) have addressed how more accomplished participants socialize novices, as, for example, in parent–child or teacher–student interaction. Work by Schieffelin (1990) and others (Burdelski 2010, this volume; Clancy 1986; Rabain-Jamin 1998) has examined prompting as an important resource for 'socialization to use language' (Schieffelin and Ochs 1986: 163), as well as socialization into particular relationships. In Kaluli a specific grammatical form, *a:la:ma*

The Handbook of Language Socialization, First Edition. Edited by Alessandro Duranti, Elinor Ochs, and Bambi B. Schieffelin.
© 2014 John Wiley & Sons, Ltd. Published 2014 by John Wiley & Sons, Ltd.

or 'say like that,' is used to help establish the gender identity of girls. Generational identity of young children is established through the term *o:mina*, meaning 'having chewed, give' (Ochs and Schieffelin 2006: 183). In Samoa, the term *sau* helps to build the directive meaning 'to come,' establishing the identity of the speaker as relatively higher status than the addressee.

Instead, here our focus is on how child participants, either members of a peer group or sibling multiage group – socialize one another. Western-influenced notions of 'peer groups' have conceptualized children's groups as consisting of same-age peers who are not related to one another. However, many children's groups in neighborhoods and nonschool settings (Goodwin 1990; Thorne 1993) in Western cultures, and in non-Western cultures in which older children spend large periods of the day caring for younger kin (de León 2007; Reynolds 2002; Rogoff 1981; see Goodwin and Kyratzis 2007 for a review), do not consist of same-age members or children unrelated to one another. We acknowledge that both 'peer groups' and 'sibling-kin groups' are important arenas where language socialization occurs, and include both in the scope of this chapter.

Children's negotiations of how they stand vis-à-vis one another – that is, their 'identities-in-interaction' (Antaki 1994; Antaki and Widdicombe 1998) – are made relevant in the midst of their naturally occurring conduct with one another. In the course of talk, as Pomerantz and Mandelbaum (2005: 153) argue, participants achieve and renew their relationships with one another through the act of 'talking and acting in ways that are recognizably bound with relationship categories.' In this chapter we investigate a number of systematic practices and resources through which children in concert with one another build the phenomenal and social worlds they inhabit as the situated product of interactive practices: evaluating their playmates, ascribing particular categorizations to one's interlocutors, creating differentiation and hierarchy, constructing a pretend world, and using practices of language alternation.

While evaluating group members through storytelling, assessments, insults, or categorizations of person, children take up either common or divergent stances towards the target, socializing appropriate forms of behavior. Such practices thus lie at the heart of processes of achieving intersubjective understanding (Goodwin and Goodwin 1987). In order to come to terms with these practices, we investigate evaluative commentary as well as members' categories (which often carry an affective valence) that occur in the midst of such activities. We also explore how children utilize members' categories, as well as directives, as resources for building social organization in pretend play, and how children use features of different registers, voices, and genres during play as means to both explore and comment on social roles, categories, and relationships from the adult world and to negotiate social order (see also Aronsson, this volume). Finally, we examine how children growing up in multilingual communities make use of practices of language alternation to build opposition and alignments as well as to define 'social places' (Schieffelin 2003: 158) for their language varieties during play.

Evaluative Commentary

In the midst of talk, peers police the local social landscape and make evaluative commentary to one another with respect to what they consider the valued signs in their larger social universe – ones that are linked to social status. Through linguistic practices such as gossip, assessments (Goodwin and Goodwin 1987; Pomerantz 1984), and storytelling, group members continuously define and redefine the social situation and hold one another accountable to it. Participants making evaluative commentary link what Sacks (1972, 1995b) has called 'category-bound activities' or 'members' categories' with the target being assessed. By taking up stances with respect to the target or stance object (Du Bois 2007), they not only locate and reference the peer group's notion of culturally appropriate moral behavior, but also negotiate their alignments to one another and position one another in the local social group or community of practice (Bucholtz 1999, 2002) – an aggregate of people who develop shared 'ways of doing things, ways of talking, beliefs, values, power relations' (Eckert and McConnell-Ginet 1992: 464).

Gossip

Within storytelling, play, and gossip, peers learn appropriate ways of interacting in the local social group (Eder 1995; Goodwin 1990; Loyd 2011; Shuman 1986). Goodwin (1990) analyzes the 'he-said-she-said' gossip event in which neighborhood girls aged between 7 and 12 tell stories leading to future confrontations of two against one that reorganize and realign the local social organization. Girls make use of multiple types of stories – instigating stories, retold stories, hypothetical stories, and harvested parallel stories – to elicit a statement from an offended party that leads to her confronting an offending party (Goodwin 1990: 187) to take action against the offense of having said something about someone behind her back. These are important ways of dealing with real and imagined offenses concerning someone having put herself above others; failure to confront one's offender is thought to result in loss of social face. The focus is on both prior and future interactions, dealing with what someone in fact said, or would say in a future meeting between the offended and offending parties.

Researching Latina gang girls in Northern California, Mendoza-Denton (2008: 181) discusses 'talking shit,' a form of gossip that has an optional confrontational denouement: 'it is either a third-person account where the speaker portrays the third party unfavorably or a narrative where one brags about one's own factual or imaginary victory against an absent one.' In the he-said-she-said disputes that Shuman (1986, 1992) examined among a group of African American, European American, and Puerto Rican inner-city junior high-school students in Philadelphia, the role of the instigator, rather than the original offending party, was critical. Shuman states (1992: 140): 'In many cases the message-bearer was held responsible for instigating the conflict, and the antagonisms shifted from the original offense to a challenge against the person who was not entitled to talk about someone else's offense.' In high-school years and beyond, responsibility for instigating becomes a key issue when gossip turns into 'rumor' (Morgan 2002: 60).

Evaldsson (2002), investigating gossip among working-class preadolescent Swedish boys, finds that boys' alignments of two against one (against girls as well as boys) result in confrontations in the present encounter rather than in a future one. As in the Maple Street, Philadelphia boys' stories studied by Goodwin (1990), the child animated as principal character in a telling is present. Through practices such as format tying, boys demonstrate highly collaborative intimate stances in support of talk by a group member about someone who positions her/himself above others. Evaldsson (2002: 211) finds that 'the participant structure of the gossip telling itself simultaneously allows the boys to solicit support, seek affiliation, and strengthen solidarity – features prominent in all-female groups.' Because the party being talked about in a degrading fashion is present, he may counter the negative assessment; nevertheless, each successive counter by the target leads to further confirmations by others of their collective alignment against him. Boys thus can establish relations of power and hierarchy in the midst of collectively showing support in aligning against a present target.

Evaldsson's work problematizes easy gender dichotomies. However, offences among boys do not concern what an intermediary party reportedly said behind one's back, as occurs in girls' groups. Rather, the social categories that are invoked deal with male cultural concerns: 'anxieties about being excluded, associated with physical vulnerability, emotional weakness, and cowardice' such as crying, sulking, wetting one's pants, or calling for a teacher's intervention (Evaldsson 2002: 199).

Assessments

Bucholtz (2007: 378) has noted that discernment (Bourdieu 1984), or the ability to distinguish between what is desirable and what is not, is fundamental to groups as a way to index social status. Goodwin's (2006) fieldwork among elementary-school girls in Los Angeles aged between 10 and 12 found that peers hold one another accountable for recognizing the meaning of signs that index wealth, such as cars that are luxurious, foreign travel, or elite sports, and being able to produce appropriate moves that show understanding of relative value within a language game.

Newon (2006), studying assessments (Goodwin and Goodwin 1987; Goodwin 2007; Pomerantz 1984) during storytelling among a multiethnic middle-class group of 14–16-year-old cheerleaders in an all-girl Catholic school in suburban California, observed that girls create their own local culture by defining what to aspire to and what to avoid. Girls evaluated body image, physical and mental ability, maturity, and popularity. In small groups, girls who produced self-deprecations – negative assessments about themselves – received in response moves of disagreement (supportive commentary about the initial speaker).

However, in larger groups negative assessments about nonpresent girls, often framed with laughter, were frequently ratified.

Forms of discernment have also been investigated by Henderson (2009), who studied a multicultural group of tweens aged between 10 and 12 in an after-school computer club. Henderson found that tweens explored a range of diverse identities online as they played 'Whyville.' They styled online avatars through forms of assessments that were used to evaluate 'the good body' and a savvy Los Angeles style. Eckert's (1987) study of jocks (students oriented towards middle-class aspirations) and burnouts (students identifying with working-class culture) in suburban Detroit found polar differences in how adolescents style forms of coolness. Mendoza-Denton examined *norteña* and *sureña*, embodied styles that index complex ideologies through multiple semiotic resources of difference (music, dress, makeup, body image, and phonetic pronunciations) (2008: 208, 212). Analyzing the language and culture of South Asian American teens or 'Desis' in three Silicon Valley high schools, Shankar (2008) compares hip, cosmopolitan 'popular' styles with what popular teens term 'FOB' ('fresh-off-the-boat') styles. Bucholtz (2011) examined the semiotic practices used to construct the youth cultural styles of preppy mainstream white hip hop fans, and nerds among youth of European American descent at Bay City High, un urban multiracial public school in the San Francisco Bay Area.

Looking at telephone conversations between 14–16-year-old girlfriends in southwest Germany, Kotthoff (2010) found the valued signs of these girls were romantic relationships with boys. She analyzed how girls socialize one another to deal with relatively unstable romantic contacts, characterized by both attraction and repulsion, simultaneously positioning themselves in their friendship groups and the larger cross-sex social world as they discuss these relationships. As Eckert (2003: 386) notes, positioning can also be accomplished through compliments, which she argues constitute the 'verbal means by which girls monitor progress in the accomplishment of new norms of feminine behavior and adornment.' Eckert (2003: 386) maintains that 'sincere compliments to players in the market add value to the receiver as evidence of her quality, and to the giver as evidence of her possession and exercise of cultural knowledge.'

Critiques of girls who imagine themselves as occupying a particular category that ranks them above others are constructed through the use of mental-state verbs ('think she popular' or 'think she cute'). For example, among a Los Angeles clique, when critiquing a girl named Janis for bragging about her Spice Girls artifacts and trendy clothing, Aretha stated, 'Janis thinks she's popular because she stays up to date.' The preface 'she think' displays how the girls, as cognitively complex actors, read the intentionality or status claims that underlie the use of particular signs (in this case, wearing clothes that are trendy) and assess the character of the person making such claims.

Spreckels (2008), conducting a two-year study with German adolescent girls during their leisure activities, discusses a similar framing for complaints against someone, with utterances such as 'He thinks he's X just because of Y': 'Now he thinks he's listening to rock music just because he listened to ACDC somewhere.'

Music is important in the culture of German adolescents (and hence in identity construction). Knowledge of musical style (e.g. *gangsta* and *hip hopper*) is used to index those who are hip (affiliate with the youth culture) from those who are not. Such framings as 'he thinks he's doing X' are often used to project the category of someone who is a 'wannabe' (as in 'wannabe hippie' or 'wannabe film star') and cannot appropriately occupy the category. Similarly, Henderson (2009), in her study of Southern California tweens who construct virtual-world identities while playing 'Whyville,' noted distinctions that children made between groupies ('emos') and actual band members (someone who is 'rockish').

Ritual insult and negative assessments

Evaldsson (2005: 765–6) reviews work on ritual insulting (talk that concerns a pejorative attribute of the target not known as literally true), including alternative ways that participants sequence next turns, pointing out that 'there is always a danger that the boundary between playful and real aggression will begin to blur'(Evaldsson 2005: 765). As physical fights are a possible next move to personal insults (Kochman 1983; Labov 1972), jocular abuse is used to prevent aggression (Eder 1995; Rampton 1995) while laughter breaks tension. Evaldsson (2005: 769) sees insult as emerging from mocking, ridiculing, and gossiping, resulting from games as well as isolated insult sequences. Evaldsson (2005: 770) argues that fighting back and 'being able to take it' are important to everyday masculine experience (Danby and Baker 1998; Eder 1995; Morgan 2002; Thorne 1993), promoting 'toughness' and competition (Evaldsson 2002; Willis 1981). Studying female peer groups in the Quartieri Spagnoli (inner city Napoli), Loyd (2011) found that 5–12-year-old girls construct their moral and social order in everyday performances of argumentation. In response to living in a world where peers constantly monitor and police each other in attempts to gain respect and rise in their dominance hierarchies, girls learn the art of quick, theatrical, witty comebacks to gain leverage in everyday relations.

In her discussion of 'playing the dozens,' a form of ritualized (Labov 1972) insult, Morgan (2002: 58) finds that a particular format is used: 'Your mother (is) so adjectival . . . (that),' where the adjectival phrase is followed by a clause. Examples include 'Your mother is so fat that when she sits on a quarter she gets two dimes and a nickel' and 'Your mother is so old that when she read(s) the Bible she reminisces' (Morgan 2002: 59). Insults not only allow practice of verbal skill; through insults peers learn the cultural categories that are relevant to their social group.

In the activity of 'clowning,' older adolescent Latina gang girls studied by Mendoza-Denton (2008: 187) make use of the structure 'Your (possession/relation of the interlocutor) is so (unflattering adjective) that (outrageous result)' to make comparisons with one another; for example, 'Your mama is so tiny that she could hang-glide on a dorito.' The retort to a clowning insult must be a funnier, more creative and more daring insult than the first, improvised in the local interaction and targeting the co-participant's undesirable features. This practice is related to ritual or mock insults in African American English as well as the vernacular Mexican Spanish verbal art form *albur*, which typically entails double entendre rhyming references with 'ambiguous sexual innuendo' (Mendoza-Denton 2008: 188); for example, *Guera, guera, ¿Quién te encurea?* ('Blondie, Blondie, who'll disrobe you?') Among French adolescents of Algerian descent, parental name-calling, which makes use of potentially face-threatening acts, is used not only to insult but also to tease and flirt (Tetreault 2010).

Forms of social aggression rather than verbal play can occur when ritual insults are responded to with personal insults. Goodwin (2006) found that a working-class African American girl (Angela) who directed a playful ritual insult to someone of a predominantly upper-middle-class clique could quickly become the target of return comments portraying being poor as a degraded status: girls described Angela as unable to find a job when she grew up, working as a cleaning woman, unable to afford braces, needing to be on welfare, and without friends. Goodwin and Alim (2010) describe practices of 'transmodal stylization' during such insult sequences. A member of the clique openly mocked what the targeted African American girl was saying by using features of talk associated with white *'Clueless'* Valley girls while simultaneously producing stereotypical gestures (neck roll, suck teeth, and eyeball roll) associated with black 'ghetto' girls.

Children make use of locally relevant and culturally specific categories and category-bound activities to provide negative depictions of those positioned as transgressors. Negative category-bound activities in Evaldsson's (2007) studies of girls' groups, including fighting, blaming, exploiting others, lying, and talking behind people's backs, were associated with the category 'bad friend.' Being poor (not having Pokemon cards, wearing old clothing, or lacking material goods more generally), having limited Swedish language proficiency, dressing like a girl, and being labeled a 'Gypsy' (rather than the in-group label 'Romany' commonly used in school) were negative person descriptors among boys of working-class or immigrant background in multiethnic elementary school groups in Sweden (Evaldsson 2005: 771). Such terms were used during character contests (Goffman 1967: 237). Evaldsson (2005) closely examines the sequential environments in which multiparty consensus (see also Evaldsson 2002; Goodwin 1990) is created to ratify particular depictions, through upgrades, laughter, recycles, repetitions, new linked evaluations, and so on that frame the acts of the offending party as disgusting. Evaldsson's point is that we cannot ascribe meaning to members' categories without conducting extended fieldwork. Assessment adjectives, pejorative person descriptors, and negative categorizations of activities and actors all point to implicit cultural values that the children invoke and orient to as they accomplish their alignments to one another in the interaction.

Membership Categorizations

Goodenough's (1965) notion of identity as situated, local, and occasioned and his idea that culture consists of an underlying body of structures, practices, and procedures, much like the grammar of a language (1981: 102–3), was influential in Harvey Sacks' formulation of notions of identity selection and membership categorization devices. Sacks (1972) argued that membership categorization devices provide ways of allowing people to understand categories as sets or standardized relational pairs (e.g. mother and child belong to the category 'family'). Membership categorizations consist of particular actions or category-bound activities that are constitutive of a specific category; members' categories are what people make use of to describe events in the world.

Games, Sacks (1995a) argued, provide ways of 'mapping members' or locating participants in relevant occasion-specific categories. Applying Sacks' notion of membership categorization to analysis of children's games and pretend play, Butler and Weatherall (2006) studied six-to-seven-year-old children in two inner-city Australian schools during recess. They examined members' categories in broadcasting games, playing 'treasures' (a game that involved follow-the-leader – with the leader having the right to judge what counted as real treasure, where the treasure was, and the proper order of game events and players (2006: 455)), playing families, and 'fairy club.'

Ethnography and studies of members' categorizations

Current work on talk-in-interaction, which combines ethnographic studies with close sequential analysis of conversation and membership categorization devices, permits investigation not only of how the local situated activity is organized but also how actions and stances (du Bois 2007; Jaffe 2009) taken across a range of interactions are consequential for participants' lives and help to construct more enduring forms of social organization. Through examining stance-taking, we can come to grips with the concerns that deeply animate participants. Evaldsson (2007) explored how 'relationship work' is accomplished among a multiethnic group of immigrant Swedish girls aged between 11 and 12. She was concerned with moral ordering by peers, achieved through both sequential analysis *and* category membership. Challenging a unitary view of female morality, Evaldsson found that one member of the group of girls she studied was repetitively subject to being made accountable for negative category-bound activities (fighting, blaming, exploiting others, lying, talking behind people's backs, and being disloyal, insane, and friendless). The targeted girl openly resisted responsibility through denials, justifications, recyclings, substitutions, and counter-accusations, which only intensified attributions of negative category membership ('bad friend') and eventually resulted in her being friendless rather than mitigating conflict.

Evaldsson (2005: 764) has argued that, by combining analysis of members' social categories with an examination of talk-in-interaction, we can explore 'the constitutive role of talk for local social organization and how issues associated with wider social structures and discourses can be located, observed, and described within situated action.' Person formulations are articulated in concert with what Zimmerman (1998: 90–1) has discussed as situated identities that emerge out of the particular action at hand. Goodwin (2011) found that gendered terms such as 'girl' and 'boy,' for example, can be mobilized both in the midst of disputes (as a component of a turn taking up an oppositional stance to a prior move interpreted as argumentative – in essence, an epithet) as well as in mutual congratulatory exclamations during assessment sequences (where a stance of affiliation is being performed). Tarım (2007, 2008) similarly observed four- and five-year-old children in Turkey orienting to gendered terms such as 'girl' and 'boy' during peer play. They invoked the terms to index category-bound behaviors and hold peers accountable to them during group disputes.

In her analysis of categorizations among a multiethnic peer group in Sweden, Evaldsson (2005) finds it essential to make use of ethnographic knowledge of the children and school setting to understand children's categorizations during insults. She argues that 'categorizations are bound up with particular actions (category-bound activities) or characteristics (natural predicates) that both constitute and reflect conventional expectations of normative behaviours within a specific group and setting' (2005: 768). Evaldsson found that, in making negative assessments, such things as possessions, clothing, limited language proficiency in Swedish, ethnicity, and sexuality were important topical concerns relevant within the frame of insults. In order to understand why particular aspects of self were viewed in a negative light – for example, why Swedish language proficiency was evaluated in a particular way – she found it important to understand the local language ideology of the school. Indeed, Stokoe and Smithson (2002: 84) argue that, contrary to accusations of an 'unmotivated "analytic mentality,"' researchers working within the conversation-analysis framework 'use their background knowledge, either acknowledged or unacknowledged, in the process of doing analysis.'

Members' categorizations in pretend play

Several researchers (Berentzen 1984; Goodwin 2011; Griswold 2007; Kyratzis, Marx, and Wade 2001; Kyratzis 2007) have noted children's use of membership categorization (Sacks 1995a) for organizing local social order during pretend play. Enacting stratified roles in pretend play provides children with resources for constituting hierarchical relationships among themselves and constructing the local social order of the peer group. For example, Goodwin (2008) noted how girls display 'best friend' relations through roles they select in pretend play, such as twins married to twins. The membership categorization devices twin sisters and twin brothers provided a resource for two girls to display alignments to one another while simultaneously differentiating themselves from other clique members, thereby also constructing asymmetrical relationships. Kyratzis (2007) observed a peer group of five-year-old girls who constructed their pretend play as news reporting (Butler and Weatherall 2006). Through their labels and interaction, they oriented to the category of 'news reporter/announcer' and divided this category into hierarchical levels, with a lead announcer/news reporter and subordinate announcers. This role division and allocation enabled the children to construct distinctions in their own local social order.

Game roles and categories can also provide children with resources for constructing positive alignments. For example, Hoyle (1998) described two boys displaying affiliation to one another through aligning to one another's characters' (sports announcer) speech in pretend play. In peer pretend play, young children can index their social alignments to one another indirectly through the membership categorizations they orient to in their play. By indexing an orientation to playing 'getting married' (Sheldon 1996), for example, two preschool girls were able to display an orientation to one another and were simultaneously able, consistently with the frame, to exclude a third girl by telling her that she was the baby brother but that she wasn't born yet.

Accomplishing Local Social Order with Directives in Pretend Play

Pretend play presents children with several resources for constructing social organization within the peer group (Goodwin 1993) in addition to membership categorizations. As Ervin-Tripp (1996: 33) has argued, 'Children's subtle observation of the background features of adult speech is never revealed so fully as in their role play.' Directives provide one major way through which children realize positions of dominance and submission between characters (Goodwin 1990: 127). (See also Andersen 1990; Aronsson and Thorell 1999; Corsaro 1985; Ervin-Tripp, Guo, and Lampert 1990; Evaldsson and Tellgren 2009; Mitchell-Kernan and Kernan 1977).

In pretend play, children show a keen awareness of how different social identities can be presented as distinct 'voicings' (Goldman 1998: 155). Away from adult presence, children 'exploit their understandings of [...] power hierarchies at familial, local, national, and global levels' (Paugh 2005: 65) and in so doing 'create alternative social realities in which THEY hold the positions of authority, power, and control' (Paugh 2005: 65). Goodwin (1990) showed how the African American working-class girls she observed enacted asymmetry in their own social relationships through directives in games of 'house.' While girls enacting the role of mother delivered imperatives loudly with emphatic stress to their 'children,' girls playing the role of subordinates made excuses to the girls enacting the role of mother, thereby ratifying the right of the girls in the mother role to command them (Goodwin 1990: 127–9).

Subsequent ethnographic studies showed girls' agentive use of the social organizational affordances provided by directives to differentiate themselves in interactions within their peer group. Griswold (2007) illustrated how six-to-eight-year-old Russian girls used directive forms (permission, information, and assistance requests), often produced in crouched bodily positions, to enact a subordinate position vis-à-vis a girl who peers constructed as occupying a leadership position in the group. They also requested that the girl in the leadership position, including 'mother,' make decisions about role assignments of other group members; the girl playing mother ratified this position through moves of her own. Kyratzis, Marx, and Wade (2001) observed four-year-old girls and boys project leadership roles in their respective peer groups by using assertive directive forms while receiving deferent forms – permission and information requests – from other group members. For example, one girl projected a leadership role by instructing other group members how to climb and by assuming the role of the oldest sister ('I'm 99') in pretend play; the other girls made permission requests and information requests of this girl, deferring to her superior knowledge and ratifying her dominant role in the interaction. Kyratzis (2007) demonstrated how asymmetry was accomplished by one five-year-old member of a friendship triad of preschool girls in a game of news reporter play. The girl enacting main reporter used in-role directives with discourse markers such as 'well,' 'so,' and 'now' ('Now we return back to our weather report'). The projected right of this lead announcer to determine transition points of the activity was repeatedly ratified in the sequence of interaction by the other group members.

In studying directive-response sequences in pretend play and other exchanges, an ethnographic perspective permits us to examine how the social orchestration of an activity can change over time (Goodwin 2006: 155) as well as over other situational features (de León in press b; Evaldsson 2004; Kyratzis and Guo 2001; Kyratzi, Marx, and Wade 2001; Nakamura 2001). De León (in press a, in press b), for example, observing directive-response sequences among siblings in caregiving situations in a Mayan township in Chiapas, Mexico, found that siblings' social organization was emergent and varied, depending on the age composition of the dyad and other features of the 'sibling developmental niche.' Flores Nájera (2009), examining children's games (*columpio* or 'swing') among bilingual Nahuatl-Spanish speakers in Tlaxcala, Mexico, describes how older siblings, in their caretaking roles, use honorific forms to mitigate both directives and justifications towards younger siblings. In the pretend game of *dueñas y criadas* ('owners and maids'), modeled after urban Mexican culture, however, cross-situational variation is evident in how authority is displayed during play. Girls in positions of power code-switch from Nahuatl to Spanish to intensify negative evaluation of inappropriate behavior (exclusion of group members). Such actions are accompanied not only by response cries, grammatical intensifiers, and reduplication that registers negative assessment but also by glances displaying annoyance.

Several of the studies mentioned earlier documented children's sensitivity to status relationships in the adult world as seen in directive use during pretend play (Andersen et al. 1999; Aronsson and Thorell 1999; Corsaro 1985; Ervin-Tripp 1996; Ervin-Tripp, Guo, and Lampert 1990; Evaldsson and Tellgren 2009; Mitchell-Kernan and Kernan 1977). The studies reviewed in this section document that positions of leadership are in addition constituted through the way in which requests from others are responded to, either ratifying or challenging the stance taken by a child proposing to act as leader in sequences of interaction. These studies consider how children use directives and other forms agentively to construct asymmetries in their own local social order.

Play with Voicing, Stylization, Genre, and Participation Frameworks – Taking Stances

Another set of resources that child peers can utilize in building their social worlds and identities includes the 'voicing' (Bakhtin 1981; Vološinov 1973), 'stylization' (Rampton 2003, 2006), and 'performance' (Bauman and Briggs 1990) of particular roles and speakers and the manipulation of participation frameworks during these stylized performances. Citing Goffman's work on frame analysis (Goffman 1974), Goodwin (1990: 230) argues that 'by telling a story a speaker is able to bring alive in the midst of ordinary conversation what is in essence a vernacular theatrical performance; the teller enacts the characters whose exploits are being recounted, and, with talk of a different type [...] comments on their meaning.' She notes Vološinov's (1973) point that 'a speaker never simply reports the talk of another but instead, in the very process of animating that talk, comments on it and shows his or her own alignment to it' (Goodwin 1990: 245). How the animator enacts the quoted speech of the author is critical for determining how others who view the performance align with the animator and evaluate the animated speaker.

Animating and stylizing others in stories

Children and teens are provided with a powerful means of disaligning from a speaker and their moral views when they animate that speaker and use his/her own words against them (Eder 1998; Goodwin 1990). When boys animate peer-group members as speaking in a high-pitched, cowardly fashion (Evaldsson 2002) or themselves as speaking assertively and challenging adult authority (Cheshire 2000), they index appropriate and inappropriate behavior for the peer group, projecting a value that boys should not act cowardly.

Teens 'use language and dialect in discursive practice to appropriate, explore, reproduce or challenge influential images and stereotypes of groups that they *don't* themselves (straightforwardly) belong to' (Rampton 1999: 421; emphasis in original). Rampton conducted 'micro-discursive analysis of particular episodes in which youngsters put on exaggerated posh and Cockney accents' (Rampton 2003: 76). These 14-year-olds, attending a multiethnic school serving low-income students in inner-city London, made use of these accents in 'stylised performances' (Rampton 2003: 67) to produce evaluative commentaries on others, frame comebacks to playful accusations, and achieve other effects in the local interaction. Rampton concluded that adolescents engage with, comment on, and 'denaturalize' cultural associations and stereotypes indexed by the accents and language varieties. Over time, such practices have the power to '*change* the associative meaning potential of a particular language form or variety' (Rampton 2006: 343).

Studying interaction during focus groups, Keim (2008) observed a group of adolescent girls of Turkish heritage in Germany (i.e. the 'Turkish Powergirls') switching into playful performances and caricatures using features of dialects of various social groups that they did not consider themselves to belong to. For example, they used *Gastarbeiterdeutsch* ('migrant workers' German') to evoke 'the negative social category of the "backward Turk"'(Keim 2008: 219). However, they also used *Gastarbeiterdeutsch* to evoke the German monolingual speaker's 'stereotypes about migrants and force him/her interactively to cope with these stereotypes' (Keim 2008: 219) in the moment. The ways in which children and teens style, stylize, and animate others in play, disputes, and stories allow them to render social commentary and construct local social and moral order in peer-group interactions.

Play with register, genre, and participation frameworks: Making social commentary

In pretend play, children play with register and genre and playfully perform, combine, delete, and juxtapose features from different registers/genres (Minks 2006, 2010; Reynolds 2002, 2008, 2010). These playful exploratory combinations provide children with a resource for exploring relations among different social roles, settings, and discourses (Briggs and Bauman 1992); for delivering powerful moral messages, and for negotiating and subverting existing social order (de León 2007; Kyratzis 2007; Loyd 2006, 2011; Minks 2006; Paugh 2005; Reynolds 2002, 2007, 2008, 2010). Even children in the early childhood years show agency in using such resources. For example, Reynolds (2007) examined how two-to-fourteen-year-old children from an extended kin network group in a highland Guatemala Kaqchikel Maya town 'entextualized' (Bauman and Briggs 1990) a formulaic politeness routine, the greeting *Buenos días*, combined it with another genre of respect, a military salute, and utilized it to negotiate the local social order of kin group exchanges. By extending use of the genre to contexts other than that in which it canonically occurs, as 'a respectful greeting routine' (Reynolds 2007: 447), and by mockingly tying it to the format of and elaborating (with insult terms) other group members' uses of the greeting, the children subverted existing hierarchical relations among members of the kin group, conveyed disrespect, and negotiated local social order.

Age hierarchies were also observed to be subverted by children in an ethnographic study conducted by de León (2007) in Zinacantan, Chiapas, Mexico. She observed a pair of young Tzotzil Mayan siblings, a two-year-old and a four-year-old, embedding a politeness routine, an invitation to eat ('Do you want to eat?'), in inappropriate contexts. The invitation or call is usually uttered by children with an evidential (i.e. 'do you want to eat, it is said') when they are calling other children in to eat for an adult, acting as the adult's messenger. The evidential indexes their role as 'animators' (Goffman 1974) of an adult-authored message. However, the children subverted the form, leaving off the evidential. They uttered it in the presence of their grandfather and format-tied to his posings of the invitation/question to them, thereby subverting existing age hierarchies.

In another analysis, Reynolds (2010) examined how two children, a six-year-old and an 11-year-old, enacted *el Desafío* ('the Challenge') performances that they had observed being performed in the streets of their Kaqchikel Maya town. This is a Spanish reconquest genre that pits *el Rey Cristiano* (the Christian king) against *el Rey Moro* (the Moorish king). The children combined poetic forms from this genre with forms that indexed a caretaking register. Reynolds argued that, by so doing, the children were able to draw an analogy between varieties of authority encompassed in the two kinds of roles, thereby providing them with a resource for exploring and subverting their own unequal social positions within the sibling–kin group. Tetreault (2009) observed teenagers of Algerian descent in France playfully appropriating and 'entextualizing' French television host register, thereby 'capitaliz[ing] on the primary power of television hosts: to contextualize guests within interactions that the host primarily orchestrates' (Tetreault 2009: 205). The peers exploited and arranged participant frameworks, enabling them to 'create a generalized footing that facilitates embedded rumors about their tutors and peer[s]' (Tetreault 2009: 217). The ironic footing also facilitated embedded commentary on the broader French society where they lived. Kyratzis (2007) observed members of a peer group of American preschool children exploiting features of announcer/news reporter register to bring on, present, and remove other characters (e.g. guest announcers) from the stage, to build local social order among group members.

Poveda and Marcos (2005) documented Gitano children (i.e. children living in Romany or Gypsy communities) teasing and animating non-Gitano children living in the same public housing project in a community in Spain during a stone fight. The Gitano children were observed animating the non-Gitano children as saying things ('I am a baby') that indexed what were, from the perspective of the children's cultural worlds (Corsaro 1997), child-based ideologies regarding age; that is, 'social categories that are problematic (face threatening) for [...] recipient[s]' (Poveda and Marcos 2005: 344). By drawing on their own child-based cultural ideologies and resources, the children were able to 'transform and reinterpret sociogeographical arrangements that have been put into place primarily by adults' (Poveda and Marcos 2005: 346).

Even young toddlers have been observed appropriating formulaic expressions from adult caregivers and embedding them in new contexts for rhetorical effect. Köymen (2008, 2010; Köymen and Kyratzis 2009) observed 24–30-month-old children appropriating the expressions of caregivers ('I don't like it when you . . .'), provided to children as part of an institutional, curriculum-based mandate to 'use your words' and make their affective states known to peers in negotiating conflicts. The children embedded and 'recontextualized' (Ochs 1996) these formulaic utterances in new contexts that were not the idealized uses of the expressions. In one example, a child used the formula to provoke a conflict with a peer rather than to resolve one, thereby perpetuating conflict and subverting the adult intention of the practice. In an ethnographic study conducted in Nicastro, southern Italy, Loyd (2006) observed children, including a three-year-old, appropriating adult-like expressions and enacting 'adult personas' in their conflicts with peers. These shifts in footing enabled children to project moral authority and influence local social order during the disputes. In another study, Reynolds (2008) examined how young children in a Kaqchikel Maya town countered attempts by older members of the sibling/kin group to author words for them during teasing routines. The authored words were intended to put down other, older members of the sibling–kin group. By 'choosing sides and authoring their own words' (Reynolds 2008: 96), the children were able to take their own stances and subvert local age hierarchies.

Howard (2009), observing a peer group of Thai boys, noted how the youngest, a five-year-old, created a space for himself to participate by appropriating a game role and game speech that were more typical of expert participants in a riddle game; through manipulating the game-embedded participation framework (by answering the riddle rather than repeating the question he was prompted to ask by an older boy), he subverted local age hierarchies. Minks observed Nicaraguan Miskitu children living on Corn Island engaging in pretend play by juxtaposing 'genres such as recitation, note-taking, testing, teacher talk, and a particular kind of subversive reading and writing called "copying" or "cheating" (Minks 2006: 118). In so doing the children were able to render commentary on peers, 'act out unsanctioned forms of behavior,' and explore and challenge the limits of such unsanctioned behavior among themselves (Minks 2006: 123). They were also provided with a venue to draw links between different 'bodies of discourse' in their multicultural experience (Minks 2006: 122; see also Bauman and Briggs 1990). Through varied means, children animate, entextualize (Bauman and Briggs 1990), enact, stylize, and 'recontextualize' (Ochs 1992) the expressions of others. By making 'artful use of speech in expressive performance' (Rampton 2006: 16) and by embedding register and genre elements agentively in new contexts, as well as exploiting participation frameworks in interaction with peers and kin, they explore and evaluate social relations in the adult world, challenge and subvert existing hierarchies, and negotiate their places in the local social order.

Juxtaposing Resources from Multiple Languages

A considerable body of research has examined how code-switching functions as a 'contextualization cue' (Gumperz 1982) during children's peer-group conversations, serving to 'alert participants in the course of the ongoing interaction to the social and situational context of the conversation' (Li 1998: 164; see also Auer 1998; Ervin-Tripp and Reyes 2005; Gumperz and Cook-Gumperz 2005). Code-switching can be used to negotiate shifts in alignment, 'footing' (Goffman 1979), or kind of talk (Ervin-Tripp and Reyes 2005; Gumperz and Cook-Gumperz 2005; Zentella 1997); in 'participation framework' (Cromdal and Aronsson 2000; Kyratzis, Tang, and Köymen 2009); or 'production format' (Cromdal and Aronsson 2000). Code-switching can serve as a resource for displaying speakers' shifting or competitive orientation to an exchange and for resolving overlap (Cromdal 2001), as an 'interactional resource in the sequential construction of oppositional stances' (Cromdal 2004: 53), and for disaligning with others' talk and suggestions during episodes of 'power-wielding' (Jorgensen 1998).

Researchers taking a language socialization perspective examine how, in areas of language contact, through their language practices in play, children 'draw on and reproduce more broadly held ideologies about the relationship and meanings of the two languages' (Schieffelin 2003: 158). (See also Garrett 2005, this volume; Garrett and Baquedano-López 2002; Kyratzis, Reynolds, and Evaldsson 2010; Paugh 2005, this volume; Zentella 1997). Paugh (2005) followed children's code-switching and play practices in peer/kin groups in Dominica. Through their selection of codes to enact particular adult roles in role-play, the children, including three-year-olds, could 'transform the associations with the languages through using them in their play' (Paugh 2005: 80), which in certain ways could contribute to the maintenance of Patwa in the region. Minks found Miskitu children on Corn Island moving very 'easily across social and linguistic boundaries' (2006: 125) in peer-group interactions. With such practices, children 'socialize heteroglossia' within the peer group (Minks 2010), possibly supporting the maintenance of indigenous languages such as Miskitu in areas undergoing language shift.

However, children's peer- and sibling/kin-group practices can also contribute to language shift and language loss in a community. Quichua-Spanish-speaking children in a highland Ecuadorian community did not play together in Quichua, preferring Spanish, despite Quichua being used among adults in the community (Rindstedt and Aronsson 2002). In immigrant communities, practices within children's peer groups can also reproduce or challenge dominant societal discourses (Garrett and Baquedano-López 2002; see also Baquedano-López and Mangual Figueroa, this volume; García-Sánchez, this volume). Cekaite and Evaldsson (2008) and Evaldsson and Cekaite (2010) followed multiethnic peer groups in two schools in Sweden, examining how group members reproduced monolingual norms of the school by criticizing their peers for uses of languages other than Swedish. At alternative moments, however, the children challenged these same norms through using code-switching and crossing, indexing bilingual identities, and defying monolingual institutional norms. García-Sánchez (2010) observed how members of a peer group of immigrant Moroccan girls in Spain made use of bilingual practices, using both Moroccan Arabic and Spanish during pretend play with their dolls. In the bilingual community in which they were growing up, bilingual play provided a space in which group members explored conflicting forms of gender identification. Garrett (2007) observed older St. Lucian boys to use Kwéyòl in 'unsupervised peer contexts,' in contrast to most everyday, adult-supervised contexts, in which they used English. Garrett concluded that Kwéyòl was used by these boys to 'index adult masculinity' and work out their own domain associations and 'subjectivities' for English and Kwéyòl (Garrett 2007: 249). Kyratzis (2010) observed members of a peer group of Mexican-heritage immigrant girls in a bilingual preschool classroom in California. Through code-switching, the children negotiated shifting activity frames, inscribed domain associations for their two languages (Garrett 2005; Paugh 2005; Schieffelin 2003), and challenged institutionally inscribed discourses. A peer group of New York Puerto Rican children (Zentella 1997) and a peer group of Dominican American youths in Providence, Rhode Island (Bailey 2007) used code-switching and 'heteroglossic' language practices (Bakhtin 1981) to effect changes in the local interactive context in group interactions, simultaneously challenging language ideologies of the dominant US society. Through their language practices within the peer group, children challenge, 'draw on, and reproduce more broadly held language ideologies' (Schieffelin 2003: 158) of the multilingual communities in which they grow up, as they act to accomplish their local social organization.

Conclusion

Kulick and Schieffelin have recently argued that missing from Bourdieu's formulations of habitus and Judith Butler's claims about the performative power of language are accounts of 'how' it is that individuals are socialized into a habitus; thus, 'processes of becoming a culturally intelligible subject are assumed and asserted more than they are actually demonstrated' (Kulick and Schieffelin 2004: 351–2). This chapter has documented embodied language practices entailed in peer-based social control and negotiation that children – across an array of diverse cultures and physical locales – make use of to build local social organization within their own peer-group communities and index appropriate and inappropriate behavior for the local peer group through (universal) language practices. Schieffelin and Ochs have argued that an important goal of language socialization research 'has been to articulate a model that reconciles what is particular and what is universal about the communicative practices of novices and of experts' (Schieffelin and Ochs 1996: 257). We have demonstrated that, within their own same- and near-age group communities, in neighborhoods, schoolyards, and separated areas of children's interaction, away from the influence of adults, children socialize one another.

Like previous bodies of research on children's peer cultures and socialization of one another (Blum-Kulka and Snow 2004; Cook-Gumperz and Kyratzis 2001; Cook-Gumperz and Corsaro 1986; Corsaro 1985, 1997; Eder 1995; Ervin-Tripp and Mitchell-Kernan 1977; Gaskins, Miller, and Corsaro 1992) and as discussed in prior reviews (Cook-Gumperz and Kyratzis 2001; Goodwin and Kyratzis 2007; Kyratzis 2004), the studies reviewed here focus on how children 'creatively use cultural resources' (Gaskins, Miller, and Corsaro 1992: 7) in building their own social worlds, ones that can be very different from the life worlds of adults. However, this body of studies differs from other peer socialization research in giving special emphasis to (1) children's agency in attending to and building local hierarchy and social organization; (2) the importance of examining moment-to-moment, embodied, and situated practices in sequences of interaction; and (3) the relevance of using ethnography to provide broader perspectives on the resources drawn upon by children in moment-to-moment interactions. Importantly, the studies also expand the types of children's peer groups studied to include age-graded groupings in which older siblings and kin care for younger children (de León 2007, in press b; Minks 2010; Reynolds 2007, 2010; Rogoff 1981). Moreover, as many of the world's children currently grow up in postcolonial and transnational societies, the studies expand the types of children's peer groups to include peer and kin groups in multicultural and multilingual communities. The research reported on was conducted in Denmark, Dominica, England, France, Germany, Guatemala, Italy, Mexico, Nicaragua, Spain, St. Lucia, Sweden, Thailand, Turkey, and diverse US communities. The comparative perspective taken in this review revealed differences across communities and cultures in practices and ideologies that children could draw upon. For example, children freely invoked differing cultural images and ideologies of gender, age-based, or language groups that were salient in their communities. They did so by using various indexical signs (Ochs 1996). These included members' category terms – such as 'girl' and 'boy' (Goodwin 2011), 'Gypsy' versus 'Romany' (Evaldsson 2005) – as well as practices such as parental name-calling, as used among French adolescents of Algerian descent (Tetreault 2010). These terms and practices were freely invoked and challenged by children for their own purposes. However, the studies also revealed universals, such as the agency shown by children in utilizing these cultural resources towards constituting their local social order, as well as the potential importance of these children's group practices for the larger communities' cultural reproduction and change.

Many of the studies reviewed here examine how children utilize a variety of resources to build, manage, and monitor local hierarchies. These include selecting and enacting pretend roles privileged to speak with high- (and low-) status control act forms (Kyratzis 2007), and utilizing positionings of the body (Griswold 2007) as well as forms of sanctioning and exclusion (Evaldsson and Tellgren 2009; Goodwin 2006). A central finding was that positions of power and subordination emerge and unfold in sequences of interaction. A child who projects a position of control over the actions of others in the group through directives and positioning of the body, or who projects another child as being in control, must have that position ratified by other group members in sequences of interaction. The studies document that hierarchy, rather than being a byproduct of the age make-up of the group, is emergent and interactionally achieved. Hierarchy is negotiated in the moment, and a child who is constructed as a lower-status member in one context can challenge that status in another through their language practices in the peer or kin group, as seen in many of the studies reviewed here (e.g. de León in press b; Goodwin 2006; Griswold 2007; Howard 2009, this volume; Kyratzis, Marx, and Wade 2001; Reynolds 2010). As noted by Bucholtz (2007), power is also indexed by discernment; therefore, forms of assessment (e.g. gossip, ritual insult, and portrayals of others in compliments, games, and stories) become primary resources through which children build their social worlds. Children were observed to be continually defining and redefining the moral order through assessment and evaluation and to hold others accountable to the important social categories of the group.

Although the studies reviewed here were concerned with how participants constituted their social and moral order through publicly available resources in sequences of interaction during talk-in-interaction, an ethnographic perspective was also needed to understand children's categorizations and assessments. An ethnographic perspective reveals the 'wider social structures and discourses' (Evaldsson 2005: 764) that are available in the broader community of which the peer group is a part and also how the children agentively draw on, reproduce, and resist those ideologies available to them (Ochs 1996; Schieffelin 2003). The studies therefore show how children (even quite young children), not only adults, can be agents of cultural reproduction and change, thereby expanding the language socialization paradigm.

Several of the studies reviewed underscore the ingenuity of teens and children, not only in evoking negative characteristics of peers and others in situated interaction but in doing so through indirect, veiled, and humorous means. They index negative (and positive) social categories of their peers or tutors, or of the societies in which they live, through exploiting footings and participation frameworks and through appropriating others' words in pretend games, disputes, and stories. Enactments in the frame of play allow children to assume authoritative roles and stances and to explore relations among different voices of authority, sometimes allowing them to subvert those same relations. Through the evaluations and categorizations of person that they make in different situated activities (Goffman 1961: 96) of storytelling, ritual insult, and pretend play, children take up either common or divergent stances towards the target, building social alignments and local social order. In multilingual settings, children also show agency in assigning roles and places to their two (or more) languages in their talk and play (Paugh 2005; Schieffelin 2003) and in drawing on dominant discourses (Cekaite and Evaldsson 2008; Evaldsson 2005; Kyratzis, Reynolds, and Evaldsson 2010) in situated action with their peers.

In summary, the studies reviewed in this chapter examine linguistic practices entailed in child-based social control and negotiation that children across an array of diverse cultures make use of to build local social organization within their own 'arenas of action' (Hutchby and Moran-Ellis 1998) and hold one another accountable for the social activity in progress. The work reviewed here provides ethnographic examples of empirically grounded studies of how local identities and forms of moral and social order (which through time evolve into more enduring forms) are constituted by children as the product of moment-to-moment interactive practices within their peer and sibling/kin groups.

REFERENCES

Andersen, E. S., Brizuela, M., Dupuy, B., and Gonnerman, L. (1999) Cross-linguistic evidence for the early acquisition of discourse markers as register variables. *Journal of Pragmatics* 31(10): 1339–51.

Andersen, E. S. (1990) *Speaking with Style: The Sociolinguistic Skills of Children*. London: Routledge.

Antaki, C. (1994) *Explaining and Arguing: The Social Organization of Accounts*. London: Bantam.

Antaki, C. and Widdicombe, S. (1998) Identity as an achievement and as a tool. In C. Antaki and S. Widdicombe (eds.), *Identities in Talk*. 1–14. London: Sage.

Aronsson, K. and Thorell, M. (1999) Family politics in children's play directives. *Journal of Pragmatics* 31: 25–48.

Auer, P. (1998) Introduction: Bilingual conversation revisited. In P. Auer (ed.), *Code-Switching in Conversation: Language, Interaction, and Identity*. 1–24. London: Routledge.

Bailey, B. (2007) Heteroglossia and boundaries. In M. Heller (ed.), *Bilingualism: A Social Approach*. 257–74. New York: Palgrave Macmillan.

Bakhtin, M. (1981) M. Holquist (ed.), *The Dialogic Imagination: Four Essays.* Austin, TX: University of Texas Press.

Bauman, R. and Briggs, C. L. (1990) Poetics and performance as critical perspectives on language and social life. *Annual Review of Anthropology* 19: 59–88.

Berentzen, S. (1984) Children constructing their social world: An analysis of gender contrast in children's interaction in a nursery school. *Bergen Occasional Papers in Social Anthropology, No. 36.* Bergen, Norway: University of Bergen.

Blum-Kulka, S. and Snow, C. E. (2004) Introduction: The potential of peer talk. *Discourse Studies* 6(3): 291–306.

Bourdieu, P. (1984) *Distinction: A Social Critique of the Judgment of Taste.* Cambridge, MA: Harvard University Press.

Briggs, C. L. and Bauman, R. (1992) Genre, intertextuality, and social power. *Journal of Linguistic Anthropology* 2: 131–72.

Bucholtz, M. (1999) 'Why be normal?': Language and identity practices in a community of nerd girls. *Language in Society* 28: 203–23.

Bucholtz, M. (2002) Youth and cultural practice. *Annual Review in Anthropology* 31: 525–52.

Bucholtz, M. (2007) Word up: Social meanings of slang in California youth culture. In L. Monaghan and J. E. Goodman (eds.), *A Cultural Approach to Interpersonal Communication: Essential Readings.* 243–67. Malden, MA: Blackwell Publishing.

Bucholtz, M. (2011) *White Kids: Language, Race, and Styles of Youth Identity.* Cambridge: Cambridge University Press.

Burdelski, M. (2010) Socializing politeness routines: Multimodality and social action in a Japanese preschool. *Journal of Pragmatics* 42: 1606–21.

Butler, C. and Weatherall, A. (2006) 'No, we're not playing families': Membership categorization in children's play. *Research on Language and Social Interaction* 39(4): 441–70.

Cekaite, A. and Evaldsson, A.-C. (2008) Staging linguistic identities and negotiating monolingual norms in multiethnic school settings. *International Journal of Multilingualism* 5: 177–96.

Cheshire, J. (2000) The telling or the tale? Narratives and gender in adolescent friendship networks. *Journal of Sociolinguistics* 4(2): 234–62.

Clancy, P. M. (1986) The acquisition of communicative style in Japanese. In B. B. Schieffelin and E. Ochs (eds.), *Language Socialization across Cultures.* 213–50. Cambridge: Cambridge University Press.

Cook-Gumperz, J. and Kyratzis, A. (2001) Child discourse. In D. Schiffrin, D. Tannen, and H. Hamilton (eds.), *The Handbook of Discourse Analysis.* 590–611. Oxford: Blackwell.

Cook-Gumperz, J. and Corsaro, W. (1986) Introduction. In J. Cook-Gumperz, W. A. Corsaro, and J. Streeck (eds.), *Children's Worlds and Children's Language.* 1–11. Berlin: Mouton de Gruyter.

Corsaro, W. A. (1985) *Friendship and Peer Culture in the Early Years.* Norwood NJ: Ablex.

Corsaro, W. A. (1997) *The Sociology of Childhood.* Thousand Oaks, CA: Pine Forge Press.

Cromdal, J. (2004) Building bilingual oppositions: Code-switching in children's disputes. *Language in Society* 33: 33–58.

Cromdal, J. (2001) Overlap in bilingual play: Some implications of code-switching for overlap resolution. *Research on Language and Social Interaction* 34(4): 421–51.

Cromdal, J. and Aronsson, K. (2000) Footing in bilingual play. *Journal of Sociolinguistics* 4(3): 435–57.

Danby, S. and Baker, C. (1998) How to be masculine in the block area. *Childhood* 5(2): 151–75.

de León, L. (2007) Parallelism, metalinguistic play, and the interactive emergence of Zinacantec Mayan siblings' culture. *Research on*

Language and Social Interaction 40(4): 405–36.

de León, L. (in press a) 'Calibrando' la atención: Directivos, adiestramiento, y responsabilidad en el trabajo doméstico de los Niños Mayas Zinacantecos. In V. Zavala and S. Frisancho (eds.), *Aprendizaje, Cultura y Desarrollo*. Lima, Peru: Fondo Editorial de la Universidad Católica Pontificia.

de León, L. (in press b) 'The *J'lk'al* is coming!' Triadic directives and emotion in socialization of Zinacantec Mayan Children. In A. Breton and P. Nondedeo (eds.). *Proceedings of the 13th European and Maya Conference. Acta Mesoamericana* 21.

Du Bois, J. W. (2007) The stance triangle. In R. Englebretson (ed.), *Stance in Discourse: Subjectivity in Interaction*. 13–182. Amsterdam, The Netherlands: Benjamins.

Eckert, P. (1987) *Jocks and Burnouts: Social Categories and Identity in the High School*. New York: Teachers College Press.

Eckert, P. (2003) Language and gender in adolescence. In J. Holmes and M. Meyerhoff (eds.), *The Handbook of Language and Gender*. 381–400. Malden, MA: Blackwell.

Eckert, P. and McConnell-Ginet, S. (1992) Think practically and look locally: Language and gender as community-based practice. *Annual Review of Anthropology*, 21: 461–90.

Eder, D. (1995) *School Talk: Gender and Adolescent Culture*. New Brunswick, NJ: Rutgers University Press.

Eder, D. (1998) Developing adolescent peer culture through collaborative narration. In S. M. Hoyle and C. T. Adger (eds.), *Kids Talk: Strategic Language Use in Later Childhood*. 82–94. Oxford: Oxford University Press.

Ervin-Tripp, S. M. (1996) Context in language. In D. I. Slobin, J. Gerhardt, A. Kyratzis, and J. Guo (eds.), *Social Interaction, Social Context, and Language: Essays in Honor of Susan Ervin-Tripp*.

21–36. Mahwah, NJ: Lawrence Erlbaum.

Ervin-Tripp, S. M., Guo, J., and Lampert, M. D. (1990) Politeness and persuasion in children's control acts. *Journal of Pragmatics* 14(2): 307–31.

Ervin-Tripp, S. M. and Reyes, I. (2005) Child code-switching and adult content contrasts. *International Journal of Bilingualism* 9(1): 85–102.

Ervin-Tripp, S. and Mitchell-Kernan, C. (1977) Introduction. In S. Ervin-Tripp and C. Mitchell-Kernan (eds.), *Child Discourse*. 1–26. New York: Academic Press.

Evaldsson, A.-C. (2002) Boys' gossip telling: Staging identities and indexing (unacceptable) masculine behavior. *Text* 22(2): 199–225.

Evaldsson, A.-C. (2004) Shifting moral stances: Morality and gender in same-sex and cross-sex game interaction. The situational relevance of rules in same sex and cross sex games. *Research on Language and Social Interaction* 37(3): 331–63.

Evaldsson, A.-C. (2005) Staging insults and mobilizing categorizations in a multiethnic peer group. *Discourse & Society* 16(6): 763–86.

Evaldsson, A.-C. (2007) Accounting for friendship: Moral ordering and category membership in preadolescent girls' relational talk. *Research on Language and Social Interaction* 40(4): 377–404.

Evaldson, A.-C. and Cekaite, A. (2010) Subverting and reproducing institutionalized norms for language use in multilingual peer groups. *Pragmatics* 20(4): 587–605.

Evaldsson, A.-C. and Tellgren, B. (2009) 'Don't enter – it's dangerous': Negotiations for power and exclusion in preschool girls' play interactions. *Educational and Child Psychology* 26(2): 9–18.

Flores Nájera, L. (2009) *Los Directivos en la Organización Social del Grupo de Pares de Niños Bilingües de San Isidro Buensuceso*,

Tlaxcala: Un Enfoque Interactivo, Maestria en Lingüística Indoamericana. Mexico City, Mexico: CIESAS.

García-Sánchez, I. (2010) Serious games: Code-switching and gendered identities in Moroccan immigrant girls' pretend play. *Pragmatics* 20(4): 523–55.

Garrett, P. B. (2005) What a language is good for: Language socialization, language shift, and the persistence of code-specific genres in St. Lucia. *Language in Society* 34(3): 327–61.

Garrett, P. B. (2007) Language socialization and (re)production of bilingual subjectivities. In M. Heller (ed.), *Bilingualism: A Social Approach.* 233–56. New York: Palgrave Macmillan.

Garrett, P. B. and Baquedano-López, P. (2002) Language socialization: Reproduction and continuity, transformation and change. *Annual Review of Anthropology* 31: 339–61.

Gaskins, S., Miller, P. J., and Corsaro, W. A. (1992) Theoretical and methodological perspectives in the interpretive study of children. In W. A. Corsaro and P. J. Miller (eds.), *Interpretive Approaches to Children's Socialization.* 5–24. San Francisco, CA: Jossey-Bass.

Goffman, E. (1961) *Encounters: Two Studies in the Sociology of Interaction.* Indianapolis, IN: Bobbs-Merrill.

Goffman, E. (1967) *Interaction Ritual: Essays in Face to Face Behavior.* Garden City, NY: Doubleday.

Goffman, E. (1974) *Frame Analysis: An Essay on the Organization of Experience.* New York: Harper and Row.

Goffman, E. (1979) Footing. *Semiotica* 25: 1–29.

Goldman, L. R. (1998) *Child's Play: Myth, Mimesis, and Make-Believe.* Oxford: Berg.

Goodenough, W. H. (1965) Rethinking 'status' and 'role': Toward a general model of the cultural organization of social relationships. In M. Banton (ed.), *The Relevance of Models for Social Anthropology.* 1–24. London: Tavistock.

Goodenough, W. H. (1981) *Culture, Language and Society.* Menlo Park, CA: The Benjamin/Cummings Publishing Company.

Goodwin, C. and Goodwin, M. H. (1987) Concurrent operations on talk: Notes on the interactive organization of assessments. *IPrA Papers in Pragmatics* 1(1): 1–52.

Goodwin, M. H. (1990) *He-Said-She-Said: Talk as Social Organization Among Black Children.* Bloomington, IN: Indiana University Press.

Goodwin, M. H. (1993) Accomplishing social organization in girls' play: Patterns of competition and cooperation in an African-American working-class girls' group. In S. T. Hollis, L. Pershing, and M. J. Young (eds.), *Feminist Theory and the Study of Folklore.* 149–65. Urbana, IL: University of Illinois Press.

Goodwin, M. H. (2006) *The Hidden Life of Girls: Games of Stance, Status, and Exclusion.* Oxford: Blackwell.

Goodwin, M. H. (2007) Participation and embodied action in preadolescent girls' assessment activity. *Research on Language and Social Interaction* 40(4): 353–76.

Goodwin, M. H. (2008) The embodiment of friendship, power, and marginalization in girls' interactions. *Girlhood Studies: An Interdisciplinary Journal* 1(2): 72–94.

Goodwin, M. H. (2011) Engendering children's talk. In E. H. Stokoe and S. A. Speer (eds.), *Conversation and Gender.* 251–71. Cambridge: Cambridge University Press.

Goodwin, M. H. and Alim, H. S. (2010) 'Whatever (neck roll, teeth suck, eyeball roll)': Transmodal stylization and stance display in preadolescent girls' argumentative talk. *Journal of Linguistic Anthropology.* 20(1): 179–94.

Goodwin, M. H. and Kyratzis, A. (2007) Children socializing children: Practices for negotiating the social order among peers. *Research on Language and Social Interaction* 40(4): 279–89.

Griswold, O. (2007) Achieving authority: Discursive practices in Russian girls' pretend play. *Research on Language and Social Interaction* 40(4): 291–320.

Gumperz, J. J. (1982) *Discourse Strategies.* Cambridge: Cambridge University Press.

Gumperz, J. J. and Cook-Gumperz, J. (2005) Making space for bilingual communicative practice. *Intercultural Pragmatics* 2(1): 1–24.

Henderson, J. (2009) Flirting with Fashion: Anticipatory Socialization in a Tween Virtual World. Masters Thesis. University of California, Los Angeles.

Howard, K. M. (2009) Breaking in and spinning out: Repetition and decalibration in Thai children's play genres. *Language in Society* 38(3): 339–63.

Hoyle, S. M. (1998) Register and footing in role play. In S. M. Hoyle and C. T. Adger (eds.), *Kids Talk: Strategic Language Use in Later Childhood.* 47–67. New York: Oxford University Press.

Hutchby, I. and Moran-Ellis, J. (1998) Introduction. In I. Hutchby and J. Moran-Ellis (eds.), *Children and Social Competence: Arenas of Action.* 1–25. London: Falmer Press.

Jaffe, A. (2009) Introduction: The sociolinguistics of stance. In A. Jaffe (ed.), *Stance: Sociolinguistic Perspectives.* 3–28. Oxford: Oxford University Press.

Jorgensen, J. N. (1998) Children's acquisition of code-switching for power-wielding. In P. Auer (ed.), *Code-Switching in Conversation: Language, Interaction, and Identity.* 237–58. London: Routledge.

Keim, I. (2008) Linguistic variation, style of communication, and sociocultural identity: Case study of a migrant youth group in Mannheim, Germany. In V. Lytra and J. N. Jorgensen (eds.), *Multilingualism and Identities Across Contexts: Cross-Disciplinary Perspectives on Turkish-Speaking Youth in Europe. Copenhagen Studies in Bilingualism, Vol. 45.* 178–226. Copenhagen, Denmark:

Faculty of Humanities, University of Copenhagen.

Kochman, T. (1983) The boundary between play and nonplay in black verbal dueling. *Language in Society* 12: 329–37.

Kotthoff, H. (2010) Constructions of the romantic market in girls' talk. In N. Jorgensen (ed.), *Current Perspectives in the Study of Youth Language.* 43–74. Frankfurt: Peter Lang.

Köymen, S. B. (2008) 'Use your words': Tying to and commenting on the speech of others in toddlers' peer interactions in daycare. Paper presented at the American Anthropological Association. San Francisco, CA.

Köymen, S. B. (2010) 'I said "I don't want him do it"': Toddlers' usage of complement constructions within interactions in daycare. Doctoral Dissertation. University of California, Santa Barbara.

Köymen, S. B. and Kyratzis, A. (2009) Format tying and the acquisition of syntax in toddlers' peer interactions. *Proceedings of the 35th Annual Meeting of the Berkeley Linguistics Society.* 202–10. Berkeley: Berkeley Linguistics Society.

Kulick, D. (1992) *Language Shift and Cultural Reproduction: Socialization, Self, and Syncretism in a Papua New Guinean Village.* Cambridge: Cambridge University Press.

Kulick, D. and Schieffelin, B. B. (2004) Language socialization. In A. Duranti (ed.), *A Companion to Linguistic Anthropology.* 349–68. Malden, MA: Blackwell.

Kyratzis, A. (2004) Talk and interaction among children and the co-construction of peer groups and peer culture. *Annual Review of Anthropology* 33: 625–49.

Kyratzis, A. (2007) Using the social organizational affordances of pretend play in American preschool girls' interactions. *Research on Language and Social Interaction* 40(4): 321–52.

Kyratzis, A. (2010) Latina girls' peer play interactions in a bilingual Spanish–

English U.S. preschool: Heteroglossia, frame-shifting, and language ideology. *Pragmatics* 20(4): 557–86.

Kyratzis, A. and Guo, J. (2001) Preschool girls' and boys' verbal conflict strategies in the US and China: Cross-cultural and contextual considerations. *Research on Language and Social Interaction* 34: 45–74.

Kyratzis, A., Marx, T., and Wade, E. R. (2001) Preschoolers' communicative competence: Register shift in the marking of power in different contexts of friendship group talk. *First Language* 21: 387–433.

Kyratzis, A., Reynolds, J., and Evaldsson, A.-C. (2010) Introduction: Heteroglossia and language ideologies in children's peer play interactions. *Pragmatics* 20(4): 457–66.

Kyratzis, A., Tang, Y.-T., and Köymen, S. B. (2009) Codes, code-switching, and context: Style and footing in peer group bilingual play. *Multilingua: Journal of Cross-Cultural and Interlanguage Communication* 28(2–3): 265–90.

Labov, W. (1972) Rules for ritual insults. In *Language in the Inner City: Studies in the Black English Vernacular*. 297–353. Philadelphia, PA: University of Pennsylvania Press.

Li, Wei. (1998) The 'why' and 'how' questions in the analysis of conversational code-switching. In P. Auer (ed.), *Code-Switching in Conversation: Language, Interaction, and Identity*. 156–76. London: Routledge.

Loyd, H. (2006) Children's use of dialect and theatricality in creating spaces of autonomy and authority in Nicastro, Italy. Paper presented at the American Anthropological Association Annual Meetings. San Jose, CA.

Loyd, H. (2011) Growing up Fast: Girls' Rhetorical Practices of Resilience in Inner City Napoli. Doctoral Dissertation. University of California, Los Angeles.

Mendoza-Denton, N. (2008) *Homegirls: Symbolic Practices in the Making of Latina Youth Styles*. Oxford: Blackwell.

Minks, A. (2006) Mediated intertextuality in pretend play among Nicaraguan Miskitu children. *Texas Linguistic Forum (SALSA)* 49: 117–27.

Minks, A. (2010) Socializing heteroglossia among Miskitu children on the Caribbean coast of Nicaragua. *Pragmatics* 20(4): 495–522.

Mitchell-Kernan, C. and Kernan, K. T. (1977) Pragmatics of directive choice among children. In S. Ervin-Tripp and C. Mitchell-Kernan (eds.), *Child Discourse*. 189–208. New York: Academic Press.

Morgan, M. (2002) *Language, Discourse, and Power in African American Culture*. Cambridge: Cambridge University Press.

Nakamura, K. (2001) Gender and language use in Japanese preschool children. *Research on Language and Social Interaction* 34(1): 15–44.

Newon, L. (2006) *Sugar, Spice, and Everything Nice: A Linguistic Study of How Adolescent Girls Formulate Notions of Culture Through Evaluative Commentary*. Honors Thesis. Los Angeles, CA: University of California, Los Angeles.

Ochs, E. (1992) Indexing gender. In A. Duranti and C. Goodwin (eds.), *Rethinking Context: Language as an Interactive Phenomenon*. 335–58. Cambridge: Cambridge University Press.

Ochs, E. (1996) Linguistic resources for socializing humanity. In J. J. Gumperz and S. C. Levinson (eds.), *Rethinking Linguistic Relativity*. 407–37. Cambridge: Cambridge University Press.

Ochs, E. and Schieffelin, B. B. (1984) Language acquisition and socialization: Three developmental stories and their implications. In R. Shweder and R. LeVine (eds.), *Culture Theory: Essays on Mind, Self and Emotion*. 276–320. New York: Cambridge University Press.

Ochs, E. and Schieffelin, B. B. (2006) The impact of language socialization on grammatical development. In C. Jourdan and K. Tuite (eds.), *Language,*

Culture, and Society: Key Topics in Linguistic Anthropology. 168–86. Cambridge: Cambridge University Press.

Paugh, A. (2005) Multilingual play: Children's code-switching, role play, and agency in Dominica, West Indies. *Language in Society* 34(1): 63–86.

Pomerantz, A. (1984) Agreeing and disagreeing with assessments: Some features of preferred/dispreferred turn shapes. In J. M. Atkinson and J. Heritage (eds.), *Structures of Social Action: Studies in Conversation Analysis.* 57–101. Cambridge: Cambridge University Press.

Pomerantz, A. and Mandelbaum, J. (2005) Conversation analytic approaches to the relevance and uses of relationship categories in interaction. In K. L. Fitch and R. F. Sanders (eds.), *Handbook of Language and Social Interaction.* 149–71. Mahwah, NJ: Lawrence Erlbaum.

Pontecorvo, C., Fasulo, A., and Sterponi, L. (2001) Mutual apprentices: The making of parenthood and childhood in family dinner conversations. *Human Development* 44: 340–61.

Poveda, D. and Marcos, T. (2005) The social organization of a 'stone fight': Gitano children's interpretative reproduction of ethnic conflict. *Childhood* 12(3): 327–49.

Rabain-Jamin, J. (1998) Polyadic language socialization strategy: The case of toddlers in Senegal. *Discourse Processes* 26(1): 43–65.

Rampton, B. (1995) *Crossing: Language and Ethnicity among Adolescents.* London: Longman.

Rampton, B. (1999) Styling the other: Introduction. *Journal of Sociolinguistics* 3/4: 421–7.

Rampton, B. (2003) Hegemony, social class, and stylisation. *Pragmatics* 13(1): 49–84.

Rampton, B. (2006) *Language in late modernity: Interaction in an urban school.* Cambridge, UK: Cambridge University Press.

Reynolds, J. F. (2002) Maya children's practices of the imagination: (Dis)playing childhood and politics in Guatemala. Doctoral dissertation. Los Angeles, CA: University of California, Los Angeles.

Reynolds, J. F. (2007) 'Buenos días/((military salute))': the natural history of a coined insult. *Research on Language and Social Interaction* 40(4): 437–65.

Reynolds, J. F. (2008) Socializing *puros pericos* (little parrots): The negotiation of respect and responsibility in Antonero Mayan sibling and peer networks. *Journal of Linguistic Anthropology* 18(1): 82–107.

Reynolds, J. F. (2010) Enregistering the voices of discursive authority in Antonero children's socio-dramatic play. *Pragmatics* 20(4): 467–93.

Rindstedt, C. and Aronsson, K. (2002) Growing up monolingual in a bilingual community: The Quichua revitalization paradox. *Language in Society* 31: 721–42.

Rogoff, B. (1981) Adults and peers as agents of socialization: A highland Guatemala profile. *Ethos* 9: 18–36.

Sacks, H. (1972) On the analyzability of stories by children. In J. J. Gumperz and D. Hymes (eds.), *Directions in Sociolinguistics: The Ethnography of Communication.* 325–45. New York: Holt, Rinehart and Winston.

Sacks, H. (1995a) On some formal properties of children's games. In Gail Jefferson (ed.), *Lectures on Conversation, Vol. I.* 489–506. Oxford, UK: Blackwell.

Sacks, H. (1995b) Category-bound activities: 'The baby cried:' Praising, warning, and challenging; tautological proverbs. In G. Jefferson (ed.), *Lectures on Conversation, Vol. I.* 584–9. Oxford: Blackwell.

Schieffelin, B. B. (1990) *The Give and Take of Everyday Life: Language Socialization of Kaluli Children.* Cambridge: Cambridge University Press.

Schieffelin, B. B. (2003) Language and place in children's worlds. *Texas Linguistics Forum* (SALSA) 45: 152–66.

Schieffelin, B. B. and Ochs, E. (1986) *Language Socialization across Cultures*. Cambridge: Cambridge University Press.

Schieffelin, B. B. and Ochs, E. (1996) The microgenesis of competence: Methodology in language socialization. In D. I. Slobin, J. Gerhardt, A. Kyratzis, and J. Guo (eds.), *Social Interaction, Social Context, and Language: Essays in Honor of Susan Ervin-Tripp*. 251–63. Mahwah, NJ: Lawrence Erlbaum.

Shankar, S. (2008) *Desi Land: Teen Culture, Class, and Success in Silicon Valley*. Durham, NC: Duke University Press.

Sheldon, A. (1996) You can be the baby brother, but you aren't born yet: Preschool girls' negotiation for power and access in pretend play. *Research on Language and Social Interaction* 29(1): 57–80.

Shuman, A. (1986) *Storytelling Rights: The Uses of Oral and Written Texts by Urban Adolescents*. Cambridge: Cambridge University Press.

Shuman, A. (1992) 'Get outa my face': Entitlement and authoritative discourse. In J. H. Hill and J. T. Irvine (eds.), *Responsibility and Evidence in Oral Discourse*. 135–60. Cambridge: Cambridge University Press.

Spreckels, J. (2009) 'Now he thinks he's listening to rock music': Identity construction among German teenage girls. In A.-B. Stenstrom and A. M. Jorgensen (eds.), *Youngspeak in a Multilingual Perspective*. 31–53. Amsterdam: John Benjamins.

Stokoe, E. H. and Smithson, J. (2002) Gender and sexuality in talk-in-interaction: Considering conversation analytic perspectives. In P. McIlvenny (ed.), *Talking Gender and Sexuality*. 79–110. Amsterdam, The Netherlands: John Benjamins.

Tarım, Ş. D. (2007) *Turkish Preschool Children's Gender Practices in Peer Play*. Master's Thesis. University of California, Santa Barbara, CA.

Tarım, Ş. D. (2008) Turkish preschool children's gender practices in peer play. Paper presented at the Ninth Biennial Conference of the Center for Language, Interaction and Culture. University of California, Los Angeles, CA.

Tetreault, C. (2009) *Cité* teens entextualizing French TV host register: Crossing, voicing, and participation frameworks. *Language in Society* 38(2): 201–31.

Tetreault, C. (2010) Collaborative conflicts: Teens performing aggression and intimacy in a French *cité*. *Journal of Linguistic Anthropology* 20(1): 72–86.

Thorne, B. (1993) *Gender Play: Boys and Girls in School*. New Brunswick, NJ: Rutgers University Press.

Vološinov, V. N. (1973) *Marxism and the Philosophy of Language*. Cambridge, M. A. and London: Harvard University Press.

Willis, P. (1981) *Learning to Labor: How Working Class Kids Get Working Class Jobs*. New York: Columbia University Press.

Zentella, A. C. (1997) *Growing Up Bilingual: Puerto Rican Children in New York*. Oxford: Blackwell Publishers.

Zimmerman, D. H. (1998) Identity, context, and interaction. In C. Antaki and S. Widdicombe (eds.), *Identities in Talk*. 87–106. London: Sage.

17 Language Socialization and Exclusion

INMACULADA M. GARCÍA-SÁNCHEZ

Introduction

Whether one feels a sense of belonging to a particular social group depends to a large extent on the treatment received by others in public domains of social life (Appiah 2006; Levinas 1998; Taylor 1994), specifically whether one is allowed to assume and develop social identities compatible with sanctioned membership in a social group (Ochs 2002). In understanding how children and other novices are apprenticed through language practices and activities into specific childhood identities associated with other community identities that will help them to become competent members of a given social group, language socialization researchers to date have mostly focused on socially organized practices designed to socialize children into ways of acting, feeling, and knowing that are consistent with membership in that social or cultural group (e.g. Ochs and Schieffelin 1984; Schieffelin and Ochs 1986). Little is still known, however, about the socially organized practices that are inconsistent with fully fledged membership in a community and that may render certain groups of novices as 'outsiders' and as a second-class members of the social group. Based on a larger linguistic ethnographic study of Moroccan immigrant children in a rural community in southwestern Spain, this chapter discusses the everyday micro-genesis of social exclusion through the examination of naturally occurring interactions of young Moroccan immigrant children with their Spanish peers and teachers during the school day.

This chapter applies a language socialization perspective on social exclusion by documenting the interactional features of negative differential positioning through which Spanish peers construct marginalized social identities for Moroccan immigrant children. By laying out the linguistic and nonverbal displays that organize the complex architecture of exclusionary acts, activities, and stances, this

The Handbook of Language Socialization, First Edition. Edited by Alessandro Duranti, Elinor Ochs, and Bambi B. Schieffelin.
© 2014 John Wiley & Sons, Ltd. Published 2014 by John Wiley & Sons, Ltd.

chapter describes how Moroccan immigrant children, in being made the 'other,' are socialized into marginalized identities. In addition, the chapter considers how the cumulative effect of these negative daily experiences with peers may be consequential to Moroccan immigrant children's development of a more enduring sense of alienation. The examination of children's daily school life provides a window through which we can catch a glimpse of how Moroccan immigrant children in Spain may grow up with a feeling of not belonging, and also, most importantly, of how some of these processes of exclusion start in early- to mid-childhood – a crucial age in child development at which children start to navigate their own ways through societal structures and institutions (Garcia Coll and Szalacha 2004).

Moroccan Immigrant Children in Contemporary Spain

Contemporary migratory trends have led to the emergence of large Moroccan immigrant communities in Spain that have taken strong and visible roots in the country (Chacón Rodriguez 2003; López García and Berriane 2004). The visibility of these communities has grown on par with increasing levels of racialization and intense scrutiny directed towards Muslim and North African immigrants. This current climate of problematization and suspicion has also gone hand in hand with a growing sense of alienation and marginalization on the part of children and youths of immigrant families, who often feel less at home in the country than their parents, who emigrated to Spain as adults. Against this backdrop, the discourse that dominates contemporary political discussion surrounding immigration in Spain is that of a crisis of inclusion or a crisis of 'integration models.' Education has emerged as one of the primary spaces in which these critical questions about the inclusion, integration, and belonging of Moroccan immigrant children are debated and negotiated (Carbonell, Simó, and Tort 2002; Carrasco 2003; Franzé 1995; Mijares 2004; Pàmies-Rovira 2006). In this chapter, I raise important questions about the meanings of 'inclusion' in the everyday school lives of a group of Moroccan immigrant children in a small Spanish town.

One way of looking at the dynamics between inclusion and exclusion is through the understanding of educational laws and the school-stated curricular goals. Spanish educational and immigration laws state that all children under the age of 16 have a right to public and free education regardless of their parents' legal status. Moreover, in the town under study, because of the high concentration of Moroccan immigrants, the school launched a major revision of its curricular programs in 2000 to address issues of diversity. The main tenets of the new curriculum centered around creating a strong sense of community and a spirit of tolerance and respect for the cultural and linguistic heterogeneity of the students. In addition, the school instituted a set of core values – such as dialogue, friendship, and cooperation – intended to regulate the social life of the school; these were enacted through school-wide activities. Although the importance of these policies and educational practices is undeniable, previous linguistic anthropological studies of the inclusion of children with marginalized identities, such as children with autism and economically disadvantaged students, have emphasized that beyond laws and educational programs members of the school community – that is, teachers and peers – are crucial agents in the successful inclusion of marginalized children into the social life of the school (Goodwin 2002, 2006; Ochs et al. 2001). Positive relationships with peers, in particular, have been shown to be essential in the successful inclusion and socialization of those children most vulnerable to social distancing: 'Successful inclusion depends upon recipiently designed procedures for maximizing participation and understanding [...] the practice of inclusion rests primarily on unaffected schoolmates rather than teachers, who typically are occupied monitoring academic progress and disciplinary transgression across a range of children' (Ochs et al. 2001: 400). These findings about the importance of peers are consistent with those of educational research focusing specifically on ethnic-minority and/or immigrant children (Baquedano-López and Mangual Figueroa, this volume; Gil Conchas 2006; Suárez-Orozco, Suárez-Orozco, and Todorova 2008). Moreover, Goodwin's (2006) work on practices of peer exclusion in relation to social class has highlighted the schism that often exists between institutional ideologies and curricular goals and children's actual comportment towards peers with marginalized identities.

In this chapter, the systematic analysis of Moroccan immigrant children's relations with Spanish children and teachers at the public school of this rural community reveals how Moroccan immigrant children are constituted as the 'other' through routine participation in everyday interactions in which these children are consistently put into positions in which they are treated differently.

Language and Prejudice: Articulating the 'Other' in Discourse

Language has always been considered an important mechanism through which immigrants and other minorities can be consistently categorized as 'outgroups' and excluded from participation in many areas of social life. Certain speech practices have been deemed to play a pivotal role in the symbolic means of (re)production of ethnic prejudice and articulation of 'otherness,' as well as to function as important coercive mechanisms in a vast repertoire of practices of rejection of outgroups (Blommaert and Verschueren 1998; Verkuyten 1998, 2001). Over the last 20 years, a booming literature has examined everyday and institutional ways of talking about the 'other' in both discursive psychology and critical discourse analysis (Augoustinos and Every 2007), focusing on language about ethnic-minority groups, immigration, and race in political campaigns (Mehan 1997), textbooks (van Dijk 1987), parliamentary debates (Martín-Rojo 2000; Wodak and van Dijk 2000), the media (van Dijk 1991), and other forms of public discourse (Santa Ana 1999). These studies have generally adopted a top-down approach to the study of language and prejudice that casts language as a means of symbolic domination and reproduction of hegemonic ideologies and discursive regimes.

The analyses presented in this chapter, however, are concerned with the generation of social exclusion in the everyday-situated practices of individuals, more specifically in daily naturally occurring interactional practices of young Moroccan immigrant children with their Spanish peers and teachers during the school day. Special attention is paid to the discursive and linguistic practices that not only justify, rationalize, or normalize social exclusion but that also, in and of themselves, constitute practices of exclusion and 'othering.' Without trying to obscure or undermine the weight of the political, economic, historical, and cultural dimensions of the social life of Moroccan children and their families, the analysis presented below attempts to capitalize on the analytic richness of everyday interaction in discerning the emergent, moment-to-moment creation of social life and social relations. By laying out the complex architecture of exclusionary interactions and by describing Moroccan immigrant children's socialization into marginalized identities, this chapter considers how the origin of the experience of exclusion is a social interactional achievement that must be understood at the micro level of everyday interaction as well as at the sociohistorical level of the conditions and effects of contemporary migration and ideologies of otherness.

Becoming the 'Other': Socialization into Marginalized Identities

Although there was variation in the behavior of individual children, the relations between Spanish children and their Moroccan immigrant peers in the school were characterized by rejection and a systematic pattern of avoidance. Most obvious was the Spanish children's reluctance to have physical contact with their Moroccan immigrant peers. In addition, the behavior of Moroccan immigrant children in the school was constantly monitored by their Spanish peers, rather than by their teachers. In the fourth-grade class that I recorded and observed on a weekly basis, Moroccan immigrant children were often the targets of tattling and policing. Focusing more specifically on the practices of monitoring and policing that characterized a significant amount of the interaction between the Spanish and Moroccan children, a systematic analysis of the field data yielded a recurrence of three interrelated interactional practices: *acusar* ('tattling'), *mandatos* ('peer directives'), and *echar leña al fuego* ('fueling the fire'). In the following analyses, I will show that there is both an observable numerical difference in the frequency with which these practices occur between, for example, Spanish perpetrator–Spanish target and Spanish perpetrator–Moroccan target, and, more importantly, a difference in the way in which these practices are enacted in actual interaction. I have identified three linguistic and interactional dimensions that are critical in understanding how these interactional practices play a major role in the construction of social exclusion:

(1) *Linguistic encoding*: The role of grammar and linguistic encoding in the formulation of one's own and other people's actions is critical in the constitution of degrees of personal agency, responsibility, and ethical worlds.

(2) *Interactional positioning*: The architecture of participation frameworks is crucial in understanding how the differential ways in which targeted Moroccan and targeted Spanish children are positioned by others in these interactions also echo children's differential access to claims and rights in the larger social order.

(3) *Alignment*: Whether the teacher and the child's peers do or do not align with the action performed towards the targeted child and the way in which this alignment is displayed (positively or negatively) are important in the constitution, maintenance, and subversion of social identities and relations.

Acusar *(tattling)*

Tattling, as a cultural practice, is prevalent in the social organization of many children's groups, particularly in early- to mid-childhood. In spite of it being common, children soon learn that tattling is an activity that is socially frowned upon because it jeopardizes the social cohesion of peer groups and subjects them to the often problematic intrusion of adult authority figures. Given that tattling can be socially detrimental for the perpetrator, children were strategic about tattling when they resorted to it. As Figure 17.1 illustrates, Spanish children were twice as likely to tattle on their Moroccan immigrant peers than on other Spanish children. In addition, those Spanish children who were the victims of a tattletale were the most marginalized children of the group.

These numerical differences are underscored by the way in which tattling was realized in actual interactions, depending on whether the target child was

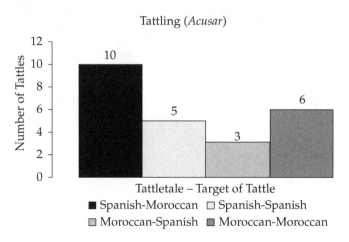

Figure 17.1   Instances of tattling.

Moroccan or Spanish. These differences will be analyzed in the following two examples.[1] In Example 17.1, students are individually reviewing the homework that they were supposed to have completed at home. The target of the tattling is Ana, a Spanish student, and the tattletale is her classmate Rosa, also a student of Spanish origin.

Example 17.1

Participants: Ana (A), Mimon (M), Rosa (R), and teacher (T).

1   R: *Ana no sabe hacer el ejer-el dos de la:::-dos~de~la~ficha*
         'Ana doesn't know how to do exer-number two of the- two in the handout'
2   T: *Qué no sabe hacer el dos de la ficha?*
         'That she doesn't know how to do number two in the handout?'
3   A: *Sí   [sé, Rosa*
         'Yes I [do, Rosa'
4   R: *[No::::*
                 ['No::::'
5   T: *Vamo' a ver, Rosa. Y TÚ por qué me dices que ella no sabe hacerlo?*
         'Let's see, Rosa. And why do YOU tell me that she doesn't know how to do it?'
6   R: *Porque lo estaba haciendo mal*
         'Because she was doing it wrong'
7   M: *No te importa*
         'It's none of your business'
8   T: *Ana ahora te lo veo yo y te lo explico*
         'Ana I'll look at it now and I'll explain it to you'

In Example 17.2, children are individually working on a math handout. The target of the tattling is a Moroccan student named Karim and the tattletale is a Spanish classmate.

Example 17.2

Participants: Karim (K), Spanish student 1 (SS1), Spanish student 2 (SS2), and teacher (T).

1   SS1:   *Maestra?*
           'Teacher?'
2   T: *Qué?*
           'What?'
3   SS1:   *Karim no está haciendo los deberes*
           Se está t-se está pintando con los rotuladores en la cremallera=
           'Karim is not doing his homework.

He's t-he is painting on his zipper with markers='

4 K: =°*En qué cremallera?*
        =°'On what zipper?'

5 SS1: *No:: mira*
          'No:: look'

6 T: *Karim, Karim* =
        'Karim, Karim'

7 SS1: = *Está así*
          = 'He's doing like this'

Figure 17.2 Peer demonstrates Karim's infraction by pointing at his jacket zipper.

Figure 17.3 Peer replays Karim's infraction.

8 T: *Tú comprendes que la ropa está para pintársela con rotuladores?*
        'Do you think that clothes are to be painted on with markers?'

9 T: KARIM (2.0) Karim.
        Mírame~que~te~estoy~ha   [*blando*
        'KARIM (2.0) Karim.
        Look at me I'm talking to
            you'

10 SS2:   [*Que desastre*
                                         ['What a disaster'

11   T: *Hoy vienes un poco tonto* (1.5) *U::mmm?*
            'Today you're acting a bit foolish (1.5) Hu::mm?'
12   T: *Karim, venga a trabajar y deja de tontear ya*
            'Karim, come on, work and stop fooling around already'

In analyzing the two previous examples according to the three key dimensions identified earlier, the first striking difference can be located in the grammatical structure of the tattle itself. Whereas in the first example of tattling (Spanish child–Spanish child) we have the structure 'X doesn't know Y' ('Ana doesn't know how to do exer-number two- two in the handout' (line 1)), in the second example of tattling (Spanish child–Moroccan child) the grammatical structure is '(X doesn't do Y) X does Z' ('Karim isn't doing his homework. He's t-he's painting on his zipper with markers' (line 3)). 'Y' refers to what the child should have been doing (his homework) while 'Z' refers to a violation of normative behavior and rules of self-comportment in this community ('he's painting on his zipper with markers'). The role of grammar is crucial in the moral characterization of people and in constituting varying degrees of responsibility, as well as in the formulation of different versions of reality (Duranti 2004, 2005). By unpacking the grammatical framing of speakers' versions of events, it is possible to ascertain participants' stances to those events, to other participants, and to social values and relations important in the community. In these particular examples, the semantic and grammatical structures of the verbs 'to know,' 'to paint,' and 'to do homework' require an actor. However, in Example 17.1, this participant role cannot be filled by an agent but by an experiencer, since there is no 'do' in the semantic structure of the verb 'to know' (van Valin and Wilkins 1996). In this way, whereas the targeted Spanish child is positioned as a passive experiencer who has, at most, epistemic responsibility, the targeted Moroccan child is positioned as an active agent and, therefore, assigned full moral responsibility for the infraction.

The negative characterization of the event as a 'wrongdoing' and of the Moroccan child as a fully responsible agent in Example 17.2 is further underscored by the tattletale's deployment of multimodal sentences (Goodwin, Goodwin, and Yaeger-Dror 2002) consisting of linguistic prompting – 'He's doing like this' – and embodied demonstrations of the infraction (see Figure 17.2 and Figure 17.3). The replay of Karim's infraction allows the perpetrator to orient to a notion of objectivity by showing that her tattling is the result of a norm-oriented evaluation of Karim's behavior. Thus, through the interplay of language and gesture, these multimodal sentences convey a 'negative affective embodied alignment' and a 'negative oppositional stance' not only toward the actions of the Moroccan boy but also toward the Moroccan boy himself (Goodwin 1998; Goodwin and Goodwin 2000; Ochs 1993).

This distinct grammatical pattern of unmitigated versus mitigated agency, depending on whether the target of tattling is a Moroccan or Spanish child, is not only constitutive of 'facts' and the personal character of their 'agents' but also moral and political statements organized around the differentiation of out-group and in-group membership. In other cases in which the grammar of blaming has been investigated, the mitigation of agency is usually the norm and the direct, negative, and unmitigated mention of the 'agent-referent' found in the examples of tattling targeting Moroccan immigrant children is very rare (Pomerantz 1978).

Finally, there is also a difference in alignment towards the action of *acusar*. In Example 17.1, when the victim of the tattling is another Spanish girl, both teacher and peers align negatively with the tattletale. In line 5, the teacher scolds the tattletale, 'Let's see, Rosa. And why do YOU tell me that she doesn't know how to do it?' The disaffiliation stance is further marked by the increased volume of *TÚ* ('YOU'). Then, in line 8, the teacher addresses Ana, the victim of the tattling, in a reassuring way ('Ana I'll look at it now and I'll explain it to you'). In addition, on line 7 one of the classmates also aligns negatively with the tattling, boldly disapproving of the action ('It's none of your business') while at the same time questioning Rosa's right and authority to be doing such reporting. In Example 17.2, however, when the target of tattling is one of the Moroccan immigrant children in the class, both teacher and peers align positively with the tattletale. The teacher proceeds to scold Karim; this scolding both sanctions the action of the tattletale and ratifies the negative moral identity that has been ascribed to the child. Moreover, although negative assessments are dispreferred and tend to be mitigated in conversation (Goodwin and Goodwin 1992; Pomerantz 1975, 1984), in the midst of the teacher's telling-off, one of the Spanish classmates produces an upgraded negative assessment of the Moroccan child ('What a disaster!' line 10). With this assessment, the classmate also ratifies the negative moral character of Karim and sanctions the actions of the tattletale.

Mandatos *(peer directives)*

Directives are overwhelmingly associated with an indexical feature of hierarchical and unequal social relations of power (Brown and Levinson 1978, 1979). Indeed, directives in educational settings, such as classrooms, are usually the prerogative of teachers. The directives analyzed in this section, however, are commands and other aggravated forms of corrections among children themselves, and are hence 'peer directives' (*mandatos*).

The vast majority of these directives targeted the Moroccan immigrant children in the classroom. The numerical differences in the case of *mandatos* are even more pronounced than in the tattling examples, since, as Figure 17.4 clearly shows, Moroccan peers were over three times more likely to be the victim of these forms of correction than their Spanish peers. These disparities are accentuated by the distinct way in which acts and stances organize the practice of *mandatos*, depending on whether the target child is Moroccan or Spanish. Example 17.3 and Example 17.4 are representative of these linguistic and affective differences.

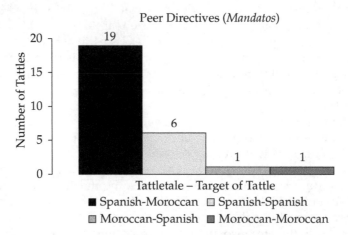

Figure 17.4   Instances of peer directives.

Before the sequence starts in Example 17.3, the music teacher had asked students to individually compose a rhythmic scheme. After finishing their compositions, the teacher had asked volunteers to come up to the front of the class and perform their rhythmic schemes using only hand claps and the syllables *ta* and *ti*. The rest of the class had to be attentive to the performance in order to identify the specific rhythmic pattern underlying their classmates' composition when they had finished. If the selected student in the audience offered the right rhythmic pattern, s/he was given the opportunity to go up to the front of the class and perform his/her composition. Since these types of activities were fairly popular among the children, there was often fierce competition for the floor. Because of the problems this competition generated, the teacher had enforced a rule that those students who wanted to be considered and selected to give the answer must raise their hands first. It was important to raise a hand as quickly as possible after the completion of the classmate's performance since usually those students who raised their hands first had more opportunities to be selected. In the following sequence, a Spanish student named Estrella is performing her rhythmic scheme for the class. No sooner is Estrella done with the first part of her composition than Roberto, another Spanish student, raises his hand conspicuously. Gloria, another Spanish student who also wanted to participate, sees Roberto's actions and issues a command directing Roberto to lower his hand.

Example 17.3

  Participants: Estrella (E), Gloria (G), Roberto (R), and teacher (T).

  1   ((Roberto raises his hand in the middle of Estrella's performance))

Figure 17.5   Roberto raises his hand while Estrella performs.

2	G:	*Na más ha dicho una o sea que baja la mano* ((to Roberto))
		'She has only said one so lower your hand'
3	T:	*Muy bien, Gloria, [eh? Te voy a poner aquí conmigo*
		'Very nice, Gloria, [ah? I'm going to put you here with me'
4.	E:	[*Ta-ta-ta-ta-ti* ((while clapping her hands))
		['Ta-ta-ta-ta-ti'

Example 17.4 is also extracted from one of the music classes. In this instance, a Moroccan student named Miriam is performing a task related to musical scales and is found out by her classmates to be chewing gum. The target of the peer directive is Miriam and the initiator of the command is one of her Spanish peers.

Example 17.4

Participants: Miriam (M), Spanish student 1 (SS1), Spanish student 2 (SS2), and teacher (T).

1	SS1:	*Tira ese chicle, Miriam*
		'Throw away that chewing gum, Miriam'
2	T:	*Miriam ese chi:::cle*
		'Miriam that chewing gum'
		((Miriam continues to perform the task))
3	SS2:	*Miriam, el chicle*
		'Miriam, the chewing-gum'
4	M:	*Vale::*
		Okay

((After completing her task, Miriam gets up and throws the chewing gum away while being scrutinized by two of her peers to make sure that she had actually thrown the chewing gum in the trash can))

Figure 17.6   Peers scrutinize Miriam's behavior.

Pragmatically speaking, performing a directive in interaction can be quite a delicate undertaking, since bald imperatives can threaten the social face of all participants involved, namely the speaker, intended recipient, and other hearers. A number of politeness strategies have been documented as being employed by social actors to perform such actions in as un-face-threatening a way as possible and to soften as much as possible their illocutionary force (Brown and Levinson 1978). The linguistic encoding of the directive in Example 17.3, 'justification + do X,' is an example of one of the ways in which that softening or mitigation is accomplished ('She has only said one so lower your hand,' line 2). The directive itself is preceded by a justification ('She has only said one'), which occupies the turn-initial position and therefore delays as much as possible the directive within the boundaries of the turn. This deferral of the directive speaks in itself to the dispreferred nature of this kind of social act. In addition to mitigating the directive, the justification provides a reason that socially validates Gloria's claims and rights to subsequently perform such a bald action. The rationalizing function of the justification is further underscored by the phrase *o sea que* ('so,' 'therefore,' 'thus,' etc.) between the justification and the directive proper.

In Example 17.4, however, the basic grammatical form is 'do X' with the name of the child either preceding or following the directive ('Throw away that chewing gum, Miriam,' line 1). This kind of unmitigated directive, which has been termed 'bald-on-record,' is one the most aggravated and negative-affect-laden social acts that can be performed in interaction. Moreover, according to Brown and Levinson (1978), a speaker performs acts baldly on record without redress when the speaker is vastly superior to the hearer or when the speaker is certain to be able to enlist audience support to destroy the hearer's face without losing his own. Therefore, this type of directive can be seen as indexically consequential in the interactional construction of hierarchical social relations, as well as in the constitution of firm boundaries of in-group and out-group membership in this community.

Following the pattern already described in tattling practices, there is also a significant difference in the ways in which other participants align with the peer directive in Example 17.3 and Example 17.4. Although at first glance it may seem that the teacher aligns positively with Gloria's directive to Roberto, a closer analysis of the turn reveals that, in fact, not only does the teacher disalign but also that, embedded in the disalignment, there is a subtle rebuke of Gloria's behavior ('Very nice, Gloria, ah? I'm going to put you here with me,' Example 17.3, line 3). After the apparent praise that initiates the turn ('Very nice, Gloria'), the teacher makes a comment that effectively questions and undermines Gloria's authority to reprimand her classmates by means of a directive. By stating that he's going to put Gloria by his side – that is, *in the position of the teacher* – he is also insinuating that it is not Gloria's prerogative to monitor peers' behavior and engage in admonitions. Thus, Gloria's directive is both nonratified interactionally and treated as inappropriate.

In Example 17.4, however, we find positive alignment of both teacher and other peers towards the *mandato* targeting Miriam. Following the peer's directive in line 1 ('Throw away that chewing-gum, Miriam'), the teacher publicly validates the directive in the official space of the classroom by repeating an elliptical version of the command in line 2 ('Miriam, that chewing gum'). In this shortened version, the focus is 'that chewing-gum,' which highlights the cause of Miriam's infraction and upholds her negative social identity as someone who does not comply with classroom norms of behavior. Similarly, another Spanish peer echoes both the original peer directive and the teacher's recasting of it by reiterating the command in line 3. It is important to note that the directive is adamantly repeated by peers and teacher alike until finally in line 4 Miriam acquiesces verbally – *Vale:::* ('Okay') – and then complies by getting up to throw away the chewing gum. It is also significant that, even when Miriam gets up to throw the chewing gum away, her behavior is closely monitored by two other Spanish girls in the class, who follow Miriam attentively with their gaze to verify that she has indeed thrown the chewing gum in the trash can (see Figure 17.6), since, often, children in the class would only pretend to throw the chewing gum away in similar situations. In this way, the Moroccan child's marginal social positioning is ratified by both the teacher and other peers.

Peer directives, in that they amount to aggravated forms of correction and public shaming, position Moroccan immigrant children in a very precarious and delicate position in the social structure of the school. Certainly, language socialization research has established that censure and shaming routines are an integral part of novice members' socialization into the conventional expectations of any given community (Brown 2002; de León 2005; Fung 1999; Lo and Fung, this volume; Ochs 1988; Schieffelin 1990). In discussing how shaming socialization routines are designed to include children in the larger community rather than to set them apart, two crucial elements have been identified cross-culturally: (1) a playful affective key achieved through the deployment of linguistic resources and the horizontal structuring of the participation frameworks and (2) the lack of negative consequences for children following these routines. As the analysis has already made clear, however, neither of these features are present in the practices of peer directives, nor in tattling or fueling the fire practices. Not only are negative disciplinary consequences likely to befall Moroccan immigrant children as a result of these practices, but also the affective key of these interactions is characterized as severe, oppositional, and disapproving.

With directives that target Moroccan children – particularly when censure is repeatedly voiced by classroom peers in an unmitigated, public, and direct way – we have a socialization routine in which children are positioned not only as uncouth classmates but also as nonmembers of the community; that is, those who have to be consistently reminded of rules and other norms of social behavior. Unlike shaming routines of young children by family members documented in other socialization studies, the shaming practices that Moroccan immigrant children encounter in school on a daily basis serve to exclude and not to include. Rather than a means of socialization into identities that are congruent with competent membership in the community, such practices realize Moroccan immigrant children's socialization into deviant and negative identities.

Echar leña al fuego *(fueling the fire)*

The practice of fueling the fire can be described as an aggravated variant of tattling in that fueling the fire is designed to call teachers' attention to the non-normative nature of the actions or behavior of another peer. Unlike tattling, however, fueling the fire sequences are initiated by the child who will eventually become the target of this practice with either an announcement of a problematic event or a particularly sensitive request to the teacher. In these announcements and requests, actions are strategically formulated in as benign a way as possible. What characterizes these sequences as fueling the fire is that these announcements and requests are followed by inflammatory comments from other peers. These comments constitute attempts at subverting the benign or accidental character of the original speaker's actions.

As Figure 17.7 illustrates, Moroccan immigrant children are almost twice as likely to be victims of these types of inflammatory remarks as Spanish peers. Further, the extent of the aggravation of these remarks in actual interactions is higher when the target of fueling the fire practices is a Moroccan child, as the analyses of Example 17.5 and Example 17.6 will show.

Example 17.5 is extracted from a music class. On the day of this recording, the children were going to rehearse a composition with half of the class playing instruments and the other half singing. In order to decide which children would get the instruments, the teacher carried out an impromptu oral review of the main concepts that they had been studying. Only those children who responded with two questions correctly were initially given instruments. However, at the end of the review, there were still a few instruments to give out. While the teacher is trying to decide the best way to hand out those instruments, María, a Spanish student, approaches him.

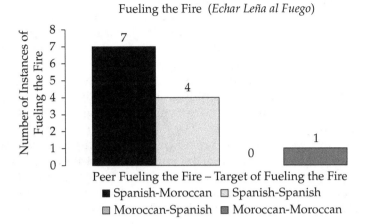

Figure 17.7   Instances of fueling the fire.

Example 17.5

Participants: David (D), María (M), and teacher (T).

1   M: (*xxx*) (*también*) *he dicho dos cosas bien* =
         '(xxx) (also) I have said two things right ='

2   T: *Has dicho dos cosas bien?*
         'You have said two things right?'

3   M: ((nods)) *Cuando has dicho tú* [(*xxx*)
         ((nods)) 'When you said   [(xxx)'

4   D: [*Sí pero no- no ha terminao de de* [*cirlas*
                                       ['yes but she didn't- she didn't finish
                                           [saying them'

5   T: [*No has rematao, María*=
                                       ['You didn't finish them off, María='

6   T: = *Venga coge un instrumento*
         = 'Come on, pick up an instrument'

Maria states that she has also answered two things right (line 1). The teacher responds in line two by repeating her claim with rising intonation ('You have said two things right?'), questioning María's statement and signaling the problematicity of her implied request for an instrument. When María tries to convince the teacher that she deserves an instrument, David intrudes in the middle of her turn with a comment directed to the teacher that is designed to persuade him of the opposite, namely that María does not deserve the instrument after all ('Yes but she didn't- she didn't finish saying them,' line 4). Although the turn is initially shaped as an agreement by the insertion of the agreement token *sí* ('yes') at the beginning of the turn, in the *pero* ('but') that follows, the *sí* ('yes') already fore-shadows what is indeed a negative refashioning of María's claim, namely that she has not provided two correct answers but only partially correct answers. The upshot is that she has not fulfilled the conditions for being granted an instrument. In terms of alignment, the teacher initially displays agreement with David's comment in line 5 ('You didn't finish them off, María'). In spite of his agreement, almost immediately the teacher continues in line 6 with 'Come on, pick up an instrument.' By granting María an instrument, the teacher disaligns with the fueling the fire practice.

Example 17.6 is extracted from a math class. Before this exchange takes place, students are getting ready to correct the homework that they were assigned the day before. The sequence initiator is a Moroccan student named Mimon, who announces that he has left his homework at home. Even before the teacher proceeds to scold him, his peers start making inflammatory comments.

Example 17.6

Participants: Karim (K), Mimon (M), Spanish student 1 (SS1), Spanish student 2 (SS2), Spanish student 3 (SS3), Spanish student 4 (SS4), and Students (Ss).

1   M: *Seño (.) Seño el ejercicio me lo he olvidao en casa*
          'Miss (.) Miss I left the exercise at home'
2   Ss: *Aahhg Aahhg*
          'Aahhg Aahhg'
3   SS1: *Pos ya sabes lo que dijo la otra semana la señorita*
          que el que no trajera los esos se iba pa casa
          'Well, you already know what Miss said the other week he who
              didn't bring the things would go home'
4   T: *Qué hacemos, Mimon? (1.0) Te mando a tu casa?*
          'What do we do, Mimon? (1.0) Do I send you home?'
5   T: *Hombre*
          'Please!'
6   K: *No te rías*
          'Don't laugh'
7   SS2: *Seño siempre se le olvida algo*
          'Miss he always forgets something'
8   T: *Bueno, los demás también callaros, vale?*
          'Well, the rest of you be quiet, too, ok?'
9   T: *Mimon, qué hacemos? (3.5) No, explícame (2.0)*
          Cuándo va a venir tu padre o tu madre a hablar conmigo?
          'Mimon, what do we do? (3.5) No, explain it to me (2.0)
          When is your father or your mother going to come to talk to
              me?'

10	M:	*No sé*	
		'I don't know'	
11	SS3:	*No sabes?*	
		'You don't know?'	
12	T:	*Hace ya mucho tiempo que te lo estoy diciendo*	
		'I've been telling you for a long time'	
13	SS4:	*Pos*	[*de:::sde-desde el año pasao*
		'Well'	[si:::nce- since last year'
14	T:		[*Ummm?*
			['Hmmm?'
15	T:	*Si:::*	
		'Yes'	
16	SS1:	*Es verdad desde el año pa* [*sao*	
		'It's true since last' [year'	
17	T:		[*Y tú en vez de arreglar las cosas y*
			portarte-y trabajar
			['And you instead of fixing things and
			behave-and work'

18   T: *Mimon, así no podemos seguir, e:h? Te voy a prestar el material yo hoy pero así no podemos seguir.*
'Mimon, we can't go on like this, eh? I'm going to lend you the materials today but we can't go on like this.'
((Mimon nods repeatedly))

19   T: *NO. Sí pero SÍ, no sí para que me calle, VALE?*
'NO. Yes means YES, not yes so that I keep quiet, OK?'

20   T: *ENTENDIDO?*
'UNDERSTOOD?'

21   T: *Mañana martes tengo yo e::h tutoría. Así que dile a tu papá o a tu mamá que vengan a hablar conmigo mañana, vale? (.) Vale, Mimon?*
'Tomorrow, Tuesday, I have e::h tutoring day. So tell your dad or your mom to come to talk to me tomorrow, ok (.) Ok, Mimon?'

22	T:	*Déjame tu agenda que*	[*te lo voy a apuntar*
		'Let me have your	[I'm going to write it down'
		daily planner that	
23	SS4:		[*Seño, no tienen muchas ganas de hablar*
			contigo
			['Miss, they are not too eager to talk
			to you'
24	T:	*Sssss* ((to SS4))	
		'Shhhh' ((to SS4))	

Figure 17.8   Gaze of child speaker directed at the teacher.

As soon as Mimon announces that he has left his homework at home ('Miss I left the exercise at home,' line 1), there is a series of scandalized exclamations performed in a choral, polyphonic manner by many of Mimon's peers ('Aahhg Aahhg,' line 2). These exclamations lay the foundations for the escalation that is to come in the following turns, since they are designed to draw other participants' attention (including, of course, the teacher's) to Mimon's infraction as a serious violation worthy of a stern reprimand. Then, in line 3, one of Mimon's Spanish peers produces the first inflammatory comment in ('Well, you already know what Miss said the other week he who didn't bring the things would go home'). This first comment is interesting not only due to its inciting nature but also because of its grammatical structure vis-à-vis its delivery. In particular, the gaze direction of the child speaker while delivering this utterance is crucial for escalation (see Mimon, circled, on the right side of Figure 17.8, and the child speaker looking at the teacher in the foreground on the left).

Although this sentence is produced with Mimon as the grammatical addressee, as is clear from the second person singular of the verb *sabes* ('you know') and the reference to the teacher in the third person ('what Miss said the other week'), the speaker is directly looking at the teacher, to the left, and not at Mimon when he speaks. The gaze direction then ratifies the teacher as the intended recipient of this utterance, which is in effect an attempt to instigate the teacher to suspend Mimon. In addition, with the verb form *sabes* ('you know') and the preposition *ya* ('already'), the Moroccan child is cast as a cognizant actor who is aware of both class rules and consequences and who has broken those rules knowingly.

The negative identity ascribed to Mimon is both ratified and amplified by another inflammatory comment produced soon after by another classmate. This comment does directly address the teacher ('Miss, he always forgets something,' line 7). By the use of the intensifier adverb *siempre* ('always'), the classmate effectively questions the accidental nature indexed by the verb 'forget' with which Mimon had characterized his own action. The use of modalizing terms, such as 'always,' to modify descriptions and formulations of action constitutes 'extreme case formulations.' Their use is prevalent in accusations and attributions of blame

(Pomerantz 1986) and is a common discursive means for constructing the behavior of immigrants and other minorities as deviant in everyday interactions (Verkuyten 2001). With the extreme case formulation, the second classmate manages to increase the escalation of the interaction by rendering ineffective Mimon's attempt to present his own action as an isolated accident and by characterizing him as essentially an irresponsible student.

This is not, however, the only instance of other peers' positive alignment with the action of *echar leña al fuego*. Other classmates continue to intervene and deploy inflammatory comments until the end of the sequence, in spite of the teacher's request for them to be quiet. In line 9, for instance, the teacher asks Mimon when his parents are going to come to talk to her and Mimon responds that he doesn't know (line 10). Immediately after this response, a third classmate repeats Mimon's response with a rising intonation ('You don't know?' line 11). The questioning, slightly ironic tone of the repetition casts doubt over Mimon's response and also helps to construct a negative moral identity for the Moroccan child. Furthermore, when in line 12 the teacher reminds Mimon that she has been telling him for a long time that she wants to talk to his parents, another classmate comes in specifying exactly how long it has been ('Well si:::nce- since last year,' line 13). Then, another peer also comes in to bear witness to the veracity of what the previous speaker had said, stating 'It's true since last year' (line 16). Throughout these instances of escalation, the Moroccan child and his parents are targeted and constructed as a certain kind of moral personae: the child is portrayed as a liar and as an irresponsible student who ignores class rules and his teacher's requests; the parents are portrayed as people who do not have any interest in the educational problems of their son ('Miss, they are not too eager to talk to you,' line 23).

Unlike the positive alignment of other peers, the teacher's position is this interaction is much more ambivalent than in previous examples. Certainly, the severity of her reprimand increases throughout the sequence and is congruent with the escalation trajectory of the children's inflammatory comments. However, although eventually Mimon is given a parental note with a request for an emergency parent–teacher conference, in the end he is allowed to continue to work in class with replacement handouts and materials. In addition, on two occasions the teacher tells the rest of Mimon's peers to be silent. In fact, although these examples are small in number, there are a handful of instances in which the teachers display ambivalence in aligning positively with the practices of *acusar* (tattling), *mandatos* (peer directives), and *echar leña al fuego* (fueling the fire) targeting Moroccan immigrant children, particularly when there are high levels of aggravation in the enactment of these practices, like in Example 17.6.

The architecture of social exclusionary practices experienced daily by Moroccan immigrant children at this school setting may be far more subtle and complex than blunt cases of verbal or physical abuse and rejection. As the previous examples evidence, construction of exclusion is a complex social act in terms of participation frameworks and the participants' alignments with respect to the speaker, the practice, and the target of the practice. In particular, when the target of the three practices analyzed is a Moroccan immigrant child, the participation frameworks and alignments that sustain them can be summarized as follows:

(1) In *acusar* (tattling), the intended recipient and addressee is always the teacher. Due to its public character, however, *acusar* is meant to be overheard by the Moroccan child and by other Spanish peers, who usually then ratify the actions and the stance of the tattletale.
(2) In *mandatos* (peer directives), Moroccan immigrant children are the main addressees. Yet, like tattling and fueling the fire, *mandatos* are designed to incite the teacher into taking disciplinary action. Therefore, teachers are crucial overhearers of the *mandatos*. As in the case of *acusar*, teachers as well as other Spanish peers regularly align positively with the speaker of the directive.
(3) In *echar leña al fuego* (fueling the fire), teachers are most commonly the intended recipients of the comments, although sometimes they can also have Moroccan children as addressees. This action, however, requires the participation of other Spanish peers who, although initially participating as overhearers, very often become active co-constructors of the action.

Figure 17.9 is a visual representation of the complex architecture involved in the constitution of exclusionary practices through language use in interaction. Social exclusion cannot be reduced to a directive or an accusation targeting a Moroccan child. Rather, social exclusion as an interactional achievement is accomplished by the ratification of the acts and stances of the original speaker by other participants in these interactions, namely teachers and other peers. In this sense, the diagram is meant to convey that the only one who is consistently excluded

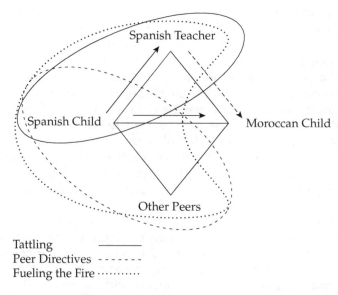

Tattling ————
Peer Directives - - - - - -
Fueling the Fire ··········

Figure 17.9 Alignment and participation frameworks.

from these alignments and differentially positioned in the participation frameworks of these interactions is the Moroccan child.

Moroccan immigrant children's reactions to practices of exclusion

Given the importance that the cumulative effect of these repeated constructions of negative social identities may have for children's sense of who they are, whether Moroccan immigrant children accept, resist, challenge, or try to subvert the negative social identities that they are habitually ascribed and the marginal positions they are frequently degraded to is significant.

Compliance and silence   There was individual variation in the observed reactions of Moroccan immigrant children to peers' practices of exclusion. Nonetheless, one of the most pervasive reactions was acceptance and cessation of the problematic behavior. In many cases, Moroccan immigrant children remained silent during these exchanges. It is important to contextualize children's acquiescence and silence in light of the strong alignments among Spanish classmates and teachers that were common in the enactment of the practices analyzed above. In fact, the higher the number of Spanish peers that joined in these actions and the clearer the positive alignment of the teacher towards the practices of *acusar* (tattling), *mandatos* (peer directives), and *echar leña al fuego* (fueling the fire), the more likely Moroccan immigrant children were to comply silently. It would be a mistake, however, to portray Moroccan children as impervious to these practices of exclusion or as passive victims, since in examples of apparent compliance there are indexes of resistance and opposition.

For instance, in Example 17.4, Miriam stopped chewing gum and got up to throw it away in the trash after two peer directives and the teacher's reprimand. Nevertheless, Miriam did not do so immediately and waited until she had fully completed the music task that she was supposed to be performing. Moreover, when Miriam's delay in action after the first peer directive and the teacher's reproof prompted a second peer directive, she turned to her peers, saying *Vale:::* ('Okay,' line 4) with a marked, elongated vowel length and a tinge of frustration in her tone of voice. Phonological features such as exaggerated vowel length, marked intonation contours, and voice quality are prime resources in the expression of emotion (e.g. Goodwin and Goodwin 2000; Ochs and Schieffelin 1989). While complying with peers' and teacher's directives, the suprasegmental features of Miriam's turn concurrently denote a negative affective reaction, conveying simultaneously her exasperation with and oppositional stance to the treatment she has just received.

Similarly, instances in which Moroccan immigrant children remain silent for many turns in these sequences can also be analyzed as having this double value of compliance imbued with a negative affective key. Indeed, children's silence has been analyzed as an interactional form of resistance, noncompliance, and even opposition, particularly in social situations when they feel threatened or under surveillance by adult authority figures, such as in parent–teacher conferences or medical interactions (Pillet-Shore 2001; Silverman, Baker, and Keogh 1998; van Dulmen 1998). It is not surprising that Moroccan children signal their resistance and their unwillingness to comply by staying silent and refusing to participate in interactions in which they may feel harassed and vulnerable. The more aggravated the actions and the more intense the complicity of peers and teachers, the more likely Moroccan immigrant children are to adopt silence as their interactional response. This is, for instance, the case in Example 17.6. Although this is the longest sequence analyzed in this chapter, Mimon, after announcing that he has left his homework at home, is virtually silent throughout the rest of the turns, minimally responding with nods to the stern scolding of the teacher and sometimes not even responding at all, as the repeated questions and long interactional silences in these two turns of the teacher evidence:

4   T: *Qué hacemos, Mimon?* (1.0) *Te mando a tu casa?*
        'What do we do, Mimon? (1.0) Do I send you home?'
9   T: *Mimon, qué hacemos?* (3.5) *No, explícame* (2.0)
        Cuándo va a venir tu padre o tu madre a hablar conmigo?
        'Mimon, what do we do? (3.5) No, explain it to me (2.0)
        When is your father or your mother going to come to talk to me?'

Another important dimension of analyzing these silences is the gestures and kinesic behavior of the children during these interactions. It is in the embodied displays of the children that their negative emotions regarding these practices of exclusion become most obvious. The children's kinesic behavior is characterized by grave and serious facial expressions; lowered heads, which are sometimes half-covered with their hands; and averted gaze, which often remain fixed on some item on the desk. The two framegrabs in Figure 17.10 illustrate these embodied reactions. The left-hand panel is from Example 17.6 at precisely the moment when Mimon is being severely reprimanded by the teacher in the midst of peers' inflammatory comments. The right-hand panel is from when, in Example 17.2, after having been the target of an accusation Karim's behavior is being censured by the teacher and negatively evaluated by one of his peers.

These embodied displays, which are congruent with reactions typically associated with shame, embarrassment, and humiliation, are good indicators of the children's distress and of the impact that their peers and teachers' negative assessments of them may have on Moroccan immigrant children's feelings about themselves.

Denial and confrontation   Sometimes Moroccan immigrant children displayed overt, verbal reactions to counter their peers' allegations. One of the most common responses of this sort found in the examples is the denial of the accusations. An instance of denial can be found in Example 17.2, when, after one of Karim's peers reports that he is painting on his zipper with markers, Karim defies the accusation by saying 'On what zipper?' (line 4) while looking at his jacket zipper with surprise (Figure 17.11).

Figure 17.10   Mimon's and Karim's embodied reactions.

Figure 17.11   Karim acting surprised.

More commonly, however, children would oppose their classmates' comments and accusations by producing the negative response cry *No:::* in the immediate next turn in a phonologically salient way. This type of response cry is commonly used by children in countermoves when managing conflict and disagreement within their peer groups (Goodwin 1998) and can be characterized by indexing a negative affective stance of opposition and defiance toward the action to which they are responding. Yet, Moroccan immigrant children's attempts to oppose the actions of their classmates by denying their accusations were often not successful because peers would respond to these denials with accounts and/or elaborate demonstrations, which often involved the replay of the Moroccan child's infraction (see, for instance, Example 17.2).

In a small number of cases, Moroccan immigrant children responded to their peers' actions in an even more oppositional way, verbally confronting their classmates and questioning the appropriateness of their behavior. In Example 17.7, for instance, Wafiya successfully manages to subvert an attempt at tattling by one of her Spanish classmates.

Example 17.7

Participants: Spanish Student 1 (SS1), teacher (T), and Wafiya (W).

1   SS1   *Qué haces Wafiya?*
           'What are you doing Wafiya?'
2   T: *Sssssssss. Ya:* ((proceeds to continue teaching the lesson))
           'Shhhhhhh. Enough'
3   W: *Qué te importa?*
           'What do you care?'

The sequence opens with a loud question by the Spanish girl ('What are you doing Wafiya?' line 1). At that moment, Wafiya was in fact misbehaving by playing at her desk with a small toy. However, Wafiya's actions were within the visual range of the Spanish girl, who happened to be sitting next to Wafiya. Thus, the question was not deployed to find out about Wafiya's activities at that moment but, rather, can be analyzed as a covert accusation designed to bring the teacher's attention to Wafiya's misbehavior – playing in class – while avoiding going on record with a tattle. The accusatory nature of the question is underscored by its public nature, since the Spanish student asks the question loudly enough for everyone else – including the teacher – to hear it, in spite of her physical proximity to Wafiya. In line 3, Wafiya responds to the Spanish girl's question in a confrontational way by posing another equally *false* question, in that it is not a request for information either but another covert accusation and an attempt to shame the Spanish girl for her action. Wafiya's question ('What do you care?' line 3) not only questions the Spanish girl's right and authority to police her peers' behaviors but also effectively deflects the negative identity the Spanish girl tried to ascribe to Wafiya by alternatively insinuating a negative social identity for the Spanish classmate, that of a tattletale or a teacher's pet. Wafiya's confrontational response follows an explicit disalignment by the teacher with the action performed by the Spanish classmate. Unlike in the majority of the examples found in the corpus, in this case the teacher neither acknowledges nor ratifies the covert accusation, but, after requesting silence, proceeds to continue with the lesson ('Shhhhhhh. Enough,' line 2). It is significant that such an explicit disalignment by the teacher occurs within one of the few examples in which Moroccan children verbally confront their peers and overtly challenge their classmates' attempts to portray them in a negative light. This example speaks to the decisive role of teachers in the social inclusion/exclusion of Moroccan immigrant children at school.

Like other responses discussed in this section – namely behavioral compliance, silence, embodied displays of emotion, and verbal denials – Moroccan children's overt challenges to their classmates' actions speak to the degree to which they are sensitive to and affected by these practices of exclusion. Moroccan immigrant children's confrontational responses are also indicative of their awareness of the indexical meanings of acts, actions, and stances and of their competence to counter them when participation frameworks allow, for example when the teacher or the rest of their peers do not align positively with the tattletale.

Overt oppositional responses are crucial in considering the impact these practices may have in Moroccan immigrant children's sense of not belonging. Example 17.8 is extracted from a longer fueling the fire sequence, in which, after severely admonishing Mimon, the teacher asks him to write a note to his parents in his daily planner about what has happened in class. A classmate asks the teacher whether she should write the note for Mimon:

Example 17.8

Participants: María (Ma), Mimon (M), and teacher (T).

1 Ma: *Maestra (.) Maestra Se lo apunto?*
              'Teacher (.) Teacher do I write it down for him?'
2 T: *Él sabe*
              'He knows'
3 M: *Qué te crees-*   [*qué te crees que yo soy tonto?*
              'What do you   [what do you think that I am dumb?'
                think-
4 T: [*Él sabe*
                        ['He knows'

When his classmate addresses the teacher, Mimon turns to his classmate with visible anger and responds 'What do you think- what do you think that I am dumb? (line 3). Responses such as this indicate that Moroccan immigrant children are distressed by these negative inclusion experiences and that they are aware of being regarded as different – or, worse, as inferiors – by their own classmates.

Conclusion

This chapter has analyzed the complex social and linguistic architecture of exclusionary practices and Moroccan immigrant children's socialization into marginalized identifications through routine ascription of negative identities. In considering the origins of the experience of exclusion and alienation as a social interactional achievement, this chapter has important implications for expanding current understandings of the role of language as an instrument of power and control, as well as the power of language to perpetuate social and ethnic inequalities. It also provides important insights for other lines of research that examine the role of language in the sociocultural and political processes through which 'otherness' and exclusion are constructed at macro-social levels. In trying to understand these complex phenomena – exclusion, alienation, and discrimination – the two levels of analysis must be viewed as symbiotic rather than dialectical.

In terms of the impact these practices may have in Moroccan immigrant children's sense of not belonging, it is important to understand how immigrant children are put into positions of being treated differently. Paths to exclusion and alienation involve a complex set of teacher and student social practices; apart from the differential way in which Moroccan immigrant children are positioned by their Spanish peers in these interactions, we must also take into account that these positionings are sanctioned more or less passively by the teachers. This may become an aggravating factor in immigrant children's feelings of school alienation: it is one thing to be victimized by peers, but when sanctioned by the teacher the practice acquires an institutional character for immigrant children, who do not find support among school professionals in positions of authority. In fairness to the teachers at this school, some of these practices of social exclusion are so subtle that they may be difficult to detect by school professionals (Goodwin 2006). Fights, insults, and racial slurs are easier to detect and, therefore, to address. Certainly, when violent or abusive behavior occurred (either verbal or physical), it was immediately stopped and addressed by the teachers. The Spanish children in the school were so aware of this fact that they would go to great lengths to avoid displaying openly racist behavior in front of teachers and administrators. One of the main implications of this work is that, beyond insults and fights, there is a need for teachers and administrators to take into account the complexities of children's social worlds and the dynamics of power and social control that exist within them.

It is of particular importance to recognize peer linguistic and communicative behavior as an effective form of social control and exclusion (see Goodwin and Kyratzis, this volume). The conclusions of this chapter challenge assumptions about children's unsophisticated knowledge of and contributions to sociopolitical realities concerning ethnic relations. While teachers and other adults may view children's racist behavior as naive (assuming that they do not understand what they are doing) or as merely mimicking what they hear at home, ethnographic work has begun to show that children have very sophisticated understandings of ethnic marginality (Devine and Kelly 2006; van Ausdale and Feagin 2001) and are able to perpetuate with their actions larger sociopolitical realities concerning ethnic relations in their immediate environment.

NOTES

1   The examples presented here were chosen because they are simultaneously compact in length and fairly representative of the ways in which these practices would usually unfold in the context of this classroom.

REFERENCES

Appiah, K. A. (2006) The politics of identity. *Daedalus: Journal of the American Academy of Arts and Sciences* Fall: 15–22.

Augoustinos, M. and Every, D. (2007) The language of 'race' and prejudice: A discourse of denial, reason, and liberal-practical politics. *Journal of Language and Social Psychology* 23: 123–41.

Blommaert, J. and Verschueren, J. (1998) *Debating Diversity: Analyzing the Discourse of Tolerance.* London: Routledge.

Brown, P. (2002) Everyone has to lie in Tzeltal. In S. Blum-Kulka and C. Snow (eds.), *Talking to Adults.* 214–75. Mahwah, NJ: Lawrence Erlbaum.

Brown, P. and Levinson, S. (1978) Universals in language use: Politeness phenomena. In E. N. Goody (ed.), *Questions and Politeness Strategies in Social Interaction.* 56–311. Cambridge: Cambridge University Press.

Brown, P. and Levinson, S. (1979) Social structure, groups, and interaction. In K. Scherer and H. Giles (eds.), *Social Markers in Speech.* 291–341. Cambridge: Cambridge University Press.

Carbonell, J., Simó, N., and Tort, A. (2002) *Magribins a Les Aules.* Vic (Barcelona), Spain: Eumo Editorial.

Carrasco, S. (2003) La escolarización de hijos e hijas inmigrantes y de minorías etnico-culturales en España. *Revista de Educación* 330: 99–136.

Chacón Rodríguez, L. (2003) La inmigración en España: Los desafíos de la construcción de una nueva sociedad. *Migraciones* 14: 219–304.

de León, L. (2005) *La Llegada del Alma: Lenguaje, Infancia y Socialización entre los Mayas de Zinacantán.* México: Publicaciones de la Casa Chata.

Devine, D. and Kelly, M. (2006) 'I just don't want to get picked on by anybody': Dynamics of inclusion and exclusion in a newly multi-ethnic Irish primary school. *Children and Society* 20(2): 128–39.

Duranti, A. (2004) Agency in language. In A. Duranti (ed.), *Companion to Linguistic Anthropology.* 451–73. Malden, MA: Blackwell Publishing.

Duranti, A. (2005) *Lingua, Cultura e Intercultural: L'italiano e le Altre Lingue. Copenhagen Studies in Language, 31.*

Copenhagen, Denmark: Samfundslitteratur Press.

Franzé, A. (1995) La población infantil marroquí en la escuela española. In *Atlas de la Inmigración Magrebí en España. Taller de Estudios Internacionales Mediterráneos.* 218–20. Madrid, Spain: UA Ediciones.

Fung, H. (1999) Becoming a moral child: The socialization of shame among young Chinese children. *Ethos* 27(2): 180–209.

Garcia Coll, C. and Szalacha, L. A. (2004) The multiple contexts of middle childhood. *The Future of Children* 14(2): 91–7.

Gil Conchas, G. (2006). *The Color of Success: Race and High-Achieving Urban Youth.* New York: Teachers College Press.

Goodwin, C. and Goodwin, M. H. (1992) Assessments and the construction of context. In A. Duranti and C. Goodwin (eds.), *Rethinking Context: Language as an Interactive Phenomenon.* 147–89. Cambridge: Cambridge University Press.

Goodwin, C. and Goodwin, M. H. (2000) Emotion within situated activity. In N. Budwig, I. C. Uzgiris, and J. V. Wertsch (eds.), *Communication: An Arena of Development.* 33–54. Mahwah, NJ: Lawrence Erlbaum.

Goodwin, M. H. (1998) Games of stance: Conflict and footing in hopscotch. In S. Hoyle and C. Temple Adger (eds.), *Kids' Talk: Strategic Language Use in Later Childhood.* 23–46. New York: Oxford University Press.

Goodwin, M.H. (2002). Building power asymmetries in girls' interaction. *Discourse & Society* 13(6): 715–30.

Goodwin, M. H. (2006) *The Hidden Life of Girls: Games of Stance, Status, and Exclusion.* Malden, MA: Blackwell Publishing.

Goodwin, M. H., Goodwin, C., and Yaeger-Dror, M. (2002) Multi-modality in girls' game disputes. *Journal of Pragmatics* 34: 1621–49.

Levinas, E. (1998) *Entre Nous: Thinking-of-the-Other*. New York: Columbia University Press.

López García, B. and Berriane, M. (eds.) (2004) *Atlas de la inmigración marroquí en España*. Madrid, Spain: Universidad Autónoma de Madrid.

Martín-Rojo, L. (2000) Spain, outerwalls of the European Fortress: Analysis of the parliamentary debates on the immigration policy in Spain. In R. Wodak and T. A. van Dijk (eds.), *Racism at the Top. Parliamentary Discourses on Ethnic Issues in Six European States*. 169–220. Klagenfurt, Austria: Drava Verlag.

Mehan, H. (1997) The discourse of the illegal immigration debate: A case study in the politics of representation. *Discourse & Society* 8: 249–70.

Mijares, L. (2004) *Aprendiendo a Ser Marroquíes. Inmigración y Escuela en España*. Doctoral Dissertation. Madrid, Spain: Universidad Autónoma de Madrid.

Ochs, E. (1988) *Culture and Language Development: Language Acquisition and Language Socialization in a Samoan Village*. Cambridge: Cambridge University Press.

Ochs, E. (1993) Constructing social identity: A language socialization perspective. *Research on Language and Social Interaction* 26(3): 287–306.

Ochs, E. (2002) Becoming a speaker of culture. In C. Kramsch (ed.), *Language Socialization and Language Acquisition: Ecological Perspectives*. 99–120. New York: Continuum Press.

Ochs, E., Kremer-Sadlik, T., Solomon, O., and Sirota, K. G. (2001). Inclusion as a social practice: Views of children with autism. *Discourse Studies* 10(3): 399–419.

Ochs, E. and Schieffelin, B. B. (1984) Language acquisition and socialization: Three developmental stories. In R. Shweder and R. LeVine (eds.), *Culture Theory: Mind, Self, and Emotion*. 276–320. Cambridge: Cambridge University Press.

Ochs, E. and Schieffelin, B. B. (1989) Language has a heart. *Text* 9(1): 7–25.

Pàmies-Rovira, J. (2006) *Dinámicas Escolares y Comuntarias de los Hijos e Hijas de Familias Inmigradas de la Yebala en la Periferia de Barcelona*. Doctoral Dissertation. Barcelona, Spain: Universitat Autònoma de Barcelona.

Pillet-Shore, D. M. (2001) *'Doing Pretty Well': How Teachers Manage the Interactional Environment of Unfavorable Student Evaluation in Parent–Teacher Conferences*. Master's Thesis. Los Angeles, CA: University of California, Los Angeles.

Pomerantz, A. M. (1975) *Second Assessments: A Study of Some Features of Agreements/Disagreements*. Doctoral Dissertation. Irvine, CA: University of California, Irvine.

Pomerantz, A. M. (1978) Attributions of responsibility: Blamings. *Sociology* 12: 115–21.

Pomerantz, A. M. (1984) Agreeing and disagreeing with assessments: Some features of preferred/ dispreferred turn shapes. In M. Atkinson and J. Heritage (eds.), *Structures of Social Action: Studies in Conversation Analysis*. 57–101. Cambridge: Cambridge University Press.

Pomerantz, A. M. (1986) Extreme case formulations: A way of legitimizing claims. *Human Studies* 9: 219–30.

Santa Ana, O. (1999) 'Like an animal I was treated': Anti-immigrant metaphor in US public discourse. *Discourse & Society* 10: 191–224.

Schieffelin, B. B. (1990) *The Give and Take of Everyday Life: Language Socialization of Kaluli Children*. Cambridge: Cambridge University Press.

Schieffelin, B. B. and Ochs, E. (eds.) (1986) *Language Socialization across Cultures*. Cambridge: Cambridge University Press.

Silverman, D., Baker, C., and Keogh, J. (1998) The case of the silent child: Advice-giving and advice-reception in parent–teacher interviews. In I. Hutchby and J. Moran-Ellis (eds.), *Children and Social Competence: Arenas of Action*. 222–40. London: Falmer.

Suárez-Orozco, C., Suárez-Orozco, M. M., and Todorova, I. (2008). *Learning a New Land: Immigrant Students in American Society*. Cambridge, MA: Harvard University Press.

Taylor, C. (1994) The politics of recognition. In A. Gutman (ed.), *Multiculturalism: Examining the Politics of Recognition*. 25–73. Princeton, NJ: Princeton University Press.

van Ausdale, D. and Feagin, J. R. (2001) *The First R: How Children Learn Race and Racism*. Lanham, MD: Rowman and Littlefield Publishers, Inc.

van Dijk, T. (1987) *Communicating Racism: Ethnic Prejudice in Thought and Talk*. Newbury Park, CA: Sage Publications.

van Dijk, T. A. (1991) *Racism and the Press. Critical Studies in Racism and Migration*. London: Routledge.

van Dulmen, A. M. (1998) Children's contributions to pediatric outpatient encounters. *Pediatrics* 102: 563–8.

van Valin, R. D. and Wilkins, D. P. (1996) The case for 'effector': Case roles, agents, and agency revisited. In M. Shibatani and S. A. Thompson (eds.), *Grammatical Constructions. Their Form and Meaning*. Oxford: Clarendon Press.

Verkuyten, M. (1998) Personhood and accounting for racism in conversation. *Journal for the Theory of Social Behavior* 28(2):147–67.

Verkuyten, M. (2001) 'Abnormalization' of ethnic minorities in conversation. *The British Psychological Society* 40: 257–78.

Wodak, R. and van Dijk, T. (eds.) (2000) *Racism at the Top. Parliamentary Discourses on Ethnic Issues in Six European States*. Klagenfurt, Austria: Drava Verlag.

Part IV Aesthetics and Imagination

The studies presented in this handbook demonstrate in detail that language is an important instrument for directing new members' attention and guiding their actions so that they behave in socially and culturally acceptable ways. Language is also shown to be a goal of socialization: those who enter a new community must do so by acquiring particular linguistic skills so as to make their communication culturally meaningful and contextually appropriate. As both instrument and goal of socialization, language cannot but be a locus of normativity. Children and other novices are encouraged to conform to societal norms and members' expectations through the ways in which they are talked to and about. In turn, these novices contribute to the reproduction of such norms and expectations by learning the ways of speaking that will get them what they need or want.

But something is left out of this description of language socialization, as stated by Elinor Ochs and Bambi B. Schieffelin (this volume), who reject the exclusively normative interpretation of the term 'socialization.' Citing Edward Sapir's view of the importance of individual creativity and Margaret Mead's statement that predictability and plasticity always coexist in society, Ochs and Schieffelin emphatically recognize the agency that children and novices enact and display in their own development. Given this theoretical stance, there remains a challenge for the language socialization paradigm: how are creativity and conformity integrated into the lives of children and novices as well as into our theory of their development? As always in the study of human behavior, one possible path toward answering this question is to look at what people do in their everyday lives. If, indeed, human development is based upon or even made possible by both the individual's creative impulse and society's call for conformity, we should be able to find these two poles of the human experience in the phenomena that have been documented and analyzed over the last several decades of research on the 'context of culture' of human development. In particular, we should be able to identify acts, activities, and situations where creativity is displayed or even encouraged.

The Handbook of Language Socialization, First Edition. Edited by Alessandro Duranti, Elinor Ochs, and Bambi B. Schieffelin.
© 2014 John Wiley & Sons, Ltd. Published 2014 by John Wiley & Sons, Ltd.

This is precisely the assumption that guides the three chapters in Part IV. The chapters focus on phenomena that reveal the roles and uses of imagination, creativity, and spontaneity across cultural activities and social settings. In so doing, each chapter presents data and analytical distinctions that further refine our understanding of language socialization.

In 'Language Socialization in Art and Science,' Shirley Brice Heath (Chapter 18) invites us to shift the attention almost exclusively given to language development and language practices towards activities that demonstrate the importance of observation, experimentation, and discovery, all forms of engagement with the surrounding world that can happen without language. One of her contributions is to foreground aspects of human cognition, interaction, and communication that are often taken for granted in developmental studies. Citing research in neuroscience as well as ethnographic studies of everyday life in what she calls 'remote indigenous communities,' Heath underscores the importance of visualization in cognitive and social development, arguing that seeing provides access to a wealth of information that children and novices need in order to achieve joint attention, a precondition for the development of children's ability to coordinate, cooperate, and communicate. A review of the literature on socialization among Aborigines in Australia shows that in their communities children are expected to use their observational skills at an early age to engage in hunting, acquire the vocabulary for talking about the natural world, make up toys, and draw scenes that represent creation stories known under the name of 'the Dreaming' (Myers 1991). All of these skills become relevant in the school context, where they are reframed within European notions of art and science, which favors linguistic competence over visualization and dexterity. In her discussion of the activities and skills that are potentially relevant for developing artistic and scientific competence, Heath returns to the theme of continuity and discontinuity between primary socialization and secondary socialization that characterized her earlier groundbreaking research on literacy events in three different communities in the United States (Heath 1983).

'Language Socialization and Verbal Improvisation,' by Alessandro Duranti and Steven P. Black (Chapter 19), explores a theme, improvisation, that is relatively new to the field of language socialization and, more generally, to the study of human development. The interest in the role and place of improvisation in language socialization originates from two sets of observations. The first is that in all kinds of daily activities children and adults are confronted with situations that require them to do something in new and unscripted ways. The second is that when we review the literature on language acquisition and language socialization we discover that variation is very common. This means that children like to both repeat and vary what they hear others say and what they themselves come up with. Duranti and Black explore verbal improvisation in play and other creative activities and distinguishes between situations in which improvisation is encouraged or at least expected and situations in which it is negatively sanctioned. Drawing from the literature in the arts, especially music, the chapter also dispels the idea that improvisation is random or completely unpredictable behavior, arguing that it typically consists of patterned actions that can be interpreted by others, whether coperformers or audience members. This is also true of verbal improvisation, not only in established artistic genres such as 'free style,' hip hop, or the Tuscan *contrasto*, but also in spontaneous creative behavior such joking among adults as well as among young children. Two examples taken from pretend play among a group of Samoan children show that new contributions to a series of joking turns are built upon a skillful alternation of repetition and variation. Furthermore, the same examples show that each line is being evaluated on the spot by co-participants in the exchange. Building on these and other cases, the chapter ends with a working definition of socialization into verbal improvisation that recognizes the practical, aesthetic, and moral evaluations that all performers are subject to.

The third and last chapter of this part, 'Language Socialization and Verbal Play,' by Karin Aronsson (Chapter 20), explores the implications and outcomes of the interactions that produce playful verbal acts. Aronsson makes the important point that to think about the aesthetics of talk means to understand the type of participation that a given verbal performance makes possible or requires. Children seem to be aware early on of the need to linguistically frame – for example, through repetition – certain interactions as playful. Over time, as shown by a number of socialization studies, children acquire more subtle ways of using language to signal the nature of their activity to each other and to any bystanders. In addition to requiring joint attention, the play activities discussed by Aronsson are also subject to timely and rapid evaluation in a manner similar to that illustrated in the examples provided by Duranti and Black (this volume). Thus, commentary and evaluation during computer games must conform to the rhythm and speed of the game that is being played, thereby showing a subordination of some aspects of meta-talk to the primary play activity. Another connection with the chapter on improvisation is that play can be quite 'serious.' This point is demonstrated by a number of studies that focus on games that involve teasing, a practice that is built on the tension between pleasure and fear, two emotions whose exploitation across contexts has been subject to psychoanalytic, developmental, social, and cultural interpretations. From Aronsson's discussion we learn that, instead of proving itself to be a liminal space where societal distinctions and tensions are suspended, children's play activities can reproduce and in some cases accentuate the forms of inequality found in the society at large (see also Goodwin and Kyratzis, this volume). The hierarchical organization and unequal distribution of roles is largely exhibited through language by means of the speaking roles that children have access to, the labeling of the characters they enact, the registers used in the exchange, and the stereotyping that they draw from and reproduce through their talk. Of course, children may try to resist or subvert society's normative order through their actions. Resistance to linguistic and other societal norms is indeed common in play activities, where mislabeling, insulting, threatening, gossiping and other usually negatively sanctioned acts are accepted and sometimes even rewarded as instances of virtuoso performance. The maxim 'to be entertaining' proposed by Aronsson as a guiding principle of children's verbal interactions across social situations captures an impulse that has universal appeal and is channeled into culture-specific activities with great implications for socialization.

Overall, these three chapters can be read as an invitation to foreground creativity and aesthetics in the study of children's and novices' socialization, with the somber reminder that in playing with words, roles, hierarchies, and institutions, children and novices, like adults and experts, continue to be part of social worlds that are highly structured and often unforgiving.

REFERENCES

Heath, S. B. (1983) *Ways with Words: Language, Life and Work in Communities and Classrooms*. Cambridge: Cambridge University Press.

Myers, F. (1991) *Pintupi Country, Pintupi Self: Sentiment, Place, and Politics Among Western Desert Aborigines*. Berkeley, CA: University of California Press.

18 Language Socialization in Art and Science

SHIRLEY BRICE HEATH

Introduction

With the exception of mathematics, which relies on numeral and other symbol systems and thus needs verbal explication for initiates, scientific and artistic activities have throughout history depended primarily on the capacity of the human species to observe, experiment, imagine, and explore. From infancy through the life course, individuals undertake initiatives aesthetic in their design and delivery and reflective of the need of humans to know their natural surroundings, to figure out how things work, and to discover what lies beyond the immediate horizon. In this chapter I argue that across societies, outside of formal education settings, language plays a relatively minor role in children's socialization into art and science. Other human resources – visual, gestural, olfactory, and tactile – precede, override, or complement the linguistic throughout the early years as the young prepare to advance their skills and knowledge in science and art.

Definitions of art and science differ significantly across societies. Some languages have no general term that refers to either art or science. In this chapter, 'art' refers to any purposefully created form of representation to which its creators assign an aesthetic and communicative valuation. 'Art' includes painting, drawing, and other visual arts; sculpture; oral and written literature; dance; music (including instrument creation); video films and still photographs; architecture; and garden development. All these forms have some permanence, but 'art' may also refer to temporary forms of creation, such as ice sculpture, presentation of food, and sand painting. 'Science' is taken to be the conceptualization of systems of process and categorization in the physical and natural world for which science-makers believe an objective reality exists. Across societies, art and science carry

The Handbook of Language Socialization, First Edition. Edited by Alessandro Duranti, Elinor Ochs, and Bambi B. Schieffelin.
© 2014 John Wiley & Sons, Ltd. Published 2014 by John Wiley & Sons, Ltd.

close relationships with cosmology, religion, and beliefs about human origin and destiny.

This chapter suggests that a human universal in early learning of science and art is reliance on seeing and doing and that verbal instruction and explication have come only in recent centuries to be essential complements to vision and action for older learners being socialized into art and science. Briefly considered here are historical perspectives on the inextricable ties between art and science across the ages and how this bond is facilitated by visuospatial and motor capacities. A review of socialization patterns surrounding science and art for children in several indigenous settings follows. Here formal schooling has a limited relationship to identity development and future economic potential for the young. Finally, we examine language forms that advance knowledge and skills of art and science in planned learning environments – school-oriented homes, classrooms, studios, rehearsal zones, and laboratories.

The Unity of Art and Science: A Historical Perspective

From the time that humans invented tools and created drawings on cave walls, art and science have been interdependent. Both played essential roles in the evolving complexity of social groups (Deacon 1997, 2006; Donald 1991, 2001, 2006). Early governments relied on artists and scientists to design and invent technologies that made architectural monuments possible and enabled dynasties to record their histories, calendrical cycles, and astronomical and meterological anomalies. Architects of city walls, temples, and state buildings of the ancient kingdoms of Africa, the Middle East, and Latin America worked as artist scientists or as scientist artists. The aesthetic and wondrous were inseparable from the pragmatic and analytical.

The evolutionary course of biological functions and social needs brought to human consciousness a sense of inquiry and aesthetic sensibility beyond immediate survival needs. Humans learned to explore the world visually, searching out degrees of similarity and difference in details of space, color, form, and motion. By the Middle Ages, arenas of knowledge to which we now give names such as astronomy, botany, climatology, geology, physics, physiology, and zoology emerged. Between the Medieval period and the eighteenth century, visual representation of newly discovered species, processes, and systems travelled around the world in diagrams, navigational charts, models, sketches, and paintings (Bender and Marrinan 2010). As special interests in science developed, art forms represented these in surgical theatres, architectural monuments, dramatic portrayals, and illustrated books. Verbal supports through nomenclature, taxonomies, map legends, and other classification systems of science increased in length and complexity as formal instruction in art and science developed. European philosophers and statesmen expressed art and science as a one-breath phrase. The earliest surgeries took place in theatres; around the world, the planetarium doubled as hall of science and architectural monument. From the fifteenth century, when artists came to be known as individuals, they relied on science in their development of color, perspective, and constructions of space and image. Leonardo da Vinci (1452–1519), Johannes Vermeer (1632–1675), and Carl Linnaeus (1707–1778) saw no distinction between art and science.

In the Western world, as formal education became possible for those beyond the most privileged, separate arenas of study developed for art and science. The Enlightenment pulled the two apart into distinct disciplines within higher education, foreshadowing art museums and science centers as entirely separate entities. The distinct and increasingly distanced professional identities of 'scientist' and 'artist' came about (Kemp 1990; Stafford 1994). Each splintered into subfields with extensive naming and explaining. This division paralleled the split of seeing as a modality from other senses. This shift is noted as a time when 'seeing produces as its cultural endpoint a unified visual and ideological field' (Wolf 2001: 11). 'Art' came to mean literature, visual illustration, music, sculpture, architecture, dance, film, and dramatic performance. Each of these developed its own subdivisions that different cultural groups, formal education institutions, and governmental agencies continued to rank order and to target for specific social and economic classes. 'Science' created and erased subfields, relying on technology to encompass what had in previous eras been merely the 'art' within science. Model-building, graphic design, charting and mapping, along with interpretation of electronic images, came to live almost entirely within departments of science and technology. Professional applied fields of science, such as medicine, oceanography, astrophysics, and biomedical engineering, brought new technologies of sight and sound firmly into the realm of the 'scientific' – no longer to be viewed as 'artistic.'

Curiously, art and science have remained linked in forms of entertainment. In eighteenth-century European society, optical cabinets, illustrations in children's books and popular literature, architectural models, machines that provoked amusement and marvel, and often outrageous displays of artifacts collected by explorers of distant cultures and regions of the globe came to be viewed as means to educate and entertain children. The leisure industry that developed during the eighteenth century brought children and adults together in various forms of entertainment that depended on visual as well as verbal dimensions of 'artful science' and the 'science of art' (Kemp 1990; Stafford 1994). Since that time, the two have remained bonded through developments of science fiction, animation, graphic design, and video games, and in websites and kits for building robots and developing home-based artful science enterprises (Stafford 2007).

Neuroscience's Contributions to Language Socialization Research

Neuroscience researchers, using functional magnetic resonance imaging (fMRI) and magnetoencephalography (MEG) technologies, provide insights into the role of visualization in development of fluency with complex language, especially that related to science (Ramadas 2009). Reading and interpreting visual images, such as maps, graphs, charts, and photographs, coordinate with verbal reasoning (Berger, Roloff, and Roskos-Ewoldsen 2009; Suwa and Tversky 1997). Visuospatial thinking accelerates inquiry around concepts and enables transfer of mental images into verbal forms. Visuospatial thinking also works as mnemonic for verbal material and as aid to reasoning with mental models (Kosslyn, Ganis, and Thompson 2006; Schnotz 2002; Uttal and O'Doherty 2008).

Neuroscientists explicate the high overlap in neural networks between language comprehension and visual perception of details in images. This work adds support to the importance of bringing image, word, and action together in learning environments of children (Hari and Kujala 2009). Critical to understanding children's reading of written language is the linkage between visual imagery and the motor system during reading (Pfeifer and Bongard 2006; Speer et al. 2009). Thus, if readers already know about or have experienced motor actions represented in what they read, their brains reflect motor neuronal activity. In other words, readers 'embody' or simulate through motor neuronal activity what is described in the words they read. Knowledge of how language learning works in relation to conscious imagery changes as neuroscientists understand more about neural representations of modalities of simulation, situated action, and bodily states in the brain (Barsalou 2008; Meltzoff et al. 2009).

Theories of grounded cognition emphasize the role of 'mirror neurons' on the contingent motor practice that results from seeing another person perform an action (Meltzoff and Prinz 2002; Rizzolatti and Craighero 2004). Behavioral scientists have long studied the circuit of joint attention or intersubjectivity of adult and infant simultaneously viewing and manipulating an object and the infant 'checking in' on the eye gaze of the adult during imitative behavior (Brown, this volume; Finnegan 2002: Kulick 1992; Rogoff 2003; Schieffelin 1990). Neuroscientists have expanded our understanding of the creative potential of this imitative behavior by pointing out how humans, unlike other higher-order primates, do not merely imitate – they adapt and create. The capacity of humans to take the perspective of the other and to collaborate in jointly enacted scenes appears to be critical to the effectiveness with which humans move beyond imitation to creativity (Meltzoff 2005).

Children observe caregivers, perform to draw their attention, and explore new objects in their environments by checking in visually with caregivers. This ability to pay attention to self and other in the perception and exploration of an object develops in the first year of life and appears to be intimately tied to infants' fundamental social nature and their ability to pick up on the communicative intentions of others (Kuhl 2007). The sensitivity of the young to joint visual attention and their ability to imitate and extend (often through improvisation) the actions of elders is critical to language learning (Bruner 1983). The 'double exposure' of learner looking, expert looking, and both perceiving the scene or action as a model for memory toward subsequent action coalesce to instill a sense of reciprocity integral to the intersubjectivity upon which relations for learning build (Heath 2000, forthcoming). Such learning is critical to the work of artists and scientists across societies and institutions.

Socialization to Art and Science within Remote Indigenous Communities

Nowhere is the alliance of performative, visuospatial, and experiential learning in relation to language socialization more evident than in remote indigenous settings (such as those of Australia and Alaska). Here learning centers on the art and science of heritage and ecological space (Gibson 1979; Ingold 2000). Formal schooling holds little relevance for an economic future in communities where employment opportunities are limited in number and range to government and commerce and often held by outsiders who identify with the national government. Moreover, formal schooling does not define parental interactions and expectations for the young with regard to their aesthetic and practical scientific understanding of the local environment (Watson-Verran and Turnbull 1995). Studies of child and adolescent language socialization in these communities expose the priority of observation and experience over verbal instruction and explanation that holds within literate-oriented families, classrooms, and laboratories.

Acquisition of knowledge of the natural environment by young children

In Australia during the 1970s and 1980s, the Central Desert and Top End of the Northern Territory were primary sites for studies of children's language socialization by linguists and anthropologists. From within one of the most linguistically diverse regions of the world, the Maningrida region in north central Arnhem Land, Hamilton (1981) provides for one group, the Gidjingali, an extensive examination of verbal interaction of adults with children from birth through age nine. Three patterns emerge: (1) young children receive as many gestural messages as they do verbal ones; (2) language support comes through brief comment, warnings, and instructional commands; and (3) open questions occur relatively rarely between adults and children. Information content centers on names of persons and their kinship status. Labels for animate beings, human and nonhuman, matter far more than labels for inanimates. Sharp age-grading and gender segregation are in effect by the time the children reach five years of age. Between the ages of five and nine years, both girls and boys learn to follow adult expectations through observing and following facial expressions and deictic gestures as well as brief verbal commands. In terms of language socialization, the bulk of lexical knowledge young children acquire for plants, animals, insects, and reptiles, as well as land formations, comes through observing the actions of others and through narratives from elders. No decontextualized labels or verbal instruction guide children in their repeated practice of technical skills involved in tracking, spearing fish, catching small animals, and gathering plant materials. Youngsters watch actions, imitate, construct small versions of tools used by their elders, and listen to stories. Children hear recounts of hunting trips, places and land formations, and wet-season practices that go on in informal camp settings. These broad features of language behavior continue as children learn to categorize flora and fauna as well as movements of the sea and signs of imminent climatic changes.

Resource managers and wildlife rangers working with elders and young people in this region three decades later report similar ways of learning and categorizing local wildlife and ecological conditions (Fordham et al. 2010). Indigenous ecological knowledge sometimes surpasses in complexity and comprehensiveness the taxonomies and understanding of life cycles held by biologists and wildlife resource scientists from universities. Multiple approaches acknowledge the co-dependence of both types of ecological knowledge and value the close observation of indigenous peoples, as well as their long history of cumulative and dynamic information built across generations (Berkes 1999).

Australian linguists have described for many Aboriginal languages the extent to which young children's learning of morphology and lexicon, in particular, are interdependent with their close observation of the natural world. Nouns that refer to animate beings include information not only about sex, but also age and kin relationship. Those that refer to inanimate objects include reference to size, dimension, shape, habitat, and texture. Aboriginal languages are rich in directional and locational terms and make fine distinctions among different types of hitting, cutting, breaking, holding, placing, and carrying (Meggitt 1962; Walsh and Yallop 1993; Yallop 1982).

Changes in socialization patterns

In the 1990s, the national push for assimilation of Aboriginal people into an English-speaking secular, literate, capitalist, and alcohol-tolerant society forcibly disrupted remote communities (Sutton 2009). Linguists and anthropologists turned their attention to documenting how the Australian indigenous viewed the world in the hope of conveying this information to policymakers and educators whose policies were destroying traditional ways of life in remote regions. Recommendations for two-way immersion and bilingual programming resulted (Malcolm, Königsburg, and Collard 2007; Simpson and Wigglesworth 2008; Walsh and Yallop 1993).

These studies also provided substantial subtextual evidence of changing patterns of language socialization, particularly in remote regions (Blake and Dixon 1991; Dixon 1984, 2002). For example, among language groups (such as the Yolngu languages of northeast Arnhem Land) where young children had attended school for at least a decade, adults took up the questioning patterns of school (cf. Simpson and Wigglesworth 2008). They asked questions not to gain information but to elicit from the child information the adults already knew. Rarely did adults address children with open questions ('why,' 'how,' 'when') that required syntactically complex responses. Children, however, addressed such questions to adult visitors to their settlements (Moses and Yallop 2008).

Adaptation of traditional ways of using language by children who attend school appears not only in conversational interactions but also in particular narrative art forms. Skilled narrators, often children, create sand stories in Arandic areas of Central Australia. Creators draw their stories in cleared areas in the sand and accompany their gestures with speech and gestures that delineate scenes and episodes (Green 2010). In Ernabella in the Central Desert, children, especially girls, imitate and adapt the storytelling and sand-drawing practices of their elders (Eickelkemp 1999). Traditionally focused on ancient history and beliefs, these stories in recent years have been transformed by Ngaanyatjarra girls and others living in the region (speaking Pitjantjatjara or Yankunytjatjara) to relate local events unlikely to be talked about in the village. The word *walka* (Pitjantjatjara usage to mean any meaningful mark) has referred to categories of art-making, such as sketch, print, paint, and draw, as well as markings on animal skins, ceremonial body marking, and the patterns of a bird's feather (Eickelkemp 1999, 2008abc; Myers 2002). These symbolic markings in a past era of tracking, hunting, and gathering, as well as eating bush tucker, conveyed multiple layers of meaning for the verbalized sand stories of children in ways analogous to illustrations in children's literature of the Western world.

The visual arts

Visual arts production by Aboriginal children, going back as far as early missionary schools, aids our understanding of how their art reflects ways of blending image, language, and memories related to scientific and artistic concepts. Records of Aboriginal children's art exist in two forms: narratives and reproductions by early missionaries and ethnographers plus current accounts of locally traditional forms adapted by the young, many of whom now grow up knowing the commercial value that Aboriginal arts can have (Barrett and Croll 1943; Miller 1952; Myers 2002; Thomson 1983; Wallace and Wallace 1968). In the first instance, children's drawings and hand-made toys (in collections such as those of the National Museum of Australia in Canberra and the South Australian Museum in Adelaide) suggest the extent to which children committed to visual memory highly specific features of the natural environment of their remote settlements. In boarding schools and mission schools far away from bush country, indigenous children reflected in their two-dimensional drawings features of ancient wall paintings that can still be found in parts of northern Australia. These drawings invariably portray aspects of the Dreaming, the belief system surrounding the creation of the world, the wandering of ancestral totemic beings to form land and country, and the initiation of cycles of life (Sutton 1988).

Teachers' records from boarding and mission schools report that the children told Dreaming stories in brief form to 'explain' their paintings. English translations of these retellings are filled with inclusive first-person-plural pronouns ('They [the Spirits] gave us hunting things, they gave each clan their land, they gave us our totems, and they gave us our Dreaming' (Aboriginal Arts Board 1977: 11). These children had watched their elders make bark paintings, and, in some cases, sand paintings. Into their drawings, the children brought the same kinds of two-dimensional stylized figures of animals and humans within the landscape that they had seen in art created by adults and heard about in songs and stories.

However, unlike most well-known art works (including paintings on canvas) by adult Aboriginals, the earliest paintings of Aboriginal children tend to fill the entire space on their paper and represent the sky, sea, and landscape, with animals and humans placed on top of these backdrops (Wallace and Wallace 1968). In their paintings, Central Desert children reflect with precision the range of shadings of ochre in their desert landscape. Their painted renderings of 'real' historical incidents generally portray highly stylized human figures without attention to musculature, facial features, or precise skin coloring.[1]

Museum collections of toys of indigenous Australian children reflect their keen visual memory and adeptness in adapting found objects (e.g. animal knucklebones used as stones and tin cans for kick-the-tin games; Kartinyeri 2003). Materials at hand, discarded, discovered, reshaped, and integrated, have traditionally found their way into children's play and toy-making. Aboriginal toys and games documented through artifacts and ethnographic information reflect a preponderance of games requiring visual precision and physical dexterity (Haagen 1994).

Adolescent Language

The few sources reporting language use by indigenous adolescents living in remote regions of Australia and Alaska center on patterns of adaptation and incorporation of internet technologies into daily existence. Three studies illustrate ways in which adolescents living with one foot in traditional life and the other in the world of entertainment via the internet and television use language in their learning of art and science. These teens take part intermittently in formal education, but persistently move toward a syncretism of old and new in habits, skills, values, and self-identity in the bulk of their time into their late twenties. Many view themselves in an orbit between remote settlement and urban centers through which they will move back and forth in their adult lives (Sutton 2009).

The first of the studies of adolescent language was carried out among Areyonga teenage Pitjantjatjara speakers in the Central Australian Desert (Langlois 2004). Teenagers appear to be replacing kin terms in local languages with lexical items from English. However, contrary to general expectations in language shift, these loans allow the teenagers to add distinctions and to express new concepts pertaining to relationships (e.g. terms that distinguish younger male sibling from older male sibling). Thus, teenage speakers of Pitjantjatjara borrow to fill lexical gaps for these traditional relations as well as for the latest technologies that come into their community. Among Areyonga teenage Pitjantjatjara speakers, stories tend to show continuity of actions, one after the other, past action followed by yet another, rather than embedding of actions within an act and consequence chain. A chaining linearity appears to dominate in their narratives; in other words, a priority in time need not be morphologically marked as either temporal or causal. These changes within indigenous language accounts of science and art parallel the focus in school recitation on given-state and in-the-moment descriptions, but depart from processes of both arts production the young have witnessed and natural life cycles recounted in traditional narratives.

A second account from Aboriginal adolescents in the Central Desert and Northern Australia relays the adaptive learning skills of artists in social enterprise, dance, and music (Kral 2007, 2008). In Beswick or Wugularr in the Northern Territory, a community of some 450 people who retain Roper River Kriol as their usual language, young people have created a community art project, Djilpin Arts. The young manage the enterprise as a culture center and, in doing so, they set out to learn from their elders traditional means of collecting natural bush medicines and plants. Intergenerational links are forged in the collection of sugar bag honey, experimentation with soap production, and design of packaging. Joint socialization toward economic ends motivates old and young to combine their areas of specialization, open channels of talk, and bring graphic design together with text production. The young and their elders work together to make soap, lip balm, and candles to sell during festivals at the culture center. The group employs local young men to film the arts and cultural activities of the community. Here science and art merge. The young people use Kriol for their own group interactions when editing one another's work, for example, but they speak English when they engage with visitors during festival times and in their musical performances.

In the Western Desert, young people who work in a community center established in Wingellina in 1992 produce CDs and regularly post performances to YouTube. Older youths teach younger peers, introducing them to a wide array of skills for searching internet sites. Without verbal directives or specific instructions, young people lay down tracks sequentially and create CDs that they rework repeatedly in subsequent sessions. As festival time approaches, they finalize their CDs, develop a sleeve with their artwork, and provide bilingual lyrics of their songs (Kral 2008; for a comparative analysis with urban Aboriginals in Western Australia, see Malcolm, Königsberg, and Collard 2002).

Margaret Mead's (1970) prefigurative, postfigurative, and co-figurative socialization all come together in these indigenous communities. Mead defined 'post-figurative' socialization as that in which elders teach the young, 'cofigurative' socialization as that in which children and adults learn from their peers, and 'prefigurative' socialization as that in which the young instruct their elders. Peers demonstrate and, when asked, explain to one another technical strategies, and the young are available to demonstrate and narrate processes with their elders. In the studios of community arts centers of remote communities, Aboriginal youths and their elders (generally males only) share the recording space and equipment. Female elders travel into the bush with the young to collect plants and herbs and retell narratives from their childhood; male elders advise the young on traditional dance and song and sometimes take part in production of the CDs. The young work with their peers and also with elders as festival times approach. Among adolescents, co-figurative peer-to-peer socialization takes place around effective use of software, writing of songs, production of text for CD covers, and creation of instructive CDs on how to use specific software programs. New genres, necessary to bringing their local product in line with the style of commercially available products, come into use. Ingredient lists for beauty products made of local herbs and plants motivate elders not only to tell stories of the past but to relate descriptions of appropriate stages of plant development for harvesting in order to ensure the best-quality product. Market requirements for quality and presentation press young and old to plan carefully their combinations of graphic design, printed instructions, ingredient lists, and brief traditional histories of these ingredients. These initiatives begin to address the void of decades in which no local economic opportunities or educational motivation existed in remote indigenous locations. Community centers, festivals, and sale of products and services through the internet bring young and old together in meaningful work that draws on traditional art and science and links to relevant development of literacy, management, and mathematical skills (Kral 2008).

A third study of adolescent indigenous language speakers comes from Yupik speakers in remote Alaskan villages. Wyman (2004), studying these speakers from middle childhood into young adulthood, shows how descriptions of sequenced actions, such as a seal hunt, find their way into narratives told primarily within specific times and places. Young people among the Yupik tell one another stories about their individual and shared experiences with subsistence, redistributing and underscoring information they gain about the environment along with their own perspectives on undertaking adult roles, relationships, and risks over time (L. Wyman, personal communication). Stories told among young people making exploratory excursions at the margins of approaching hunting or fishing seasons appear to allow the young to test theories for and about themselves and their standing as future subsistence participants and adult members of their society. The frequency and content of these stories vary by gender and also by stage of season, as well as in relation to a sense of endangerment about the future of the society. Contrary to the many oversimplifications of how indigenous learners living in remote regions learn ecological knowledge, initiates undertake multiple means of taking in information on a vast array of highly technical subjects and skills (Lomawaima and McCarty 2006).

Planned Learning Environments and the Separation of Art and Science

Social scientists of several disciplines have described both formal and informal learning environments that advance knowledge about and applications of skills in science and art. These range from literate-oriented families to classrooms, museums, marine life centers, laboratories, studios, and rehearsal spaces.

The language of learning science and art in school-oriented families

As a result of their focus on preparing their children for academic success, upper- and middle-income families direct their children from infancy forward to name, describe, sequence, and compare objects. Multiclausal sentences, past and future tense usage, and questions characterize parental talk to children (Hart and Risley 1995, 1999; Lareau 2003; Vernon-Feagans 1996). During visits to museums, exhibitions, and parks, along with participation in sports and hobbies, parents link current experiences to school topics (Bell, Zimmerman, and Reeve 2008; National Research Council 2009).

In these families, picture books and early story books include fictional and nonfictional topics related to science and art. Bedtime stories ensure attention to illustrative representations of animals, seasonal change, and famous painters and their subjects. Museums sponsor scores of children's books that link science and art and their common processes. During middle childhood, families watch television programs and visit museums and parks that address current topics in scientific exploration and discovery. Parents talk with their children about practices and technologies that make predictions and advances in science possible. This 'concerted cultivation' of children looks ahead to formal education, while free play and family projects inspired by curiosity and implemented without commercial products fall out of favor in comparison with learning opportunities that help the young to envision themselves studying science or seeking employment in science-related fields (Chabon 2009; Heath 2006, 2008; Louv 2006; National Research Council 2009; Tai et al. 2006).

Formal study of science and art

Studies of art and science classrooms reveal the importance of learning labels and taxonomies and of handling instruments and technologies. Complementing oral and written language instruction, especially of primary students, are dramatic role-play, visuospatial activities, and spectator events (e.g. videos) (e.g. Fleer 2009). For adolescents, instructors have found highly effective increased use of gesture to demonstrate concepts or to focus on metacognitive processes or mnemonic strategies (Roth 2000).

The younger the learner, the more likely there are to be opportunities for 'taking part' in discovery, creation, and experimentation in both art and science classes. Young learners are also more likely than their older peers to hear narratives about art and science and to be asked to create their own stories about their work (Heath and Wolf 2004). Both art and science presuppose a theory of mind that grasps the intentions and ways of knowing of others distant from the current scene, a realization that primary teachers take into account when they devise means for children to embody roles in which they can 'be' scientists and artists' (Heath and Wolf 2005). Sociodramatic play and narrative development help young learners to bridge from colloquial, narrative, and informal language to the formal language demands of science (Lemke 1990).

As levels of study advance through formal education, the language socialization that instructors undertake increasingly emphasizes defining, identifying, explaining, hypothesizing, and critically reviewing. In both science and art, visual representations in a wide variety of forms (e.g. videos, photographs, diagrams, graphs, charts, timelines, paintings, and demonstrations) figure centrally in text-books and assessments. Accurate interpretation of these materials with their verbal supports (oral and written) determines competency. Often students must demonstrate specific levels of linguistic competency before they may take part in scientific or artistic activities in clubs, after-school programs, and high-level classes.[2]

With advancement in formal education, learners must also master specific processes of investigation, verification, invention, critique, and discovery (Bowker and Star 1999; Soep 2006). In art, they have to learn processes and techniques as well as historical and aesthetic dimensions of various forms, artists, and schools. In science, they must know and practice a readily recognized form of scientific objectivity and be able to offer theories as rationales for the universality of science (Star and Griesemer 1989). Artists and scientists alike constantly engage with the hypothetical. Laboratories, studios, and rehearsal spaces reflect similar frequencies in their use of technical lexicon, modal verbs, questions related to process, and hypothetical propositions (Heath, Paul-Boehncke, and Wolf 2007).

Language in workplaces

The interdependence of gesture, oral language, and forms of representation (e.g. diagrams, photographs, models) is ubiquitous in workplaces of scientists. In the laboratory, physicists set up visual domains through combinations of gesture, talk, sketches, and diagrams in their attempts to achieve mutual understanding and a working consensus around experimental findings (Ochs, Gonzales, and Jacoby 1996). Gestural moves reinforce verbal deictics (e.g. 'here,' 'there') and create narrative and envisoned worlds of work being represented – whether from past experiments or toward performances projected (see Heath (forthcoming) on the three major functions of discourse 'chunks' in collaborative production and rehearsal of scientific work). Speakers blend the identity of scientist and the arena of inquiry or joint planning and thus capture 'the animate physicist and the inanimate physical entity undergoing some change of state' (Ochs, Gonzales, and Jacoby 1996: 348).

Sociologically oriented studies of science laboratories have shown the ideological and verbal character of participants' collaborative work (Latour 1986, 1987; Latour and Woolgar 1986). Talk surrounds and often depends on 'artifact' either currently present or referenced from past experiments (Lynch 1985). Visuospatial resources – graphs, charts, models – have to be read in detail by all. Gestures and deictic references attune visual focus to props and support and extend verbal work. Laboratories operate as 'think collectives' in which participants have 'ideovisions' (stylized ideograms) as well as unique uses of language (Fleck 1979 [1935]). French sociologist Bruno Latour underscores self-reports of scientists and artists who point to the expectation that initiates learn to read interactions, numerous symbol systems, and signals for conformity to the ethic of individual responsibility in the life of the laboratory (Latour 1987; Latour and Woolgar 1986). The lives of those working in art studios are similarly 'joined,' and creative collaborators depend on common definitions of problems, deliberative approaches to solutions, and willingness to present evidence in a host of ways to support deliberation and even argument in the midst of action (John-Steiner 2000; Tharp 2003).

The interdependence of spatial alignment, gesture, and verbal interaction in the work of science comes not only from laboratory studies but also from analyses of how indigenous and Western-trained scientists, such as pilots and air traffic controllers, navigate their everyday worlds of work (Gladwin 1970). Much of the 'expertise' on which navigators now depend comes from inanimate objects (robots, computer transmissions, etc.) that communicate to human interpreters, whose visual observations translate into collaborative action to steer a ship into harbor or manage take-off and landing of a plane or space capsule on earth, in space, or on the moon or Mars (Goodwin 1994, 1995; Hutchins 1995; Hutchins and Klausen 1995). These and other studies of discourse in workplaces devoted to uses of science and technology stress the need for initiates to become fluent users of particular grammatical forms, agreed-upon 'unique' naming practices, and group-specific ways to defuse potential interactional difficulties (e.g. Drew and Heritage 1992).

Conclusions

As advanced nations move their economic base from manufacturing to finance, electronic technologies, and service industries, formal education – especially higher-education institutions – will be the most visible environment to support invention, discovery, and exploration in both science and the arts. However, informal modes of socialization into art and science will also grow rapidly as schools urge museums, botanical parks, and zoos to complement the curricular work of formal education (National Research Council 2009). The push around the world for environmental conservation and sustainability, healthy living, and indigenous resource management will ensure that 'researchers beyond the university walls' sharpen the vision and resolve of individuals and groups for science and art (Finnegan 2005). This promotion is likely to draw increasing attention to the dominant role of long-standing fundamentals in the learning of art and science – looking, tracing, re-enacting, and playing, which are essential supports for language socialization.

ACKNOWLEDGMENTS

This chapter went through its penultimate version while I was a visiting professor in the Centre for Aboriginal Economic Policy Research at the Australian National University in the spring of 2010. I am grateful to staff of the centre for their contributions and critical editing of this chapter. The chapter also benefitted considerably from the editorial suggestions of Alessandro Duranti.

NOTES

1   I am indebted to Nancy Michaelis, formerly within the curatorial department of the National Museum of Australia, for access in 2008 to the museum's collection of children's drawings and paintings. I also remember with appreciation the access that Peter Sutton, curator with the South Australian Museum, gave me at several points during the 1980s to that museum's collections of children's art work.

2   These generalizations are derived from review of state standards in the United States for science and art between 2000 and 2005 and from introductory descriptions of science teaching in nations included in the PISA international comparisons of subject-matter achievement levels.

REFERENCES

Aboriginal Arts Board. (1977) *The Aboriginal Children's History of Australia*. Adelaide, Australia: Rigby Publishers.

Barrett, C. and Croll, R. (1943) *Art of the Australian Aboriginal*. Melbourne, Australia: The Bread and Cheese Club.

Barsalou, L. W. (2008) Grounded cognition. *Annual Review of Psychology* 59: 617–45.

Bell, P., Zimmerman, H., and Reeve, S. (2008) Distributed expertise in a science center: Social and intellectual role-taking by families. *Journal of Museum Education* 33(2): 143–52.

Bender, J. and Marrinan, M. (2010) *The Culture of Diagram*. Stanford, CA: Stanford University Press.

Berger, C., Roloff, M., and Roskos-Ewoldsen, D. (eds.) (2009) *The Handbook of Communication Science*. 2nd ed. Thousand Oaks, CA: Sage.

Berkes, F. (1999) *Sacred Ecology: Traditional Ecological Knowledge and Resource Management*. Philadelphia, PA: Taylor and Francis.

Blake, B. and Dixon, R. (eds.) (1991) *Handbook of Australian Languages*. Oxford: Oxford University Press.

Bowker, G. and Star, S. (1999) *Sorting Things Out: Classification and Its Consequences*. Cambridge, MA: MIT Press.

Bruner, J. (1983) *Child's Talk: Learning to Use Language*. New York: W. W. Norton.

Chabon, M. (2009) *Manhood for Amateurs*. New York: Harper Collins.

Deacon, T. (1997) *The Symbolic Species: The Co-Evolution of Language and the Brain*. New York: Norton.

Deacon, T. (2006) The aesthetic faculty. In M. Turner (ed.), *The Artful Mind: Cognitive Science and the Riddle of Human Creativity*. 21–57. New York: Oxford.

Dixon, R. (1984) *Searching for Aboriginal Languages: Memoirs of a Field Worker*. St. Lucia, Australia: University of Queensland Press.

Dixon, R. (2002) *Australian Languages: Their Nature and Development*. Cambridge: Cambridge University Press.

Donald, M. (1991) *Origins of the Modern Mind: Three Stages in the Evolution of Culture and Cognition*. Cambridge, MA: Harvard University Press.

Donald, M. (2001) *A Mind So Rare: The Evolution of Human Consciousness*. New York: Norton.

Donald, M. (2006) Art and cognitive evolution. In M. Turner (ed.), *The Artful*

Mind: Cognitive Science and the Riddle of Human Creativity. 3–20. New York: Oxford University Press.

Drew, P. and Heritage, J. (eds.) (1992) *Talk at Work: Interaction in Institutional Settings*. New York: Cambridge University Press.

Eickelkamp, U. (1999) *'Don't Ask for Stories…' the Women from Ernabella and Their Art*. Canberra, Australia: Aboriginal Studies Press.

Eickelkamp, U. (2008a) 'I don't talk story like that': On the social meaning of children's sand stories at Ernabella. In J. Simpson and G. Wigglesworth (eds.), *Children's Language and Multilingualism: Indigenous Language Use at Home and School*. 79–102. London: Continuum Press.

Eickelkamp, U. (2008b) Play, imagination, and early experience: Sand storytelling and continuity of being among Anangu Pitjantjatjara girls. In G. Robinson, U. Eickelkamp, J. Goodnow, and I. Katz (eds.), *Contexts of Child Development: Culture, Policy and Intervention*. 138–52. Darwin, Australia: Charles Darwin University.

Eickelkamp, U. (2008c) (Re)presenting experience: A comparison of Australian Aboriginal children's sand play in two settings. *International Journal of Applied Psychoanalytic Studies* 5: 12–50.

Finnegan, R. (2002) *Communicating: The Multiple Modes of Human Interconnection*. London: Routledge.

Finnegan, R. (ed.) (2005) *Participating in the Knowledge Society: Researchers Beyond the University Walls*. New York: Palgrave Macmillan.

Fleck, L. (1979 [1935]) *Genesis and Development of a Scientific Fact*. Chicago, IL: University of Chicago Press.

Fleer, M. (2009) Supporting scientific conceptual consciousness or learning in 'a roundabout way' in play-based contexts. *International Journal of Science Education* 31(8): 1069–89.

Fordham, A., Fogarty, W., Corey, B., and Fordham, D. (2010) *Knowledge Foundations for the Development of Sustainable Wildlife Enterprises in Remote Indigenous Communities of Australia*. Canberra, Australia: ANU Centre for Aboriginal Economic Policy Research Working Paper No. 62.

Gibson, J. (1979) *The Ecological Approach to Visual Perception*. Boston, MA: Houghton Mifflin.

Gladwin, T. (1970) *East Is a Big Bird: Navigation and Logic on Puluwat Atoll*. Cambridge, MA: Harvard University Press.

Goodwin, C. (1994) Professional vision. *American Anthropologist* 96: 606–33.

Goodwin, C. (1995) Seeing in depth. *Social Studies of Science* 25: 237–74.

Green, J. A. (2010) *Between the Earth and the Air: Multimodality in Arandic Sand Stories*. Doctoral Dissertation. Melbourne, Australia: Melbourne University.

Haagen, C. (1994) *Bush Toys: Aboriginal Children at Play*. Canberra, Australia: Aboriginal Studies Press.

Hamilton, A. (1981) *Nature and Nurture: Aboriginal Child-Rearing in North-Central Arnhem Land*. Canberra, Australia: Australian Institute of Aboriginal Studies.

Hari, R. and Kujala, M. (2009) Brain basis of human social interaction: From concepts to brain imaging. *Physiological Review*. 89(2): 453–79.

Hart, B. and Risley, T. R. (1995) *Meaningful Differences in the Everyday Experience of Young American Children*. Baltimore, MD: Brookes.

Hart, B. and Risley, T. R. (1999) *The Social World of Children Learning to Talk*. Baltimore, MD: Brookes.

Heath, S. B. (2000) Seeing our way into learning. *Cambridge Journal of Education* 30(1): 121–32.

Heath, S. B. (2006) Commentary 2. Building the micros toward seeing the macro. *Text: Special Issue: Family Discourse, Framing Family* 26(4/5): 627–34.

Heath, S. B. (2008) Foreword. In J. Simpson and G. Wigglesworth (eds.), *Children and*

Multilingualism: Indigenous Language Use at Home and School. ix–xiii. London: Continuum International.

Heath, S. B. (forthcoming) Seeing our way into learning science in informal environments. In W. Tate and C. Yeakey (eds.), *Research on Schools, Neighborhoods and Communities: Toward Civic Responsibility*. Washington, DC: AERA.

Heath, S. B., Paul-Boehncke, E., and Wolf, S. (2007) *Made for Each Other: Creative Sciences and Arts in the Secondary School*. London: Creative Partnerships.

Heath, S. B. and Wolf, S. (2004) *Visual Learning in the Community School*. London: Creative Partnerships.

Heath, S. B. and Wolf, S. (2005) *Dramatic Learning in the Primary School*. London: Creative Partnerships.

Hutchins, E. (1995) *Cognition in the Wild*. Cambridge, MA: MIT Press.

Hutchins, E. and Klausen, T. (1995) Distributed cognition in an airline cockpit. In Y. Engestrom and D. Middleton (eds.), *Cognition and Communication at Work*. 15–34. Cambridge: Cambridge University Press.

Ingold, T. (2000) *The Perception of the Environment: Essays on Livelihood, Dwelling, and Skill*. New York: Routledge.

John-Steiner, V. (2000) *Creative Collaboration*. New York: Oxford University Press.

Kartinyeri, D. (2003) *Bush Games and Knucklebones*. Broome, WA: Magabala Books.

Kemp, M. (1990) *The Science of Art: Optical Themes in Western Art from Brunelleschi to Seurat*. New Haven, CT: Yale University Press.

Kosslyn, S. M., Ganis, G., and Thompson, W. L. (2006) Neural foundation of imagery. *Nature Reviews Neuroscience* 2: 635–42.

Kral, I. (2007) *Writing Word – Right Way! Literacy and Social Practice in the Ngaanyatjarra World*. Doctoral Dissertation. Canberra, Australia: Australian National University.

Kral, I. (2008) Youth, learning and enterprise in remote Aboriginal Australian communities. Unpublished paper. Canberra, Australia: Australian National University.

Kuhl, P. K. (2007) Is speech learning 'gated' by the social brain? *Developmental Science* 10(1): 110–20.

Kulick, D. (1992) *Language Shift and Cultural Reproduction: Socialization, Self, and Syncretism in a Papua New Guinean Village*. New York: Cambridge University Press.

Langlois, A. (2004) *Alive and Kicking: Areyonga Teenage Pitjantjatjara. Pacific Linguistics 561*. Canberra, Australia: ANU Research School of Pacific and Asian Studies.

Latour, B. (1986) Visualization and cognition: Thinking with eyes and hands. *Knowledge and Society* 6: 1–40.

Latour, B. (1987) *Science in Action: How to Follow Scientists and Engineers through Society*. Cambridge, MA: Harvard University Press.

Latour, B. and Woolgar, S. (1986) *Laboratory Life: The Construction of Scientific Facts*. Beverly Hills, CA: Sage.

Lareau, A. (2003) *Unequal Childhoods: Class, Race and Family Life*. Berkeley, CA: University of California Press.

Lemke, J. (1990) *Talking Science: Language, Learning, and Values*. Norwood, NJ: Ablex.

Lomawaima, T. and McCarty, T. (2006) *To Remain an Indian: Lessons in Democracy from a Century of Native American Education*. New York: Teachers College Press.

Louv, R. (2006) *Last Child in the Woods: Saving Our Children from Nature-Deficit Disorder*. Chapel Hill, NC: Algonquin Books.

Lynch, M. (1985) *Art and Artifact in Laboratory Science*. Boston, MA: Routledge and Kegan Paul.

Malcolm, I. G., Königsberg, P., and Collard, G. (2002) *Umob Deadly: Recognized and Unrecognized Literacy Skills of Aboriginal Youth*. Mount Lawley, WA: Centre for Applied Language and Literacy Research, Edith Cowan University.

Mead, M. (1970) *Culture and Commitment: A Study of the Generation Gap*. London: The Bodley Head Ltd.

Meggitt, M. J. (1962) *Desert People: A Study of the Walbiri Aborigines of Central Australia*. London: Angus and Robertson.

Meltzoff, A. (2005) Imitation and other minds: The 'like me' hypothesis. In S. Hurley and N. Chater (eds.), *Perspectives on Imitation: From Neuroscience to Social Science, vol. 2*. 55–77. Cambridge, MA: MIT Press.

Meltzoff, A., Kuhl, P. K., Movellan, J., and Sejnowski, T. J. (2009) Foundations for a new science of learning. *Science* 325: 284–8.

Meltzoff, A. and Prinz, W. (eds.) (2002) *The Imitative Mind: Development, Evolution and Brain Bases*. Cambridge: Cambridge University Press.

Miller, M. D. (1952) *Child Artists of the Australian Bush*. London: G. G. Harrap.

Moses, K. and Yallop, C. (2008) Questions about questions. In J. Simpson and G. Wigglesworth (eds.), *Children's Language and Multilingualism: Indigenous Language Use at Home and School*. 30–56. London: Continuum Press.

Myers, F. R. (2002) *Painting Culture: The Making of an Aboriginal High Art*. Durham, NC: Duke University Press.

National Research Council of the National Academies (2009) *Learning Science in Informal Environments: People, Places and Pursuits*. Washington, DC: The National Academies Press.

Ochs, E., Gonzales, P., and Jacoby, S. (1996) 'When I come down I'm in the domain state': Grammar and graphic representation in the interpretive activity of physicists. In E. Ochs, E. Schegloff, and S. Thompson (eds.), *Interaction and Grammar*. 328–69. Cambridge: Cambridge University Press.

Pfeifer, R. and Bongard, J. C. (2006) *How the Body Shapes the Way We Think: A New View of Intelligence*. Cambridge, MA: MIT Press.

Ramadas, J. (2009) Visual and spatial modes in science learning. *International Journal of Science Education* 31(3): 301–18.

Rizzolatti, G. and Craighero, L. (2004) The mirror-neuron system. *Annual Review of Neuroscience* 27: 169–92.

Rogoff, B. (2003) *The Cultural Nature of Human Development*. New York: Oxford University Press.

Roth, W.-M. (2000) From gesture to scientific language. *Journal of Pragmatics* 32: 1683–714.

Schieffelin, B. B. (1990) *The Give and Take of Everyday Life: Language Socialization of Kaluli Children*. Cambridge: Cambridge University Press.

Schnotz, W. (2002) Towards an integrated view of learning from text and visual displays. *Educational Psychology Review* 14(1): 101–19.

Simpson, J. and Wigglesworth, G. (2008) *Children's Language and Multilingualism: Indigenous Language Use at Home and School*. London: Continuum.

Soep, E. (2006) Critique: Assessment and the production of learning. *Teachers College Record* 108(4): 748–77.

Speer, N. K., Reynolds, J., R. Swallow, K. M., and Zacks, J. M. (2009) Reading stories activates neural representations of visual and motor experiences. *Psychological Science* 20(8): 989–99.

Stafford, B. (1994) *Artful Science: Enlightenment Entertainment and the Eclipse of Visual Education*. Cambridge, MA: MIT Press.

Stafford, B. (2007) *Echo Objects: The Cognitive Work of Images*. Chicago, IL: University of Chicago Press.

Star, S. L. and Griesemer, J. (1989) Institutional ecology, translations, and boundary objects: Amateurs and professionals in Berkeley's Museum of

Vertebrate Zoology. *Social Studies of Science* 19: 387–420.

Sutton, P. (2009) *The Politics of Suffering.* Melbourne, Australia: Melbourne University Press.

Sutton, P. (ed.) (1988) *Dreamings: The Art of Aboriginal Australia.* New York: The Asia Society Galleries.

Suwa, M. and Tversky, B. (1997) What architects and students perceive in their sketches: A protocol analysis. *Design Studies* 18: 385–403.

Tai, R. H., Liu, C., Maltese, A., and Fan, X. (2006) Planning early for careers in science. *Science* 312: 1143–4.

Tharp, T. (2003) *The Creative Habit: Learn It and Use It for Life.* New York: Simon and Schuster.

Thomson, D. (1983) *Children of the Wilderness.* South Yarra, Australia: Curry O'Neil Ross.

Uttal, D. and O'Doherty, K. (2008) Comprehending and learning form 'visualization': A developmental perspective. In J. K. Gilbert, M. Reiner, and M. Nakhleh (eds.), *Visualization: Theory and Practice in Science Education.* 53–72. New York: Springer.

Vernon-Feagans, L. (1996) *Children's Talk in Communities and Classrooms.* Cambridge, MA: Blackwell.

Wallace, P. and Wallace, N. (1968) *Children of the Desert.* Melbourne, Australia: Thomas Nelson.

Walsh, M. and Yallop, C. (1993) *Language and Culture in Aboriginal Australia.* Canberra, Australia: Australian Studies Press.

Watson-Verran, H. and Turnbull, D. (1995) Science and other indigenous knowledge systems. In S. Jasanoff, G. E. Markle, J. C. Petersen, and T. Pinch (ed.), *Handbook of Science and Technology Studies.* Rev. ed. 115–39. Thousand Oaks, CA: Sage.

Wolf, B. J. (2001) *Vermeer and the Invention of Seeing.* Chicago, IL: University of Chicago Press.

Wyman, L. (2004) Language shift, youth culture and ideology: A Yup'ik example. Doctoral Dissertation. Stanford, CA: Stanford University.

Yallop, C. (1982) *Australian Aboriginal Languages.* London: Andre Deutsch.

19 Language Socialization and Verbal Improvisation

ALESSANDRO DURANTI AND STEVEN P. BLACK

Introduction

In this chapter, we suggest that verbal improvisation is a human universal even though its manifestation is subject to contextual variation and conventionalization. Communities and social units of various kinds and size (e.g. family, peer group, school, workplace) vary in how they recognize, encourage, and tolerate verbal improvisation. On the basis of the existing evidence, we hypothesize that (1) children and other novices must acquire the ability to discern when and to what extent they may vary their performance of any culturally recognizable activity and, more generally, be creative in the way they carry out a task; (2) given that much of human action is conceived, executed, and interpreted by others as within culturally established paths, novices' creativity does not imply a general expectation for completely novel acts: in other words, verbal improvisation – like musical improvisation – is also subject to cultural constraints; and (3) despite degrees and types of variation in the execution of tasks allowed or prescribed in different communities, cross-cultural similarities in patterns of verbal improvisation and in their evaluation are possible and not uncommon.

Improvisation is common in certain types of music and theater as well as in certain genres of oral poetry, from the ancient Homeric epics as reconstructed by Milman Parry and his student Albert Lord to contemporary 'free style' hip hop – Ruth Finnegan's (1977: 18) term 'composition-in-performance' captures an important quality of these genres. The ability to improvise is also necessary in children's linguistic play and other creative activities that have been studied by researchers in a variety of fields. Even though the importance of improvisation has been recognized in Bourdieu's influential notion of habitus (1977: 79) and in

The Handbook of Language Socialization, First Edition. Edited by Alessandro Duranti, Elinor Ochs, and Bambi B. Schieffelin.

Giddens' (1979: 18) interpretation of Chomsky's notion of 'rule-governed creativity,' there has been little use of the notion of improvisation in the study of children's language use or language acquisition. In this chapter, we identify a number of activities in which children are exposed to or engage in verbal improvisation. We start with repetition as the basis of variation and continue with analysis of various forms of creative behavior, including verbal play and joking. We also stress the ubiquity of improvisation as an art form that emerges out of everyday interaction. Verbal improvisation is also constantly evaluated, like all human creative activities. A distinction must be made between situations and genres where improvisation is tolerated or even encouraged and those in which it is negatively sanctioned. Adult prompting and metapragmatic instructions (e.g. 'say it this way!') can thus be seen as attempts to control and regulate the type and degree of verbal improvisation that children and novices are allowed.

We start our discussion by looking at variation as a basic type of creative behavior that includes improvised elements. We then continue with 'performed improvisation'; that is, situations in which speakers are engaged in exhibiting their spontaneous verbal creativity (e.g. in joking, pretend play). Finally, we examine how improvisation is tolerated, encouraged, or negatively sanctioned. The attention to improvisation as behavior that calls for a practical, aesthetic, and ethical evaluation informs the definition of socialization into improvisation provided at the end of the chapter.

Repetition versus Variation

Although language socialization studies often stress children's role in their own socialization (echoing Jean Piaget's view of children as agents in their understanding of their world), there has been a tendency in the discipline to focus on normative behavior and, more specifically, on the ways in which children are taught to conform to expected social norms in terms of speaking, acting, and feeling (but see Kulick and Schieffelin 2004 for an argument in favor of the need for 'bad subjects'). This tendency is well-represented by the focus on routines, a recurrent theme of language socialization studies, which suggests that not only members but researchers as well have generally assumed that repetition is a key strategy for getting novices to acquire a given skill, for example how to greet, how to make a request, or how to pray (see Moore, this volume). But the empirical study of routines has also revealed variation, in at least two senses of the term: (1) variation as an end result – that is, how much variability the child ends up mastering – and (2) variation in performance – that is, how closely a child is able or willing to follow a given model provided by peers or adults.

Variation as an end result

The study of children's participation in routines has shown that over time rigid or fixed structures may give way to looser ones in which 'the child is [...] allowed to take on roles other than the one originally assigned to him or her' (Peters and Boggs 1986: 91). In other words, it can be shown that the social system in place for scaffolding children's meaningful actions expects conformity to a given model or pattern while leaving room for some variation. In fact, when we look at children's own renditions of adult ritual performances, we may find that they expand significantly on the range of linguistic features found in the adult versions. This is carefully documented in Jennifer Reynolds' research in the Kaqchikel Maya town of San Antonio Aguas Calientes, Guatemala, where she recorded children re-enacting at home the ritual performance of *El Desafío* ('the Challenge') (between Christians and Moors) that is yearly performed in public by the adult Catholic parishioners in the town. She shows that, in playing the traditional roles of *Rey Moro* (Moor King) and *Rey Cristiano* (Christian King), the children, differently from the adults, hybridize the speech genre and register of the public performance in order to play out moral characters and stances that make sense to them (Reynolds in press).

These observations on the relationship between variation and improvisation lead us to a distinction between two possible meanings of the term 'improvisation' as applied to human development and socialization: improvisation as flexibility and improvisation as performance.

Improvisation as Flexibility in Execution of Tasks

The first and broader meaning of improvisation is flexibility in the ways of carrying out a task. This is made explicit by some authors. For example, in her work on apprenticeship, Rogoff (1990: 8–9) recognized that problem solving involves 'flexible improvisation towards goals as diverse as planning a meal, writing an essay, convincing or entertaining others, exploring the properties of an idea or unfamiliar terrain or objects, or remembering or inferring the location of one's keys.' In this first sense, improvisation is 'one hallmark of expertise' (Pressing 1998: 50) and is expected to be a feature of all those situations in which participants must select among various aspects of individual or collective competence to solve novel problems. As pointed out by students of everyday interaction (e.g. Goffman 1967; Schegloff 2007), one of the problems that all people are called to solve countless times during any one day is the assessment of the situation at hand in order to decide one course of action among the many possible ones. In order to face this kind of daily challenge, memory and imitation alone are not sufficient and therefore children (and other novices) around the globe must be allowed – probably more often than we have been able to document – to show initiative and inventiveness at the right time and place. The search for patterns in children's actions – typically interpreted as the reproduction of adult ways of doing (e.g. speaking, gesturing, posturing, grasping, walking, using tools) – has often obscured the ways in which children are called upon to introduce variations and innovations in daily routines. Sawyer's (1996) proposal for a continuum from ritualized to improvisational performance is a way of accounting for the ongoing tension between predictability and innovation that characterizes children's and, more generally, novices' meaningful actions (see also Paugh, this volume; Sawyer 2003).

Among social theorists, Pierre Bourdieu is noted for explicitly relying on the notion of improvisation as a key aspect of what he called the 'practical logic' of social life. As made clear by his adoption of the medieval notion of 'habitus,' for Bourdieu the kind of improvisation that social agents engage in is both 'regulated' and the product of 'intentionless invention' (1977: 79). This means that what appears 'natural' in someone's actions may in fact turn out to be the product of a long, implicit, and partly forgotten apprenticeship, as when a musician's ability to improvise is interpreted as 'pure inspiration.' Jean-François Dortier (2002) eloquently captured this aspect of the musician's habitus in the following passage (Dortier 2002: 5, translated by A. D.):

> The *habitus* is in the first place the product of an apprenticeship that has become unconscious and is understood therefore as a seemingly natural attitude freely evolving in a given context. Thus, musicians can freely improvise at the piano only after having spent a long time practicing their scales, acquiring the rules of composition and harmony. It is only after having internalized musical codes and constraints (the *"structured structures"*) that a pianist can then compose, create, invent, and transmit her music (the *"structuring structures"*). Authors, composers, artists thus live their creations as due to a freedom to create, to pure inspiration, because they are no longer aware of the codes and the styles that they have deeply internalized. Such is the case for music as well as, in general, for language, writing, and thinking. We believe them all to be free and disembodied, whereas they are the product of deeply rooted constraints and structures. (Dortier : 2002 : 5, translation by A.D.)

This conceptualization of how creativity is made possible by routinization recognizes what child language studies have long argued for; namely, the crucial role of repetition in development and apprenticeship. It also recognizes the fact that creativity is to be found in most task accomplishment, even though the degree of freedom of execution varies across situations and speech genres (see below). To better understand this variation, we examine verbal improvisation as performance.

Play and Other Creative Behaviors

We have evidence that there is variation across societies and contexts in the extent to which children are expected to closely follow the model offered to them by experts. In some activities, children are required to repeat *exactly* what the adult or local expert is modeling for them. This is often the case in those school contexts where rote learning is the dominant teaching paradigm. For example, in Maroua, Northern Cameroon, both the Qur'anic and the public schools follow a pattern that Leslie Moore called 'guided repetition,' a way of teaching that 'involves modeling by an expert and imitation by a novice, followed by rehearsal and performance by the novice' (Moore 2006: 110; this volume). In some other types of activities, it has been shown that children are allowed more room for creative contributions. This is particularly the case in play activities, which may require and thus foster improvisational skills. For example, in Thailand, as documented by Kathryn Howard, children engage in humorous play with an aesthetic that 'requires being able to capitalize on fleeting opportunities, by utilizing complex contextual and pragmatic knowledge about the cultural frameworks and expectations that are in play in a particular interaction' (2009: 340). Howard explicitly mentions improvisation, drawing a parallel with jazz performance (see also Howard, this volume).

Even though the term 'improvisation' was not used in the study of language development before Keith Sawyer's study of children's pretend play (1993, 1997), instances of children spontaneously improvising can be found in the early literature on children's discourse. It was in particular the study of child–child as opposed to adult–child communication that showed that children interacting among themselves seem to *naturally* engage in creative behavior that we could now recast as verbal improvisation. Thus, Elinor [Ochs] Keenan (1974) showed that her twins David and Toby at two years and nine months, in addition to engaging in long sequences of conversational exchanges that were referentially interpretable, also exchanged long sequences of 'sound play' that were cooperative and (sound-wise) coherent.

In reporting that exchanges of this sort are common in her data, [Ochs] Keenan also noted that sound play sequences can start in response to utterances that have a clear referential meaning. In other words, her recorded examples show that for her children it was 'often acceptable to reply to a comment, command, question or song with an utterance which attends only to the form of that talk' (Keenan 1974: 176):

Example 19.1a

- *wake up/ wake up/*
- [he:kʌt] (laughing)
- [he:kʌt]
- [be:kʌp]
- [bre:kʌt] [bre:kʌp]
- *wake up* [wi:kʌp] (laughing) [wi:kʌp]

Example 19.1b

- *black sheep* (4 sec)/
- *black/* [bakji] (?)
- [badijotj] (2 sec)
- [badzots]
- [batji] [batjiotj]

As Keenan points out, this kind of non-sense response and its uptake over several more turns of sound play would not normally be acceptable among adults (see also Keenan 1974: 176n). This comparison between children's and adults' discourse highlights another important factor in the study of socialization into improvisation; namely, that although children seem naturally prone to certain forms of verbal improvisation and engage in it when left to their own devices, adults may not be as prone to indulge in it. More importantly, adults and older siblings hold and use the right to approve, disapprove, or regulate various kinds of verbal creativity in a number of ways.

When we expand the population to include school-aged children all the way up to teenagers, we find that children's playful communication has been the subject of a considerable number of studies, which have shown that peer-group interactions are full of verbal improvisation. An important contribution in this area is Labov's (1972) discussion of 'ritual insults,' a type of highly creative verbal dueling common in black communities and referred to at the time by such terms as 'sounding, signifying, woofing, cutting' (see also Abrahams 1962; Kochman 1970; Mitchell-Kernan 1972; Smitherman 1977, 2007; Spears 2007). Labov and his research team documented that the group they studied ('the Jets') engaged in sequences of insults full of semantic shifts and other rhetorical devices. When subjected to formal analysis, this type of verbal competition revealed complex inferential processes at work in quickly improvised lines. Similar joking, playful rhyming, and sound symbolism have been described in a number of contexts including freestyle rap battles among hip hop artists (Alim 2006; Alim, Lee, and Mason 2010; Morgan 2009) and second language classrooms (Cetaike and Aronsson 2004, 2005; Rampton 1999). The linguistic innovations found in contemporary hip hop lyrics have also been shown to be a resource for the acquisition of a wide range of literacy skills (Alim 2004, 2007; Smitherman 2007). These and other sources suggest that, although improvisation and play tend to be equated in the popular literature (e.g. Nachmanovitch 1990), improvisation is by no means always 'playful.' It is possible to conceive and practice improvisation as a serious activity or as 'serious play' (Turner 1982). This is the case, for example, in most musical traditions, including jazz and other genres where the ability to improvise is seen as the result of strenuous and protracted practice and training (see Berliner 1994).

Verbal improvisation as performed creative behavior

There is another sense of improvisation that includes and at the same time goes beyond flexibility of task execution or variation in routine: scripted activities. In this other sense of the term, improvisation is no longer just a means to an end (e.g. for problem solving) but an end in itself. This second kind of improvisation can emerge spontaneously in any context but it is typically found in activities in which participants are expected to act in novel ways, displaying through their actions their own understanding of what is or should be going on. Improvisational theater and jazz have been shown to be such activities (Sawyer 2001, 2003). This interpretation of improvisation places it within the domain of performance, an important focus of interest for linguistic anthropologists. In particular, this second type of improvisation shares a key feature of Richard Bauman's conceptualization of verbal art as performance; namely, the performers' assumption of responsibility to an audience for the display of their competence (Bauman 1975: 168–9; see also Hymes 1975). As pointed out by Harris Berger and Giovanna del Negro (2002), this type of commitment to an audience is a reflexive type of mutual understanding and thus a key element in the construction of a complex type of intersubjectivity (Husserl 1960): performers act knowing that the audience knows that they (the performers) know that they are being evaluated not only for what they do but also for the way they do it, as well as, in some cases, for the fact that they are doing it at all (as made explicit in comments such as 'it was courageous of you to give such a speech!'). If we accept the idea that evaluation is a key component of agency (e.g. Duranti 2004; Taylor 1985), we can recognize the domain of performance in the sense proposed by Bauman as a reflexive kind of agency; namely, the acting in the world of agents who know they are being agentive.

Verbal improvisation: Joking   Joking is an everyday activity that fits the definition of verbal performance as reflexive agency. Spontaneous jokes are also pivotal moments in an interaction when the mood and content shift, unexpectedly pulling bystanders into the jokes or transforming them into an evaluating audience (Sherzer 2002: 44). In several respects, jokes in conversational interaction have properties that are similar to improvised music. Without being professional performers, those who engage in these verbal exchanges are able to rapidly and smoothly construct speech actions that build on what has just been said (or done) while adding a new point of view that evokes or imposes a different stance with respect to what has just happened. Spontaneous jokes provide an arena for displaying fast thinking and a person's sense of humor while also testing out recipients' or bystanders' moral stance with respect to a given issue or problem. To illustrate this point, we will draw from Black's research project in Durban, South Africa, where he followed a gospel choir comprised of isiZulu-speaking individuals living with HIV/AIDS. Black (2010) found that, among choir members, in the context of extreme societal stigmatization of the disease, joking about HIV was not unusual (see also Black forthcoming). It could, in fact, be interpreted in two ways: (1) a transformation of a broader community-wide pattern of stigmatized humor about HIV and (2) part of a shared attitude that enabled them to carry on maintaining semblance of a normal life. Typically, choir members' joking was highly improvisational and often constituted a form of support and their way of facing HIV.

Example 19.2 captures an interaction in isiZulu that occurred before the start of a choir rehearsal, when group members and the researcher were cleaning up the garage in which the choir rehearsed, moving things around to make space and setting up the keyboard, bass, and drum set (see also Black 2010: 275–7). To understand what is going on among the participants, it is important to remember that tuberculosis infection (TB) is often correlated with HIV in South Africa, a fact that has led many South Africans to conceptualize the two diseases as inexorably linked.

Example 19.2:   05–11–2008 Tape 1: 11min 10sec

Bongiwe (B), Ndumiso (N), and other participants including Dumisile and the researcher.

1 B: ((sweeping)) *sima lapha vele*? (('it' refers to a small bench))
         'is it [the bench] supposed to be here?'
2 N: *yah sima lapha. noma uzosidonsa uhambe naso.*
         'Yeah, it's supposed to be here. or you'll drag it and go (home)
            with it.'
3 B: *hhayibo. ngiyaphuquza mina.*
         'Hey (no). Me, I am making dust.'
4 N: *sizoba ne TB*
         'We will get TB'
5 B: *kade ngingashaneli benginiphathisa ngethi- ehh. nge TB.*
         'I wasn't sweeping I was just infecting you all with- ehh. with TB.'
6 N: *mmm* ((high-pitched start, drops down))

The excerpt began with Bongiwe sweeping and asking about where to position a small bench upon which choir members sometimes sat (line 1). In line 2, Ndumiso responded 'yeah,' and then established a play frame (Bateson 1955) with his exaggerated claim that if Bongiwe did not leave the bench where it was she would 'drag it and go home with it' (line 2). Recognizing this play frame, Bongiwe then explained that she was 'making dust' – the opposite of what one should do when sweeping (line 3). Ndumiso next expanded on Bongiwe's statement, perhaps perceiving an implicit indexical entailing (Silverstein 1976) of TB through the verb meaning 'making dust.' Ndumiso said outright, 'we will get TB' (line 4). After this, Bongiwe made the link between making dust and TB explicit, saying that she 'wasn't sweeping' but instead was infecting nearby individuals with TB (line 5). The instance of joking concludes with Ndumiso's 'mmm' (line 6), which we take to be a minimal and yet effective evaluation.

In Example 19.2, each next move built off of the indexical entailments of the previous moves, with the shared presupposition that both Bongiwe and Ndumiso are HIV-positive; the joking was 'emergent,' in the sense that each conversational turn developed from the previous turn and the course of the joking could not have been predicted prior to its conclusion (Mead 1932; Sawyer 1997: 41).

The Ubiquity of Improvisation

Both improvisation as flexibility in the execution of tasks and improvisation as performed creative behavior are ubiquitous dimensions of human life. They remain, however, little recognized or theorized in the study of human development[1] and language socialization. Sawyer is an unusual scholar in having devoted a number of publications to exploring the similarities between children's conversations and improvisational genres such as jazz and improvisational theater. On the basis of his observations of pretend play in a preschool classroom with 24 children between the ages of three and five, Sawyer (1997) proposed a model that draws from a number of authors but ends up converging on three main concepts: the emergent nature of children's pretend play, the importance of the frame established by previous interactions, and the role of the indexical properties of speech, whereby each contribution (e.g. turn) both presupposes what has just been said and entails possible future directions.

A good example of the tension between making one's contribution relevant to what was just said and proposing something new is provided by the following interaction from a 1981 film of Samoan children engaged in pretend play on the beach, where the sand becomes cement and rocks and little sticks are transformed into trucks, boats, or firewood.[2]

Example 19.3: 'Boys on the beach' – *from Sound Super 8 Film*[3]

Participants: Amato (A) , Iaone (I), Manuele (Ma), and Siʻi (S).

4	A:	*mai kaloge!*
		'bring (a) gallon (of cement)!'
5		(*e loʻo ma ʻau / / ? le uila*)
		'there it is with me/my . . . the toilet'
6	S:	*kākou ō sa kae (gi) ele (i le) sami!*
		'let's go to wash in the sea!'
7	A:	*ʻuma fai laʻu pū faleuila.*
		'I finished making my toilet hole.'
8		*ʻuma.*
		'finished.'
9		*ʻuma fai laʻu faleui / / la*
		'finished doing my restroom'
10	I:	*fai VAʻA!* ((LG)) *hehe-he//he!*
		'make BOATS!' ((laughing)) 'hehe!'
11	A:	*e eli pū::!*
		'. . . to dig a hole!'
12	Ma:	*fai VAʻA!*
		'make BOATS!'
13	I:	*faʻa VAʻA! alu. kope.*
		'make BOATS! Go. quick.'
14		*e ō ʻuma (le) fa (i / le) vaʻa.*
		'to go finish (the) making (of) boats.'
15	S:	*//sole!*
		brother!
16	A:	*ʻo le vaʻa A :: FI. : !*
		'An ELECTRIC boat!'

17   *// e ola le va`a afi.*
            'the electric boat works.'
18   I: *(`uma) le va`a afi.*
            'the electric boat (is finished).'
19   *alu. alu. alu. //((softer)) alu-alu-alu-alu.*
            'go. go. go. go-go-go-go.'

While seven-year-old Ameto is still working at making his own pretend toilet, six-year-old Si`i proposes to go to wash in the sea, but the suggestion is ignored by the rest of the group. Only after Ameto has repeatedly announced (lines 7–9) that he has finished making the toilet does the older boy, Ioane (nine years), propose a new task, building a boat (*fai va`a*) (line 12). The proposal is accepted by four-year-old Manuele (line 12), who, however, continues to dig into the sand. Ioane immediately expands his own proposal into a more complex directive that includes the same verb (*`uma* ('finish')) previously used by Ameto (line 14). The latter accepts and further expands Ioane's proposal, making the boat 'electric' (*va`a afi*); that is, with a motor.

At the end of the excerpt, the pretend play turns into a quickly uttered series of individual proposals with the same rhythm and sing-song prosody. The play frame (Bateson 1955) has acquired recognizable features of 'verbal performance' – in the sense described by Bauman (1975) – as made evident by the frequent use of parallelism in the form of complete or partial repetition of the immediately preceding utterance, within or across turns. This type of performance is related to but different from the notion of performance used by Goffman (1959) to describe everyday interaction as a stage where individuals assume particular roles and work at managing the impression they give about themselves as moral characters. In the exchange among the Samoan children, one of the goals of each contribution is to keep the exchange going, or 'make it last,' as suggested by Elinor [Ochs] Keenan's (1983) study of the spontaneous verbal play of her twins. The practical, action-oriented aspect of the interaction among the Samoan boys is – phenomeno-logically speaking – repeatedly 'suspended' as participants become an audience and verbal contributions are explicitly evaluated not only by whether or not there is an uptake of a given proposal – as we saw, Si`i's proposal of going to wash in the sea (line 6) is ignored all the others – but also by a standard feedback signal such as laughter, which suggests that each proposal is being judged not so much on the basis of whether it will be carried out but in terms of whether it is funny, clever, or original as well as in terms of its contribution to keeping the verbal exchange going as a goal in itself.

Example 19.4 is a continuation of the previous interaction:

Example 19.4:   'Boys on the beach'

20   S: *fai MAUGA! fai MAUGA!*
            'make HILLS! make HILLS!'

21   A: *fai le FU.: (G)`A :. fai FU`A!*
          'make a FLAG. make FLAGS!'
22   (1.0)
23   I: ī. fai fu`a=
          'yeah. make flags'
24   Ma: *=fai KA`AVALE!*
          'make cars!'
25   A: *fai fu`a. `uma fu`a.*
          'make flags. finish flags.'
26   S: *FAI-FAI!*
          do (it) do (it)!
27   Ma: *(sa // u / fa // i) KA`AVALE!*
          '(comes/do) (the) cars'
28   ((unclear)) (? ?)
29   A: *fai le (alaisa. //alaisa. alaisa.)*
          'make the (rice // rice. rice.)'
[...]

This extended exchange shows that children not only improvise the content of their verbal exchanges by entering and sustaining the frame of 'pretend play,' 'make believe,' or 'role-play' (see Bretherton 1984), but also cleverly produce verbal contributions that are matched against an in-progress collectively evoked and sustained aesthetic, as defined, among other things, by such nonreferential features as the length, volume, rhythm, and prosody of their contiguous utterances and turns.

Improvisation as Patterned Behavior

From previous studies of improvisation in music and other art forms, we learn that typically improvisation does not mean random behavior – as in doing something that is out of the ordinary, completely unpredictable, or unexplainable. Rather, it consists of the production of meaningful actions that follow patterns or principles – what Pressing (1984) calls 'the referent' – that are both sufficiently specific to provide guidelines and constraints on what to do (and what to expect) and sufficiently generic to allow for individual and collective creativity (Berliner 1997). From the point of view of socialization, the study of improvisational genres in music has shown that performers undergo a long and arduous period of training in which repetition, daily routines, and imitation play a major role. This is true of the most diverse genres, from Indian classical music (Neuman 1990) to jazz (Berliner 1994).

Improvisation always implies a combination of conformity and innovation and the extent to which and the areas in which an individual or group is allowed to do something in a novel way vary from one context to another within and across communities. In many improvised musical genres, for example, there is freedom 'only within a rigorous and tightly knit system of structural principles' (Nettl and Riddle 1998: 391). For these reasons, it is not innovation *per se* that defines improvisation but the combination of recognizable variation (from an expected pattern), culture-specific acceptable degree of innovation, and its evaluation (Barontini and Nardini 2009; Duranti and Burrell 2004; Martin 2002). In genres that include multiple performers improvising simultaneously, there are also conventions that shape how performers attend to and respond to others' improvisational contributions (Berger 1999; Black 2008; Duranti 2009; Monson 1996; Pagliai 2010; Sawyer 2001; Tiezzi 2009).

The Evaluation and Sanctioning of Improvisation

In some cases the evaluation of improvisation will be explicit, as when it is the object of verbal comments or gestures, including nodding, laughter, or applauding; in other cases it will be implicit, as when children are allowed to do something in their own way instead of being corrected and forced to follow the pattern that is expected in the given situation. The tension between conformity to expectations and negotiation of the rules on the ground is captured by Marcyliena Morgan in her study of freestyle at 'Project Blowed' in Los Angeles (2009: 96–7):

> While the rules of freestyle are well defined, the grounds for battle are not explicitly stated. Rather, they have been established through long-term socialization in hiphop skill development and assessment. The Project Blowed freestyle of rapid-fire, extemporaneous, articulate delivery is known throughout LA's underground. Members usually follow each other without missing a beat. Their style is the modification and reworking of the American English sound and word system – with Jamaican Creole and Mexican and Chicano Spanish thrown in for added measure. The Project Blowed style stands out in that it is a linguistic exercise in the juxtaposition of meaningful and meaningless sounds, words, and grammatical structures that create fissures that erupt into new meanings.

These playful linguistic innovations documented by Morgan are also used to deliver social and political messages (2009: 97). More generally, she shows that in performing freestyle there are both aesthetic and ethical standards. The latter are expressed in sayings such as 'those who rhyme – represent; those who lack game – complain' (Morgan 2009: 101), which must be understood as a warning against MCs who focus too much on 'dissing' or shaming an opponent. In these contexts, the aesthetic canons – for example, rhyming, keeping the rhythm, and being funny in ways that keep the audience engaged – are also instrumental to a type of problem-solving that has existential as well as political and moral meanings. This is made evident by Alim, Lee, and Mason (2010), who show that hip hop verbal competition can function as a way of working out speakers' own racial, ethnic, and gender identities.

Degree of tolerance toward improvisation

The degree to which improvisation is encouraged versus discouraged in a given context or activity contributes to an analytical distinction between the notion of verbal art as performance and the notion of verbal improvisation. The two do not necessarily imply one another. It is possible to be in the domain of performance in the sense defined above while not being in the domain of improvisation (Sawyer 1995). A good example for clarifying this distinction is found in Paul Kroskrity's (1993, 1998) study of verbal performance among the Arizona Tewa. Kroskrity illustrates a contrast between two speech genres that we could recast as a difference between a speech genre in which improvisation is devalued and a (related) speech genre in which improvisation is tolerated and even expected. In the kiva, the center of ritual life for the Tewa and several other Native American groups in the southwest of the United States, exact reproduction of the ancestral language is demanded: 'In the kiva, ritual performers rely on fixed prayer and song texts, and innovation is neither desired nor tolerated. Ritual performance should replicate past conventions; if such repetition is impossible, the ritual should not be performed at all' (Kroskrity 2000: 336). Indeed, Frank Hamilton Cushing (1957–1900), a pioneer anthropologist practicing participant-observation among the neighboring Zuni, was severely hit with a large wooden pole for uttering a Spanish word in a kiva and thus violating the purist language ideology of the community (2000: 337). As Kroskrity explains, though, other closely related genres, most notably storytelling, share only some of the features of kiva speech 'regimentation' (2009: 47–8), a fact recognized by some Tewa speakers themselves: 'Though [Tewa storytellers] recognize the need for authority-conferring connections, they know their stories are not the fixed-text prayers of [kiva] ritual performance' (2009: 48). In particular, stories are subject to the aesthetics of 'carrying it here'; that is, the need to adapt them to the unique needs and interests of the audience (Kroskrity, personal communication). The degree of similarity between the two genres, along with a performer's leeway in reproducing authoritative texts, is a site of recent ideological contestation (2009: 51). From this and other examples provided by Kroskrity, we conclude that, even though kiva speech is an instance of speech in the domain of performance, in it improvisation is explicitly devalued.

From the point of view of socialization, it is important to document in what activities and to what extent children of various ages and novices (of varying levels) are allowed to improvise. One genre that shows a great deal of variation in this respect is prayer. At one end of the continuum we find 'guided repetition,' for example from the Qur'an (Moore 2006, this volume) or other religious texts. At the other end of the continuum, we find both tolerance and encouragement of improvisation to such an extent that the very boundaries of the genre and even the nature of the activity risk being violated. Example 19.5 is taken from a study of socialization into prayer in the United States (Capps and Ochs 2002).[4] Five-and-a-half-year-old Laurie volunteers to say grace. Her mother lets her do it after making sure that the condition of having everyone sitting at the table is satisfied.

Example 19.5:   Jessup Dinner 1

Participants: Jimmy (4;4), Laurie (5;7), Annie (7;10), Roger (10;8), and mother.

Laurie:	I wanna pray ((clasps her hands)) – Jesus?
Mother:	((to Roger)) ( ) ((adjusting Laurie's chair))
Roger:	((mumbled, to Mom)) ( )=
Laurie:	=Jesus?
Mother:	Wait a minute Laurie ((irritated, throwing arms up in semi-despair)) I'm not sitting down
	((Mother sits))
Laurie:	'kay – Jesus? – plea:?se – um – help us to love and .hh um – Thank you for letting it be a n:ice day and for taking a fun nap? .hh – a:nd – for (letting) Mommy go bye and I'm glad that I cwied to[day? cuz I [like cwying .hh and
Annie:	[((snicker))
Roger:	[((snicker))
Laurie:	I'm glad (that anything/everything) happened today in Jesus name ((claps hands)) A:-MEN!
Roger:	[amen ((clapping lightly))
Mother:	[amen
Jimmy:	[A:MEN
	(1.0) ((Laurie starts licking fork))
Jimmy:	amen bay?be.! ((baby))
Mother:	hohoho
	((general laughter – Mom, then Roger and Annie; Mom gets up))
Jimmy:	[amen
Annie:	[amen honey bunch? ((with Southern accent))
	(1.0)
Annie:	[amen dahling? ((with glamor accent))
Jimmy:	[amen!
Jimmy:	A:MEN bay?be.
	((Mom begins bringing cups and milk container to table and begins pouring))

As pointed out by Capps and Ochs (2002: 47), despite the positive framing of the events ('I'm glad'), 'the recounted events themselves ('Mommy go bye,' 'I cwied today') appear to clash with these sentiments. […] Whereas Laurie's earlier account of pleasant events fits well with the design features of thanksgiving, the evolving problem-centered narrative is dramatically discrepant.'

From the point of view of improvisation, this exchange provides us with a rich example of both creativity and tolerance. The responses by Laurie's siblings display some of the verbal features we previously noticed among the Samoan children playing on the beach and the South African friends joking about their own very serious medical condition. In Example 19.5, the inappropriate and, to the children, humorous verbal additions to the closing 'amen' shift the frame, turning the activity of praying into a playful performance of verbal dexterity. As documented by Capps and Ochs, the breaking of the prayer frame is also found in institutional contexts, for example in the Sunday school. But in that context the teacher tries to bring the children back into assuming the expected behavior. This study shows that children are socialized into being sensitive to the contexts in which playful improvisation is allowed.

Adults and experts may also try to control in advance the amount of freedom of execution that children and novices can have. This is particularly the case when adults are afraid that a younger person acting as messenger might not be able to convey the right message or the appropriate attitude, thereby putting at risk the relationship with the sender or the principal (Goffman 1981). An example of this kind of metapragmatic control is found in the following exchange where two Samoan *matai* ('titled people'), SA and F, order a young man, M, to go and ask the senior orator Iuli for some kava roots ('ava) to be used to prepare the ceremonial drink with the same name.

Example 19.6: 'Some kava for the chiefs'; Western Samoa, May 1981

1	F:	*sau!*
		'come!'
2		(5.0)
3	SA:	*alu fai iā Iuli po 'o iai soga 'ava.*
		'go tell Iuli if he has any kava.'
4		(1.8)
5	F:	*alu fai iā Iuli e-*
		'to tell Iuli to-'
6		(0.3)
7	SA:	*fa'amolemole pe:-*
		'please if-'
8		(0.4)
9	F:	*iai soga 'ava e 'aumai 'o-*
		'(he) has kava to bring - '
10		(2.0)
11		*'o lea kāk-*
		'now that we-'
12		*e- e pokopoko lo kākou pikogu'u!*
		'(that) our subvillage is assembling'
13		(5.0)

14   F: *(o) le (a) maua fo`i fa`apea e::- e: lava mai.*
          '(we) heard also that (he) said (he) would come.'
15   (1.0)
16   F: *`a e `aumai muamua se `ava se`i-*
          'but to give (us) first some kava so that-'
17   ?:   (?)
18   F: *se`i sāugiugi ai.*
          'so that it can be prepared.'
19   (2.2)
20   SA: *fai iai fa`amolemole `ua lee ai so makou `ava*
          'say to him "please we have no kava"'
21   *pe iai soga `ava e:,*
          'if he's got kava, okay?'
22   (0.2)
23   M: *ia`.*
          'okay.'

The collaborative reformulation of what should be said to Iuli shows that both SA and F are concerned with the younger man's ability to show respect and explain the reason for the request. The embedded request in lines 3 and 5 is enriched by SA in line 7 with the addition of the directly quoted term 'please' (*fa`amolemole*) that M should use, which is then, in turn, followed by another embedded request initiated by SA and completed by F as an indirect if- clause (*pe-*) in the third person: 'if- if he has some kava' (lines 7 and 9). F continues by providing M with the lines that can be used to explain to Iuli the reason for the request; namely, that the representatives of the (i.e. Iuli's) subvillage are (already) gathered (line 12) and that they have heard that he had planned to attend (line 14). In anticipation of the response that Iuli might be bringing the kava himself, M is provided with the additional motivating factor for why he has been sent; namely, that the kava roots are needed as soon as possible so that the kava drink can be prepared in time for the gathering (line 18). At this point, chief SA wraps it up with a final reformulation of the request that, if properly delivered, should make Iuli feel sorry for the other chiefs, who do not have any kava of their own. With his 'okay' (*ia`*), M agrees to carry out the task and the exchange comes to completion.

It is the inherently improvised quality of everyday life that worries the two adult speakers in Example 19.6. This exchange shows that, even in a society where children, teenagers, and young adults are routinely asked to perform tasks on behalf of older and more experienced people, there is concern not only with making the request clear but also with its motivation and the manner in which it is delivered. In other words, in sending young M to ask Iuli to provide kava roots for the meeting, the Samoan *matai* F and SA want to do everything they can to control the practical, aesthetic, and moral sense of the request. M must achieve (1) the practical goal of getting the kava roots from Iuli immediately so that he can bring them back before Iuli arrives, (2) the aesthetic goal of asking with a language that displays respect, and (3) the moral goal of making a request that is perceived as just and reasonable and not as an imposition.

Conclusions

In this chapter we have reviewed existing literature in the study of child language, language socialization, and improvisational art genres such as jazz and freestyle in hip hop to provide a general framework for socialization into verbal improvisation and, in turn, for the role of improvisation in socializing children to interact with others in ways that are not only culturally appropriate but also valuable. We know from language acquisition studies that children start out being exposed to and engaging in a high dose of verbal repetition. This repetition, however, also provides the basis of verbal variation, including the variation found in verbal play. As reflected in Bourdieu's use of the notion of habitus, it is when repetition becomes routinization that creativity becomes possible. Rather than being pure invention or random behavior, improvisation in the arts (e.g. in jazz music) as well as in everyday life is founded on established and familiar patterns. This is evident in the ways in which adults and children improvise jokes and in the ways in which children engage in artful verbal play at all stages of development. At the same time, the ability to diverge from established patterns and be creative is itself subject to social control (cf. Csikszentmihalyi 1996). We can therefore say that communities vary in the ways in which they favor improvised verbal behavior in children as well as in adults. In addition, we find varying degrees of tolerance of improvisation depending on the types of activities (e.g. reciting a memorized religious prayer versus saying grace) and the types of participants (e.g. mother versus teacher).

The cases presented in this chapter and the general observations drawn from the literature suggest that we should think of socialization into verbal improvisation as the process whereby novices are allowed, expected, or even encouraged to engage in actions that are locally recognized as different from what they have previously experienced as witnesses or participants. These actions are in turn subject to evaluation for the degree to which they manage to (1) appear seamless, fluid, or effortless; (2) be effective (with respect to the goal of the activity); and (3) be appropriate from the point of view of the aesthetics and ethics of the activity as recognized in the community.

In other words, in addition to being oriented toward the accomplishment of something new or at least partly different from what was previously done by themselves or others, verbal improvisation is guided by practical, aesthetic, and moral canons that are specific to the cultural tradition that gives meaning to the ongoing activity.

ACKNOWLEDGMENTS

We thank Anna Corwin, Paul Kroskrity, Elinor Ochs, and Jason Throop for their comments and suggestions on earlier drafts of this chapter. Any errors in interpretation or representation of other people's work remain, of course, our own.

NOTES

1   Griffin and Mehan (1981) are an exception in their proposal that we should think of classroom interaction as spontaneous improvisation.
2   These data are drawn from a larger corpus of sound Super 8 films and audio recordings that are part of a project on children's activities supported in the Spring of 1981 by the (then) Research School of Pacific Studies at The Australian National University while Alessandro Duranti and Elinor Ochs were postdoctoral fellows at that university.
3   In the Samoan transcripts, we follow the traditional orthographic conventions originally introduced by British missionaries in the nineteenth century: the macron on vowels (e.g. ā, ē) indicates a long vowel, the inverted comma (') stands for a glottal stop, and the letter 'g' stands for a velar nasal, as in the 'ng' of the English word 'sing.' The latter convention was economical given that Samoan does not have the voiced palatal sound /g/ – and borrowings such as the English 'guitar' are pronounced /kitala/ – but it has had the disastrous effect that people who are not familiar with the language do interpret the 'g' as a /g/), and thus mispronounce it, for example reading Pago Pago, the name of the capital of American Samoa, as if it should be pronounced /pago pago/ instead of /paŋo paŋo/.
4   We thank Elinor Ochs for providing us with a fuller version of the original transcript used for the analysis given in Capps and Ochs (2002).

REFERENCES

Abrahams, R. D. (1962) Playing the dozens. *Journal of American Folklore* 75: 209–20.

Alim, H. S. (2004) Now *you Know my Steez: An Ethnographic and Sociolinguistic Study of Styleshifting in a Black American Speech Community.* Durham, NC: American Dialectical Society and Duke University Press.

Alim, H. S. (2006) *Roc the Mic Right: The Language of Hip Hop Culture.* London and New York: Routledge.

Alim, H. S. (2007) 'The Whig party don't exist in my hood': Knowledge, reality, and education in the hip hop nation. In H. S. Alim and J. Baugh (eds.), *Talking Black Talk: Language, Education, and Social Change.* 15–29. New York: Teachers College.

Alim, H. S., Lee, J., and Mason, L. C. (2010) 'Short' fried-rice-eating Chinese MCs and good-hair-havin Uncle Tom niggas: Performing race and ethnicity in freestyle rap battles. *Journal of Linguistic Anthropology* 20(1): 116–33.

Barontini, C. and Nardini, P. (eds.) (2009) *Improvisar Cantando. Atti Dell'incontro Di Studi Sulla Poesia Estemporanea in Ottava*

Rima. Roccastrada, Italy: Biblioteca Comunale.

Bateson, G. (1955) A theory of play and fantasy. *Psychiatric Research Reports* 2: 39–51.

Bauman, R. (1975) Verbal art as performance. *American Anthropologist* 77: 290–311.

Berger, H. M. and Del Negro, G. P. (2002) Bauman's verbal art and the social organization of attention: The role of reflexivity in the aesthetics of performance. *Journal of American Folklore* 115: 62–91.

Berger, H. M. (1999) *Metal, Rock, and Jazz: Perception and the Phenomenology of Musical Experience*. Hanover, NH: University Press of New England.

Berliner, P. (1994) *Thinking in Jazz: The Infinite Art of Improvisation*. Chicago, IL: Chicago University Press.

Berliner, P. (1997) Give and take: The collective conversation of jazz performance. In R. K. Sawyer (ed.), *Creativity in Performance*. 9–41. Greenwich, CT: Ablex.

Black, S. P. (2008) Creativity and learning jazz: The practice of 'listening'. *Mind, Culture, and Activity* 15: 1–17.

Black, S. P. (2010) Facing HIV/AIDS stigmatization in South Africa through language and music. Doctoral Dissertation. Los Angeles, CA: University of California, Los Angeles.

Black, S. P. (forthcoming) Laughing to Death: Joking as Support Amidst Stigmatization for isiZulu-Speaking South Africans Living with HIV/AIDS. *Journal of Linguistic Anthropology*.

Bourdieu, P. (1977) *Outline of a Theory of Practice*. R. Nice, transl. Cambridge: Cambridge University Press.

Bretherton, I. (ed.) (1984) *Symbolic Play: The Development of Social Understanding*. Orlando, FL: Academic Press.

Capps, L. and Ochs, E. (2002) Cultivating prayer. In C. Ford, B. Fox, and S. A. Thompson (eds.), *The Language of Turn and Sequence*. 39–55. Oxford: Oxford University Press.

Cekaite, A. and Aronsson, K. (2004) Repetition and joking in children's second language conversations: Playful recyclings in an immersion classroom. *Discourse Studies* 6(3): 373–92.

Cekaite, A. and Aronsson, K. (2005) Language play, a collaborative resource in children's L2 learning. *Applied Linguistics* 2(2): 169–91.

Csikszentmihalyi, M. (1996) *Creativity: Flow and the Psychology of Discovery and Invention*. New York: Harper Collins Publishers.

Dortier, J.-F. (2002) Les idées pures n'existent pas. *Sciences Humaines Special Issue: Pierre Bourdieu* 3–8.

Duranti, A. (2004) Agency in language. In A. Duranti (ed.), *A Companion to Linguistic Anthropology*. 451–73. Malden, MA: Blackwell.

Duranti, A. (2009) The relevance of Husserl's theory to language socialization. *Journal of Linguistic Anthropology* 19(2): 205–26.

Duranti, A. and Burrell, K. (2004) Jazz improvisation: A search for hidden harmonies and a unique self. *Ricerche di Psicologia* 27(3): 71–101.

Finnegan, R. (1977) *Oral Poetry: Its Nature, Significance and Social Context*. Bloomington, IN: Indiana University Press.

Giddens A. (1979) *Central Problems in Social Theory: Action, Structure and Contradiction in Social Analysis*. Berkeley, CA: University of California Press.

Goffman, E. (1959) *The Presentation of Self in Everyday Life*. Garden City NY: Doubleday.

Goffman, E. (1967) *Interaction Ritual: Essays in Face to Face Behavior*. Garden City, New York: Doubleday.

Goffman, E. (1981) Footing. In E. Goffman (ed.), *Forms of Talk*. 124–57. Philadelphia, PA: University of Pennsylvania Press.

Griffin, P. and Mehan, H. (1981) Sense and ritual in classroom discourse. In F. Coulmas (ed.), *Conversational Routine: Explorations in Standardized Communication*

Situations and Pre-patterned Speech. 187–213. The Hague: Mouton.

Howard, K. M. (2009) Breaking in and spinning out. *Language in Society* 38: 339–63.

Husserl E. (1960) *Cartesian Meditations: An Introduction to Phenomenology.* The Hague: Nijhoff.

Hymes, D. (1975) Breakthrough into performance. In D. Ben-Amos and K. S. Goldstein (eds.), *Folklore: Performance and Communication.* 11–74. The Hague: Mouton.

Keenan, E. Ochs. (1974) Conversational competence in children. *Journal of Child Language* 1: 163–83.

Keenan, E. Ochs. (1983) Making it last: Repetition in children's discourse. In E. Ochs and B. B. Schieffelin (eds.), *Acquiring Conversational Competence.* 26–39. Boston, MA: Routledge and Kegan Paul.

Kochman, T. (1970) Toward an ethnography of black American speech behavior. In N. E. Whitten Jr. and J. F. Szwed (eds.), *Afro-American Anthropology.* 145–62. New York: Free Press.

Kroskrity, P. (1993) *Language, History and Identity: Ethnolinguistic Studies of the Arizona Tewa.* Tuscon, AZ: University of Arizona Press.

Kroskrity, P. (1998) Arizona Tewa kiva speech as manifestation of a dominant language ideology. In B. B. Schieffelin, K. Woolard, and P. V. Kroskrity (eds.), *Language Ideologies: Practice and Theory.* 103–22. New York: Oxford University Press.

Kroskrity, P. (2000) Language ideologies in the expression and representation of Arizona Tewa identity. In P. Kroskrity (ed.), *Regimes of Language: Ideologies, Polities, and Identities.* 329–59. Santa Fe, NM: School of American Research Press.

Kroskrity, P. (2009) Narrative reproductions: Ideologies of storytelling, authoritative words, and generic regimentation in the village of Tewa. *Journal of Linguistic Anthropology* 19(1): 40–56.

Kulick, D. and Schieffelin, B. B. (2004) Language socialization. In A. Duranti (ed.), *A Companion to Linguistic Anthropology.* 349–68. Malden, MA: Blackwell.

Labov, W. (1972) Rules for ritual insults. In *Language in the Inner City: Studies in the Black English Vernacular.* 297–353. Philadelphia, PA: University of Pennsylvania Press.

Martin, P. J. (2002) Spontaneity and organization. In M. Cooke and D. Horn (eds.), *The Cambridge Companion to Jazz.* 133–52. Cambridge: Cambridge University Press.

Mead, G. H. (1932) *The Philosophy of the Present.* Chicago, IL: University of Chicago Press.

Mitchell-Kernan, C. (1972) Signifying and marking: Two Afro-American speech acts. In J. J. Gumperz and D. Hymes (eds.), *Directions in Sociolinguistics: The Ethnography of Communication.* 161–79. New York: Holt, Rinehart and Winston.

Monson, I. (1996) *Saying Something: Jazz Improvisation and Interaction.* Chicago, IL: Chicago University Press.

Morgan, M. (2009) *The Real Hiphop: Battling for Knowledge, Power, and Respect in the LA Underground.* Durham, NC: Duke University Press.

Moore, L. C. (2006) Learning by heart in Qur'anic and public schools in northern Cameroon. *Social Analysis* 50(3): 109–26.

Nachmanovitch, S. (1990) *Free Play: Improvisation in Life and Art.* New York: Penguin.

Nettl, B. and Riddle, R. (1998) Taqsim Nahawand revisited: The musicianship of Jihad Racy. In B. Nettl and M. Russell (eds.), *In the Course of Performance: Studies in the World of Musical Improvisation.* 369–93. Chicago, IL: University of Chicago Press.

Neuman, D. M. (1990) *The Life of Music in North India: The Organization of an Artistic Tradition.* Chicago, IL: University of Chicago Press.

Pagliai, V. (2010) Conflict, cooperation, and facework in *contrasto* verbal duels. *Language in Society* 20(1): 87–100.

Peters, A. M. and Boggs, S. T. (1986) Interactional routines as cultural influences upon language acquisition. In B. B. Schieffelin and E. Ochs (eds.), *Language Socialization Across Cultures*. 80–96. Cambridge: Cambridge University Press.

Pressing, J. (1984) Cognitive processes in improvisation. In R. Crozier and A. Chapman (eds.), *Cognitive Processes in the Perception of Art*. 345–63. Amsterdam, The Netherlands: North Holland.

Pressing, J. (1998) Psychological constraints on improvisational expertise and communication. In B. Nettl and M. Russell (eds.), *In the Course of Performance: Studies in the World of Musical Improvisation*. 47–67. Chicago, IL: University of Chicago Press.

Rampton, B. (1999) Inner London Deutsch and the animation of an instructed foreign language. *Journal of Sociolinguistics* 3: 480–504.

Reynolds, J. F. (2010) Enregistering the voices of discursive figures of authority in Antonero children's socio-dramatic play. *Pragmatics* 20(4): 467–93.

Rogoff, B. (1990) *Apprenticeship in Thinking*. New York: Oxford University Press.

Sawyer, R. K. (1993) The pragmatics of play: Interactional strategies during children's pretend play. *Pragmatics* 3(3): 259–82.

Sawyer, R. K. (1995) Creativity as mediated action: A comparison of improvisational performance and product creativity. *Mind, Culture, and Activity* 2(3): 172–91.

Sawyer, R. K. (1996) The semiotics of improvisation: The pragmatics of musical and verbal performance. *Semiotica* 108(3/4): 269–306.

Sawyer, R. K. (1997) *Pretend Play as Improvisation: Conversation in the Preschool Classroom*. Mahwah, NJ: Lawrence Erlbaum.

Sawyer, R. K. (2001) *Creating Conversations: Improvisation in Everyday Discourse*. Cresskill, NJ: Hampton Press.

Sawyer, R. K. (2003) *Group Creativity: Music, Theater, Collaboration*. Mahwah, NJ: Lawrence Erlbaum.

Schegloff, E. A. (2007) *Sequence Organization in Interaction: A Primer in Conversation Analysis, Vol. 1*. Cambridge: Cambridge University Press.

Sherzer, J. (2002) *Speech Play and Verbal Art*. Austin, TX: University of Texas Press.

Silverstein M. (1976) Shifters, linguistic categories, and cultural description. In K. H. Basso and H. A. Selby (eds.), *Meaning in Anthropology*. 11–56. Albuquerque, NM: University of New Mexico Press.

Smitherman, G. (1977) *Talkin and Testifyin: The Language of Black America*. Detroit, MI: Wayne State University Press.

Smitherman, G. (2007) The power of the rap: The black idiom and the new black poetry. In H. S. Alim and J. Baugh (eds.), *Talking Black Talk: Language, Education, and Social Change*. 77–91. New York: Teachers College.

Spears, A. (2007) African American communicative practices: Improvisation, semantic license, and augmentation. In H. S. Alim and J. Baugh (eds.), *Talking Black Talk: Language, Education, and Social Change*. 100–11. New York: Teachers College.

Taylor, C. (1985) *Human Agency and Language*. Cambridge: Cambridge University Press.

Tiezzi, G. (2009) La pratica dell'improvvisazione in ottava rima in Maremma. Forme dell'interazione nella poetica estemporanea. In C. Barontini and P. Nardini (eds.), *Improvisar Cantando. Atti dell'incontro di Studi Sulla Poesia Estemporanea in Ottava Rima*. 81–104. Roccastrada, Italy: Biblioteca Comunale.

Turner, V. (1982) *From Ritual to Theater: The Seriousness of Human Play*. New York: Performing Arts Journal Publication.

20 Language Socialization and Verbal Play

KARIN ARONSSON

Play Hierarchies and Language Socialization

In a broad review of anthropological studies of play, Helen Schwartzman (1978) discusses the role of culture in play and ways in which play often involves extended discussions about who will play, with whom, and in what ways. Young children successively engage in complex biddings and other negotiations, displaying political skills and mutually socializing each other into participation rights and other aspects of social order (Evaldsson and Corsaro 1998; Goodwin and Kyratzis, this volume; Sheldon 1990; Whalen 1995). Complex argumentation and negotiations reflect children's growing cultural experience and can be seen as key aspects of play. What we could call children's play politics should therefore be at the foreground of theorizing on play and culture.

Even early play monologues are intrinsically cultural events in that children's play activities involve reconstructions of past encounters with important groups in their lives: siblings, peers, and various family constellations.

> Play is more nearly recollection than imagination in that it is more memory in action than a novel imaginary situation. (Vygotsky 1967: 16).

In line with Vygotsky's theorizing, verbal play echoes past events, and even solitary play is therefore essentially a cultural event. Gradually, it will include more sophisticated transformations and variations. Yet, neither Schwartzman nor Vygotsky have foregrounded the role of language and language socialization in children's play.

This chapter will foreground the role of language in children's play, focusing on ways in which language is employed both in language play and in ways in

The Handbook of Language Socialization, First Edition. Edited by Alessandro Duranti, Elinor Ochs, and Bambi B. Schieffelin.

which children verbally package play performances, teasing activities, and assessments of other players as well as play roles and objects. In their pioneering work on sibling and peer groups, Elinor Ochs and Bambi B. Schieffelin (1979, 1984) revealed two types of bias in much early research on children's socialization: an intergenerational bias, privileging the roles of parents (rather than siblings and peers), and a dyadic bias, foregrounding individual adult caretakers (notably the mother) rather than the role of groups in children's lives. This chapter will draw upon and extend their critique by presenting ways in which anthropological and other ethnographic work on children's sibling and peer play are rich sites for exploring language socialization phenomena. It will be shown that such play involves series of implicit and explicit choices and play hierarchies. Much in play is up for negotiation, for example choice of play partner (access rituals), play language, play roles, and toys. In ranking various options, children engage in teasing as well as other implicit and explicit assessments of play objects and partners. As will be shown, play hierarchies are ever-present phenomena in everyday play practices.

Participants' Perspectives – A Methodological Note

In social interaction, participants' moves may vary in terms of 'footings' (Goffman 1979); that is, their alignments toward co-participants, topics, and objects. In a play context, a choice of footing may refer to playful versus nonplayful positionings; that is, ways of constructing a target activity (e.g. teasing) as serious talk or as nonserious. This also means that there may be more than one reading or set of interpretations. What is seen as playful by one participant may be read as serious by another. Similarly, what is serious for a four-year-old may be casual, nonserious play for the same child as an eight-year-old (cf. Goffman 1972 [1961] on children in different age classes taking rides on a merry-go-round). Traditional analyses of play have often missed this multiperspective aspect of children's interactions, whether they involve intra- or intergenerational play. By the same token, what is seen as the main activity by two participants can be analyzed as by-play (Goffman 1979) from the perspective of a third participant. Multiparty encounters, such as group play, necessarily thus involve complex and equivocal relational matrices in which some parties are, in fact, marginalized or excluded from the action.

This review will draw upon some Goffmanian insights in that it will present studies that document the footings and participation frameworks of play, revealing ways in which relational positionings in play and game worlds are basic elements in the making of membership categories in specific communities, be it girls versus boys (Danby and Baker 1998; Thorne 1993), gamers versus newbies, or nerds versus mainstreamers (Blashki and Nichol 2005; Boellstorff 2008; Bucholtz 1999). When the analyst engages in detailed explorations of the interactants' moves, it is possible to determine whether something is said or done in earnest or as a nonserious move. Ethnographic work on children's socialization should therefore not be confined to interviews and observations. Video and audio recordings are needed in order to show in detail the many ways in which participants orient to each other and when and how they change footings in the direction of more playful modes. Such methods have recently become something of a standard feature of language socialization studies of children's play (Cromdal and Aronsson 2000; de León 2007; Evaldsson 2005; Goodwin 2006). Thereby, participants' perspectives are studied through what they say and do to each other and not only through interview-based ethnographic work on what they say about each other.

This means that language socialization practices are not seen as unilateral forms of transmission; the analyst has to take into account both the speaker's moves and the recipient's uptake. For instance, language socialization involves mutual influences in that parental practices shape children's ways of behaving but are, in turn, also shaped and reshaped by these very encounters. In many ways, informal learning can be seen as a type of 'mutual apprenticeship' (Pontecorvo, Fasulo, and Sterponi 2001). Such mutual apprenticeship does, of course, also pertain to play practices, both between peers and between children and caregivers.

This chapter draws on socialization practices involved in inter- and intragenerational play practices, access rituals, teasing practices, and play performance. Moreover, it will illuminate young children's language play in bilingual communities as well as adolescents' video-gaming activities: practices that separate gamers from 'newbies' and 'wannabees' and members from nonmembers (Blashki and Nichol 2005). An overriding idea is that aesthetic practices are intimately related to participation, in that performance might be seen in terms of audience design features, which are linked to the soliciting of attention in the competitive play environments of children and adolescents. Therefore, play practices also invoke and create play hierarchies.

Access Rituals

In many different parts of the world, children use specific language formats for signaling 'this is play' (Bateson 1972; Schwartzman 1978). One of the earliest and simplest ways of signaling play action is through verbalizations in the form of repetitions of the target activity or object – for example, 'cooking, cooking, cooking' or 'kiss, kiss' – which can be seen as a kind of verbal shorthand for the activity. Even very young children spontaneously use such play formats. In her doctoral dissertation on multimodal play repertoires, Tamm (1990) showed that Swedish preschoolers manage quite well at making drawings and verbal role enactments of, for example, getting dressed (signaling, for instance, 'putting on shoes, putting on shoes, putting on shoes'). Yet, only somewhat older school children managed to enact convincing pantomime versions of similar actions (without any talk). Across various semiotic modes, the children thus varied in the extent to which they could perform target play actions.

Obviously, verbal repetition forms one important mode for signaling play. In quite diverse language communities, the past tense is used for planning play – for example, 'and we were sisters' for planning to engage in playing sisters. The past tense is thus used as a kind of hypothetical mode (see Andersen 1990; Aronsson and Thorell 1999; Garvey 1993; Göncu 1993; Vygotsky 1967, who provide examples from among US, Turkish, Russian, and Swedish children).

In his analyses of peer interaction in a North American preschool environment, Corsaro (1979) has shown that young children (aged three to five years) might be quite selective about who gets to play and who does not. In a group context, such as a preschool play corner, play is set up by specific children and others are not automatically included. In order to access play, young children thus have to engage in various roundabout movements: circling around the ongoing play activity, offering to help, handing play objects, initiating mirror activities nearby, making claims on objects or areas, greeting players, commenting on play, requesting access, or just hanging around.

Computer gaming is a contemporary arena where children have developed a series of ways for soliciting the attention of co-participants. Like other games, computer games require cultural knowledge about the rules of the game. One of the special and distinctive requirements of computer gaming is the ability to maintain a rapid tempo. In work on Swedish kindergarten and school-age children's peer group gaming in home contexts, Pål Aarsand and Karin Aronsson (2009) have shown that the players designed verbal comments in such a way that they did not slow down the tempo of the game. Through response cries such as 'oh' and 'wow' (or other blurted vocalizations displaying affects such as revulsion, fear, and pleasure) (Goffman 1981), the gamers assist each other in orienting to what is risky, novel, or noteworthy in the game. Thereby, they indicate what is important (Aarsand and Aronsson 2009), socializing each other into gamers, as opposed to newbies or wannabe players, who are as yet not aware of how the gaming is organized.

Gaming and chatting activities are often also marked by so-called 'leet speak' elements (Blashki and Nichol 2005) such as established abbreviations (e.g. 'lol,' laughing out loud) or hybrid words featuring both letters and numbers – for example, 'waiting 4u' – in messages and in hybrid nicknames (Aarsand 2008; Tingstad 2003). Hybrid nicknames may for instance involve both letters and numbers or both small and capital letters and other graphic markers: for example, 'HOT girl' and 'KISS_ME,' which were nicknames adopted by two of the school-age children documented by Tingstad in her work on Norwegian chat room visitors. Such hybrid registers are also quite common in other types of contemporary youth media culture and they offer the participants ways of positioning themselves as in the know. In contrast to so-called newbies – that is, novices – gamers in the know deploy leet speak and other types of jargon as ways of positioning themselves as advanced players – people high up in the play hierarchy. In this way, play positions are intimately linked to language socialization practices.

Teasing

Some early play rituals used by parents with their infants and toddlers reveal elements of teasing (e.g. Kulick 1992; Schieffelin 1990). When teasing children, parents and other elders can be seen to play with the border between what is serious and nonserious, sensitizing them to pay attention to different types of footing. During the early part of the last century, Sigmund Freud (1959 [1926]) discussed peekaboo and how this game involves ambivalent play practices in the boundary between separation and reunion, drawing on the young child's separation anxiety; that is, its fear of being left alone by its caregivers. Between about eight months and one year of age, peekaboo is a favorite game of many infants. The child may shriek in delight as the grownup disappears, reappears, and disappears. This may be repeated again and again, and the child will be delighted each time. The Freudian explanation is that the child has just learnt that adults may disappear and it is both scared and delighted in re-enacting this fear, and Piaget (1968 [1945]) later explained that part of the delightfulness of this game is that the child has just acquired an awareness of the fact that objects, including love objects such as caregivers, do not just disappear but are still there (even when out of sight). In terms of game analysis, peekaboo can thus be seen as a type of nonverbal teasing (even if it may involve vocalizations such as laughs, giggles, or more or less articulate 'oh's or other response cries). When the grownup goes into hiding the child is being teased, and when s/he reappears the child is reassured that love objects are indeed constant.

Games of hide-and-seek have a related logic of teasing. A cherished person or object may disappear temporarily, but it is still there. On an underlying level, such games may of course take place as a type of nonverbal teasing: the grownup pretends that the object is gone, teasing the child by suggestion that s/he might loose an important toy or other cherished artifact, and, again, the child is comforted when the object reappears (thanks to the 'magical' power of the adult). Another game that plays on the boundary between pleasure and fear is the adult throwing or lifting up the child into the air. The child may shriek in delight, but it may also start to cry as the game progresses. Fear and delight are inextricably related in such nonverbal teasing games. In her autobiography, *Under My Skin*, Doris Lessing reconstrued her fear of being tossed into the air as a young child, how the hands and laughing faces of the adults were overpowering and scary, and how she dreaded being tickled, as in her family's pillow fight games before bedtime, where her father, to whom she otherwise was very close, appears somewhat threatening (1995: 31):

> By now my head is aching badly, the knocking headache of overexcitement. His great hands go to work on my ribs. My screams, helpless, hysterical, desperate. Then tears. But we were being taught how to be good sports. For being a good sport was necessary for the middle-class life. To put with 'ragging' and with being hurt, with being defeated in games, being 'tickled' until you wept, was a necessary preparation.

Pillow fight games, as well as peekaboo and hide-and-seek, all play on the boundary between pleasure and discomfort. On an underlying level, they can be seen as borderwork play, in the interface of children's impotence and adults' authority. Ultimately, adults are the ones who let go or reappear; who choose to withdraw or to show mercy.

Similarly, children's own play practices involve boundary work between pleasure and fear. Traditional notions of play, such as 'rough-and-tumble' play, suggest that young children's own play practices may seem rough but that they are basically happy and cheerful. Detailed studies of the participants' own perspectives – as displayed in children's play – reveal such happy shared delight, but they also show exclusion, competition, gatekeeping phenomena, rankings, and participants' hard work at performing in such a way that they will be included. In her ethnography of gender borderwork in a North American school setting, Thorne (1993) has documented ways in which boy–girl play chasing routines would draw on related ambivalences. All these play practices (e.g. peekaboo, rough-and-tumble play, and chasing) primarily involve nonverbal resources. Moreover, it can be argued that they involve borderwork between fear and pleasure in ways that are quite similar to what is later explored through adults' and children's joking, teasing, and related types of play.

In cultures in many parts of the world, verbal teasing similarly plays a role in adults' play routines with very young children. Drawing on recordings from fieldwork in Papua New Guinea, both Schieffelin (1990) and Kulick (1992) have documented ways in which parents and other elders engage in extended teasing activities with toddlers and very young children, including playful threats and ridicule, as in this teasing routine from Gapun, where a Tok-Pisin-speaking mother, Sopak, tells her toddler daughter Masito (1;11 years) that her sister and favorite playmate, Kama, is gone for ever (Kulick 1992: 229):

Example 20.1

Tok Pisin original is here presented in italics; Taiap is underlined.

1	*Toddler:*	Kama?	'Kama?'
2	Mother:	*Kama i go Wongan*	'Kama went to Wongan'
3	Toddler:	*Ah?*	'Ah?'
4	Mother:	*Kama i go long bus. Em i*	'Kama went into the forest.
5		*go kisim <u>oike</u>*	She went to get <u>mangoes.</u>'
6	Toddler:	*Ma, Kama?*	'Ma, Kama?'
7	Mother:	<u>*Sia aiata*</u>. *Kama indai pinis.*	'<u>Sia enough</u>. Kama died.
8		*Snek i kaikaim em na em indai.*	A snake bit her and she died.'

Through such teasing, very young New Guinean children are taught to be on the alert to what is serious and what is nonserious, and to the whereabouts of important others (where did Kama go, and where is she now? Would she normally go to fetch mangoes at this time of the day?). Thereby, playful teasing socializes children into *save* (being smart and alert), which is an important cultural virtue in the local community, linked to notions of modernity and to Tok Pisin not to the vernacular Taiap. It is different type of teasing from the nonverbal teasing of peekaboo, hide-and-seek, or pillow fights, but some of the underlying elements are the same. The child is socialized into heightened alertness and into defending herself/himself.

As can be seen in this brief review of play in the borderwork between delight and fear, both nonverbal and verbal teasing games draw on the boundary between adult authority and the child's lack thereof. In play rituals, the child may challenge adult authority within the frames of the play. Yet, ultimately, adults tend to come out as winners, as it were, in that they are stronger or more in the know.

In fieldwork with African American school-age children in Philadelphia, Marjorie Goodwin (1990) has shown that bragging, teasing, and gossiping (including *he-said-she-said*-routines) are recurrent phenomena in children's play dialogues, and that various types of such verbal challenges of co-participants are integral parts of children's assessments of each other (see also Goodwin and Kyratzis, this volume). Moreover, it can be seen that such episodes often develop in a stepwise fashion from relatively mild forms of teasing or gossiping to more elaborate and escalated forms, successively upgrading implicit criticism, as co-participants align (Evaldsson 2005; Sheldon 1990; Tholander and Aronsson 2002).

Consumption, Play Hierarchies, and Peer Assessments

As mentioned in the introduction, Schwartzman (1978) has shown that children's play often does not move beyond the planning phase. Language plays a significant role in play, as a large proportion of play time is devoted to negotiations about the projected playing, including who gets to play what role. In documentations of children playing house in US and Swedish contexts, there is prototypically only one mother and one father (Andersen 1990; Aronsson and Thorell 1999). This means that less favoured roles, such as that of the youngest child, recurrently are ascribed to someone who actually would prefer to play another role. Competition for attractive roles is thus one of the dynamic features of children's play (for other US studies see Garvey and Kramer 1989; Sheldon 1990; Whalen 1995). Often children are quite ingenious in finding mechanisms for taking turns in assuming unattractive roles, for sharing attractive ones, or for obtaining other privileges as a compensation for accepting less attractive roles. Bargaining and other negotiations are thus key elements of the planning of play.

> It is incorrect to conceive of play as activity without purpose; play is purposeful activity for a child. In athletic games you can win or lose, in a race you can come first, second, or last. In short, the purpose decides the game. It justifies all the rest. Purpose as the ultimate goal determines the child's affective attitude to play. When running a race, a child can be highly agitated or distressed and little may remain of pleasure because he finds it physically painful to run, while if he is overtaken he will experience little functional pleasure. (Vygotsky 1967: 16)

Competitive aspects of children's play can be linked to contemporary discussions of social hierarchies. Elinor Ochs (1992) has discussed how participants indicate age and gender hierarchies through the ways in which they position themselves prosodically and through other verbal and nonverbal accentuation. In his works on positions and positionings, Pierre Bourdieu (2003 [1979]) discusses ways in which participants position themselves in terms of both symbolic and economic markets.

In work on children's play with collector items, it has similarly been shown that children position themselves and their co-participants through verbal assessments that indicate implicit rankings in locally grounded symbolic and economic markets. For Swedish children, this type of identity work is an integral part of playing marbles or playing with so-called pog disks, Pokemon cards, and other commercially available collectors' items (Evaldsson and Corsaro 1998; Sparrman and Aronsson 2003). In their work on pog disks, Sparrman and Aronsson have documented some of the ways in which boys at an after-school center engaged in extended negotiations about the value of their pogs. As in Example 20.3, concerning US cars, color, glitter, and shine were important parameters, as was the fact that a pog disk was a commercial item (rather than home made); disks that featured cherished images, for example those of contemporary icons such as Spiderman, were also valued. As in the game of marbles (Evaldsson and Corsaro 1998), the players spent extensive time in trading and discussing the metrics of their play objects (marbles, pogs). In many ways, it was apparent that the pogs were important markers of the boys' positions in the local play hierarchy. Assessments (categorizations) of pogs therefore had something of a dual purpose: categorizing both the play item and its owner.

Play hierarchies are obviously related to symbolic markets, where someone's value is positioned in relation to that of other players. Yet symbolic markets are, of course, not completely independent of economic rankings. In several cases, a top position on the economic market may also be linked to a top ranking on the symbolic market.

Characters from the media and popular culture can serve as sources for fantasy play. In work on peer play at a Swedish after-school center for young children, Anna Sparrman (2002) has documented a series of play practices modeled on the singing group the Spice Girls: dancing like Spice Girls, drawing Spice Girls, and verbally engaging in fantasy play. Some of the activities involved hybrid play activities – for example, the girls actually played with wooden blocks, building roads and houses for the Spice Girls, and also engaged in fantasy play about their idols. Moreover, the girls wrote 'Spice Girls fairy tales' (*Spice Girls Sagor*) in ways that involved information about the Spice Girls' extravagant consumption patterns. One of the ways in which an idol (e.g. Posh Spice or Wild Spice) could outperform others was, for instance, by taking a novel car every time that she 'went shopping' (buying candy and groceries). Yet, the written Spice Girls fairy tales would also foreground routine activities: 'Now, we'll go shopping, then we'll go home. Emma will play the violin, Mel C is out on the town, Geri is ill. Victoria is also out on the town. Mel B is at home, eating candy, and then everybody will eat pop corn, and then they'll sleep' (Sparrman 2001). When she had finishing reading out loud, the writer commented, 'Well, this is poor!' but one of her peers laughingly joined in the telling, claiming that Mel B was also ill. The players identified with specific Spice Girls but much of the playing, including the written stories, were collaborative products, produced with some glee (Sparrman 2002: 177).

Example 20.2

Participants: girls at an after-school centre for grades one to three: Hedda, Gunhild, and another girl, playing Spice Girls with wooden blocks.

1	Hedda:	*På kvällen var de x. Då*	'In the evening, there was x.'
2		*ställer jag in mina bilar här*	'Then I put my cars in here'
3	X:	*Jag har ett garage*	'I have a garage'
4	Hedda:	*Jag har också ett garage*	'I have a garage too'
5	Gunhild:	*Jag har byggt ett jättelyxigt*	'I have built a super-luxurious garage
6		*garage och jag kör skitfort*	and I'm driving fucking fast on the road
7		*på vägen in till stan*	into town. When there are bridges, I'm
8		*När det är broar, jag bara*	just jumping across'
9		*hoppar över dem xx*	((driving a car with her hand))

The garage is 'super-luxurious,' and Gunhild/Spice Girl is driving 'fucking fast' *(skitfort)*, jumping across bridges. Fast cars, reckless driving, and super-luxurious buildings (lines 5–9) are part of the Spice Girls' lifestyle. This fantasy world is in line with media images, drawn from MTV, racing games such as 'Grand Theft Auto,' and related global media worlds. In their play patterns, the Swedish after-school girls thus made various assessments of the Spice Girls and indirectly also of each other.

In line with research on North American adolescents and preadolescent girls' playground activities, Marjorie Goodwin (2006) shows that, regardless of ethnicity or class, girls at play constantly negotiate phenomena pertaining to inclusion and exclusion. The girls in her study engage in constant comparisons, through talk, showing and showing off to each other who is high ranking and who is not. They, for instance, recurrently engage in implicit rankings even when this is not specifically discussed in terms of rankings or local hierarchies. Prestigious cars are, for instance, important resources for positioning oneself as a member who has access to important objects. What is prestigious and what is not is, at times, contested though, as shown, for instance, in a documentation [see Example 20.3] of US girls' negotiations about age, role, and (virtual) possessions.

Example 20.3:   A play dialogue between school-age girls (Goodwin 2006: 187–8; fragment of larger excerpt)

4	Lisa:	I got a Nisan convertible.
5		No I- IGOTAGREEN*MUS*TANG!
6	Janis:	I got a silver Mus-
7		I got purple- silver Mus-
8		Purple- [glitter Mustan.
9	Sharie:	[I wanna be sixteen?
10	Sarah:	I have a Miata
11	Janis:	**No** you don't ah hah hah! Heh heh
12	Lisa	[She has a Miata ((pointing to Ruth))
13	Sharie:	[I wanna be sixteen
14	Ruth:	Nope [I have a Corvet
15	Sharie:	[I wanna be sixteen
16	Lisa:	Well, you're [*not*

As can be seen, individual girls announce various identity ascriptions, linked to their roles in projected play. Yet, these plans have to be validated by their co-participants. It is, for instance, not up to someone to play a 16-year-old unless this role is also part of a shared agreement, which can be seen in Sharie's two unsuccessful attempts at playing a 16-year-old character (line 16); she is immediately opposed by Lisa, who later explains that she and Ruth are 16-year-old twins, which means that Sharie has to be younger (15).

Apparently, color, silver, and glitter, as well as brand names, are aspects of artefacts (here: cars) that are important for role identity, as is whether the car is a convertible. Within their identity choices, the girls decide who gets to play what age as well as who is allowed to play the same age and who gets to have what car. Somewhat later in the same episode, Ruth, in fact, commented on Sharie's later choice of a Miata car (the car that Sarah had chosen), tapping her shoulder and claiming 'That's the stinkiest car. The Miata' (Goodwin 2006: 188). Observably, roles and objects are recurrently negotiated, more or less successfully in that some girls get more attractive roles and others less attractive ones (e.g. that of a 15-year-old or someone who has a 'stinky' car).

Both Goodwin's US findings and the Swedish findings can be seen to document how symbolic and economic capital are linked in children's play (fancy cars matter, as does the ownership of attractive play items such as unique marbles or pogs) (Goodwin 2006; Sparman and Aronsson 2003). Yet, the precise value of glitter or fancy colors varies in ways that are constantly negotiated and renegotiated within given play communities. Within these communities and their local markets, children are also socialized into norms for sharing. In order for play to go on, participants are at times expected to give away goods, as someone may otherwise have to leave the game altogether. However, someone who gives away too much (e.g. heaps of pogs) breaks the local norms, inflating the market, as it were, as does someone who is never willing to share. As discussed by Schieffelin (1990) in her work on Kaluli patterns, local norms for the give and take of everyday life form fundamental aspects of what is a moral person. There is a moral order for play and games.

Performance, Accentuations, and Language Play

As shown in work on after-school activities among Swedish children (Evaldsson and Corsaro 1998; Sparrman and Aronsson 2003), social hierarchies are at times construed and displayed through play consumption patterns; that is, virtual consumption. Yet, age and gender hierarchies may, of course, be displayed and collaboratively shaped through any type of positioning in play or language play; identity is intimately linked to language use and language socialization practices, as revealed in various types of prosodic and other language choices (Ochs 1992).

In theorizing professional acting practices, Constantin Stanislavskij (1986) has discussed accentuations – including intonation, gesture, posture, and locomotion – and how some of these distinct modes may assist in conveying an actor's attitude. When playing house, children recurrently assume more or less similar theatrical stances, using variations of pitch, volume, tempo, and voice quality for highlighting aspects of the self-presentations of, for instance, authority figurers – a type of social stereotyping. Such variations can be analyzed as accentuations and reaccentuations (Bakhtin 1981) that reveal the speaker's stance toward others and toward specific phenomena. Moreover, dramaturgical resources, such as accentuations, invoke the important distinction between what is 'play' and 'playing at.' Two sisters may play at being two sisters, holding hands or talking in a way that exaggerates their sisterhood (Vygotsky 1967). Both preschoolers and school-age children have been found to deploy all these nonverbal resources in their parodic enactment of various authority figures such as teachers, doctors, and parents (Andersen 1990; Cekaite and Aronsson 2005; Tholander and Aronsson 2003). Social stereotyping and parodic enactments are important ways for children to form intragenerational play alignments. In play, children display and acquire subversive ways of orienting to adult authority.

In school settings, language play – including rhyming, mislabelings, alliteration, puns, and repetitions – are important resources for entertaining classmates and for sustaining their attention (Cekaite and Aronsson 2005; Broner and Tarone 2001; Sullivan 2000). What is a successful play performance is closely linked to improvisations, as in jazz improvisations (Duranti and Black, this volume; Duranti and Burrell 2004;); that is, to spontaneous collaborative play actions. In an ethnographic study of a Swedish immersion class for young refugee and immigrant children, Asta Cekaite and Karin Aronsson (2004, 2005) have documented that it is through co-participants' uptake that players jointly create a truly successful performance, as illustrated in Example 20.4.

Example 20.4

Participants: four girls, Layla (10 years), Nok (7 years), Rana (8 years), and Fusi (7 years), and two boys, Hiwa (8 years) and Sawan (9 years) (Cekaite and Aronsson 2005: 181–2).

1	Hiwa:	*Xxx Rana du pojke xx*	'Xxx Rana you a boy xx
2		pojke	boy'
3	Rana:	*Nej he he nej nej* [X	'No he he no no [X'
4	Hiwa:	[*he he du är*	['he he you
			are'
5	Layla:	*Xxxxx* ((singing in Arabic))	'Xxxxx'
6	Hiwa:	*Xxxxx* ((imitating her singing,	'Xxxxx'
7		pretend weeping))	
8	Rana	*What's this?* ((speaking in	'What's this?'
9		English))	
10	Hiwa:	((rising from his place,	
11		prepared to fight with the	
12		girls))	
13	Nok:	*Titta flicka pojke fli- ah*	'Look girl boy gi- ah'
14		((pointing at girls, and a boy,	
15		Sawan))	
16	Sawan:	*Ne: jag flicka* ((playfully	No: I girl
17		smiling at Nok))	

This episode features various types of language play: Hiwa (line 1) and Sawan (line 16) both align in playful mislabelings in that they deploy incorrect gender categories: the girl Rana is called 'boy' and the boy Sawan claims that he is a girl. These children, native speakers of Arabic and Thai, are still in an early stage of acquiring Swedish and they, for instance, fail to use the indeterminate article (*en pojke* and *en flicka*). Yet, they are capable of making simple jokes, entertaining their co-participants as in Rana's laughing uptake to her classmate's deliberate mislabeling of her, calling her 'boy' (lines 1–2). Moreover, Hiwa re-enacts Layla's singing in a mocking way, embellishing it with pretend weeping (lines 6 and 7). Through various playful variations, employing both nonverbal and verbal means, the children are able to entertain each other. As discussed in some recent work, such playful language variations are important resources in positioning oneself as someone who qualifies as a member of the local classroom community (Broner and Tarone 2001; Catharct-Strong 1986; Cekaite and Aronsson 2004). Children even engage in playful language drills, imitating teacher-style language lessons, soliciting words (Cekaite and Aronsson 2004), and systematically producing various phonological and other variations of language elements. In fact, the children themselves spontaneously engage in teaching routines. Within such improvised classroom performances, playful repetitions and language drills become important resources for establishing a classroom community of second language speakers. Catharct-Strong (1986) has, in fact, suggested that 'to be entertaining' can be seen as an important conversational maxim in children's peer interaction. Within classroom entertainment, children thus spontaneously initiate various types of language drills and other improvised lessons, where they mutually socialize each other into speakers of a second language. It can be seen that the local organization, a Swedish immersion classroom, provides something of a protected space, where children (speakers of Arabic, Kurdish, Turkish, and Thai) may engage in types of language play that would have appeared at a much younger age in the case of their first language. Yet, shared laughter, playful comebacks, and playful language drills testify to the usefulness of language play. Children's play with language – jokes, riddles, and playful mislabellings – is a cultural activity with its own aesthetics, where incongruent and unexpected speech is appreciated and rewarded (Cekaite and Aronsson 2004; Howard 2009). On another note, it can, of course, again be seen that the classroom environment is a competitive arena, where children have to find ways of soliciting their co-participants' sustained attention.

Audience design features of play in fact also seem to be part and parcel of the ways in which children and young people in different cultures face global aspects of contemporary video-game culture. As pointed out by Buckingham (2000), discussions of game cultures tend to shift between moral panics on the one hand, and Rousseauan romantic views of the 'active' child on the other. Yet, the competencies of the active child have been poorly documented. Perhaps the competencies of the 'active' child may merely involve handling of the on/off button of the television or video control (Buckingham 2000). In contrast, some recent work on children's playing in fact includes studies of what children actually do when engaging in video gaming, rather than disembodied theoretical reasoning on what they might do in their play encounters with new media. Such work concerns broad global patterns of video-game consumption, including work on performance elements of video gaming, and work that problematizes the interface between pre-structured game worlds and children's social interactions with peers and family members (cf. Aarsand and Aronsson 2009; Buckingham and Scanlon 2003;). As yet, there has not been much research on language socialization and media. However, the work of Amanda Minks (e.g. 2008) shows ways in which adolescents in Corn Island, Nicaragua, exploit song games as a legitimate public space for exploring sexually charged language.

Code-Switching and Language Shift

Code-switching is another resource for embellishing play conversations (Cromdal and Aronsson 2000; Paugh 2005). Drawing on video recordings from a Swedish–English school playground context, Jakob Cromdal and Karin Aronsson (2000), have shown that, regardless of actual mastery of the two languages, the children often code-switched as a way of embellishing and highlighting parts of the conversation. The participants thus switched to a contrasting language, just as a way of marking something as awesome or at least newsworthy (Cromdal and Aronsson 2000). Code-switching was, in fact, one of several strategies for sustaining peers' attention in play activities. Obviously, these bilingual children at times switched to a peer's best language in the rare cases where s/he had not quite mastered the language spoken. Yet, they more commonly code-switched just for aesthetic purposes, marking something as new or extraordinary or just interesting – as a type of dramaturgic summoning, indicating that upcoming talk was worthy of the listener's close attention. The mastery of a second language was thus one of the children's resources for getting access to play.

Code-switching is a phenomenon that is not restricted to languages that are mastered by the speaker. Drawing on Dominican children's play code-switches between Patwa (a French Creole language) and English, Amy Paugh (2005, this volume) has shown that peer play is a critical site for socializing one another into code-switching practices and language ideologies. In multicultural UK school settings, Ben Rampton (1999, 2002) has documented what he calls 'crossings'; that is, conversational insertions of glosses from a foreign language that is not mastered. Such crossings in a play-group environment have also been documented by Polly Björk-Willén (2007) in her documentation of a Swedish-speaking preschool girl's attempts at getting access to the play activities of two Spanish–Swedish boys. In her efforts to access play, this preschooler code-switched to the target language (Spanish) of her playmates. These 'crossings' testify to the hard work of getting access to play. Children may have to draw on both existing and emerging resources in their efforts at getting access to play. Conversely, a child who has not acquired local rules for access rituals may run the risk of being excluded from play (Corsaro 1979; Cromdal and Aronsson 2000).

Lastly, verbal play will be discussed in terms of its impact on language choice and language shift. Many of the early studies of children's play in non-Western cultures did not document detailed aspects of siblings or play (but see Schieffelin 1990). In her ethnographic work on children in Ecuador, Camilla Rindstedt (2001) shows in detailed ways how young Quichua Indian children's play is carefully monitored by older siblings. On the basis of this work in Quichua-speaking areas of Ecuador (Rindstedt and Aronsson 2002), it can be seen that sibling and peer play are important arenas for emergent language shift phenomena and, in a long-range perspective, ultimately even for language death. More specifically: it could be seen that sibling caretakers generally chose to play in the school language, Spanish, not in the indigenous language. This meant that toddlers and young children heard a lot of Quichua spoken (between their parents, and between parents and grandparents and other grownups). Yet, they played in Spanish, as school-age children were generally their main caretakers (with mothers and grandmothers as stand-by caretakers, out in the field or nearby).

Some isolated words would be spoken in the indigenous language, but, for the most part, the elder siblings' language of schooling also became the youngest children's play language, as in Example 20.5:

Example 20.5

Participants: Miriam (3;8), Geovanni (9;5), and Fanni (11 years) (Rindstedt 2001: 160). Underlined italics: words spoken in Quichua.

1	Geovanni:	*Parece <u>huahua lluchito</u>*	'She seems to be a little naked infant'
2	Miriam:	*¡Teta, teta, teta!*	'Breast, breast, breast!'
3	Geovanni:	*Cómo fue?*	'How did it go?'
4	Fanni:	*¡Haremos vuelta!*	'Let's do it again!
5		*¡Teta, teta diga!*	Say breast, breast!'
6	Miriam:	*¡Teta! ¡Teta!*	'Breast! Breast!'
7	Geovanni:	*Llora tan como*	'Then cry like a [naked infant
		[*<u>huahua</u>*	cries!'
8		*<u>lluchu</u> llora*	
9	Fanni:	[*A ver*	['Let's see
10		*llora llora!*	Cry! Cry!'
11	Miriam:	*E:: TETA TETA*	'U:H BREAST! BREAST!'
12	Fanni:	[*¡A ver¡ !Habla! ¡Habla!*	['Let's see! Speak! Speak!'
13	Geovanni:	[*<u>Huahua</u> <u>lluchu</u> no llora*	['A naked little infant does not cry
14		*así* [*Viejita está llorando*	like this [it's crying like a very old woman'
15	Miriam:	[*¡Oa oa oa, oa oa!*	['Oua oua oua oua oua!'

In this episode, two elder siblings instruct their little sister Miriam to cry like a 'little naked infant.' Apparently, neither of her two siblings is completely satisfied with her performance as a baby; Fanni instructs her through a local so-called *diga* routine (lines 4–5; say after me!), as well as through further encouragements (line 12), and Geovanni repeatedly instructs her (lines 7–8 and 13–15), criticizing her for crying like an old woman. They address their younger sister in something of a Baby Talk register: simple, short sentences and repetitions, much like mothers in this Andean community would address their babies. Moreover, they use the *diga* routine in a traditional way (as the local parents did in their upbringing practices). The children's fantasy play is thus closely aligned with real-life interactions. Yet, most of the interaction takes place in Spanish, not in Quichua, which is normally the language spoken to babies by their parents and grandparents.

While engaging in sibling caretaking and play in Spanish, the two older siblings can simultaneously be seen as agents of an emergent language shift. In the fieldwork village, Quichua is gradually fading out in children's spontaneous play and peer conversations. The sibling caretakers bring Spanish home from school and, as they spend much more time than their parents interacting with the youngest children, they are apparently also the most important language socialization agents (for related language shift phenomena in New Guinea, see Kulick 1992). In Rindsted's Ecuadorian study, very few school-age children mastered Quichua even though it was the parents' mother tongue, and the language of an intense ethnic revitalization movement. While engaging in play, the children thus simultaneously played away the minority language, Quichua.

Beyond Rousseau – Toward Models of Verbal Play Aesthetics and Play Hierarchies

Work on children's aesthetic performance in play and daily interaction tends to foreground creativity and artfulness (e.g. Sullivan 2000). Such artfulness is an important aspect of children's semiotic resources for doing accentuations, including speech, gestures, posture, locomotion, and orientation to material resources, including orientation to artifacts. The very design of playful threats requires careful planning, as do clever comebacks (Tholander and Aronsson 2002).

Moreover, even quite young children recurrently engage in name-calling, insults, and other types of verbal abuse that may aid in embellishing or escalating an argument (Maynard 1986; Rindstedt 2001; Whalen 1995). Children's play activities in Western and non-Western cultural settings – including play argumentation – recurrently involve audience design features that can be discussed in terms of local rules of aesthetics. The play practices of even very young children in various cultural contexts (in Swedish-, Arabic-Swedish-, Spanish-, and Russian-speaking parts of the world) reveal ways in which poetic repetitions, neologisms, alliterations, and other performance elements are key features in the design of mundane play interactions in both home and school settings (e.g. Cekaite and Aronsson 2005; de León 2007; Fasulo, Liberati, and Pontecorvo 2002; Jakobson 1988).

Playful threats, insults, gossiping, exaggerations, and parody can be deployed in the pursuit of sustained attention, and they may involve embellishment and successive upgradings in order to be heard (Aronsson and Thorell 1999; Evaldsson 2005; Goodwin 2006; Sheldon 1990; Whalen 1995. Yet, what is playful and what is threatening or discomforting is, again, a matter of participants' perspectives. There are always hierarchical aspects of performance, in terms of what counts and does not count in the local culture, related to co-participants' assessments, uptake, and negotiations.

In sum, verbal play is serious business. Further, it requires specific cultural and linguistic skills (cf. Danby 1999; Goffman 1972; Tholander and Aronsson 2003). Access to play is not anything to be taken for granted, and even very young children have to acquire cultural and linguistic routines for accessing play and ways of performing in order to become members of play communities. Participation also involves the acquisition of repertoires of verbal play. Children gradually have to acquire advanced entertainment skills or advanced competencies for eventually outperforming others or for at least managing to qualify for community membership.

Moreover, play, at times, takes place in the interface between delight and fear, and between what is serious and nonserious. This means that play access does not end with access rituals. Access is a never-ending affair, ranging from initial access to sustained attention, full membership status, and to strivings for higher rankings in local play hierarchies. Novices – like children and other new members of a community – are always at risk in that they may misunderstand not only what is said but also whether it is seriously meant or not (its footings). At any point, members may have to withdraw from play if they do not perform in a way that fulfils local standards of an 'authentic' play self. Participation thus involves a set of ambivalences or tensions: between pleasure and fear, and between what is serious and nonserious.

Unspoken participation rights concern inclusion–exclusion, but also local rankings of who is outperforming whom or who is not up to the mark. As has been discussed, not only Rousseauan playful explorations but also comparisons, competition, and hierarchies are central features of children's own play activities. On an underlying level, the tensions involved concern inclusion, and thereby also identity work. In play, identity is therefore at stake.

REFERENCES

Aarsand, P. (2008) Frame switches and identity performances: Alternating between online and offline. *Text & Talk* 28: 147–65.

Aarsand, P. and Aronsson, K. (2009) Response cries and other gaming moves: Toward an intersubjectivity of gaming. *Journal of Pragmatics* 41: 1557–75.

Andersen, E. (1990) *Speaking with Style: The Sociolinguistic Skills of Children*. London: Routledge.

Aronsson, K. and Thorell, M. (1999) Family politics in children's play directives. *Journal of Pragmatics* 31: 25–47.

Bakhtin, M. (1981) *The Dialogic Imagination*. Austin, TX: University of Texas Press.

Bateson, G. (1972) *Steps to an Ecology of Mind: Collected Essays in Anthropology, Psychiatry, Evolution, and Epistemology*. San Fransisco, CA: Chandler Publishing Company.

Björk-Willén, P. (2007) Participation in multilingual preschool play: Shadowing and crossing as multilingual resources. *Journal of Pragmatics* 39: 2133–58.

Blashki, K. and Nichol, S. (2005) Game geek's goss: Linguistic creativity in young males within an online university forum. *Australian Journal of Emerging Technologies and Society* 3(2): 77–86.

Boellstorff, T. (2008) *Coming of Age in Second Life: An Anthropologist Explores the Virtually Human*. Princeton, NJ: Princeton University Press.

Broner, M. and Tarone, E. (2001) Is it fun? Language play in a fifth grade Spanish immersion classroom. *The Modern Language Journal* 85(3): 363–79.

Bourdieu, P. (2003 [1979]) *Distinction: A Social Critique of the Judgement of Taste*. R. Nice, transl. New York: Routledge.

Bucholtz, M. (1999) Why be normal? Language and identity presentations in a community of nerd girls. *Language in Society* 28: 203–23.

Buckingham, D. (2000) *After the Death of Childhood: Growing Up in the Age of Electronic Media*. Cambridge: Polity Press.

Buckingham, D. and Scanlon, M. (2003) *Education, Entertainment and Learning in the Home*. Buckingham, UK: Open University Press.

Cathcart-Strong, R. (1986) Input generation by young second language learners. *TESOL Quarterly* 20: 515–30.

Cekaite, A. and Aronsson, K. (2004) Repetition and joking in children's second language conversations: Playful recyclings in an immersion classroom. *Discourse Studies* 6: 373–92.

Cekaite, A. and Aronsson, K. (2005) Language play, a collaborative resource in children's L2 learning. *Applied Linguistics* 26(2): 169–91.

Corsaro, W. (1979) 'We're friends, right?': Children's use of access rituals in a nursery school. *Language in Society* 8: 315–36.

Cromdal, J. and Aronsson, K. (2000) Footing in bilingual play. *Journal of Sociolinguistics* 4: 435–57.

Danby, S. (1999) The serious business of play. In J. Mason and M. Wilkingson (eds.), *Taking Children Seriously. Proceedings of a National Workshop.* 208–36. Sydney, Australia: Childhood and Youth Policy Research Unit, University of Western Sydney.

Danby, S. and Baker, C. (1998) How to be masculine in the block area. *Childhood* 5: 151–75.

de León, L. (2007) Parallelism, metalinguistic play, and the interactive emergence of Zinacantec Mayan siblings' culture. *Research on Language and Social Interaction* 40: 405–36.

Duranti, A. and Burrell, K. (2004) Jazz improvisation: A search for hidden harmonies and a unique self. *Ricerche di Psicologia* 27: 71–101.

Evaldsson, A.-C. (2005) Staging insults and mobilizing categorizations in peer group interaction. *Discourse & Society* 16: 763–86.

Evaldsson, A.-C. and Corsaro, W. (1998) Play and games in the peer cultures of preschool and preadolescent children: An interpretive approach. *Childhood* 5: 377–402.

Fasulo, A., Liberati, V., and Pontecorvo, C. (2002) Language games in the strict sense of the term: Children's poetics and conversation. In S. Blum-Kulka and C. E. Snow (eds.), *Talking to Adults. The Contribution of Multiparty Discourse to Language Acquisition.* 209–37. Mahwah, NJ: Lawrence Erlbaum.

Freud, S. (1959 [1926]) Inhibitions, symptoms and anxiety. In J. Strachey (ed.), *The Standard Edition of the Complete Psychological Works of Sigmund Freud, Vol. 20.* 87–175. London: Hogarth Press.

Garvey, C. (1993) Diversity in the conversational repertoire: The case of conflicts and social pretending. *Cognition and Instruction* 11: 251–64.

Garvey, C. and Kramer, T. L. (1989) The language of social pretend play. *Developmental Review* 9: 364–82.

Goffman, E. (1972 [1961]) *Encounters: Two Studies in the Sociology of Interaction.* London: Penguin.

Goffman, E. (1979) Footing. *Semiotica* 25: 1–29.

Goffman, E. (1981) *Forms of Talk.* Philadelphia, PA: University of Pennsylvania Press.

Goodwin, M. H. (1990) *He-Said-She-Said: Talk as Social Organization Among Black Children.* Bloomington, IN: Indiana University Press.

Goodwin, M. H. (2006) *The Hidden Life of Girls: Games of Stance, Status, and Exclusion.* Oxford: Blackwell.

Göncu, A. (1993) Development of intersubjectivity in social pretend play. *Human Development* 36: 185–98.

Howard, K. M. (2009) Breaking in and spinning out: Thai children's games. *Language in Society* 38: 339–63.

Jakobson, R. (1988) Children's verbal art. In *Selected Writings, Vol. VIII.* Berlin: Mouton.

Kulick, D. (1992) *Language Shift and Cultural Reproduction: Socialization, Self and Syncretism in a Papua New Guinean Village.* Cambridge: Cambridge University Press.

Lessing, D. (1995) *Under My Skin: Volume One of My Autobiography, to 1949.* New York: Harper.

Maynard, D. (1986) Offering and soliciting collaboration in multi-party disputes among children (and other humans). *Human Studies* 9: 261–5.

Minks, A. (2008) Performing gender in song games among Nicaraguan Miskitu children. *Language & Communication* 28: 36–56.

Ochs, E. (1992) Indexing gender. In A. Duranti and C. Goodwin (eds.), *Rethinking Context: Language as an Interactive Phenomenon.* 335–58. Cambridge: Cambridge University Press.

Ochs, E. and Schieffelin, B. B. (eds.) (1979) *Developmental Pragmatics.* New York: Academic Press.

Ochs, E. and Schieffelin, B. B. (1984) Language acquisition and socialization: Three developmental stories. In R. Shweder and R. LeVine (eds.), *Cultural Theories: Essays on Mind, Self, and Emotion.* Cambridge: Cambridge University Press.

Paugh, A. (2005) Multilingual play: Children's code-switching, role play and agency in Dominica. *Language in Society* 34: 63–86.

Piaget, J. (1968 [1945]) *La formation du symbole chez l'enfant. Imitation, jeu et rêve, image et representation.* Paris: Delachaux et Niestlé.

Pontecorvo, C., Fasulo, A., and Sterponi, L. (2001) Mutual apprentices: The making of parenthood and childhood in family dinner conversations. *Human Development* 44: 340–61.

Rampton, B. (1999) Inner London Deutsch and the animation of an instructed foreign language. *Journal of Sociolinguistics* 34(4): 480–504.

Rampton, B. (2002) Ritual and foreign language practices at school. *Language in Society* 31: 491–525.

Rindstedt, C. (2001) Quichua children and language shift in an Andean community: School, play, and sibling caretaking. *Studies in Arts and Science* 241.

Rindstedt, C. and Aronsson, K. (2002) Growing up monolingual in a bilingual community: The Quichua revitalization paradox. *Language in Society* 31: 721–42.

Schieffelin, B. B. (1990) *The Give and Take of Everyday Life: Language Socialization of Kaluli Children.* Cambridge: Cambridge University Press.

Schwartzman, H. (1978) *Transformations: The Anthropology of Children's Play.* New York: Plenum Press.

Sheldon, A. (1990) 'You can be the baby brother, but you aren't born yet': Preschool girls' negotiatons for power and access in pretend play. *Research on Language and Social Interaction* 29: 57–80.

Sparrman, A. (2002) Visuell kultur i barns vardagsliv. Bilder, medier och praktiker (Visual culture in children's everyday lives. Pictures, media, and practices). *Linköping Studies in Arts and Science* 250.

Sparrman, A. and Aronsson, K. (2003) Pog game practices, learning and ideology: Local markets and identity work. In G. Walford, (ed.), *Investigating Educational Policy through Ethnography.* 169–92. Amsterdam, The Netherlands: Elsevier.

Stanislavskij, C. (1986) *Building a Character.* London: Methuen.

Sullivan, P. N. (2000) Spoken artistry. Performance in second language classroom. In J. K. Hall and L. S. Verplaetse (eds.), *Second and Foreign Language Learning Through Classroom Interaction.* Mahwah, NJ: Lawrence Erlbaum.

Tamm, M. (1990) *The Semiotic Function. Studies in Children's Representations.* Umeå, Sweden: Department of Psychology, Umeå University.

Tholander, M. and Aronsson, K. (2002) Teasing as serious business: Collaborative staging and response work. *Text* 22: 559–95.

Tholander, M. and Aronsson, K. (2003) Doing subteaching in school groupwork: Positioning, resistance, and participation frameworks. *Language and Education* 17(3): 208–34.

Thorne, B. (1993) *Gender Play: Girls and Boys in School.* New Brunswick, NJ: Rutgers University Press.

Tingstad, V. (2003) *Children's Chat on the Net. A Study of Social Encounters in Two Norwegian Chat Rooms.* Trondheim, Norway: Norwegian University of Science and Technology.

Whalen, M. R. (1995) Working toward play: Complexity in children's fantasy activities. *Language in Society* 24: 315–48.

Vygotsky, L. S. (1967) Play and its role in the mental development of the child. *Soviet Psychology* 5: 6–18.

Part V   Language and Culture Contact

While anthropologists and linguists have had a long-standing interest in understanding what happens to speakers, languages, and societies in contexts of contact, it is only recently that language socialization research has been recognized for its important theoretical contributions to understanding the very processes of language shift, change, and transformation. Language socialization scholars recognize the importance of sociohistorical, political, cultural, and linguistic forces at play in contact situations, and the resulting variations in forms and valuations of bilingualism, multilingualism, and multiculturalism. The chapters in Part V focus on these contexts, articulating links between cultural and linguistic practices – mediated by language ideologies – and complex networks of informal and formal social institutions that regiment, or attempt to regiment, cultural and symbolic values associated with different linguistic varieties and discursive expressions. Language ideologies and speech practices are linked at multiple levels, and these chapters (and others in the volume) illustrate the importance of language ideological factors and the role of indexicality in language for understanding language socialization practices and outcomes.

In directly addressing issues of language shift, maintenance, and endangerment, these chapters also foreground the importance of investigating relationships of language, power, and identity, showing that, even for the youngest speakers, such associations are always indexed in talk, in what they are expected to say, and in the talk around them, underscoring the notion that attention to code or variety choice, and its associated meanings in contact settings, is not only essential but has long-term consequences for speakers, communities, languages, and researchers.

The chapters in Part V also expand the notion of zones of contact and ideas of belonging and place, established in early speech activities, for speakers and languages. Not only are issues of colonial and postcolonial language settings investigated in terms of local social and linguistic practices and transformations, but

The Handbook of Language Socialization, First Edition. Edited by Alessandro Duranti, Elinor Ochs, and Bambi B. Schieffelin.

the chapters explore the consequences of immigration and diaspora for language learners, examining 'processes and practices of continuity and identification, as well as discontinuity and *dis*-identification' (Baquedano-López and Mangual Figueroa, this volume) relevant to challenges facing heritage language and second language socialization, instruction, and use through the life cycle.

Part V also highlights the importance of speaker agency for the social and linguistic life of languages and speech varieties; language socialization research shows the possibility that in contact situations, in spite of language socialization efforts, learners may resist, transform, adopt, or reject some genres or registers of the language or speech variety, but not others, as a result of how language is taken to signal affiliation to a group or is understood to be a semiotic resource more broadly. This has consequences for notions of language boundaries and maintenance and for the assignment of codes to particular groups, ages, and activities that themselves may transform at multiple levels and be subjected to regimes of value.

Finally, the chapters in Part V show the deep connections between language socialization scholarship and research in other fields, and the potentials for a bidirectionality that is generated through this type of academic contact and exchange. In spite of their different genealogies and distinct goals, and the methods and theories associated with these separate fields, these chapters testify to the synergy between language socialization and heritage language acquisition, second language socialization, language shift, language endangerment, and language revitalization, to name but a few. We also see language socialization's impact on other disciplines, for example sociolinguistics, applied linguistics, education, anthropology, and linguistics. These chapters, and the volume more generally, demonstrate that the study of language socialization not only accounts for how particular ways of knowing, feeling, and speaking are learned, used, and even forgotten but also reveals details about linguistic and cultural practices that are often imagined as invisible and inaudible.

In 'Language Socialization and Language Ideologies,' Riley (Chapter 21) examines how language ideologies, especially those that are 'power-inflected,' shape and help make sense out of language socialization practices. To this end, she considers three dynamics: (1) how cultural beliefs about children's language linked to local notions of personhood and society shape caregivers' and educators' routines; (2) how negative and positive indexical meanings of linguistic forms are highlighted and imitated through routines that use metapragmatic markers and deictic verbs; and (3) how enduring and shifting hegemonic ideologies about language varieties including dialects, or 'ideologies about the symbolic and/or pragmatic value of linguistic forms themselves,' may have detrimental effects and lead to contradictory socialization patterns and outcomes. Riley points out the 'ethnic revitalization paradox' that takes place when contradictory ideologies concerning the dominant and minority language undermine acquisition of both the revitalized and standard language. Ideologies about language purism and syncretic forms in various speech communities, ranging from parental rejection to acceptance of code-switching, have definitive consequences for language socialization routines and the attitudes toward language(s) as a social object, as well as significant impacts on the language varieties taken up by younger speakers as markers of generation and identity.

Riley investigates connections between language ideologies and language socialization practices throughout *la francophonie*, itself a type of ideological construct of places and speech networks where French is used and recognized as central to identity construction. Drawing on her scholarship in a Parisian suburb, the Marquesas, northern Vermont, and Montreal, Riley shows that French language ideologies and socialization practices have been transformed by local histories, languages, and politics, but nonetheless exhibit three persistent preferences: (1) pedagogical techniques that ensure children will acquire 'the art of clear and precise expression'; (2) the centrality of language in mediating national or ethnic unity; and (3) a particular variety of French deemed to have clarity (*clarté*), perfect for expressing truth and conferring prestige and high status on its users.

Garrett frames 'Language Socialization and Language Shift' (Chapter 22) within broad processes of change in the context of contact at the societal level, asking what motivates shift and what inhibits it, insisting on the linkages between ideology and practice at multiple levels as central to understanding outcomes. He views contact-related phenomena in terms of complex histories of hierarchy, inequality, dominance, and subordination. Thus, in communities that use more than one code, the relation between varieties is never neutral but is embedded in some form of social hierarchy. Language shift enters into relations of inequality between social groups and social difference more broadly (see also Howard, this volume; Paugh, this volume; Riley, this volume). Children's participation in language socialization practices that discursively elaborate code choice both indexes the symbolic capital of particular forms and creates subjectivities that can explain processes of change.

To illustrate these processes, Garrett examines current language shift in St. Lucia, where Kwéyòl and varieties of English, most saliently the heavily Kwéyòl-influenced Vernacular English of St. Lucia (VESL), are spoken. In St. Lucia, 'bilingualism' refers to a broad range of variation across speakers and generations. Garrett focuses on micro-processual dynamics within interactions and their seemingly paradoxical outcomes. For example, prohibiting and stigmatizing a language variety can lead to shift as well as to revitalization, as when vernacular linguistic and traditional cultural practices become linked to custom, leading to preservation, valorization, standardization, (objectification), and revitalization. Some language ideologies assume that the vernacular is natural and that, regardless of language socialization preferences, it will be acquired. Ethnographic and sociolinguistic analyses of language socialization practices, however, reveal how codes are differentiated and regimented; the analyses make sense of the relative vitality of communicative codes, and uneven patterns of circulation. Talk about value-laden code choice and meaning is evident in everyday interactions, socialized implicitly and explicitly, even with preverbal infants.

Baquedano-López and Mangual Figueroa's 'Language Socialization and Immigration' (Chapter 23) draws attention to both macro-sociological and micro-interactional phenomena manifested in language practices and ideologies in immigrant and migrant communities. While highlighting the bidirectionality of knowledge between experts and novices, the authors also look at social barriers, ideologies, and practices that inhibit social access to knowledge. Against a background of key issues in immigration studies and linguistic anthropology, the authors review a broad range of verbal practices developed by youths living in ethnic and religious diasporic communities, including code-switching, various stylized forms, and discourse strategies. They identify early work in language socialization that locates the importance and meaning of everyday routines within the context of colonialism and missionization, which affect the organization, circulation, and flow of information and institutions.

Language socialization studies have systematically investigated the 'critical' transition from home to school and provided ethnographic and sociolinguistic evidence about the dynamics (social, linguistic, cultural) involved in this process. While Baquedano-López and Mangual Figueroa (this volume) focus on students in US immigration settings, the authors also review work on immigrant communities in Spain, detailing, for example, the translation practices of youths and adolescents, who also act more generally as language and cultural brokers (García-Sánchez, this volume), and other European communities. Youths' use of first language verbal routines in new settings, as well as role-playing, language play, and other innovative skills, assist their acquisition of local competencies. The focus on diasporic settings highlights what learners can take from both school and home, depending on the nature of the contact zone, ideas of homeland and belonging, and heritage language maintenance (see also He, this volume). Baquedano-López and Mangual Figueroa also pay attention to religious socialization as a critical context in which diasporic communities define identity and create social connections in their new home while maintaining connections to homeland. Formal (institutional) and informal (home) religious instruction, songs, religious registers and texts, orientation, and demeanors are socialized through specific speech practices. Issues of access, as well as political tensions, emerge in religious settings where the language of instruction is central to immigrant policies. As they make clear, particular religious communities (e.g. ultra-orthodox Jews, Muslims) experience local as well as transnational dilemmas that are sociohistorically specific. Language socialization studies in diasporic communities identify the converging and conflicting practices, language preferences, and social and ethnic boundaries that exist across families, schools, and communities.

Duff's 'Second Language Socialization' (Chapter 24) highlights variation in bilingual and multilingual language contact settings resulting from political, social, and economic factors, outlining how languages may be learned more or less concurrently with the first language, sequentially across the life cycle, or over a more limited span of time, and may include languages (L3, etc.) that come to assume dominant positions (see also Fader, this volume; Howard, this volume; Moore, this volume). In comparing first language and second language socialization, Duff points out that first and second language communities may share certain pedagogical preferences, while socialization into diverse varieties in the same language community may be vastly different, as between home and school language registers. Duff's theoretical orientation also extends the boundaries of what to consider as 'language,' arguing for attention to stylistic features of borrowing and accent that must be acquired as part of a second language. She analyzes how different second language learners approach politeness, gender, formality, and other stylistic issues; for example, how speaking with certain forms enacts a particular type of identity. Duff notes that second language students may have quite different 'investments' in language and literacy skills from those evidenced by their native-speaker classmates. At the same time, second language socialization in and out of school contexts is a platform for socializing much more than linguistic competence, entailing situated ideologies, dispositions, and practices. Like first language socialization, access to second language socialization settings may be constrained by gender, status, economic resources, and political conditions. Unlike first language acquirers, however, second language learners may resist using second language social indexical forms, for example female politeness forms that are seen to diminish their authority.

Of particular interest to Duff is how second language students are socialized into kinds of academic discourse and academic cultures. In US university classrooms, competence in genres of presentation and writing that are central to academic success is primarily apprenticed through modeling and face-saving indirect strategies. Less effective are socializing commentaries on written work. As such, second language socialization can be a protracted endeavor, wherein novices have piecemeal access to knowledge critical to their participation in academic, work, and informal personal settings.

The term 'heritage language' refers to a language used in or inherited from a 'home' country and that differs from the language of the mainstream society. He's 'Heritage Language Socialization' (Chapter 25) addresses the complex linguistic and cultural relationships that obtain between heritage languages and cultures, and details processes through which heritage language learners acquire their language and its associated social and symbolic meanings. Heritage language acquisition is always in competition with the dominant language of the local community and thus is implicated in identity, stance, and other issues that pertain to multilingual, multicultural, and immigrant contexts. He recommends that scholarship in heritage language socialization consider more comprehensive settings beyond schools, broader time spans beyond childhood, participant structures that go beyond the individual to include relevant generations and social networks, and a wider range of communicative resources beyond speech.

He's dynamic theoretical framework, developed out of her research on Chinese heritage language schools, addresses both temporal and spatial dimensions and is embedded in an identity-based approach, which stresses learner agency. In it, she posits ten hypotheses to describe and predict key variables for heritage language development, and presents a composite, reconstructed profile of a learner spanning kindergarten to college based on multiple types of culturally contextualized verbal and interactional data. This goes beyond cross-sectionally-based typification models and highlights diachronic and other multiperspectival analyses used in linguistics, applied linguistics, and linguistic anthropology. He's chapter also offers suggestions for how heritage language socialization research can contribute to relevant disciplines, offering notions about language and speech communities as socioculturally constructed objects (e.g. native language/target language) as well as providing more general theoretical and methodological insights into how to analyze the complexities of multiple language socialization activities through the life cycle.

Nonaka's 'Language Socialization and Language Endangerment' (Chapter 26) discusses the complex social, political, cultural, and natural factors driving language endangerment, a source of extensive debate among language activists, linguists, and anthropologists. All agree, however, on the importance of documentation and support for research aiming to understand the dynamics of language loss. After reviewing language socialization scholarship highlighting work on language shift, Nonaka concludes that most at-risk languages are found in relatively small, marginalized rural communities. Foregrounding the significance of ethnographic and linguistic anthropology methodologies, she examines multilingual settings where negative and/or ambivalent attitudes associated with a code lessen its chances of transmission and, ultimately, survival (see also Garrett, this volume; Howard, this volume; Paugh, this volume). Even when a particular code is no longer dominant, however, interactional structures associated with the lost code may survive. Cases from a range of indigenous communities illustrate complex causal links across language ecology, practices, ideologies and endangerment and language socialization showcasing unpredictable outcomes.

Sign languages are particularly vulnerable because of negative associations with those for whom they are the mode of communication. Nonaka focuses on Ban Khor Sign, a relatively recent indigenous language used in a small multilingual community in northeastern Thailand where there is an unusually high number of deaf individuals. In this community, both hearing and deaf members learn sign, which is necessary for its survival. The recent introduction of the national sign language is, however, changing the local language ecology, giving rise to code-switching and lexical borrowing. This government intervention amplifies the value of Thai Sign Language and consequently renders Ban Khor Sign less viable, indicating a significant process that threatens the future of this language.

Language revitalization (or reversing language shift) is a form of language planning associated with endangered languages. While scholarship has largely focused on macro-level factors (e.g. state language policies), recent research on activists in minority language communities and the central role of language ideologies has broadened the ways in which revitalization efforts and outcomes are understood. Friedman's 'Language Socialization and Language Revitalization' (Chapter 27) takes up a relatively new area of research, focusing on three areas in which language socialization offers theoretical links to transgenerational language outcomes.

Exploring how everyday language ideologies and socialization practices intersect those of language activists, Friedman draws on ethnographic studies and identifies factors that promote or discourage the successful revitalization of minority languages, such as cultural capital, associations with cultural identity, and increased economics and revaluation of local cultural practices. Language socialization studies demonstrate how children shape ideologies pertaining to revitalization outcomes, highlighting children's agency and their associations of the vernacular with authority. Alternatively, in certain Native American communities, language revitalization is linked to traditional culture (specialized knowledge) and high-status speakers (elders) to whom respect must be given, resulting in children viewing the indigenous language as reserved exclusively for those of high status. This practice has had a negative outcome for language revitalization. In contrast, in Rapa Nui, where several varieties of Spanish and Rapa Nui are spoken and language ideologies support code-switching and syncretic forms, teenagers are learning the language, fueling Rapa Nui's revitalization after it was almost lost.

Finally, Friedman reviews schools as sites in which children may be socialized into ideologies that subvert or support language revitalization, exploring both successful and unsuccessful programs in a range of indigenous and nonindigenous communities. She concludes with an in-depth treatment of her own scholarship on schooling in the Ukraine, which has undergone political transformations and Russian language influences. While language ideologies and routines construct Ukrainian as beautiful and regiment language purism, children often codeswitch into Russian. Thus, while a shift to Russian has been stopped, the revitalization of Ukrainian as the nation's primary language is not assured. Friedman underscores the contribution of language socialization research, which reveals through ethnographic and interactional analysis a paradox of language revitalization, in which the language ideologies of children may thwart the realization of a community's desires for a language to be maintained or revitalized.

21 Language Socialization and Language Ideologies

KATHLEEN C. RILEY

Socializing Language Ideologies . . . Ideological Language Socialization

The term 'language ideology' has been used to encompass everything from unexamined cultural assumptions to politically charged dogma about the use and acquisition of language in general and the value of specific forms of language in particular (Kroskrity 2004; Silverstein 1979; Woolard 1998). Given such a broad reading of the term, language ideologies are intrinsically implicated in all language socialization processes and vice versa – that is, language ideologies influence the sociocultural contexts that shape language socialization, and language ideologies are also among the many cultural values socialized through language use.

The theory of linguistic relativity (Lucy 1997) puts perhaps the most unconscious and disinterested spin on this relationship: given that cultural beliefs (and thus language ideologies) are encoded within linguistic forms, the acquisition of linguistic forms is in part responsible for the cognitive development of these cultural beliefs (and thus language ideologies). However, language ideologies frequently shape the socialization practices that forge the social contract between linguistic forms and meanings in ways that carry a political load, one of the most obvious types being the social evaluation of the forms themselves as well as the sociocultural norms about who has the right to acquire and use them. In the terms formulated by Bourdieu (1991), hegemonic language ideologies regiment not only the evaluation of 'distinctive' linguistic resources but also their patterns of production, distribution, and reproduction. Within particular speech economies or linguistic marketplaces, some will and some will not have access to acquiring linguistic capital – that is, the linguistic resources deemed valuable – as well as

The Handbook of Language Socialization, First Edition. Edited by Alessandro Duranti, Elinor Ochs, and Bambi B. Schieffelin.
© 2014 John Wiley & Sons, Ltd. Published 2014 by John Wiley & Sons, Ltd.

the knowledge of how to use them with whom and to what ends. As these regimenting ideologies form a part of what is acquired, endless reproduction in favor of the powers that be is assured.

While remaining sensitive to this issue of structural constraint, scholars have more recently criticized Bourdieu's paradigm as being overly deterministic and have developed a range of dynamic approaches for exploring how power-inflected language ideologies interact with the socialization of linguistic resources and strategies for using them. In this chapter, I survey studies such as these that consider not only the impact of oppressive language ideologies on language socialization but also the role of interactive agents in negotiating the language socialization contexts and practices that give rise to such powerful ideologies. After examining the feedback relationships between language ideologies and language socialization practices in general, I look at a particular imagined linguistic community, *la francophonie*, in which the political implications of these relationships are traced more closely.

The Impact of Power-Inflected Ideologies on Socialization

Cultural beliefs about language acquisition affect the language socialization routines used by caregivers and educators. Assumptions about the contextual use of language have an impact on the socialization of communicative competence. Hegemonic ideologies about specific forms of language (modes, varieties, and genres) consequentially frame the institutions and processes that shape the acquisition of valued forms. In this section, I investigate the effects of these three types of language ideology, in each case highlighting issues of power – that is, how via language socialization novices and experts sometimes confirm and sometimes resist the ideologies that govern the acquisition of their resources, rights, and strategies within a given social hierarchy.

Language acquisition ideologies

One language ideology shared by most human communities is that young children are less competent and therefore unequal partners in any communicative interaction and must be exposed over time to language in order to learn the communicative tools with which to take up the more powerful role of older sibling or adult. However, communication 'experts' (whether older siblings, parents, or salaried teachers) vary across cultures in their opinions as to how and to what degree these cultural 'novices' need to be explicitly taught to communicate. Language acquisition ideologies (LAIs) – whether these take the form of semi-conscious and fluctuating intuitions or of fully fleshed and institutionally applied theories – have more or less apparent effects on how caregivers use socialization routines to engage children in social interaction. As such, LAIs frequently index and help construct age- and gender-based hierarchies as well as sometimes ethnic or class-based social inequities.

In communities in which caregivers believe that children need to be explicitly taught the grammatically correct and pragmatically appropriate forms of language, caregivers articulate this LAI and demonstrate it through their elicitation of children's correct usage of specific words and utterances. For instance, the Kaluli of Papua New Guinea (for whom age is the primary basis of social inequality) hold that parents and older siblings must 'show' children how to speak and use 'say it' routines within triadic participant structures to engage children in the production of simple but grammatically correct and contextually suitable utterances (Schieffelin 1990). The Basotho also believe that children need to be taught to speak, use primarily triadic 'say it' routines, and directly model the requisite forms; however, unlike the egalitarian Kaluli, the rank-stratified Basotho do less correcting of ungrammatical forms and more correcting of pragmatically inappropriate formulations (Demuth 1986). Both Anglo-American working and middle-class parents in the US feel it necessary to use 'say it' routines with their children, but these parents tend to model and elicit words for things or, like the Basotho, politeness acts, rather than illustrating and requiring syntactically complete utterances – the strategies used (e.g. what-questions and dyadic participant structures) reflect the institutional LAIs and pedagogical strategies of this class-stratified society (Miller 1982; Ochs and Schieffelin 1984).

By contrast, many cultures share no such belief in the need to explicitly 'teach' their children how to talk, and this correlates in interesting ways with several parameters of social stratification. For instance, Western Samoans reject the child-centered practices of scaffolding (prompting, clarifying, and correcting) children's linguistic attempts to participate in social interaction, thus manifesting their deep investment in age hierarchy. The only time explicit 'say it' routines are employed is to inculcate the respectful etiquette formulas required in this rank-conscious society (Ochs 1988).

Adopting a similar situation-centered LAI, adults in a rural, African American community believe that children cannot be made to talk nor should their early attempts at speech be interpreted, as they will of their own accord 'come up' by imitating the talk of their elders. As a consequence, children in this community 'fail' to learn the skills explicitly taught by the socialization practices of their middle-class white counterparts (e.g. learning to label objects or to respond to questions for which the questioner already knows the answer) – that is, practices imbued with ideological knowledge about how to succeed in the educational system of this class- and ethnicity-stratified society (Heath 1983).

Nuyorican caregivers also 'fail' to simplify their own speech or interpret the speech of their children due to the explicit belief that it is not up to adults to take the child's perspective but up to children to attend to, figure out, and replicate the ways of their elders in this community sensitive to age-grading (Zentella 1997). And, yet, Zentella is careful to add that this LAI and the attendant practices vary in relationship to caregivers' differential access to mainstream models of thinking and acting with respect to raising children. In an interesting twist, LAIs such as these that inculcate age hierarchy appear to be de-emphasized in direct relationship to the acceptance of LAIs that support social stratification based on class and ethnicity.

Early language socialization paradigms concerning the impact of local LAIs on language acquisition by children within domestic settings have been adapted for application to the socialization of older novices within more diverse settings from schools to workplaces. However, the language ideologies examined in these contexts have as much or more to do with power-laden ethnotheories about which forms of languages are to be acquired and used by whom, in what way, and for what reason. Thus, the next two sections focus on local answers to these questions within specific contexts and communities of practice.

Semiotic and contextual usage ideologies

Local beliefs about the contextual use of language – that is, the semiotic association of certain linguistic forms with specific speakers, participant structures, settings, moods, and goals – shape how 'experts' model interaction and how they engage the participation of 'novices' in these interactions. In this section, I investigate the impact of the obviously power-infused and power-enforcing forms of these beliefs, or what I will refer to here as semiotic and contextual usage ideologies (SCUIs).

In relatively homogeneous cultural settings, SCUIs affect the socialization of linguistic structures that reflect the prevailing power structures in that society. For instance, Ochs (1988) and Platt (1986) show that in Samoa sociolinguistic expectations about how higher- and lower-status speakers ought to speak to one another structure domestic socialization routines between higher-status caregivers and lower-status children; this, in turn, has consequences for the order in which children develop the ability to use deictic verbs such as 'give' and 'come' and ergative case markers. Similarly, Thai SCUIs about relative speaker status shape the language socialization routines used by older caregiving siblings in ways that affect younger siblings' acquisition of Thai metapragmatic markers such as kin terms and status-indexing pronouns (Howard 2007, this volume).

By contrast, SCUIs may also shape socializing routines in ways that allow for power seepage. For instance, Antoneros Mayans believe that children are like parrots in their aptitude for imitating without understanding what is said to them and thus are easily engaged as triadic participants in teasing routines. However, as 'unequal' if amusing partners, the children do not only take away invaluable lessons about how to speak to whom and with what anticipated results; they also sometimes manifest an understanding of how to work their 'parrot' roles and subvert the teasing event to their own ends (Reynolds 2008). Elsewhere in the literature, SCUIs influence peer socializing interactions in ways that allow not only for the transference of past precedent but also for the creation of new communicative patterns (e.g. de León 2007; Paugh 2005).

It is not only in informal settings but also in more institutional domains such as schools that SCUIs are influential. For instance, in Thailand, ideologies about how to use Standard Thai politeness particles when addressing higher-status persons (e.g. teachers) are socialized by the teacher's modeling and correction routines in the classroom (Howard 2009). Further, in US law-school classrooms, SCUIs inform the initiation-reply-evaluation routines used by law professors to socialize first-year law students into the specific ways of speaking expected in courtroom exchanges (Mertz 1998).

In studies of specifically heterogeneous (e.g. colonial or ethnically segregated) contexts, contrasts between the SCUIs found in homes and schools can be extreme and have a powerful impact on the socialization of interactional resources and styles, thus undermining the apparent developmental goals and democratic ideals of public schooling (Cazden, John, and Hymes 1972; Heath 1983). But, even in contexts in which differences in cross-cultural communicative norms are apparent to all, participants may apply incorrect and stereotyping SCUIs, which result in new forms of interaction that are culturally appropriate for no one. For instance, Western orientalist ideologies about 'silent Asians' contribute to Hong Kong immigrant students' nonparticipation in classroom activities in a Toronto high school (Pon, Goldstein, and Schecter 2003). Similarly, in the multicultural workplace, the SCUI that teaching communicative routines will help immigrants to integrate does not always result in the transformations anticipated by management. For instance, Katz's research (2001) on training sessions for hotel employees in the US demonstrates that teaching Anglo-American politeness norms does not necessarily produce the 'perfect' American worker.

One more consequential SCUI is the semiotic attachment of linguistic varieties with specific power-graded identities based on gender and ethnicity. Frequently, genderlectal ideologies – notions of how men and women speak – shape the 'language ecology' within which children are socialized into their gender-specific identities and ways of speaking. Thus, Aymara children raised in bilingual households in Bolivia learn to role-play according to a model in which men are more publicly outspoken and display their knowledge of Spanish whereas Aymara-dominant women express themselves more through silence and behind-the-scenes talk (Luykx 2003). Sometimes the code ideologically associated with women takes ascendancy for the whole community because women are the primary agents of language socialization (see Cavanaugh 2006). However, where women and their ways of speaking are denigrated, language socialization practices may have the opposite impact, as in the village of Gapun in Papua New Guinea (Kulick 1998). Strange alignments may form when women occupy a secondary social status and yet speak the socially dominant language. For instance, historically deep SCUIs propel the socialization of genderlectal practices among Hasidim immigrants in New York such that school-aged girls are shifting from Yiddish-English bilingualism toward English dominance whereas boys are conserving their Hebrew-Yiddish bilingualism (Fader 2009).

Ethnolinguistic ideologies – that is, the association of linguistic varieties with cultural or ethnic identities – represent one more familiar form of politically loaded SCUI whose effects on language socialization practices need to be examined in ethnographic detail and historical particularity. For instance, Langman's research (2003) explores how a Hungarian folk dance group forges their bilingual practices and minority ethnic identity against a long historical backdrop of (Czecho-)Slovak nationalist ideologies that have relegated the use of Hungarian to private and semi-private cultural organization settings. By contrast, Rampton's work in Britain (1995) reveals how ethnolinguistic SCUIs can produce fascinating forms of hybrid usage or 'crossing' as Anglo, Afro-Caribbean, and South Asian adolescents allow each other variable access to using elements of Creole, Punjabi, and stylized Asian English – varieties to which only some of them have inheritance 'rights' according to traditional European belief systems concerning ethnolinguistic identity politics.

Ideologies of the value of linguistic forms

Implicit in many of the contexts and communities reviewed so far are ideologies about the inherent superiority of some forms of language over others and therefore the presumed superiority of the speakers associated with the dominant linguistic varieties. For instance, the dominant ideologies to which language learners are exposed is the presumption that orality is inferior to literacy or that white American middle-class communicative practices are superior to Native American, African American, or white working-class dialects and norms for interaction. However, we have not yet explicitly considered the impact of ideologies about the symbolic and/or pragmatic value of linguistic forms themselves (IVLFs) – whether mode, code, or genre – on language socialization.

Modal ideologies: Literate, oral, and manual   Those IVLFs concerning the relative value of the mode of communication – literacy over orality, oralism over manualism – have transformed dramatically over the last century in a variety of contexts and in a variety of ways that have powerfully affected language socialization patterns and the effective transmission (or not) of socially valued modes.

Language ideologies that elevate literacy practices and variably value different forms of oral performance can have a detrimental impact on the socialization of communicative competence both in and out of school settings (e.g. Heath 1983); and, as Bell's study (2003) of a Canadian job retraining program demonstrates, standard literacy ideologies may have an impact on education throughout the lifespan. However, not all societies evince such a simplistically homogeneous and hierarchical ideology – that is, high literate over low oral modes – and the resulting socializing practices are similarly complex. For instance, stereotypes about the presumed orality of Gypsy culture are contradicted by evidence that the Spanish Gitano community have a long history of developing the means for acquiring the valued resource of literacy, but all outside the mainstream educational settings in which Gitano children are still normally perceived to fail (Poveda, Cano, and Palomares-Valera 2005). As illustrated by this and other studies (e.g. Baquedano-López 2004; de la Piedra and Romo 2003; Sterponi, this volume), the acquisition of literacy is influenced by ideologies about what constitutes literacy events, how learning ought to be structured, who should be in charge, and whether or not hybrid codes are appropriate.

Complexity at the level of ideology and practice also shows up in studies of signing communities, as traditional Western stereotypes about deaf persons and their codes have given way to new forms of prestige associated with sign languages as well as tensions over emerging standards and varieties of these codes. As a result, new and contradictory socialization patterns have also been produced. The development of a sign language and linguistic community in Nicaragua (Senghas, Senghas, and Pyers 2005) provides a clear example of how modal ideologies may influence social structures and practices in ways that obstruct or facilitate the socialization of a signing code and the successful formation of a community of signers (see also Nonaka, this volume).

Varietal ideologies: Languages, dialects, and code-switching codes Those IVLFs that concern the relative status of distinct linguistic varieties and the value of multilingualism in general are woven throughout many everyday exchanges and institutional policies and have an impact on language socialization in both public and domestic spheres. The impact of these ideologies on societal language shift is taken up at length in Garrett (this volume); thus, I focus here on how evaluative ideologies affect the acquisition of multiple linguistic varieties by individuals in multilingual societies.

The power of specific codes usually correlates with the socioeconomic power of their speakers, and the construction of these sociolinguistic hierarchies is the result of political economic forces ranging from imperial expansion on the one hand to industrialization and immigration on the other. In these contexts, the dominant linguistic variety is invested with symbolic capital by direct sociopolitical oppression as well as by more subtle hegemonic forces involving trade, schooling, and employment. Codes that have attained ideological dominance are regimented by prescriptive ideologies and practices that index the standard and nonstandard forms, identify those who produce and control them, and imbue insecurity in those who do not. For instance, attitudes at a South Indian college about what is proper English and who speaks it create a learning environment in which students who have had no access to English in the home are actively 'dis-socialized' by peers and teachers – that is, stigmatized and further restricted in their attempts to acquire the power code of this postcolonial country (Atkinson 2003).

Dominant language ideologies frequently lead to the demise of minority languages as well as the denigration of their speakers. However, in some cases, covert prestige for nonstandard varieties may exist and work to subvert the impact of dominant language ideologies on language socialization practices such that both standard and nonstandard varieties may be simultaneously acquired (e.g. Paugh 2005, this volume). In still other cases, more than one high-capital language may be vying for ideological control over the hearts and minds of the speakers of one or more minority languages. For instance, the competition between English and Afrikaans in South Africa has opened up an ideological space in which Xhosa is gaining value on the local linguistic market in one community (Dyers 2008). Also common in the literature is a phenomenon conceptualized as the 'ethnic revitalization paradox' (Rindstendt and Aronsson 2002). In these cases, the official ideology favoring the revitalization of an endangered language is undermined by now-covert forces maintaining the power of the politically and economically dominant language. For instance, the Quichua children studied by Rindstendt and Aronsson are inhibited by contradictory messages about the relative value of Spanish and Quichua from acquiring a standard form of the dominant language or a fluent variety of the 'revitalizing' language.

However, socializing practices are affected not only by IVLFs concerning specific codes but also by beliefs about the value of being multilingual, of living in a multilingual community, and of mixing the codes at one's command. At one extreme, one finds purism – that is, a belief in the necessary separation of codes – and at the other end an ideological embrace of linguistic hybridity. In between lies the pragmatic acceptance of multiplicity for the sake of something else.

Addressing the purist end of the spectrum, Zentella (1997) proposes a specifically 'anthropolitical' analysis of the English-only ideology that, she says, has colonized the minds of New York Puerto Ricans. Young parents tend to denigrate their own code-switching skills (using the pejorative label 'Spanglish') and believe they must teach their children English in order to 'defend' themselves in the United States. What has been accepted is a 'subtractive bilingual' model of language acquisition (another LAI) that undermines the successful acquisition of either language, inhibits the capacity to switch between them strategically, and obstructs the articulation of multiple social identities.

By contrast, 'additive bilingualism' (i.e. the LAI that one can successfully learn a dominant language while also maintaining one's minority mother tongue) accompanies the IVLF that multilingualism is an asset in the construction of a cosmopolitan identity. But here, too, ideologies and socialization practices tend toward inconsistencies and ambiguities that undermine language acquisition. For instance, Pease-Alvarez (2003) found that, although Californians of Mexican descent express a belief in cultivating Spanish–English bilingualism in their children, they have fluctuating opinions about how bilingualism should be socialized and do not always follow through on their intentions to use Spanish with their children on a daily basis; as a result, this community of immigrants, like so many others, displays a trend toward intergenerational shift in the direction of English.

Finally, a pragmatic acceptance of code-mixing may be found influencing the socializing practices even of some communities that officially subscribe to IVLFs about the dominance of one language over the other. Here caregivers may use both languages in an effort to facilitate children's acquisition of the dominant language and/or express alternative social or emotional meanings than those carried by the dominant code (e.g. Garrett 2005; Schieffelin 1994). In these cases, the impact on socialization is not only exposure to more than one language but also a modeling of when and how to switch between multiple codes. However, at times, pragmatic code-switching tolerance verges into an actual IVLF that promotes the production and expansion of new syncretic codes. For instance, children on Rapa Nui are actively exposed to their caregivers' mix of several varieties of Chilean Spanish and Rapa Nui; under the auspices of the growing heritage tourism industry, this new syncretic style carries significant symbolic capital as it is used for the pragmatic purpose of indexing a valuable ethnic identity (Makihara 2005).

Metapragmatic ideologies: Genres, styles, registers, and voices   Speech genres, styles, registers, or voices – that is, forms of language that are metapragmatically associated with specific linguistic varieties, participant structures, speech contexts, and/ or speech act sequences – are frequently assessed as 'good' or 'bad,' especially with respect to their utility for language socialization purposes. For instance, the speech genre known as 'teasing' in English is especially valued for use with children and other newcomers to a speech community (see Schieffelin and Ochs 1986 (especially Eisenberg 1986); Reynolds 2008; Riley 2007). By contrast, swearing and insulting may be considered inappropriate (e.g. Garrett 2005). Other genres that socializing 'experts' value more or less consciously include counseling talk (Watson-Gegeo and Gegeo 1990) and narrative (Baquedano-López 1997; Miller, Cho, and Bracey 2005).

Throughout these studies, one can trace the roots of a theory of what Agha (2005) has termed 'enregisterment' – that is, the notion that certain ways of speaking are produced, delimited through entextualization, and indexically associated with particular contexts, functions, and communities of speakers via specific acts of alignment and contestation. The ideologies resulting from these metapragmatic processes could be considered a type of SCUI, as discussed in the last section; but the linguistic forms that result, once evaluated, give us a type of IVLF that in turn influences socialization patterns. For instance, Howard studies the 'speech chains' through which metapragmatic ideologies organize the socialization and enregistration of politeness features (both linguistic and nonverbal) among ethnic Muang children in Northern Thailand (2009). On the one hand, historic ideologies positively associate the use of Standard Thai honorific particles and bows of respect with national identity and social hierarchy; these in turn shape civic discourse in general and classroom practices in particular (ranging from student rules and guide books to pragmatic routines in the classroom).

In other words, ideologies about such metapragmatic forms are not fixed or homogenous but subject to social variability and change over time, and these ideologies in turn transform the socialization patterns by which language is acquired. Crago's work in northern Québec (Crago, Annahatak, and Ningiuruvik 1993) makes this argument explicit by demonstrating how younger Inuit mothers appear to be eschewing traditional Baby Talk forms and 'affectionate talk' and 'affectionate verses,' instead adopting 'say it' routines for teaching Western etiquette formulas and conversational patterns in order to prepare children for school interactions and the successful acquisition of Western-style symbolic capital – that is, the result of a genre-specific IVLF.

As should be apparent from the foregoing survey, the ideological evaluation of speech forms (IVLFs) – whether the literate channel, a hybrid code, or a particular politeness formula – is rarely disconnected from both LAI and SCLI ideologies concerning who has or ought to have access to learning specific speech forms and the subsequent right to use them at particular times, in particular places, and in particular ways. In the next section, I review studies that examine how beliefs about the value, acquisition, and social distribution of linguistic resources according to age, gender, class, and ethnicity are regularly negotiated within otherwise 'routine' socialization practices.

Power-Inflected Socialization of Politically Loaded Language Ideologies

While some politically loaded language ideologies are imposed via deterministic policies and structures, many are in fact transmitted and transformed via culturally patterned yet context-specific socializing interactions. Sometimes community members use explicit language socialization strategies to inculcate community norms in children and other community newcomers. However, in most cases participants engage in far more subtle power struggles over the reproduction and revision of these language ideologies.

According to Ochs (1991), culturally diverse responses to child–caregiver misunderstandings socialize different worldviews about the egocentric versus sociocentric nature of child–caregiver interactions – that is, beliefs about who should orient toward the perspective of whom in conversation. At the sociocentric extreme are the Inuit, who ignore children's incomprehensible utterances; at the egocentric extreme are white American middle-class caregivers, who attempt to understand and clarify everything children say; and in between are the Kaluli and Samoans, who share a dispreference for interpreting their children's speech.

Ochs and Schieffelin (1984) have hypothesized that white American middle-class socializing routines contribute to the Western ideology that demotes caregivers (i.e. women in this case) to second-class status as conversational partners and therefore in society as a whole. Expanding on these findings, Ochs and Taylor (1995) have analyzed how the gendered language ideology named after the television program 'Father Knows Best' is socialized in white American middle-class families. The organization of social interaction, especially narratives, during dinner-table talk – who speaks, who listens, who raises the topic, and who resolves it – enlists these children into the assumption that, while Mother guides the conversation, Father is the final go-to guy for answers.

While peer socialization offers children the chance to play a more active role in the production of language ideologies, they may nonetheless from a very young age contribute to the actual reproduction of the status quo. For instance, Farris (1991) looks at how Taiwanese preschool children contribute to power-inflected and gendered notions of language use through playground interactions. Not only do they display distinctive communicative styles (with boys engaging in direct competitive verbal interactions and girls enacting indirect and manipulative styles); these children also actively and explicitly maintain an ethos of hierarchically ordered genders and associated genderlects.

Studies of language socialization in Japan (e.g. Burdelski, this volume; Clancy 1986; Dunn 1999) uncover a different orientation to ideologies of power as certain linguistic forms – for example, indirect speech styles and honorific particles – are linked with a social order based on empathy for others, conflict avoidance, and respect for elders. For instance, Cook (1999) examines how Japanese schoolroom interactions promote a belief in the communal construction of knowledge rather than the ideology embedded in Western dyadic classroom exchanges, which involve the individualistic acquisition, display, and evaluation of knowledge. The socialization of Navajo communicative ideologies via everyday interactional routines with preschoolers bears some similarity to the Japanese case: through engagement in triadic directives (to help and to handle conflicts with other children), adults direct and model for children the importance of taking responsibility as a group for accomplishing tasks and for taking authoritative roles when responding to problems (Field 2001). Thus, in these cultures the notion of power appears to be communicatively shared in the interests of acquiescence to the authority of society as a whole (or its representatives).

The production of language ideologies concerning the articulation and distribution of social authority becomes even more obvious in institutionalized language acquisition contexts. For instance, He's (2001) study of a Chinese American heritage classroom explores the socializing interactions by which children acquire and demonstrate a 'preference for ambiguity' in avoiding confrontation with authority figures, even as these more powerful figures demand of the children clear and unqualified answers in return. She then asks whether these socializing processes and the resulting ideologies are specific to Chinese culture or whether similar co-constructions may be found in the socializing interactions of unequal partners in many cultures (see Eisenberg 1986 for a study of how very distinctive socializing routines and communicative styles – for example, Mexican American teasing patterns – may nonetheless produce similar ends – i.e. social control).

All too often, colonial encounters create contexts in which alien linguistic forms (both codes and pedagogic genres) are imposed on a community via schooling. For instance, Duranti and Ochs (1986) reveal the ways in which literacy instruction in Samoan village classrooms shapes the acquisition of Western-like ideologies concerning (1) the necessity of using 'good language' in school, when reading and writing and when addressing foreigners, and (2) the notion that providing correct answers is an individual accomplishment, relevant to success in the Westernized economy outside the village. Similarly, Watson-Gegeo and Gegeo (1992) explore how the Kwara'ae ideology about the importance of *fa'amanata* ('shaping the minds') of young children and adults in need of social counseling has been undermined by the imposition of Western schooling practices.

And yet, sometimes, more local socializing patterns influence the resulting language ideologies. For instance, Blommaert et al. (2005) have examined how nonstandard forms of English and the ideological appreciation of these forms are being produced in marginalized school settings in South Africa, where not only the students but also the teachers speak a nonstandard variety. These ways of speaking are inscribed as a language ideology – a semiotic link between these speakers and their locality – within the larger community.

Socialization procedures in schools and other institutional contexts also breed ideologies about the relationship between individuals' cognitive and communicative skills and their subsequent chances of success (in variously self-fulfilling fashion). For example, Harklau (2003) contrasts the practices that construct three different representations of immigrants in a high school in western New York: the 'colorblind' approach, which ignores students' ethnic backgrounds as variables of interaction; the 'Ellis Island' approach, which ennobles the tough experiences and perseverance of immigrants; and the 'linguistic deficit' approach, which assumes multilingual immigrants are operating with a handicap that produces or masks cognitive deficits. Similarly, Wortham (2005) analyzes how teachers' beliefs about 'good' and 'bad' students (who they are and what are their characteristics) are jointly produced by long-term teacher–student interactions at an American high school.

Whether considering the impact of language socialization on language ideologies or the reverse, it is necessary to remember that 'novices' are not mere passive subjects imbibing whatever is imparted by the so-called 'experts.' Instead, all learners play a more or less active part in socializing themselves, developing (both acquiring and transforming) the codes and ideologies modeled and explicitly taught by the socializing agents. This tension between individual agency and structural determinism is broached in many of the studies reviewed so far in this chapter, but will be traced in more historical and ethnolinguistic specificity in the final section on *la francophonie*.

Language Ideology and Language Socialization in *La Francophonie*

La francophonie as understood here refers to the loose affiliation of states and regions in which the French language has come to be acquired, used, and recognized as a symbolic force mobilizing identity construction. Unlike the traditional language or speech community, *la francophonie* operates like an archetypal social speech network; that is, it cannot be considered a bounded political or cultural entity but exists (to the extent that it does exist) ideologically and pragmatically as an interlocking set of speakers in an imagined community (one virtual representation of this community can be seen at http://www.francophonie.org). Binding this speech network together are the hegemonic language ideology and an array of socialization practices that were originally developed in France and later disseminated globally via colonialism and postcolonial treaties and aid programs. Yet, due to interplay with a varying set of ethnohistorical phenomena, these ideologies and practices have led to quite diverse results worldwide. Thus, *la francophonie* represents a particularly rich terrain in which to trace the power-laden relationship between language ideologies and language socialization.

The French language ideology, being one of the more powerful and prevalent of language ideologies operating in the world today, had its origins in northern France, was first enshrined by Richelieu in *l'académie française*, and was further developed during the Age of Enlightenment and the French Revolution. According to the ideology, language functions primarily as a medium for the transmission of rational thought and secondarily as a social unifier of people into a single state capable of protecting individuals' rights to freedom and equality. That many French citizens also believe that standard Parisian French is the best language for the job of communicating rationality and uniting citizens is to some degree a chauvinist and perhaps inevitable byproduct of the belief system itself (Ager 2001; Grillo 1989).

However, France is also home to one of the key theorists of the notion that ideologies such as this are produced by specific socialization strategies and structures that are in turn re-enforced by those very language ideologies. Bourdieu's writings (Bourdieu 1991; Bourdieu and Passeron 1977) on structural domination, especially by way of the educational system, have underwritten much of the politicization of the relationship between language socialization and language ideology over the past three decades. Thus, it is no wonder that much of the work influenced by and to some degree reacting against Bourdieu's theories has been conducted within *la francophonie*.

Conducted at the epicenter of the francophone sphere of influence, my recent ethnographic research in a privileged suburb of Paris (Riley 2004, 2009) demonstrates the reproduction as well as transformation of French language ideologies and domestic socialization practices. On the one hand, caregivers provide children (as well as anthropologists) with both models and explicit corrections as to how to communicate correctly in French – I refer to this process using a term taught to me by one of my parent-assistants as *encadrement* ('framing'). On the other hand, we are also encouraged to *se débrouiller* – that is, to make do, manage, or think outside the box in response to the otherwise highly structured and bureaucratic social system (sometimes referred to as the *système D*). In other words, children and foreigners are taught both the elaborate communicative codes needed to negotiate the system as well as the key to breaking or bypassing these very same codes when they turn out to be ineffective.

One step removed from the old imperial capital, we find in Jaffe's work (1999) on Corsica an example of active resistance to the imposition of French nationalist ideological standards and socializing practices. Here one sees, on the one hand, an acceptance of the language-culture-nation ideology (i.e. that defense of the culture requires defense of the Corsican language), and yet, on the other, ambivalence in response to the standard French ideological tenets that languages must be codified and competence taught through standardized means. Instead, at the level of language policy and classroom practice, plural orthographies are tolerated, phonological and morpho-syntactic variants applauded, and affiliation proven not through linguistic mastery but through sympathetic attachment.

At the margins of the old empire, one finds overseas territories, such as French Polynesia, struggling in similar ways with both francophone language ideologies and socialization practices. For instance, my study in the Marquesas (Riley 2007) has uncovered many of the ethnic revitalization paradoxes found elsewhere in colonial settings (e.g. Rindstendt and Aronsson 2002) as well as some of the pragmatic syncretic solutions found throughout the language contact world (e.g. Makihara 2005). That is, on the one hand, one finds the people making efforts to preserve the indigenous language (*'Enana*) through both daily usage and institutional codification while they in fact avoid it in interactions with young children and worry over its lack of purity in official settings. On the other hand, one also finds the beginnings of a covert celebration of the code-switching forms socialized by youths in interaction with each other and the generation of the language ideology that ethnolinguistic identity is meant to be hybrid and ever-transforming.

In a postcolonial setting such as Cameroon, one finds complex configurations in which French vies for status with multiple codes and carries with it many socializing practices in public-school settings that contradict those associated with the other dominant language, Arabic, in another educational context, the Qur'anic school (Moore 2006, this volume). Qur'anic teachers guide children in the correct repetition of the entire Arabic text (God's word) but without the goal of semantic comprehension. By contrast, French teachers use dialogues (mere pedagogical devices) as models for repetition (but not word-for-word perfection). While rote learning is used in both contexts, the different ideological frameworks result in different socialization practices and different levels of spoken competence (as well as conflicting subjective identifications as traditional Muslims and modern francophone Cameroonians).

The long-term maintenance of French language ideologies and socialization practices in North America centuries after French colonial control ended raises a host of fascinating research issues. Whereas throughout the rest of (post)colonial *francophonie* the dominance of French is assumed, in Canada and the United States, French faces daily ideological domination by English as a result of everyday socialization practices embedded in schooling, media, employment training, and recreational interactions.

In Québec, the *Révolution tranquille* of the 1960s and 1970s was founded on the tenet of French language ideology that specifies the intrinsic link between a language, culture, race, and nation. Although the French language and culture are no longer those of the homeland left 400 years earlier, *nous nous souvenons les idéologies* ('we remember the ideologies') and have felt the need to establish a bastion against the hegemony of Anglophone Canada. The effort to create an island of French monolingualism within the North American sea of English was epitomized by the passage in 1977 of *Loi 101*, which legislated the authority of the French language in schools and public signage. However, in Montréal, awash in multilingual multicultural cosmopolitanism since the 1980s, the generation referred to as the 'Children of Law 101' has led a noisy rebellion against the rigidity of the nationalist ideology and attendant socialization practices, a rebellion that has taken the form of pro-multilingual ideologies and peer socialization practices involving bivalence and code-switching.

One study of this Montréal phenomenon reveals how contrasting household ideologies concerning which and how many languages it is good to know – French, English, one or more ancestral language(s), or others – have affected the acquisition and use of these languages among allophone youths in Montreal. In some families, children are imbued with the habitus of multilingual socialization as a strategic choice, the multiple codes serving as capital in the linguistic marketplace; by contrast, in other families, multilingualism is viewed as a consequence of external forces, practical resources over which the individual exercises little agency or control (Lamarre and Paredes 2003).

Also in Montréal, Riley, Peters, and Couture (2008) have focused on the socialization experiences of immigrants from other non-European francophone countries who deal on the one hand with the racism of a people intent on defending their newly acquired bastion of identity against ethnolinguistic and even genetic adulteration and on the other with the internalized biases these immigrants acquired through French schooling elsewhere in *la francophonie* and imported with them about what constitutes grammatically proper French (they are clear that this is not the variety spoken in Québec). Against such a complex background, many such immigrants choose to emphasize quixotic fluidity – that is, the ability to learn and use whichever code will work in interaction with a given interlocutor without regard to predetermined contextual boundaries. This chameleon approach (a mix of pragmatism and play) is also to be found increasingly among the bilingual youth who have, since birth, straddled the longstanding frontiers between franco and anglo solitudes. Through the analysis of bilingual interviews and recorded speech events, I have been uncovering evidence of how these ideologies and practices are socialized and manifested (Riley 2008, forthcoming).

By contrast, in northern Québec, First Nations people have forged their own path in response to this hegemonic movement (Patrick 2003). Although English has historic priority over French due to patterns of trade and missionary contact, the political economic value of French has grown as a result of the relatively recent provincial language policy changes, such that some Inuit parents choose French language schooling for their children over English. Nonetheless, outside the classroom English is favoured over French in public contexts and with non-Inuit, while Inuktituk is used among friends and in traditional activity domains as well as newly created political formations. In other words, the tension between two rival colonial languages may be creating here (as in South Africa) a space in which revivalist ideologies may successfully support the socialization of the indigenous languages and, in this case, even undermine the socialization of the officially 'dominant' language.

Outside Québec, one finds a range of traditional French language ideologies and socialization practices surfacing and influencing the acquisition of varieties of French and ideologies about their value. As in Montréal, in Ontario, bilingual competence has come to represent a substantial form of symbolic capital as it provides access to relatively-well-paid jobs; however, access to fluency in both codes is constrained by a number of ideological and practical barriers. Heller (1994) has provided a critical examination of the difficulties of acquiring and/or retaining French in a French immersion school in Toronto. Roy (2003), by contrast, is concerned with how claims to bilingual competence may be challenged on ideological grounds as, for example, when the French spoken by Franco-Ontarians may not pass as standard in workplaces such as call centers.

Finally, in the United States, from New Orleans to Maine, one finds traces, generations removed, of both the ideologies and the socializing practices found in France. For instance, since World War II, French-Canadian immigrants to New England have begun to partake of the classic American pattern of language shift in which French is replaced by English in the third generation, and this despite deeply ingrained ideologies (now over two centuries old) concerning the importance of *la survivance* of the language–culture–faith complex and domestic socializing routines led by the rallying cry, '*Français à la maison!*' (Williams and Riley 2001).

Thus, French language ideologies and socialization practices have been transformed as they have spread throughout *la francophonie*, carrying diverse power-laden messages and triggering a variety of political ramifications. First, one finds throughout the francophone world the French LAI that the rules of any language must be codified and taught through explicit pedagogical techniques in order for children to acquire the art of clear and precise expression. Older, more heavy-handed versions of this LAI are retained as punitive methods in homes from Vermont to the Marquesas, whereas they may arrive in 'modern' liberalized form in schools in Corsica and Cameroon. Additionally, these socialization rules are frequently applied to the teaching not only of French but also of indigenous languages – as manifested by pedagogical methods and materials in the Marquesas.

Second, the SCUI that language is a powerful tool in the mediation of national or ethnic unity is evident in many francophone settings, from its origins in Republican France to its carryover in the Québécois nationalist movement. And yet this belief system (anchoring language to people), in the hands of Corsicans and Marquesans, becomes dogma in the fight to preserve their local languages from the incursions of French itself. By contrast, among Muslim Cameroonians and Inuktituk and elsewhere in Canada, it is the political-economic power of the French language that carries symbolic weight in school choice decisions whereas everyday practice may defy this ideological vector. Even in Montréal, an SCUI promoting multilingualism and contextual hybridity may be threatening the old hold of the French nationalist language ideology.

Finally, nearly ubiquitous is the inheritance of the seventeenth-century French IVLF that a particular variety of French is the best code on earth for expressing the truths of our world – whether the Parisian French spoken by the parents I worked with in the Isle-de-France or international French as spoken by Congolese immigrants to Montréal. The linguistic fact that these varieties differ is less relevant than is the semiotic fact that children continue to be socialized to believe the ideology that some varieties are better or worse than others (whether Québécois or Corsican) and that therefore the speakers of these lesser varieties are doomed to second-class citizenship (thus indefinitely reproducing seeds of linguistic insecurity throughout *la francophonie*).

Nonetheless, a love of French (francophilia) and the universal ideals of beauty and reason, liberty and equality that it symbolizes (if not actually realized in the classroom, workplace, or the republic at large, then existing still in the popular imagination) is at the heart of whatever creative claim *la francophonie* has to strategic unity on the world stage (frequently operationalized in the face of Anglo global hegemony). And if, within that speech network, miscommunications, whether at the level of ideology or socializing interaction, provide a stage for the production of transformed, sometimes transgressive, beliefs and practices that challenge the political power inhering within old ideologies and novice–expert relationships, this researcher's reaction is: *'Vive la francophonie!'*

Conclusions

Some language ideologies are unconscious and unspoken, while others are baldly stated and prescribed. Some are under metapragmatic (re)construction via every socializing interaction, and some have been fixed and codified in institutional law and handed down through careful pedagogy. Whatever their origins, once they exist these ideologies have a further impact on the ongoing socialization of the interactive strategies they reflect upon.

As demonstrated by the studies surveyed in this chapter, the consequential interplay of language ideologies and language socialization is particularly evident in multilingual, culture-contact contexts. In these speech communities, miscommunications are frequently assumed to be the consequence of a lack of linguistic competence by disempowered interlocutors; however, the 'experts' in these settings frequently teach linguistic mastery while failing to address the learning of the relevant communicative norms. Even when speech-community members share the same linguistic variety yet differ in their communicative norms, interactions may be perceived as running the gamut from mysterious to rude, and efforts to repair these communicative breakdowns – case by case or at a policy-wide level – may prove fruitless. Finally, when in contact, contrastive language ideologies not only produce miscommunications between individuals in everyday interactions but also frequently contribute to social structural inequalities in schools and work sites, and even sometimes to global-scale rifts.

If such micro and macro misunderstandings are to be resolved, interlocutors at all levels of the semiotic food chain need to understand more about how communicative ideologies are shaping the course of their own language socialization and how in turn their own speech acts are having an impact on the thoughts and feelings of others who are in the process of learning how to communicate in a given context. The possibility of constructive interpersonal communication at all levels of human contact depends on this form of metapragmatic reflection and on our universal capacity to engage in it.

ACKNOWLEDGEMENTS

This paper was made possible by the support and guidance of many institutions and individuals: Wenner-Gren and the National Science Foundation; Concordia University, Johnson State College, and Université Paris X Nanterre; my project participants, friends, and colleagues in French Polynesia, Northern Vermont, Ile-de-France, and Montréal; and the very astute editors of this volume.

REFERENCES

Ager, D. (2001) *Francophonie in the 1990s*. Clevedon, UK: Multilingual Matters.

Agha, A. (2005) Voice, footing, enregisterment. *Journal of Linguistic Anthropology* 15(1): 38–59.

Atkinson, D. (2003) Language socialization and dis-socialization in a south Indian college. In R. Bayley and S. R. Schecter (eds.), *Language Socialization in Bilingual and Multilingual Societies*. 147–62. Clevedon, UK: Multilingual Matters.

Baquedano-López, P. (1997) Creating social identities through doctrina narratives. *Issues in Applied Linguistics* 8: 1: 27–45.

Baquedano-López, P. (2004) Literacy practices across learning contexts. In A. Duranti (ed.), *A Companion to Linguistic Anthropology*. 245–68. Malden, MA: Blackwell.

Bell, J. S. (2003) Back to school: Learning practices in a job retraining community. In R. Bayley and S. R. Schecter (eds.), *Language Socialization in Bilingual and Multilingual Societies*. 251–68. Clevedon, UK: Multilingual Matters.

Blommaert, J., Muyllaert, N., Huysmans, M., and Dyers, C. (2005) Peripheral normativity: Literacy and the production of locality in a South African township school. *Linguistics and Education* 16: 378–403.

Bourdieu, P. (1991) *Language and Symbolic Power*. Cambridge, MA: Harvard University Press.

Bourdieu, P., and Passeron, J.-C. (1977) *Reproduction in Education, Society and Culture*. London: Sage.

Cavanaugh, J. (2006) Little women and vital champions: Gendered language shift in a northern Italian town. *Journal of Linguistic Anthropology* 16(2): 194–210.

Cazden, C. B., John, V. P., and Hymes, D. (eds.) (1972) *Functions of Language in the Classroom*. New York: Teachers College Press.

Clancy, P. M. (1986) The socialization of communicative style. In B. B. Schieffelin and E. Ochs (eds.), *Language Socialization across Cultures*. 213–50. Cambridge: Cambridge University Press.

Cook, H. M. (1999) Language socialization in Japanese elementary schools: Attentive listening and reaction turns. *Journal of Pragmatics* 31: 1443–65.

Crago, M. B., Annahatak, B., and Ningiuruvik, L. (1993) Changing patterns of language socialization in Inuit homes. *Anthropology and Education Quarterly* 24(3): 205–23.

de la Piedra, M. and Romo, H. D. (2003) Collaborative literacy in a Mexican immigrant household: The role of sibling mediators in the socialization of pre-school learners. In R. Bayley and S. R. Schecter (eds.), *Language Socialization in Bilingual and Multilingual Societies*. 44–61. Clevedon, UK: Multilingual Matters.

de León, L. (2007) Parallelism, metalinguistic play, and the interactive emergence of Zinacantec Mayan siblings' culture. *Research on Language and Social Interaction* 40(4): 405–36.

Demuth, K. (1986) Prompting routines in the language socialization of Basotho children. In B. B. Schieffelin and E. Ochs (eds.), *Language Socialization Across Cultures*. 51–79. Cambridge: Cambridge University Press.

Dunn, C. D. (1999) Coming of age in Japan: Language ideology and the acquisition of formal speech registers. In J. Verschueren (ed.), *Language and Ideology: Selected Papers from the 6th International Pragmatics Conference, 1*. 89–97. Antwerp, Belgium: International Pragmatics Association.

Duranti, A. and Ochs, E. (1986) Samoan literacy instruction in a Samoan Village. In B. B. Schieffelin and P. Gilmore (eds.), *Acquisition of Literacy: Ethnographic Perspectives*. 213–32. Norwood, NJ: Ablex.

Dyers, C. (2008) Truncated multilingualism or language shift? An examination of language use in intimate domains in a new non-racial working class township in South Africa. *Journal of Multilingual and Multicultural Development* 29(2): 110–26.

Eisenberg, A. R. (1986) Teasing: Verbal play in two Mexicano homes. In B. B. Schieffelin and E. Ochs (eds.), *Language Socialization Across Cultures*. 182–98. Cambridge: Cambridge University Press.

Fader, A. (2009) *Mitzvah Girls: Bringing Up the Next Generation of Hasidic Jews in Brooklyn*. Princeton, NJ: Princeton University Press.

Farris, K. S. (1991) The gender of child discourse: Same-sex peer socialization through language use in a Taiwanese preschool. *Journal of Linguistic Anthropology* 1(2): 198–224.

Field, M. (2001) Triadic directives in Navajo language socialization. *Language in Society* 30(2): 249–63.

Garrett, P. B. (2005) What a language is good for: Language socialization, language shift, and the persistence of code-specific genres in St. Lucia. *Language in Society* 34(3): 327–61.

Grillo, R. (1989) *Dominant Languages: Language and Hierarchy in Britain and France*. Cambridge: Cambridge University Press.

Harklau, L. (2003) Representational practices and multi-modal communication in US high schools: Implications for adolescent immigrants. In R. Bayley and S. R. Schecter (eds.), *Language Socialization in Bilingual and Multilingual Societies*. 83–97. Clevedon, UK: Multilingual Matters.

He, A. W. (2001) The language of ambiguity: Practices in Chinese heritage language classes. *Discourse Studies* 3(1): 75–96.

Heath, S. B. (1983) *Ways with Words: Language, Life, and Work in Communities and Classrooms*. Cambridge: Cambridge University Press.

Heller, M. (1994) *Crosswords: Language, Education and Ethnicity in French Ontario*. New York: Mouton de Gruyter.

Howard, K. (2007) Kinterm usage and hierarchy in Thai children's peer groups. *Journal of Linguistic Anthropology* 17(2): 204–30.

Howard, K. (2009) 'When meeting Mrs. Teacher, each time we should show respect': Standardizing respect and politeness in a Northern Thai classroom. *Linguistics and Education* 20(3): 254–72.

Jaffe, A. (1999) *Ideologies in Action: Language Politics on Corsica*. Berlin: Mouton de Gruyter.

Katz, M.-L. (2001) Engineering a hotel family: Language ideology, discourse, and workplace culture. *Linguistics and Education* 12(3): 309–43.

Kroskrity, P. V. (2004) Language ideologies. In A. Duranti (ed.), *A Companion to Linguistic Anthropology*. 496–517. Malden, MA: Blackwell.

Kulick, D. (1998) Anger, gender, language shift, and the politics of revelation in a

Papua New Guinean village. In B. B. Schieffelin, K. A. Woolard, and P. V. Kroskrity (eds.), *Language Ideologies: Practice and Theory*. 87–102. New York: Oxford University Press.

Lamarre, P. and Paredes, J. R. (2003) Growing up trilingual in Montreal: Perceptions of college students. In R. Bayley and S. R. Schecter (eds.), *Language Socialization in Bilingual and Multilingual Societies*. 62–80. Clevedon, UK: Multilingual Matters.

Langman, J. (2003) Growing a *bányavirág* (rock crystal) on barren soil: Forming a Hungarian identity in eastern Slovakia through joint (inter)action. In R. Bayley and S. R. Schecter (eds.), *Language Socialization in Bilingual and Multilingual Societies*. 182–99. Clevedon, UK: Multilingual Matters.

Lucy, J. (1997) Linguistic relativity. *Annual Review of Anthropology* 26: 291–312.

Luykx, A. (2003) Weaving languages together: Family language policy and gender socialization in bilingual Aymara households. In R. Bayley and S. R. Schecter (eds.), *Language Socialization in Bilingual and Multilingual Societies*. 25–43. Clevedon, UK: Multilingual Matters.

Makihara, M. (2005) Rapa Nui ways of speaking Spanish: Language shift and socialization on Easter Island. *Language in Society* 34(5): 727–62.

Mertz, E. (1998) Linguistic ideology and praxis in US law school classrooms. In B. B. Schieffelin, K. A. Woolard, and P. V. Kroskrity (eds.), *Language Ideologies: Practice and Theory*. 149–62. New York: Oxford University Press.

Miller, P. J. (1982) *Amy, Wendy and Beth: Language Learning in South Baltimore*. Austin, TX: University of Texas Press.

Miller, P. J., Cho, G. E., and Bracey, J. R. (2005) Working-class children's experience through the prism of personal storytelling. *Human Development* 48(3): 115–35.

Moore, L. C. (2006) Learning by heart in Qur'anic and public schools in northern Cameroon. *Social Analysis* 50(3): 109–26.

Ochs, E. (1988) *Culture and Language Development: Language Acquisition and Language Socialization in a Samoan Village*. New York: Cambridge University Press.

Ochs, E. (1991) Misunderstanding children. In N. Coupland, H. Giles, and J. M. Wiemann (eds.), *'Miscommunication' and Problematic Talk*. 44–60. Newbury Park, CA: Sage.

Ochs, E. and Schieffelin, B. B. (1984) Language acquisition and socialization: Three developmental stories and their implications. In *Culture Theory: Essays on Mind, Self, and Emotion*. R. A. Shweder and R. A. LeVine (eds.), 276–320. New York: Cambridge University Press.

Ochs, E. and Taylor, C. (1995) The 'father knows best' dynamic in dinnertime narratives. In K. Hall and M. Bucholtz (eds.), *Gender Articulated: Language and the Socially Constructed Self*. 97–120. New York: Routledge.

Patrick, D. (2003) Language socialization and second language acquisition in a multilingual Arctic Quebec community. In R. Bayley and S. R. Schecter (eds.), *Language Socialization in Bilingual and Multilingual Societies*. 165–81. Clevedon, UK: Multilingual Matters.

Paugh, A. (2005) Multilingual play: Children's code-switching, role play and agency in Dominica, West Indies. *Language in Society* 34(1): 63–86.

Pease-Alvarez, L. (2003) Transforming perspectives on bilingual language socialization. In R. Bayley and S. R. Schecter (eds.), *Language Socialization in Bilingual and Multilingual Societies*. 9–24. Clevedon, UK: Multilingual Matters.

Platt, M. (1986) Social norms and lexical acquisition: A study of deictic verbs in Samoan child language. In B. B. Schieffelin and E. Ochs (eds.), *Language Socialization Across Cultures*. 127–52. Cambridge: Cambridge University Press.

Pon, G., Goldstein, T., and Schecter, S. R. (2003) Interrupted by silences: The contemporary education of Hong Kong-born Chinese Canadians. In R. Bayley and S. R. Schecter (eds.), *Language Socialization in Bilingual and Multilingual Societies*. 114–27. Clevedon, UK: Multilingual Matters.

Poveda, D., Cano, A., and Palomares-Valera, M. (2005) Religious genres, entextualization and literacy in Gitano children. *Language in Society* 34: 87–115.

Rampton, B. (1995) *Crossing: Language and Ethnicity among Adolescents*. London: Longman.

Reynolds, J. F. (2008) Socializing *puros pericos* (little parrots): The negotiation of respect and responsibility in Antonero Mayan sibling and peer networks. *Journal of Linguistic Anthropology* 18(1): 82–107.

Riley, K. C. (2004) 'Encadrer' and 'se débrouiller': Socializing dialogic identity in a well-to-do suburb of Paris. Paper presented at the Language and Identity Summer School. Graduate School in Language and Communication, University of Southern Denmark, Odense.

Riley, K. C. (2007) To tangle or not to tangle: Shifting language ideologies and the socialization of *Charabia* in the Marquesas, French Polynesia. In M. Makihara and B. B. Schieffelin (eds.), *Consequences of Contact: Language Ideologies and Sociocultural Transformations in Pacific Societies*. 70–95. New York: Oxford University Press.

Riley, K. C. (2008) Language ideology and heteroglossic footing in a multilingual metropolis. Paper presented at the Annual Meeting of the Canadian Anthropological Society/Société Canadienne d'Anthropologie. Ottawa, Ontario.

Riley, K. C. (2009) Who made the soup? Socializing the researcher and shaping her data. *Language & Communication* 29(3): 254–70.

Riley, K. C. (forthcoming) L'idéologie hétéroglossique et l'identité dialogique à Montréal. In C. Trimaille and J. M. Eloy (eds.), *Idéologies Linguistiques et Discriminations, Actes du Colloque du Réseau Francophone de Sociolinguistique, Rennes, June 2009, Carnets d'Atelier de Sociolinguistique*. Paris: Harmattan.

Riley, K. C., Peters, J., and Couture, O. (2008) 'J'ai un mot à dire…' Metapragmatic cues and the projection of identity by Congolese immigrants in Montreal. Paper presented at the Annual Meeting of the American Association for Applied Linguistics. Washington, DC.

Rindstedt, C. and Aronsson, K. (2002) Growing up monolingual in a bilingual community. The Quichua revitalization paradox. *Language in Society* 31: 721–42.

Roy, S. (2003) Bilingualism and standardization in a Canadian call center: Challenges for a linguistic minority community. In R. Bayley and S. R. Schecter (eds.), *Language Socialization in Bilingual and Multilingual Societies*. 269–85. Clevedon, UK: Multilingual Matters.

Schieffelin, B. B. (1990) *The Give and Take of Everyday Life: Language Socialization of Kaluli Children*. Cambridge: Cambridge University Press.

Schieffelin, B. B. (1994) Code-switching and language socialization. In J. Duchan, L. Hewitt, and R. Sonnenmeier (eds.), *Pragmatics: From Theory to Practice*. 20–42. New York: Prentice Hall.

Schieffelin, B. B. and Ochs, E. (eds.) (1986) *Language Socialization Across Cultures*. Cambridge: Cambridge University Press.

Senghas, R. J., Senghas, A., and Pyers, J. E. (2005) The emergence of Nicaraguan sign language: Questions of development, acquisition, and evolution. In J. Langer, S. T. Parker, and C. Milbraith (eds.), *Biology and Knowledge Revisited: From Neurogenesis to Psychogenesis*. 287–306. Mahwah, NJ: Lawrence Erlbaum.

Silverstein, M. (1979) Language structure and linguistic ideology. In P. R. Clyne, W. F. Hanks, and C. L. Hofbauer (eds.), *The Elements: A Parasession on Linguistic Units and Levels*. 183–247. Chicago, IL: Chicago Linguistic Society.

Watson-Gegeo, K. and Gegeo, D. W. (1990) Shaping the mind and straightening out conflicts. In K. A. Watson-Gegeo and G. M. White (eds.), *Disentangling: Conflict Discourse in Pacific Societies*. 161–213. Stanford, CA: Stanford University Press.

Watson-Gegeo, K. and Gegeo, D. W. (1992) Schooling, knowledge, and power: Social transformation in the Solomon Islands. *Anthropology and Education Quarterly* 23(1): 10–29.

Williams, R. S. and Riley, K. C. (2001) Acquiring a slice of Anglo-American pie: A portrait of language shift in a Franco-American family. In R. D. González and I. Melis (eds.), *Language Ideologies: Critical Perspectives on the Official English Movement, Vol. 2: History, Theory, and Policy*. 63–90. Mahwah, NJ: Lawrence Erlbaum.

Woolard, K. A. (1998) Introduction: Language ideology as a field of inquiry. In B. B. Schieffelin, K. A. Woolard, and P. V. Kroskrity (eds.), *Language Ideologies: Practice and Theory*. 3–47. New York: Oxford University Press.

Wortham, S. E. F. (2005) Socialization beyond the speech event. *Journal of Linguistic Anthropology* 15(1): 95–112.

Zentella, A. C. (1997) *Growing Up Bilingual: Puerto Rican Children in New York*. Oxford: Blackwell.

22 Language Socialization and Language Shift

PAUL B. GARRETT

In a case of language shift, a community of speakers effectively abandons, not necessarily consciously or intentionally, its use of one language in favor of another. The language that speakers cease to use (in at least some domains) is typically one that has served since time immemorial as their community's vernacular and language of ethnic identity. Ultimately it may be lost altogether if it ceases to be acquired and used in everyday contexts by members of succeeding generations. Meanwhile, the language toward which the community is shifting is in most cases a language of wider communication or one that otherwise offers (or, at least, is perceived to offer) some significant advantage to those who speak it. Depending on the circumstances, that advantage may be sheer survival, socioeconomic advancement, politico-economic gain, social prestige, or some combination of these.

Language shift presupposes a situation of language contact (Garrett 2004; Thomason 2001), which may arise through a wide variety of circumstances, ranging from the hostile invasion of one group's territory by another to large-scale out-migration and formation of a diaspora. As this suggests, language shift often occurs under conditions of stark inequality, as tend to prevail in colonial and postcolonial settings as well as in those engendered by more recently emerging kinds of 'globalization' processes (Errington 2007; Pratt 1987). The study of language shift, whether from a language socialization perspective or any other, therefore requires careful attention to the workings of power both in and through language. As scholarship on political economy of language and ideologies of language has amply demonstrated, language is both a site and a resource for the constitution, reproduction, and contestation of power relations (Bauman and Briggs 2003; Gal and Woolard 2001; Kroskrity 2000; Schieffelin, Woolard, and Kroskrity 1998; Silverstein 1998; see also Riley, this volume). These intermeshing

The Handbook of Language Socialization, First Edition. Edited by Alessandro Duranti, Elinor Ochs, and Bambi B. Schieffelin.
© 2014 John Wiley & Sons, Ltd. Published 2014 by John Wiley & Sons, Ltd.

bodies of research have revealed the pervasiveness and subtlety of such processes, demonstrating that they influence even the most intimate of face-to-face interactions – including those between caregiver and child, the canonical focus of language socialization research (Schieffelin and Ochs 1986a, 1986b).

Building on these foundations, various language socialization researchers have conducted studies in communities where language shift is underway (e.g. Fader 2007; Field 2001; Garrett 2005; Kulick 1992; Makihara 2005; Meek 2007; Paugh 2005). As these studies make clear, the coexistence of two or more codes within a given community is rarely a neutral, uncontested state of affairs; it tends to be a focus of metapragmatic, discursive, and ideological elaboration and, in many cases, an enduring source of social tensions (Heller 2007). As they are socialized to use language, children and other novices are socialized into understandings of these matters and of locally preferred and dispreferred ways of dealing with them, such as restricting use of a particular language to particular domains and genres, maintaining language boundaries and standards of language 'purity,' and cultivating proficiency in a particular language as a means of coping with entrenched social hierarchies. These are precisely the kinds of practices that tend to give rise to language shift – usually without the intent, often without even the awareness, of those who engage in them.

This chapter considers some of the ways in which the distinctive configuration of methods, analytical approaches, and theoretical perspectives that constitute the language socialization research paradigm can contribute to understandings of language shift, as well as related phenomena such as language endangerment, preservation, and revitalization (Fishman 1991; Hinton and Hale 2001; Mufwene 2003; Mühlhäusler 2003; Nettle and Romaine 2000; Schmidt 1990; see also Friedman, this volume; Nonaka, this volume). This is accomplished in part through a consideration of child language socialization practices in the Caribbean island of St. Lucia, where an Afro-French creole language known as Kwéyòl is in contact with English and where language shift from the former to the latter is currently underway. The approach taken here emphasizes that bilingualism, language shift, and other contact-related phenomena, in all their social, cultural, and historical diversity, are ultimately rooted in contingent relationships of hierarchy and inequality, dominance and subordination. These contingent relationships, in turn, are ideologically mediated in ways that may not be readily discernible but are enormously consequential insofar as they guide individuals' understandings of the social world and their actions in it, including, crucially, their everyday use of language.

Codes in Contact

Working in situations where language shift is (or may be) underway has motivated language socialization researchers to re-examine certain broadly shared working concepts and theoretical premises. The need to account for hybrid, syncretic, and heteroglossic forms of communicative practice, for example, has led researchers to problematize implicit assumptions about the discreteness and boundedness of language systems (Fader 2007; Garrett 2007b, Makihara 2005; Riley 2007); these insights have been inspired in part by investigations of simultaneity and bivalency phenomena (Woolard 1998), which suggest that a given form need not be confined to a single code, discourse, or other semiotic system. On the other hand, and just as important, language socialization studies have also brought attention to the fact that, in settings characterized by sustained contact between two or more normatively differentiated codes, some of the most salient and prevalent language socialization practices may be oriented toward fostering children's awareness of the specific ways in which, and the extent to which, their community's linguistic resources are organized into distinct, separable, regimented systems (Garrett 2007b, Schieffelin 1994). In St. Lucia, for example, children are encouraged from an early age to distinguish sharply between two named codes, 'Patwa' and 'English,' and to observe fairly strict norms of age-appropriate language use. Notions of age-appropriateness prove to be somewhat fluid, however, and in practice they are subtly calibrated, affording gradually increasing opportunities for children to experiment with both of the codes and with the porous boundary between them (Garrett 2005, 2007b).

Language contact and its attendant processes, ranging from 'stable' bilingualism to language 'death,' are inherently dynamic, emergent phenomena, presenting researchers with moving targets that demand correspondingly flexible theoretical and methodological approaches. This is true both at the individual level and at the group level. Any 'bilingual' individual's proficiency in one or the other language is better conceptualized as a process than as a state, in that it is constantly strengthening or weakening, increasing or diminishing, depending upon such factors as the degree to which the language is deemed acceptable or preferable for use in particular kinds of interactions and the degree to which the individual conforms his or her usage to such expectations and preferences. Similarly, at the level of the social group, the relative stability of bilingualism in a particular community is contingent on demographic and macro-economic factors as well as less obvious ones such as ideological shifts (Meek 2007; Riley 2007, this volume). Language socialization research that links micro and macro levels of analysis by examining individual developmental trajectories in the context of broader societal trends and sociohistorical trajectories provides a means of exploring the relationship between linguistic form and communicative practice.

As noted previously, any episode of language contact occurs in what Pratt (1992: 6–7) conceptualizes as 'the contact zone': a kind of 'social space' in which human groups previously separated by geography and/or history 'come into contact with each other and establish ongoing relations, usually involving conditions of coercion, radical inequality, and intractable conflict.' Pratt notes explicitly that she borrows her notion of contact from linguistics (particularly pidgin and creole linguistics) but that it is intended 'to foreground the interactive, improvisational dimensions' of such encounters and to 'emphasiz[e] how subjects are constituted in and by their relations to each other.' The kinds of issues indicated by Pratt are central concerns for contemporary linguistic anthropological approaches to language shift and other contact-related phenomena. In any study of such phenomena that has an explicit sociohistorical or longitudinal dimension, as does any language socialization study, the consequences of language contact cannot be taken as stable states or properties of either communities or individuals. Rather, they must be regarded as ongoing processes that take quite different forms and trajectories in different sociocultural and sociohistorical settings, and may be only a relatively fleeting phase in the history of a community or in the life of an individual speaker.

Heller (2006) outlines a practice-based perspective on bilingualism (broadly conceived) that can be applied just as usefully to language shift and virtually any other language contact phenomenon. Key areas of inquiry include questions of 'who is doing what, and with what resources. This entails looking at language as a set of resources which are socially distributed, but not necessarily evenly, and so speakers have to act within certain kinds of structural constraints' (2006: 166). Of particular importance for the study of language shift are questions such as these, also raised by Heller: 'How do speakers draw on their linguistic resources in the situations they find themselves in, to accomplish what, or with what perverse or unintended consequences?' (2006: 166).

Linking Ideology and Practice

How can the study of language socialization practices contribute to these and related lines of inquiry? Researchers who have investigated language shift from the perspective of language socialization research have found it crucial, on both methodological and theoretical grounds, to examine local ideologies of language in order to elucidate the workings of power in and through language. At the most general level, notions of what language itself is, and of its relationship to locally relevant categories of identity, vary considerably across communities as well as within any given community. Local notions of what 'counts' as a language, of who counts as a speaker, and of what can (and cannot) be done with, and done to, particular languages also vary considerably, as do the specific properties and meanings associated with and indexed by different languages and differentially evaluated varieties thereof (e.g. standard and nonstandard). As Heller puts it, '[I]t is always someone's notion of what counts, and someone's ability to control access both to resources and to the definition of their value, which ultimately make a difference to people's lives' (2006: 166). Various kinds of normative and prescriptive imperatives, for example, though their points of origin may be remote in both time and space (e.g. in a former colonial metropole), are enacted, interpreted, and reinterpreted, syncretically or otherwise, at local levels and in local contexts.

Not surprisingly, certain resultant practices, such as prohibition or stigmatization of local languages or language varieties, tend to give rise to language shift, as in many postcolonial settings (Garrett 2005; Makihara 2005; Paugh 2005). But language is also used in ideologically informed ways to constitute locally salient social categories and to delineate and negotiate the boundaries thereof. Some recent language socialization studies describe various communities' more or less self-conscious efforts to achieve language maintenance or revitalization (Garrett 2007a; Makihara 2005; Meek 2007). In these cases the link between language and culture tends to be explicitly foregrounded; those involved in these efforts see themselves as preserving community and 'tradition,' or 'heritage,' as well as language. Despite such cultivated awareness of the relationship between language, culture, and everyday communicative practice, these efforts too can lead to unforeseen and undesirable outcomes; processes of preservation, valorization, standardization, and revitalization all tend to be deeply transformative of both language and social relations.

Local ideologies of language inform, organize, and in some ways constrain people's everyday communicative practices, which in turn engender specific linguistic and sociocultural outcomes that may go partially or wholly unrecognized (or misrecognized) by those whose actions and practices are bringing them about. In many cases of language shift, adults assume that their community's 'traditional' language will continue to be reproduced across the generations, just as it 'always has,' even as they are socializing their own children in such a way that the children are acquiring, at best, only partial command of the language (Garrett 2005; Meek 2007). In these and other regards, ideologies of language intersect with local notions of cultural and group identity, nationhood, personhood, childhood, and language acquisition as a developmental process.

Transforming Subjectivities

Language socialization practices may be, in some cases, one of the most important mechanisms of language shift – a point made vividly by Kulick's (1992) pioneering study of rapid shift in the small Papua New Guinean village of Gapun. Kulick's study set an important precedent for all subsequent work on language shift by demonstrating that language socialization practices, always a prime site of linguistic and sociocultural reproduction, may also be the source of far-reaching changes: in the case that Kulick examines, a community-wide shift from multilingualism to monolingualism. Particularly relevant to the present discussion is Kulick's analysis of how two languages spoken in this community, Taiap and Tok Pisin, have come to be mapped onto the villagers' dualistic notion of the self. Taiap, the traditional local vernacular, is steeped in associations with the backward, pagan ways of the ancestors, and with *hed*, the willful, selfish, backward, antisocial side of the self. Meanwhile Tok Pisin, a fairly recently introduced language of wider communication, is strongly associated with Christianity, literacy, consumer goods, and the world beyond Gapun; and it is thought to express *save*, the enlightened, sociable, cooperative, forward-looking side of the self.

In Gapuners' syncretic cosmology, which serves as the interpretive framework for what they perceive to be their current situation, dramatic, instantaneous transformations of persons and things are possible and indeed are to be expected, provided that conditions conducive to such transformations are in place. Therein lies their dilemma: at present, an overabundance of unsuppressed *hed* in the village, and a regrettable shortage of *save*, are causing Gapun to remain mired in the old, backward ways. This renders the villagers collectively unable to *kamap* – that is, to develop – and to join the rest of the developed world in enjoying a comfortable, modern way of life, filled with technological marvels and endlessly abundant consumer goods. (Significantly, the terms *hed*, *save*, and *kamap* all come from Tok Pisin, not Taiap.) The way out of this dilemma, they believe, is to suppress outward manifestations of *hed* while cultivating and prominently displaying *save*. 'In using Tok Pisin,' Kulick explains, 'villagers are thus expressing an important and highly valued aspect of self [...] But in doing this, they are also constituting a situation in which their vernacular is becoming less and less desirable and important' – a situation in which Taiap is literally 'losing its ability to express positive aspects of self' (1992: 21). The ultimate effect of this, Kulick convincingly demonstrates, is that Gapun children, due to subtle but profoundly consequential changes in language socialization practices, no longer receive sufficient exposure to Taiap to become proficient speakers of the language: '[T]here is no demand on children to speak Taiap, nor is there any reward for speaking it' (1992: 222).

Kulick stresses that Gapuners have not abandoned their traditional dualistic concept of the self. But the introduction of Tok Pisin and, crucially, of powerful exogenous cultural forms of which it is the primary medium, particularly Christianity, has resulted in a significant reworking of the Gapuners' traditional dualistic concept of the self and, in effect, a reworking of the relationship between language and subjectivity. Kulick notes that, prior to the introduction of Tok Pisin, multilingualism was highly valued in Gapun; being able to speak the vernaculars of other groups in the region (with whom there was intermittent contact) was 'the traditional cultural ideal' (1992: 69). To be a Gapuner was to be bi- or multilingual. But this was an era in which the multiple languages in question coexisted in a more or less egalitarian, nonhierarchical relationship; no particular language was regarded as being intrinsically superior to the rest, and no group sought to impose its language on other groups. This changed drastically with the introduction of Tok Pisin, a language spoken by powerful outsiders (such as plantation labor recruiters and missionaries) whose clear intent was to impose both their will and their ways on others and, in effect, to transform them into wholly new kinds of subjects, such as indentured laborers or Christians. This could not be effected through physical coercion alone; to a great extent, it was also a matter of symbolic domination, in which language always has a central role (Bourdieu 1991).

The introduction into Gapun of Tok Pisin, Christianity, wage labor, schooling, consumer goods, and related exogenous cultural forms and systems resulted in the emergence of new kinds of subjects and, hence, new kinds of subjectivities: new ways of experiencing and understanding the known world and one's place within it. This entailed, among other things, new ways of being bilingual and of experiencing bilingualism; that is, new forms of bilingual subjectivity. Gapuners' newfound conviction that suppressing *hed* would enable them to *kamap* – a collective aim that would scarcely have been conceivable prior to the introduction of Tok Pisin and the exogenous cultural forms with which it was associated – gave them a new goal to strive for, as it were, in their lives as individuals as well as in their relationships with their children and in their collective life as a community. And strive for it they did. The pursuit of this goal entailed a whole new way of being: a new experience of everyday social life in Gapun and a new sense of their place in the world, both as individuals and as a group. To suppress *hed* was to suppress Taiap – which in effect was to suppress one's own bilingualism, one's own bilingual self – all in the interest of radically changing Gapun's place in a heretofore unknown, indeed unimaginable, social and cosmological order.

Building on Kulick's work – which shows, among other things, that local cultural and ideological factors may be of considerably greater importance in accounting for language shift than the macro-sociological (e.g. political and economic) factors that are more commonly invoked – more recent studies have shown language shift to be a contingent, non-linear phenomenon in which language socialization practices play a crucial but often subtle mediating role. Paugh (2005, this volume) shows that young children in the Caribbean island of Dominica are encouraged by their parents and other adults to acquire English, which is contributing to language shift away from the local Afro-French creole. But in later years, as children spend increasing amounts of time interacting with peers beyond the supervision (and earshot) of adults, they increasingly use the creole in their play as a way of enacting adult roles and activities. Although ultimately it may not prevent language shift from running its course, at present such pretend play seems to provide older children with opportunities to develop some degree of proficiency in the creole. In an investigation of a quite similar situation in the Caribbean island of St. Lucia, Garrett (2005) examines 'code-specific genres' as the basis for socialization activities in which adults encourage young children to be verbally self-assertive. Cursing, insulting, and other locally valued self-assertive ways of speaking conventionally require use of the historically stigmatized Afro-French creole language that many St. Lucian caregivers (much like their counterparts in Dominica) otherwise discourage children from using. The persistence of socialization routines in which adults playfully urge children to use the creole in self-assertive ways favors the maintenance of such code-specific genres, which in turn may be having a retarding or dampening effect on language shift.

These and other recent studies suggest that a language socialization approach can yield a more nuanced account of ongoing changes and shifts in local communicative practice than can larger-scale, quantitatively oriented studies that are less attentive to situated interactions (particularly those occurring at the critical juncture between generations). In cases where language shift is already quite far along, for example, a language socialization approach may reveal that culturally specific ways of using language persist in speakers' use of the 'new' code. In her study of a Navajo community, Field (2001) demonstrates that, although today's bilingual caregivers often speak English to children, they continue to socialize traditional Navajo values of autonomy, self-determinacy, and respect through the use of a triadic participant structure in issuing directives. Based on this observation, Field (2001: 249–50) proposes that 'certain aspects of language use may be more conservative, or more resistant to change, than code.' She goes on to assert,

'[I]t is exactly those aspects of a speech community's interaction that are tacitly taken for granted that are also the most basic, pervasive, and resistant to change. Furthermore, they are maintained through the most mundane routines and forms of everyday communicative practice – which also happen to be the preferred context for research on language socialization.'

In settings characterized by sustained contact between two or more normatively differentiated codes, some language socialization practices may be oriented toward fostering children's awareness of the specific ways in which, and the extent to which, their community's communicative resources are organized into discrete, more or less regimented systems. Such language socialization practices in turn have discernible consequences for children's developing linguistic and communicative competence and, ultimately, for processes of sociocultural and linguistic reproduction. In the Caribbean island of St. Lucia, where an Afro-French creole language known as Kwéyòl is spoken along with (local vernacular varieties of) English, children are encouraged from an early age to distinguish sharply between these two codes and, in so doing, to abide by fairly strict norms of age-appropriate communicative practice that privilege displays of English proficiency. Yet children find ample opportunity to experiment with the two normatively differentiated codes as well as with the boundary between them, which, in practice, is often rather indistinct. Close examination of everyday interactions involving children of various ages yields insight into the ways in which socialization to use (or not to use) particular communicative resources contributes to the emergence of age-inflected subjectivities and competencies, as well as to ongoing processes of language shift.

In the following sections, I consider how language socialization practices contribute to the differentiation and regimentation of codes as well as how these practices are informed by broader historical, political, and ideological processes. In doing so, I suggest some of the ways in which language socialization research, with its characteristic close attention to face-to-face interactions and micro-level developmental processes, can enhance our understanding of codes as fuzzy sets of communicative resources, comprising forms and formations that circulate unevenly through social networks, discursive spaces, and temporal orders; and as resources the meanings and values of which are socially constructed and ideologically refracted within the constraints of particular modes of regimentation under specific (and hence specifiable) historical and politico-economic conditions. In this view, language or, more broadly, communicative practice, constitutes a terrain of social difference and, perhaps inevitably, a foundation for hierarchical social formations. Such a perspective calls for close attention to questions of who is doing what, with what resources, toward what ends, and with what consequences, intended or not. If the uneven distribution and circulation of communicative resources, both within and across communities, is understood not as random but as the product of specific, historically situated configurations of political-economic and ideological processes, then certain productive kinds of questions about the relationships among power dynamics, sociocultural formations, ideological processes, and everyday patterns of communicative practice come to the fore.

Language Shift in St. Lucia

Many language socialization studies of the second generation – that is, those of the past twenty years or so – have been centrally concerned with ideologies of language and the political economy of language; and, not surprisingly, much of the impetus for these developments has come from research conducted in language contact settings (Garrett and Baquedano-López 2002). In my own work in the Caribbean island of St. Lucia, I examine a situation in which members of the first local generation of bilinguals – young adults at the time of my fieldwork, many of them parents of young children – were socializing those children in ways that yielded a wide range of outcomes, from near-monolingualism to varying degrees of bilingualism. One of the two languages involved is an Afro-French creole language known as Patwa or Kwéyòl, a legacy of the island's French colonial period (1651–1814). The other language is St. Lucia's present-day official language, English, which became established as such during a subsequent British colonial period (1814–1979). In 1979, St. Lucia became an independent nation state and member of the Commonwealth, retaining English as its sole official language. Processes of language shift from Kwéyòl to English have been underway for several decades; consequently, increasing numbers of St. Lucia's youth speak little, if any, Kwéyòl. The English spoken by most St. Lucians, however, is actually a markedly nonstandard, heavily-Kwéyòl-influenced variety that I have described as Vernacular English of St. Lucia, or VESL (Garrett 2003).

St. Lucia is one of the Windward Islands of the Lesser Antilles, located in the eastern Caribbean. The island is about 27 miles (43 kilometers) long and 14 miles (23 kilometers) wide at its widest point, for a total land area of 238 square miles (616 square kilometers), about the same size as the city of Chicago. The terrain is mountainous, with dramatically steep peaks of volcanic origin. Due in part to this rugged landscape, St. Lucia is still largely 'undeveloped,' and the interior is thickly cloaked by one the Caribbean's last remaining rainforests. The great majority (96 percent) of St. Lucia's population of approximately 160,000 is of primarily African ancestry. Like many other Caribbean islands, St. Lucia produced sugar during the colonial era. The economy today is still heavily agricultural and still heavily dependent on a single crop, but since the early 1960s sugar cane has been replaced by bananas. Until fairly recently, St. Lucia lagged behind many of its Caribbean neighbors in integrating itself into the international tourism industry; but, in the past two to three decades, the government has taken major steps toward diversifying the economy, which has become increasingly services-oriented.

As might be expected, these developments seem to be accelerating the shift from Kwéyòl to English. At present, the majority of the population can be described as bilingual to one degree or another. As in many other societies where language shift is underway, at the present historical moment, St. Lucian 'bilingualism' actually encompasses a broad span of variation. In the small rural community where I conducted my fieldwork, Morne Carré, many of the oldest residents are still monolingual speakers of Kwéyòl. Most persons middle-aged and younger are bilingual, to varying degrees, in Kwéyòl and English, and some children are now growing up as virtually monolingual speakers of English (actually VESL, as previously noted), with only quite limited knowledge of Kwéyòl. These generational differences can be attributed in part to steadily increasing access to formal education. Many members of the eldest generation never attended school at all. But their children were able to do so, particularly after a primary school was established in Morne Carré in the mid-1970s; and for today's children, here and throughout St. Lucia, access to primary education is universal. Consequently, many children, much like their parents, are to varying degrees bilingual, their proficiency in Kwéyòl and English broadly reflecting the extent to which each language is (or is not) used with them by their primary caregivers and other members of their households. But this varies considerably: in some households, caregivers are diligent about speaking only English with children, while in others – especially in multigenerational household compounds where grandparents or other elderly relatives reside – Kwéyòl may be used almost exclusively.

Most Morne Carré households, however, fall somewhere between these two extremes, with adults speaking mostly Kwéyòl among themselves but showing a strong preference for the use of English with children. The preference for the use of English *by* children is even stronger. Most St. Lucian adults subscribe to a locally adapted notion of subtractive bilingualism: it is widely and quite firmly believed that Kwéyòl has a profoundly detrimental effect on children's acquisition of English. Because of Kwéyòl's supposedly noxious tendency to corrupt and contaminate children's developing English, adults insist that children must master English before they are allowed to begin speaking Kwéyòl. While English must be explicitly taught to children, Kwéyòl need not be taught at all – it will come naturally, adults say, and they assume that children will eventually begin speaking Kwéyòl of their own volition. But a close examination of everyday interactions between adults and children reveals that this can no longer be taken for granted.

What Comes Naturally: Chantal

Infants in Morne Carré are born into a richly verbal environment in which, from the earliest days of their lives, they are immersed in varied social gatherings involving persons of all ages: parents, siblings, grandparents, great-grandparents, aunts, uncles, cousins, godparents, and neighbors. On the whole, preverbal infants are more often spoken about than spoken to; although their caregivers and other adults do not often treat them as conversational partners in any sustained way, they do not hesitate to attribute emotional states, affective stances, and intentions to them, and to act toward them in accordance with those attributions. Often this is done in an affectionate, humorous spirit, sparking conversation among the adults present rather than between adult and infant.

An infant who fusses and struggles, or merely vocalizes or attempts to move about a little more vigorously than expected, is likely to be accused of behaving in ways that are not age-appropriate – that is, of being too willful and assertive for one so small and dependent. Almost invariably, an infant who exhibits such behavior is accused of being *twop nonm* or *twop fanm* in Kwéyòl, meaning 'too mannish' or 'too womanish,' as it is said in VESL. Such accusations may also be leveled at an infant who will not cooperate with an adult's efforts to make her smile or to make eye contact; in such cases, the infant may also be asked rhetorically whether she is *faché épi* or *veks wif* ('angry at') the adult, or at some other person toward whom her attention is being directed.

In Example 22.1, a small group of young-to-early-middle-aged adults interact with (or rather, around) the infant Chantal. Chantal is only three months old; her mother, Carlene, has been alternately cradling her in her arm and holding her on her lap while the adults have been conversing animatedly in Kwéyòl. As this excerpt begins, Carlene's friend Lucille has just leaned over and said something softly and briefly to the baby, who, as everyone knows, is too young to respond in any meaningful way, verbally or otherwise. Holding Chantal on her lap to face Lucille and the other adults, Carlene responds 'for' the infant by engaging in a bit of quasi-ventriloquism. Speaking in a petulant, infantile voice, and speaking in Kwéyòl, she attributes to the infant an antisocial sentiment and an uncooperative, disagreeable stance toward her interlocutor, Lucille.

Example 22.1:   Chantal[1]

1 Carlene → Lucille:	*M'a kay wéponn ou bonmaten-a*
	'I'm not going to answer you this morning'
	((speaking for Chantal))
2 Lucille:	*Paul, mi an ti bétjé blan*
	'Paul, here's a little white *bétjé*' (('white person'; an
	allusion to the baby's fair complexion))
3 Vernice → Chantal:	*Ay palé bay Paul*
	'Go talk to Paul'
4 Harry → Chantal:	*Chantal, waat yuu see? Yuu airii?*
	'Chantal, what [do] you say? You Irie?'
5 Carlene:	*Sa-a fanm!*
	'That one's womanish!'
6 Vernice:	*I manhé fig mi, i bwè glo,*
	'She ate ripe banana, she drank water,'
	i bwè hool yon bibon ankò . . .
	'she drank a whole other bottle...'
7 Carlene → Chantal:	*Vòwas!*
	'Greedy!'
8 Harry:	*Bonmaten-a i té vlé vin' anlè mwen pou mòdé*
	mwen
	'This morning she wanted to get on me and bite
	me'

9 Vernice:	*Lè i fini pou i ay maap èk lanng li ankò.*
	'And still she has to go and mop with her tongue some more' ((the baby's tongue is hanging out of her mouth))
10 Harry → adults:	*Mwen ha di'y si i mòdé mwen,*
	'I've told her that if she bites me,'
	mwen kay mòdé'y viyé ah, i sav sa.
	'I'm going to bite her back, eh, she knows that.'
	Mwen ha pa hayi mòdé pyès.
	'I don't hate biting at all' ((i.e. if she were to bite me, I'd bite her right back))

Speaking in the first person and attributing her words to the baby, Carlene asserts that she is 'not going to answer' Lucille (who has just spoken to Chantal, probably in a bid simply to attract the baby's attention and gaze). Refusal to respond to any form of verbal interpellation, particularly the calling-out of one's name, which is the most common form of casual greeting, is regarded by St. Lucians as a fairly grave offense, whether the offending party is an adult or a child who is old enough to know better – and any child who is old enough to respond, however minimally, is considered old enough to know better. The fact that Chantal is not yet old enough, and cannot really be held accountable for the ventriloquated response that Carlene attributes to her, is of course obvious to all present.

Rather than countering this ventriloquated utterance, Lucille makes a joking comment about the baby's fair complexion, ostensibly directing it toward me, but clearly intending it to be appreciated by everyone present (line 2). Lucille's joke is then taken up by Vernice (line 3), who suggests that Chantal 'go and talk to' the only other *bétjé* ('white person') in the group. Harry now joins in, maintaining the facetious notion that Chantal can speak, and is far more mature than she actually is, in additional ways: by speaking VESL to her, by acting as though the infant might have said something that he missed, and by asking her, *Yuu airii?* (line 4). Harry's choice of code here can be regarded as a further elaboration of the facetious notion already in play: that Chantal is old enough to interact verbally with the adults. By speaking VESL to her, as he would to an older child, Harry takes the joke a step further; and by asking her *Yuu airii?*, he takes it a bit further still. The word *airii* is strongly associated with the distinctive speechways of Rastafarians (Pollard 2000); commonly used in greeting, as it is here, it refers to a state of well-being and mutual good will. Asking someone *Yuu airii?* (or simply *Airii?*) is a typical Rastafarian greeting that is sometimes used by non-Rastafarians as well, particularly male adolescents and young adults (who use it mostly with their peers). In any case, it indexes an identity that in terms of age and other factors is clearly neither appropriate for, nor available to, this female infant.

Carlene's response to all of this (line 5) is to exclaim that Chantal is *fanm* ('womanish'). In most contexts the word *fanm* functions as the noun 'woman,' but it is also used adjectivally, as it is here, often preceded by the intensifier *twop* ('too/

too much'). Carlene's use of the rather depersonalizing pronominal form *sa-a* ('that one') in conjunction with this characterization is fairly typical; it is often used as a means of characterizing and indirectly rebuking a child who is guilty of some form of age-inappropriate behavior – especially verbal assertiveness toward an adult, such as 'talking back' when scolded. When applied to preverbal infants such as Chantal, it generally refers to some nonverbal form of willful behavior. (It is somewhat unclear here whether Carlene means it jocularly in the former sense or somewhat more seriously in the latter sense.)

Vernice takes up yet another theme by recounting the food and drink that Chantal had consumed earlier in the day, thereby suggesting (line 6) that Chantal is *vòwas* ('greedy'); it is Carlene who first says so explicitly, however (line 7). Greediness is another highly undesirable trait that older children are frequently accused of, by their peers as well as by adults. Anyone, child or adult, who is perceived as taking more than his or her share, or who has something (typically food) and doesn't offer to share it with everyone present, will invariably be accused, immediately and loudly, of being *vòwas*. Harry, evidently inspired by this talk of Chantal's greediness, now remarks that, earlier in the day, the baby had tried to bite him (line 8); likewise, Vernice's comment about the baby's tongue (line 9) is probably a continuation of the same theme. Harry then asserts, first to the adults (line 10) and then directly to Chantal (line 11), speaking to her this time in Kwéyòl, how he intends to deal with the situation if she should ever try to bite him again: he'll gladly bite her back.

In the course of this brief episode, the adults construct Chantal's social persona (with very little contribution from the preverbal Chantal herself) as assertive, greedy, antisocial, even somewhat aggressive – in short, as not yet socialized, ignorant even of how to behave in ways appropriate to her very young age. Notice that they do so almost entirely in Kwéyòl, attributing Kwéyòl utterances to the infant as well; the only exception is Harry's use of VESL to suggest jocularly that the child is considerably older and more capable than she really is.

This excerpt offers some important insights into local understandings of infants' linguistic proclivities, particularly their supposed affinity for the Kwéyòl language. Adults sometimes use Kwéyòl with preverbal infants, as in the affectionate little utterances that a mother uses to soothe or distract her baby while changing its diaper. For somewhat older but still preverbal infants, there is even a small set of Kwéyòl Baby Talk forms, such as *doudou* ('sweetie'), a term of endearment; *koko* ('genitals,' either male or female); and *sisid* ('sit down'), mostly used as an imperative. Speaking Kwéyòl to an infant is not considered undesirable or inappropriate, as it is with older children (particularly school-age children); the infant is not yet able to imitate what it hears, so addressing it in Kwéyòl is not regarded as potentially harmful. Adults differ somewhat in their opinions about the extent to which preverbal infants understand what is said to them, but there is general agreement that they attend and respond mainly to the affective tone of an utterance, rather than its referential or propositional meaning.

In the above excerpt, Carlene's attribution to Chantal of a Kwéyòl utterance that expresses a disagreeable, antisocial sentiment – natural in origin, in the sense that it is fully to be expected from an infant – is significant in at least two respects. It suggests that, if Chantal *could* express herself verbally at this moment, she would do so in Kwéyòl. It also suggests that the Kwéyòl language itself issues from, or at least is rooted in, the same primordial developmental substrate that gives rise to the presumptive emotional state and affective stance that the language both conveys and indexes. The prevailing belief is that Kwéyòl quite literally comes naturally to young children, much like the developmentally primal sentiments and behaviors that they manifest at this early age.

Having and Showing a Code Preference: Lamar

As infants begin to show signs of understanding language, and of being able to use it themselves, caregivers and other adults begin to engage with them differently, making concerted, more or less consistent efforts to foster their acquisition of English while at the same time constraining their use of Kwéyòl. A toddler whose first intelligible single-word utterances are (or are understood to be) Kwéyòl words is almost always encouraged to produce the English equivalents instead. Caregivers typically respond by modeling the corresponding English word and encouraging the child to repeat it. But, if the youngster is not receptive to such modeling-and-repetition routines, and persists in producing Kwéyòl words, this demonstrated 'preference' may be tolerated and even indulged to some extent during the preschool years. In the early stages of language acquisition, toddlers, much like preverbal infants, are expected to have a natural predisposition toward speaking Kwéyòl and to have greater facility with Kwéyòl than with English.

This could clearly be seen in the case of Lamar. Spending most of his time with only his mother and his infant sister – their tiny home was somewhat more isolated than most others in Morne Carré, both spatially and socially – Lamar was a fairly taciturn child during the early phase of my study. His mother, Violet, rarely spoke to him or encouraged him to vocalize; and, when he did so of his own volition, she rarely treated his vocalizations as meaningful by repeating, expanding, or otherwise responding to them. As Lamar began to produce recognizable words, however, Violet began to engage him in brief verbal exchanges. At first, she used English (or rather, VESL), and encouraged Lamar to do the same. But it soon became apparent that most of the recognizable single-word utterances that he was producing were Kwéyòl words. He especially favored Kwéyòl interjections such as *bondis!* ('god!') and *salop!* (quite similar in meaning to its French reflex, or like *bastard!* in English). Lamar typically produced these words at pragmatically quite appropriate moments, such as when he fell down, dropped something, or knocked something over. His first intelligible English/VESL utterance that occurs in my recordings, when his age was 1;9, was *haat!* ('hot!'). This was a word with which he had become familiar from his mother's frequent warnings that he should not touch her cooking utensils or the stones encircling the cooking fire. But otherwise, most of Lamar's early one-word utterances were Kwéyòl words, as was the first two-word utterance that I recorded, *ga' penng* ('look at [the] comb').

From time to time, Violet expressed genuine consternation at Lamar's apparent 'preference' for Kwéyòl. She was particularly dismayed by his affinity for coarse words, which he sometimes repeated gleefully over and over. But it was really not so surprising that Lamar seemed to 'prefer' Kwéyòl, as Violet used it almost exclusively with other adults as well as to herself in his presence (e.g. muttering *salop!* when she spilled something); while, at the same time, unlike children in larger households, he had relatively little exposure to English/VESL from older siblings, cousins, or anyone else with whom he regularly interacted. Even so, Violet attributed Lamar's apparent 'preference' for Kwéyòl to Lamar himself. This is not at all unusual in Morne Carré; mothers often comment that preschool-age children 'like to speak' Kwéyòl and that it is very difficult to dissuade them. By the time of my third recording, by which time Lamar had begun to produce two-word utterances, Violet had begun to speak to him much more frequently in Kwéyòl than in VESL, having resigned herself to the fact that the child just 'liked to speak' Kwéyòl. This was a source of wry amusement but also of some vexation for her, for she felt that in the preceding months she really had made her best efforts to encourage him to speak English.

Being Put to the Test: Crystal

Even those adults who, unlike Violet, maintain strict English-only policies in their interactions with children fully expect that children will eventually, inevitably, begin speaking Kwéyòl of their own accord. Such an eventuality is not regarded in a negative light. On the contrary, it is fully expected and, if it fails to manifest itself, something is thought to be amiss. At the very least, it is something worthy of comment and perhaps even a modicum of concern, as can be seen in Example 22.2, which involves two young women named Misha and Judy.

Judy is seated on a battered plastic crate, with two large washbasins and a laundry basket positioned in front of her as she launders clothes. Misha, seated on a wooden stool a few feet away, has been chatting with Judy as she supervises the play of her own two children with several others, most of them younger relatives of Judy. Both women are in their mid-twenties. As they have been chatting, they have been code-switching extensively between Kwéyòl and VESL, as is typical for Morne Carré residents of their generation. Judy and Misha are members of the last local generation to have been brought up by monolingual or near-monolingual Kwéyòl-speaking elders. But they are also members of the first generation to have gone to primary school on a regular basis, learning English to some extent in the classroom while becoming proficient speakers of VESL outside the classroom, largely though their interactions with other children, both on and off the school grounds. The two women's conversation is largely in Kwéyòl, but their Kwéyòl is liberally interspersed with VESL words and phrases, and occasionally they switch completely to VESL for a few turns. Misha has been using VESL exclusively, however, whenever she addresses her two children, who are playing nearby with a few others. This is common practice for Misha and most other mothers of young children. Judy has no children of her own, but she follows the same practice in her interactions with the several nieces and nephews to whom she is a sometime caregiver.

As this excerpt begins, Judy, who for the past few moments has been a bit more attentive than usual to the children's play, suggests that Misha's children, unlike the others, do not seem to know Kwéyòl. Misha assures her that the older of the two, five-year-old Crystal, does know Kwéyòl. But Judy has her doubts, and when Crystal approaches, Judy takes it upon herself to find out whether this is true. She does so by translating a simple utterance of Crystal's own into Kwéyòl and then prompting her to repeat it. Crystal's shy hesitation and lack of fluency elicits further commentary from Judy.

Example 22.2:   Crystal[2]

1 Judy → Misha:	*Soo do tuu smaal waanz eh noo Patwaa?*
	'So the two small ones don't know Patwa?'
2 Misha → Judy:	*Crystal aloon dat noo it*
	'Only Crystal knows it'
3 Crystal → Misha:	*Maamii, ai waan tuu goo- wif um- wif um-*
	'Mommy, I want to go- with um- with um-'
4 Judy → Crystal:	*See- See- See 'Mwen vlé alé èk- èk sé manmay-la,'*
	'Say- Say- Say "I want to go with the children,"'
	see dat, let mii he.
	'say that, let me hear.'
	Di 'Mwen vlé alé èk sé manmay-la'
	'Say "I want to go with the children"'
5 Crystal → Judy:	*Patwaa?*
6 Judy → Crystal:	*Di 'Mwen vlé alé èk sé manmay-la.' Di 'Mwen vlé,'*
	'Say "I want to go with the children." Say "I want,"'
7 Misha → Crystal:	*See it en yuu wil goo*
	'Say it and you will [be allowed to] go'
8 Judy → Crystal:	*Mwen vlé alé èk sé manmay-la*
9 Misha → Crystal:	*See 'Mwen vlé alé èk sé ma'ay-la'*
10 Crystal:	Mwen vlé èk- sé ma'ay-la ((attempts to repeat the phrase, garbling it a bit))
11 Judy:	*A:::::h ha ha!! Bondyé!*
	((guffawing loudly)) 'God!'
12 Misha → Crystal:	*See it, see it, see 'Mwen vlé alé èk sé ma'ay-la'*
13 Judy:	*Sa-la pa kay konpwann- Sa-la pa kay konpwann Patw-*
	((laughing)) 'That one won't understand- That one won't understand Patw-'
	Sa-la pa kay palé Patwa pyès!
	'That one's never going to speak Patwa <u>at all</u>!'

14 Misha → Judy: *I ni bagay i ka konpwann 'i, Judy,*
                     'There are things she understands, Judy,'
                     i ni bagay, i ka pale'y 'i
                     'there are things, she does speak it'
15 Crystal → Judy: *Ai noo 'i, ai noo 'i*
                     'I do know, I do know'
16 Judy → Crystal: *Yuu doo noo!*
                     'You don't know!'

Notice that, despite her apparent inability to repeat accurately Judy's relatively simple Kwéyòl model, it seems that Crystal understands at least the gist of what Judy and Misha say to each other in Kwéyòl in lines 13 and 14. This suggests that Crystal is following a developmental trajectory that is becoming increasingly common in Morne Carré: while acquiring full speaking proficiency in VESL, she is acquiring only some degree of passive understanding of Kwéyòl (as Misha suggests in line 14; notice also Misha's acknowledgment, in line 2, that *only* Crystal, the older of her two children, 'knows' Kwéyòl). Crystal's Kwéyòl proficiency will probably improve somewhat over the next several years, but it is unlikely that she will ever speak the language as fluently as her grandparents did, or even be able to use it in combination with VESL as extensively and as productively as her mother does.

Moments like this one, in which a child is actually called upon to speak some Kwéyòl, are few and far between. For the most part, children's relative lack of proficiency in Kwéyòl goes unnoticed and without comment. When a school-age child fails to understand something said by an elderly Kwéyòl monolingual, or has some difficulty repeating a simple model utterance, the parents and other adults are not exactly taken by surprise. They tend to treat it as some sort of passing glitch, a problem that is bound to correct itself in short order. Or they may simply brush it off as the result of momentary shyness, lack of attention, or uncooperativeness on the child's part. In any case, no one dwells on the matter, and everyone proceeds on the assumption that the child will be able to speak Kwéyòl just fine, whenever he or she is good and ready to do so, or whenever a situation really calls for it.

In the meantime, if the child is not quite comfortable with using Kwéyòl, so much the better; her English will be stronger for it, and she is that much less likely to speak out coarsely or disrespectfully. As I have described elsewhere (Garrett 2005), St. Lucians tend to regard Kwéyòl as inherently well-suited to cursing, scolding, joking, teasing, insulting, haranguing, complaining, and other kinds of self-assertive talk – the very kinds of talk that would result in a child being deemed 'mannish' or 'womanish,' not to mention being swiftly and severely punished. This is not to suggest that Kwéyòl cannot be used politely and respectfully; but it is considered to be especially well suited to these more assertive, potentially confrontational and face-threatening ways of speaking, and it is certainly considered far superior to English for such purposes. A child, of course, should not be speaking in these potentially inflammatory ways at all; so, in some sense, limiting the child's opportunities to speak Kwéyòl is as much a matter of common sense and good child-rearing as is restricting her access to kerosene and matches.

Toward a Human-Developmental Perspective on Language Shift

As Example 22.1 and Example 22.2 suggest, children in Morne Carré are both implicitly and explicitly socialized to distinguish between two normatively differentiated codes, Kwéyòl and English, and to observe fairly strict norms of age-appropriate use of those two codes. Ultimately, the ability to draw on both English and Kwéyòl as communicative resources, and to deploy the forms and features associated with these two codes in socially and pragmatically appropriate ways, is a salient aspect of locally preferred, culturally intelligible adult subjectivities – a hallmark of which, at the present sociohistorical moment in Morne Carré (and in St. Lucia more generally), is bilingualism. But, as these excerpts suggest, this particular form of bilingualism is not necessarily a stable or sustainable one, and adults' zeal for separating and regimenting their community's communicative resources as two distinct, age-graded codes, particularly where children are concerned, may be contributing to the dissipation and decline of one of them, Kwéyòl, and the steady morphing of the other, English, into a profoundly nonstandard vernacular that, just beneath its carefully patrolled lexical and phrasal surface, is heavily influenced by Kwéyòl and incorporates numerous Kwéyòl-derived features.

Kulick and Schieffelin (2004: 351–2) remark that an important shortcoming of certain influential works of contemporary social theory is that 'the socialization of habitus, or the early reiterations of language that initiate processes of becoming a culturally intelligible subject, are assumed and asserted more than they are actually demonstrated [...] [W]e know *that* they happen [...] but we don't know *how*.' In settings where children's acquisition and use of two or more codes is a value-laden, ideologically charged, discursively elaborated process – as seems to be the case more often than not – language socialization research can yield important insights into the ways in which local, face-to-face interactions are impinged upon (often orthogonally or indirectly) by extralocal factors. In the St. Lucian case, these include recent and still-ongoing changes in the relationship between English and Kwéyòl in St. Lucian society, the imperatives of nation-building (Garrett 2007a), and the ongoing shift from a primarily agricultural to a primarily service-based economy – which, in Morne Carré, has implications for the relevance of formal education, for household subsistence strategies, and for the life chances and personal aspirations of members of the younger generations.

As the St. Lucian case suggests, processes of language shift are virtually always rooted in relations of inequality between social groups, and these relations constitute fertile ground for the encoding, elaboration, and performance of social difference. Language socialization research provides a useful perspective on language shift in that it avoids conceptualizing human development as a matter of individuals somehow internalizing pre-existing, self-contained bodies or systems of linguistic forms and cultural knowledge. Rather, languages, cultures, and social formations, and likewise the developmental processes whereby individuals can be said to 'acquire' knowledge of them, are conceptualized in relational terms, emphasizing their symbolically mediated, co-constructed, discursively emergent qualities (Kramsch 2002). Similar concerns inform language socialization researchers' nonteleological perspectives on the outcomes of socialization; individual developmental trajectories are considered to be variable, non-linear, and ultimately open-ended. Guided by these and related concerns, language socialization research illuminates the complex linkages between locally situated, micro-level developmental processes and broader, macro-level processes of sociocultural reproduction, transformation, and change.

ACKNOWLEDGMENTS

Research in St. Lucia was supported by a Fulbright Fellowship (and an extension thereof), a National Science Foundation Dissertation Research Grant (SBR-9522567), a Wenner-Gren Foundation Predoctoral Grant, and a Spencer Foundation Dissertation Fellowship for Research Related to Education. I am grateful to these organizations and, above all, to the residents of Morne Carré, without whose generosity, assistance, and good humor my work would not have been possible.

NOTES

1 The orthographic system used here for Kwéyòl is the now widely accepted one that was originally set forth in Louisy and Turmel-John (1983).
2 VESL utterances are rendered here in the phonemic orthography used by Rickford (1987) for Guyanese; Rickford's system, in turn, is based on that originally devised by Cassidy (1961) for Jamaican.

REFERENCES

Bauman, R. and Briggs, C. (2003) *Voices of Modernity: Language Ideologies and the Politics of Inequality*. Cambridge: Cambridge University Press.

Bourdieu, P. (1991) *Language and Symbolic Power*. Cambridge, MA: Harvard University Press.

Cassidy, F. G. (1961) *Jamaica Talk: Three Hundred Years of the English Language in Jamaica*. London: Macmillan.

Errington, J. (2007) *Linguistics in a Colonial World: A Story of Language, Meaning, and Power*. Oxford: Blackwell.

Fader, A. (2007) Reclaiming sacred sparks: Linguistic syncretism and gendered language shift among Hasidic Jews in New York. *Journal of Linguistic Anthropology* 17(1): 1–22.

Field, M. (2001) Triadic directives in Navajo language socialization. *Language in Society* 30(2): 249–63.

Fishman, J. (1991) *Reversing Language Shift: Theoretical and Empirical Foundations of Assistance to Threatened Languages.* Clevedon, UK: Multilingual Matters.

Gal, S. and Woolard, K. (eds.) (2001) *Languages and Publics: The Making of Authority.* Manchester, UK: St. Jerome Publishing.

Garrett, P. B. (2003) An 'English creole' that isn't: On the sociohistorical origins and linguistic classification of the vernacular English of St. Lucia. In M. Aceto and J. Williams (eds.), *Contact Englishes of the Eastern Caribbean.* 155–210. Amsterdam, The Netherlands: John Benjamins.

Garrett, P. B. (2004) Language contact and contact languages. In A. Duranti (ed.), *A Companion to Linguistic Anthropology.* 46–72. Oxford: Blackwell.

Garrett, P. B. (2005) What a language is good for: Language socialization, language shift, and the persistence of code-specific genres in St. Lucia. *Language in Society* 34(3): 327–61.

Garrett, P. B. (2007a) 'Say it like you see it': Radio broadcasting and the mass mediation of creole nationhood in St. Lucia. *Identities: Global Studies in Culture and Power* 14(1–2): 135–60.

Garrett, P. B. (2007b) Language socialization and the (re)production of bilingual subjectivities. In M. Heller (ed.), *Bilingualism: A Social Approach.* 233–56. New York: Palgrave Macmillan.

Garrett, P. B. and Baquedano-López, P. (2002) Language socialization: Reproduction and continuity, transformation and change. *Annual Review of Anthropology* 31:339–61.

Heller, M. (2006) Bilingualism. In C. Jourdan and K. Tuite (eds.), *Language, Culture, and Society: Key Topics in Linguistic Anthropology.* 156–67. Cambridge: Cambridge University Press.

Heller, M. (2007) *Bilingualism: A Social Approach.* New York: Palgrave Macmillan.

Hinton, L. and Hale, K. (2001) *The Green Book of Language Revitalization in Practice.* San Diego, CA: Academic Press.

Kramsch, C. (ed.) (2002) *Language Acquisition and Language Socialization: Ecological Perspectives.* New York: Continuum.

Kroskrity, P. V. (2000) *Regimes of Language: Ideologies, Polities, and Identities.* Santa Fe, NM: School of American Research Press.

Kulick, D. (1992) *Language Shift and Cultural Reproduction: Socialization, Self, and Syncretism in a Papua New Guinean Village.* Cambridge: Cambridge University Press.

Kulick, D. and Schieffelin, B. B. (2004) Language socialization. In A. Duranti (ed.), *A Companion to Linguistic Anthropology.* 349–68. Malden, MA: Blackwell.

Louisy, P. and Turmel-John, P. (1983) *A Handbook for Writing Creole.* Castries, St. Lucia: Research St. Lucia Publications.

Makihara, M. (2005) Rapa Nui ways of speaking Spanish: Language shift and socialization on Easter Island. *Language in Society* 34: 727–62.

Meek, B. A. (2007) Respecting the language of elders: Ideological shift and linguistic discontinuity in a northern Athapascan community. *Journal of Linguistic Anthropology* 17(1): 23–43.

Mufwene, S. S. (2003) Language endangerment: What have pride and prestige got to do with it? In B. D. Joseph, J. Destafano, N. G. Jacobs, and I. Lehiste (eds.), *When Languages Collide: Perspectives on Language Conflict, Language Competition, and Language Coexistence.* 324–45. Columbus, OH: Ohio State University Press.

Mühlhäusler, P. (2003) Language endangerment and language revival. *Journal of Sociolinguistics* 7(2): 232–45.

Nettle, D. and Romaine, S. (2000) *Vanishing Voices: The Extinction of the World's Languages*. Oxford: Oxford University Press.

Paugh, A. L. (2005) Acting adult: Language socialization, shift, and ideologies in Dominica, West Indies. In J. Cohen, K. McAlister, K. Rolstad, and J. MacSwan (eds.), *ISB4: Proceedings of the Fourth International Symposium on Bilingualism*. 1807–20. Somerville, MA: Cascadilla Press.

Pollard, V. (2000) *Dread Talk: The Language of Rastafari*. Kingston, Jamaica: Canoe Press University of the West Indies.

Pratt, M. L. (1987) Linguistic utopias. In N. Fabb et al. (eds.), *The Linguistics of Writing: Arguments Between Language and Literature*. 48–66. Manchester, UK: Manchester University Press.

Pratt, M. L. (1992) *Imperial Eyes: Travel Writing and Transculturation*. London: Routledge.

Rickford, J. R. (1987) *Dimensions of a Creole Continuum: History, Texts, and Linguistic Analysis of Guyanese Creole*. Stanford, CA: Stanford University Press.

Riley, K. C. (2007) To tangle or not to tangle: Shifting language ideologies and the socialization of *Charabia* in the Marquesas, French Polynesia. In M. Makihara and B. B. Schieffelin (eds.), *Consequences of Contact: Language Ideologies and Sociocultural Transformations in Pacific Societies*. 70–95. Oxford: Oxford University Press.

Schieffelin, B. B. (1994) Code-switching and language socialization: Some probable relationships. In J. F. Duchan et al. (eds.), *Pragmatics: From Theory to Practice*. 20–42. Englewood Cliffs, NJ: Prentice Hall.

Schieffelin, B. B. and Ochs, E. (1986a) Language socialization. *Annual Review of Anthropology* 15: 163–91.

Schieffelin, B. B. and Ochs, E. (eds.) (1986b) *Language Socialization Across Cultures*. Cambridge: Cambridge University Press.

Schieffelin, B. B., Woolard, K. A., and Kroskrity, P. V. (eds.) (1998) *Language Ideologies: Practice and Theory*. Oxford: Oxford University Press.

Schmidt, A. (1990) *Young People's Dyirbal: An Example of Language Death from Australia*. Cambridge: Cambridge University Press.

Silverstein, M. (1998) Contemporary transformations of local linguistic communities. *Annual Review of Anthropology* 27: 401–26.

Thomason, S. G. (2001) *Language Contact: An Introduction*. Washington, DC: Georgetown University Press.

Woolard, K. A. (1998) Simultaneity and bivalency as strategies in bilingualism. *Journal of Linguistic Anthropology* 8: 3–29.

23 Language Socialization and Immigration

PATRICIA BAQUEDANO-LÓPEZ AND ARIANA MANGUAL FIGUEROA

Overview

Recent theoretical and methodological debates in the social sciences have called for the development of more comprehensive approaches to investigating the dynamics between the local and the global and the micro- and the macro-level processes that shape and influence practices of migration and immigration (Burawoy et al. 2000; Inda and Rosaldo 2002; Kearney 1995). Ongoing discussions about globalization and its flows of material, symbolic, and human resources afford us possibilities to develop more inclusive ways to understand identity formation processes among individuals who either physically travel or ideologically straddle geopolitical borders and boundaries (Agamben 1998; Alvarez 1995; Appadurai 1996, 2003; Clifford 1994; Ong 1999; Safran 1991). The study of these phenomena calls for anthropological methods that include multiple cultural and interactional sites that more comprehensively examine processes and practices of continuity and identification, as well as discontinuity and *dis*-identification, of those who experience migration (Brah 1996; Clifford 1994; Levy 2000;[1] Marcus 1995). Language socialization research offers an empirical grounding to these theoretical and methodological aims with its strong focus on the analysis of linguistically mediated socializing interactions. This focus, by design, engages the broader experiences, historical and sociological, of the participants in those interactions. This is partly due to the growth of the language socialization paradigm under the field of linguistic anthropology, a field that employs linguistic methods to understand sociocultural processes. The language socialization approach draws on the work of social theorists, significantly Bourdieu (1977) and Giddens (1979), to analyze the relationship between a social actor's orientations to others and to social institutions. The contexts of interaction of immigrant populations are thus

The Handbook of Language Socialization, First Edition. Edited by Alessandro Duranti, Elinor Ochs, and Bambi B. Schieffelin.
© 2014 John Wiley & Sons, Ltd. Published 2014 by John Wiley & Sons, Ltd.

important sites for understanding how immigrant groups negotiate participation in and influence new communities and social institutions. The term 'immigration' is defined here as the processes and practices of an individual or a group when they enter and settle in another region, country, or nation. The term 'migration' refers more broadly to the movement of people (physical and/or ideological) in relation to the processes that generate that movement (e.g. colonization, globalization, and temporary or permanent labor, to name a few). The related concept of 'diaspora' is used to indicate the movement (whether by force or by choice) of people from one nation (or nation state) to another, and the ways in which this movement affords ideological, social, and economic links to the homeland or community of origin.

This chapter reviews language socialization research that has engaged the study of language mediated interactions and experiences at the intersection of migration. It also examines how these studies have contributed to the development of a more integrated approach to the study of immigration. The chapter is organized as follows: first, it provides an overview of the key issues and general trends in the study of immigration with an emphasis on work carried out in the United States. It discusses concepts and approaches relevant to the study of language and the context of immigration, including the concepts of 'speech community' (Fishman 1972; Gumperz 1968) and 'competence' (Chomsky 1965; Hymes 1972). Second, the chapter charts the development and influence of the Language Socialization[2] paradigm on our understanding of immigration and cultural and linguistic change. In this section, the concept of 'language contact' in relation to practices of migration is briefly discussed. This discussion is included given that recent work in the field of Language Socialization has been carried out in postcolonial, transnational, and globalized settings (see Garrett, this volume). The following section reviews the research on migration and language socialization that addresses (1) the relationship between home and community socialization, (2) the transitions between home and school, and (3) the relationship between homeland and diaspora, and then focuses on the practices of religious socialization in diaspora. Finally, this chapter concludes with a discussion of current trends and possible trajectories for language socialization research in immigration.

Approaches to the Study of Immigration

The unique history of the United States, from its beginnings as part of the process of European expansion, its participation in the slave trade of Africans, its large-scale immigration from Europe during the 1800s and 1900s, and the more recent immigration from Latin American and Asian countries, has prompted scholars in a variety of fields to examine why different groups come to have such disparate experiences upon arrival (and even beyond settlement) in this country. In their book on immigrant adaptation, *Immigrant America: A Portrait*, Portes and Rumbaut (1996) classify immigrant groups into four categories: first, labor migrants who cross the border into the United States by land; second, professional immigrants who enter the United States to work in highly specialized fields and who may bring their spouses and children; third, entrepreneurial immigrants who often have previous business experience in their native countries and have access to capital and labor in the United States; and, fourth, refugees and asylees who are classified as such by governmental bodies based upon the dire conditions they experience in their home country. Many of the studies that we will review in this chapter examine the social and cultural phenomena of immigrant groups that fall into these categories; and while this typology may be expanded or revised, it provides a useful starting point for this discussion.

One of the most significant theories of immigration to surface in the late 1990s, one that remains a centerpiece in today's US immigration scholarship, is based on the notion of 'segmented assimilation' (Kasinitz et al. 2008; Zhou 1997). The notion of segmented assimilation was developed in response to decades of immigration scholarship that assumed that all immigrant groups shared the same linear assimilation trajectory (Bean and Stevens 2003; Zhou 1997). The theory's innovative claim was that immigrant groups' assimilation processes were dynamic and were influenced by a variety of pressures that immigrants faced within workplace and educational institutions, as well as peer groups and neighborhood enclaves. From this perspective, immigrants do not follow a linear path to assimilation but instead select from a variety of social statuses and practices that they encounter in US society. The success of the immigrant group depends upon which attributes members choose to assimilate, ranging from the underclass of 'native minorities' to the white upper class (Portes and Zhou 1993; Zhou and Xiong 2005). Immigration scholars from the sociological tradition have continued to focus on the ways in which institutions in the host country influence group behavior. Today, they rely on traditional methodologies of population surveys and interviews, while also beginning to incorporate ethnographic observations in immigrant communities in order to capture the nuances of how group members' cultural practices and national affiliations shift across institutions and over time (Kasinitz et al. 2008).

Another significant approach to the study of immigration has examined how individual behaviors are influenced by interactions with people and institutions in the immigration context. These studies have done important work to illustrate how key concepts in the study of culture and development, including 'cultural models' (d'Andrade 1992) and 'typologies of incorporation' (Ogbu 1987), as well as 'ecological systems' (Bronfenbrenner 1979) and 'cultural mediation' (based on the ideas of Vygotsky 1978), are enacted in the daily lives of immigrant communities. Studies following this approach have focused on the school (Azmitia and Brown 2002; Suárez-Orozco, Suárez-Orozco, and Todorova 2008) and the family (Buriel 1993; Delgado-Gaitan 1992; García-Coll, Meyer, and Brillon 1995; Goldenberg and Gallimore 1995) as the primary contexts that organize human behavior into activities that in turn influence an individual's developmental trajectory. The overlapping fields of immigration and education have also benefitted from research in Cultural Historical Activity Theory, which takes a Neo-Vygotskian approach (where learning is socially mediated) to the study of learning and development in minority and immigrant communities (González, Moll, and Amanti 2005; Gutiérrez and Rogoff 2003; Lee and Smagorinsky 1999).

The segmented assimilation and developmental frameworks have greatly contributed to our current understandings of the dynamic social and cultural processes that US immigrants experience, and thus continue to challenge notions of group homogeneity. We know that the diversity of immigrant groups and the politics of identity *within* immigrant groups are not new phenomena; rather, they have become the focus of attention that was not always salient in earlier scholarship. As US immigration policy shifted from a national quota system to a system of refugee relocation and family reunification in the middle of the twentieth century, scholars also readjusted their focus away from the linear assimilation of immigrants into a homogenous white middle class and towards an understanding of the diverse identities and experiences of new immigrants from Asia, Africa, and Latin America (Bean and Stevens 2003; Zhou 1997). In emphasizing cross-group and cross-generation comparisons, however, scholars working within these frameworks may continue to assume a one-to-one correspondence between language code and community membership and the focus on shared patterns of group behavior can lead to typified understandings of communities and convey implicit beliefs about how the 'competent' or 'successful' immigrant assimilates into the US mainstream.

The speech community revisited

Language socialization scholarship has pointed us towards a more dynamic notion of social integration and of language or code use as central to participation in community. The cornerstone concept of 'speech community' in the study of language in society designates a group of people socially bound by language (Bloomfield 1984 [1933]). The earlier, more narrow focus of this definition, which correlated either geographical proximity or shared language code to community membership, has shifted to account for the fact that, as individuals in society, we participate in and are members, often simultaneously, of more than one speech community (Baquedano-López and Kattan 2007; Garrett 2005; Garrett and Baquedano-López 2002; Morgan 2004). It was not until the work of Gumperz (1968) and Hymes (1972) that the notion of speech community began to include and account for the inherent diversity and complexity of social context and language use. Breaking free from models that mapped a one-to-one correspondence between a speaker and a group, the speech community became a notion that captured the gradient nature of cultural and linguistic membership. This membership is fluid and dynamic, and, at times, manifests itself in contradictory ways.

Silverstein (1998) has argued for a distinction between the terms 'language community' and 'speech community' in his insightful essay 'Contemporary transformations of local linguistic communities.' A language community shares both a language repertoire and communicative norms, both prerequisites for shared denotational meanings. A speech community, on the other hand, can comprise multiple language communities with shared indexical meanings that unite them socially and politically but do not necessarily entail shared meaning-making processes. Silverstein's review of 'ethnographically based, and historically informed work,' which features discourse as the medium that both constitutes community and contributes to interaction among communities, illustrates the interplay between key terms in the study of language and society: purity and mixing, change and persistence, and the local and the global (1998: 403). He cited as examples the work of Duranti and Ochs (1986), Schieffelin (1995), and others to illustrate how language use in missionary contexts has been shown to be a rich site for contact between the local language communities of Samoa and Papua New Guinea and the broader speech communities that encompassed Western religious and colonizing ideologies, institutions, and individuals. As Silverstein claims, and as the studies reviewed in this chapter show, these points of contact and the tensions that are inherent in them are central to our understanding of speech and language communities in the current geopolitical context of mass media and mass migration.

Notions of 'competence' have also become more encompassing, expanding from notions of having knowledge of the language (Bloomfield 1984 [1933]; Chomsky 1965) to having the ability to use language in its appropriate context and domain (Hymes 1972). Language socialization researchers and linguistic anthropologists have also advanced the notion that the acquisition of linguistic competence is not a neutral or value-free process; rather, it is conditioned by the ideologies we hold about ourselves and about the languages we speak (Schieffelin, Woolard, and Kroskrity 1998). The tensions between the knowledge and use of linguistic codes and the more global, technologically mass-mediated popular culture symbols create fluid notions of community and language that defy earlier, narrower assumptions concerning the location of and membership in community (Alim 2003, 2004, 2006; Garrett 2007; Spitulnik 1996, 1998). As a result, recent studies have demonstrated that displays of competence in dynamic community formations are diverse and multiply mediated. Mendoza-Denton's (2008) study of the linguistic and cultural practices of young Latina gang members in Northern California examined the complex layers of meanings created and recreated in the familiar and proximal notions of 'localism' and 'territory,' and advanced a notion that captures multiple ideological locations in her concept of 'hemispheric localism.' Hemispheric localism is a 'projection of neighborhood-based, spatialized discourses of "turf" onto broader domains that play out debates over race, immigration, modernity, and globalization' (2008: 104). Symbolism and other embodied representations of place and identity among gang members illustrate how the indexical property of language, the ability to name and resignify in one word – for example, *sur* ('south,' indexing Mexico) or *norte* ('north,' indexing the United States) – references, with impending social consequences, speakers' language background, possible immigration status, gender, ethnicity, and gang affiliation (see also Rymes 1996, 2001).

Such complex understandings of community and competence invite new ways to study how interactions in an immigrant context reconcile macro-sociological categories of belonging with micro-interactional negotiations of group membership and identity. Hall (2002, 2004) has provided a multidimensional approach for anthropologists studying immigrant incorporation in ways that capture the transformation processes that occur not just at the individual level (as in an immigrant incorporating to the larger society) but also at the societal level (the processes of nation formation). Ethnographers cannot just focus on the local, the everyday negotiations; they must attend to the broader public discourses that construct 'nationhood' (Hall 2002, 2004). Drawing from her work among Sikh youths in London who construct identities for themselves as British yet are held to Indian standards by elder and recent immigrants, Hall suggests that a shift away from the description of levels of accommodation to the identification of how sites of power operate across social scales may provide a productive way to understand the tension between the individual and the group. In short, the shift would permit examination of not only how one negotiates belonging to a community but also why belonging to a particular community seems important to an individual. Rampton's (2001) ethnographic study of Indian and Pakistani youths born in England, in diaspora, echoes Hall's work by illustrating how the macro-politics of social power relations emerge in micro-interactions between Indian students and their British teachers. The Indian and Pakistani adolescents employed 'stylized Asian English' (Rampton 2001: 404), code-switching from vernacular English into a form of English contoured with Indian accents in interactions with teachers. The students' use of stylized Asian English in these interactions accomplished two goals: first, it indexed broader societal relationships between dominant and majority communities, and, second, it rejected or tested the teachers' assumptions about youths of immigrant descent in the school. Language socialization research has been offering a way to productively study the tensions between macro-political and micro-interactional social phenomena. By tracing the development of individuals' participation in a group, made observable through their use of discourse strategies, talk, and other forms of language to co-construct social norms and manage locally contingent criteria for membership, language socialization scholars study culture and identity as they are organized and enacted during interactions in both the daily lives of individuals and in the lives of institutions. Language socialization research thus provides a nuanced approach to the study of immigration experiences with its conflicts, tensions, and resolutions.

Intersections of Language, Movement, and Power: How Language Socialization Research Contributes to the Study of Immigration

Language socialization researchers study and analyze developmental language data obtained through sustained ethnographic fieldwork.[3] Language socialization research is thus longitudinal – it involves the observation and analysis of language data over time and, in many cases, across sites and contexts of interaction. A careful analysis of any ethnographic field site also necessarily engages a historical and contemporary study of that setting. Such engagement traces a line of human activity and movement – its resources, disruptions, and divergences across time and space. From this perspective, facts and accounts of migration experiences are not just used as a backdrop for building the ethnographic context for the analysis of language data; these migration experiences actually, directly or indirectly, influence the language socialization practices being observed and analyzed by the ethnographer. This has been demonstrated in much of the earlier language socialization research conducted in geographical areas that had experienced large-scale cultural and linguistic contact (Kulick 1992; Ochs 1988; Schieffelin 1990). These studies analyzed language use that reflected the development of hybrid and syncretic ideologies and practices of socialization that signaled the transformation of the social order in non-Western, traditional societies. In many instances, such change was the result of European colonization or missionization campaigns.

While largely stemming from interests in human and language development, several of the earlier language socialization studies (Schieffelin and Ochs 1986), focused on interactions of members of communities that were part of, or were at least influenced by, migration processes. Thus, while not analytically focusing on these actors in an immigration context, the work examined socializing interactions that were constructing diaspora and enacting transnational flows. For example, the socialization practices of members of immigrant families in Northern California were analyzed among first- and second-generation Spanish-speaking Mexican immigrants (Eisenberg 1986). This study highlighted how the context of immigration and the ongoing cultural, linguistic, and racial contact it afforded organized and framed the interactions of family members. In an excerpt of a teasing exchange (the focus of Eisenberg's study), the adults and children in a family were discussing whether the children would dress up in Halloween costumes and participate in door-to-door 'trick or treat' practices. Another teasing routine involved imagining romantic relations between a young Mexican girl and a white, American boy of the neighborhood. Teasing exchanges in this case served to discursively examine the boundaries and possibilities of living in a multicultural and multiracial environment. As will be discussed below, teasing routines among Mexican immigrants continue to be a rich site to study the politics of diaspora and the ways in which broader concerns, including the presence of state authority, pervade daily interactions (Bhimji 2005; Mangual Figueroa in press).

Language socialization research in Pacific communities has examined how migration and contact led to linguistic and cultural change (Duranti and Ochs 1986; Kulick 1992; Ochs 1988; Schieffelin 1990). In a remarkable line of work, now spanning over 25 years of research, Schieffelin has continued to examine the ways in which Australian missionaries and the establishment of Christian churches transformed local worldviews and their representation among the Kaluli in Bosavi, Papua New Guinea. The initial focus of her studies centered on Kaluli family routine interactions and described the linguistic structure of gender role socialization and of young children's participation in multiparty interactions. This focus expanded to include the effects of literacy socialization (including religious literacy) and the shifting worldviews of this community (Schieffelin 1995, 2000). This is the only language socialization study that has captured, in one generation, the process and outcome of colonization in a modern-day society and the profound transformations that this has had on ideologies of self and other in that community (Makihara and Schieffelin 2007; Schieffelin 1990, 2000, 2002, 2008). In another study in Papua New Guinea, Kulick (1992) investigated language shift in the community of Gapun. Much internal and external migration had taken place across Papua New Guinea as men were contracted for labor away from their communities. In Gapun, the shift from the local vernacular Taiap to Tok Pisin (an English-based contact language) was also related to the extended processes of migration in Papua New Guinea, even though there was little migration into and out of the community. The effects of this shift created an ideological and domain-regulated separation of the languages in which Taiap became the less desirable code as the language of the village, of the elders, and a language of emotion, and Tok Pisin began to be seen as the language of progress, Christianity, and reason (Kulick 1992, 1998). The effects of Western expansion and migration were also documented in other Pacific societies. In Duranti and Ochs' (1986) study of literacy practices in Falefa, a community in Western Samoa, letter writing was a common practice between community members and their relatives working or living outside Samoa in New Zealand, Australia, or the United States. This practice suggested the existence of an established community of Samoans outside the islands. Perhaps most telling of the influence of Western culture on the socialization practices of young children in Samoa is Duranti and Ochs' description of the teaching of a printed syllabary that included superimposed images from non-Samoan contexts (an elephant, a ship, a sedan car) that illustrated representations of Samoan words that begin with a particular letter of the Roman alphabet. The children in these lessons were learning to represent the sounds of their language invoking an imaginary of Western concepts.

The above research is foregrounded to indicate that, while immigration was not the sole focus of their analyses, these language socialization researchers necessarily brought into relief the fact that the study of the everyday interactions they observed occurred in a larger, complex societal context. Many of the linguistic and cultural practices that were analyzed in these studies were also the result of the flows of religious ideologies and the economic expansion of more dominant groups in the region. There is now strong and sustained interest in understanding these dynamics across a variety of contexts of immigration and this work is reviewed in the next section. It is important to note that language socialization research on Creoles is also becoming a rich and robust area for understanding the effects of language contact phenomena. Led by Garrett's (2003, 2005, 2007) research in St. Lucia, Paugh's (2001, 2005) in Dominica; Riley's (2001, 2007) in the Marquesas; and Schieffelin and Doucet's (1994) on Haiti, these researchers collectively illustrate how negotiations involving multiple codes/languages and registers cannot be understood without attention to the histories that generated linguistic and cultural contact, including migration. These language socialization researchers' studies have focused more centrally on the experiences of young children growing up in contexts where they have to negotiate more than one language and role across speech events and activities with multiple interlocutors. The practices of children and their caregivers in these studies motivate us to reconsider notions of linguistic competence and the long-standing concepts of 'speech community' and of language specificity in its social domain (Fishman 1972). Other language socialization researchers have been studying second language socialization processes in foreign language education and in English-as-a-second-language (ESL) classes. With a focus on language learning and acquisition in formal schooling settings and in the workplace, these researchers have also expanded the scope of earlier studies to include adolescents and adult immigrant populations (see Duff, this volume; see also Duff and Hornberger 2008 and Zuengler and Cole 2005 for comprehensive reviews).

Home and community socialization

This section reviews selected recent language socialization studies that directly address the immigration context. It reviews research that has focused on language socialization interactions in the home and that also addressed community membership (cultural or ethnic[4]). The socialization studies described here examined linguistic and cultural practices in which interlocutors created and maintained speech communities through code choice that conformed to social, historical, and ideological conventions and expected patterns of language use. In her book, *Growing Up Bilingual* (1997), Ana Celia Zentella examined, through ethnographic and detailed analyses of naturally occurring data, English and Spanish code-switching practices among members of a New York Puerto Rican neighborhood that she called *el bloque.* Her study analyzed how social, political, and economic variables influenced the ways that cultural and linguistic participation in *el bloque* was negotiated. The choice of language – English, Spanish, or 'Spanglish' – revealed that locally situated norms for displaying competence, role-taking, and identity formation shifted in different locations within *el bloque* in response to perceptions of language use by community members. The ways in which members of *el bloque* used 'Spanglish,' for example, itself a linguistic practice of migration and language contact from Puerto Rico (the island) to the United States (the mainland), illustrated how its use was subjected to the social conventions of the local community, including when it was appropriate for speakers to use it (see also Urciuoli 1996). Such norms of use and appropriateness are central to second language development as well. Schieffelin's (1994) analysis of the verbal environments and everyday household routines of immigrant Haitian Kreyòl-speaking families in New York City illustrated how young children code-switched to elicit a host of linguistic strategies and expansions that furthered their acquisition of English as their second language. These strategies involved other participants and caretakers (who were Kreyòl speakers but who also spoke to varying degrees English, Spanish, and French) in the use of paraphrases, repetitions, repair sequences, and clarification requests to expand local linguistic repertoires.

The intermediary role of youths and young children in immigrant contexts is varied and complex. Drawing on a longitudinal and comprehensive corpus of language data on bilingual practices of young adolescents in Illinois (mostly Latino youths), Orellana et al. (2003) and Orellana and Reynolds (2008) examined the linguistic repertoires of youths who translate and interpret for family members.[5] Through analyses of texts and interpreting activities, the researchers analyzed the linguistic and ideological competencies that children and youths displayed while engaging a number of genres, including letters, official jury summonses, and advertisements. The authors argued that these higher-order competencies contrasted sharply with the activities that the same youths carried out in school settings, where the full range of their linguistic abilities was not always utilized[6] (see also Valdés 2003). In a south central Los Angeles study of low-income immigrant Mexican families' interactions with school and preschool-age children in the home, Bhimji (2005) pointed out the ways in which the young children not only learned to become adept at language and cultural practices of the home during adult–child interactions but also learned to mediate and be intermediaries in adult–adult teasing routines (see also Eisenberg 1986; Farr and Domínguez Barajas 2005). Through teasing exchanges, these children were also taught to become aware of the politics of immigration affecting immigrant Latinos in California. As an illustration of this last point, in the context of a teasing exchange, a young child, Esmeralda (2 years old), is encouraged by her mother (Carmen) to respond to an adult (her godmother, *madrina*), who was teasing her, with the threat of deportation.

Example 23.1:   *Example layout modified from Bhimji (2005: 74).*

Madrina:	*Mocosa.*
	'Snoot nose'
	((to Esmeralda))
Carmen:	*Dile. La Migra. Dile*
	'Tell her. Immigration police. Tell her.'
	((to Esmeralda))
Esmeralda:	**La miga.** [sic]
	'Immigration police'
Carmen:	*Dile. Te lleva la migra. Van a venir*
	'Tell her. The immigration police will take you. They're going to come.'

This exchange illustrates the role that children play as 'conduits' of teasing and humorous exchanges among adults. But, as the interaction between Esmeralda and her godmother and mother shows, the seriousness of the difficulties of the immigrant experience is palpable and *teachable*. The threat of deportation and the fear of surveillance invoked by the words '*la migra*' can shape the daily contexts of interaction for many immigrant families and youths (see also Mendoza-Denton 2008). Teasing routines and other speech events that invoke and reference immigration policies or dominant public discourses on immigration become opportunities, however difficult to negotiate, to make sense of exclusionary experiences. Such discussion of immigration policies and experiences are also common outside the home.

Home and school socialization

This section reviews studies on the transition from home to school that may also include the transition from the home language to the language of the school. The studies reviewed here also illustrate the entanglement between educational policy and ideologies of immigration. More often than not, both policy and ideology frame immigrant students as deficient learners, which can severely limit these students' participation across educational contexts. The focus on linguistic strategies of the language socialization studies reviewed here illustrates the complex practices that families and youths engage in as they negotiate the overlapping, yet at times disconnected, contexts of socialization between the home and school.

In a series of studies looking at transitions between home and school and their impact on language skill development, Pease-Alvarez and Vásquez (1994) and Vásquez, Pease-Alvarez, and Shannon (1994) examined practices of linguistic and cultural continuity among the children of Mexican immigrant families of a community in Northern California. In response to the perception that the academic failure of Mexican immigrant students in schools stemmed from deficiencies in the home that largely resulted from a lack of extended, directive, and expansive conversational routines with peers and family members (see also Heath 1982), these researchers set out to ethnographically observe and examine the linguistic and interactional contexts of home and school. Their studies showed that adults' uses of 'contingent queries' at home in response to children's requests served as productive scaffolding strategies that worked to clarify and elaborate on those requests. Such queries also served as deliberate strategies to enforce maintenance of the home language and delay the shift from Spanish to English. These studies were the first to provide longitudinal, ethnographic evidence to support an additive model of learning for bilingual Mexican immigrant children in schools (see also González 2001). The authors contended that children had the strategies in the home language to engage academic content in the school. Yet, having the linguistic skill is only one aspect of children's successful integration in school; they still have to contend with the expectations that teachers and schools have of their abilities.

In a study of a first-grade ESL classroom, Willett (1995) documented the second language socialization experiences of four immigrant students. The students, three girls (Palestinian, Maldivian, and Israeli) and one boy (Mexican American), were students at a school that was attended primarily by children of university graduate students. The boy, who was part of the focal group, was the child of a laborer at the campus stables. Several factors influenced the ways in which students demonstrated communicative competence during interactional routines in the classroom. These factors primarily included gender and class – preferred participation frameworks in teacher(s)-to-student(s) and peer-to-peer interactions – and the teachers' presumptions about the students' cognitive abilities. These criteria, and the practices that they supported, reproduced contexts and ideologies that reinforced gender, class-based, and ethnic group expectations that positioned the four immigrant children on a differential path to academic success. During the course of the observations, the three girls displayed, and were rewarded for, their linguistic competencies, peer support, and academic success, while the boy increasingly became singled out as a problematic learner as he tried unsuccessfully to position himself as socially competent in the class. Rymes and Pash (2001) examined the literacy and language practices of René, a second-grade boy from Costa Rica who was also an English language learner. In the second-grade class that René attended, he learned to 'pass' as a competent speaker during classroom routines, in part to enact a desirable male behavior among his peers and gain social approval. At the same time, however, he was also being designated for special education classes and entering a different academic track in school.

Kyratzis, Tang, and Koymen's (2009) research on peer socialization during play activities at a Head Start program for low-income and mostly Mexican immigrant children challenged the assumption that working-class children were more likely to use restricted codes (rich in paralinguistic strategies but without much verbal elaboration) and that they lacked the linguistic skills for successful participation in the language of the school, with its reliance on elaborated codes (explicit and explanatory language practices) (see also Bernstein 1974). The bilingual children in the study employed a range of productive communicative resources that included strategic switches between English and Spanish, the use of paralinguistic cues to indicate joint engagement, and the use of complex referential practices. Thus, rather than falling strictly within a dichotomy between the use of elaborated and restricted codes, these children's use of peer group language, with its varied rules and conventions, can facilitate entry into the complex language practices of the school.

Expanding on the research of young translators and interpreters discussed above, García-Sánchez and Orellana (2006) examined parent–teacher conferences in which children were also present. Narratives that teachers constructed about their students' progress were illustrative of the socialization of institutional expectations of behavior, including the moral identities that were desired by schools. Remarkably, in these parent–teacher meetings, children were not simply translators and interpreters for the events; they were also the main co-participants as well as the actual objects of behavioral scrutiny and evaluation. The discussions and teacher narratives in these parent–teacher conferences tended to absolve teachers of problems arising in the development of the children and placed the greater moral weight on the children themselves to become responsible for their learning. These studies are mentioned to illustrate the ways in which attention to the transition from home and school by language socialization researchers has served to identify the first 'critical' transitions (from home to school) that are also constructed as the first indicators of academic success and failure.

Recent work studying the critical transition across higher levels of education points to yet another point of contact where academic success depends on more than just having the institutional structure to facilitate that transition. Solís' language socialization study (2009) of a cohort of recent immigrant Latino students in Northern California (all designated English language learners) transitioning from two middle schools to one high school points to the need to examine the linguistic practices that go along with structures of academic transitions. The rigid administrative structuring of this institutional change (the shift from eighth to ninth grade), which is sometimes arranged independently of actual language learning or proficiency, follows district policies. Solís argues that these critical academic transitions may maintain the linguistic, and thus power, asymmetries experienced in the students' schools of origin through continued English-language-learner labeling and via limited educational supports throughout high school. This is a situation that becomes exacerbated in the new and often larger and more complex educational context.

Institutional labels given to immigrant language learners do not only shape the process of socialization; they frame it from a perspective of deficit and undesirability (García-Sánchez 2009, this volume; Lucko 2007; Talmy 2005, 2008). In his study of a Hawaiian school that served a varied population of ESL students from various countries of origin covering a wide span of US residency (from six months to ten years), Talmy discussed the process that created the near impossibility of becoming a different kind of learner once an ESL learner has been given that identity. Drawing on his two-and-a-half-year-long study, Talmy described this process as the result of 'the cultural productions of ESL students' (2008: 621). This process constructed a school-sanctioned version of an ESL student (through programs and educational policies) and a more oppositional 'generation 1.5' version illustrated through student behaviors that reinforced school beliefs about ESL instruction as academically inferior (students came unprepared for class or did not do their homework).

Although the focus of this review has been primarily on US immigration so far, ongoing immigration processes in other countries have also been subjects of study from language socialization and related perspectives. Lucko (2007) has investigated the formation of ethnic identity among Ecuadorian immigrant teenagers in a working-class neighborhood in Madrid, Spain. Based on 16 months of ethnographic research, the relationship between academic success and failure and the Ecuadorian students' understanding of their ethnic identity as distinct from that of their Spanish classmates was examined. Through multisited observations at a school for immigrant students (at an *escuela concertada*, which is a system partly funded by the state), at an Evangelical Church, and during activities of Latino gangs, Lucko discussed how essentialist discourses gave way to unbridgeable cultural differences that positioned Ecuadorian youths as problematic, untrainable, and different. García-Sánchez (2009, this volume) drew on her 20 months of fieldwork in a community in southwestern Spain to illustrate complex linguistic and cultural practices of Moroccan Muslim immigrants, who in the course of everyday activities negotiate for themselves and their families the meanings of a politics of exclusion that has historically positioned them as an inferior 'other.' These expressions of exclusion seem especially incomprehensible when it is remembered that the host country's ideological efforts to integrate and include linguistic and cultural minorities in the mainstream now amount to special, if only ideologically, inclusive schools. Under the increasing surveillance of Arab groups, these immigrant children demonstrate, in spite of the exclusionary practices they experience (and not unlike those experienced by the children in the Orellana et al. studies), a tremendous sense of responsibility, managing to translate and interpret complex situations, including taboo topics, for adult family members during medical visits. These youths learn, at an early age, to act as buffers to ameliorate the tensions and differences of the cultural worlds they inhabit and, in so doing, they still manage to uphold the moral standards of their home communities.

Di Lucca et al. (2008) reported on a larger study of Moroccan adolescents in Italian schools where rapid linguistic shift from Arabic to Italian (within the same generation) and a redistribution of these languages across genres and domains were taking place. Moroccan Arabic became confined to oral genres in the community, while Italian (and affiliation to Italian identities) permeated these students' educational and social activities. The process of early childhood incorporation into the routine practices of schools has also been examined from a language socialization perspective. Pallotti (2000, 2002) documented for eight months the language development of a Moroccan girl, Fatima, at a nursery school in an Italian city. Building on repetition and format tying as linguistic and interactional scaffolding, Fatima borrowed key words from ongoing conversations with peers and teachers and managed to achieve coherence across turns, which positioned her as an engaged interlocutor in multiparty interactions. In another study addressing second language socialization, Cekaite and Aronsson (2004) examined first-to-third-grade (seven to ten years of age) Swedish 'reception classrooms' or immersion classrooms for refugee and immigrant children. The children, who were immigrants from Iraq, Lebanon, Thailand, and Turkey, demonstrated innovative skills at participating in humorous, joking activities (including producing a great deal of language play) as a way to use the second language meaningfully and become proficient in it (see also Aronsson, this volume). Since much of these children's activities involved role-playing and role-appropriation, the opportunities to animate voices other than their own were particularly conducive to learning registers and taking on stances not usually their own.

There is much we can learn from examining language socialization processes from a cross-cultural perspective, an earlier approach favored in language socialization research; yet, as the studies discussed here illustrate, the nuances of each immigration context might only explain the social and historic dynamics of that setting. Collectively, however, these studies illustrate that children and youths can, when it is possible to do so, engage fully with the linguistic and cultural resources available to them at home and at school.

Homeland and diaspora

The relationship between 'homeland' and 'diaspora' has been central to anthropological studies and related disciplines addressing immigrant populations with social and ideological ties across geographical and political regions. The notions of home and dispersion create a tension that engages transnational networks and practices of identification (Brah 1996). As Clifford (1994: 317) noted, 'diaspora cultures work to maintain community, selectively preserving and recovering traditions, "customizing," and "versioning" them in novel, hybrid, and often antagonistic situations.' Such work is evident in the findings of language socialization research in both new and established diasporas as participants in studies negotiate notions of homeland and the creation of individual and collective identities.

Education in the New Latino Diaspora: Policy and the Politics of Identity (Wortham, Murillo, and Hamman 2002) comprises studies that analyze the ways in which educational institutions in the US South (a relatively recent immigration context for Latinos) have begun to socialize newly emerging communities of Central American and Mexican immigrants. The volume includes Villenas' two-year ethnographic study of the cultural contact and debate over child-rearing practices in a city in North Carolina and Hamman's and Martínez's studies of bilingual policy in the South and Midwest. Each chapter of the volume identifies a different component of the US public educational system and illustrates its impact on the socialization and education of Latinos in diaspora communities, reminding us that socializing sites produce conflicting ideological positions. For the new Latino communities in the South and Midwest, the history of the more established sites of Latino immigration such as the Southwest and the East Coast provides continued public debate and is generating new immigration policies. As the work in this volume shows, much of the research in diaspora is concerned with questions of authenticity, acceptability, and adaptability of immigrant populations in the host country's mainstream institutions. Mangual Figueroa's 23-month ethnographic study of a mixed-status Mexican community living in the New Latino Diaspora of the US Rust Belt follows four mixed-status families from home to school and into the public space in order to track the moments when juridical categories of citizenship status are taken up, reproduced, and contested during routine interactions between family and community members (Mangual Figueroa 2010). She finds that adults and children of all ages develop appropriate understandings of the significance of Mexican and US citizenship that are expressed during talk in everyday activities such as homework completion routines (Mangual Figueroa in press), family discussions about the family's future plans, and peer interactions among adults and children. Like other language socialization research reviewed here, this work is fundamentally concerned with the ways in which micro interactions are shaped by and indexical of macro-sociopolitical phenomena, and how these phenomena converge in the daily language socialization experiences of immigrant communities.

Kattan (2009) has been studying the language socialization and development of young children of families of Israeli origin who are temporary immigrants to the United States. The *shlichim*, emissaries of the Jewish Agency for Israel, relocate to the United States for short periods of time (two to three years) to recruit diaspora Jews (those living outside of Israel) to move to Israel, establish and support Zionist or pro-Israel communities, and raise funds for the agency's work.

Kattan's work on the experiences of these temporary immigrant families helps us to appreciate the complex nature of notions such as nation, immigration, homeland, and diaspora. While adopting cosmopolitan ideals vis-à-vis transnationalism and bilingualism, the children in the study (all living in or near New York City) also develop strong (and more favorable) ideological and linguistic identifications with Israel in ways that help to construct at an early age desirable forms of ethno-religious identity. In interactions at home and in school settings, the children explore the boundaries of proper or authentic forms of Hebrew (as the desired language spoken by Israelis) in comparison to inauthentic uses of Hebrew by non-Israeli Jews. The children of *shlichim* learn to parody US pronunciations of Hebrew to indicate the less desirable identity of 'American,' while simultaneously asserting their ability to pass as 'Americans.' This boundary work (between Israeli, Jewish, American, and transnational identities) draws on the historical relationship between the Israeli state, the Jewish Diaspora, and the United States, and the significance of Hebrew, as the ideal code, within that relationship. In simultaneously recognizing the prestige of English while derogating its speakers – and in acclaiming Hebrew and its speakers – *shlichim* and their children reconfigure the values of languages often positioned in hierarchical relation to each other.

Shankar's (2008, 2009) research among South Asian American teens (Desi) in Northern California illustrates how, in another diasporic setting, the use of speaking styles converged with perceived class statuses and shaped linguistic and social norms for these youths. The South Asian American teens in this study were from more upwardly mobile Punjabi families who had settled and benefitted from the economic and technological boom of Silicon Valley. Depending on prior histories of class and education in India and the United Sates, Desi youths and their families would speak English or Punjabi at home. The study described the use of two styles of English: the popular or more mainstream style and the 'fresh off the boat' style that represented the marginalized second- or third-generation immigrant Sikh Punjabi. The marginalized group resignified the features of the more popular and mainstream speech to disaffiliate with it and with the social group it purportedly represented. Lo's (2009) study of Korean heritage speakers in Northern California is significant here for the dynamics of moral desirability inculcated by teachers in their students, who were Korean heritage language learners (see also Lo and Fung, this volume). This multisited language socialization study of interactions across the weekend heritage language school, a tae kwon do studio, an art school, and an after-school program that taught English and math, examined how moral judgments of persons and actions were conveyed across these settings in ways that reified Korean norms and expectations and that positioned children as morally worthy Korean people. The identities that were being constructed for the students incorporated the present experiences of these children as Korean American youths but were also emblematic of a past and present history of immigration to the United States by Koreans.

In a linguistic and educational study of an immigrant Yemeni community, Sarroub (2002, 2005) discussed the tensions that young Yemeni women experience as they negotiated new literacy and linguistic worlds as Muslims at an American public school. Based on two years of ethnographic research in a Yemeni community in southeastern Michigan, the study examined the educational experiences of adolescent women as they negotiated learning to become Americans while remaining Yemeni. The women were also learning to grow up as daughters of immigrant families and students at the public school and to straddle the difference between being teenagers and being women. For many of these students, the school provided a safe space without the demands placed on them by virtue of the gender norms and expectations of the home community. Yet, these conflicting experiences (which can run counter to community norms) were not easy to resolve in a context that was not always welcoming of women wearing the *hijabat* in post-9/11 times. The pressure on these students sometimes produced moments of anxiety that created perceptions of themselves as having failed to uphold the expectations of them at home and at school.

Religious socialization in diaspora

Religious socialization has been a growing area of language socialization research and inquiry that has centered more recently on immigrant and diasporic communities in the United States. A main focus of attention in the research on religious socialization has been to study the inculcation and teaching of literacy practices. For example, Duranti, Ochs, and Ta`ase (1995) expanded the scope of the Samoan studies discussed above (Ochs 1988) and examined the literacy practices of a Samoan American community in Southern California during Sunday School lessons. The same syllabary that served as a literacy tool in Samoa (with its Western features) was also being used at the Californian church to index experiences, worldviews, and identities present in the Samoan islands prior to Western colonization. These discourses of identity, and even more of nostalgia, socialized young Samoan American children to adopt bicultural and bilingual identities that promoted the use of established formal and informal registers, as well as the development of linguistic innovations that the new immigrant context afforded (see also Duranti and Reynolds 2000). Admonitions to learn and retain the home language permeated the lessons at church and, like many other religious contexts for children, repetition of religious text, while in many cases unintelligible, was the vehicle for acquiring and displaying desired knowledge and practices.

Ethnographic studies of transnational practices of Mexican immigrants in both Chicago and Michoacán identified the *doctrina* (Catholic catechism for young children) educational setting for young children as a site of cultural and linguistic continuity for immigrant communities in Chicago (Farr 1994). Baquedano-López's studies of *doctrina* classes at two parishes in California analyzed a range of literacy practices from narrative tellings of the religious icon of *Nuestra Señora de Guadalupe* (Our Lady of Guadalupe) – which socialize children to affiliate with a collective identity of dark-skinned Mexicans living in the United States (1997, 2000) – to the interpretation of prayers, Bible stories, and parish events with moralizing messages relevant to their identities as Mexicans and US immigrants (Baquedano-López 2004, 2008; Baquedano-López, Leyva, and Barretto 2005). Additionally,

sermons and Bible lessons at a Pentecostal church in Southern California socialized youths to stay on a Christian path, or *El Camino*, and to not choose the sinful
ways of the world, or *El Mundo* (Ek 2002, 2005). The stronghold of such moral
exhortations also created a sense of belonging not to an ethnic community, as was
the case in the *doctrina* studies, but to a broader Latino Christian community. This
illustrates the fact that the choices that immigrant youths make, such as learning
to remain visible or hidden and to affiliate with the larger ethnic group (Mexican
in California, for example) instead of claiming an ethnic-minority identity (e.g.
Salvadorian or Guatemalan) are not without consequence. These decisions are
part of the everyday socialization experiences that many Central American immigrant youths experience in situations that require identity work (e.g. when youths
are challenged by other youths in the schoolyard or on the street to identify with
a particular ethnic group) (Lavadenz 2005). Depending on context, these youths
must enact norms of behavior that align with an ideological position that goes
along with a particular ethnic affiliation.

Access to religious contexts is not always problem-free. Political tensions also
surface in ways that illustrate how larger discourses of immigrant fear or rejection
articulate exclusionary practices. Baquedano-López (1997, 2004) and Baquedano-
López and Ochs (2002) report on the parish debates concerning the possible
elimination of *doctrina* instruction in favor of English-only instruction at a parish
in Los Angeles. These debates took place during and after the passing of anti-
immigrant policies (in particular the passing of Proposition 187 in 1994, a ballot
initiative that denied social services, including public education, to undocumented
workers and their families).[7] The tensions among parishioners indexed conflicting
views of Catholicism, ethnic identity, and cultural practice that were resolved by
invoking English-only ideologies and practices. In other cities in Southern
California, parishioners have experienced a range of negative emotional consequences during church services in English. As reported in Relaño Pastor's (2005)
study of immigration stories among Latina mothers, parishioners found services
in English to be insulting when the majority of the congregation spoke Spanish.
These mothers' responses to such practices, such as leaving church during religious services, served to moralize their younger children to learn and take stances
on church politics. Young children learned to see that language use in religious
settings was one place in which immigrants could construct a sense of belonging,
but they also learned how the politics of immigration shaped immigrant reception
in these contexts.

The tension and conflict in the socialization of religious and social identity are
also difficult to resolve (Aminy 2004; Fader 2001, 2007, 2008; Klein 2009; see also
Sarroub 2002). Fader's research in Hasidic communities in New York City has
examined the relationship between linguistic boundaries and community boundaries and how they are shaped by religious beliefs about gender and difference.
Processes of language shift and the creation of syncretic registers and practices
of Yiddish and English indexed an ethno-religious identity that allowed some
members of the community to participate in secular contexts outside the community. Young girls learned at an early age to shift to English and engage in

multilingual literacy practices as they prepared for their roles as cultural brokers for the men of the community, who are mainly speakers of Hebrew and Yiddish. Aminy's (2004) research in a Muslim religious community in Northern California that included many recent immigrants from Pakistan, Afghanistan, Palestine, and Morocco examined the revivalist nature of religious instruction in this community. In her multisited ethnographic study of two Islamic schools and of a study group for women (*halaqa*), Aminy described the diversity of practices within the Islamic community even as the US public responses to the events surrounding 9/11 constructed a negative public image of a homogenous religious community. The practices of the religious community were shaped by discourses of insider/outsider and reflected the tensions created by the moral weight of being Muslim in the United States. In a study that also explored the tensions of minority religious socialization, Klein's (2009) analysis of the narratives around turban (*dastaar*) wearing and religious affiliation among Punjabi Sikh youths in Los Angeles examined these youths' conflicting stances on religion, dress, and identity. While wearing a turban would index a moral commitment to community and religious belief, it could also evoke negative perceptions about Sikh identity and a misrecognition of the group (or an individual) as Muslim, which in America's post 9/11 context continues to elicit reactions of terrorist fear (see also Sarroub 2005).

Conclusions

The research reviewed here integrates the complex macro-sociological and micro-interactional phenomena that are enacted through language use and that have an impact on a range of socialization practices in immigrant and migrant communities. Each of the studies presented here examined the historical trajectories and contemporary sociopolitical conditions of interlocutors, a particularly exigent task in the study of cultural contact, transmission, and shift. Language socialization research on immigration supports longstanding assertions about the bidirectionality of expert and novice roles across the lifespan. For example, children who are more proficient than their parents in the language of the host country often take up expert roles in relation to their parents. In these cases, we see that children, who are perceived to be novices in family dynamics, assume new responsibilities as they take on expert roles in high-stakes translating situations at school, in the hospital, and during legal encounters. The research presented here also highlights the existence of social barriers that continue to prevent children from fully integrating into educational contexts. These social barriers stifle children's learning and participation in multiple discursive worlds and the societal mainstream, and, more poignantly, prevent them from being appreciated for their skills across various educational contexts in which they participate and, in many cases, help mediate.

The voices of immigrant children in social institutions, which have been animated in the research reviewed here, demand a departure from the way in which we do and understand research on child development. In the work examined in this chapter, ethnographers have documented and analyzed the many cases of children's acts of innovation, convention, and norm-breaking – for example, the linguistic and morally complex work young children do as interpreters for adults across social institutions. Yet, mainstream ideologies surrounding linguistically diverse communities and assumptions regarding limited cultural competence continue to be reproduced in institutions, such as schools, through policies and practices that hinder the full incorporation of many immigrant groups into the larger society. In other words, verbal practices and repertoires are not devoid of value within the social hierarchies of class and race. This point could become a catalyst for directing us to study the politics and consequences of language choice or, even more poignantly, the responsibility and politics involved in conducting research in contexts of language use often fraught with social inequities. There is much that language socialization research can do to continue to upgrade the status of immigrant children. A step toward this would be to continue to document the ways in which children are very much social actors who produce culture in the course of everyday activities, actively figuring out how to be competent members of multiple communities. This documentation could in turn be used to influence institutional policies that could make reception contexts for immigrant children more inclusive.

New studies of bidirectional socialization could shed light on how immigrant groups are socialized to the vast array of participation frameworks and settings available across their contexts of migration. We have learned from language socialization research how schools influence immigrant parents and children, but we know very little about how immigrant groups socialize one another and even less about how immigrant groups influence the cities and locales they inhabit. As such, a strong call is put forth for studies that foreground the bidirectional nature of socialization and that expand the socialization sites studied to include events across the multiple sites of cultural and linguistic contact, including host and home communities.

This review began by citing key research in sociology and anthropology that has started to document immigrant–immigrant and immigrant–city socialization processes. Language socialization research can offer a complex understanding of the role of language and interaction across and within these processes. As noted at the start of this chapter, recent theorizations on diaspora and globalization now permit us to engage in more integrated approaches to the study of immigration, where a focus on language provides a much-needed lens through which to understand the complexities and affordances of this ever-present and evolving process.

ACKNOWLEDGMENTS

The authors wish to thank the editors and reviewers for their insights and thoughtful suggestions. Thanks are also extended to Shlomy Kattan for helpful comments on earlier drafts. The authors are responsible for any errors that remain.

NOTES

1   André Levy (2000) critiques anthropologists' traditional commitment to (one) fieldsite as a narrow focus of attention in the study of diaspora. The essay was written as a review of Pattie (1997).
2   This term is capitalized when referring to the research paradigm.
3   We also direct the reader to Baquedano-López and Kattan (2008), Garrett (2006), and Garrett and Baquedano-López (2002) for reviews of language socialization methodology.
4   For a linguistic anthropological study investigating the differences between the racial and ethnic identity constructions reported by Dominican Republic youth immigrants in Providence, Rhode Island and US racial categories, see Bailey (2001).
5   See also Orellana (2009) for a broader treatment of Mexican immigrant youths and their interpreting practices.
6   The youths, however, were occasionally asked by teachers to use those skills on behalf of the institution, for example by serving as translators for others on school grounds. Children often provide these services and labor for schools without remuneration.
7   This proposition was later deemed unconstitutional.

REFERENCES

Agamben, G. (1998) *Homo Sacer: Sovereign Power and Bare Life*. Stanford, CA: Stanford University Press.

Alim, H. S. (2003) On some serious next millennium rap ishhh. *Journal of English Linguistics* 31(1): 60–85.

Alim, H. S. (2004) *You Know My Steez: An Ethnographic and Sociolinguistic Study of Styleshifting in a Black American Speech Community*. Durham, NC: Duke University Press.

Alim, H. S. (2006) *Roc the Mic Right: The Language of Hip Hop Culture*. New York: Routledge.

Alvarez Jr., R. R. (1995) The Mexican–US border: The making of an anthropology of borderlands. *Annual Review of Anthropology* 24: 447–70.

Aminy, M. (2004) *Constructing the Moral Identity: Literacy Practices and Language Socialization in a Muslim Community*. Doctoral Dissertation. Berkeley, CA: University of California, Berkeley.

Appadurai, A. (1996) *Modernity at Large: Cultural Dimensions of Globalization*. Minneapolis, MN: University of Minnesota Press.

Appadurai, A. (2003) *Globalization*. Durham, NC: Duke University Press.

Azmitia, M. and Brown, J. R. (2002) Latino immigrant parents' beliefs about the 'path of life' of their adolescent children. In J. M. Contreras, K. A. Kerns, and A. M. Neal-Barnett (eds.), *Latino Children and Families in the United States: Current Research and Future Directions*. 77–105. Westport, CT: Praeger.

Bailey, B. (2001) Dominican-American ethnic/racial identities and United States social categories. *International Migration Review* 35(3): 677–708.

Baquedano-López, P. (1997) Creating social identities through *doctrina* narratives. *Issues in Applied Linguistics* 8(1): 27–45.

Baquedano-López, P. (2000) Narrating community in *doctrina* classes. *Narrative Inquiry* 10(2): 1–24.

Baquedano-López, P. (2004) Traversing the center: The politics of language use in a Catholic religious education program for immigrant Mexican children. *Anthropology and Education Quarterly* 35(2): 212–32.

Baquedano-López, P. (2008) The pragmatics of reading prayers: Learning the Act of Contrition in Spanish-based religious education classes (*doctrina*). *Text & Talk* 28(5): 582–602.

Baquedano-López, P. and Kattan, S. (2007) Growing up in a bilingual community: Insights from language socialization. In P. Auer and L. Wei (eds.), *New Handbook of Applied Linguistics*. 57–87. Berlin: Mouton de Gruyter.

Baquedano-López, P. and Kattan, S. (2008) Language socialization in schools. In N. Hornberger and P. Duff (eds.), *Encyclopedia of Language and Education, Vol. 8: Language Socialization*. 2nd ed. 161–73. New York: Springer/Kluwer Academic Publishers.

Baquedano-López, P., Leyva, R. L., and Barretto, T. (2005) Strategies for linguistic and cultural continuity in Spanish-based Catholic religious education programs (doctrina). In *Proceedings of the 4th International Symposium on Bilingualism*. 199–209. Somerville, MA: Cascadilla Press.

Baquedano-López, P. and Ochs, E. (2002) The politics of language and parish storytelling: Nuestra Señora de Guadalupe takes on English-only. In P. Linell and K. Aronsson (eds.), *Selves and Voices: Goffman, Viveka, and Dialogue*. 173–91. Linköping, Sweden: Linköping University.

Bean, F. and Stevens, G. (2003) *America's Newcomers and the Dynamics of Diversity*. New York: Russell Sage Foundation.

Bernstein, B. B. (1974) *Class, Codes, and Control, Vol. 1: Theoretical Studies Towards a Sociology of Language*. London: Routledge.

Bhimji, F. (2005) Language socialization with directives in two Mexican immigrant families in south central Los Angeles. In A. C. Zentella (ed.), *Building on Strength: Language and Literacy in Latino Families and Communities*. 60–76. New York: Teachers College.

Bloomfield, L. (1984 [1933]). *Language*. Chicago, IL: University of Chicago Press.

Bourdieu, P. (1977) *Outline of a Theory of Practice*. R. Nice, transl. Cambridge, UK: Cambridge University Press.

Brah, A. (1996) *Cartographies of Diaspora: Contesting Identities*. London and New York: Routledge.

Bronfenbrenner, U. (1979) *The Ecology of Human Development: Experiments by Nature and Design*. Cambridge, MA: Harvard University Press.

Burawoy, M. (2000) *Global Ethnography: Forces, Connections, and Imaginations in a Postmodern World*. Berkeley, CA: University of California Press.

Buriel, R. (1993) Childrearing orientations in Mexican American families: The influence of generation and sociocultural factors. *Journal of Marriage and the Family* 55: 987–1000.

Cekaite, A. and Aronsson, K. (2004) Repetition and joking in children's second language conversations. *Discourse Studies* 6: 373–92.

Chomsky, N. (1965) *Aspects of the Theory of Syntax*. Cambridge, MA: MIT Press.

Clifford, J. (1994) Diasporas. *Cultural Anthropology* 9(3): 302–38.

d'Andrade, R. G. (1992) Schemas and motivation. In R. G. d'Andrade and C. Strauss (eds.), *Human Motives and Cultural Models*. 23–44. Cambridge: Cambridge University Press.

Delgado-Gaitan, C. (1992) School matters in the Mexican-American home: Socializing children to education. *American Educational Research Journal* 29(3): 495–513.

di Lucca, L., Masiero, G., and Pallotti, G. (2008) Language socialisation and language shift in the 1b generation: A study of Moroccan adolescents in Italy.

International Journal of Multilingualism 5(1): 53–72.

Duff, P. and Hornberger, N. (eds.) (2008) *Encyclopedia of Language Education and Education, Vol. 8: Language Socialization*. New York: Springer.

Duranti, A. and Ochs, E. (1986) Literacy instruction in a Samoan village. In B. B. Schieffelin and P. Gilmore (eds.), *The Acquisition of Literacy: Ethnographic Perspectives*. 213–32. Norwood, NJ: Ablex.

Duranti, A., Ochs, E., and Ta`ase, E. K. (1995) Change and tradition in literacy instruction in a Samoan American community. *Educational Foundations* 9: 57–74.

Duranti, A. and Reynolds, J. F. (2000) Phonological and cultural innovations in the speech of Samoans in Southern California. *Estudios de Sociolingüística* 1: 93–110.

Eisenberg, A. (1986) Teasing: Verbal play in two Mexicano homes. In B. B. Schieffelin and E. Ochs (eds.), *Language Socialization Across Cultures*. 182–98. Cambridge: Cambridge University Press.

Ek, L. D. (2002) *Language, Identity, and Morality in an Immigrant Latino Pentecostal Church*. Doctoral Dissertation. Los Angeles, CA: University of California, Los Angeles.

Ek, L. D. (2005) Staying on God's path: Socializing Latino immigrant youth to a Christian Pentecostal identity in southern California. In A. C. Zentella (ed.), *Building on Strength: Language and Literacy in Latino Families and Communities*. 77–92. New York: Teachers College.

Fader, A. (2001) Literacy, bilingualism, and gender in a Hasidic community. *Linguistics and Education* 12(3): 261–83.

Fader, A. (2007) Reclaiming sacred sparks: Linguistic syncretism and gendered language shift among Hasidic Jews in New York. *Journal of Linguistic Anthropology* 17(1): 1–22.

Fader, A. (2008) Reading Jewish signs: The socialization of multilingual literacies among Hasidic women and girls in Brooklyn, NY. *Text & Talk* 28(5): 621–41.

Farr, M. and Dominguez Barajas, E. (2005) Mexicanos in Chicago: Language ideology and identity. In A. C. Zentella (ed.), *Building on Strength: Language and Literacy in Latino Families and Communities*. 46–59. New York: Teachers College.

Farr, M. (1994) En los dos idiomas: Literacy practices among Mexicano families in Chicago. In B. Moss (ed.), *Literacy Across Communities*. 9–47. Cresskill, NJ: Hampton Press.

Fishman, J. A. (1972) Domains and the relationship between micro- and macrosociolinguistics. In J. Gumperz and D. Hymes (eds.), *Directions in Sociolinguistics*. 435–53. New York: Holt, Rinehart and Winston.

Garcia Coll, C., Meyer, E. C., and Brillon, L. (1995) Ethnic and minority parenting. In M. Bornstein (ed.), *Handbook of Parenting, Vol. 4: Social Conditions and Applied Parenting*. 189–209. Mawah, NJ: Lawrence Erlbaum.

García-Sánchez, I. (2009) *Moroccan Immigrant Children in a Time of Surveillance: Navigating Sameness and Difference in Contemporary Spain*. Doctoral Dissertation. Los Angeles, CA: University of California, Los Angeles.

García-Sánchez, I. and Orellana, M. F. (2006) The construction of moral and social identities in immigrant children's narratives-in-translation. *Linguistics and Education* 17(3): 209–39.

Garrett, P. B. and Baquedano-López, P. (2002) Language socialization: Reproduction and continuity, transformation and change. *Annual Review of Anthropology* 31: 339–61.

Garrett, P. B. (2003) An 'English creole' that isn't: On the sociohistorical origins and linguistic classification of the vernacular English of St. Lucia. In M. Aceto and J. Williams (eds.), *Contact Englishes of the*

Eastern Caribbean. 155–210. Amsterdam, The Netherlands: John Benjamins.

Garrett, P. B. (2005) What a language is good for: Language socialization, language shift, and the persistence of code-specific genres in St. Lucia. *Language in Society* 34(3): 327–61.

Garrett, P. B. (2006) Language socialization. In K. Brown (ed.), *Encyclopedia of Language and Linguistics*. 2nd ed. 604–13. Oxford: Elsevier.

Garrett, P. B. (2007) 'Say it like you see it': Radio broadcasting and the mass mediation of creole nationhood in St. Lucia. *Identities: Global Studies in Culture and Power* 14(1–2): 135–60.

Giddens, A. (1979) *Central Problems in Social Theory: Action, Structure and Contradiction in Social Analysis*. London: Macmillan.

Goldenberg, C. and Gallimore, R. (1995) Immigrant Latino parents' values and beliefs about their children's education: Continuities and discontinuities across cultures and generations. *Advances in Motivation and Achievement* 9: 183–228.

González, N. (2001) *I Am My Language: Discourses of Women and Children in the Borderlands*. Tucson, AZ: University of Arizona Press.

González, N., Moll, L. C., and Amanti, C. (eds.) (2005) *Funds of Knowledge: Theorizing Practice in Households, Communities, and Classrooms*. Mawah, NJ: Lawrence Erlbaum.

Gumperz, J. J. (1968) The speech community. In D. L. Sills (ed.), *International Encyclopedia of the Social Sciences*. 381–6. New York: Macmillan.

Gutiérrez, K. and Rogoff, B. (2003) Cultural ways of learning: Individual traits or repertoires of practice. *Educational Researcher* 32(5): 19–25.

Hall, K. D. (2002) *Lives in Translation: Sikh Youth as British Citizens*. Philadelphia, PA: University of Pennsylvania Press.

Hall, K. D. (2004) The ethnography of imagined communities: The cultural production of Sikh ethnicity in Britain.

Annals, American Academy of Political and Social Science 595: 108–21.

Heath, S. B. (1982) What no bedtime story means: Narrative skills at home and at school. *Language in Society* 11(2): 49–76.

Hymes, D. (1972) On communicative competence. In J. B. Pride and J. Holmes (eds.), *Sociolinguistics: Selected Readings*. 269–93. Harmondsworth, UK: Penguin.

Inda, J. X. and Rosaldo, R. (eds.) (2002) *The Anthropology of Globalization: A Reader*. Malden, MA: Blackwell.

Kasinitz, P., Mollenkopf, J. H., Waters, M. C., and Holdaway, J. (2008) *Inheriting the City: The Children of Immigrants Come of Age*. Cambridge, MA: Harvard University Press.

Kattan, S. (2009) 'Because she doesn't speak real Hebrew': Accent and the socialization of authenticity among Israeli Shlichim. *Crossroads of Language, Interaction, and Culture* 7: 65–94.

Kearney, M. (1995) The local and the global: The anthropology of globalization and transnationalism. *Annual Review of Anthropology* 24: 547–65.

Klein, W. L. (2009) Turban narratives: Discourses of identification and difference among Punjabi Sikh families in Los Angeles. In A. Reyes and A. Lo (eds.), *Beyond Yellow English: Toward a Linguistic Anthropology of Asian Pacific America*. 111–30. Oxford: Oxford University Press.

Kulick, D. (1992) *Language Shift and Cultural Reproduction: Socialization, Self, and Syncretism in a Papua New Guinean Village*. Cambridge: Cambridge University Press.

Kulick, D. (1998) Anger, gender, language shift, and the politics of revelation in a Papua New Guinean village. In B. B. Schieffelin, K.A. Woolard, and P. V. Kroskrity (eds.), *Language Ideologies: Practice and Theory*. 87–102. New York: Oxford University Press.

Kyratzis, A., Tang, Y.-T., and Koymen, B. S. (2009) Codes, code-switching, and context: Style and footing in peer group bilingual play. *Multilingua* 28: 265–90.

Lavadenz, M. (2005) Como hablar en silencio (like speaking in silence): Issues of language, culture, and identity of Central Americans in Los Angeles. In A. C. Zentella (ed.), *Building on Strength: Language and Literacy in Latino Families and Communities*. 93–109. New York: Teachers College.

Lee, C. and Smagorinsky, P. (eds.) (1999) *Vygotskian Perspectives on Literacy Research: Constructing Meaning through Collaborative Inquiry*. Cambridge: Cambridge University Press.

Levy, A. (2000) Diasporas through anthropological lenses: Contexts of postmodernity. *Diaspora* 9(1): 137–58.

Lo, A. (2009) Evidentiality and morality in a Korean heritage language school. In A. Reyes and A. Lo (eds.), *Beyond Yellow English: Toward a Linguistic Anthropology of Asian Pacific America*. 63–83. New York: Oxford University Press.

Lucko, J. D. (2007) *God, Gangs, and Grades: Constructing Identity and Difference among Ecuadorian Students in Madrid, Spain*. Doctoral Dissertation. Berkeley, CA: University of California, Berkeley.

Makihara, M. and Schieffelin, B. B. (eds.) (2007) *Consequences of Contact: Language Ideologies and Sociocultural Transformations in Pacific Societies*. Oxford/New York: Oxford University Press.

Mangual Figueroa, A. (2010) *Language Socialization Experiences of Mixed-Status Mexican Families Living in the New Latino Diaspora*. Doctoral Dissertation. Berkeley, CA: University of California, Berkeley.

Mangual Figueroa, A. (in press). Citizenship and education in the homework completion routine. *Anthropology and Education Quarterly*.

Marcus, G. (1995) Ethnography in/of the world system: The emergence of multi-sited ethnography. *Annual Review of Anthropology* 24: 95–117.

Mendoza-Denton, N. (2008) *Homegirls: Language and Cultural Practice among Latina Youth Gangs*. Malden, MA: Blackwell.

Morgan, M. (2004) Speech community. In A. Duranti (ed.), *A Companion to Linguistic Anthropology*. 3–22. Oxford: Blackwell.

Ochs, E. (1988) *Culture and Language Development: Language Acquisition and Language Socialization in a Samoan Village*. Cambridge: Cambridge University Press.

Ogbu, J. (1987) Variability in minority responses to schooling: Nonimmigrant vs. immigrants. In G. Spindler and L. Spindler (eds.), *Interpretive Ethnography of Education at Home and Abroad*. 255–78. Mahwah, NJ: Lawrence Erlbaum.

Ong, A. (1999) *Flexible Citizenship: The Cultural Logic of Transnationality*. Durham, NC: Duke University Press.

Orellana, M. F., Reynolds, J. F., Dorner, L., and Meza, M. (2003) In other words: Translating or 'paraphrasing' as a family literacy practice in immigrant households. *Reading Research Quarterly* 38(1): 12–34.

Orellana, M. F. and Reynolds, J. F. (2008) Cultural modeling: Leveraging bilingual skills for school paraphrasing tasks. *Reading Research Quarterly* 43(1): 50–65.

Orellana, M. F. (2009) *Translating Childhoods: Immigrant Youth, Language and Culture*. New Brunswick, NJ: Rutgers University.

Pallotti, G. (2000) External appropriation as a strategy for participation in intercultural multiparty conversations. In A. di Luzio, S. Günthner, and F. Orletti (eds.), *Culture in Communication*. 295–334. Amsterdam, The Netherlands: John Benjamins.

Pallotti, G. (2002) Borrowing words: Appropriations in child language discourse. In J. J. Leather and J. van

Dam (eds.), *Ecology of Language Acquisition*. 1–20. Amsterdam, The Netherlands: Kluwer.

Pattie, S. (1997) *Faith in History: Armenians Rebuilding Community*. Washington, DC: Smithsonian Institution Press.

Paugh, A. (2001) Dominica. In M. Ember and C. R. Ember (eds.), *Countries and their Cultures*. 637–45. New York: Macmillan Reference.

Paugh, A. (2005) Multilingual play: Children's code-switching, role play, and agency in Dominica, West Indies. *Language in Society* 34(1): 63–86.

Pease-Alvarez, C. and Vasquez, O. (1994) *Language socialization in ethnic minority communities*. In F. Genesee (ed.), *Educating Second Language Children: The Whole Child, the Whole Curriculum, the Whole Community*. 82–102. Cambridge: Cambridge University Press.

Portes, A. and Rumbaut, R. (1996) *Immigrant America: A Portrait*. Berkeley, CA: University of California Press.

Portes, A. and Zhou, M. (1993) The second generation: Segmented assimilation and its variants. *Annals, American Academy of Political and Social Science* 530: 74–96.

Rampton, B. (2001) Youth, race, and resistance: A sociolinguistic perspective on micropolitics in England. In M. Heller and M. Martin-Jones (eds.), *Voices of Authority: Education and Linguistic Difference*. 403–18. Westport, CT: Ablex.

Relaño Pastor, A. M. (2005) The language socialization experiences of Latina mothers in southern California. In A. C. Zentella (ed.), *Building on Strength: Language and Literacy in Latino Families and Communities*. 148–61. New York: Teachers College.

Riley, K. C. (2001) *The Emergence of Dialogic Identities: Transforming Heteroglossia in the Marquesas, French Polynesia*. Doctoral Dissertation. New York: City University of New York.

Riley, K. C. (2007) To tangle or not to tangle: Shifting language ideologies and the socialization of *Charabia* in the Marquesas, French Polynesia. In M. Makihara and B. B. Schieffelin (eds.), *Consequences of Contact: Language Ideologies and Sociocultural Transformations in Pacific Societies*. 70–95. New York: Oxford University Press.

Rymes, B. R. (1996) Naming as social practice: The case of Little Creeper from Diamond Street. *Language in Society* 25(2): 237–60.

Rymes, B. R. (2001) *Conversational Borderlands: Language and Identity in an Alternative Urban High School*. New York: Teachers College Press.

Rymes, B. R. and Pash, D. (2001) Questioning identity: The case of one second language learner. *Anthropology and Education Quarterly* 32(3): 276–300.

Safran, W. (1991) Diasporas in modern societies. *Diaspora* 1(1): 83–99.

Sarroub, L. K. (2002) In-betweenness: Religion and conflicting visions of literacy. *Reading Research Quarterly* 37(2): 130–48.

Sarroub, L. K. (2005) *All-American Yemeni Girls: Being Muslim in a Public School*. Philadelphia, PA: University of Pennsylvania Press.

Schieffelin, B. B. (1990) *The Give and Take of Everyday Life: Language Socialization of Kaluli Children*. New York: Cambridge University Press.

Schieffelin, B. B. (1994) Code-switching and language socialization: Some probable relationships. In J. F. Duchan, L. Hewitt, and R. M. Sonnenmeier (eds.), *Pragmatics: From Theory to Practice*. 20–42. Englewood Cliffs, NJ: Prentice Hall.

Schieffelin, B. B. (1995) Creating evidence: Making sense of written words in Bosavi. *Pragmatics* 5(2): 225–44.

Schieffelin, B. B. and Doucet, R. (1994) The 'real' Haitian creole: Ideology, metalinguistics and orthographic choice. *American Ethnologist* 21(1): 176–200.

Schieffelin, B. B. and Ochs, E. (eds.) (1986) *Language Socialization across Cultures*. Cambridge: Cambridge University Press.

Schieffelin, B. B., Woolard, K., and Kroskrity, P. V. (eds.) (1998) *Language Ideologies: Practice and Theory*. Oxford: Oxford University Press.

Schieffelin, B. B., (2000) Introducing Kaluli literacy: A chronology of influences. P. Kroskrity (ed.), *Regimes of Language*. 293–327. Santa Fe, NM: School of American Research.

Schieffelin, B. B. (2002) Marking time: The dichotomizing discourses of multiple temporalities. *Current Anthropology* 43: 5–17.

Schieffelin, B. B. (2008) Speaking only your own mind: Reflections on talk, gossip, and intentionality in Bosavi (PNG). *Anthropological Quarterly* 81(2): 431–41.

Shankar, S. (2008) Speaking like a model minority: 'FOB' styles, gender, and racial meanings among Desi teens in Silicon Valley. *Journal of Linguistic Anthropology* 18(2): 268–89.

Shankar, S. (2009) Reel to real: Desi teens' linguistic engagements with Bollywood. In A. Reyes and A. Lo (eds.), *Beyond Yellow English: Toward a Linguistic Anthropology of Asian Pacific America*. 309–24. New York: Oxford University Press.

Silverstein, M. (1998) Contemporary transformations of local linguistic communities. *Annual Review of Anthropology* 27: 401–26.

Solís, J. L. (2009) *Theorizing Educational Transitions: English Language Learners (ELLs) across Academic Settings*. Doctoral Dissertation. Berkeley, CA: University of California, Berkeley.

Spitulnik, D. (1996) The social circulation of media discourse and the mediation of communities. *Journal of Linguistic Anthropology* 6(2): 161–87.

Spitulnik, D. (1998) The language of the city: Town Bemba as urban hybridity.

Journal of Linguistic Anthropology 8(1): 30–59.

Suárez-Orozco, C., Suárez-Orozco, M., and Todorova, I. (2008) *Learning a New Land: Immigrant Students in American Society*. Cambridge: Belknap Press of Harvard University Press.

Talmy, S. (2005) *Lifers and Fobs, Rocks and Resistance: Generation 1.5, Identity, and the Cultural Productions of ESL in a High School*. Doctoral Dissertation. Honolulu, HI: University of Hawaii.

Talmy, S. (2008) The cultural production of the ESL student at Tradewinds High: Contingency, multidirectionality, and identity in L2 socialization. *Applied Linguistics* 17(1): 1–22.

Urciuoli, B. (1996) *Exposing Prejudice: Puerto Rican Experiences of Language, Race, and Class*. Boulder, CO: Westview.

Valdés, G. (2003) *Expanding Definitions of Giftedness: The Case of Young Interpreters from Immigrant Communities*. Mahwah, NJ: Lawrence Erlbaum.

Vásquez, O. A., Pease-Alvarez, L., and Shannon, S. M. (1994) *Pushing Boundaries: Language in a Mexicano Community*. Cambridge: Cambridge University Press.

Vygotsky, L. S. (1978) *Mind in Society*. Cambridge, MA: Harvard University Press.

Willett, J. (1995) Becoming first graders in an L2: An ethnographic study of L2 socialization. *TESOL Quarterly* 29(3): 473–503.

Wortham, S., Murillo, E. G., and Hamman, E. T. (eds.) (2002) *Education in the New Latino Diaspora: Policy and the Politics of Identity*. Westport, CT: Ablex.

Zentella, A. C. (1997) *Growing Up Bilingual: Puerto Rican Children in New York*. Malden, MA: Blackwell.

Zhou, M. (1997) Segmented assimilation: Issues, controversies, and recent research on the new second generation. *International Migration Review* 31(4): 975–1008.

Zhou, M. and Xiong, Y. S. (2005) The multifaceted American experiences of the children of Asian immigrants: Lessons for segmented assimilation. *Ethnic and Racial Studies* 28(6): 1119–52.

Zuengler, J. and Cole, K.-M. (2005) Language socialization and L2 learning. In E. Hinkel (ed.), *Handbook of Research in Second Language Teaching and Learning*. 301–16. Mahwah, NJ: Lawrence Erlbaum.

24 Second Language Socialization

PATRICIA A. DUFF

Introduction: Second Language Socialization

Although formal and informal socialization into more than one language, culture, and community has been a common experience throughout human history, systematic research on second language, bilingual, or multilingual socialization is relatively recent. Second language (L2) socialization represents a process by which non-native speakers of a language, or people returning to a language they may have once understood or spoken but have since lost proficiency in, seek competence in the language and, typically, membership and the ability to participate in the practices of communities in which that language is spoken. Their experiences may take place in a variety of language contact settings: in settings where the additional language is widely spoken and may be the dominant language of society (e.g. L2 learners of English in the United States); where it is used in more isolated or confined contexts, such as a high school or university foreign language classroom (e.g. learners of French in Mexico); in diaspora settings where minority groups who speak the target language exist (learners of Yiddish or Vietnamese in New York or Melbourne); or in virtual communities mediated by digital communication technologies (e.g. non-native learners and users of Mandarin in various parts of the world connected through online learning, gaming, or discussion sites, often with the intention of improving their Mandarin). The languages may be learned more or less concurrently with the first language (L1), in bilingual contexts, or sequentially.

Alongside this additional-language socialization, learners normally continue their linguistic socialization into and through their first (and perhaps other) languages because language socialization is both a lifelong process and a 'life-wide' process across communities and activities or speech events at any given time in

The Handbook of Language Socialization, First Edition. Edited by Alessandro Duranti, Elinor Ochs, and Bambi B. Schieffelin.
© 2014 John Wiley & Sons, Ltd. Published 2014 by John Wiley & Sons, Ltd.

one's life (Garrett and Baquedano-López 2002; Ochs 1986; Ochs and Schieffelin 2008). The word 'second' in 'second language socialization' is a cover term that is sometimes controversial precisely because of the multiple languages (i.e. more than two) and varied sequences (e.g. L1 → L2 → L3 → L1) involved in language learning for many people in multilingual societies; that is, the stark contrast between 'first' and 'second' is often much less apparent or clear-cut than these labels or arrows suggest; what was once an L1 might lose ground, functionally, to an additional language, which then may become the person's dominant language. Another distinction, between 'second' and 'foreign' language, can also be problematic, in addition to the 'othering' or alienation inherent in the word 'foreign' itself. Foreign language learning or socialization generally refers to learning a language not widely spoken in the local community or country, and is often associated with a required subject at school or university although it may be a leisure activity. But what might have been learned initially as a 'foreign' language might later be learned and used in a 'second language' context, with migration to a location in which the language is widely used (which might be in one's own country, hardly a 'foreign' community).

Heritage language learning often constitutes L2 socialization in that the ancestral language being learned may be neither the children's L1 nor their dominant language at the time of study, due to language shift or loss, for example, within their generation or in earlier generations (He 2008). Within immigrant communities, specifically, two or more languages may be present and inculcated to a greater or lesser extent such as in the case of Generation 1.5 children; over time, however, cross-generational shift in languages may occur as learners' L2 receives more attention and support and enjoys a higher local social status. Second language socialization may also occur in language revitalization settings, particularly in indigenous communities in which a colonial language or lingua franca (formerly an L2) has displaced or supplanted one or more local languages (L1s) but efforts are being made to preserve the endangered languages and to socialize new generations into the linguistic and cultural traditions of elders and previous generations. The contrast between linguistic, political, and other ideologies associated with the languages being revitalized and what are perceived to be hegemonic colonial languages and practices has also received attention by applied linguists, psycholinguists, and anthropologists (e.g. Friedman 2010b; Howard 2008; Pesco and Crago 2008).

'Second language (L2) socialization' is used in this chapter to refer generically to socialization beyond one's first, or dominant, language and encompasses second, foreign, and (concurrent) bilingual and multilingual learning contexts. Because L2 socialization is associated with L2 acquisition and education, much of the research is done by scholars in applied linguistics, education, and bilingualism, although some of the work comes out of anthropology and linguistics more directly. There is also a natural overlap between aspects of L2 socialization and sociolinguistics (e.g. Duff 2010a). Like most L1 socialization research, L2 socialization research and theorizing is usually grounded in aspects of sociocultural (cultural-historical) theory and activity theory (Duff 2007a; Duff and Talmy 2011).

Mediation and expertise in second language socialization

As in the case of L1 socialization (Schieffelin and Ochs 1986), L2 socialization is usually mediated by those who are more knowledgeable about and proficient in the language and familiar with the culture (the 'experts' or 'oldtimers') for those with less proficiency (relative 'novices' or 'newcomers'). The mentors or agents of socialization typically include teachers, tutors, peers, relatives, or co-workers who have a desire to assist learners to become more proficient not only in normative target language forms but also in the values, ideologies, identities, stances, affective states, and practices associated with the language and its users in particular communities of practice. However, the level of proficiency of 'experts' (whether teachers, parents, or caregivers) in either the learners' L1 or L2 may vary considerably, particularly when the language being taught is not widely or commonly spoken in local contexts (e.g. Latin or Khmer in Canada) and when the socializers (instructors) themselves have had limited opportunities to become highly proficient in it or to maintain whatever linguistic and cultural proficiency they once may have attained. Expertise may as a result be negotiated to some extent through various kinds of power dynamics and interaction (Bronson and Watson-Gegeo 2008; Duff 1995, 2002, 2003; Kramsch 2002). Furthermore, as discussed in the following section, learners themselves may seek different levels of expertise in the L2, some aspiring to high levels of proficiency and community engagement (which they may or may not achieve) and others seeking functional, but relatively low, levels depending on their circumstances. Their actual levels of attainment depend on a number of other factors as well, such as the age at which they begin to study or learn the language, the duration, intensity, and effectiveness of instruction or socialization, and their motivation and opportunities to use it (Ellis 2008).

To give an example, the hearing parents of deaf children may have limited or no knowledge of sign language until their children begin to learn it at school or in Deaf clubs. The children may subsequently begin to socialize their parents and siblings into their Deaf language and culture, but those family members may reach only modest levels of L2 proficiency relative to their children, who are more immersed and engaged in the community, usually from a younger age (Erting and Kuntze 2008). On the other hand, the hearing children of Deaf parents proficient in sign language may easily learn the home signed language as their L1 and be socialized into Deaf culture, in addition to learning the oral language spoken in the wider community (e.g. English).

Other issues and challenges in second language socialization

Beyond issues of language choice itself (e.g. Garrett 2007; Guardado 2009; Rymes 1997), L2 socialization often poses interesting challenges for immigrants and transnational sojourners, who may have quite complex histories of prior language exposure and socialization, conflicted identities, and often uncertain future trajectories and/or investments in the target language and its community(ies) (e.g. Bayley and Schecter 2003; Duff et al., forthcoming; Watson-Gegeo 2004). Similarly, it may differ considerably from L2 socialization in 'foreign' language education contexts with learners whose goals and intentions may not include living in a community of target-language speakers or adopting all (or many) of the cultural and linguistic norms associated with such communities or becoming integrated within a more dispersed community of L2 users; and yet they are, regardless, being socialized into the new language and aspects of culture (often by a sole native or near-native speaker from that language and culture) through curriculum materials, interaction patterns, sociocultural activities, and the language itself.

Therefore, as a locus of both cross-linguistic and cross-cultural contact and learning, L2 socialization offers many interesting avenues for research. It also raises new theoretical considerations and potentially a wider range of linguistic and nonlinguistic learning outcomes than might typically be found in L1 socialization research (Duff 2003). In addition to the possibility of high levels of L2 achievement and acculturation, outcomes and attitudes might include ambivalence; defiance; resistance to or rejection of the target language, culture, or community (or aspects thereof); or prematurely terminated or suspended L2 learning (perhaps returned to many years later, again with no expectation of integration or membership in communities of target-language speakers outside the language classroom). Conversely, there may be a strong desire on the part of newcomers for successful L2 socialization but too few opportunities for interaction with appropriate socializing agents and interlocutors or too little support from them (Duff 2010a). Another outcome might be learning to play the game of 'doing being a student,' or getting by without actually internalizing the necessary linguistic and substantive content (Rymes and Pash 2001). Innovative syncretic or hybrid practices and identities may also be prevalent, blending primary language and culture practices and additional ones or imposing L2 forms, practices, or identities on those associated with the L1 (or vice versa). Such syncretic processes and outcomes exist in L1 socialization as well (e.g. Garrett and Baquedano-López 2002; Kulick and Schieffelin 2004) but may be especially salient in the context of globalization, migration, multilingualism, transnationalism, and lingua franca use, in which the language learners or users may affiliate to different degrees with the nonprimary languages and communities they are connected with and those affiliations and allegiances may change radically, frequently, and unpredictably over time for social, economic, political, and other, more personal, reasons. However, even in classroom L2 learning (e.g. studying German in London; Rampton 1999) learners may be invested in the target language and culture and in literacy practices to quite different degrees than might typically be the case in L1 learning and they may exert their agency, creativity, and subversiveness in different ways as well, sometimes avoiding the target language entirely and aligning with highly stylized vernacular languages of peers instead (Rampton 1995, 2006). Thus, the complexities of language socialization are manifold in L2 contexts, potentially compounding those in L1 socialization.

Similarities and differences between first language and second language socialization

As in L1 socialization, L2 socialization occurs in home, community, and other settings and not exclusively in formal educational domains. Second language socialization research frequently examines the practices of adolescent and adult learners and their interlocutors and not the experiences of young children primarily, which would be more common in L1 socialization research.

However, the inevitable contrasts implied between L1 and L2 socialization may obscure the fact that socialization *within* a given language – that is, into one or more of its many oral and written forms, genres, registers, speech acts, and the social meanings they index – is also highly differentiated and diverse. This differentiation typically increases as people move from home to school uses of language and then into a host of vocational, professional, technical, and other specialized social spheres (Duff 2010a; Roberts 2010). In that sense, L1 and L2 socialization into school discourses and routines connected with questioning patterns, such as routine initiation-response-evaluation (IRE) interaction between teachers and students, may have much more in common structurally and pragmatically (apart from the actual lexical, grammatical, and phonological realizations) across certain cultures than socialization into vernacular versus scientific or legal discourse in the *same* language. Similarly, diglossic situations involving socialization into both 'low' (e.g. unofficial, informal, home) and 'high' (official, formal, public) versions of the same language have some parallels with bilingual and L2 socialization (see Heath 1983).

Benor (2004), for example, describes the second 'style' acquisition of newly orthodox Jews in Philadelphia, who, along with adopting new forms of dress, home décor, food, faith, and music, must also learn to understand and use loanwords from Hebrew and Yiddish and adopt linguistic patterns (grammatical, phonological) in their English that show traces of those languages, even when the newcomers do not have general proficiency in the source languages. Children growing up in other American subcultures, such as Hasidic communities in Brooklyn, or returnees to such cultures, similarly must learn the interactional routines sanctioned and socialized within those faith communities (signifying 'discourses of difference' and 'boundary maintenance') instead of those of the secular mainstream (Fader 2006, this volume), a situation found in many other religious enclaves as well. Thus, whereas the focus of such studies may not be L2 socialization *per se* (although liturgical Hebrew and Yiddish may be present and highly valued), this kind of socialization shares many features with socialization into a new language (L2), culture, and set of communicative and semiotic practices, ideologies, identities, and so on, even when mediated by English.

In what follows, I review studies of L2 socialization involving children, adolescents, and adults in Western and non-Western societies. Many of the studies are situated in schools, universities, or comparable educational programs involving European languages; fewer involve Asian languages or languages of other regions.

I explore theoretical issues that emerge when learners who have already acquired or are still in the process of acquiring a primary language and the cultural knowledge and practices associated with that language are expected to internalize the norms, preferences, and expectations associated with additional language(s) and culture(s) (Ochs and Schieffelin 2008). Some of the studies focus on certain indexical linguistic forms (e.g. address terms and honorifics; the use of deictic pronouns related to nation or group) or IRE sequences inculcated in learning communities (Ohta 1999; Rymes 2008). Others examine broader processes of how newcomers learn to participate more fully and competently in new communities, frequently drawing on Lave and Wenger's (1991) work on communities of practice (Duff 2007a).

Review of Research on Second Language Socialization

Because of the breadth of research in L2 socialization, which spans many continents (e.g. Africa, Europe, Asia, North America), age groups, educational contexts, and combinations of languages and cultures, and which in turn might focus on an ever-growing range of aspects of socialization (e.g. respect, identity, taste, morality, pragmatic routines, gender ideologies), this review is necessarily selective. Furthermore, several edited volumes and review articles describe L2 socialization processes and contexts in some detail, typically chronologically, from childhood to adolescence and adulthood, and across formal versus informal educational communities (Bayley and Schecter 2003; Baquedano-López and Kattan 2008; Duff 2003, 2008b, 2010a; chapters in Duff and Hornberger 2008; Duff and Talmy 2011; Watson-Gegeo 2004; Watson-Gegeo and Nielsen 2003; Zuengler and Cole 2005). Zuengler and Cole's (2005) review, for example, presents 17 studies of L2 socialization (broadly construed), 15 of which take place in formal education settings, typically in Canada or the United States and generally at the elementary and secondary-school levels. Many of the studies are ethnographies of communication that focus on the interactional routines that newcomers must internalize and learn to engage in well in order to succeed within the new cultures.

Negotiating competing linguistic ideologies, identities, and practices

A number of studies have examined the macro-societal contexts, ideologies, and processes of language socialization in bilingual and multilingual communities generally or in relation to specific micro-linguistic practices (e.g. Howard 2008). They have also looked at how L2 socialization in turn affects L1 socialization, and vice versa. It is important, therefore, not to examine L2 socialization in complete isolation or as independent from L1 socialization; indeed, as suggested earlier, at some stages it may be very difficult to determine which language is a person's L1 and which is their L2.

From their larger study of 40 Mexican-descent Hispanic families in California and Texas, Schecter and Bayley (1997) sought to uncover the language ideologies and practices of four families in relation to Spanish language and culture socialization. Language choice itself was considered identity work in light of the dominance and cachet of English in schools, wider society, and the media; the seemingly 'low-quality' Spanish and code-switching found within the local Mexican American community (according to parents); and the more sophisticated Spanish varieties that some families tried to preserve in their homes to offset the influence of either of these other linguistic codes and what they represented symbolically. Thus, the families' L1 socialization practices had to be seen in light of more pervasive L2 socialization practices and ideologies related to English and the children's academic trajectories and future possibilities in the United States as well as their links to their home country and language. In addition, because of the different levels of competence in L1 (Spanish) and L2 (English), children often had to act as brokers, helping to socialize their parents into English-medium activities and transactions.

Also related to Spanish socialization, but in a western Canadian context, Guardado (2008, 2009) examined how many parents in a Scouts group and in other grassroots sociocultural Spanish-medium organizations in metropolitan Vancouver actively reinforced language ideologies, identities, and language and literacy practices related to Spanish language maintenance by contrasting the relative benefits of using Spanish in home and group activities with use of English, the local dominant language. Sometimes the ideologies and practices were inconsistent, however – a phenomenon reported in other studies as well. Parents acting as group leaders might, for example, insist on the use of one language (Spanish), because of its beauty, as an act of resistance to English domination and for Hispanic community-building purposes but then proceed to use English for high-status speech activities such as reciting the Scouts' pledge, thereby inadvertently reproducing the dominance of English.

Other studies revealing the juxtaposition of L1 maintenance practices and L2 socialization have also described them in terms of national ideologies and identities (e.g. being 'good' Mexicans or Koreans or Chinese students, even when they had become US nationals) as well as linguistic ideologies. These studies have sometimes also documented how the newcomers (e.g. children learning Chinese or Korean) have tried to impose L2-related socializing practices and ideologies (of openness, fun, distributed power, American identity) on the so-called experts, their more conservative first-generation immigrant heritage language teachers, based on the children's English–L2-mediated schooling experiences in the United States (He 2004; Lo 2006). Tensions between national and classroom ideologies and identities associated with the two or more languages present in L2 socialization therefore manifest themselves in numerous ways. He and Lo revealed, for example, how the teachers in their studies positioned their students as Chinese or Korean (respectively), rather than American, using oppositional pronouns equivalent to 'us versus them,' even though the students were US citizens and often had been born and raised in the US as well.

Friedman (2006) similarly documented how children in post-Soviet Ukraine were being inducted by Ukrainian teachers into discourses and codes of difference and of 'correctness' (and Ukrainian purity and sovereignty) driven by Ukrainian nationalism also reflecting an 'us versus them' mentality. These ideologies opposed Russian language use in class, which indexed the legacy of Soviet occupation. Yet Russian was the home language (L1) or was used together with Ukrainian by many of the students and their families, in addition to having formerly been the official language of public schooling. Only one third of the students participating in Friedman's study were from 'homes where Ukrainian was used exclusively' (2006: 22). The socialization was part of what Friedman called (re)imagining the nation, socialization into the sort of idealized 'imagined community' described by Anderson (1991). Friedman (2010a) examined how teachers attempted to use classroom error correction routines, an important and ubiquitous mechanism for both L1 and L2 socialization, to eradicate Russian in favor of Ukrainian, in order to help children 'speak correctly,' thereby reinforcing the local ideologies.

In the same vein, Duff (1995, 1996) described how post-Soviet-era Hungarian students were being socialized into Hungarian versus 'Western' (i.e. Anglo-American) ideologies and discourse practices in Hungarian (L1)-medium and English (L2)-immersion classes, respectively, in the same subject areas (especially in history) within the same bilingual schools. Thus, the L1 and L2 socialization students may simultaneously experience can pull them in different philosophical and discursive directions and position them differently in other ways as well, beyond providing them simply with a wider repertoire of code choices and new forms of cultural knowledge.

One of the earliest publications on classroom L2 socialization, by Poole (1992), looked at ideologies of accommodation toward L2 learners, following the seminal early L1 research examining caregiver talk and issues of accommodation in speech directed at children in different cultures (Schieffelin and Ochs 1986). Poole examined how white middle-class English-as-a-second-language (ESL) instructors in an introductory-level US university course accommodated and socialized students through various interactional activities in English. Examples included certain question-answer routines and interactions in which teachers gave novices credit for tasks jointly accomplished by the teacher and student (using inclusive first-person pronouns as tasks were scaffolded by teachers followed by second-person pronouns to give credit to the students for completing the work that the teacher had actually assisted with). For example, a teacher would set up an activity saying 'describe the picture and see if we can make a story out of it' but then would evaluate students' contributions with 'Good work, you guys! That's hard! You did a good job' (1986: 605). Poole also documented the avoidance of 'overt displays of asymmetry' in teacher–student interaction in that culture, where inclusiveness, positive feedback, and experiences of success were valued.

A more recent study in Korean foreign language classes, also in the United States, shows how the opposite ideology of hierarchism and social asymmetry can prevail, as seen in an example of the socialization of students through highly stratified language forms in Korean (Byon 2006). In the first-year university classroom, the Korean teacher used particular sentence-final suffixes, assertive directives, and occupational titles (in lieu of a pronoun) whereas students were expected to produce humble first-person pronouns. Through implicit as well as more explicit socialization into the forms and functions of Korean honorifics, students were expected to learn the underlying cultural values of Korean politeness, formality, and social stratification.

Language socialization in multilingual communities

Some fascinating research has examined multilingual socialization in postcolonial settings, such as in the mountainous region of Northern Cameroon known as Maroua (Moore 1999, 2004). There, Fulbe children are socialized into multiple community languages, ideologies, and subjectivities; principal among these languages is Fulfulde (L1), the language of the home, which is complemented by French, the colonial language of public schooling, and Classical Arabic, taught at Qur'anic schools, which offer daily lessons in the morning, afternoon, or evening, depending on the public school schedule. In this community and across these three settings – domestic, secular, and religious – Moore focused on rote learning (guided repetition or recitation), or 'learning by heart'; how it was organized; and the cultural meanings it had for students (since they typically did not understand the literal meanings of the Arabic sacred texts or the French secular texts) and for their language socialization. Interestingly, each language also has a different orthography, which students needed to become literate in, and the content and form of the language socialization also differed: through folktales (at home), dialogues (at public school), and Koranic texts (at religious school). Each activity was accorded a great deal of time and apprenticeship, reflecting its importance in the lives and curriculum of the Fulbe. As the year progressed, the young students began to engage in the activities more capably as well.

Unfortunately, too little research on multilingual socialization, and particularly classroom L2 socialization, has examined non-European languages and cultures (Moore 2008). In that respect, Moore's work paves the way for more studies examining a potentially much wider range of speech events, participants, and languages. Other studies have examined, say, socialization into and through L2 Japanese either in North America or Japan (e.g. see review by Cook 2008a, 2008b; Kanagy 1999; Ohta 1994, 1999, 2001) or through Korean in the US (e.g. Byon 2006; Lo 2006), or into aspects of Indonesian related to taste for study-abroad students in Indonesia (Dufon 2006), but not typically in as linguistically, culturally, and ethnically as diverse a community as Maroua.

Yet, much recent work in urban areas of North America and the UK reflects a great deal of multilingual and multicultural diversity, as in Talmy's (2008) study of Micronesian students in Hawaii from various L1 and cultural backgrounds. Many of the students had already adopted Hawaii Creole English as their L2 lingua franca or vernacular but needed to learn Standard English in their secondary-school classes. Their observed resistance to classroom instruction and to ESL coursework was in part due to the way they felt positioned and stigmatized as 'fresh off the boat,' 'infantilized,' ESL speakers, outsiders or newcomers, or as remedial low-achieving students, even though many had been in Hawaii for many years and they were not newcomers at all. Talmy therefore characterizes the processes of students' L2 socialization in one particular school program as highly contingent and multidirectional (toward different norms, preferences, and expectations, particularly toward those of local Hawaiian islanders) and manifesting a variety of oppositional practices vis-à-vis the official curriculum and the essentialist subject position of 'ESL' present in the school and in their coursework (with ESL students in the same class treated as homogeneous in level and needs through an undifferentiated curriculum despite their enormous heterogeneity). Their oppositional practices, however, undermined their chances of succeeding either in institutionally valued Standard English linguistic and literacy genres and registers or in the school curriculum. Rymes and Anderson's (2004) case study of a young Spanish-speaking Costa Rican immigrant student in the United States and his African American classmate, who spoke a local vernacular of African American English, also illustrated how the two boys were differentially positioned linguistically and culturally through classroom interaction patterns to the detriment of the AAE-speaking student. The Spanish-speaker's background was validated but those of the local English-speaking minority students and their repertoires, identities, and desires were not, despite the teacher's commitment to creating a more educationally inclusive classroom.

Gender, social stratification, and second language socialization

Issues related to gender and L2 or bilingual socialization often come up in research, especially when the target language and culture gender norms and practices contrast dramatically with those in students' L1 or when their new ways of speaking (in L2) and their new social groups might position them unfavorably in gendered terms or their gendered cultural sensibilities might preclude greater levels of participation in particular social practices (e.g. mixed-sex language classrooms for learners accustomed to segregation). Contemporary gendered language socialization research and theory eschew reified or essentialized norms, practices, and categories associated with gender, although such categories may in fact emerge emically and interactionally from discourse practices (Kyratzis and Cook-Gumperz 2008). Yet, within the confines of their social groups, participants may nonetheless knowingly transgress norms and stereotypes related to language and gender for various social reasons.

Fader (2000, 2001) describes gendered expectations concerning language choice and ideology in US Hasidic girls' and boys' learning, maintenance, and use of Yiddish – and also notes school-aged girls' resistance to Yiddish as their working vernacular instead of English. Girls maintain Yiddish as a formal, respectful, religious register (or register of Baby Talk and code directed to Yiddish-dominant males) and accommodate increasingly to English. English, the dominant (and secular) societal language, is also typically their mothers' and female peers' dominant language, marking nonreproduction across generations but also conservativism – to index differences between them and males, who are more immersed in the everyday study and use of Yiddish and Hebrew. The boys, conversely, attempt to socialize their mothers into greater use of Yiddish in the home as a marker of piety, Jewish (Hasidic) identity, morality, and tradition, based on the boys' religious schooling in Yiddish.

Willett (1995), in her year-long ethnography of the English–L2 socialization of young first-grade boys and girls in a US school, noted how gender norms seemed to affect one Mexican American boy's opportunities for success with English in that classroom. They also had an impact on his social status with boys in the class because the teacher expected him to do phonics work with two local girls he was seated between, which he did not want to do. Girls in the class preferred to talk, work, and play with other girls, and boys with boys, and crossing those boundaries was scorned by peers. Isolated, he therefore sought out more assistance from the teacher or assistants, thus positioning him as a 'needy' child. Conversely, the three focal girls in Willett's study who worked together productively earned high praise from their teacher for their resourcefulness and independence and their close friendships were viewed favorably by their female peers. Willett also noted how the research practices themselves inadvertently became constrained by gender because boys in the study refused to wear micro tape recorders in a harness device that the girls had begun to call their 'ET baby.'

In languages highly differentiated for gender and other aspects of social membership and hierarchy (such as Korean, as we saw earlier), L2 learners may face other challenges and dilemmas. For example, in Siegal's (1994) study of adult Western women learning Japanese in Japan, she noted that some of the learners resisted the highly feminized polite forms of language involving high pitch and other feminized intonation and lexical and grammatical conventions as well as nonlinguistic dispositions (e.g. bowing deeply). Normally these aspects of Japanese sociolinguistics would be required at advanced levels in formal public interactions. However, the Western learners opted for simpler, more gender-neutral language instead. They believed that the practices expected of Japanese women clashed with language and gender ideologies from their own cultural backgrounds and experiences and that independent, strong Western women should not adopt and perform aspects of a language and culture that would position them as subordinate. Many Japanese women, for precisely that reason, choose to study L2 English as adults because it offers them gender identities and opportunities often unavailable to them in Japanese study or work contexts (Duff and Uchida 1997; Kobayashi 2002).

Some learners of Japanese, however, may be less conscious of either their adoption or non-use of socially significant discourse markers or morphology. Cook's (2008b) book on Japanese L2 learning, *Socializing Identities through Speech Style*, examines the levels of formality, politeness, and honorifics (particularly as indexed by the *–masu* verbal suffix or the *desu* copula versus 'plain forms' found in informal conversations) that students of Japanese are expected to emulate but often misuse. Cook tracked nine students in their year abroad studying Japanese in Japan and living with host families, focusing on the families' and students' Japanese dinnertime conversations in particular. She examined the (indexical) social functions played by *–masu* and students' differential appropriation of (and metalinguistic awareness of) correct usage by means of their formal and informal socialization in foreign language study contexts in the United States and then in Japan, relating usage ultimately to aspects of identity as well.

Other reviews of L2 socialization and gender (e.g. Gordon 2008; Pavlenko and Piller 2008) point to challenges for L2 learners not related to *formal* aspects of language but to *access* to L2 social interaction and assistance at school, work, or in other social spheres, particularly for women (Norton 2000). In some cases, however, women may have opportunities for access to a high-status L2 but may not avail themselves of those opportunities. One deterrent might be fear of negative perceptions of them within their home culture if they become too proficient in their L2. Goldstein (1997), for example, found that Portuguese-Canadian women at a Toronto-area manufacturing company commonly opted *not* to participate in English L2 socialization through workplace programs that might offer them opportunities for advancement precisely because it would endanger the solidarity they enjoyed with their Portuguese female co-workers, their 'sisters' on the factory floor. Moreover, courses might inadvertently also position female L2 learners in disadvantageous ways, for example as 'homemakers' rather than 'professionals' (Menard-Warwick 2007). Access to L2 socialization is by no means constrained by gender issues and social roles alone, though; it may also be constrained by perceived status and positioning in society and a sense of entitlement and legitimacy, by proficiency, and by resource constraints (time, money, social capital, child care).

Second language socialization through virtual communities and online practices

A burgeoning area of research for children, adolescents, and adult L2 learners in both diaspora and nondiaspora settings examines how digital technologies and virtual interaction mediate the learning of language and culture. Sometimes the digital practices in L2 contexts involve code-switching and innovative multimodal literacy practices. Lam (2004), for example, observed how immigrant Chinese L1 students in the United States joined an online community of other Chinese-background users of English worldwide that incorporated English and different varieties of oral and written Chinese (and other semiotic systems, such as emoticons) in their chatroom discussions. Over time, the two focal participants in her study became socialized into hybrid identities and linguistic and textual practices as a result, to their great satisfaction. (See Lam (2008) for a review of other studies of online L2 socialization.)

Thorne, Black, and Sykes (2009) described socialization through the affordances of digital tools for L2 learners into voluntary (or, as they call them, 'digital vernacular') 'fan fiction and virtual diaspora community spaces' or virtual worlds (e.g. 'Second Life') as well as through online games in the Web 2.0 environment. They describe a number of studies illustrating how English L2 learners can be socialized into and through digital narratives based on popular culture (e.g. based on fan fiction; Black 2005). Often, like Lam's learners, they incorporate a variety of other linguistic forms, symbol systems, and orthographies from their L1 to create hybrid texts, reflecting and performing their hybrid linguistic identities and investments.

Second language socialization and discourse at work

As is the case in the L1 socialization literature, less L2 socialization research to date has been conducted with adults in or seeking entry into workplaces (see Duff 2008a for a review) than of L2 socialization of youths in formal educational contexts. Roberts (2010) synthesized several decades of workplace-oriented language socialization research, much of it conducted by her and her colleagues. For example, research on people seeking employment in England identified the 'institutional' and 'personal' discourses and contextualizing cues that foreign-born workers need to master (i.e. be socialized into) to succeed in job interviews (Campbell and Roberts 2007). But Li (2000), based on her research on L2 pragmatic socialization in a US Chinatown workplace context, noted that the native-speaker co-workers who would otherwise be expected to serve as a helpful resource to newcomers sometimes behaved inconsistently and in a sociolinguistically inappropriate manner by acting rudely to their novice co-workers, demonstrating that they themselves were not pragmatically sophisticated in workplace language use, although they did assist the learners with some aspects of their L2 use, such as requesting behaviors. Vickers (2007) demonstrated how workplace ideologies and cultures related to social practices (project work, team interaction) inculcated in the engineering profession affected how new engineering students were being socialized through their L2 into the valued discourse, interaction, and identities by students senior to them.

Second language socialization and academic discourse

One major area of my own (and others') L2 socialization research over the last two decades has been socialization into academic discourse in bilingual (especially 'foreign language') and multilingual (L2) settings, typically in content-area classrooms (as opposed to language courses) mediated by the L2 (see review in Duff 2010b). Some of this work has been at the secondary-school level (e.g. Duff 1995, 1996, 2002, 2003, 2004) and some of it at the postsecondary level (Duff, Wong, and Early 2000; Duff 2007a, 2007b). The earlier work (1990s) was situated in Hungary and the more recent work in a western Canadian high school and university. Underlying this research is the desire to understand the kinds of academic cultures or discourse communities newcomers enter into that are mediated, and indeed discursively constructed by, oral and written language and other semiotic tools, and the linguistic and nonlinguistic forms and practices students need to participate successfully in the new communities according to local norms and expectations. I have focused on particular speech events, such as oral recitations, presentations, and discussions of classroom films and of current events, to see how students are socialized over time and often across course contexts with respect to language, discourse, and content (Duff 1995, 2002, 2009).

Academic discourse in this work is part of dynamic, situated sociocultural processes that are often multimodal and also multilingual. It is characterized by variable amounts and uptake of modeling and feedback, variable levels of investment and agency on the part of learners, behind-the-scenes (out-of-class) as well as in-class power-plays, and variable outcomes – both in the shorter and longer term (see Duff 2007b). My (former) graduate students (e.g. Kobayashi 2003; Morita 2000, 2004; Morita and Kobayashi 2008; Zappa-Hollman 2007a, 2007b) and I first examined *oral* discourse but then turned to *written* discourse as well, both in written online communication in mixed-mode graduate courses (Yim 2005, 2011; see also Potts 2005) and in more traditional textual practices in undergraduate and graduate courses, such as written assignments, which instructors must assess (Séror 2008; 2009).

The basic sorts of questions this research addresses are: how do newcomers to an academic culture, especially L2 learners, learn how to participate appropriately in the oral and written discourse and related practices associated with that discourse community? How are they explicitly or implicitly inducted or socialized into these local discursive practices? How does interaction with their peers, instructors, tutors, and others facilitate the process of gaining expertise in those practices? And how do the practices and norms themselves evolve over time and across practitioners, given the cultural and historical context of the local community of practice? Our methodology has usually involved an ethnography of communication with an analysis of discourse from observations, interviews, and other document sources although some studies have been more interview-based.

Depending on the course context and educational culture, within the sphere of oral discourse in a formal presentation mode students may be socialized, explicitly, to present concise and fluent summaries of course content or news reports (Duff 1996, 2009) or, rather, they may be asked to slow their pace of presentation so other students are better able to understand them, seek clarification, and take notes (Duff 1995); they are thus accommodating to their peers. They may be asked to explain why a particular topic (e.g. a newsworthy current event, an academic article to critique) is meaningful to them, to explain its larger social (or intellectual) significance and possible controversies associated with it, or to explain how it relates to the course content (Duff 2009). They may be socialized into a presentation mode that requires striking a careful balance between (1) conveying their role as a novice in a graduate student program with particular interests and experiences and (2) fulfilling the expectation that they should be able to demonstrate adequate authority and expertise with respect to the material they are presenting (without appearing arrogant), based on their careful preparation, even when an article being presented and critiqued may be written by the instructor herself (Morita 2000). In some disciplinary contexts students might need to be very

tentative in their conclusions, whereas in others they might need to be very definitive and authoritative (Zappa-Hollman 2007a). They must find ways to establish
and demonstrate rapport with the audience (their peers) throughout the presentation and the ensuing discussion phase but also meet the demands or instructional
objectives of their instructor. Finally, they must be able to use both language and
media effectively, whether in PowerPoint presentations, slides, or using other
tools, but not normally with recourse to a full written script (which they nonetheless must also prepare as another part of the assignment); therefore, the ability to
move seamlessly between oral, written, and graphic texts effectively while still
maintaining an appropriate physical presence and eye contact with the audience
is key. Most of all, they must often perform these activities in another language
and possibly in a genre that is completely unfamiliar to them based on their prior
(e.g. L1) academic socialization. However, without explicit socialization about
how best to manage the activity and without adequate feedback on performances,
students may invest large amounts of time with relatively little payoff in terms of
actual learning or success (Duff 2010b; Zappa-Hollman 2007a).

    Although much of the research our team has conducted, collectively, has
involved solo presentations across a wide range of academic content areas and
levels of study (high school, undergraduate, graduate; neuroscience, history, engineering), group presentations have also been examined (Duff and Kobayashi
2010). Group activity increases the social complexity of the undertaking because
students must first choose partners or be assigned to groups, confirm the nature
of the task before them, then negotiate their roles (identities), responsibilities,
expertise, and preferences with others in advance of the presentation (Kobayashi
2003, 2004), often using more than one language. In Duff and Kobayashi (2010),
for example, we describe how, in a study of Japanese university students' pair or
small-group presentations at a Canadian university, students were socialized by
their instructor and by one another into certain practices related to L1 versus L2
use, into effective PowerPoint slide preparation including the joint production of
accurate English grammar, and into the pragmatics of building rapport with the
instructor and their classmates through the use of humor, irony, and rhetorical
questions, in addition to other substantive aspects of the content being presented.
Such activities (speech events) therefore embody a large amount of sociocultural,
linguistic, and discursive knowledge as well as procedural knowledge about effective enactments and interpersonal pragmatics before, during, and after the presentation. They also entail a great deal of identity work and social positioning (see
also Morita 2000, 2004).

    One of the common findings in our research has been the contingencies involved
in oral academic socialization: how previous students' presentations affect the
present ones; how one's presentation last time, or in another course, may affect
the current performance; how the point in the term or the point in that day's class,
and how the number of other presentations scheduled the same day, and many
additional factors (allocated time, rehearsal, success memorizing a script in some
cases) may also affect the resulting performance. As Zappa-Hollman's (2007a) and
Morita's (2000) research shows, L2 socialization and expectations regarding
optimal performance may vary considerably across courses within the same

department and field (e.g. in applied linguistics) and across disciplines (e.g. history and anthropology versus neuroscience and biochemistry) in different faculties, each with their own traditions (cf. Jacoby 1998). Second language students often find such presentations intimidating and very challenging. As one graduate student, a first-year MSc student in biochemistry from India in Zappa-Hollman's research, reported (2007a: 481, emphasis added by Zappa-Hollman: interview, Sohan):

> For me, presentation in this seminar meant huge – it's like a thesis defense. *Life or death.* If today I would have screwed up there, maybe there would have been a negative effect on my psyche which would have never permitted me in giving other lectures, no matter how well prepared I am.

Related to oral presentations, and often a necessary segment following a presentation and a normal part of classroom lectures as well, is teacher- or student-led discussion. Interactionally, leading or participating in class discussion requires an entirely different repertoire of skills and resources and – whether it is for a class situation, a thesis defense, or a conference presentation – requires socialization into the relevant disciplinary norms and practices of the discourse community. In my high-school-based research in Canada (Duff 2002, 2004), the discussion phase seemed inevitably to incorporate quick-paced, apparently freewheeling nonacademic references to a wide variety of pop culture texts, from television (e.g. *The Simpsons, Friends*), music, sports, the internet, and other media. Thus, students were being socialized into highly intertextual discourse, involving the lamination of academic and nonacademic texts, content, and references. Again, considerable identity work was involved. For L2 students, especially relative newcomers to Canada, this form of discourse was particularly difficult to comprehend and engage in since it was such an unfamiliar, blended genre and register, and presupposed a great deal of knowledge of Anglo-Canadian and US popular culture as well as proficiency in English.

Another form of discussion into which students may need to be socialized involves not just in-class synchronous oral interaction but online asynchronous threaded discussion via course bulletin boards and websites. Second language newcomers to this mode of participation may be socialized by the instructor, but practices are also often based on the development of the preferences of classmates about appropriate genres, social roles, and other conventions (length and frequency of posting, degree of formality, degree of interactivity) (see Yim 2005; 2011). These practices, conventions, and preferences may also change over time (Potts 2005). The blending of aspects of both oral and written language in such discourse and its interdiscursivity as well as intertextuality provides many possibilities for L2 (and L1) socialization research (Duff 2004).

Finally, our team has more recently examined aspects of written discourse socialization (Duff 2010b), following earlier work by Atkinson and Ramanathan (1995), Casanave (2002), Prior (1998), and Spack (1997), among many others. We are particularly interested in the formal and informal socialization provided by instructors on students' assignments (e.g. in the margins or at the end of texts, whether handwritten, typed online, or delivered orally through face-to-face writing conferences). However, the quality, quantity, and potential effectiveness of this socialization must be seen in light of the institutional sociopolitical and economic constraints on what feedback can be provided and also the messages the feedback conveys (when legible) about the student's ideas, language, discourse, and discipline, and about what it means to be a competent student in that course and domain. Unfortunately, as Séror (2008) has demonstrated, this 'socialization in the margins' is all too often ineffective for L2 learners: when handwritten, the feedback might be inaccessible (illegible, incomprehensible, or long delayed) and comments often position students as incompetent or illegitimate (e.g. as 'non-native speakers') without providing scaffolding that would help them to become more competent or without attending to the substance of their ideas rather than superficial linguistic aspects.

Conclusion

Research on L2 socialization occurs in many of the same domains and involves issues similar to those in L1 socialization but often compounded by multiple modes of communication, by the interplay of multiple languages, by a variety of media, and by a great deal of prior lived experience. More of the L2 research seems to be situated in educational settings, the typical context in which students learn an additional language and must use it for other kinds of learning, including in higher education. Second language socialization is yet one other dimension of learning across the lifespan for many people in modern society (as well as in more traditional multilingual societies), one that is often assumed by nonspecialists and by learners themselves, initially, to be a relatively straightforward linear process that can be completed within a short period of time. As research has shown, however, for many learners it is a frustrating, complicated, and often unexpectedly protracted process that they have inadequate resources to assist them with: insufficient numbers of willing and competent experts to socialize and apprentice them effectively into the communities or networks of practice they seek membership and competence in; insufficient time to devote to additional linguistic and cultural challenges on top of other academic, vocational, or personal ones; and multiple, sometimes competing, roles and identities in society that preclude a greater investment in the process or greater parsimony across the activities and languages of their complex lives. Given more positive conditions, however, L2 socialization can open up new worlds, new practices, and new possibilities.

REFERENCES

Anderson, B. R. (1991) *Imagined Communities: Reflections on the Origin and Spread of Nationalism*. 2nd ed. London: Verso.

Atkinson, D. and Ramanathan, V. (1995) 'Cultures of writing': An ethnographic comparison of L1 and L2 university writing programs. *TESOL Quarterly* 29: 539–68.

Baquedano-López, P. and Kattan, S. (2008) Language socialization and schooling. In P. A. Duff and N. H. Hornberger (eds.), *Encyclopedia of Language and Education, Vol. 8: Language Socialization.* 161–73. New York: Springer.

Bayley, R. and Schecter, S. (eds.) (2003) *Language Socialization in Bilingual and Multilingual Societies.* Clevedon, UK: Multilingual Matters.

Benor, S. B. (2004) *Second Style Acquisition: The Linguistic Socialization of Newly Orthodox Jews.* Doctoral Dissertation. Palo Alto, CA: Stanford University.

Black, R. W. (2005) Access and affiliation: The literacy and composition practices of English-language learners in an online fanfiction community. *Journal of Adolescent and Adult Literacy* 49(2): 118–28.

Bronson, M. and Watson-Gegeo, K. A. (2008) The critical moment: Language socialization and the (re)visioning of first and second language learning. In P. A. Duff and N. H. Hornberger (eds.), *Encyclopedia of Language and Education, Vol. 8: Language Socialization.* 43–56. New York: Springer.

Byon, A. S. (2006) Language socialization in Korean-as-a-foreign-language classrooms. *Bilingual Research Journal* 30: 265–91.

Campbell, S. and Roberts, C. (2007) Migration, ethnicity and competing discourses in the job interview: Synthesizing the institutional and personal. *Discourse & Society* 18: 243–72.

Casanave, C. P. (2002) *Writing Games: Multicultural Case Studies of Academic Literacy Practices in Higher Education.* Mahwah, NJ: Lawrence Erlbaum.

Cook, H. M. (2008a) Language socialization in Japanese. In P. A. Duff and N. H. Hornberger (eds.), *Encyclopedia of Language and Education, Vol. 8: Language Socialization.* 313–26. New York: Springer.

Cook, H. M. (2008b) *Socializing Identities Through Speech Style: Learners of Japanese as a Foreign Language.* Bristol, UK: Multilingual Matters.

Duff, P. A. (1995) An ethnography of communication in immersion classrooms in Hungary. *TESOL Quarterly* 29: 505–37.

Duff, P. A. (1996) Different languages, different practices: Socialization of discourse competence in dual-language school classrooms in Hungary. In K. M. Bailey and D. Nunan (eds.), *Voices from the Language Classroom: Qualitative Research in Second Language Acquisition.* 407–33. New York: Cambridge University Press.

Duff, P. A. (2002) The discursive construction of knowledge, identity, and difference: An ethnography of communication in the high school mainstream. *Applied Linguistics* 23: 289–322.

Duff, P. A. (2003) New directions in second language socialization research. *Korean Journal of English Language and Linguistics* 3: 309–39.

Duff, P. A. (2004) Intertextuality and hybrid discourses: The infusion of pop culture in educational discourse. *Linguistics and Education* 14: 231–76.

Duff, P. A. (2007a) Second language socialization as sociocultural theory: Insights and issues. *Language Teaching* 40: 309–19.

Duff, P. A. (2007b) Problematising academic discourse socialisation. In H. Marriott, T. Moore, and R. Spence-Brown (eds.), *Discourses of Learning and Learning of Discourses.* 1–18. Sydney, Australia: Monash University e-Press/ University of Sydney Press.

Duff, P. A. (2008a) Language socialization, higher education, and work. In P. A. Duff and N. H. Hornberger (eds.), *Encyclopedia of Language and Education, Vol. 8: Language Socialization.* 257–70. New York: Springer.

Duff, P. A. (2008b) Language socialization, participation and identity: Ethnographic approaches. In M. Martin-Jones, A.-M.

de Mejia, and N. H. Hornberger (eds.), *Encyclopedia of Language and Education, Vol. 3: Discourse and Education*. 107–19. New York: Springer.

Duff, P. A. (2009) Language socialization in a Canadian secondary school: Talking about current events. In R. Barnard and M. Torres-Guzman (eds.), *Creating Communities of Learning in Schools*. 165–85. Clevedon, UK: Multilingual Matters.

Duff, P. A. (2010a) Language socialization. In N. H. Hornberger and S. McKay (eds.), *Sociolinguistics and Language Education*. 427–55. Bristol, UK: Multilingual Matters.

Duff, P. A. (2010b) Language socialization into academic discourse communities. *Annual Review of Applied Linguistics* 31: 169–92.

Duff, P., Anderson, T., Ilnyckyj, R., Lester, E., Wang, R., and Yates, E. (forthcoming) *Learning Chinese: Linguistic, Sociocultural, and Narrative Perspectives*. Berlin and New York: De Gruyter Mouton.

Duff, P. A. and Hornberger, N. H. (eds.) (2008) *Encyclopedia of Language and Education, Vol. 8: Language Socialization*. New York: Springer.

Duff, P. A. and Kobayashi, M. (2010) The intersection of social, cognitive, and cultural processes in language learning: A second language socialization approach. In R. Batstone (ed.), *Sociocognition and Second Language Learning*. 75–93. Oxford: Oxford University Press.

Duff, P. A. and Talmy, S. (2011) Language socialization approaches to second language acquisition: Social, cultural, and linguistic development in additional languages. In D. Atkinson (ed.), *Alternative Approaches to Second Language Acquisition*. 95–116. London: Routledge.

Duff, P. A. and Uchida, Y. (1997) The negotiation of sociocultural identity in post-secondary EFL classrooms. *TESOL Quarterly* 31: 451–86.

Duff, P. A., Wong, P., and Early, M. (2000) Learning language for work and life: The linguistic socialization of immigrant Canadians seeking careers in healthcare. *Canadian Modern Language Review* 57: 9–57.

Dufon, M. (2006) The socialization of taste during study-abroad in Indonesia. In M. Dufon and C. Eton (eds.), *Language Learners in Study Abroad Contexts*. 91–119. Clevedon, UK: Multilingual Matters.

Ellis, R. (2008) *The Study of Second Language Acquisition*. 2nd ed. Oxford: Oxford University Press.

Erting, C. J. and Kuntze, M. (2008) Language socialization in Deaf communities. In P. A. Duff and N. H. Hornberger (eds.), *Encyclopedia of Language and Education, Vol. 8: Language Socialization*. 287–300. New York: Springer.

Fader, A. (2000) *Gender, Morality, and Language: Socialization Practices in a Hasidic Community*. Doctoral Dissertation. New York: New York University.

Fader, A. (2001) Literacy, bilingualism, and gender in a Hasidic community. *Linguistics and Education* 12: 261–83.

Fader, A. (2006) Learning faith: Language socialization in a community of Hasidic Jews. *Language in Society* 35: 205–29.

Friedman, D. (2006) *(Re)Imagining the Nation: Language Socialization in Ukrainian Classrooms*. Doctoral Dissertation. Los Angeles, CA: University of California, Los Angeles.

Friedman, D. (2010a) Speaking correctly: Error correction as a language socialization practice in a Ukrainian classroom. *Applied Linguistics* 31(3): 346–67.

Friedman, D. (2010b) Becoming national: Classroom language socialization and political identities in the age of globalization. *Annual Review of Applied Linguistics* 31: 193–210.

Garrett, P. B. (2007) Language socialization and the (re)production of bilingual subjectivities. In M. Heller (ed.), *Bilingualism: A Social Approach.* 233–56. New York: Palgrave Macmillan.

Garrett, P. B. and Baquedano-López, P. (2002) Language socialization: Reproduction and continuity, transformation and change. *Annual Review of Anthropology* 31: 339–61.

Goldstein, T. (1997) *Two Languages at Work: Bilingual Life on the Production Floor.* New York: Mouton de Gruyter.

Gordon, D. (2008) Gendered second language socialization. In P. Duff and N. H. Hornberger (eds.), *Encyclopedia of Language and Education, Vol. 8: Language Socialization.* 231–42. New York: Springer.

Guardado, M. (2008) *Language Socialization in Canadian Hispanic Communities: Ideologies and Practices.* Doctoral Dissertation. Vancouver, BC: University of British Columbia.

Guardado, M. (2009) Speaking Spanish like a boy scout: Language socialization, resistance and reproduction in a Spanish language scout troop. *Canadian Modern Language Review* 66: 101–29.

He, A. W. (2004) CA for SLA: Arguments from the Chinese language classroom. *Modern Language Journal* 88: 568–82.

He, A. W. (2008) Heritage language learning and socialization. In P. A. Duff and N. H. Hornberger (eds.), *Encyclopedia of Language and Education, Vol. 8: Language Socialization.* 201–13. New York: Springer.

Heath, S. B. (1983) *Ways with Words: Language, Life, and Work in Communities and Classrooms.* New York: Cambridge University Press.

Howard, K. M. (2008) Language socialization and language shift among school-aged children. In P. A. Duff and N. H. Hornberger (eds.), *Encyclopedia of Language and Education, Vol. 8: Language Socialization.* 187–99. New York: Springer.

Jacoby, S. (1998) *Science as Performance: Socializing Scientific Discourse through the Conference Talk Rehearsal.* Doctoral Dissertation. Los Angeles, CA: University of California, Los Angeles.

Kanagy, R. (1999) The socialization of Japanese immersion kindergartners through interactional routines. *Journal of Pragmatics* 31: 1467–92.

Kobayashi, M. (2003) The role of peer support in students' accomplishment of oral academic tasks. *Canadian Modern Language Review* 59: 337–68.

Kobayashi, M. (2004) *A Sociocultural Study of Second Language Tasks: Activity, Agency, and Language Socialization.* Doctoral Dissertation. Vancouver, BC: University of British Columbia.

Kobayashi, Y. (2002) The role of gender in foreign language learning attitudes: Japanese female students' attitudes toward learning English. *Gender and Education* 14: 181–97.

Kramsch, C. (ed.). (2002) *Language Acquisition and Language Socialization: Ecological Perspectives.* London: Continuum.

Kulick, D. and Schieffelin, B. B. (2004) Language socialization. In A. Duranti (ed.), *A Companion to Linguistic Anthropology.* 349–68. Malden, MA: Blackwell.

Kyratzis, A. and Cook-Gumperz, J. (2008) Language socialization and gendered practices in childhood. In P. A. Duff and N. H. Hornberger (eds.), *Encyclopedia of Language and Education, Vol. 8: Language Socialization.* 145–57. New York: Springer.

Lam, W. S. E. (2004) Second language socialization in a bilingual chat room: Global and local considerations. *Language Learning and Technology* 8: 44–65.

Lam, W. S. E. (2008) Language socialization in online communities. In P. A. Duff and N. H. Hornberger (eds.), *Encyclopedia of Language and Education, Vol. 8: Language Socialization.* 301–11. New York: Springer.

Lave, J. and Wenger, E. (1991) *Situated Learning: Legitimate Peripheral Participation.* New York: Cambridge University Press.

Li, D. (2000) The pragmatics of making requests in the L2 workplace: A case study of language socialization. *Canadian Modern Language Review* 57: 58–87.

Lo, A. (2006) Becoming 'Korean people': Socializing and challenging ethnonational identities at a Korean heritage language school. Paper presented at the American Association for Applied Linguistics. Montreal, QC.

Menard-Warwick, J. (2007) 'Because she made beds. Every day.' Social positioning, classroom discourse, and language learning. *Applied Linguistics* 29: 267–89.

Moore, L. C. (1999) Language socialization research and French language education in Africa: A Cameroonian case study. *Canadian Modern Language Review* 56: 329–50.

Moore, L. C. (2004) *Learning Languages by Heart: Second Language Socialization in a Fulbe Community*. Doctoral Dissertation. Los Angeles, CA: University of California, Los Angeles.

Moore, L. C. (2008) Language socialization and second/foreign language and multilingual education in non-Western settings. In P. A. Duff and N. H. Hornberger (eds.), *Encyclopedia of Language and Education, Vol. 8: Language Socialization*. 175–85. New York: Springer.

Morita, N. (2000) Discourse socialization through oral classroom activities in a TESL graduate program. *TESOL Quarterly* 34: 279–310.

Morita, N. (2004) Negotiating participation and identity in second language academic communities. *TESOL Quarterly* 38: 573–603.

Morita, N. and Kobayashi, M. (2008) Academic discourse socialization in a second language. In P. A. Duff and N. H. Hornberger (eds.), *Encyclopedia of Language and Education, Vol. 8: Language Socialization*. 243–56. New York: Springer.

Norton, B. (2000) *Identity and Language Learning: Gender, Ethnicity, and Educational Change*. Harlow, UK: Pearson Education.

Ochs, E. (1986) Introduction. In B. B. Schieffelin and E. Ochs (eds.), *Language Socialization Across Cultures*. 1–13. New York: Cambridge University Press.

Ochs, E. and Schieffelin, B. B. (2008) Language socialization: An historical overview. In P. A. Duff and N. H. Hornberger (eds.), *Encyclopedia of Language and Education, Vol. 8: Language Socialization*. 3–15. New York: Springer.

Ohta, A. (1994) Socializing the expression of affect: An overview of affective particle use in the Japanese as a foreign language classroom. *Issues in Applied Linguistics* 5: 303–25.

Ohta, A. (1999) Interactional routines and the socialization of interactional style in adult learners of Japanese. *Journal of Pragmatics* 31: 1493–512.

Ohta, A. (2001) *Second Language Acquisition Process in the Classroom: Learning Japanese*. Mahwah, NJ: Lawrence Erlbaum.

Pavlenko, A. and Piller, I. (2008) Language education and gender. In S. May and N. H. Hornberger (eds.), *Encyclopedia of Language and Education, Vol. 8: Language Policy and Political Issues in Education*. 57–69. New York: Springer.

Pesco, D. and Crago, M. (2008) Language socialization in Canadian Aboriginal communities. In P. A. Duff and N. H. Hornberger (eds.), *Encyclopedia of Language and Education, Vol. 8: Language Socialization*. 273–85. New York: Springer.

Poole, D. (1992) Language socialization in the second language classroom. *Language Learning* 42: 593–616

Potts, D. (2005) Pedagogy, purpose, and the second language learner in on-line communities. *Canadian Modern Language Review* 62: 137–60.

Prior, P. A. (1998) *Writing/Disciplinarity: A Sociohistoric Account of Literate Activity in the Academy*. Mahwah, NJ: Lawrence Erlbaum.

Rampton, B. (1995) *Crossing: Language and Ethnicity Among Adolescents*. London: Longman.

Rampton, B. (1999) Deutsch in inner London and the animation of an instructed foreign language. *Journal of Sociolinguistics* 3/4: 480–504.

Rampton, B. (2006) *Language in Late Modernity: Interaction in an Urban School.* Cambridge: Cambridge University Press.

Roberts, C. (2010) Language socialization in the workplace. *Annual Review of Applied Linguistics* 31: 211–27.

Rymes, B. (1997) Second language socialization: A new approach to second language acquisition research. *Journal of Intensive English Studies* 11(1/2): 143–55.

Rymes, B. (2008) Language socialization and the linguistic anthropology of education. In P. Duff and N. H. Hornberger (eds.), *Encyclopedia of Language and Education, Vol. 8: Language Socialization.* 29–42. New York: Springer.

Rymes, B. and Anderson, K. (2004) Second language acquisition for all: Understanding the interactional dynamics of classrooms in which Spanish and AAE are spoken. *Research in the Teaching of English* 39(2): 107–35.

Rymes, B. and Pash, D. (2001) Questioning identity: The case of one second-language learner. *Anthropology and Education Quarterly* 32: 276–300.

Schecter, S. R. and Bayley, R. (1997) Language socialization practices and cultural identity: Case studies of Mexican-descent families in California and Texas. *TESOL Quarterly* 31: 513–42.

Schieffelin, B. B. and Ochs, E. (eds.) (1986) *Language Socialization Across Cultures.* Cambridge: Cambridge University Press.

Séror, J. (2008) *Socialization in the Margins: Second Language Writers and Feedback Practices in University Content Courses.* Doctoral Dissertation. Vancouver, BC: University of British Columbia.

Séror, J. (2009) Institutional forces and L2 writing feedback in higher education. *Canadian Modern Language Review* 66: 203–32.

Siegal, M. (1994) *Looking East: Learning Japanese as a Second Language in Japan and the Interaction of Race, Gender and Social Context.* Doctoral Dissertation. Berkeley, CA: University of California, Berkeley.

Spack, R. (1997) The acquisition of academic literacy in a second language: A longitudinal case study. *Written Communication* 14: 3–62.

Talmy, S. (2008) The cultural productions of ESL student at Tradewinds High: Contingency, multidirectionality, and identity in L2 socialization. *Applied Linguistics* 29: 619–44.

Thorne, S. L., Black, R. W., and Sykes, J. (2009) Second language use, socialization, and learning in internet interest communities and online games. *Modern Language Journal* 93: 802–21.

Vickers, C. (2007) Second language socialization through team interaction among electrical and computer engineering students. *Modern Language Journal* 91: 621–40.

Watson-Gegeo, K. A. (2004) Mind, language, and epistemology: Toward a language socialization paradigm for SLA. *The Modern Language Journal* 88: 331–50.

Watson-Gegeo, K. A. and Nielsen, S. (2003) Language socialization in SLA. In C. Doughty and M. Long (eds.), *The Handbook of Second Language Acquisition.* 155–77. Malden, MA: Blackwell.

Willett, J. (1995) Becoming first graders in an L2: An ethnographic study of language socialization. *TESOL Quarterly* 29: 473–503.

Yim, Y. K. K. (2005) *Second Language Speakers' Participation in Computer-Mediated Discussions in Graduate Seminars.* Doctoral Dissertation. Vancouver, BC: University of British Columbia.

Yim, Y. K. K. (2011) Second language students' discourse socialization in academic online communities. *Canadian Modern Language Review* 67: 1–27.

Zappa-Hollman, S. (2007a) Becoming socialized into diverse academic communities through oral presentations. *Canadian Modern Language Review* 63: 455–85.

Zappa-Hollman, S. (2007b) *The Academic Literacy Socialization of Mexican Exchange Students at a Canadian University*. Doctoral Dissertation. Vancouver, BC: University of British Columbia.

Zuengler, J. and Cole, K.-M. (2005) Language socialization and L2 learning. In E. Hinkel (ed.), *Handbook of Research in Second Language Teaching and Learning*. 301–16. Mahwah, NJ: Lawrence Erlbaum.

25 Heritage Language Socialization

AGNES WEIYUN HE

Locating Heritage Language Development in a Research Tradition

The term 'heritage language' (HL) refers to a language that is often used at or inherited from home and that is different from the language used in mainstream society. A HL may delight, enrich, or comfort us or it may embarrass or annoy us. It may provide valuable personal, familial, and national resources or become a linguistic and cultural liability. There have been substantive debates at social and political as well as cultural and linguistic levels on whether HLs should be maintained (Brecht and Ingold 2002; Fishman 1964, 1989, 1991; Hornberger 2004; Peyton, Ranard, and McGinnis, 2001), whether the loss of HLs is part of the price to be paid for becoming acculturated into the mainstream society (Wong Fillmore 1996), and whether 'citizenship' and 'citizens' should be a uniform concept (Rosaldo 1994). Heritage language research is such a fledgling area that there are many more unknowns with respect to HL development. Does HL acquisition follow a natural sequence of development in the same way as native language? What are the decisive factors for the success of HL development and maintenance? Why is it that we often witness a resistance to HL learning when learners are young but subsequently an embrace of HL after learners come of age?

Researchers do not share a consensus as to a precise definition of an HL learner (Wiley and Valdés 2000). The term 'heritage language' has generally been used to refer to an immigrant, indigenous, or ancestral language with which a speaker feels personal relevance and desire to (re)connect (Cummins 2005; Fishman 2001;

The Handbook of Language Socialization, First Edition. Edited by Alessandro Duranti, Elinor Ochs, and Bambi B. Schieffelin.
© 2014 John Wiley & Sons, Ltd. Published 2014 by John Wiley & Sons, Ltd.

Wiley 2001). In the United States, Canada, and the UK, where the vast majority of relevant research is conducted, the term 'heritage language' has often been used synonymously with 'community language,' 'home language,' 'native language,' and 'mother tongue' to refer to a language other than English used by immigrants and their children. In addition, HL students have been referred to as 'native speakers,' 'quasi-native speakers,' 'residual speakers,' 'bilingual speakers,' and 'home-background speakers' (Valdés 1997). The range of terms reflects the diversity in proficiency and linguistic status among HL speakers.

While some have highlighted the level of language proficiency, others such as Fishman (2001: 69), have emphasized the 'particular family relevance' and the affiliation with and allegiance to an ethnolinguistic group. Valdés (2001: 38) defines the HL learner broadly as a language student who is raised in a home where a non-English target language is spoken and who speaks or at least understands the language and is to some degree bilingual in the HL and in English. Van Deusen-Scholl (2003: 221) characterizes HL learners as 'a heterogeneous group ranging from fluent native speakers to non-native speakers who may be generations removed, but who may feel culturally connected to a language.' She distinguishes heritage learners from learners with a heritage motivation. The former are those who have achieved some degree of proficiency in the home language and/or have been raised with strong cultural connections, while the latter are 'those that seek to reconnect with their family's heritage through language, even though the linguistic evidence of that connection may have been lost for generations' (van Deusen-Scholl 2003: 222).

This chapter follows the definitions proposed by Valdés (2001) and van Deusen-Scholl (2003) and considers HL learners as those who have an ethnolinguistic affiliation to the heritage but may have a broad range of proficiency in oral or literacy skills. Furthermore, the HL learner manifests a set of ambiguities and complications that are perhaps less salient in the second language, foreign language, or mother-tongue learner and that can be sources of both challenges and opportunities (He and Xiao 2008). I propose that the process of how these learners acquire and maintain their HLs and the symbiotic social and cultural processes that accompany HL learning can be fruitfully enlightened by the analytic framework of language socialization.

Grounded in ethnography, language socialization, as a branch of linguistic anthropology, focuses on the process of becoming a culturally competent member through language use in social activities. As formulated by Ochs and Schieffelin (Ochs 1990, 1996; Ochs and Schieffelin 2008; Schieffelin and Ochs 1986, 1996), language socialization is concerned with (1) how novices are socialized to use language and (2) how novices are socialized to be competent members in the target culture through language use. It tells us that language and culture are reflexively and systematically bound together and mutually constitutive of each other. This approach focuses on the language used by and to novices (e.g. children, language learners) and the relations between this language use and the larger cultural contexts of communication – local theories and epistemologies concerning social order, local ideologies and practices concerning socializing the novice, relationships between the novice and the expert, the specific activities and tasks at hand, and so forth. Work using language socialization as theoretical guidance has focused on analyzing the organization of communicative practices through which novices acquire sociocultural knowledge and interactional competence and on the open-ended, negotiated, contested character of the interactional routine as a resource for growth and change (Garrett and Baquedano-López 2002). In this line of work, both the forms of language (e.g. word order, sentence-final particles, intonation, modal verbs, turn-taking routines) and the sociocultural contexts of language use become important research objects and sites. A language socialization approach to language development promises to provide a synthesis between cognitivist and sociocultural approaches, where cognition is reconsidered to originate in social interaction and is shaped by cultural and social processes (Watson-Gegeo 2004). It enables us to conceptualize HL and heritage culture, the relations between them, and their acquisition and development as follows.

Given that the heritage culture is by definition a complex, developing, transnational, intergenerational, intercultural, cross-linguistic, and hybrid one, to learn an HL means not merely to command the phonetic and lexico-grammatical forms in both speech and writing and to master a static set of discourse rules and norms, but also to understand or embrace a set of continually evolving norms, preferences, and expectations relating linguistic structures to multifaceted, dynamic, and fluid contexts. Heritage language learners' acquisition of linguistic forms thus requires a developmental process of delineating and organizing complex contextual dimensions in continuingly evolving, culturally sensible ways. A language socialization model views learners as tuned into certain indexical meanings of grammatical forms that link those forms to, for example, the social identities of interlocutors and the types of social events. This model relates a learner's use and understanding of grammatical forms to complex yet orderly and recurrent dispositions, preferences, beliefs, and bodies of knowledge that organize how information is linguistically packaged and how speech acts are performed within and across socially recognized situations. In this view, HL learning involves acquiring repertoires of language forms and functions associated with complex and changing contextual dimensions (e.g. evolving and shifting role relationships, identities, acts, and events) over developmental time and across space (He 2006).

Like foreign language and second language learners, HL learners often exhibit varying degrees of investment (Norton 2000) and complex but compatible identities that may appear blended or blurred through their language learning process. Unlike mother-tongue acquisition or foreign/second language acquisition in a monolingual environment, however, HL learning, by its very definition, takes place in multilingual, multicultural, immigrant contexts where the HL is in constant competition with the dominant language in the local community. As a result, HL learner motivations are derived not merely from pragmatic, instrumental, utilitarian concerns but also from the intrinsic cultural, familial, affective, and aesthetic values of the language. Under these circumstances, language socialization's position on the indexical relationship between language form and sociocultural meaning becomes particularly suitable and robust when it comes to the analysis of how different displays of and reactions to certain acts and stances construct different identities and relationships.

Since existing research on HL is still scarce and few have explicitly adopted a language socialization approach, what is presented next can be seen as an emerging body of work that lays the empirical foundation for a conceptualization of HL development from a language socialization perspective and suggests possibilities for language socialization to enrich and expand research on HL from related paradigms.

Review of the Literature

Research that focuses on socialization to use heritage languages

Research that focuses on the various linguistic components and language skills – pronunciation, grammar, lexicon, listening, reading, writing, narrative skills, register, literacy, etc. – is just emerging. In almost all cases, research is being carried out in comparison with either monolingual speakers or foreign language learners (see Duff, this volume for a more detailed, comparative account).

Godson (2004) investigated whether the age at which English becomes dominant for heritage speakers of Western Armenian in the United States affects their vowel production in Western Armenian. Participating in the study were 10 Western-Armenian bilinguals who learned English before age eight, 10 bilinguals who did not learn English until adulthood, and one Western Armenian monolingual. Vowel production was measured using recordings from oral reading of a list of sentences. Results showed that English affects the Western Armenian vowel system but only for those vowels that are already close to English. This bifurcation of vowel behavior indicates that a single across-the-board principle that governs the influence of a dominant language on a minority language is too general. Other forces such as universal tendencies, normal diachronic change, and sociolinguistic pressures must be considered.

Jia and Bayley (2008) investigated the (re)acquisition of the Mandarin Chinese perfective aspectual marker *–le* by 36 children and adolescents who either initially acquired Mandarin as an first language or were acquiring it as an HL. The results of several different measures indicate that, as expected, participants who were born in China outperformed their US-born counterparts, as did participants who reported using primarily Mandarin at home. Results for age show a more complicated picture, with younger speakers outperforming older speakers on a narrative retelling task but older speakers outperforming younger speakers on cloze and sentence completion tasks. Finally, the results of multivariate analysis of the narratives show that use of the perfective verbal suffix *–le* was significantly constrained by its position in the sentence and by whether it is optional or obligatory.

Using both proficiency tests and self-assessment measures, Kondo-Brown (2005) investigated (1) whether Japanese HL learners would demonstrate language behaviors distinctively different from those of traditional Japanese as a foreign language learners and (2) which domains of language use and skills would specifically exhibit such differentiation. Her findings suggest that there were striking similarities between the foreign language learner group and HL students with at least one Japanese-speaking grandparent but without a Japanese-speaking parent and HL students of Japanese descent without either a Japanese-speaking parent or grandparent. In contrast, HL students with at least one Japanese-speaking parent proved to be substantially different from other groups in (1) grammatical knowledge, (2) listening and reading skills, (3) self-assessed use or choice of Japanese, and (4) self-ratings of a number of can-do tasks that represented a wide range of abilities.

Achugar (2003) and Schwartz (2003) address the areas of register and genre in Spanish HL use. Their work indicated that Spanish HL learners need to make adjustments in their speech as they move from informal oral settings to formal settings or to written communication such as oral presentations in academic settings and writing assignments. While the way they speak Spanish among friends and family is completely appropriate for that setting, what they lack is the ability to modify their speech for other settings, audiences, and purposes.

Koda, Zhang, and Yang (2008) addresses literacy development in Chinese as a heritage language (CHL) among school-age students. These children typically use Chinese at home, receive primary literacy instruction in English at school, and pursue ancillary literacy in Chinese at a weekend school. As such, their primary literacy tends to build on underdeveloped oral proficiency, and secondary literacy reflects heavily restricted print input and experience. Hence, their literacy learning in both languages lacks sufficient linguistic resources. Despite these inadequacies, however, many children succeed in their primary literacy, and some even in HL literacy. Based on theories of cross-language transfer, reading universals, and metalinguistic awareness, their study explores what additional resources – metalinguistic and cognitive – are available to these children and how such resources might offset the limited linguistic support.

In addition to phonology, grammar, reading, writing, register, and genre, broader features of narration and interaction of HL learners have also been researched. Kaufman (2005) investigated narratives produced by speakers of Hebrew as an HL. Compared to Hebrew monolingual norms, the HL narrative data showed considerable fragmentation in all aspects of the language. The HL learners lacked communicative fluency, grammatical accuracy, and lexical specificity, as evidenced in their use of developmental forms characterized by present-tense temporal anchoring, frequent pauses, false starts, repairs, lexical substitution, simplification, redundancy, and circumlocution.

Many researchers agree that HL maintenance is profoundly connected to speakers' attitudes and values. Jeon (2008) explored the role of language ideology in the maintenance of Korean. In a three-year, multisited ethnographic study she examined the range of language ideologies espoused by individuals in different phases of life. Drawing upon data from three separate venues – a university Korean language class of mostly heritage Korean speakers, a community-based English-as-a-second-language program for Korean American senior citizens, and the home of a recent Korean immigrant family with teenage children – Jeon examined and compared the language attitudes of the mostly Korean-speaking elders in the community, those of the largely English-speaking second generation, and those of a recently emigrated father who insisted that his children speak only English. Jeon concludes that language ideologies are continuously shaped by changing life circumstances and that promoting bilingualism at the societal level is a critical requirement in any language maintenance effort (see also Friedman, this volume; Garrett, this volume; Riley, this volume).

Even though most of the above studies are not directly informed by the theoretical model of language socialization (with the exception of Jia and Bayley 2008), collectively they document the challenges HL learners face across a spectrum of linguistic components and language skills. The language socialization model could inspire future work to reveal and specify the culturally situated ways in which these and other linguistic forms are learned and taught along different developmental stages.

Research on heritage language as a resource

There is a long tradition of conceptualizing language as an integral part of the development of the self, of the mind, and of society that complements language socialization. When language is seen not as a self-contained system but as a context-specific tool for achieving our purposes, identity is structured in the everyday flow of language and stabilized in the pragmatic narratives of our day-to-day, fluid social life. For HL learners, HL acquisition is thus constitutive of identity, which is accomplished in everyday social interactions. From a language socialization perspective, the indexical relationship between language and sociocultural dimensions of language use (including identity) is achieved through a two-step process. Ochs (1990) argues that 'affective and epistemological dispositions' are the two contextual dimensions that are recurrently used to constitute other contextual dimensions. In accordance with this line of thought, researchers have focused on HL as intricately woven with learner identity formation or transformation.

Tse (1997) attempts to explain the relationships among ethnic identity, attitudes, and motivations, and HL development. Based on a study of US-born Asian American adults, Tse concluded that language acquisition is facilitated when an individual has positive attitudes toward the language and feels positively about her or his ethnic group. In a further study, Tse (2000) examined published narratives of Asian Americans to discover whether feelings of ethnic ambivalence or evasion extend to the HL and, if so, how they affect language beliefs and behaviors. The results suggest that, for many, the HL is closely associated with the ethnic group so that attitudes toward the ethnic group and its language speakers also extend to the narrators' own language ability and their interest (or lack of interest) in maintaining and developing their HL.

Similarly, Li (1994) posits that HL proficiency correlates positively with a well-developed sense of ethnic identity and network with the speaker's ethnic group, such that group members have a greater understanding and knowledge of their group's cultural values, ethics, and manners. The same is echoed in Bernhard, Freire, and Pacini-Ketchabaw (2001), Chinen and Tucker (2005), Cho (2000), Kaufman (2005), Kondo-Brown (2005), and Lee (2002), all of whom suggest that, in addition to internal factors such as attitudes, motivation, and social identity, ethnic identity is also a key factor in HL development in the case of adult learners.

In addition to learner identities, other researchers have examined how the use of HL socializes cultural values and speech roles. Lo (2004) demonstrates how expressions of epistemic stance relate to moral evaluations by looking at cases in which teachers at a Korean HL school claim to read their students' minds with a high degree of certainty. Lo argues that Korean HL learners are socialized to portray their access to the thoughts and sensations of other individuals differently depending upon who these individuals are. If the individuals are perceived as morally worthy, then the access is portrayed as distant; if they are perceived as morally suspect, then the access is presented as self-evident. He (2000) details the discourse processes by which young CHL learners are socialized to values of respect for authority and group conformity through teachers' directives in weekend Chinese language schools, where teachers do not merely impart knowledge and facts but also function as moral guides to the students.

Park (2008) investigates how parents and grandparents in three-generational Korean American households socialize young children through their use of a particular linguistic feature in Korean, the verb suffix *–ta*. Drawing on naturally occurring interaction in the household, Park shows that utterances ending in *–ta* are used mostly by Korean adults to socialize children into the distinction between culturally desirable and culturally dispreferred behavior, thereby reconstructing the hierarchical relationships among different generations. Park highlights the importance of three-generational Korean households in making it possible for children to observe and imitate the culturally appropriate verbal behavior of their parents as the latter are engaged in interactions with the children's grandparents. In Park's study, the verb suffix *–ta* is not the end of socialization (i.e. children are not expected to use this form in their own speech) but the means to socialize children into cultural norms and values.

Some proposals for future research

We have seen an increasingly large body of empirical studies documenting the various formal and functional aspects of HL socialization, as reviewed in the previous sections, that are concerned with different subgroups of HL learners.

Some studies have looked at developmental traits in learners who have minimal proficiency in the HL, whereas others have focused on maintenance issues in the case of highly proficient HL learners. These studies (but see Jeon 2008) largely focus on one language proficiency level of the subjects at one life stage in one specific life circumstance. It is proposed here that, alternatively, the successful socialization of HL has to do with the role of school systems, social institutions, and the historical experiences of particular language communities, as well as language ideologies, proficiency assessments that are suitable for heritage speakers, and adequate literacy development (Campbell and Christian 2003). We have learned from previous research that a range of variables may influence language maintenance, including the social prestige of the language, the number of speakers, affinity to the native country, the vitality of HL schools, learners' social and ethnic positionings, the degree of family bond, and discourse and interactional practices (Baker 2006; Creeze and Martin 2006; Fishman 1991, 2001; Gibbons and Ramirez 2004; He 2006; He and Xiao 2008; Shin 2005; Zentella 1997). Given our definition of HL, neither the HL classroom nor the family is the only domain relevant to HL development or maintenance. Efforts to understand HL will be most fruitful if we take into account not only formal, institutional settings such as schools (e.g. Byon 2003; He 2000; Lo 2004) but also patterns of HL use in informal settings such as homes and communities (Bayley and Schecter 2003; Park 2008; Xiao 2008), and not only the impact of face-to-face interaction but also the role of technology and popular culture (Lam 2008; Lee 2006). Temporally, like socialization in other domains (Markee 2008; Wortham 2005), HL socialization is not limited to any specific given period of time; HL competencies, choices, and ideologies change over the HL learner's lifespan, reflecting changing motivations, social networks, opportunities, and other variables. Research needs to examine the different stages as well as different domains of HL development.

Heritage language socialization research also needs to expand its focus from individual language learners to other co-participants. It will be important to realize that expert guidance in HL socialization may be multiple, conflicting, and contested. The HL learner is engaged in multiple speech events in multiple settings for multiple purposes. The learning of an HL, for example, takes place through the learner's interactions with multiple participants including language instructors, parents, grandparents, siblings, and peers, each of whom positions the learner in unique speech and social roles and each of whose reactions and responses to the HL learner help to shape the path of his language development. Future HL socialization research will highlight the co-constructed, interactive nature of HL socialization activities.

Case in Point: Chinese as a Heritage Language

In the past 10 years, my work has centered on delineating the complexity of HL socialization along temporal and spatial dimensions, with a focus on CHL. Along the temporal dimension, I underscore the nonlinear, iterative, dynamic nature of HL development (He 2006). Along the spatial dimension, my research highlights the multiagency and multidirectionality of HL development. I have proposed a general identity-based approach that looks at how HL learning takes place as the learner moves across time and space. Given the multiplicity of connotations and usages of the term 'identity' (Brubaker and Cooper 2000), it is necessary to clarify that my overall objective is to locate learner identity as the centerpiece rather than the background of HL development. Identity is to be understood in association with its verb form, 'to identify,' and thus as identification. In other words, identity is treated not as a collection of static attributes or as a mental construct existing prior to and independent of human actions, but rather as a process of continually emerging and becoming, a process that identifies what a person becomes and achieves through ongoing interactions with other persons (Bucholtz and Hall 2004; He 1995; Ochs 1993). In the words of Lemke, 'What else is an *identity* but the performance, verbally and nonverbally, of a possible constellation of attitudes, beliefs, and values that has a recognizable coherence by the criteria of some community?' (2002: 72, emphasis in original). I ask whether CHL development places learners in interactional conditions of cultural and linguistic ambiguity that they are prepared to handle and whether the growing cultural complexity of communication as a result of CHL development leads to the withering away or the emergence of certain types of identity constructs. Conceptualizing HL development as a socialization process with multiple agencies, multiple directions, and multiple goals, I have put forth 10 hypotheses to describe and predict the key variables responsible for HL development, as follows.

(1) *The rootedness hypothesis.* The degree of success in CHL development correlates positively with the learner's desire to be rooted in his or her heritage culture and to accentuate similarities with members of the CHL community. This explains why CHL students in university CHL classes often claim that they disliked taking Chinese lessons when they were young and did not have the desire to remain connected with their family background whereas, now that they are fully grown and ready to embrace their cultural heritage, they are eager to learn CHL seriously.

(2) *The benefits hypothesis.* The degree of success in CHL development correlates positively with the learner's envisaged benefits and rewards (social and economic) in the future. In today's world, Mandarin Chinese is clearly the language of literacy linked to not only literary activities but also economic opportunities. Learning the language well makes practical, functional sense.

(3) *The interaction hypothesis.* The degree of success in CHL development correlates positively with the learner's desire to communicate successfully in a moment-by-moment fashion. Existing research, though limited, has confirmed our hunch that strong long-term motivations may not necessarily lead

to success in CHL learning (Lu and Li 2008; Tse 2002). A very important aspect of motivation comes from the reward of communicating in situated activities (e.g. understanding a comic strip in a magazine or a letter from grandparents; being able to talk to relatives or to travel independently in Chinese-speaking worlds). This hypothesis is particularly applicable to child CHL learners when the rootedness hypothesis and the benefits hypothesis are indeterminate.

(4) *The positive-stance hypothesis.* The degree of success in CHL development correlates positively with the positive stance the English-speaking community has towards the Chinese language. For a long time, China was poor and Chinese language was not considered important in US schools. But that is no longer the case. With more and more students learning Chinese as a foreign language, CHL students will feel inspired and compelled to master the language, especially in contexts and on campuses where cultural tolerance and diversity are promoted and celebrated.

(5) *The by-choice hypothesis.* The degree of success in CHL development correlates positively with the frequency with which the learner's family uses CHL by choice. It has been observed anecdotally that, when families use CHL by necessity (i.e. parents speak CHL because their English is limited), learners are likely to see CHL as limiting rather than enriching. By contrast, when parents speak CHL because they choose to, learners see a model of the development or maintenance of CHL 'where the motive is linguistic, cognitive, and cultural enrichment – the creation of citizens of the world' (Hakuta 1986: 229–30). This perhaps also explains to some extent why there seems to be pride for school-attained CHL on the one hand and sometimes uneasiness about home-acquired CHL on the other.

(6) *The diverse-input hypothesis.* The degree of success in CHL literacy development correlates positively with the extent to which the learner has access to rich and diverse CHL input. Input includes not only various reading and audiovisual materials at home and school but also spoken and cultural input from interacting with Chinese-speaking family members as well as from frequent visits to places where Chinese is used natively (e.g. parents' home towns in China, Taiwan, etc.).

(7) *The discourse-norms hypothesis.* The degree of success in CHL development correlates positively with the extent to which the discourse norms (ways of speaking, patterns in turn-taking, allocation of speech roles, preferences in conversational topics, etc.) in CHL-speaking contexts (home, classroom, or community) are sensitive to the discourse norms in the English-speaking community.

(8) *The enrichment hypothesis.* The degree of success in CHL development correlates positively with the extent to which the learner has created a niche (linguistic, social, cultural) in the English-speaking community. This explains why adult CHL learners tend to be more enthusiastic about and committed to CHL learning than children as the former have found their own place, so to speak, in the English-speaking world, a place where they see themselves as linguistic and social equals to others and where they feel free to ground,

enrich, and expand their experiences. It can be predicted that children who speak only CHL before school age are more likely to develop a negative attitude towards CHL when they start school than early bilinguals (those using two languages from infancy). The former group see CHL as holding them back and as the cause of not understanding English (and its various ramifications) whereas the latter, who are already comfortable with English, do not see the need to resist CHL in order to position themselves fittingly in the English-speaking world.

(9) *The multiplicity hypothesis.* Neither in the temporal nor spatial sense is identity singular, unitary, or noncontradictory. The CHL learner's identity is complex in that he or she assumes multiple identifications that may be overlapping and/or competing. The salience of various identifications varies contextually and relationally (Goffman 1959; Rampton 1995; Reyes and Lo 2009). The degree of success in CHL development correlates positively with the ease with which the learner is able to manage differences and discontinuities presented by multiple speech roles in multiple, intersecting communities.

(10) *The transformation hypothesis.* As the CHL learner copes with the multiple linguistic codes in the contexts of family, peer groups, and school institutions, s/he is engaged in a double process of socialization into given speech communities and of acquisition of literacy as a means of asserting personal meanings that have the potential to transform the speech community. In other words, CHL can be used both to inherit heritage practices and to transform the very practices that motivated CHL learning in the first place.

Below, I will present a quasi-ergodic, composite profile of a CHL learner based on interactional, interview, reported, and published data collected from a period spanning kindergarten to college (He 2006). Then, I will examine the developmental stages and diverse spaces of the prototype learner to gain insight into how CHL socialization takes place as the learner moves across time and space. The 'quasi-ergodic' approach adopted here enables one to go beyond the HL learner's language use in different domains and settings and also to include the temporal aspect of the analysis, examining how the learner's behavior changes according to his different developmental stages by defining time as an additional coordinate. As integral parts of the study, relevant demographic and ethnographic data will complement the interactional, linguistic data.

A brief explanation of the term 'quasi-ergodic' is in order here. The notion of 'ergodicity' was originally used in statistical physics and refers to, for turbulent flow, the property of having the spatial, temporal, and ensemble averages all converge to the same mean. This can only be true if the flow is stationary and homogenous. Since we are concerned with determining what the most common pattern of CHL development is, one way is to take a momentary snapshot: to see how many CHL learners are at this moment doing X, how many are doing

Y, and so on. Another way is to look at one individual CHL learner and to follow him or her for a certain period of time. We then observe when and how often this individual does X, when and how often she or he does Y, and so on. Thus, we obtain two different results: one analysis over the entire ensemble of CHL learners at a certain moment in time and one analysis for one CHL learner over a certain period of developmental time. The first result may not be representative for a longer period of time while the second may not be representative for all the CHL learners. The idea is that an ensemble is 'ergodic' if the two types of analysis yield the same result. My plan is to build a master CHL learner profile by gathering data from different subjects who are in different stages and different domains of CHL development. However, since human populations are, scientifically and technically speaking, not ergodic, I call the approach I take 'quasi-ergodic.' This approach differs from a 'typification' approach that is based cross-sectional data in that the former pays special attention to change and development over time. In some ways, it parallels the diachronic reconstruction approach used in linguistics (Givón 2009), the meta-analysis argument advanced in applied linguistics (Norris and Ortega 2000), as well as the effort to examine socialization beyond a single speech event in linguistic anthropology (Wortham 2005).

A composite master profile of a heritage language learner

Jason Chen is a 19-year-old student in a beginning-level CHL class in a university. He can speak Cantonese and understands Mandarin but does not know how to read or write in Chinese. He was born in Canton and immigrated with his family to Queens, New York, when he was three. Before he started kindergarten at age six, he spoke Cantonese at home with his parents, his grandmother, and his aunt, all of whom speak Cantonese, comprehend Mandarin, and have limited command of English. He had some knowledge of English from television and from the children he played with, who spoke a mixture of English, Vietnamese, Cantonese, Fujianese, Chaozhou dialect, and Mandarin. When Jason started school, his teacher thought his English was weak and placed him in extra help sessions taught by teachers' aids who were bilingual in Cantonese and English. It didn't take him long to pick up English language skills. Very soon, Jason was speaking English fluently and became one of the highest-achieving students in his class, all the way through high school. However, as his abilities in English grew, his interaction with his family became less frequent and more insignificant. Since a time he no longer recalls, he has been speaking English to his parents and his aunt at home too; the only person he still speaks Cantonese to is his grandmother, with whom he keeps up a minimum level of communication. In his own words, 'I love my family. But I don't talk to them. Well, I'd like to talk to them, but there's such a language barrier.' At some point during his formative years, his parents sent him to a community-based weekend Chinese language school, where he was taught Mandarin. He went for a year but felt 'the teacher was just totally boring' and he 'didn't learn anything.' His best friends are Bob, his roommate at the dorm, who is from a Jewish family background, and Jim, a transfer student from Korea who shares his interests in business and finance, basketball, and video games. He is also seriously dating a girl from a Mandarin-speaking family background. When asked why he is taking CHL, Jason said, 'I am Chinese. I feel stupid not knowing the language. Plus I'd like to do business in China, some day.'

Jason Chen would be a rather typical student in a university-level CHL classroom. He was raised in a home where an HL was spoken and he speaks or at least understands the language and is to some degree bilingual in the HL and in English (Valdés 2001: 38). He sees the HL as having 'a particular family relevance' (Fishman 2001: 169) and he is English-dominant with no or very limited reading and writing ability in his HL. In order to understand the complexities of Jason's HL development, I attempted to reconstruct his life by collecting data from a wide range of subjects in settings and situations that Jason has experienced at various stages of his life from Kindergarten to university. The end result is a composite 'Jason,' representing an 'ergodic' model of his life experiences with respect to his HL development.

As noted previously, before entering school, Jason's exposure to English was limited. At the beginning of his formal schooling, he was usually only seen but not heard. He rarely responded to the teacher or other students verbally, as can be in Example 25.1.

Example 25.1:   Kindergarten classroom [field notes, classroom interaction 2004]

Mrs. B: My friends, let's get ready. It's center time.
((Jason doesn't move.))
Mrs. B: Jason, which center do you wanna go?
((Jason doesn't respond. Mrs. B takes his hand and brings him to the art center next to an easel.))
Mrs. B: You like to paint? I know you are a good artist.
((Jason looks at the easel and then at other kids who are at the number center working with numbers 0 through 9. Jason joins the number center. Mrs. B leaves.))

On the one hand, Jason's parents were concerned with his lack of English language competence and were doing their best to talk to him in English in spite of their own limited command of the language. But, on the other hand, they also wanted Jason to keep Chinese and to develop literacy in Chinese. As a result, the parents increased their use of English at home and at the same time sent Jason to a weekend Chinese language school in their community. Example 25.2 illustrates what may have happened in the classroom at the language school.

Example 25.2:   *Chinese language school [audio and video recorded data, 4.5–9 age group 2001]*

((in the context of '孔融让梨'– Kong Rong Yields Pears)).

7 Teacher: 要把– 应该 把 玩具让:: 给   弟弟   妹妹
should ought BA toy yield DIR younger brother younger sister
Should– Ought to yie::ld the toys to younger brothers and sisters

8   (.2)

9 Teacher: 谦::让:(.) 懂   吗? 谦让 就 是 这 个   意思
Yield understand Q yield just be this CL. meaning
Yield (.) Understand? This is what yield means.

10 Jason: 让 给 他? 我们share就 可以了。
yield DIR he we share just ok CRS
Yield to him? We can share.

11 Teacher: Share (.) 噢:: share 是 不   错
Share PRT share be NEG wrong
Share (.) uh:: share is not wrong

12   (.4)

13 Teacher: 可是能 让   更好=
But able yield even better
But being able to YIELD will be EVEN better.

14 Jason: =Oh:: no::: Do I really have to?

15 Teacher: 不是– 不是说   非– 不是说   <必须得 让>
NEG NEG say have to– NEG say must must yield
I'm not saying you have to– not saying that you MUST yield

16   能   让(.)   最:好啊
Able yield best PRT
Being able to yield is THE BEST ok

Here the teacher is leading a discussion of the Chinese cultural preference of 'yielding' in the context of a widely circulated folk story of 'Kong Rong Yields Pears' (a moral story teaching children the virtue of putting others' needs before their own), which apparently requires more from a child than the US notion of 'sharing,' which Jason has brought to the Chinese class from his daytime regular school. That the two cultural norms could not be reconciled with each other most likely played a role in Jason's perception of the Chinese language school as 'boring' (for lack of a better descriptor) and the fact that he eventually dropped out.

From fourth grade onward, Jason became a very confident and consistently successful student at school. His sixth-grade school report card read, 'Jason is a superior student who excels across all subject areas.' However, he was speaking less and less at home. Example 25.3 is illustrative of the kind of interaction he had at home at that stage, keeping his speech at the dinner table to a minimum and, when he did have to speak, doing so in English.

Example 25.3:   Sixth grade: At dinner table [audio recorded data, Spring 2007]

((This interaction took place when Jason's Mandarin-speaking maternal grandmother was visiting around Chinese New Year.))

Grandma: 吃，来，吃，来
          Eat come eat come
          eat, come, eat, come
          ((Grandma pushes Jason to dinner table))
Grandma: 那么瘦！多吃多吃不吃怎么胖
          So skinny much eat much eat NEG eat how fat
          So skinny! Eat a lot eat a lot if you don't eat how can you gain
          weight
          只长个儿不长肉
          Only grow height NEG grow flesh
          [You] only gain height but not weight.
          啊哟：：你看看他们拿来这么多吃的
          PRT you look they bring-COMP this much food
          ayo ::: you see they brought this much food
          想吃什么？
          Want eat Q
          What do you want to eat?
Mother: 姥姥跟你说话呢
          Maternal grandma with you speak PRT
          Grandma is talking to you
          这孩子=哎别拿了够了够=
          This child=PRTNEG bring LE enough LE enough
          This kid=ai don't bring anything more enough enough
Jason: =I'm not hungry.

During high school, Jason was perceived differently by different people in his life, as can be seen in Example 25.4. At this point, he was speaking English almost exclusively. His aunt and grandmother no longer lived with them. His parents were doing better in their business and they were also speaking much more, and better, English themselves.

Example 25.4:   High school: Others' perceptions of Jason [Spring 2005]

- Guidance counselor: 'He is the kind of student we all dream to have.'
- Schoolmate: 'Oh that Chinese guy? Or is he Vietnamese or some other kind of Asian? He is okay. Never bothers me. But what is he doing here? I think people like him should go back to China or wherever they came from.'
- Neighbor: 'Nice young man! He will have a great future. I wish my son more like him. You know, my son only play with people like him, you

know, only Chinese. Too narrow, you know. You live in America, you want to be American, you know.'

- An elderly woman at temple:
  '这孩子不错。他父母人很好，可他从来也不叫我奶奶。都美国化了。(He is a good kid. His parents are very nice people, but he never calls me 'Grandma.' He is Americanized.)'
- Mother: 'He study not bad. Has good grades. He like computer. Play computer game all the time. Never stop. Spend a lot money too. He like brand. Waste money!'
- Sister: 'He talks to me but he really doesn't talk to anyone else [in the family] that much. He's real busy'n stuff.'

By the time Jason entered the university, he had decided that he would like to seriously learn Chinese. Due to his language background and language proficiency, it was not immediately clear which track of the elementary Chinese language class Jason should be placed in – the foreign language track or the HL track. In Example 25.5, an instructor was interviewing Jason for the purpose of his placement.

Example 25.5:   University: With CHL instructor [Spring 2005]

Professor: Ok if I– I speak Mandarin, do you follow me well?
Jason: I mean (.) >I underSTAND Mandarin.< At home my mom'n my aunt the– they sometimes speak Mandarin b't (.) not all that well. .hhh Most of the time everybody (.) jus speak Canto [nese.
Professor: [Ok,=
Jason: =I like Mandarin. Sounds better than other dialects. >Don't know why jus feels that way.< I mean if I want to find a jo:b like (.) in China I wanna be in big (cities/places) like <Beijing> or something=
Professor: =Uhuh,
             (.2)
Jason: I don't wanna be (.) like (.) you know (.) where THEY. came from.

One might think that to learn one's HL is to (re)establish similarities with members of one's heritage culture and/or to (re)establish differences from members of mainstream American culture. However, as can be seen in Example 25.5, to learn CHL appears to mean not merely to inherit one's HL and maintain one's heritage cultural identity but also to transform the HL (in terms of changes in dialect, script, accent, discourse norms, etc.) and recreate one's identity. When Jason walks into the CHL classroom, he brings with him linguistic and behavioral patterns that were formed when he was six or twelve and that remain active or that await reactivation; he brings with him richly textured experiences from interacting with his Cantonese- and Mandarin-speaking family members; his English-, Vietnamese-, Cantonese-, Fujianese-, Chaozhou dialect-, and Mandarin-speaking neighbors; his English-speaking but multiethnic peers and teachers; and his English- and Mandarin-speaking girl friend. He brings with him ways of speaking and being that mirror those of these diverse groups of people. He brings with him memories of his past experience learning CHL as well as expectations and anticipations about the verbal and nonverbal behavior of his present CHL teacher and CHL classmates. He also brings with him dreams of working in China some day and ideas of what being a Chinese American means. In a nutshell, Jason embodies elements that are both hetero-temporal and hetero-spatial. He has learned and is still learning to cope with, to understand, to accept or reject, and to model or modify the language and cultural behaviors of every community he has encountered throughout his lifespan. Learning CHL will enable him to inherit some of the 'Chineseness' from his family and his neighborhood but will also enable him to become a very different kind of Chinese American from his family and his neighbors.

Most interestingly, whereas Jason may consider himself a beginning learner of the Chinese language, his best friend Brad, who is from a non-Chinese family background and who is learning Chinese as a foreign language, sees him differently, as illustrated in Example 25.6.

Example 25.6:   University: Best friend Brad (who is taking CFL) [Spring 2005]

Jason: When's your oral?
Brad: Friday, (.) I think, (.) .hhh oh no actually I don think she's told us
         yet. I'm gonna fail hhahaha=
Jason: =no you won't,
Brad: C'mon ((hhh I'm gonna)) say '我· (.) 觉··得 (.2) 发·音 (.) 很··难'(('I
         think pronunciation is hard')) hhahhhaha
Jason: Oh yea you can do it, you just did it hhuhuhuh
Brad: Easy for YOU ((it's)) your (.) lan [guage
Jason: [ne::: my mom– I don=
Brad: =but s[till
Jason: [I guess.

Here, regardless of Jason's minimal level of proficiency in Chinese, he is perceived by Brad as 'possessing' the language ('Easy for YOU ((it's)) your (.) language'). After a brief and unsuccessful protest of such a characterization, Jason acquiesces.

Earlier, I discussed the central role of identity formation and transformation in the development and maintenance of HLs. Most often, the connection between language and identity is tacit and requires inferences. The segment in Example 25.7, however, caught an extremely rare moment when language and identity were explicitly marked and linked.

Example 25.7:   University: With math teaching assistant [Spring 2005]

((Jason is seeking help in the teaching assistant (TA)'s office. TA is a native of China who arrived in the US not long ago for graduate school. 'ABC' stands for 'American-born Chinese.'))

TA: This– this is the rule, the equation. What I tell you (.2) you mus
          must follow. The right way.
          ((Jason is still confused))
TA: Are you Chinese?
          ((Jason stares at TA))
TA: I tell you in Chinese.
          (.2)
Jason: uh:: my Chinese isn't that good=
TA: =So you are ABC. No problem. I tell you again...

What is noteworthy in Example 25.7 is that Jason does not seem to be prepared for any explicit discussion of his ethnic identity. When the TA first inquires about his ethnicity, Jason gives a blank answer (both verbally and visually). When the TA assumes that he is an American-born Chinese, Jason does not correct the TA's mistake (Jason was in fact born in China). This is a revealing moment where Jason is compelled to confront the issue of identity and yet he appears ambivalent and inadequate in handling the matter.

I argued earlier that HL socialization concerns and transforms all parties involved. As the years went by, Jason's parents were speaking more and better English. His father does not speak much in general. By the time Jason is in college, his mother has become quite comfortable talking to him in English, as seen in Example 25.8.

Example 25.8:   University: With mother [Spring 2005]

Jason: I'm also (.2) taking uh Chinese history.
          (.4)
Jason: It's hard.
Mother: Hard? You study hard (.) it's easy.
Jason: Ma you don't get it.
          ((pause))
Mother: Why– why Chinese history? Economy major need Chinese
          history? I study my major I never study history=
Jason: =Ma you never get it. 你不懂啦·· (('You don't understand this'))
          I'm taking it cus I want to. Nobody asks me to.

Two items are worthy of particular mention. First, at this stage, Jason is, out of his own initiative, trying to learn as much Chinese language and history as possible, to an extent that is surprising and perplexing to his mother. Second, in interaction with mother, it is in this instance Jason who code-switches to Chinese from English, while his mother uses English consistently.

Jason's change of attitude toward the Chinese language certainly has something to do with the changing climate of the overall culture he is in. At institutions of learning, especially the university, foreign languages have enjoyed an increasingly higher status and the Chinese language in particular has undergone phenomenal changes in its prestige. Persons with the ability to use Chinese have become objects of admiration and respect, as illustrated in Example 25.9.

Example 25.9: University: With supervisor [Spring 2005]

((Jason is studying for a CHL quiz in between part-time work at a university photocopy center))

Supervisor:	That's Chinese?
Jason:	Yeah (.) the professor sh– she said we have to (.) memorize all this stuff it's killing me=
Supervisor:	=it sure looks pretty har::d (.2) but it's cool I wish (.) I could read something like that. You must be smart.

To sum up, I have taken as an anchor position for my research that HL development is grounded in the learner's participation in social practice and continuous adaptation to the unfolding, multiple activities and identities that constitute the social and communicative worlds that s/he inhabits. This work also compels us to take a more dialectical, dialogical, and ecological perspective on socialization, in the sense that the process should be viewed as reciprocal. Heritage language learners are not merely passive, uniform recipients of socialization. As the HL learner's allegiances and competencies evolve, the language choices and competencies of their parents, siblings, neighbors, and friends will also change, consequently and/or concurrently. In other words, it is important to keep in mind that the HL learner contributes to the HL socialization process of the very people who socialize him or her to use the HL. Heritage language learning has the potential to transform all parties involved in the socialization process.

It can also be expected that HL research will contribute to the very disciplines that have served as its theoretical or methodological guidance in terms of fundamental theoretical constructs, research methods, and units of analysis. For example, HL learning provides fertile grounds for us to reconsider dichotomous concepts such as native language versus target language, native speech community versus target speech community, instrumental versus integrative motivations, and basic interpersonal communication skills versus cognitive academic language proficiency. In Jason's case, Mandarin Chinese is part of his native speech repertoire but is also a language that he clearly needs explicit instruction if he is to command its full range of use in both speech and writing. There is certainly Chinese culture in Jason's family, but that culture is shifting and evolving as the family's immigrant experience unfolds in time. Further, Jason is motivated to learn Chinese by a variety of factors along his academic and personal developmental path. Last but not least, HL research will challenge us to re-evaluate our unit of analysis from single snapshots of one-on-one, unidirectional interactional processes to trajectories of growth and change over space and time for all participants. The nature of an HL is such that its acquisition requires sustained (though not necessarily continuous or routinized) exposure and input over time in ways that are meaningful and consequential to not only the learner but also all those who invoke for and impart to him or her a sense of cultural lineage, affinity, or investment. In this sense, HL development presents a test case for language socialization research.

REFERENCES

Achugar, M. (2003) Academic registers in Spanish in the US: A study of oral texts produced by bilingual speakers in a university graduate program. In A. Roca and M. C. Colombi (eds.), *Mi Lengua: Spanish as a Heritage Language in the United States.* 213–34. Washington, DC: Georgetown University Press.

Baker, C. (2006) *Foundations of Bilingual Education and Bilingualism.* Clevedon, UK: Multilingual Matters.

Bayley, R. and Schecter, S. (eds.) (2003) *Language Socialization in Bilingual and Multilingual Societies.* Clevedon, UK: Multilingual Matters.

Bernhard, J. K., Freire, M., and Pacini-Ketchabaw, V. (2001) Struggling to preserve home language: The experiences of Latino students and families in the Canadian school system. *Bilingual Research Journal* 25 (1–2): 115–45.

Brecht, R. D. and Ingold, C. W. (2002) www.ericdigests.org/2003-1/ tapping.htm. *Eric Digests* ED464515.

Brubaker, R. and Cooper, F. (2000) Beyond 'identity.' *Theory and Society* 29: 1–47.

Bucholtz, M. and Hall, K. (2004) Language and identity. In A Duranti (ed.), *A Companion to Linguistic Anthropology.* 369–94. Oxford: Blackwell.

Byon, A. (2003) Language socialization and Korean as a heritage language: A study of Hawaiian classrooms. *Language, Culture and Curriculum* 16(3): 269–83.

Campbell, R. and Christian, D. (eds.) (2003) Directions in research: Intergenerational transmission of heritage languages. *Heritage Language Journal* 1(1): 1–44.

Chinen, K., and Tucker, G. R. (2005) Heritage language development: Understanding the role of ethnic identity and Saturday school participation. *Heritage Language Journal* 3(1): 27–59.

Cho, G. (2000) The role of heritage language in social interactions and relationships: Reflections from a language minority group. *Bilingual Research Journal* 24(4): 369–84.

Creeze, A. and Martin, P. (2006) (eds.), Interaction in complementary school contexts. *Language and Education Special Issue* 20(1).

Cummins, J. (2005) A proposal for action: Strategies for recognizing heritage language competence as a learning resource within the mainstream classroom. *Modern Language Journal* 89: 585–92.

Fishman, J. A. (1964) Language maintenance and language shift as a field of inquiry. *Linguistics* 9: 32–70.

Fishman, J. A. (1989) *Language and Ethnicity in Minority Sociolinguistic Perspective.* Clevedon, UK: Multilingual Matters.

Fishman, J. A. (1991) *Reversing Language Shift.* Clevedon, UK: Multilingual Matters.

Fishman, J. A. (2001) 300-plus years of heritage language education in the United States. In J. K. Peyton, D. A. Ranard, and S. McGinnis (eds.), *Heritage Languages in America. Preserving a National Resource.* 81–9. McHenry, IL and Washington, DC: Delta Systems/Center for Applied Linguistics.

Garrett, P. B. and Baquedano-López, P. (2002) Language socialization: Reproduction and continuity, transformation and change. *Annual Review of Anthropology* 31: 339–61.

Gibbons, J. and Ramirez, E. (2004) *Maintaining a Minority Language: A Case Study of Hispanic Teenagers.* Clevedon, UK: Multilingual Matters.

Givón, T. (2009) *The Genesis of Syntactic Complexity: Diachrony, Ontogeny, Neuro-Cognition, Evolution.* Philadelphia, PA: John Benjamins.

Godson, L. (2004) Vowel production in the speech of western Armenian heritage speakers. *Heritage Language Journal* 2(1): 1–26.

Goffman, E. (1959) *The Presentation of Self in Everyday Life.* New York: Doubleday.

Hakuta, K. (1986) *Mirror of Language: The Debate on Bilingualism.* New York: Basic Books.

He, A. W. (1995) Co-constructing institutional identities: The case of student counselees. *Research on Language and Social Interaction* 28(3): 213–31.

He, A. W. (2000) Grammatical and sequential organization of teachers'

directives. *Linguistics and Education* 11(2): 119–40.

He, A. W. (2006) Toward an identity theory of the development of Chinese as a heritage language. *Heritage Language Journal* 4(1): 1–28.

He, A. W. and Xiao, Y. (eds.) (2008) *Chinese as a Heritage Language: Fostering Rooted World Citizenry.* Honolulu, HI: University of Hawaii Press.

Hornberger, N. (2004) The continua of biliteracy and the bilingual educator: Educational linguistics in practice. *International Journal of Bilingual Education and Bilingualism* 7 (2–3): 155–71.

Jeon, M. (2008) Korean heritage language maintenance and language ideology. *Heritage Language Journal* 6(2): 54–71.

Jia, L. and Bayley, R. (2008) Perfective aspect marking by CHL learners. In A. W. He and Y. Xiao (eds.), *Chinese as a Heritage Language.* 205–24. Honolulu, HI: National Foreign Language Resource Center/University of Hawaii Press.

Kaufman, D. (2005) Acquisition, attrition, and revitalization of Hebrew in immigrant children. In D. Ravid and H. B.-Z. Shyldkrot (eds.), *Perspectives on Language and Language Development.* 407–18. Dordrecht, The Netherlands: Kluwer.

Koda, K., Zhang, Y., and Yang, C.-L. (2008) Literacy development in Chinese as a heritage language. In A. W. He and Y. Xiao (eds.), *Chinese as a Heritage Language.* 125–36. Honolulu, HI: National Foreign Language Resource Center/University of Hawaii Press.

Kondo-Brown, K. (2005) Differences in language skills: Heritage language learner subgroups and foreign language learners? *The Modern Language Journal* 89: 563–81.

Lam, W. S. E. (2008) Language socialization in online communities. In P. Duff and N. Hornberger (eds.), *Encyclopedia of Language and Education, Vol. 8: Language Socialization.* 301–12. New York: Springer.

Lee, J. S. (2002) The Korean language in America: The role of cultural identity and heritage language. *Language, Culture, and Curriculum* 15(2): 117–33.

Lee, J. S. (2006) Exploring the relationship between electronic literacy and heritage language maintenance. *Language Learning and Technology* 10(2): 93–113.

Li, W. (1994) *Three Generations, Two Languages, One Family*. Clevedon, UK: Multilingual Matters.

Lemke, J. (2002) Language development and identity: Multiple timescales in the social ecology of learning. In C. Kramsch (ed.), *Language Acquisition and Language Socialization*. 68–87. New York: Continuum.

Lo, A. (2004) Evidentiality and morality in a Korean heritage language school. *Pragmatics* 14(2–3): 235–56.

Lu, X. and Li, G. (2008) Motivation and achievement in Chinese language learning. In A. W. He and Y. Xiao (eds.), *Chinese as a Heritage Language: Fostering Rooted World Citizenry*. 89–108. Honolulu, HI: University of Hawaii Press.

Markee, N. (2008) Toward a learning behavior tracking methodology for CA-for-SLA. *Applied Linguistics* 29(3): 404–27.

Norris, J. M. and Ortega, L. (2000) Effectiveness of L2 instruction: A research synthesis and quantitative meta-analysis. *Language Learning* 50(3): 417–528.

Norton, B. (2000) *Identity and Language Learning: Gender, Ethnicity, and Educational Change*. Harlow, UK: Longman.

Ochs, E. (1990) Indexicality and socialization. In J. W. Stigler, R. Shweder, and G. Herdt (eds.), *Cultural Psychology: Essays on Comparative Human Development*. 287–308. Cambridge: Cambridge University Press.

Ochs, E. (1993) Constructing social identity. *Research on Language and Social Interaction* 26: 287–306.

Ochs, E. (1996) Linguistic resources for socializing humanity. In J. J. Gumperz and S. L. Levinson (eds.), *Rethinking Linguistic Relativity*. 407–37. Cambridge: Cambridge University Press.

Ochs, E. and Schieffelin, B. B. (2008) Language socialization: A historical overview. In P. Duff and N. Hornberger (eds.), *Encyclopedia of Language and Education, Vol. 8: Language Socialization*. 3–16. New York: Springer.

Park, E. (2008) Intergenerational transmission of cultural values in Korean American families: An analysis of the verb suffix -ta. *Heritage Language Journal* 6(2): 21–53.

Peyton, J. K., Ranard, D. A., and McGinnis, S. (eds.) (2001) *Heritage Languages in America: Preserving a National Resource*. McHenry, IL and Washington, DC: Delta Systems/Center for Applied Linguistics.

Rampton, B. (1995) *Crossing: Language and Ethnicity Among Adolescents*. New York: Longman.

Reyes, A. and Lo, A. (eds.) (2009) *Beyond Yellow English*. New York: Oxford University Press.

Rosaldo, R. (1994) Cultural citizenship and educational democracy. *Cultural Anthropology* 9(3): 402–11.

Schieffelin, B. B. and Ochs, E. (eds.) (1986) *Language Socialization Across Cultures*. New York: Cambridge University Press.

Schieffelin, B. B. and Ochs, E. (1996) The microgenesis of competence. In D. Slobin, J. Gerhardt, A. Kyratzis, and J. Guo (eds.), *Social Interaction, Social Context, and Language*. 251–64. Mahwah, NJ: Lawrence Erlbaum.

Shin, S. J. (2005) *Developing in Two Languages: Korean Children in America*. Clevedon, UK: Multilingual Matters.

Schwartz, A. M. (2003) *No me suena!*: Heritage Spanish speakers' writing strategies. In A. Roca and M. C. Colombi (eds.), *Mi Lengua: Spanish as a Heritage Language in the United States*. 235–56.

Washington, DC: Georgetown University Press.

Tse, L. (1997) *Ethnic Identity Development and the Role of the Heritage Language.* Doctoral Dissertation. Los Angeles, CA: University of Southern California.

Tse, L. (2000) The effects of ethnic identity formation on bilingual maintenance and development: An analysis of Asian American narratives. *International Journal of Bilingual Education and Bilingualism* 3: 185–200.

Tse, L. (2002) Heritage language literacy: A study of US biliterates. *Language, Culture, and Curriculum* 14(3): 256–68.

Valdés, G. (1997) The teaching of Spanish to bilingual Spanish-speaking students: Outstanding issues and unanswered questions. In M. C. Colombi and F. X. Alarcón (eds.), *La Ensenanza del Español a Hispanohablantes: Praxis y Teoría (Teaching Spanish to Spanish Speakers: Practice and Theory).* 93–101. Boston, MA: Houghton Mifflin.

Valdés, G. (2001) Heritage language students: Profiles and possibilities. In J. K. Peyton, D. A. Ranard, and S. McGinnis (eds.), *Heritage Languages in America. Preserving a National Resource.* 37–80. McHenry, IL: Center for Applied Linguistics.

van Deusen-Scholl, N. (2003) Toward a definition of heritage language: Sociopolitical and pedagogical considerations. *Journal of Language, Identity, and Education* 2(3): 211–30.

Watson-Gegeo, K. A. (2004) Mind, language, and epistemology: Toward a language socialization paradigm for SLA. *The Modern Language Journal* 88(3): 331–50.

Wiley, T. (2001) On defining heritage languages and their speakers. In J. K. Peyton, D. A. Ranard, and S. McGinnis (eds.), *Heritage Languages in America: Preserving a National Resource.* 29–36. McHenry, IL and Washington, DC: Delta Systems/Center for Applied Linguistics.

Wiley, T. and Valdés, G. (2000) Heritage language instruction in the United States: A time for renewal. *Bilingual Research Journal* (24)4: i–v.

Wong Fillmore, L. (1996) What happens when languages are lost? An essay on language assimilation and cultural identity. In D. Slobin, J. Gerhardt, A. Kyratzis, and J. Guo (eds.), *Social Interaction, Social Context and Language: Essays in Honor of Susan Ervin-Tripp.* 435–46. Mahwah, NJ: Lawrence Erlbaum.

Wortham, S. (2005) Socialization beyond the speech event. *Journal of Linguistic Anthropology* 15(1): 95–112.

Xiao, Y. (2008) Home literacy environment in CHL development. In A. W. He, and Y. Xiao (eds.), *Chinese as a Heritage Language: Fostering Rooted World Citizenry.* 259–66. Honolulu, HI: University of Hawaii Press.

Zentella, A. (1997) *Growing Up Bilingual.* Oxford: Blackwell.

26 Language Socialization and Language Endangerment

ANGELA M. NONAKA

Introduction

Language socialization and language endangerment are two topics of central interest to linguistic anthropologists, sociolinguists, and others doing fieldwork-based research at the nexus of language and society. 'Though the term "endangered languages" is of recent (post-1980) origin,' recording, describing, and preserving threatened linguistic diversity is a long-standing scholarly practice (Moore 2001: 60). Language socialization, by contrast, is a relatively new domain of inquiry interested in 'the relationship between communication and culture from the perspective of the acquisition of language and socialization through language' (Ochs and Schieffelin 1984: 276).

As real-world phenomena, language socialization and language endangerment have a profound impact on each other, although as fields of academic research they have developed along separate trajectories and tend to be practiced by scholars in different disciplines. Consequently, the full extent of the mutual interplay and influence of language socialization and language endangerment remains something of a mystery – an irony given that language acquisition, use, transmission, and vitality are inextricably linked.

Language endangerment is occurring on a larger scale and at a faster pace than ever before. If current trends continue, experts predict that at least 50 percent of extant languages are at risk of disappearing within the next century.[1] Those statistics have given pause as well as cause for concern internationally, and in recent years there has been a revival of interest not only in preserving but also in rejuvenating endangered languages (see Friedman, this volume).

The Handbook of Language Socialization, First Edition. Edited by Alessandro Duranti, Elinor Ochs, and Bambi B. Schieffelin.

Contemporary work on language endangerment differs from previous research in two significant ways. Whereas earlier studies diagnosed endangerment, current research attempts early detection of language tip[2] by assessing language and speech community vitality (Lewis 2008; Nonaka 2009; UNESCO 2003); and, whereas previous language documentation efforts were largely academic exercises in salvage linguistics, contemporary documentary linguistic fieldwork is often conducted – at the behest of and in cooperation with local communities – with the goal of reversing language shift (Fishman 1991) and revitalizing threatened languages (Hinton and Hale 2001; Munro 2002; Reyhner et al. 1999; Yamamoto, Linn, and Peter 2004). These expanded, new approaches to language endangerment are benefitting from dialogue with and also enriching language socialization studies (Leonard 2007; Morris and Jones 2008).

Although language endangerment and language socialization are inseparable phenomena, scholarly studies about them have developed independently – an intellectual historical consequence of the reconstitution of anthropology and linguistics as separate intellectual disciplines after World War II. This chapter brings together relevant literatures from language endangerment and language socialization studies. A summary of current discussions and debates about language endangerment is provided, followed by a review of the modest but growing body of research that elucidates language socialization's complex, multifaceted relationship(s) to language endangerment.

Despite growing awareness of and concern about language endangerment, most discussions of the phenomenon focus on spoken languages and ignore imperiled manual-visual languages. By contrast, this chapter concludes with a case study analysis of an endangered sign language in Thailand. Sign language isolates such as Ban Khor Sign Language are among the world's least documented but most threatened languages. The Ban Khor case study highlights the efficacy of holistic ethnographic language socialization research for explicating the vitality or vulnerability of this rare type of language variety and also underscores the utility of a language socialization approach for expanding endangered language archives.

Language Endangerment

Languages have appeared and disappeared since time immemorial. Long-lost languages such as Akkadian, Phrygian, Ugaritic, and many other languages of antiquity attest to this fact. This vanishing process – which entails many different causes, domains of use, speeds, and phases – is referred to variously as 'language shift' (Fishman 1964; Weinreich 1953: 68–9); 'language obsolescence' (Dorian 1989; Jones 1998; Swadesh 1948); 'language death' (Crystal 2000; Cust 1899; Dressler and Wodak-Leodolter 1977; Sasse 1990); 'language extinction' (Nettle and Romaine 2000); and so forth.[3]

Language endangerment is a complex phenomenon, one that exists on a continuum and therefore is a matter of degree. Precise and concise definitions are difficult to come by, for there are numerous classifications, scales, and typologies that attempt to gauge the phenomenon. 'Unfortunately, however, they do not always distinguish different types of criteria, and consequently, the classifications proposed are sometimes inconsistent and confusing' (Tsunoda 2005: 19). Nevertheless, one widely accepted and oft-quoted definition is the following (UNESCO 2003):

> A language is in danger when its speakers cease to use it, use it in an increasingly reduced number of communicative domains, and cease to pass it on from one generation to the next. That is, there are no new speakers, either adults or children.

Language shift can occur gradually or quickly, unintentionally or deliberately, willingly or unwillingly (see Garrett, this volume). Multiple factors – demographic, economic, environmental, historical, ideological, pedagogical, political, psychological, and social – operating at different levels (micro and macro, local or national, international or supranational), usually simultaneously, contribute to language endangerment. Languages are threatened for many complex reasons, including but not limited to migration, population decline, industrialization, economic mobility, natural disasters, plague epidemics, local language ideologies, national language policies, formal education, warfare, colonization, shame, stigma, secularization, and urbanization. Scores of case studies of at-risk languages around the world reveal how complicated and multifaceted the phenomenon of language endangerment is (e.g. Bobaljik, Pensalfini, and Storto 1996; Bradley and Bradley 2002; Brenzinger 1992, 2007; Broderick 1999; Fase, Jaspaert, and Kroon 1992; Garrett 2006; Grenoble and Whaley 1998; Hill 1983; Hill and Hill 1977; Ishtiaq 1999; Janse and Tol 2003; Matsumura 1998; Mougeon 1976; Nonaka 2004; Robins and Uhlenbeck 1991; Shoji and Janhunen 1997; Timm 1973).

Language endangerment has been an enduring concern since the advent of anthropology in the United States (e.g. Bloomfield 1927; Boas 1911; Haas 1968; Hoijer 1933; Sapir 1922). Indeed, the specter of linguistic, and by extension cultural, loss was a primary motivation for the early American(ist) emphasis on widespread language documentation and description – work that predominated throughout the first half of the twentieth century (Darnell 2001; Moore 2001). That research focus shifted after World War II, however, as linguistics and anthropology split into separate disciplines with ever-greater intradisciplinary differentiation and with increasingly specialized and distinct(ive) methodologies, theories, and scholarly research agendas. Disciplinary divergence coincided with a surge of new approaches to the study of language – that is, ethnography of speaking, speech act theory, conversation analysis, language ideologies, and, of course, formal linguistics – all of which resulted in a trend away from traditional documentary linguistics (Ahlers and Wertheim 2009; Duranti 2003; Woodbury 2011).

In recent decades, however, there has been a revival of interest in and concern about language endangerment. Languages are disappearing on an unprecedented scale and at an unparalleled speed – a magnitude and pace that may further diminish linguistic diversity by disrupting linguistic differentiation through normal processes of historical linguistic change. Whereas in past millennia there was a continual process of contraction and expansion of linguistic diversity as 'agricultural and pastoralist societies created large regions occupied by a single linguistic family' that subsequently became internally diverse, 'the situation now is that linguistic diversity is simply being lost without languages being replaced'; thus, current patterns of language disappearance are 'more desperate now' than ever before (Ash, Fermino, and Hale 2001: 19).

Within the last 15 years, the rapidly escalating problem of disappearing languages has received both professional and popular attention and concern. Organizations ranging from the United Nations to the Linguistic Society of America have adopted policy stands emphasizing the value and importance of documenting and preserving linguistic diversity around the world (Linguistic Society of America 1994; UNESCO 2003). Funding for such work has followed, provided by a number of public institutions and private foundations – for example, the National Endowment for the Humanities, the National Science Foundation, the EuroBabel Initiative, the Endangered Language Fund, the Foundation for Endangered Languages, and the Hans Rausing Endangered Languages Project. This has resulted in a recent explosion of research on the subject of language endangerment.

Inevitably, renewed scholarly interest in language endangerment has generated debate and controversy. For example, when languages vanish, is it a natural process or a threat to biocultural diversity? And, by extension, when languages are threatened, should research be motivated strictly by scientific observation (e.g. nonintervention) or by humanitarian concerns (e.g. activism)? These questions are at the heart of a debate over how best to conceptualize the phenomenon of disappearing languages and how best to respond to it (see Dorian 1993; Hale 1992; Hale et al. 1992; Harrison 2007; Krauss 1992; Ladefoged 1992; Maffi 2001; Romaine 2008). Another area of controversy involves critical approaches to discourses about language endangerment, including the applications, implications, and consequences of those discourses for professional linguists and anthropologists researching and publishing on issues of language endangerment; for native speakers and local communities that (do not) use endangered languages; and for nation states' language policies and ideologies (de Swaan 2004; Dorian 2002; Duchêne and Heller 2007; England 2002; Fishman 2002; Hill 2002; Hinton 2002).

Debates notwithstanding, there is now broad professional consensus about the importance of documenting existing linguistic diversity, 'with highest priority given to the many languages which are closest to becoming extinct, and also to the many languages which represent the greatest diversity' (Linguistic Society of America 1994: 181–2). 'At the same time, a broader public of educators, students, politicians, activists, and indigenous communities have been engaged in a dialogue about the value of languages, cultures and human diversity in the face of encroaching globalization' (Harrison, Rood, and Dwyer 2008: 3).

According to United Nations' estimates, 'About 97 percent of the world's people speak about 4 percent of the world's languages; and conversely about 96 percent of the world's languages are spoken by about 3 percent of the world's people. Most of the world's language heterogeneity, then, is under the steward-ship of a very small number of people' (UNESCO 2003). The prognosis for many 'small' languages (as measured by number of speakers) is grim. Nevertheless, there is growing enthusiasm for keeping such languages alive. Individuals, fami-lies, and communities are undertaking documentation not just for preservation but also for revitalization of endangered languages. Their efforts can benefit from dialogue with as well as further enrich language socialization studies.

Language Socialization Studies

The temporary decline and recent resurrection of concern for language endanger-ment is but one of a myriad outcomes of the disciplinary transformation that began in the second half of the twentieth century and led to the establishment of separate departments of linguistics and anthropology. Language socialization focuses on 'both linguistic form and sociocultural context, [which] allows the researcher to integrate micro and macro levels of investigation' – that is, everyday language practices and ideologies and large-scale socioeconomic and historical events and trends – to elucidate and explain 'broader issues of sociocultural change and reproduction,' which is highly relevant to language maintenance and endangerment (Garrett 1999: 9).

Language socialization – the process of acquiring language and becoming a competent member of society through the use of language (Ochs and Schieffelin 1984) – arose as a new domain of study in anthropology during the 1980s. At the time, the discipline was experiencing an identity crisis of sorts. Interpretive, post-modern, critical, deconstructionist approaches were problematizing a founda-tional pillar of anthropological study – the notion of 'culture' (e.g. Clifford 1988; Clifford and Marcus 1986; Geertz 1973; Ortner 1984). As previous descriptions and theories of culture came under fire, accused of being ahistorical, monolithic reifica-tions, the search began for more nuanced accounts sensitive to historicity, hetero-geneity, and agentive change. Yet the foundational anthropological holistic challenge remained: explaining the existence and persistence of patterned, sys-tematic cultural coherence built from elements of particularism, variation, and change.

In the case of linguistic anthropology, this led to investigations of the mutually constitutive nature of language and lived social life and, in that vein, building on their earlier work in *Developmental Pragmatics* (1979), Ochs and Schieffelin prof-fered language socialization – an approach that offers 'a comprehensive and synthetic treatment [. . .] of research on language acquisition and cultural trans-mission through language learning' (Shweder 1984: 22–3). Language socialization constitutes both theory and method. Firmly rooted in the ethnographic tradition, it focuses on the study of language and language use *in situ*. Language socializa-tion research involves rich and rigorous case study description that can support both specific and comparative analysis.

In the classic article that started it all, Ochs and Schieffelin (1984) examined the socialization practices and ideologies of everyday talk and interaction between children and adult caregivers in three societies: among Western Samoans, the Kaluli of Papua New Guinea, and white middle-class Americans. Ochs and Schieffelin advocated analyzing linguistically and culturally specific instances of language socialization as 'developmental stories' that share basic overarching goals and functions (i.e. promoting linguistic and communicative enculturation) but vary significantly in form (i.e. particular values and practices). The developmental story was a comparative model that organized early language socialization work (Heath 1983; Ochs 1988; Schieffelin 1990; Schieffelin and Ochs 1986b). Subsequently, however, the research paradigm expanded dramatically, and now examines not only adult–child interactions but also expert–novice language socialization generally (Duff and Hornberger 2008; Garrett and Baquedano-López 2002; Ochs and Schieffelin 1995; Schieffelin and Ochs 1986a).[4]

Within the language socialization literature, a few works have examined issues of language endangerment and shift. These studies began appearing in the 1990s and continue to proliferate. Undertaken in geographically, linguistically, and culturally diverse communities around the world, they include ethnographic case studies of small-scale societies in Papua New Guinea (Kulick 1992); Polynesia (Makihara 2005); the Caribbean (Garrett 1999, 2005; Paugh 2001, 2005); indigenous American communities (Augsburger 2004; Field 1998; Meek 2001, 2007; Philips 1983); and villages in Thailand (Howard 2003, 2004; Nonaka 2004). With the exception of Fader's (2006, 2007, 2009) project on Hasidic Jews in New York City, research on language socialization and language endangerment has focused on relatively small, marginalized, rural communities – perhaps because at-risk languages are often found in such settings.

Continuing in the tradition of descriptively rich and grounded ethnography, this subset of language socialization literature has broken important, new theoretical ground in the study of language endangerment, for 'although language shift is geographically and historically widespread,' for a long time, there were 'no ethnographic descriptions of it' and thus 'the process by which it occurs' was not well understood (Gal 1979: 1–2). The publication of two seminal studies, Gal's (1979) examination of language shift in bilingual Austria and Dorian's (1981) account of the life cycle of an obsolescing Scottish Gaelic dialect, drew attention to dynamics of change. While not language socialization studies, both deserve mention here because they provided ethnographically grounded case study evidence for macro-sociological correlates, and thereby offered insight into actual large-scale historical and socioeconomic processes involved in language shift or loss. Language socialization studies of language endangerment, however, go further: documenting everyday linguistic and cultural practices and local language ideologies; illustrating their delicate and complex interplay as manifested in the process of language socialization; and locating those micro-practices and ideologies of language socialization within the context of larger historical, economic, and social forces that are also operating and contributing to language endangerment.

Kulick (1992) was one of the earliest language socialization studies to address issues of language endangerment. Focusing on the first generation of non-vernacular-speaking children in a Papua New Guinea community, Kulick takes up a question that was perplexing Gapun villagers: why are local children no longer speaking Taiap but instead using the lingua franca, Tok Pisin? According to local language ideology, small children choose to use one language and not another, but Kulick illustrates that it is change in adult linguistic input, altered in the light of dynamic sociopolitical realities, that accounts for the decline of Taiap. Kulick documents 'the intricate ways in which people's interpretations of change affect how they talk to one another in mundane, day-to-day interactions and how these patterns of interaction results over time in language shift' (1992: 257–8).

The fact that language endangerment results from a complex intermeshing and interplay of local cultural beliefs and micro-practices within a larger, dynamic sociolinguistic ecology is further illustrated by two case studies of island communities in the Caribbean. Read together, these studies provide in-depth and long-term insight into processes of language shift.

Garrett's (1999) research on St. Lucia examines a case of language contact, change, convergence, and shift: the attrition of Patwa or Kwéyòl (a French lexicon Creole language), which is in sustained contact with English, and the emergence of Kwéyòl-ized English or the Vernacular English of St. Lucia (VESL). Combining macro- and micro-level approaches, he establishes the local, national, and international context(s) within which these linguistic processes are happening and within which local language socialization occurs. Garrett documents 'the culturally specific ways in which caretakers interact verbally with young children, and the ways in which children are taught, both explicitly and implicitly, to think about and to use the languages of their community' (1999: 2). Among his many findings, Garrett notes that St. Lucians are ambivalent about the different codes and their appropriate domains of use, but, as a general rule, adult caregivers believe that it is better for children to learn English and that learning Patwa interferes with learning English – language ideologies with profound consequences for intergenerational language transmission.

Paugh's (2001, 2005, this volume) study in Dominica also tracks local language ideologies and their relationship to language socialization. She too found language ambivalence about Patwa, as evidenced not only in the general, ongoing process of shift away from the language but also in 'Creole Day,' a state and urban elite-led one-day celebration of Patwa and of 'traditional culture,' festivities with artificial links to everyday life and with little real utility for language preservation or revitalization.

In a more recent publication about language shift in St. Lucia, Garrett (2005) illustrates that, while Patwa is declining in general use, it persists in code-specific genres such as children's cursing. Persistence of this sort raises interesting and complex issues that ultimately reify negative ideologies about the code that in turn continue to erode its overall viability.

Howard's (2003, 2004) study of children's language socialization in Northern Thailand offers another, albeit different, example of how code-specificity, genre, and language endangerment can intersect. In the bilingual community where Howard works, children acquire two languages: Kam Muang and Standard Thai. Standard Thai is the dominant, prestige code used for official governmental business and for formal pedagogical instruction. At school, children are actively socialized into expressing respect in and through Thai (see Howard, this volume). Thus, it is increasingly associated with politeness, while Kam Muang is not. This link between code and register reinforces language ideologies about, power relations between, and (non-) use of Kam Muang versus Thai.

Language socialization studies of endangered languages have also shed light on matters of communicative competence beyond code. A compelling illustration of this point is found in Field's (1998) study of a Native American Indian community where language shift is occurring. She has observed that, despite language shift away from Navajo to English at the level of code, 'other indigenous aspects of communicative practices, or ways of speaking,' persist, as evidenced through the use of a triadic participation structure to issue directives, use of silence as a response, and use of English language directives that are grammatically influenced by Navajo directives (1998: iii).

More manifestations of this type of 'invisible culture' are discussed by Philips (1983) in her ethnography of communication at a school on the Warm Springs Indian Reservation in Oregon. Although English is the dominant language used in the classroom on the reservation, Philips found striking evidence for the persistence of indigenous communicative practices related to use of auditory and visual channels of communication and socialization into the social structuring of attention. She examines differences between Native American and Anglo-American pragmatics and considers the implications of those difference for the educational experiences and outcomes of Indian children.

Gender is also a critical factor in language outcomes and socialization activities. Fader's (2007, 2009, this volume) ethnographic and sociolinguistic research in a New York Hasidic Jewish community analyzes the communal attitudes and beliefs that undergird intragroup notions of masculinity and femininity and discusses the links between those ideologies and quotidian activities that reinforce the distinct(ive) Hasidic male–female 'gendering of languages and persons' (Fader 2009: 127). This gendering process begins early in life and intensifies across the lifespan.

From preschool, Hasidic children's formal education is strictly sex-segregated. Hasidic boys spend the entire day in Yiddish-medium classrooms where they become fluent in both spoken and written Yiddish, in addition to developing literacy in Hebrew and Aramaic, the 'holy' languages of religious texts. As adults, men's communicative interactions are highly circumscribed, taking place primarily within the community.

Among girls, by contrast, Yiddish is 'a register increasingly associated with restricted contexts of use' (Fader 2007: 16). Their primary language of daily use is a type of syncretic English known as Yiddish English, a variety of Jewish English. 'Teachers and mothers' attribute this language shift to the fact that girls think English is 'fancy, sophisticated, ladylike, and *shtotty*, high-class or cosmopolitan,' but, as an everyday practicality, it is women who, for religious reasons, manage the communicative interface with the non-Hasidic community, most of which occurs in English (Fader 2009: 135).

Community members recognize that this process is underway, but intracommunity ideologies about and socialization into gender and gendered language use normalize, or perhaps render inevitable, language shift. As Fader explains, 'Hasidic girls' shift from Yiddish fluency' provides 'visible and audible evidence of divinely ordained gender differences between Hasidic males and females' (2007: 16).

The complex causal links between language ecology, language practices, language ideologies, and language endangerment are further illustrated by two indigenous North American case studies. Following the organization of a fairly classic language socialization study, Barbra Meek's (2001) dissertation examines language (de-)acquisition of Kaska, the ancestral language of the Liard River First Nation, located in the Yukon Territory of Canada. In a more recent article, Meek (2007) elucidates the subtle but striking ways in which changing language ideologies exacerbate language endangerment by constraining children's use of the local indigenous language. More specifically, her micro-analysis of children's and adolescents' attitudes about, comments on, and practices involving Kaska language reveals that

> while elders retained their status as intellectual authorities responsible for passing their knowledge on to younger community members, their knowledge became limited to practices conceptualized as 'traditionally Kaska.' [...] As a result, the acquisition of Kaska became subject to the same social practices that organized other forms of 'traditional indigenous' or specialized knowledge such that speaking Kaska became the domain of elders. (Meek 2007: 23)

Augsburger's (2004) analysis of a Diidxazá-speaking community in rural Mexico also highlights the critical role(s) that language ideologies play in language socialization, and, by extension, in indigenous language vitality or endangerment. She observes that 'the history of indigenous languages in Mexico has been one largely of gradual displacement by Spanish; nevertheless, many communities persist in using their ancestral language despite widespread ideological forces favoring the national language, Spanish' (Augsburger 2004: viii). 'Resistance' is identified and explored as a characteristic theme in local language ideologies that sustain indigenous languages, and Augsburger traces the origins, development, and interplay of Zapotecan language ideologies of resistance vis-à-vis the larger socioeconomic and political historical context of the nation. Then, she examines discourses about, as well as the strategies of, language socialization, comparing and contrasting talk about language socialization with real-world manifestations of the phenomenon *in situ* and its long-term consequences for language shift or maintenance. Augsburger identifies

> important contradictions between the expressed ideological support for Zapotec and everyday practices that support language shift. [For example,] parents attempt to

reconcile the competing pressures by sequencing the acquisition of the two languages so as to produce eventual bilingualism; [however], the practical realities of the family and the community keep this strategy from producing the expected results and in present form ultimately cannot deflect the steady pressure towards Spanish. As a result, parental strategies designed to promote bilingualism are contributing to the unintended consequences of language shift. (2004: viii–ix)

Another example of language shift from an indigenous language to Spanish is found in Makihara's (2005) research on Easter Island. This case study identifies a fairly predictable constellation of macro-factors and trends (e.g. colonial annexation, an influx of Spanish-speaking immigrants, integration into the world economy) that have occurred within the last half century and have led to dramatic intergenerational language shift away from Rapa Nui (Polynesian) to Spanish. At the same time, however, countervailing forces – for example, an active indigenous movement promoting elevation of the symbolic value of the local language and culture and the practical politico-economic realization of those gains due to the spread of heritage tourism – have resulted in a revival of Rapa Nui. This linguistic renaissance manifests in particular ways, though, namely in the creation of Rapa Nui Spanish and of syncretic Rapa Nui speech styles.

By attending to local sites, practices, and ideologies of language socialization, Makihara illustrates the central role that marginally bilingual children and young people are playing in the diversification of Rapa Nui speech styles. These new ways of speaking, in turn, index a new ethnic identity, both of which are emerging through active linguistic and cultural reclamation efforts.

> An observer of the macro-sociolinguistic change that has taken place on Rapa Nui might remark on the ironic and 'contradictory' way in which these children's linguistic choices, motivated by their wish to belong to their ethnic language community, are nonetheless contributing to the loss of their ethnic language. Yet, at the micro-interactional and semiotic level, these children are making rational choices to use their dominant language, Spanish, in interactions and in the performance of their Rapa Nui identity. (Makihara 2005: 755).

The full implications of these changing language ideologies and practices over time is difficult to predict, for, as Makihara explains, 'these developments will contribute to yet further transformation of the local language community, perhaps slowing or even reversing language shift and loss' (2005: 755).

Sign Languages and Language Endangerment

Anthropological language socialization studies of language shift, like the linguistic literature on language endangerment, historically have focused exclusively on imperiled spoken languages, inadvertently excluding an entire class of languages from discussions of language disappearance. Sign languages are 'the forgotten endangered languages' (Nonaka 2004). Threatened for the same reasons that spoken languages are, sign languages are at additional risk due to pathologized social constructions of deafness, negative language ideologies about sign languages, and widespread biomedical and pedagogical efforts to eradicate hearing loss and manual communication (Johnston 2004; Meier 2000).

The exact number of extant manual-visual languages is unknown, but they cluster into three types: 'national,' 'original,' and 'indigenous' or 'village' sign languages (Woodward 2000; Zeshan 2004). Endangerment is acute among languages of the third variety.

'Indigenous' or 'village' sign languages emerge in restricted settings: small, face-to-face communities with labor-intensive, nonindustrial economies; low intracommunity occupational and educational differentiation between deaf and hearing people; and high degrees of kinship (biological or nonbiological). This language variety corresponds with a special kind of speech community that shares the essential characteristics and functions of any other speech community but that also evinces distinctive characteristics and dimensions. The *conditio sine qua non* of a 'speech/sign community' is 'moral *habitus*,' which resides in the social praxis of deafness (Nonaka 2007, 2009). In villages where indigenous sign languages spontaneously develop, significant numbers of hearing people acquire and use the local sign language with deaf residents. Sign language fluency among the former fosters social integration of the latter, which begets better attitudes toward deaf people and sign language. This interactional dynamic maintains the local sign language and transforms the speech community into a speech/sign community.

As I have previously stated, 'the sociolinguistic ecologies of village sign languages and speech/sign communities are delicate and fragile. Indigenous sign languages tend to arise suddenly, spread rapidly, and disappear quickly' (2009: 214). Their compressed life cycles render them vulnerable to extinction. A case in point is Ban Khor Sign Language, an imperiled village sign language in Thailand. Illustrating the utility of holistic ethnographic language socialization research for elucidating indigenous sign language endangerment, the next section reviews the conditions that supported the spontaneous emergence of Ban Khor Sign Language; describes the particular language ideologies and practices that sustain it; and identifies the changes in language ecology that now threaten the language.

Language Socialization and Endangerment of Ban Khor Sign Language[5]

Ban Khor is a village like many others in northeastern Thailand: a Theravada Buddhist community of subsistence rice agriculturalists who supplement their daily diets by foraging or fishing and who augment their annual incomes by conducting small-scale economic activities or by working as seasonal migrant laborers outside the village. Demographically, Ban Khor is unremarkable, save for the number of deaf residents. There are 16 (formerly 17) deaf individuals in a population of 2,741, a number that is 6 to 11 times greater than the expected incidence of congenital hearing loss.

The linguistic anthropological impact of Ban Khor's deaf population, proportional to its size, has been great. The appearance of 'hereditary' deafness (understood locally as a karmic rather than a genetic phenomenon) was the precipitating event for creation of a new sign language and speech/sign community.

Ban Khor Sign Language (BKSL) arose *de novo* around 75 years ago. It began as a home sign system[6] among members of the family to whom the first two deaf individuals were born but quickly became a full-fledged sign language that is now three generations deep and used by more than 400 people.

While deaf people were crucial for the emergence of BKSL, both deaf and hearing villagers are vital for its maintenance. Unlike most speech communities, where deaf people are expected to make linguistic accommodations (e.g. learning to speak or write the dominant language, using an interpreter, or forming a distinct deaf community), in speech/sign communities linguistic accommodation is made by hearing people who acquire the local sign language.

Hearing villagers' willingness to learn and use BKSL is consistent with broader concessionary linguistic accommodations they routinely make. With the exception of Thai, all four of the vernacular languages spoken in Ban Khor are sociolinguistically marginal (Smalley 1994). The prospect of learning one more – BKSL – is unproblematic in a community where multilingualism is the norm.

The two patterns of accommodation described above derive from more basic Thai patterns of enculturation. 'Accommodation,' as it is classically understood in language socialization studies, refers to the tendency of adults in a society to adapt themselves, their language, and the interactional situation to the needs and abilities of the child, while 'nonaccommodation' implies the opposite, an expectation that children should adjust their communicative interactions to the requirements of the situation (Ochs and Schieffelin 1984). Comparative ethnographic research outlines a cross-cultural continuum of accommodation versus nonaccommodation, and Ban Khor falls somewhere midway on that continuum.

In their communicative interactions with babies, Ban Khorians tend to let them be. Infants are carefully monitored and lovingly attended, but if they are not nursing or in need of immediate attention they are often left bundled in blankets under mosquito netting. Babies are seldom constructed as conversational partners, although this changes as they grow. Thus, accommodation is evident in the primary language socialization of children aged 9–24 months. BKSL has a Baby Talk register. Its classic characteristics mirror those of Baby Talk in American Sign Language and include '(i) heightened affect, (ii) active physical stimulation of the child, (iii) signing more slowly than usual, (iv) signing close to the child to maximize visual attention, (v) signing on the child's body, and (vi) repetition' (Nonaka 2004: 754). Adults often talk/sign to toddlers using Baby Talk or other child-directed utterances. Playing peek-a-boo and other linguistic games is common too.

By age three, however, use of Baby Talk with children ceases in Ban Khor. Child-rearing in Thailand is permissive (Piker 1964) in most ways, save one. Thai society is quite hierarchical, and early on children are socialized to begin adjusting their communicative interactions to conform to the cultural norms of hierarchy. They should be polite and demonstrate respect, both linguistically and nonlinguistically (Howard 2003).

Cooperation is also highly valued in rural Thai society. Ban Khorians expect and are expected to help one another; they do so often and, usually, reciprocally. Mutual assistance is extended to family members, neighbors, and friends but also to community members at large. This cooperative ethos is manifested in everyday practices and cultural patterns of caregiving that have contributed to the maintenance and spread of BKSL.

In Thailand the basic family unit is the nuclear family. Kinship and descent are bilateral and, ideally, postmarital residence is matrilocal. Upon marriage, the groom moves into his wife's natal home (or her mother's family compound), where the newlyweds live for a few years or permanently. Thus, when the new couple becomes parents, they have abundant social support.

Most children are born at home, and for a few days or weeks after giving birth the new mother is literally expected to 'lie by the fire' – a postpartum tradition that is both a curative practice and a rite of passage whereby a woman 'cooks/ripens' or fully matures (Hanks 1963). While she lies by the fire, the new mother is exempted from all work. Her only duties are to nurse the newborn, to drink special hot herbal water that promotes richer breast milk production, and to heal her genitals by washing them with another special herbal water. During this period of recuperation, her husband and kinsmen assume all of her normal household responsibilities and also attend to the needs of the baby. Extended family members are in charge of bathing the child, changing and washing soiled clothing and bedding, arranging a Buddhist 'christening' ceremony, and even taking the newborn to the health center to register its birth.

Distributed, multiparty caregiving is the norm in Ban Khor. Once a child is weaned, it is quite common for others in the household (e.g. young, unmarried aunts or cousins) to assume primary childcare responsibilities. When they are slightly older, children sometimes choose to live at other homes in their grandmother's compound or at the houses of other relatives. Flexible caregiving of this sort influences language socialization in interesting ways. For example, in several instances, a deaf aunt became the primary caregiver for a hearing niece or nephew who grew up to be fluent in BKSL.

As in other societies, Ban Khorian children are first exposed to the language(s) of their community at home. Many of the best hearing BKSL signers are the close relatives (e.g. children or siblings) of deaf people with whom they live. Prototypical primary language socialization among coresident family members is insufficient, however, to explain the spread of BKSL to 15~26 percent of all villagers within less than a century, because in Ban Khor there are only nine households with deaf residents, who total less than 20 village-wide. Yet there are hundreds of people who can sign.

The rapid transmission of BKSL has not occurred randomly. Of those who know BKSL, 73 percent reside in the same area of the village where most deaf Ban

Khorians live. Signers also draw almost exclusively from one social class; they are farmers, as are all the deaf people and their families. Relatives and neighbors of deaf people are likely to acquire BKSL. In short, there are clear correlations between a hearing person's proximity (e.g. relational links) to and interactions with deaf people and his/her signing ability – the closer and more frequent, the better.

Ban Khor Sign Language has thrived for several decades, but now it is increasingly threatened by contact with the country's national sign language. Thai Sign Language (TSL) is entering the village speech/sign community by several means. Unlike earlier generations, young deaf Ban Khorians attend residential deaf schools outside the village where TSL is the language of instruction. New community outreach adult education initiatives also promote TSL by distributing free dictionaries. Greater contact with the national Deaf community, however, is the primary reason for TSL's growing influence in Ban Khor. More deaf villagers are participating in activities of the National Association of the Deaf; seeking employment outside the village; and marrying deaf people from other communities.

These changes in the local language ecology have intensified language contact and triggered language shift. During the last decade, lexical borrowing from TSL into BKSL has risen dramatically, and code-switching has started too. Contrary to existing theories of language maintenance of national sign languages, in Ban Khor hearing signers are becoming the critical 'keepers' of BKSL.

For deaf Ban Khorians, TSL is both a lingua franca (for communication with other deaf people) and a prestige code (for potential social, economic, and political mobility). Hearing villagers, by contrast, have no incentive to learn the language. Their continued use of BKSL is slowing language shift but is unlikely to prevent or reverse it because hearing people acquire sign language in order to communicate with deaf Ban Khorians who are increasingly motivated to learn TSL due to its relative sociolinguistic power and utility. Regrettably, this dynamic, projected over time, bodes ill for the continued viability of BKSL.

Conclusion

Like other village sign languages, BKSL is a young language but already an imperiled one. Widespread endangerment of this language variety is regrettable because study of indigenous sign languages and speech/sign communities enriches our collective knowledge of both linguistics and anthropology, underscoring the extent of the world's linguistic (signed as well as spoken) and cultural (deaf as well as hearing) diversity.

Language socialization's efficacy for illuminating matters of language endangerment has been demonstrated in several communities with threatened spoken languages. The approach is especially promising, however, for study of imperiled indigenous sign languages and other severely under-documented languages because, in addition to holistically elucidating processes of language shift, language socialization research generates robust and internally diverse data corpora that are currently missing from most endangered language archives. Lamenting the 'frustrating gaps' caused by the dearth of video-recorded data of real-world language use in everyday contexts, documentary linguists note that 'relatively few speech communities have been studied in this way, and for many it will soon be too late (Hinton 2001: 11). Language socialization's emphasis on study of language *in situ* captures precisely these types of data, which are useful not only for the preservation but for the revitalization of endangered languages.

ACKNOWLEDGMENTS

I thank the following individuals and groups for their assistance and support: Alessandro Duranti, Elinor Ochs, Bambi Schieffelin, Merav Shohet, Heather Loyd, Inma García-Sánchez, Chiho Sunakawa, Ana Luisa Gediel, Enrique Rodriguez, Deborah Bolnick, Beth Pomeroy, Yasmine Beale-Rosana-Rivaya, the National Science Foundation, the Wenner-Gren Foundation, IIE Fulbright, the Thai–US Educational Foundation, Ratchasuda College, Ratchasuda Foundation, and the community of Ban Khor.

NOTES

1   Many predictions are higher, between 50 and 90 percent.
2   A precise term for a nebulous process, 'language tip' has been defined thusly: 'In terms of possible routes toward language death, it would seem that a language which has been demographically highly stable for several centuries may experience a sudden 'tip,' after which the demographic tide flows strongly in favor of some other language' (Dorian 1981: 51).
3   Many terms are used to describe the phenomenon of language disappearance. Some authors use the various terms synonymously, while others do not. Tsunoda (2005) provides a detailed list and a useful discussion of the various terminologies.
4   The terms 'primary' and 'secondary' socialization (Duranti 2003: 330–1), respectively, have also been used to refer to adult caregiver–child and expert–novice socialization relationships, activities, and contexts.
5   Findings in this section derive from over a decade of ethnographic fieldwork in Ban Khor. Diverse qualitative and quantitative methods were used, including systematic videographic observation of five children's language development and socialization for 11 consecutive months during 2003.
6   Home sign' refers to 'the gestural communication that typically develops within a family or limited social sphere where one member is deaf and no pre-existing signed language is available' (Kegl, Senghas, and Coppola 1999: 183).

REFERENCES

Ahlers, J. and Wertheim, S. (2009) Introduction: Reflecting on language and culture fieldwork in the early 21st century. *Language & Communication* 29: 193–8.

Ash, A., Fermino, J. L. D., and Hale, K. (2001) Diversity in local language maintenance and restoration: A reason for optimism. In L. Hinton and K. Hale (eds.), *The Green Book of Language Revitalization in Practice*. 19–35. San Diego, CA: Academic Press.

Augsburger, D. (2004) *Language Socialization and Shift in an Isthmus Zapotec Community of Mexico*. Doctoral Dissertation. Philadelphia, PA: University of Pennsylvania.

Bloomfield, L. (1927) Literate and illiterate speech. *American Speech* 2: 432–9.

Boas, F. (1911) *Handbook of American Indian Languages*. Washington, DC: Bureau of Indian Affairs Government Printing.

Bobaljik, J. D., Pensalfini, R., and Storto, L. (eds.) (1996) *Papers on Language Endangerment and the Maintenance of Linguistic Diversity*. MIT Working Papers in Linguistics 28. Cambridge, MA.

Bradley, D. and Bradley, M. (eds.) (2002) *Language Endangerment and Language Maintenance*. London: Routledge Curzon.

Brenzinger, M. (ed.) (1992) *Language Death: Factual and Theoretical Explorations with Special Reference to East Africa*. New York: Mouton de Gruyter.

Brenzinger, M. (ed.) (2007) *Language Diversity Endangered*. Trends in Linguistics Studies and Monographs 181. Berlin and New York: Mouton de Gruyter.

Broderick, G. (1999) *Language Death in the Isle of Man: An Investigation Into the Decline and Extinction of Manx Gaelic as a Community Language in the Isle of Man*. Tübingen, Germany: Max Niemeyer.

Clifford, J. (1988) *The Predicament of Culture: Twentieth-Century Ethnography, Literature, and Art*. Cambridge, MA: Harvard University Press.

Clifford, J. and Marcus, G. E. (eds) (1986) *Writing Culture: The Poetics and Politics of Ethnography*. Berkeley, CA: University of California Press.

Crystal, D. (2000) *Language Death*. Cambridge: University of Cambridge Press.

Cust, R. N. (1899) *Language its I. Birth, II. Development and Life, and III. Decay and Death*. London: Spottiswoode and Company.

Darnell, R. (2001) *Invisible Genealogies: A History of Americanist Anthropology*. Lincoln, NE: University of Nebraska Press.

de Swaan, A. (2004) Endangered languages, sociolinguistics, and linguistic sentimentalism. *European Review* 12(40): 567–80.

Dorian, N. (1981) *Language Death: The Life Cycle of a Scottish Gaelic Dialect*. Philadelphia, PA: University of Pennsylvania Press.

Dorian, N. (ed.) (1989) *Investigating Obsolescence: Studies in Language Contraction and Death*. Cambridge: Cambridge University Press.

Dorian, N. (1993) A response to Ladefoged's other view of endangered languages. *Language* 69: 75–9.

Dorian, N. (2002) Commentary: Broadening the rhetorical and descriptive horizons in endangered language linguistics. *Journal of Linguistic Anthropology* 12: 134–40.

Dressler, W. and Wodak-Leodolter, R. (eds.) (1977) *Language Death (Special Issue of International Journal of the Sociology of Language 12)*. New York: Mouton.

Duchêne, A. and Heller, M. (eds.) (2007) *Discourses of Endangerment: Ideology and Interest in the Defence of Languages*. London and New York: Continuum.

Duff, P. A. and Hornberger, N. H. (eds.) (2008) *Encyclopedia of Language and Education, Vol. 8: Language Socialization*. New York: Springer.

Duranti, A. (2003) Language as culture in US anthropology. *Current Anthropology* 44(3): 323–47.

England, N. (2002) Commentary: Further rhetorical concerns. *Journal of Linguistic Anthropology* 12: 141–3.

Fader, A. (2006) Learning faith: Language socialization in a Hasidic community. *Language in Society* 35(2): 207–29.

Fader, A. (2007) Reclaiming sacred sparks: Linguistic syncretism and gendered language shift among Hasidic Jews in New York. *Journal of Linguistic Anthropology* 17(1): 1–22.

Fader, A. (2009) *Mitzvah Girls: Bringing Up the Next Generation of Hasidic Jews in Brooklyn*. Princeton, NJ: Princeton University Press.

Fase, W., Jaspaert, K., and Kroon, S. (eds.) (1992) *Maintenance and Loss of Minority Languages*. Amsterdam, The Netherlands/Philadelphia, PA: John Benjamins.

Field, M. (1998) *Maintenance of Ways of Speaking in a Community Undergoing Language Shift: Language Socialization in a Navajo Preschool*. Doctoral Dissertation. Santa Barbara, CA: University of California, Santa Barbara.

Fishman, J. (1964) Language maintenance and language shift as a field of inquiry. *Linguistics* 9: 32–70.

Fishman, J. (1991) *Reversing Language Shift: Theoretical and Empirical Foundations of Assistance to Threatened Languages*. Bristol, PA: Multilingual Matters.

Fishman, J. (2002) Commentary: What a difference 40 years makes! *Journal of Linguistic Anthropology* 12(2): 144–9.

Gal, S. (1979) *Language Shift: Social Determinants of Linguistic Change in Bilingual Austria*. New York: Academic Press.

Garrett, P. B. (1999) *Language Socialization, Convergence, and Shift in St. Lucia, West Indies*. Doctoral Dissertation. New York: New York University.

Garrett, P. B. (2005) What a language is good for: Language socialization, language shift, and the persistence of code-specific genres in St. Lucia. *Language in Society* 34: 327–61.

Garrett, P. B. (2006) Contact languages as 'endangered' languages: What is there to lose? *Journal of Pidgin and Creole Languages* 21(1): 175–90.

Garrett, P. B. and Baquedano-López, P. (2002) Language socialization: Reproduction and continuity, transformation and change. *Annual Review of Anthropology* 31: 339–61.

Geertz, C. (1973) *The Interpretation of Cultures*. New York: Basic Books.

Grenoble, L. A. and Whaley, L. J. (eds.) (1998) *Endangered Languages: Current Issues and Future Prospects*. Cambridge: Cambridge University Press.

Haas, M. R. (1968) The last words of Biloxi. *International Journal of American Linguistics* 34: 77–84.

Hale, K. M. (1992) Language endangerment and the human value of linguistic diversity. *Language* 68(1): 1–3.

Hale, K. M., Krauss, M., Watahomigie, L. J., Yamamoto, A. Y., Craig, C., LaVerne, M. J., and England, N. C. (1992) Endangered languages. *Language* 68(1): 1–42.

Hanks, J. R. (1963) *Maternity and Its Rituals in Bang Chan*. Cornell University Southeast Asia Program, Data Paper 51. Ithaca, NY: Cornell University.

Harrison, K. D. (2007) *When Languages Die: The Extinction of the World's Languages and the Erosion of Human Knowledge*. Oxford: Oxford University Press.

Harrison, K. D., Rood, D. S., and Dwyer, A. (2008) A world of many voices: Editors' introduction. In K. Harrison, D. S. Rood, and A. Dwyer (eds.) *Lessons from Documented Endangered Languages*.

1–11. Amsterdam, The Netherlands: John Benjamins.

Heath, S. B. (1983) *Ways with Words: Language, Life, and Work in Communities and Classrooms*. New York: Cambridge University Press.

Hill, J. H. (1983) Language death in Uto-Aztecan. *International Journal of American Linguistics* 49(3): 258–76.

Hill, J. (2002) 'Expert rhetorics' in advocacy for endangered languages: Who is listening, and what do they hear? *Journal of Linguistic Anthropology* 12: 119–33.

Hill, J. and Hill, K. (1977) Language death and relexification in Tlaxcalan Nahuatl. *International Journal of the Sociology of Language* 12: 55–69.

Hinton, L. (2001) Language revitalization: An overview. In L. Hinton and K. Hale (eds.) *The Green Book of Language Revitalization in Practice*. 3–18. San Diego, CA: Academic Press.

Hinton, L. (2002) Commentary: Internal and external language advocacy. *Journal of Linguistic Anthropology* 12: 150–6.

Hinton, L., and Hale, K. (eds.) (2001) *The Green Book of Language Revitalization in Practice*. San Diego, CA: Academic Press.

Hoijer, H. (1933) *Tonkawa: An Indian language of Texas*. New York: Columbia University Press.

Howard, K. M. (2003) *Language Socialization in a Northern Thai Bilingual Community*. Doctoral Dissertation. Los Angeles, CA: University of California, Los Angeles.

Howard, K. (2004) Socializing respect at school in Northern Thailand. *Working Papers in Educational Linguistics* 20(1): 1–30.

Ishtiaq, M. (1999) *Language Shifts Among the Scheduled Tribes in India: A Geographical Study*. Delhi: Motilal Banardsidass Publishers Private Limited.

Janse, M. and Tol, S. (eds.) (2003) *Language Death and Language Maintenance: Theoretical, Practical and Descriptive Approaches. (Series IV—Current Issues in Linguistic Theory)*. Amsterdam, The Netherlands and Philadelphia, PA: John Benjamins.

Johnston, T. (2004) W(h)ither the deaf community? Population, genetics, and the future of Australian sign language. *American Annals of the Deaf* 148(5): 358–75.

Jones, M. C. (1998) *Language Obsolescence and Revitalization: Linguistic Change in Two Sociolinguistically Contrasting Communities*. Oxford: Oxford University Press.

Kegl, J., Senghas, A., and Coppola, M. (1999) Creation through contact: Sign language emergence and sign language change in Nicaragua. In M. DeGraff (ed.) *Language Creation and Language Change: Creolization, Diachrony, and Development*. 179–237. Cambridge, MA: MIT Press.

Krauss, M. (1992) The world's languages in crisis. *Language* 68(1): 4–10.

Kulick, D. (1992) *Language Shift and Cultural Reproduction: Socialization, Self, and Syncretism in a Papua New Guinean Village*. Cambridge: Cambridge University Press.

Ladefoged, P. (1992) Another view of endangered languages. *Language* 68: 809–11.

Leonard, W. Y. (2007) *Miami Language Reclamation in the Home: A Case Study*. Doctoral Dissertation. Berkeley, CA: University of California, Berkeley.

Lewis, M. P. (2008) Evaluating endangerment: Proposed metadata and implementation. In K.A. King, N. Schilling-Estes, L. Fogle, J.J. Lou, and B. Soukup (eds.) *Sustaining Linguistic Diversity: Endangered and Minority Languages and Language Varieties*. 35–9. Washington, DC: Georgetown University Press.

Linguistic Society of America, Committee on Endangered Languages (1994) The need for the documentation of linguistic diversity. *LSA Bulletin* 144 (June): 5.

Maffi, L. (ed.) (2001) *On Biocultural Diversity: Linking Language, Knowledge, and the Environment*. Washington, DC: Smithsonian Institution Press.

Makihara, M. (2005) Rapa Nui ways of speaking Spanish: Language shift and socialization on Easter Island. *Language in Society* 34: 727–62.

Matsumura, K. (ed.) (1998) *Studies in Endangered Languages. (ICHEL Linguistic Studies Vol. 1.)* Tokyo: Hituji Syobo.

Meek, B. A. (2001) *Kaska Language Socialization, Acquisition, and Shift*. Doctoral Dissertation, Tucson, AZ: University of Arizona.

Meek, B. A. (2007) Respecting the language of elders: Ideological shift and linguistic discontinuity in a northern Athapascan community. *Journal of Linguistic Anthropology* 17(1): 23–43.

Meier, R. (2000) Diminishing diversity of signed languages (letter to the editor). *Science* 288: 1965.

Moore, R. E. (2001) Endangered. In A. Duranti (ed.) *Key Terms in Language and Culture*. 60–3. Malden, MA: Blackwell Publishing.

Morris, D. and Jones, K. (2008) Language socialization in the home and minority language revitalization in Europe. In P. A. Duff and N. H. Hornberger (eds.), *Encyclopedia of Language and Education, Vol. 8: Language Socialization*. 127–43. New York: Springer.

Mougeon, R. (1976) Bilingualism and language maintenance in the Gaspe Peninsula, Quebec, Canada. *Anthropological Linguistics* 18: 53–69.

Munro, P. (2002) *Making Dictionaries: Preserving Indigenous Languages of the Americas*. Berkeley, CA: University of California Press.

Nettle, D. and Romaine, S. (2000) *Vanishing Voices: The Extinction of the World's Languages*. New York: Oxford University Press.

Nonaka, A. M. (2004) The forgotten endangered languages: Lessons on the importance of remembering from Thailand's Ban Khor sign language. *Language in Society* 33: 737–67.

Nonaka, A.M. (2007). *Emergence of an indigenous sign language and a speech/sign community in Ban Khor, Thailand*. Doctoral Dissertation. Los Angeles, CA: University of California, Los Angeles.

Nonaka, A. M. (2009) Estimating size, scope, and membership of the speech/sign communities of undocumented indigenous/village sign languages: The Ban Khor case study. *Language & Communication* 29: 210–29.

Ochs, E. (1988) *Culture and Language Development: Language Acquisition and Language Socialization in a Samoan Village*. New York: Cambridge University Press.

Ochs, E. and Schieffelin, B. B. (eds.) (1979) *Developmental Pragmatics*. New York: Academic Press.

Ochs, E. and Schieffelin, B. B. (1984) Language acquisition and socialization: Three developmental stories and their implications. In R. A. Shweder and R. A. Levine (eds.), *Culture Theory: Essays on Mind, Self, and Emotion*. 276–320. New York: Cambridge University Press.

Ochs, E. and Schieffelin, B. B. (1995) The impact of language socialization on grammatical development. In P. Fletcher and B. MacWhinney (eds.), *The Handbook of Child Language*. 73–94. Cambridge, MA: Blackwell.

Ortner, S. B. (1984) Theory in anthropology since the sixties. *Comparative Studies in Society and History* 26(1): 126–66.

Paugh, A. L. (2001) *Creole Day Is Every Day: Language Socialization, Shift, and Ideologies in Dominica, West Indies*. Doctoral Dissertation. New York: New York University.

Paugh, A. (2005) Acting adult: Language socialization, shift, and ideologies in Dominica, West Indies. In K. T. Cohen, K. R. McAlister, and J. MacSwan (eds.), *Proceedings of the 4th International*

Symposium on Bilingualism. 1807–1820. Somerville, MA: Cascadilla Press.

Philips, S. (1983) *The Invisible Culture: Communication in Classroom and Community on the Warm Springs Indiana Reservation*. New York: Longman.

Piker, S. (1964) *An Examination of Character and Socialization in a Thai Peasant Community*. Doctoral Dissertation. Seattle, WA: University of Washington.

Reyhner, J., Cantoni, G., St. Clair, R. N., and Yazzie, E. P. (eds.) (1999) *Revitalizing Indigenous Languages*. Flagstaff, AZ: Northern Arizona University Press.

Robins, R. H. and Uhlenbeck, E. M. (eds.) (1991) *Endangered Languages*. New York: St. Martin's.

Romaine, S. (2008) Linguistic diversity, sustainability, and the future of the past. In K.A. King, N. Schilling-Estes, L. Fogle, J.J. Lou, and B. Soukup (eds.) *Sustaining Linguistic Diversity: Endangered and Minority Languages and Language Varieties*. 7–21. Washington, DC: Georgetown University Press.

Sapir, E. (1922) *The Fundamental Elements of Northern Yana*. Berkeley, CA: University of California Press.

Sasse, H.-J. (1990) *Theory of Language Death and Language Decay and Contact-Induced Change: Similarities and Differences*. Koln, Germany: Institut für Sprachwissenshaft.

Schieffelin, B. B. (1990) *The Give and Take of Everyday Life: Language Socialization of Kaluli Children*. New York: Cambridge University Press.

Schieffelin, B. B. and Ochs, E. (1986a) Language socialization. *Annual Review of Anthropology* 15: 163–91.

Schieffelin, B. B. and Ochs, E. (eds.) (1986b) *Language Socialization Across Cultures*. Cambridge: Cambridge University Press.

Shoji, H. and Janhunen, J. (eds.) (1997) *Northern Minority Languages: Problems of Survival*. Osaka, Japan: National Museum of Ethnology.

Shweder, R. A. (1984) Preview: A colloquy of culture theorists. In R. A. Shweder and R. A. Levine (eds.) *Culture Theory: Essays on Mind, Self, and Emotion*. 1–24. New York: Cambridge University Press.

Smalley, W. A. (1994) *Linguistic Diversity and National Unity: Language Ecology in Thailand*. Chicago, IL: University of Chicago Press.

Swadesh, M. (1948) Sociological notes on obsolescent languages. *International Journal of American Linguistics*. 14: 226–35.

Timm, L. A. (1973) Modernization and language shift: The case of Brittany. *Anthropological Linguistics* 15: 281–98.

Tsunoda, T. (2005) *Language Endangerment and Language Revitalization. (Trends in Linguistics Studies and Monographs 148)*. Berlin and New York: Mouton de Gruyter.

UNESCO. (2003) *Language Vitality and Endangerment (Document Prepared for the Intangible Cultural Heritage Unit of U NE SCO by the Ad Hoc Expert Group on Endangered Languages; A. Y. Yamamoto and M. Brenzinger, Co-Chairs)*. Adopted by UNESCO March 2003. Available from http://portal.unesco.org/culture/en/files/35646/12007687933Language_Vitality_and_Endangerment.pdf/Language%2BVitality%2Band%2BEndangerment.pdf

Weinreich, U. (1953) *Languages in Contact: Findings and Problems*. New York: Columbia University Press.

Woodbury, A. (2011) Language documentation. In P. K. Austin and J. Sallabanks (eds.) *The Cambridge Handbook of Endangered Languages*. 159–86. Cambridge: Cambridge University Press.

Woodward, J. C. (2000) Sign languages and sign language families in Thailand and Vietnam. In K. Emmorey and H. Lane (eds.), *The Signs of Language Revisited*. 23–47. Mahwah, NJ: Lawrence Erlbaum.

Yamamoto, A., Linn, M. S., and Peter, L. (2004) *Awakening Our Languages: Designing Curriculum*. ILI Handbook 8. Santa Fe, NM: Indigenous Language Institute.

Zeshan, U. (2004) Interrogative constructions in signed languages: Cross-linguistic perspectives. *Language* 80(1): 7–39.

27 Language Socialization and Language Revitalization

DEBRA A. FRIEDMAN

The last two decades have seen increasing scholarly interest in 'language revitalization,' the effort by governments, political organizations, or community activists to revive a language perceived to be under threat. Language revitalization (also referred to as 'language revival,' 'language regenesis,' 'language renewal,' or 'language maintenance') is a form of language planning, involving 'deliberate efforts to influence the behavior of others with respect to the acquisition, structure, or functional allocation of their language codes' (Cooper 1989: 45). It is most often associated with what Fishman (1991) has termed 'reversing language shift'; that is, reversing the process in which speakers abandon a minority language in favor of a dominant one (see Garrett, this volume). However, it may also address other aspects of language change, such as 'language loss' (a term variously used to describe speakers' decreased level of linguistic competence or a reduction in the structural, lexical or pragmatic complexity of the language), 'language convergence' (when language contact results in extensive change to a linguistic system), or constriction in the range of social functions of a language.

Language revitalization is a relatively new field of scholarly inquiry that emerged in the early 1990s as sociolinguists and anthropologists studying endangered languages (see Nonaka, this volume) began to turn from merely documenting the process of language shift and death to considering what could be done to halt or reverse it (Fishman 1991; Hale et al. 1992). Fishman's work has been particularly influential in the field, and his Graded Intergenerational Disruption Scale

The Handbook of Language Socialization, First Edition. Edited by Alessandro Duranti, Elinor Ochs, and Bambi B. Schieffelin.

(GIDS), a model measuring language vitality on a scale from stage 8 (most threatened) to stage 1 (relatively secure), has been widely adopted by both researchers and language revitalization activists. However, some researchers have questioned the suitability of this model to account for language revitalization in indigenous communities (e.g. Henze and Davis 1999; Hinton 2001), while others have criticized it for problematizing the linguistic choices of minority language speakers and overlooking community perspectives (Reynolds 2009).

Much language revitalization research has focused on macro-level factors such as state language policy or measurement of language attitudes and practices through large-scale surveys (e.g. Fishman 1991, 2001). However, this literature has been supplemented by edited volumes highlighting the role of minority language communities as active agents in the process of language revitalization (e.g. Grenoble and Whaley 1998; Hinton and Hale 2001; Hornberger 1997) as well as book-length ethnographic studies of language planning, maintenance, and revitalization at the levels of family, school, and community (e.g. Davis 1994; Heller 1999; Jaffe 1999). Another trend has been increased attention to the role of language ideologies in determining the trajectory and outcomes of language revitalization campaigns (e.g. England 2003; Gal 1993; Hornberger 1994; Jaffe 1993, 1996, 2003; King 2000; Kroskrity and Field 2009; Schieffelin and Doucet 1998). By shaping understandings of what a language is and how, by whom, and when different codes are to be used, language ideologies have been shown to contribute to a range of factors – such as the relative status of dominant and minority languages, associations between language and cultural identities, judgments regarding the authenticity of a language variety, and attitudes towards bilingualism, code-switching, and code-mixing – that can have an impact on language maintenance and revitalization.

With its emphasis on language use as a set of ideologically mediated cultural practices, the language socialization approach is well positioned to elucidate how such language ideologies are produced, reproduced, transmitted, or transformed through everyday socialization routines (Riley, this volume). Although relatively little language socialization research has focused expressly on language revitalization, studies conducted in communities in the midst of ongoing language or cultural revival projects have revealed how both local and dominant language ideologies can shape or be shaped by socialization practices, with serious, if often unintended, consequences for the success of these projects. Drawing upon a number of these studies, this chapter will highlight the findings of language socialization research in three key areas: (1) how everyday language ideologies and socialization practices interact with and, at times, counteract those promulgated by language activists, (2) the role of children in shaping ideologies that impact revitalization, and (3) the classroom as a potential site for socializing children into ideologies that support or undermine language revitalization efforts. The chapter will conclude with a review of the contributions made by language socialization research to understandings of language revitalization and the implications for the future direction of language socialization research in this area.

Language Socialization and Ideologies of Language Revitalization

The study of language ideologies involves the social (i.e. indexical) meanings of linguistic signs and the processes through which these signs come to be seen as both embodying and constituting social phenomena such as group membership, political allegiance, prestige, or moral worth (Dorian 1989; Irvine 1989; Kroskrity 2000; Silverstein 1996; Woolard and Schieffelin 1994). Language ideologies assigning value to language varieties within multilingual communities have been identified as key factors in determining code choice and language vitality (e.g. Crystal 2000; Dorian 1998; Woolard 1985). Evaluation of a language as more or less prestigious arises from indexical associations between linguistic forms and particular social identities, institutions, or functions, whose qualities come to be seen as inherent qualities of the language itself and of those who speak it. A primary task of language revitalization movements is therefore to revalue a subordinate language and grant it prestige through promotion of ideologies such as those representing the language as an emblem of ethnic or cultural identity or establishing it as a medium for valued functions such religious practices, literacy, or 'high culture' (Crystal 2000; Dorian 1998; Jaffe 1999). Yet these ideologies, often originating with a cultural elite, may be at odds with those governing everyday language practices. Language socialization studies by Paugh (2001), Fellin (2001), and Bunte (2009) demonstrate how multiple language ideologies interact with larger social forces to shape language practices and attitudes that may enhance or counter the rhetoric and goals of revitalization movements.

Paugh's research (2001, this volume) in a rural village in the Caribbean island nation of Dominica illustrates how associations between language, culture, and identity are differentially constructed at the local and national levels. Since Dominican independence from Britain in 1978, Patwa, a once-distained French-based Creole spoken in rural areas, has been seized upon by some intellectuals as a symbol of the nation's distinct cultural identity and become the focus of revitalization efforts through projects such as festivals celebrating island culture and traditional genres of verbal art; documentation of Patwa in dictionaries and grammars; and Creole Day on which everyone is supposed to speak the language. However, while these activities may have helped to revalue Patwa from a backward dialect to a positive cultural symbol, they have not challenged the dominance of English, which remains the language of government, education, and business.

Paugh contrasts these discourses of language and national identity with the ideologies prevailing within a Patwa-speaking village. Tracing the historical and socioeconomic roots of community ideologies regarding Patwa and English, she reveals how the two codes have come to index dichotomies related to settings (rural versus urban), social identities (farmer versus office worker), aspects of personhood (assertiveness versus politeness), social values (traditional versus modern), and group membership (community versus nation). She further demonstrates how positive associations with English interact with local theories of language learning that view English as something that needs to be explicitly taught (as opposed to Patwa, which is naturally acquired through living in a Patwa-speaking community) to lead to language socialization practices in which both teachers and parents consciously promote English language acquisition by endeavoring to speak only English to children and proscribing children's use of Patwa, which is thought to interfere with the acquisition of English.

In sum, the positioning of Patwa as the emblem of an imagined unified Dominican identity and a supposedly shared language that transcends class and urban/rural divisions runs counter to the experiences of rural residents, for whom Patwa is a mark of difference, something that distinguishes them from urban residents and excludes them from full participation in national life. The language use and socialization practices of rural adults reflect and reproduce the values of this local speech economy. Thus, despite the fact that villagers associate Patwa with village identity and positive aspects of traditional rural life, they are socializing children into speaking English while retaining Patwa for a limited set of affective and pragmatic functions.

In contrast, Fellin's (2001) work on language revitalization in a northern Italian village explores how a revaluation of local identity has led to a revival in the use of the local dialect, Nones. In the 1970s and 1980s, more mechanized farming practices (resulting in less need for children's participation on the family farm) and deepening connections to the national economy had encouraged an orientation towards what locals referred to as 'the outside' (2001: 68). In the presence of dominant language ideologies associating Italian with desirable attributes such as education, urban sophistication, modernity, and economic progress, this orientation had given rise to home language socialization practices promoting Italian rather than Nones as the language that would best prepare children for schooling and participation in the world beyond the village, leading to a decrease in the number of local children who could fluently speak the vernacular.

However, by the time Fellin began her fieldwork, the successful marketing of local apples (and the consequent rise in the economic and social status of farmers) as well as increased attention to minority languages and cultures (encouraged by the European Union) had altered the local speech economy. In interviews Fellin found that, while Italian continued to be valued, there had also been a revaluation of Nones by many young parents, who embraced it as an emblem of their distinctive and vital local culture and expressed a determination to raise their children to be Nones–Italian bilinguals. Fellin further reveals how use of Nones in the home had become part of these individuals' own social identities, not only as members of a Nones-speaking community but as progressive and concerned parents who had discarded outmoded ideologies advocating home use of Italian as necessary for children's school success in favor of what they saw as more enlightened attitudes regarding the cognitive benefits of bilingualism and the need to take personal responsibility for transmitting the vernacular to their children.

In addition, Fellin observed that, even in settings in which Italian dominated (e.g. in school or in Italian-speaking homes), caregivers and children frequently code-switched into the vernacular, especially during affect-laden activities such as teasing, joking, or disciplining children's problematic behavior, a practice that she interprets as making salient children's membership in the local community with its attendant obligations, values, and behavioral norms. While these patterns of code-switching associating the vernacular with local identity are similar to those noted by Paugh (2001) in Dominica, in this case these associations were being socialized in a context in which residents were coming to identify themselves primarily as members of a local community rather than a national one, a trend reflected in the rising political fortunes of regional parties such as the Northern League. As a result, Nones was invested with considerable symbolic capital, a circumstance that bodes well for its future survival.

Drawing from fieldwork conducted over the course of 27 years among the San Juan Southern Paiute tribe, Bunte (2009) offers further illustration of how evolving ideologies linking language and identity interact with local theories of child rearing and personhood to have an impact on language revitalization. A small tribe living within the territory of the Navajo reservation, the community has long asserted a distinct Paiute identity. However, although community members expressed pride that the tribe had maintained the Paiute language, the language itself did not seem to be a vital part of this identity. While caregivers engaged in socializing interactions with children in Paiute, the emphasis was on instilling knowledge of culturally appropriate behavior, and the fact that children were increasingly using English when engaging in these interactions did not excite any immediate concern.

However, by the early 1990s a dispute with the Navajo over land rights, which made it essential to gain federal recognition of a distinctive tribal identity, engendered a shift in the ways that community members identified themselves, and the ability to speak the language emerged as a primary means of claming a Paiute identity. At the same time, however, younger members of the tribe were shifting to English even in families in which Paiute was the primary language. Bunte traces this dichotomy to the interplay between two ideologies regarding learning and personhood. First was the belief that children learn through listening to instructions and suggestions provided by caregivers regarding proper ways to behave; even though children may not produce the desired behavior immediately, it is assumed that they will be able to act upon this information later in life. For example, while Bunte frequently observed caregivers telling children that they 'should speak Paiute' (2009: 177), there appeared to be no expectation that the children do so at that particular moment. Rather, it was believed that the ability to speak Paiute would eventually come to them 'on the wind' (2009: 175) as long as they had developed a passive knowledge of it in childhood. Second, Bunte noted that this reluctance to insist upon children's immediate compliance arose from the belief that all individuals, including young children, are autonomous beings who cannot be forced to act in particular ways but must make the decision to do so themselves.

As a result, despite the growing tendency to link a Paiute identity to the Paiute language and increasing community awareness and concern regarding language shift, many of the remedies promoted in language revitalization workshops conducted by outsiders were viewed with skepticism as incompatible with Paiute cultural beliefs and socialization practices. Bunte concludes that the future of Paiute depends on how the community is able to reconcile multiple and sometimes conflicting ideologies to find culturally appropriate ways of encouraging children to speak the language.

Language Revitalization and Children's Agency

While children are ostensibly the focus of language revitalization projects, they are rarely the focus of language revitalization research, which tends to depict them as passive recipients of language or ideologies transmitted by adults. This perspective runs counter to that of the language socialization approach, which regards children as active participants in the co-construction and reconstruction of social and cultural knowledge (e.g. Ochs and Schieffelin 1986). In studies conducted in diverse settings, Paugh (2005), Meek (2007, 2010), and Makihara (2005) argue for attending to children's agency in the process of language revitalization. By examining the language practices and ideologies of children in language minority communities, these studies reveal how children take up, transform, or challenge the ways of speaking and thinking that are promoted through socialization practices.

Drawing from her study of language socialization in Dominica, Paugh (2001, 2005) offers an example of how children interpret and transform indexical associations between language, social identity, and social status. As noted above, the English-only rule that adults enforce when speaking to children is largely governed by perceptions of English as the language of power and social mobility and the desire to ensure that children are able to acquire this valuable form of cultural capital without interference from the local vernacular, Patwa. While it might be assumed that such practices would lead to children devaluing Patwa, Paugh's observation of children's code-switching during imaginary play suggests that the patterns of language usage to which they are exposed are socializing them into different understandings.

Although children are forbidden to speak Patwa at home or in school, Paugh notes that they frequently code-switch into the language when outside of adult supervision. Peer interactions among children are primarily conducted in English, but children use Patwa when cursing, intensifying their directives, or criticizing others, thus mirroring adult practices. However, the most extensive use of Patwa occurs when children are engaged in imaginary play in which they enact certain adult roles, such as farmer or bus driver, that are associated with the vernacular. From these observations, Paugh draws two conclusions regarding the future of Patwa. First, children's use of the language in defiance of attempts to socialize them into speaking only English demonstrates that they are not passively accepting the language practices or ideologies imposed on them by others, but actively shaping the process of their own socialization. Second, through their play, they are transforming associations with the language, linking it to positive values such as adult authority, status, and autonomy. Paugh concludes by suggesting that the positive valuations of Patwa being built through play may provide a foundation for future maintenance of the language.

Meek's (2007, 2010) study of an endangered language community in Yukon Territory, Canada, reveals a similar ideological transformation through which children come to associate their ancestral language, Kaska, with an authoritative social identity – that of community elders. However, because of a confluence of social and ideological factors, this revaluation of Kaska seems to be contributing to language shift rather than to language revitalization. Meek situates children's ancestral language socialization at the nexus of three prevailing discourses: those linking Kaska language revitalization to preservation of traditional cultural practices, those conferring status to possessors of specialized traditional knowledge, and those related to respect. As is common in indigenous communities, Kaska language revitalization is embedded within a larger project of cultural revival that seeks to recover and transmit knowledge regarding traditional cultural practices. As the only community members with direct experience of these practices, elders have achieved status within and outside of the community as the experts on what it means to 'be Kaska.' They have also been charged with primary responsibility for transmitting both cultural and linguistic knowledge to the younger generation through activities such as narrating traditional stories to children in Kaska.

Association of a language with high-status speakers is usually assumed to lead to increased usage, as people equate acquisition of social status with speaking a prestigious language (e.g. Dorian 1998). However, Meek's analysis of children's use of and talk about the language reveals that, while a revaluation of Kaska has indeed taken place, it has not had the expected results. First, the association of Kaska with traditional culture has removed it from the realm of everyday life and incorporated it into a body of specialized traditional knowledge associated with the social status of elder. Second, these associations have been filtered through the discourse of respect, which socializes children to show deference to authority by remaining silent and passively observing experts until they themselves have fully mastered a skill. From the children's perspective, the increased value of Kaska has turned the language into something reserved for high-status speakers, such as elders, and forbidden for low-status community members, such as children.

Like their Dominican counterparts (Paugh 2005), Kaska children occasionally used Kaska words or expressions to claim authority over other children. However, Meek also observes that, because of the discourses of respect, children appeared to be avoiding engaging with competent older speakers in Kaska, thus minimizing their opportunities to learn the language. Children also expressed the belief that Kaska language competence, like other forms of traditional knowledge, is something that comes with age and increased social status. Meek concludes that, despite official rhetoric in favor of revitalizing the language, Kaska children are implicitly being socialized into not speaking Kaska until they have achieved the status of elder.

Makihara's (2005) research on the isolated Pacific island of Rapa Nui (Easter Island) examines the emergence of a new Rapa Nui Spanish speech style among children and considers its potential effect on the future of the Rapa Nui language. In recent decades, increased integration with the outside world since establishment of air links has profoundly affected the linguistic repertoire of local residents. Most adults are bilingual in Rapa Nui and Chilean Spanish, and syncretic (i.e. mixed) varieties of both languages are commonly used in informal contexts. More recently, however, the value of the local culture and language in the tourist industry as well as the influence of a strong indigenous rights movement have increased the symbolic capital of Rapa Nui and established it as a emblem of a distinct island identity.

Nevertheless, increased use of Spanish in the home as well as Spanish-medium schooling and television mean that most children are Spanish-dominant. Yet Makihara's observations of caregiver–child interactions reveal that children receive considerable exposure to syncretic Rapa Nui in the home, both through listening to adult conversations and participating in nonreciprocal interactions in which the adult speaks Rapa Nui while the child speaks Spanish. That is, children appear to be developing a passive knowledge of Rapa Nui even though they cannot speak it. She further notes that, while children are speaking Spanish rather than Rapa Nui, their Spanish is neither Chilean Spanish nor the Rapa Nui Spanish spoken by adults. Rather, they appear to have developed their own Rapa Nui Spanish speech style that incorporates Rapa Nui lexical items. Makihara interprets this speech style as a creative response that enables children to harness the symbolic function of Rapa Nui to index a Rapa Nui ethnolinguistic identity despite limited competence in the language. Given socialization practices in which adults accommodate children's linguistic choices, this speech style is implicitly validated and may possibly transform the way that language is used to index ethnic identity.

The effect of this transformation on the future of Rapa Nui language revitalization is uncertain. To the extent that speaking Rapa Nui Spanish becomes an acceptable means of attaining membership in the local community it may contribute to loss of Rapa Nui. Yet Makihara also points to countervailing forces, such as the interest of teenagers and young adults in improving their competence in Rapa Nui and the recent establishment of Rapa Nui immersion education, that may further affect the language choices of the younger generation and thus shape future development of the island's linguistic repertoire.

Language Revitalization and Schooling

The role of schooling in language revitalization has been the focus of an ongoing debate among revitalization activists. Many see acceptance by the educational system as a means of enhancing the status of a language through associations with valued knowledge and literacy as well as promoting continued linguistic development (e.g. Hornberger 1997, 2006). In addition, in situations in which intergenerational transmission has already broken down, some system of formal schooling may be the only means of passing the language on to the younger generation. Thus, language revitalization campaigns are often accompanied by calls for teaching the endangered language in school or promotion of bilingual education for language minority children. However, the role of formal schooling in language revitalization remains controversial, particularly in indigenous communities in which Western pedagogical practices may conflict with local beliefs and traditions and remove the language from its social and cultural context (e.g. Gómez de García, Axelrod, and Lachler 2009; Henze and Davis 1999). The following discussion will explore this issue in a range of educational contexts, including an extended discussion of my own work on language socialization and revitalization in two fifth-grade classrooms in Ukraine (Friedman 2006, 2010).

Language revitalization and schooling in indigenous communities

Nevins's (2004) account of a failed project to develop computer-based language teaching materials in a White Mountain Apache community in Arizona provides a thought-provoking analysis of the varying ways in which notions of communicative competence are constructed in dominant and minority speech communities and the challenges this presents to those seeking to legitimate a threatened language within the educational system. Seeking to explain why these materials, on which she herself had worked as a consultant, had ultimately been rejected by the community, Nevins contrasts the practices of language pedagogy prevalent in schools, which emphasize explicit teaching of grammar rules, pronunciation, and literacy skills, with the language socialization practices that she observed in Apache homes. In the community, language acquisition was closely intertwined with development of social relationships and instilling in children a sense of their responsibilities as members of the community. There was little explicit teaching; rather, as was the case in the Paiute community observed by Bunte (2009), it was believed that children learn by listening and participating in activities with other family members. Caregivers also used teasing as a means of making children aware of how their behavior was viewed by others, thus encouraging them to alter that behavior.

While in schools the Apache language was treated as a decontextualized object of study. From the community perspective it was part of daily life and could only be learned through the performance of activities that constituted this life, such as baking bread or chopping wood. For many community members, transferring responsibility for Apache language transmission away from the family to the schools was viewed as a further weakening of already fragile social bonds and thus a threat to the survival of the Apache way of life. Nevins concludes with a call for devoting more attention to local ideologies and pedagogical practices when developing language revitalization programs as well as ceding a higher degree of control of such programs to local communities.

While the efficacy and appropriateness of school-based language programs in indigenous language revitalization remains an open question, a number of alternative, community-based language education programs have been successful in producing a new speakers and generating a sense of pride and connection to a threatened indigenous language. Most notable among these are the preschool programs or 'language nests' designed to revive Māori in New Zealand (*Te Kōhanga Reo*) and Hawaiian in Hawai'i (the *Pūnana Leo*). What distinguishes these programs from other forms of language education is the attempt to replicate traditional home socialization practices within the context of schooling. Rather than being taught the language as a subject, as was the case in the Apache program described by Nevins (2004), children are taught *through* the language as they participate in activities that evoke and socialize traditional family relationships, responsibilities, and behaviors. The schools also require parental involvement, both as facilitators and as language learners, in the hopes of engaging the parents in their children's indigenous language development and encouraging further socialization in the home environment.

The language nests represent a potentially rich site for the study of socialization into appropriate ways of speaking, feeling, and acting as Māori or Hawaiian in contexts in which the language and traditional practices had all but disappeared. Yet, while research on these programs has generated an informative descriptive literature detailing their goals, practices, and achievements (e.g. King 2001; Wilson and Kamana 2001), there are some lingering questions regarding their long-term effects on family language socialization practices and reversing language shift (e.g. Benton and Benton 2000), especially given entrenched ideologies and practical necessities promoting use of English and relegating languages such as Māori and Hawaiian to peripheral roles in the larger society. Longitudinal ethnographic studies examining children's indigenous language socialization across the contexts of school, home, and community could enrich our understanding of the role that schooling can play in revitalizing such languages.

Language revitalization and schooling in Ukraine

Unlike the other languages discussed in this chapter, Ukrainian has long enjoyed the status of a literary language as well as some degree of institutional support. Under Russian imperial rule, Ukrainian was regarded as a dialect of Russian and at one time was banned from public use. However, during the Soviet period it became an official language of the Ukrainian Soviet Socialist Republic, was taught in schools, and for a brief time in the 1920s was actively promoted (Martin 2001; Wexler 1974). Nevertheless, positive associations with Russian as the language of government, higher education, science, and the Communist Party (and thus of upward mobility) furthered the shift to Russian that had been ongoing since the nineteenth century. Today, although Ukrainian is the sole official language of an independent nation state, it is far from hegemonic in its titular nation; in addition to a substantial ethnic Russian population, many ethnic Ukrainians speak Russian as their primary language (Pavlenko 2006) and Russian continues to dominate in popular culture. As part of its nation-building project, the state has embarked on a campaign to cleanse the language of perceived Russian influences and encourage its more widespread use. A primary site for this effort is the nation's schools, all of which teach Ukrainian as an obligatory subject.

My research, conducted in two fifth-grade classrooms in a small city in central Ukraine (Friedman 2006, 2010), explores the language classroom as a site for socializing children into dominant language ideologies that support state-sponsored language revitalization projects. The language classroom represents a potentially rich context for the study of language revitalization in this setting, as Ukrainian language revitalization has long been centered on ideologies promoting literary (i.e. Standard) Ukrainian and what is called *čysta mova* ('pure language') as the sole legitimate variety suitable for representing the nation (e.g. Wexler 1974). In interviews and informal conversations with teachers and parents, I found general agreement that extensive language contact with Russian had, in the words of one of my interviewees, 'polluted' the local variety of Ukrainian with Russianisms, and that mastery of pure Ukrainian therefore required explicit school-based teaching and extensive effort, even for those who grew up in Ukrainian-speaking homes.

Both Ukrainian teachers involved in this study expressed allegiance to the language revitalization project, seeing their role as not simply teaching the mechanics of good grammar or spelling but instilling in children a sense of pride in Ukraine as well as a sense of responsibility towards maintaining the Ukrainian language. As the first generation growing up in independent Ukraine, these children were considered to be at the forefront of the effort to revitalize and develop the language, and teachers often reminded them that, in the words of one teacher, '[Ukrainian's] stature depends exactly on the extent that we speak it and how we foster it.' During lessons, both teachers routinely referred to *naša ridna mova* ('our native language') or *naša ukrajins'ka mova* ('our Ukrainian language'), even though many of the children came from Russian-speaking families.

In addition to such explicit affirmations, many classroom practices and activities were implicitly socializing children into dominant language ideologies that positioned Ukrainian as a pure and beautiful language that the children should be proud to speak. Predominant among these were error-correction routines that targeted children's use of Russian words (Friedman 2010). Teachers regularly interrupted children to replace a word deemed to be Russian with a Ukrainian word or to prompt children to correct themselves, even when the focus of the interaction was not on language. Children were well socialized into their roles in these routines; I noted few instances in which children failed to respond to a correction, either by taking up the teacher's replacement word or correcting themselves, and on occasion they self-selected to correct their classmates as well. These error-correction routines were not only teaching children to speak Ukrainian 'correctly' but also socializing them into ideologies that defined what 'speaking correctly' means. Through participation in these routines, teachers and students collaboratively constructed and displayed understandings that the norms of Ukrainian usage included allegiance to ideologically mediated standards of correctness that proscribe language mixing as a violation of the natural boundaries between languages, thus preserving a distinct Ukrainian language as a emblem of a distinct Ukrainian nation.

Another common interactional routine revolved around whole-class discussions initiated by a question such as 'What do you think?' that invited children to take a stance vis-à-vis some feature of the language. While this question might appear to be soliciting children's individual opinions, teachers' responses to children's answers revealed the expectation that children were to answer not as individuals but as members of a community that valued language in particular ways. For example, on one occasion a teacher asked his class, 'What do you think. On what depends the beauty of any language?' He then led them through a lengthy sequence involving incorrect guesses by children and further hints by the teacher that ended only when a child finally provided the answer that he had been seeking: vowels. After accepting the answer he closed the sequence by declaring, 'Language sounds beautiful when in every word there are a few more vowel sounds.' He then went on to establish the connection between this fact and that day's lesson on simplification of consonant clusters in Ukrainian spelling by pointing out that, since Ukrainian has a built-in mechanism for minimizing consonants (and thus maximizing vowels) it is recognized as one of the most beautiful languages in the world.

Although the teacher's closing statement could have been made from the beginning, thereby obviating the need for this extended sequence, by posing this issue as a problem for the children to solve and scaffolding the process through which they collectively arrived at a solution he pushed them to engage actively and methodically with the concept of beauty in language. The answer, when it finally emerged, was collaboratively achieved through contributions from the teacher and several children, making the teacher's final statement a confirmation of what the children had discovered rather than an assertion of his own opinion. Such routines can therefore be seen as a means of socializing children into doing a 'proper' evaluation consistent with dominant ideologies, with teachers guiding the discussion until this proper evaluation is achieved and then aligning with the children's stance, thus affirming its validity and incorporating it into the store of common knowledge of the classroom.

Through activities such as these, teachers endeavored to socialize children into speaking and thinking about Ukrainian in ways congruent with dominant language ideologies of pure and beautiful language. Overall, evidence from children's behavior in the classroom confirmed the children's appropriation of these ideologies. Children readily took up the corrections offered by their teachers and used the standards of pure language to correct or challenge classmates' use of Russian words. They also responded to questions such as 'What do you think?' by voicing the language ideologies of their community, thus reifying the validity and relevance of these ideologies.

Yet, the ultimate effect of these ideologies on children's actual language practices and thus on the future of Ukrainian remains unclear. Although the hegemony of pure Ukrainian was established within the classroom, children often switched to Russian or used mixed language during breaks between lessons, a practice that both teachers and administrators deplored but did not prohibit, feeling that such action would conflict with the values of free choice and respect for other languages and cultures that the state and the educational system currently espouse. Moreover, in interviews conducted on a recent follow-up visit to the site of the original research, many these same children (then 15 years old) told me that they more often use Russian in their daily lives outside of the classroom, even as they unanimously expressed positive attitudes towards Ukrainian and asserted that all Ukrainians should know the national language. As one young woman expressed it, 'It's possible to speak any language but we must know Ukrainian since we're citizens of Ukraine (we live) on Ukrainian territory and its our native language.' In other words, while voicing the ideologies linking Ukrainian national identity to knowledge of the Ukrainian language, she simultaneously claimed the right to linguistic choice. And, for many young people, that choice remains Russian. Despite the increased status of Ukrainian and allegiance to language ideologies supporting its use, Russian retains symbolic capital as an international language and the lingua franca of the former Soviet Union, and its entrenchment as a family language in many Ukrainian homes has enabled Russian to maintain a formidable presence in Ukraine, even in the absence of official recognition. Thus, while it appears that Ukrainian language revitalization efforts have succeed in halting language shift to Russian and increasing the level of Ukrainian language proficiency among the younger generation, the ultimate goal of reversing language shift in Ukraine – restoration of intergenerational transmission and establishment of Ukrainian as the primary language of all of the country's citizens – remains elusive.

Language Socialization and Language Revitalization

The language socialization studies summarized above confirm the findings of other research that has highlighted the challenges of maintaining or revitalizing minority languages even in the context of community and institutional support. But, while these studies have not provided definitive answers to what has been termed 'the revitalization paradox' (Rindstedt and Aronsson 2002), they have contributed a number of insights and raised some intriguing issues that could inform future research.

First, although intergenerational transmission of the language within families is the ultimate goal of many language revitalization efforts (e.g. Fishman 1991, 2001), there has been little systematic investigation into local theories of language learning and child rearing or how these theories relate to other cultural practices and ideologies (see Paugh, this volume). By situating language acquisition within a web of cultural, social, and ideological beliefs and practices, the language socialization paradigm provides a useful framework for investigation of this issue. For example, Paugh (2001) has shown that the tendency of caregivers to socialize children into speaking the dominant language does not necessarily represent a rejection of the local vernacular but may rather be an attempt to promote bilingualism, with caregivers focusing efforts on the valuable (but difficult to learn) dominant language while assuming that children will naturally acquire the local language without any intervention. Similarly, Meek (2007, 2010) and Bunte (2009) have revealed how socialization practices are shaped by cultural expectations regarding the role of children in learning. In both of these communities it is believed that children learn by observing and listening to experts, and this belief affects the degree to which caregivers expect children to interact in the local language. In contrast, in Ukrainian classrooms (Friedman 2006, 2010) children's participation is actively solicited by teachers, who structure discussions to involve children in the co-construction of knowledge (albeit under the teacher's strict control). This increased role for children was consistent with claims expressed by teachers and other community members that mastery of Ukrainian required effort and attention and also reflected the high degree of responsibility placed on children as the first generation of post-Soviet Ukrainians to preserve and develop the language for future generations.

Some of these beliefs (e.g. that learning the local language is easy for group members) have been noted by other researchers (e.g. Dauenhauer and Dauenhauer 1998; Dorian 1999), and one sometimes hears calls by language revitalization activists for educating the local populace as to the incorrectness and potential dangers of such attitudes. Yet, to the extent that these beliefs are deeply engrained within local cultural systems, they may be difficult to eradicate. Studies by Meek (2007, 2010) and Bunte (2009) that unpack the many layers of cultural beliefs involving learning, respect, and autonomy offer particularly compelling examples of the complexity of this issue. In some cases, the very cultural beliefs and practices that activists seek to preserve or revive may be contributing to the challenges of language revitalization.

In addition, these studies have pointed to the need to reconsider the role of children in the process of language revitalization. As studies by Paugh (2005), Meek (2007, 2010), and Makihara (2005) have demonstrated, children may be actively transforming, not merely passively absorbing, the ideologies and practices promoted by caregivers and other adults. In this regard, one issue deserving further attention is the impact of peer socialization (Goodwin and Kyratzis, this volume) on language revitalization. As Paugh (2005: 80) points out, studying children as they interact with each other outside of adult supervision can lead to insights regarding language choice and language change that might not be visible in other contexts. Similarly, my conversations with Ukrainian young people have suggested that forces operating outside of the contexts of home and school, such as peer social networks and popular culture, may provide the most powerful socialization contexts for adolescents in terms of language practices.

These observations lead to a final recommendation to extend the scope of this research to encompass a broader range of age groups as they participate in activities across multiple contexts. For example, adolescents are often seen as crucial to the success of language revitalization, as language choices made at this age will likely influence how they socialize their own children (e.g. Crystal 2000). Yet, with a few exceptions, little socialization research on language revitalization has focused on this population. Furthermore, studies such as those by Bunte (2009), Makihara (2005), and Nevins (2004) point to the value of extensive long-term engagement in the field and examination of socialization across a range of contexts in capturing the multiplicity and evolving nature of ideologies governing language socialization and revitalization. Taking to heart the insight that language socialization occurs across the lifespan and involves socialization into multiple communities of practice may enable us to make further progress towards unraveling the mysteries of the language revitalization paradox.

REFERENCES

Benton, R. and Benton, N. E. (2001) RLS in Aotearoa/New Zealand 1989–1999. In J. Fishman (ed.), *Can Threatened Languages be Saved?* 423–50. Clevendon, UK: Multilingual Matters.

Bunte, P. A. (2009) 'You keep not listening with your ears!' Language ideologies, language socialization, and Paiute identity. In P. V. Kroskrity and M. Field (eds.), *Native American Language Ideologies: Beliefs, Practices, and Struggles in Indian Country*. 172–89. Tucson, AZ: University of Arizona Press.

Cooper, R. L. (1989) *Language Planning and Social Change*. Cambridge: Cambridge University Press.

Crystal, D. (2000) *Language Death*. Cambridge: Cambridge University Press.

Dauenhauer, N. M. and Dauenhauer, R. (1998) Technical, emotional, and ideological issues in reversing language shift: Examples from southeast Alaska. In L. A. Grenoble and L. J. Whaley (eds.), *Endangered Languages: Language Loss and Community Response*. 57–98. Cambridge: Cambridge University Press.

Davis, K. A. (1994) *Language Planning in Multilingual Contexts: Policies, Communities, and Schools in Luxembourg*. Amsterdam, The Netherlands: John Benjamins.

Dorian, N. C. (ed.) (1989) *Investigating Obsolescence: Studies in Language Contraction and Death*. Cambridge: Cambridge University Press.

Dorian, N. C. (1998) Western language ideologies and small language prospects. In L. A. Grenoble and L. J. Whaley (eds.), *Endangered Languages: Language Loss and Community Response*. 3–21. Cambridge: Cambridge University Press.

Dorian, N. C. (1999) Linguistic and ethnographic fieldwork. In J. A. Fishman (ed.), *Handbook of Language and Ethnic Identity*. 25–41. New York: Oxford University Press.

England, N. C. (2003) Mayan language revival and revitalization politics: Linguists and linguistic ideologies. *American Anthropologist* 105(4): 733–43.

Fellin, L. (2001) *Language Ideologies, Language Socialization, and Language Revival in an Italian Alpine Community*. Doctoral Dissertation. Tucson, AZ: University of Arizona.

Fishman, J. A. (1991) *Reversing Language Shift*. Clevendon, UK: Multilingual Matters.

Fishman, J. A. (ed.) (2001) *Can Threatened Languages be Saved?* Clevendon, UK: Multilingual Matters.

Friedman, D. (2006) *(Re)Imagining the Nation: Language Socialization in Ukrainian Classrooms*. Doctoral Dissertation. Los Angeles, CA: University of California.

Friedman, D. (2010) Speaking correctly: Error correction as a language socialization practice in a Ukrainian classroom. *Applied Linguistics* 31(3): 346–67.

Gal, S. (1993) Diversity and contestation in linguistic ideologies: German speakers in Hungary. *Language in Society* 22(3): 337–59.

Gómez de García, J., Axelrod, M., and Lachler, J. (2009) English is the dead language: Native perspectives on bilingualism. In P. V. Kroskrity and M. Field (eds.), *Native American Language Ideologies: Beliefs, Practices, and Struggles in Indian Country*. 99–122. Tucson, AZ: University of Arizona Press.

Grenoble, L. A. and Whaley, L. J. (eds.) (1998) *Endangered Languages: Language Loss and Community Response*. Cambridge: Cambridge University Press.

Hale, K., Krauss, M., Watahomigie, L. J., Yamamoto, A. Y., Craig, C., LaVerne, M. J., and England, N. C. (1992) Endangered languages. *Language* 68(1): 1–42.

Heller, M. (1999) *Linguistic Minorities and Modernity: A Sociolinguistic Ethnography*. London/New York: Longman.

Henze, R. and Davis, K. A. (eds.) (1999) Authenticity and identity: Issues from indigenous language education. *Anthropology and Education Quarterly* 30(1): 3–21.

Hinton, L. (2001) Language revitalization: An overview. In L. Hinton and K. Hale (eds.), *The Green Book of Language Revitalization in Practice*. 3–18. San Diego, CA: Academic Press.

Hinton, L. and Hale, K. (eds.) (2001) *The Green Book of Language Revitalization in Practice*. San Diego, CA: Academic Press.

Hornberger, N. H. (1994) Five vowels or three?: Linguistics and politics in Quechua language planning in Peru. In J. W. Tollefson (ed.), *Power and Inequality in Language Education*. 187–205. Cambridge: Cambridge University Press.

Hornberger, N. H. (ed.) (1997) *Indigenous Literacies in the Americas: Language Planning from the Bottom Up*. Berlin/New York: Mouton de Gruyter.

Hornberger, N. H. (2006) Voice and biliteracy in indigenous language revitalization: Contentious educational practices in Quechua, Guarani, and Maori contexts. *Journal of Language, Identity, and Education* 5(4): 277–92.

Irvine, J. (1989) When talk isn't cheap. Language and political economy. *American Ethnologist* 16: 248–67.

Jaffe, A. (1993) Obligation, error and authenticity: Competing cultural principles in the teaching of Corsican. *Journal of Linguistic Anthropology* 3(1): 99–114.

Jaffe, A. (1996) The second annual Corsican spelling contest: Orthography and ideology. *American Ethnologist* 23(4): 816–35.

Jaffe, A. (1999) *Ideologies in Action: Language Politics on Corsica*. Berlin/New York: Mouton de Gruyter.

Jaffe, A. (2003) Talk around text: Literacy practices, cultural identity and authority in a Corsican bilingual classroom. *International Journal of Bilingual Education and Bilingualism* 6(3/4): 202–20.

King, J. (2001) Te Kōhanga Reo: Māori language revitalization. In L. Hinton and K. Hale (eds.), *The Green Book of Language Revitalization in Practice*. 119–28. San Diego, CA: Academic Press.

King, K. A. (2000) Language ideologies and heritage language education. *International Journal of Bilingual Education and Bilingualism* 3(3): 167–84.

Kroskrity, P. V. (2000) Regimenting languages: Language ideological perspectives. In P. V. Kroskrity (ed.), *Regimes of Language: Ideologies, Polities, and Identities*. 1–34. Santa Fe, NM: School of American Research.

Kroskrity, P. V. and Field, M. (eds.) (2009) *Native American Language Ideologies: Beliefs, Practices, and Struggles in Indian Country*. Tucson, AZ: University of Arizona Press.

Makihara, M. (2005) Rapa Nui ways of speaking Spanish: Language shift and socialization on Easter Island. *Language in Society* 34: 727–62.

Martin, T. (2001) *The Affirmative Action Empire: Nations and Nationalism in the Soviet Union 1923–1939*. Ithaca, NY: Cornell University Press.

Meek, B. (2007) Respecting the language of elders: Ideological shift and linguistic discontinuity in a northern Athapascan community. *Journal of Linguistic Anthropology* 17(1): 23–43.

Meek, B. (2010) *We are Our Language: An Ethnography of Language Revitalization in a Northern Athabascan Community*. Tucson, AZ: University of Arizona Press.

Nevins, M. E. (2004) Learning to listen: Confronting two meanings of language loss in the contemporary White Mountain Apache speech community. *Journal of Linguistic Anthropology* 14(2): 269–88.

Ochs, E. and Schieffelin, B. B. (1986) *Language Socialization Across Cultures*. Cambridge: Cambridge University Press.

Paugh, A. (2001) *'Creole Day Is Every Day': Language Socialization, Shift, and Ideologies in Dominica, West Indies*. Doctoral Dissertation. New York: New York University.

Paugh, A. (2005) Multilingual play: Children's code-switching, role play, and agency in Dominica, West Indies. *Language in Society* 34: 63–86.

Pavlenko, A. (2006) Russian as a lingua franca. *Annual Review of Applied Linguistics* 26: 78–99.

Reynolds, J. F. (2009) Shaming the shift generation: Intersecting ideologies of family and linguistic revitalization in Guatemala. In P. V. Kroskrity and M. Field (eds.), *Native American Language Ideologies: Beliefs, Practices, and Struggles in Indian Country*. 213–37. Tucson, AZ: University of Arizona Press.

Rindstedt, C. and Aronsson, K. (2002) Growing up monolingual in a bilingual community: The Quichua revitalization paradox. *Language in Society* 31: 721–42.

Schieffelin, B. B. and Doucet, R. C. (1998) The 'real' Haitian creole: Ideology, metalinguistics, and orthographic choice. In B. B. Schieffelin, K. A. Woolard, and P. V. Kroskrity (eds.), *Language Ideologies: Practice and Theory*. 271–316. New York: Oxford University Press.

Silverstein, M. (1996) Monoglot 'standard' in America: Standardization and metaphors of linguistic hegemony. In D. Brenneis and R. K. S. Macaulay (eds.), *The Matrix of Language: Contemporary Linguistic Anthropology*. 284–306. Boulder, CO: Westview Press.

Wexler, P. N. (1974) *Purism and Language: A Study in Modern Ukrainian and Belorussian Nationalism (1840–1967)*. Bloomington, IN: Indiana University Press.

Wilson, W. H. and Kamana, K. (2001) 'Mai loko mai o ka 'i'ini: Proceeding from a dream': The 'Aha Pūnana Leo connection in Hawaiian language revitalization. In L. Hinton and K. Hale (eds.), *The Green Book of Language Revitalization in Practice*. 147–76. San Diego, CA: Academic Press.

Woolard, K. A. (1985) Language variation and cultural hegemony: Toward an integration of sociolinguistic and social theory. *American Ethnologist* 12: 738–48.

Woolard, K. A. and Schieffelin, B. B. (1994) Language ideology. *Annual Review of Anthropology* 23: 55–82.

Index

The Handbook of Language Socialization, First Edition. Edited by Alessandro Duranti,
Elinor Ochs, and Bambi B. Schieffelin.
© 2014 John Wiley & Sons, Ltd. Published 2014 by John Wiley & Sons, Ltd.

CPSIA information can be obtained
at www.ICGtesting.com
Printed in the USA
BVHW010904250920
589200BV00058B/119